Good Clinical Practice: A Question & Answer Reference Guide

May 2005

Edited by
Mark P. Mathieu
PAREXEL International Corporation

DISCLAIMER

This reference guide is not intended to provide specific regulatory or legal advice. Readers should consult their company's standard operating procedures (SOP), clinical and regulatory departments, and legal counsel for guidance when applying GCP standards in clinical research.

Table of Contents

Introduction

At its core, good clinical practice (GCP) is a set of broad FDA regulatory requirements, standards, and recommendations that apply to thousands of highly specific tasks, processes, and roles in the conduct of clinical research. Given the disparity between the specificity of clinical trial processes and tasks and the general GCP requirements and standards under which they occur, it is not surprising that interpreting and implementing GCP standards continue to represent challenges for the pharmaceutical, biotechnology, and medical device industries.

As is true of any area in which interpretation plays such a central role, the GCP discipline is today, as much as it has ever been, characterized by many long-standing and emerging questions regarding how broad GCP standards should be applied in the real world of clinical trials. Today, emerging questions in such areas as pharmacogenomic testing, possible conflict-of-interest disclosures, Part 11 and electronic clinical trials, as well as the Privacy Rule and its implications for clinical research are taking their places aside long-standing GCP gray areas, including how FDA GCP standards intersect with ICH GCP principles and the federal government's Common Rule.

Recognizing this, we set out to systematically collect, catalog, and answer the most important, emerging, and difficult questions regarding the interpretation and implementation of GCP standards today. In doing so, it is our hope that the resultant work, *Good Clinical Practice: A Question & Answer Reference Guide (Third Edition),* will represent the next step in GCP training and instruction—one that begins where all others leave off. Through this text's question-and-answer format, we attempt to highlight, explore, and address a vast array of GCP-related questions, some of which have persisted for many years without definitive answers and some of which have emerged in response to new clinical trials- or regulatory-related developments.

In creating this work, we selected a few hundred questions culled from a much larger list developed with the help of more than 100 industry and FDA experts, ranging from clinical research associates to QA auditors, from clinical trainers to regulatory attorneys, and from study investigators/coordinators to FDA field inspectors. In addressing these questions, we had one clear and overriding goal: To provide definitive answers where they exist, and to provide informed, thoughtful, and well-researched answers where they do not. In developing these answers, we called upon our own experiences in clinical research, reviewed hundreds of regulatory documents, and consulted directly with dozens of FDA officials and a network of colleagues, opinion leaders, attorneys, and clinical researchers.

In developing the new third edition, we have captured the changes and regulatory implications brought by many newly released FDA and NIH guidance documents. We have also added dozens of new questions on topics ranging from pharmacogenetics research to HIPAA enforcement and from electronic patient-reported outcomes to conflict-of-interest disclosures. This new text also features key contributions from several recognized experts in the field, including Mark Barnes of Ropes & Gray, James Nickas of Genentech, John McKenney of SEC Associates, John Serio of Brown Rudnick Berlack Israels LLP, and Laura Owens of Alston & Bird, among others.

We have developed the answers in this reference guide to reflect the multiple layers of standards that may be applied under GCP. In many areas, for example, emerging industry "best-practice" standards or international standards (e.g., ICH) may surpass those mandated or recommended by FDA GCP.

We ask that, in using this text, readers keep in mind that many areas lack an absolute consensus in approach, and that there is no perfect knowledge in the GCP discipline. After all, GCP is a complicated, evolving discipline that intersects with several other complex and evolving disciplines, including ethics, medicine and nursing, health systems, regulatory, administrative and case law, management science, information technology, biostatistics, risk analysis, public health, and health policy. Reasonable GCP practitioners with varied backgrounds can, and sometimes do, disagree about how best to interpret and implement GCP standards and guidelines.

Given the nature and premise of this work, we fully anticipate that not all readers will agree with all of the answers provided in this reference guide. Put simply, we could not have endeavored to provide meaningful answers without assuming such a risk. It is our fondest hope, however, that this work can spark new discussions or further existing dialogue that will, in the end, lead to more clarity and consensus in those areas in which they are so badly needed.

The reference guide itself categorizes questions and answers into 22 different areas, ranging from clinical monitoring to investigators/sites, from source data/ documentation to quality assurance activities/study auditing/FDA inspections, and from Part 11/electronic clinical trials to informed consent. Because we also wanted this reference guide to capture as wide a variety of GCP-related questions as possible, we have also integrated the FDA's frequently asked GCP-related questions and answers (see Section 20), which the agency released in its IRB and Investigator Information Sheets (1998). Finally, the appendix includes 2004-2005 updates to key FDA and international GCP-related regulations and guidances, including: Title 21 CFR Parts 11 (electronic records/signatures), 50 (informed consent), 54 (financial disclosure by clinical investigators), 56 (IRBs), and 312 (INDs/sponsor and investigator responsibilities); the ICH's Consolidated Guideline on Good Clinical Practice (E6); the ICH's Guideline on Clinical Safety Data Management (E2A); and the European Union's Clinical Trials Directive.

It is important to note that this reference guide addresses GCP as it applies to clinical research on human beings. It does not discuss GCP as it might apply to the practice of medicine or nursing, to health care administration, to veterinary or non-clinical studies or to non-U.S. laws or customs.

This reference guide is not intended to provide specific regulatory or legal advice. Readers should consult their company's standard operating procedures (SOP), clinical and regulatory departments, and legal counsel for guidance when applying GCP standards in clinical research.

We wish to thank those colleagues who took the time and made the effort to compose and submit questions for this reference manual.

Readers who have additional questions that might be addressed in future editions or who have comments on the existing text may forward them to mark.mathieu@parexel.com.

Section 1:
GCP Regulations, Standards and Guidelines
for Clinical Research

1.1 *Q. In addition to the FDA's GCP regulations and guidelines, several other documents are often mentioned in the context of clinical research standards, including the Declaration of Helsinki, the ICH's GCP guideline, the Department of Health and Human Services' (HHS) so-called "Common Rule," and the World Health Organization GCP guidelines. What is the specific applicability of each document to clinical research in the United States, and how do these documents, and the standards embodied within them, interact and intersect with the FDA's GCP standards?*

A. The general discussions below profile each of the various clinical research standards and its applicability:

The "Common Rule" (also called the HHS regulations, or the "Basic DHHS Policy for Protection of Human Subjects"). The "common rule" refers to a U.S. federal policy that provides regulations (Subpart A of Part 46 of Title 45, CFR (45 CFR 46)) for human subject protections in research conducted, supported, or otherwise subject to regulation by a federal government agency that has formally adopted the policy. Sixteen government agencies—including the National Institutes of Health (NIH), the Department of Justice, the Department of Education, the Department of Energy, and the National Aeronautics and Space Administration—that conduct, regulate or fund human research have signed on to comply with the provisions of the common rule. When studies involving FDA-regulated products are funded/supported by HHS, the research must comply with both FDA GCP standards and the common rule. The common rule, which focuses on IRB standards and informed consent, is similar to FDA requirements for IRBs (21 CFR Part 56) and informed consent (21 CFR 50), and is in many cases identical to FDA GCP standards in these areas. In fact, under an April 2001 interim rule, the FDA formally adopted (i.e., with certain changes to reflect differences in FDA and HHS regulatory authority) Subpart D of the common rule pertaining to special protections for children in clinical research (see Q5.33).

Although the common rule, which is administered by the HHS Office for Human Research Protection (OHRP), has no direct applicability to purely commercial research regulated by the FDA (i.e., that does not involve federal funding or is not conducted directly by a federal agency), industry sponsors should be aware that many of the institutions at which they are conducting trials will, as a matter of policy, be operating in compliance with the requirements in the common rule. As part of the so-called "assurance process," under which institutions and clinical sites conducting HHS-supported research provide HHS with an assurance that they will comply with the common rule for those research projects, the institutions are specifically asked if they will be applying the common rule standards to just the HHS-supported research or all research at the institution. According to some estimates, the vast majority of institutions voluntarily agree to conduct all research—including commercial research not otherwise subject to the common rule—in compliance with the common rule and all its subparts (Subpart B-Protections for Pregnant Women, Human Fetuses, and Neonates; Subpart C-Protections for Prisoners; and Subpart D-Protections for

Children), even though such a commitment is not necessary under the assurance process.

It is also worth noting that members of Congress have, in recent years, introduced several bills proposing that all human research be conducted under a single federal standard. Some lawmakers continue to promise new legislation that will mandate a single standard for U.S.-based clinical trials. The FDA has published a comparison of its GCP provisions with those of the common rule (www.fda.gov/oc/gcp/comparison.html).

The Declaration of Helsinki. At a June 1964 meeting in Helsinki, Finland, the World Medical Association first adopted the so-called Declaration of Helsinki, which comprises "a statement of ethical principles to provide guidance to physicians and other participants in medical research involving human subjects." GCP standards throughout the world note openly that they derive largely from the Declaration of Helsinki, which has been revised five times since its 1964 adoption, most recently in October 2000. In fact, the ICH's consolidated GCP guideline notes, under Section 2-The Principles of ICH GCP, that "clinical trials should be conducted in accordance with the ethical principles that have their origin in the Declaration of Helsinki, and that are consistent with GCP and the applicable regulation requirement(s)."

Through 21 CFR 312.120(c)(1), the FDA actively uses the Declaration of Helsinki as a standard for accepting data from certain foreign clinical studies in support of the safety and efficacy claims for drugs and biologics. Under this section, the FDA will accept a foreign clinical drug or biologic study that was not conducted under a U.S. IND (i.e., U.S. standards) only if the study conforms to whichever of the following provides greater protection for the human subjects: (1) the ethical principles contained in the 1989 version of the Declaration of Helsinki; or (2) the laws and regulations of the country in which the research was conducted. Therefore, when there is a non-U.S. study that was not conducted in accordance with the FDA's GCP standards (i.e., because an IND was not submitted) and the sponsor subsequently wants to use the study in support of U.S. approval, then the FDA may be willing to accept the study if it, at a minimum, meets the principles outlined in the Declaration of Helsinki.

After first incorporating the 1964 Declaration of Helsinki into its regulations (21 CFR 312.120(c)(4)) for such foreign trials in 1975, the agency has evaluated two subsequent revisions to the Declaration of Helsinki (i.e., the 1975 revisions and the 1989 revisions) before incorporating them into its regulations. Although the Declaration of Helsinki was most recently modified in 2000, the agency is unlikely to adopt this version, due to the amended document's dramatic shift away from the use of placebos in most clinical trials, a shift that put it at odds with the FDA's long-standing preference for placebo controls in many circumstances. Paragraph 29 of the 2000 amendment states that "the benefits, risks, burdens and effectiveness of a new method should be tested against those of the best current prophylactic, diagnostic, and therapeutic methods. This does not exclude the use of placebo, or no treatment, in studies where no proven prophylactic, diagnostic or therapeutic method exists." Although the World Health Association's General Assembly added a clarification to Paragraph 29 in 2002 seemingly liberalizing the 2000 amendment's stance on placebo controls at least to some degree, FDA officials were not swayed by the clarification and are unlikely to adopt the latest version of the Declaration of Helsinki.

This does not mean that the Declaration of Helsinki ceased to have relevance as an FDA standard for the acceptance of foreign trials that are not conducted under an IND. For now, the agency, in its regulations at 21 CFR 312.120, simply continues to reference the 1989 version of the Declaration of Helsinki, rather than the newest version as amended in 2000.

Under a June 2004 proposed regulation, however, the FDA is seeking to replace the Declaration of Helsinki with its existing GCP requirements as the standard applicable to foreign clinical trials not conducted under an IND. In the proposed rule, the FDA states that U.S. GCP is now considered a better standard because "it provides more detail and enumeration of specific responsibilities of various parties, including monitoring of the trial and reporting adverse events" (see Q1.2).

The ICH GCP Guideline. As a party to the ICH GCP guideline, the FDA has formally adopted the ICH GCP guideline (E6) in the United States. When it released the document in 1997, the FDA stated that the ICH GCP guideline "represents the agency's current thinking on good clinical practices." FDA officials have steadfastly maintained that the ICH GCP guideline is entirely consistent with the agency's existing GCP regulations/standards. Many have pointed out, however, that the ICH GCP guideline is more specific in several areas, and some claim that it provides additional standards to ensure data quality and subject protection in certain areas (see discussions below).

Over time, the differences in emphasis and specificity between the FDA standards and ICH GCP guideline should become less evident. FDA officials have stated that the agency will "take into account the ICH GCPs" in developing new or revising existing regulations and guidance as part of routine GCP program maintenance activities. In the meantime, FDA officials maintain that they will "consider clinical studies conducted under ICH GCP as meeting GCP standards acceptable to FDA."

WHO Guidelines for Good Clinical Practice. In 1994, the World Health Organization issued its Guidelines for Good Clinical Practice (GCP) for trials on pharmaceutical products "to set globally applicable standards for the conduct of such biomedical research on human subjects." Based on GCP standards implemented in a number of "highly developed countries, including Australia, Canada, European Community countries, Japan, Nordic Countries (Denmark, Finland, Iceland, Norway and Sweden) and the United States," the WHO guidelines were not designed to challenge or replace existing national regulations or requirements, only "to provide a complementary standard that can be applied worldwide."

Although WHO's GCP guideline has no applicability in countries that have their own national or regional (e.g., ICH) GCP standards, it is relevant in many developing countries that may lack or have limited standards for clinical research. "In countries where national regulations or requirements do not exist or require supplementation, relevant government officials may designate or adopt, in part or in whole, the [WHO] guidelines as the basis on which clinical trials will be conducted," says the WHO. The WHO GCP guideline is perceived as more general and flexible than many other GCP standards, which some credit for its adoption in many developing countries.

1.2   *Q. If the FDA finalizes the June 2004 proposal in which it proposes to replace the Declaration of Helsinki with existing GCP requirements as the standard*

applicable to foreign studies that are not conducted under a U.S. IND, will the Declaration of Helsinki cease to have formal relevance in U.S. regulations?

A. It appears so, except that the Declaration of Helsinki will continue to have at least indirect relevance given that current FDA GCP, ICH GCP, and related standards around the world derived from the Declaration of Helsinki. By eliminating CFR Section 312.120 of its regulations, the FDA's proposal would eliminate both the mention of the Declaration and the full text of the Declaration itself (i.e., the 1989 version).

In its discussion of the proposed rule, the FDA provided some insights as to its rationale for eliminating a reliance on the Declaration in its regulations. "The Declaration is a document that is subject to change independent of FDA authority," the agency wrote. "As a result, it could be modified to contain provisions that are inconsistent with U.S. laws and regulations. Although revisions to the Declaration could not supersede U.S. laws and regulations, such changes could create the potential for confusion about the requirements for nonIND foreign studies."

1.3 *Q. Given the dramatic increase in foreign clinical studies, what is the HHS policy regarding non-U.S. clinical studies that they regulate or support and whether such foreign studies should operate under Common Rule standards?*

A. Interestingly, as the FDA moves to require its own GCP standards for more foreign clinical studies that will produce data for U.S. regulatory submissions, HHS in many ways appears to be moving in the opposite direction. Although the HHS is now supporting growing numbers of foreign clinical studies, its current position is that any HHS-regulated or supported foreign clinical study must be conducted in a manner consistent with the standards and patient protections specified in the Common Rule and its relevant subparts. This is so despite that fact that the Common Rule, at 45 CFR 46.101(h), states that, "if a Department or Agency head determines that the procedures prescribed by the [foreign] institution afford protections that are at least equivalent to those provided in this policy, the Department or Agency head may approve the substitution of the foreign procedures in lieu of the procedural requirements provided in [the Common Rule]." HHS has not issued any "formal findings of equivalent protection" since the Common Rule was finalized in 1991.

In a March 2005 notice, however, HHS requested public comment on a working group's July 2003 recommendations regarding criteria that the HHS should employ in making such equivalence determinations on foreign patient protection standards. HHS will consider such comments in deciding whether, and if so how, it will proceed in instituting "equivalence protection" assessments and determinations for foreign studies.

1.4 *Q. Given that the FDA now has its long-standing GCP standards and then, in 1997, adopted the ICH GCP guideline as representing "the agency's current thinking on good clinical practices," what standards should a clinical trial sponsor, its monitors, and clinical trial sites follow in conducting a clinical study—the U.S. GCP regulations/guidances or the ICH GCP guideline? Or does it matter?*

A. Since the ICH GCP guideline is more specific than—some would say goes further than—the FDA GCP regulations/guidances in selected areas (see Q1.5), conventional wisdom suggests that a company should use the ICH GCP standards for clinical studies that it intends to use in regulatory submissions globally. Adherence to this guideline, as well as additional regulatory standards of the other ICH regulatory parties, can only be expected to promote the acceptance of the clinical studies in the other ICH regions as well as other countries that subscribe to ICH standards despite not being ICH parties (e.g., Canada).

For studies to be submitted exclusively in the United States, either standard should suffice. It is important to note that FDA officials have stated that the agency will "consider clinical studies conducted under ICH GCP as meeting GCP standards acceptable to FDA."

Agency officials emphasize, however, that studies conducted under an IND must always, at a minimum, meet FDA regulatory requirements. It is also worth noting that, under the FDA's Bioresearch Monitoring Program, agency inspectors continue to assess sponsors, monitors, and investigators against FDA GCP standards exclusively (see Q10.12). Since the ICH GCP provisions are generally seen as being consistent with—and in some cases being more specific than—the FDA GCP regulations/guidelines, FDA inspectors, in theory, should not discover compliance problems when the ICH GCP standards are employed.

FDA officials emphasize that agency inspectors will inspect sponsors, monitors, or investigators exclusively for compliance with FDA GCP standards, regardless of the GCP standard implemented in a trial.

According to CDER's Division of Scientific Investigations (DSI), the center's Bioresearch Monitoring Program (BIMO) is focused primarily on finding deviations from FDA GCP regulations, and *not* deviations from either FDA or ICH GCP guidelines. Following an FDA inspection of a clinical investigator, sponsor/monitor, or CRO, the Form 483-Inspectional Observations that an inspector may leave with the sponsor/monitor, investigator, or CRO should, according to CDER policy, identify ONLY observed deviations from FDA GCP regulations. [Editor's Note: an FDA inspector leaves a Form 483 only if deviations are discovered.] Although deviations from FDA guidelines *should* be identified and discussed in the later-developed establishment inspection report (EIR) and *may* be discussed in a subsequent inspection-related FDA letter (e.g., untitled letter, warning letter) to the firm or investigator, these deviations will be identified separately from the deviations from FDA regulations. DSI staffers do not recall having seen any EIR or inspection-related CDER letter that identified or discussed any deviation specifically from the ICH GCP guideline.

Over time, the differences in emphasis and specificity between the FDA standards and ICH GCP guideline should become less evident. FDA officials have stated that the agency will "take into account the ICH GCPs" in developing new or revising existing regulations and guidance as part of routine GCP program maintenance activities.

1.5   Q. While FDA officials maintain that the ICH's GCP guideline is entirely consistent with the agency's GCP regulations and guidances, there are clearly areas in which the ICH guideline is more detailed or specific, and other areas in which FDA standards are more detailed. What are the most important differences in detail and specificity between FDA GCP and ICH GCP provisions?

A. Although there are differences in specificity, level of detail, and emphasis, the regulatory significance of these differences to clinical research efforts is likely negligible. FDA officials have stated, for example, that the agency will "consider clinical studies conducted under ICH GCP as meeting GCP standards acceptable to FDA."

Further, over time, the differences in emphasis and specificity between the FDA standards and ICH GCP guideline should become less evident. FDA officials have stated that the agency will "take into account the ICH GCPs" in developing new or revising existing regulations and guidance as part of routine GCP program maintenance activities.

Still, since the ICH GCP guideline was released in 1997, several differences have been noted, including the following:

- Unlike FDA regulations and guidances, the ICH GCP guideline recommends that a patient's primary care physician be notified that the patient is enrolling in a clinical trial.
- The ICH GCP guideline states that any source documentation recorded directly on the CRF should be specified in the protocol. FDA regulations and guidances have no such provisions.
- The ICH GCP guideline calls for the completion of a staff delegation of responsibility form. The form is not mentioned in FDA regulations or guidances.
- The ICH GCP guideline explicitly states that the copy of the informed consent form provided to the subject following the informed consent procedure should be a copy of the signed form, while FDA GCP regulations state only that a copy of the form should be provided. In its 1998 information sheets for investigators and IRBs, however, the FDA recommends that the copy provided to subjects be a signed copy.
- The ICH GCP guideline calls for an "impartial witness" to be present in those cases in which an informed consent document is read to a trial subject/legally authorized representative (e.g., when the subject/legally acceptable representative cannot read). FDA regulations require that a "witness" be present during the oral presentation of the elements of informed consent when the short form is used, but do not specify that the witness be impartial. [*Editor's note:* because the short form is so rarely used in the United States, the relevance of these requirements is limited.]
- FDA regulations require that investigators responsible for key clinical studies complete a financial disclosure form, and that the clinical sponsor collect such information and report on the relevant financial interests of, and compensation paid to, such investigators in premarketing applications (e.g., NDAs, BLAs). The ICH GCP guideline has no such provisions, although it does state that the sponsor's agreements with the investigator/institution and/or with any other parties involved with the clinical trial should be in writing, either as part of the protocol or in a separate agreement.
- Although both FDA regulations and ICH GCP provisions for the informed consent process call for the disclosure of appropriate alternative procedures or courses of treatment that may be advantageous to subjects, only ICH GCP calls for the disclosure of the important potential benefits and risks of the alternatives.

- As part of the informed consent process, ICH GCP calls for a statement that monitors, auditors, the IRB and regulatory authorities will be granted direct access to medical records, and for a statement that, by signing the consent, the subject is authorizing such access. FDA regulations require only a statement that notes the possibility that the agency may inspect the records. It is worth noting that the Privacy Rule, which took effect in April 2003 in the United States, calls for a document that informs the subject of the persons, classes of persons, and organizations that will create, disclose, and/or receive protected health information during research (see Section 14).
- When a subject can only be enrolled with the consent of a legally acceptable representative (e.g., minors, patients with severe dementia), ICH GCP states that the subject should be informed about the trial to the extent compatible with the subject's understanding and, if capable, the subject should assent, sign and personally date the written informed consent. FDA regulations have no such specific provisions. However, the FDA's regulations do require that, when children are involved in a trial, the child's assent is required unless the child is not capable of providing assent or the intervention or procedure is intended to provide direct benefit that is important to the child's well being. Further, FDA regulations require additional safeguards to protect the rights and welfare of subjects who are vulnerable to coercion or undue influence. While not specifically required by the regulation, the IRB may determine that the assent of those subjects not able to decide for themselves is an appropriate safeguard.
- In the informed consent process, ICH GCP calls for an explanation as to whether any compensation and any medical treatments will be available if injury occurs for all studies. FDA regulations require such statements only for studies that involve more than minimal risk.
- ICH GCP specifically calls for all informed consents to be signed and dated by the person who conducts the informed consent discussion. In most cases, FDA regulations require only one signature—that of the subject or the legally authorized representative. When a short form written consent document is used to establish that the elements of informed consent have been presented orally to the subject or the subject's legally authorized representative, however, FDA regulations require three signatures: the person conducting the consent interview, the witness to the oral presentation, and the subject or legally authorized representative. In such cases, the subject/legally authorized representative signs the short form, the witness signs the short form and a copy of the summary of what was said to the subject/legally authorized representative, and the person obtaining consent shall sign the copy of the summary. [Editor's note: because the short form is so rarely used in the United States, the relevance of these requirements is limited].
- The ICH guideline specifically calls for an IRB review of subject recruitment procedures, the investigator's brochure, payments and compensation to study subjects, and the curriculum vitae of the investigators. FDA regulations require IRBs to review "all research activities," which is generally understood to include all these elements. FDA guidance documents also call for IRB review of certain recruitment materials and practices.

- While the ICH GCP guideline calls on IRBs to review investigator qualifications, FDA regulations do not explicitly include such a provision.
- FDA regulations allow an expedited initial review of certain types of studies involving no more than minimal risk. The ICH GCP guideline has no such provision.
- The ICH GCP guideline calls on IRBs, when asked, to provide copies of their written procedures and membership lists to investigators, sponsors, or regulatory authorities. FDA regulations require only that IRBs provide such information to regulatory authorities upon request.
- With few exceptions, ICH GCP specifically calls for nontherapeutic trials (i.e., studies in which there is no anticipated direct clinical benefit to the subject) to be conducted only in those subjects who personally provide their consent. FDA regulations have no such provision.
- While, in general, both FDA and ICH GCP set the records retention period at three years for IRBs and two years for sponsors and investigators, the records retention standards differ in some ways, particularly in the starting point for the retention period. The FDA requires sponsors and investigators to retain required records and reports for two years after a marketing application is approved for the drug or, if an application is not approved for the drug, until two years after shipment and delivery of the drug for investigational use is discontinued and the FDA has been so notified. Under the ICH GCP guideline, investigators and sponsors should retain "essential documents" until at least two years after the last approval of a marketing application in an ICH region and until there are no pending or contemplated marketing applications in an ICH region, or at least two years have elapsed since the formal discontinuation of clinical development of the investigational product. It should be noted that some localities and regions have longer retention requirements than either the FDA or ICH.

1.6 Q. Some have pointed out that the versions of ICH GCP guidelines, as adopted in the European Union, United States, and Japan, have differences in wording that may affect the way in which GCP is implemented within the regions. To what degree is this true?

A. It is true that, in making late-stage and minor "edits" to the final ICH GCP guideline before releasing the document in their respective regions, the ICH regulatory bodies, particularly the FDA, revised the guideline in minor ways. After the final GCP guideline was released in all three regions, for example, the European Agency for the Evaluation of Medicinal Products (EMEA) issued a September 1997 release highlighting some of the editorial differences in the regions, although it focused primarily on differences in the U.S. and European versions.

The minor editorial differences between the ICH guidelines as issued in the three regions, however, are not expected to have a material impact on the harmonized ICH standards as applied to clinical trials. As the EMEA's September 1997 release stated, "Regulatory compliance does not depend on a comma or one word but on the overall implementation of the GCP standard."

1.7 Q. While the FDA and other regulatory bodies set basic GCP standards, can sponsors and IRBs establish standards for their studies that are more stringent than established regulatory standards?

A. Sponsors and IRBs can and do establish standards that are more stringent than those set out in FDA GCP and ICH standards. In fact, it can be argued that, while FDA GCP regulations set a minimum "bar" for clinical trial sponsors and investigators, a set of "best research practices" and/or "generally accepted good research practices" that go beyond FDA and ICH standards have been developed in many areas. As one clinical research maxim goes, "GCP standards represent the floor, not the ceiling, of the standards that clinical trial conduct should meet."

Best research practices sometimes develop in response to specific trends or controversies, as seems to be happening most recently with regard to changes in the worldwide attitude toward the use of placebos in clinical research and researcher conflict of interest (see Section 13). The following are examples of common best practice standards that go beyond the provisions of FDA and/or ICH GCP requirements:

- If subjects are being given a drug designed to prevent a disease or prevent the progression of a disease, they should be informed of the chances—in the absence of the study drug or the presence of a placebo—of acquiring the disease or having the disease progress.
- Risks and benefits of alternative approved drugs should be specified in the informed consent.
- If subjects are medically injured by a study drug or procedure, all of the resulting care should be provided at no charge to the subject, and the consent document should so state.
- Sites that conduct more than one study at the same time should have a fair and equitable method for allocating patients across studies.
- Investigators should ensure that medical records for serious adverse events, especially those located off-site, are obtained and thoroughly reviewed. The same principle applies to medical histories—relevant records should be reviewed, and investigators should not rely on patient-completed history forms administered just before consenting to determine study eligibility.
- Decisions on early study discontinuation and withdrawal should be mutually agreed upon by physician and subject.

In many cases, an IRB will have to enforce compliance with institutional policies or state or local requirements that are more stringent than those embodied in the FDA's GCP.

1.8 Q. In terms of key study-related tasks, which ones are likely to be governed specifically by state and local laws?

A. Areas of clinical research that are often affected by state and local laws include the following:

- drug dispensing and administration;
- certain elements of informed consent (e.g., child's assent, capacity to consent, age of consent);

- recording and reporting requirements for sexually transmitted diseases and other communicable diseases, including HIV;
- requirements associated with HIV, fetal, and pregnancy tests, the distribution of contraception to minors, and pregnancy termination;
- patient/medical records confidentiality;
- circumstances requiring autopsy;
- newborn tests for abnormalities, including genetic testing;
- physician supervision and independent practice of clinical staff (e.g., NPs, PAs, RNs, midwives, emergency medical technicians);
- the provision of care/decision-making in emergency and terminal conditions;
- requirements for health care institutions to report care provider fraud and misconduct to state regulatory agencies;
- protections for whistleblowers; and
- indemnification/insurance coverage/compensation for research subjects and investigators.

It is important to note that this is a brief and non-exhaustive list of the clinical research areas that state and local laws can affect. Some specific state requirements, such as California's "Experimental Subjects Bill of Rights," which must be presented to patients in California-based studies, are well known, while others are more obscure. In rare instances, clinical trials may be subject only to state law, provided that they are investigator-sponsored and do not involve interstate commerce (California, for example, has regulations governing such studies).

In general, FDA requirements should be viewed as a minimum standard, and clinical research should meet higher standards when state/local requirements or IRB/medical institution requirements call for them. As the FDA's informed consent regulations (21 CFR 50.25(d)) state, for example, "the informed consent requirements in these regulations are not intended to preempt any applicable Federal, State, or local laws which require additional information to be disclosed for informed consent to be legally effective." As a general rule, if a state law for a particular area listed above is more restrictive or stringent, then this state law preempts federal law, and *vice versa.*

ICH states emphatically that its GCP guidance recognizes state and local laws, and that the GCP guidance is not intended to supersede these laws. For all intents and purposes, GCP best practices include adherence to all state and local laws as they apply to the conduct of clinical research (see Section 22).

[For more information on state-specific laws and regulations, refer to the *State-by-State Clinical Trial Requirements Reference Guide* (September 2004), which is available through www.barnettinternational.com]

1.9   Q. Specifically, who is responsible—the investigator, site/institution, IRB, or sponsor—for ensuring that a clinical study complies with state and local regulations and requirements? Is a clinical sponsor/monitor responsible for being aware of, or monitoring to, the state and local regulations for every state and locality in which clinical sites participating in the company's studies are located?

A. In recent informal correspondence on this issue, the FDA stated that, "all of the parties mentioned have responsibility for complying with state and local laws. For example, the issue of who is a legally authorized representative to sign a consent form in lieu of the subject is controlled by state law. The IRB and the clinical investigator are responsible for ensuring that a consent form is signed by the subject or the subject's legally authorized representative; each, therefore, would have a responsibility for ensuring that state law is followed in this regard.

"Of course, the practice of medicine itself is a matter of state law . . . FDA, of course, is a Federal agency and only has jurisdiction over matters within the scope of federal law. Likewise, states have jurisdiction over matters within the scope of their jurisdiction. It would probably be prudent for a sponsor to be aware of and comply with state and local laws that may cover their activities within a particular jurisdiction."

1.10 Q. Given the proliferation of postmarketing studies for approved drugs (e.g., Phase 4 studies), questions regarding when new IND submissions are necessary for such studies persist. Under FDA law and regulation, when is the submission of an investigational new drug application (IND) required?

A. This is a complex question that requires a correspondingly complex answer. To further complicate the issues relevant to this question, the FDA is said to be in the midst of re-examining situations in which an IND submission is and is not mandatory (see Q 1.13).

In general terms, FDA regulations require sponsors that want to study a new drug or biological product in a clinical investigation to submit a "notice of claimed investigational exemption for a new drug," or IND, to the FDA. The agency defines clinical investigation as "any experiment in which a drug is administered or dispensed to, or used involving, one or more human subjects. For the purposes of this part, an experiment is any use of a drug except for the use of a marketed drug in the course of medical practice."

The IND itself provides an "exemption" from the legal prohibition against the shipping of unapproved drugs in interstate commerce. An approved IND (i.e., an IND that has been reviewed and not placed on clinical hold by the FDA), therefore, constitutes the FDA's tacit permission to do something that would otherwise be a violation of the law—that is, shipping an unapproved new drug across state lines for the purpose of clinical research.

The "investigational use" of approved, marketed products in Phase 4 studies differs from the use of a marketed drug in the course of medical practice, the agency states in an Information Sheet entitled, "Off Label and Investigational Use of Marketed Drugs, Biologics, and Medical Devices." "'Investigational use' suggests the use of an approved product in the context of a clinical study protocol [see 21 CRF 312.3(b)]," the agency states. "When the principal intent of the investigational use of a test article is to develop information about the product's safety or efficacy, submission of an IND [for drugs and biologics] or IDE [for devices] may be required."

FDA regulations, however, provide for certain exemptions from the IND requirements for clinical investigations meeting specific criteria. Agency regulations (21 CFR 312.2(b)) specifically exempt several types of clinical investigations, including some Phase 4 studies, from the need for an IND submission:

1. A clinical investigation of a drug product that is lawfully marketed in the United States, provided that ALL of the following conditions apply:

- The investigation is not intended to be reported to the FDA as a well-controlled study in support of a new indication for use nor intended to be used to support any other significant change in the labeling for the drug.
- If the product is a prescription drug, the investigation is not intended to support a significant change in the product's advertising.
- The investigation does not involve a route of administration or dosage level or use in a patient population or other factor that significantly increases the risks (or decreases the acceptability of the risks) associated with the use of the drug product. In the preamble to the IND regulations published in March 1987, the FDA wrote that an exemption was not necessarily intended to tie the investigator to the doses and routes of administration and patient population(s) described in the approved labeling, but to permit deviations from the approved labeling to the extent that such changes are supported by the scientific literature and generally known clinical experience. In an April 2002 draft guidance (see discussion below), the FDA established that it "recognizes that a considerable amount of professional judgment is exercised in determining whether the conditions significantly increase the risk associated with the use of the drug." Further, in the preamble to its March 1987 regulation, the FDA maintained that, because the assessment of risks involved in a therapeutic procedure is an everyday part of the practice of medicine, the individual investigator should usually be able to determine the applicability of the exemption.
- The investigation is conducted in compliance with the FDA's IRB and informed consent requirements.
- The sponsor/investigator does not represent in a promotional context that an investigational new drug is safe or effective for the purposes for which it is under investigation or otherwise promote the drug, does not "commercially distribute" or "test market" the investigational new drug, or charge for the investigational drug in a clinical trial without prior written approval from the FDA (21 CFR 312.7).

Because Phase 4 studies initiated by a drug manufacturer are, in the majority of cases, designed for commercial purposes and are likely to affect a product's labeling (e.g., comparative claims) or advertising, the FDA has stated that IND submission exemptions for investigations involving drugs lawfully marketed in the United States "will apply primarily to researchers in academia or other institutions."

2. A clinical investigation involving a product from any one of three specific classes of *in vitro* diagnostic biological products—blood grouping serum, reagent red blood cells, and anti-human globulin—provided: (a) it is intended to be used in a diagnostic procedure that confirms the diagnosis made by another, medically established, diagnostic product or procedure; and (b) it is shipped in compliance with FDA regulations applicable to drugs for investigational use in laboratory research animals or *in vitro* tests (21 CFR 312.60).

3. A drug intended solely for tests *in vitro* or in laboratory research animals, provided it is shipped in accordance with FDA regulations applicable to drugs for investigational use in laboratory research animals or *in vitro* tests (21 CFR 312.60).

4. A clinical investigation involving the use of a placebo is exempt, provided the investigation does not otherwise trigger the IND submission requirement.

5. *In vivo* bioavailability and bioequivalence studies are exempt, except that FDA regulations state that INDs are required for *in vivo* bioavailability or bioequivalence studies in humans if the test product is a radioactively labeled drug product, is a cytotoxic drug product, or contains a new chemical entity. Further, INDs are required for the following types of human bioavailability studies that involve a previously approved drug that is not a new chemical entity: (1) a single-dose study in normal subjects or patients when either the maximum single or total daily dose exceeds that specified in the labeling of the approved product; (2) a multiple-dose study in normal subjects or patients when either the single or total daily dose exceeds that specified in the labeling of the approved product; or (3) a multiple-dose study on a controlled-release product for which no single-dose study has been completed.

Finally, FDA regulations provide a mechanism under which sponsors of studies otherwise ineligible for IND exemptions can obtain an agency waiver from IND submission requirements. The agency can grant a waiver if certain criteria are met, including that the sponsor's noncompliance will not pose a significant or unreasonable risk to human subjects (21 CFR 312.10).

In discussing IND exemptions, FDA regulations make clear that IND submission requirements do not apply to the use of an approved drug or biologic for an unlabeled indication "in the practice of medicine." Further, the regulations establish that a clinical investigation that involves an IRB-approved exception from informed consent requirements (21 CFR 50.24) is not eligible for an exemption from IND submission requirements.

The agency concedes that there has been, over the years, considerable uncertainty and confusion over these exemptions, particularly with regard to the use of approved products in Phase 4 clinical studies. Because certain sponsors, particularly practicing physicians, continued to submit hundreds of unnecessary INDs for studies involving approved cancer drugs, the FDA specifically addressed uncertainty in this area, first through the 1996 Reinventing the Regulation of Cancer Drugs initiative and then through a September 2003 guidance entitled, *"IND Exemptions for Studies of Lawfully Marketed Cancer Drug or Biological Products"* (since updated in January 2004, see below). While these documents address IND exemption issues specific to oncology drugs, many of the agency's statements within them are instructive for other classes of drugs as well, and shed light on the agency's interpretations of the requirements highlighted above (see Q1.11).

Under the 1996 initiative, the agency revealed that many physician-investigators submitted INDs for exploratory studies for so-called "off-label indications" for two reasons: (1) IRBs incorrectly believed that an IND was required for such studies; or (2) the pharmaceutical manufacturer agreed to provide a drug free of charge, but mistakenly concluded that the FDA would view this as a promotional activity. In response, the agency established "that providing a drug for study would not, in and of itself, be viewed as a promotional activity if the manufacturer or distributor provides the product for a physician-initiated, bona fide clinical investigation. [FDA also] explained that it is the responsibility of the investigator to determine whether or not an IND is necessary."

1.11 Q. Has the FDA provided specific examples of the applicability of the IND submission exemption to specific types of studies involving marketed drugs in the United States?

A. Although the FDA does not generally believe it is "desirable" to indicate specific situations in which an IND is not required, it offered several examples of such situations in the 1987 IND regulations and the January 2004 guidance entitled, "IND Exemptions for Studies of Lawfully Marketed Cancer Drug or Biological Products" (first published in September 2003). In the former, the agency addresses several case examples about which it was asked directly in response to the proposed regulation:

- "In general, the use in a clinical investigation of a drug in capsule form that is lawfully marketed in tablet form should not, in itself, raise safety concerns necessitating submission of an IND. Of course, there may be exceptions. For example, the agency can foresee circumstances in which reformulation to capsule form of a drug product might so affect its bioavailability as to raise safety concerns warranting submission of an IND. There might also be significant problems involved in grinding up and encapsulating enteric-coated or film-coated tablets. Apart from these exceptions, however, FDA believes that the change from tablet to capsule should rarely result in the removal of a study from the terms of the . . . exemption."
- "FDA would presume that any change from one dosage form to an intravenous (I.V.) dosage form (including a change from an intramuscular (I.M.) dosage form to an I.V. dosage form) would significantly increase the risk so as to warrant an IND."
- "The substitution of an investigational label for an approved label should rarely, if ever, raise safety concerns triggering the need to submit an IND. Similarly, modifications in packaging and labeling that do not impair a drug's stability or quality should not remove a product from the terms of the exemption. Indeed, because the study will be investigational, it is expected that the labeling for the drug will be changed to some extent for purposes of the investigation."
- "There would appear to be few situations in which use of an OTC drug at a dosage level lower than the marketed level would raise safety concerns. However, where a drug is used to treat a life-threatening illness or to prevent irreversible damage, safety concerns might appropriately trigger the need to submit an IND."

In its January 2004 guidance on IND exemptions for approved cancer drugs and biologics, the FDA provides several examples to illustrate the types of oncology studies that are—and that are not—exempt from IND submission requirements. Since the principles upon which these examples are based should be similar across therapeutic categories, the agency's discussions of these study examples may be instructive for other studies as well. It is important to note, however, that just because a study is exempt from IND submission requirements does not mean that the study is exempt from informed consent, IRB, or related GCP requirements.

Studies That Are Generally Exempt

"1. Single-arm, Phase 2 trials using marketed drugs to treat a cancer different from that indicated in the approved labeling and using doses and schedules similar to those in the marketed drug labeling are usually exempt. An exception may exist when standard therapy in the population to be studied is very effective (e.g., is associated with a survival benefit); in that case, use of another regimen may expose patients to the risk of receiving an ineffective therapy and an IND would be necessary.

2. Phase 1 oncology trials of marketed drugs may be considered exempt if such therapy is appropriate for the patient population (i.e., if patients have residual cancer) and if there is no effective therapy (i.e., therapy producing cure or a documented increase in survival) that the patients have not yet received. It remains the investigator's responsibility to use starting doses that appear safe based on approved labeling or detailed literature reports, use incremental changes in dose or schedule, and carefully evaluate toxicity prior to dose escalation.

3. The study of new combinations of drugs would not ordinarily constitute a significant risk if these combinations have been described in the professional medical literature. Even when the regimen described in the literature does not use exactly the doses planned for study, incremental differences in doses from those described in the literature would not normally pose a significant risk and would not require an IND. Because of the danger of synergistic toxicity (i.e., enhanced effects from the combination) occurring with a new drug combination, if there are no data from the literature on its safety, the initial study of a new drug combination should ordinarily be performed under an IND. Synergistic toxicity may be anticipated when one agent interferes with the metabolism or elimination of the other agent; when both agents target the same metabolic pathway or cellular function; or when one agent targets signaling pathways that are reasonably expected to modulate sensitivity to the other agent. If it is determined that synergistic toxicity is likely, animal studies should be considered for determining a safe starting dose for the drug combination in humans.

4. Studies of new routes or schedules of administration not described in the approved labeling are generally exempt if there is sufficient clinical experience described in the literature documenting safety to determine that treatment is safe. On the other hand, initial experience with a new route of administration should be based on studies in animals, and an IND should be submitted.

5. Studies of high-dose therapy in cancer patients are likely to be considered exempt if the studies use adequately evaluated regimes that appear to have an acceptable therapeutic ratio for the population being studied. Similarly, Phase 1 studies involving incremental changes from such well-described regimens are generally exempt."

Studies That Are Generally Not Exempt

"1. Studies of cytotoxic drugs are normally not exempt in patients for whom cytotoxic therapy would not be considered standard therapy and would require special justification. Any use of cytotoxic agents in non-malignant disease (e.g., rheumatoid arthritis, multiple sclerosis) would, most likely, be considered to alter the acceptability of the risk of the agent.

2. Studies of adjuvant chemotherapy (chemotherapy given after surgery to remove cancer) are likely not exempt for the following reasons:
- If the population studied has a low risk of cancer recurring after surgery, treatment with any toxic therapy may indicate a significantly increased risk.

- If standard adjuvant therapy is available and produces a survival benefit, substitution of new therapy for standard therapy poses a significant risk that the new therapy will not produce the same survival benefit.
- If adjuvant trials are properly designed, they usually will be able to demonstrate whether the new therapy is safe and effective, and such results may lead to a marketing application. As discussed earlier, under regulations at 21 CFR 312.2(b)(1), all investigations intended to support marketing of a new product indication, significant change in product labeling, or a significant change in the advertising for a product require an IND. During FDA review of INDs intended to support marketing applications, the Agency will provide feedback about the acceptability of trial design for this purpose.

3. Studies involving substitution of a new agent of unproven activity are generally not exempt in settings where standard therapy provides a cure or increase in survival. For instance, in the first-line treatment of testicular cancer, ovarian cancer, breast cancer, leukemia, and lymphoma, studies of new agents without proven efficacy would likely not be exempt. In this case, the critical judgment is whether it is ethical to withhold standard therapy while testing a new agent.

4. Studies are generally not exempt in settings where animal studies should be conducted to determine a safe starting dose or schedule. For example:

- Initial studies of a marketed drug given by a new route of administration are not likely exempt.
- Unless adequately described in the literature, initial studies of new drug combinations should usually be performed under an IND because of the possible occurrence of synergistic toxicity. As noted earlier, synergistic toxicity may be anticipated when one agent interferes with the metabolism or elimination of the other agent; when both agents target the same metabolic pathway or cellular function; or when one agent targets signaling pathways that are reasonably expected to modulate sensitivity to the other agent.
- Initial studies in humans of changes in the schedule of drug administration should generally be submitted in an IND. Some drugs have demonstrated significantly greater toxicity when given by an alternative schedule (e.g., methotrexate demonstrates much more hematologic toxity when given by prolonged administration compared to intermittent administration).
- Initial studies of drugs intended to be chemosensitizers, radiosensitizers, or resistance modulators should generally be submitted in an IND. Animal studies should be used to estimate the effect of the modulator on toxicity and to allow estimation of a safe starting dose in humans.

5. Studies intended to support approval of a new indication, a significant change in the product labeling, or a significant change in advertising are not exempt (21 CFR 312.2(b)(1)(i), (ii))."

In January 2004, the FDA amended the industry guidance on IND exemptions for cancer therapies specifically to revise its reference to the last group of studies (i.e., in item 5) above. The September 2003 version of the guidance included an additional statement that the FDA deleted in the January 2004 version: "FDA believes that most randomized studies of a size that could support a labeling supplement would fall in this category." In explaining its rationale for the revision, the FDA stated:

"In the September 2003 version, the Agency's final statement was that it believed that most randomized studies of a size that could support a labeling supplement would likely **not** be exempt from IND regulation under 21 CFR 312.2(b)(1)(i), (ii). This is because they would be intended to support approval of a new indication, a significant change in the product labeling, or a significant change in advertising. Experience has shown that this interpretation was formulated too broadly and inappropriately referred to size alone. The Agency has decided to revise this guidance by removing that statement . . . Whether a study could support a change in labeling is a complex determination, based on study design, size, and other factors."

1.12 Q. One of the conditions of an IND exemption is that the sponsor or investigator does not intend to use the results to support significant changes in a product's labeling. But does this mean that, if the sponsor or investigator changes his or her mind, those results cannot later be submitted in a marketing application?

A. Assuming that the sponsor or investigator acted in good faith in taking the IND exemption, those results can be submitted in a marketing application. In the preamble to the 1987 IND regulations, the agency states that, "FDA advises that a study that is conducted in good faith under the terms of the exemption in [FDA regulations] (i.e., without the filing of an IND) will later be acceptable to the agency in support of an IND or marketing application. Therefore, where the agency finds that a study was conducted under the exemption on the reasonable belief that each of the significant elements of the exemption applied, the FDA will not subsequently raise any objections to its acceptance, assuming adequate guarantees of the ethical propriety and scientific validity of the study. On the other hand, where there is evidence that the sponsor had no reasonable basis for concluding that a study should have been exempted, FDA may take other regulatory action, as appropriate . . . As FDA is willing to discuss and advise sponsors on the applicability of the exemption to planned clinical investigations, the agency believes there should be few occasions for determining after the fact that a study did not qualify for the exemption, but should have been conducted under an IND."

1.13 Q. There were rumors that the FDA could be reconsidering when IND submissions will be required in specific circumstances, and when certain types of studies are considered exempt from IND submission requirements. What is happening in this area, specifically?

A. Following the death of a healthy patient in a clinical study in which a researcher administered the unapproved drug hexamethonium bromide, the FDA inspected and subsequently issued a March 2003 warning letter to Alkis Togias, M.D., of the Johns Hopkins Asthma & Allergy Center. In the warning letter, the FDA charged that Togias violated the Federal Food, Drug and Cosmetic Act and FDA regulations by initiating a clinical investigation involving an unapproved new drug without submitting an investigational new drug application.

At the time, some analysts held that the warning letter to the Johns Hopkins University researcher could signal the beginning of an FDA and government effort to re-examine and even tighten its IND exemption criteria for certain types of studies. In fact, during July 2003, the FDA reportedly formed an internal group to re-examine when current regulations require that clinical investigators who serve as study sponsors must submit INDs. While CDER officials acknowledge that an internal committee has considered releasing guidance on the topic, other priorities likely mean that no guidance will be developed or released in the near term.

In its June 2004 regulatory agenda, the FDA did confirm its plans to develop a proposed regulation that will outline criteria for a variety of experimental drug access options for patients not enrolled in formal clinical trials. To be entitled, "Treatment Use of Investigational Drugs," the proposed regulation will propose to permit the treatment use (i.e., the "compassionate use") of investigational drugs in individual patients (including in emergencies), intermediate size patient populations, and larger populations under a treatment protocol or IND.

1.14 Q. So in cases in which an investigator submits an IND (i.e., an "investigator IND") to initiate a study with an approved drug, or in which the investigator determines that the study is exempt from IND submission requirements, what are the regulatory responsibilities of the drug company that manufacturers the drug?

A. In the simplest terms, the investigator is the study sponsor, also called the "sponsor-investigator," in such cases, and he or she would bear all the burdens of the study sponsor. Therefore, the drug firm would not have regulatory responsibilities associated with such studies.

FDA regulations (21 CFR 312.3(b)) emphasize this in defining the term "sponsor-investigator": "an individual who both initiates and conducts an investigation, and under whose immediate direction the investigational drug is administered or dispensed. The term does not include any person other than an individual. The requirements applicable to a sponsor-investigator under this part include both those applicable to an investigator and a sponsor."

The ICH guideline's definition of sponsor-investigator (1.54) is equally clear on the regulatory responsibilities of this individual: "An individual who both initiates and conducts, alone or with others, a clinical trial, and under whose immediate direction the investigational product is administered to, dispensed to, or used by a subject. The term does not include any person other than an individual (e.g., it does not include a corporation or an agency). The obligations of sponsor-investigator include both those of a sponsor and those of an investigator."

1.15 Q. In April 2005, the FDA released a new draft guidance on "exploratory INDs" and "early phase 1 exploratory approaches." What is behind this initiative, and how does it stand to change the agency's long-standing IND requirements?

A. During the last few years, most recently as part of the March 2004 release of the agency's Critical Path initiative, FDA officials have promised the release of a new guidance to help companies bring experimental products into early-stage clinical trials, what some FDA officials initially called "pre-Phase I" human studies. As the document's arrival moved closer, growing numbers of terms—proof-of-mechanism, screening, microdose, exploratory—were being used to characterize the studies that it would authorize or address.

In the April 2005 draft guidance for industry, investigators, and agency reviewers entitled, "Exploratory IND Studies," the FDA encourages industry to exploit the existing flexibility of the current IND regulations (i.e., in terms of the amount of data necessary) to "move ahead more efficiently with the development of promising candidate products while maintaining needed human subject protections." Specifically, the guidance supports what it calls "exploratory IND studies," which it defines as limited studies that occur very early in phase 1, involve very limited human exposure, have no therapeutic intent (e.g., screening studies, microdose studies) and that are "conducted prior to the traditional dose escalation, safety, and tolerance studies that ordinarily initiate a clinical drug development program." Although the agency notes that exploratory IND studies can have multiple goals (e.g., understanding mechanism of action, pharmacokinetics, lead product selection), it claims that the "studies can help identify, early in the process, promising candidates for continued development, and eliminate those lacking promise. As a result, exploratory IND studies may help reduce the number of human subjects and resources, including the amount of candidate product, needed to select promising drugs."

As noted, the draft guidance claims that no change or liberalization of IND standards is necessary to facilitate the exploratory IND. Because they involve dosing a limited number of subjects with a limited dose range for a limited period of time, "limited exploratory IND investigations in humans can be initiated with less, or different, preclinical support than is required for traditional IND studies," the agency emphasizes. Although the draft guidance highlights how all the key elements of the exploratory IND can differ from those of a traditional IND (i.e., clinical development plan, chemistry/manufacturing/controls, and pharmacology/toxicology), it focuses most intently on the "more limited toxicology evaluation recommended for an exploratory IND application," and provides a number of safety program designs based on different study objectives.

1.16 Q. Does it appear that there are any GCP-related implications regarding these so-called "exploratory IND studies"? Given that some of these studies will be undertaken with "more limited" preclinical testing programs to support them, for example, should the potential additional risks be disclosed in the informed consent process?

A. The FDA's April 2005 draft guidance on exploratory IND studies makes no reference to GCP-related issues. In theory, however, the types of issues that such exploratory Phase 1 studies raise should not be any different than those raised by more traditional early-stage Phase 1 studies. In fact, given that most exploratory IND studies will involve the administration of sub-therapeutic doses of a candidate product or products over a limited duration (e.g., 7 days), the FDA states in the draft guidance that "the potential risks to human subjects are less than for a traditional phase 1 study." The agency also claims that the exploratory study approach can reduce risks in other ways, including the number of human subjects needed to select promising drugs.

1.17 Q. FDA officials and agency guidance documents frequently use the term "clinical equipoise" when discussing the development of policy regarding GCP issues. What does this term mean, and how is it applied to current thinking at the agency?

A. The agency employs certain guiding principles in developing policy. In this case, the principle of "clinical equipoise" is used in developing policy in certain GCP-related areas—for example, in the conduct of studies in emergency settings and Year 2000 revisions to the Declaration of Helsinki (see Q1.1 and Q1.2).

The principle of clinical equipoise was defined by Dr. Benjamin Freedman:

"At the start of the trial, there must be a state of clinical equipoise regarding the merits of the regimens to be tested, and the trial must be designed in such a way as to make it reasonable to expect that, if it is successfully conducted, clinical equipoise will be disturbed."

Clinical equipoise means a genuine uncertainty on the part of the expert medical community about the comparative therapeutic merits of each arm of a clinical trial. The tenet of clinical equipoise provides a clear moral foundation to the requirement that the health care of subjects not be disadvantaged by researchers and other study staff. In other words, there should be a "balance" or relative "equality" between the arms of a study before it is conducted. Therefore, a study subject might be indifferent as to which arm he or she is randomized.

As the FDA states in its information sheet entitled, "Exception from Informed Consent for Studies Conducted in Emergency Settings: Regulatory Language and Excerpts from the Preamble," "when the relative benefits and risks of the proposed intervention, as compared to standard therapy are unknown, or thought to be equivalent or better, there is clinical equipoise between the historic intervention and the proposed test intervention" (60 FR 49086 at 49093, September 21, 1995, preamble to Protection of Human Subjects, Informed Consent; Proposed Rule).

The purpose of randomized controlled trials is to test a hypothesis regarding a proposed intervention (a study drug or device). It would not be good clinical practice to conduct a trial:

- if it were known with a reasonable degree of certainty that the study drug's risks outweighed its benefits; or
- if it were known with a reasonable degree of certainty that the study drug's efficacy was inferior to other approved treatments.

The basic principle is that it would not be ethical to randomize patients to a treatment known to be inferior.

Thus, when considering trial designs (acceptability of controls), proposed study subpopulations (children, the aged, childbearing women), study conditions (comatose patients, serious outcomes), and specific interventions (thrombolytics, other potent drugs), agency officials apply this principle in their decision-making.

Although clinical equipoise is now considered to be an important consideration in the ethical conduct of medical research, there continues to be active debate regarding the use of equipoise analysis in evaluating the ethics of a particular study and in evaluating international research conducted in third world countries (see Hellman, D. "Evidence, Belief and Action: The Failure of Equipoise to Resolve the Ethical Tension in the Randomized Clinical Trial," *J Law Med Ethics* 30:375-80, Fall 2002;

London, A.J. "Equipoise and International Human-Subjects Research," *Bioethics* 15:312-32, August 2001; and Crouch, R.A. "Eligibility, Extrapolation, and Equipoise: Unlearned Lessons in the Ethical Analysis of Clinical Research," *IRB* 23:6-9, July-August 2001).

1.18 Q. In discussing sponsor versus investigator GCP responsibilities and liabilities, the concept of "learned intermediaries" is sometimes used. In general, how does this concept differentiate responsibilities between the two entities?

A. Historically, the legal doctrine of "learned intermediaries" was protective of drug manufacturers in product liability actions, given that prescription medicines could not be dispensed without a physician's prescription, which is based on the examination of a patient, medical history, diagnosis, and related factors. The physician was "learned" in both the practice of medicine and his or her patient's condition, and served as an intermediary between the manufacturer of the drug and the patient. In essence, the manufacturer relied on the "learned intermediary" to help ensure the proper use of the drug.

In defending drug manufacturers against suits involving clinical trials, defense attorneys sometimes use the "learned intermediaries" doctrine among other defenses. To the extent that the doctrine is relevant in this context, the investigator is the learned intermediary and has the legal responsibility to evaluate each study patient and to exercise medical judgment in the use of treatment interventions, including the study drug (although, given the study protocol, etc., he or she has less flexibility in doing so than in general practice). The informed consent document is, in part, meant to explain differing study responsibilities to a patient by clarifying the limits of the physician's role and ability in the study to be a "learned intermediary"—that is, the clinical investigator/trial subject relationship does not represent and conform to the conventional treating physician/patient relationship.

Decided in 2001, the case of *Kernke v. The Menninger Clinic* established an important precedent in delineating the responsibilities of study sponsors and clinical investigators. Mr. Kernke, who had a medical history of schizophrenia and unnatural behavior, including several hospital admissions resulting from suicide attempts, agreed to participate in both a clinical study for an investigational schizophrenia treatment and an open-label follow-on study of the same drug, both of which were sponsored by Hoechst Marion Roussel. During the second study, Mr. Kernke wandered off and died in a wooded area. His family sued the Menninger Clinic, three of its physicians, and Aventis Pharmaceuticals, the successor-in-interest to Hoechst Marion Roussel.

Ultimately, defense attorneys for Aventis were successful in arguing that the learned intermediary doctrine applies to clinical drug studies. The court held that the sponsor had warned the study physicians that patients were at risk of worsening schizophrenic symptoms, depression, and suicidal thoughts, and that it was the physicians' responsibility—and not the sponsor's—to conduct the study, a ruling consistent with FDA GCP regulations. In its decision, the court recognized that the study sponsor does not actually conduct the investigation, and that it is the investigator or subinvestigator who is responsible for all trial-related medical decisions.

[For further insights on this case, see Kuckelman, John, "Patient Safety in Clinical Trials: Whose Legal Duty of Care?" *GCPj* 10:21-23, January 2003.]

Further Reading

Meinert, Curtis L., *Clinical Trials: Design, Conduct and Analysis,* New York: Oxford University Press, 1986.

Code of Federal Regulations, Title 21–Food and Drugs Good Clinical Practice Parts 11, 50, 54, 312, 314.

ICH Good Clinical Practice: Consolidated Guideline (E6), 1997.

DiJohnson, Celeste, "Successful Design and Conduct of a Treatment IND Program," *Drug Information Journal,* 34:165-72, 2000.

Parascandola, Mark, "The History of Clinical Research in the United States," *J Clinical Research Practice* 1:7-20, Spring 1999.

Friedman, Lawrence M., Furberg, Curt, and Demets, David L., *Fundamentals of Clinical Trials,* New York: Springer Verlag, 3rd Ed., 1998.

Acknowledgments

Douglas Mackintosh, DrPH, MBA, MS Hyg, and Vernette Molloy, MBA, RN, of GCPA, Inc.; John Serio, JD, Brown, Rudnick, Berlack Israels, LLP, Boston, MA.

Section 2:
Investigators/Sites

2.1 Q. When is an individual considered "qualified" to conduct a clinical trial? For example, can non-physicians, such as Ph.D.s, Pharm.D.s, D.O.s, or D.D.S.s, be considered qualified to serve as principal investigators?

A. FDA GCP regulations at 21 CFR 312.53(a) require that investigators be "qualified by training and experience as appropriate experts to investigate the drug." The ICH GCP guideline adds that an investigator "should be qualified by education, training, and experience to assume responsibility for the proper conduct of the trial and should meet all the qualifications specified by the applicable regulatory requirements."

Although the FDA's GCP regulations make no reference to a medical degree or other specific education or training necessary to qualify as an investigator, the ICH GCP guideline is somewhat more definitive. In Section 2.7 of "The Principles of ICH GCP," the guideline states that "the medical care given to, and medical decisions made on behalf of, subjects should always be the responsibility of a qualified physician or, when appropriate, of a qualified dentist."

In recent informal correspondence on this question, the FDA stated that, "while technically a non-physician can be a principal investigator, this requires that the non-physician be qualified to personally conduct or personally supervise all aspects of the study. In practice, we have found it very rare that a non-physician can comply with this requirement. In general, where we have seen non-physicians listed on the 1572 as a principal investigator we usually would find an M.D., as a subinvestigator, to perform those study functions requiring the appropriate level of medical expertise. For example, a Ph.D. pharmacologist may be listed as a principal investigator on a pharmacokinetic study with an M.D. as a subinvestigator. Another example might be a clinical psychologist principal investigator with an M.D. subinvestigator."

As a general rule, a non-M.D. can be listed on the Form FDA 1572 as the principal investigator, provided that there is an M.D. involved in the study to assume medical responsibility for enrolled subjects.

Frequently in the past, the FDA has been asked specifically about whether non-physicians can serve as investigators. One of the more definitive declarations of FDA's policy on this subject came in an October 4, 1989, memo (see exhibit below) from Office of Drug Evaluation I (ODE I) Director Robert Temple, M.D., and then-ODE II Director James Bilstad, M.D., which stated:

"Qualified individuals who are not M.D.'s can participate in clinical trials either as principal investigators or sub-investigators provided that an M.D. or D.O. (or D.D.S. depending upon the study) is either a sub-investigator or is listed in the IND as an individual who will be responsible for drug administration and evaluation of patient safety."

In a 1983 response to a letter addressing the participation of clinical pharmacists as principal investigators, then-FDA Associate Commissioner for Health Affairs Stuart Nightingale wrote:

"In [your] letter you posed the question whether Doctors of Pharmacy (Pharm.D.) may serve as investigators in clinical pharmacological studies of investigational drugs. You noted that you have received varying interpretations of our regulations on

M E M O R A N D U M   DEPARTMENT OF HEALTH AND HUMAN SERVICES
PUBLIC HEALTH SERVICE
FOOD AND DRUG ADMINISTRATION
CENTER FOR DRUG EVALUATION AND RESEARCH

DATE: October 4, 1989

FROM: Director, Office of Drug Evaluation I, HFD-100
Director, Office of Drug Evaluation II, HFD-500

SUBJECT: Non-M.D.'s as Clinical Investigators and Monitors

TO: Division Directors

At the June 1, 1989 Division Directors' Policy Meeting, one of the topics was
FDA policy on qualifications of principal investigators. It was agreed that
FDA policy should continue to be as stated in the July 16, 1980 memorandum
from Dr. Finkel, but that the memo should be updated to reflect the wording of
the IND Rewrite as follows:

Clinical Investigators

Qualified individuals who are not M.D.'s can participate in clinical
trials either as principal investigators or sub-investigators provided
that an M.D. or D.O. (or D.D.S. depending upon the study) is either a
sub-investigator or is listed in the IND as an individual who will be
responsible for drug administration and evaluation of patient safety.

Clinical Monitors

Qualified individuals who are not M.D.'s can serve as monitors of clinical
trials provided that an M.D., D.O., or D.D.S. is involved in the review
and evaluation of the ensuing clinical data and the adverse reactions.

Please remind division staff of the above policy.

Robert Temple, M.D.

James Bilstad, M.D.

DEPARTMENT OF HEALTH & HUMAN SERVICES

Public Health Service

Food and Drug Administration
Rockville MD 20857

MAY 1 0 1983

Peter H. Vlasses, Pharm.D.
Associate Director, Clinical Pharmacology Unit
Thomas Jefferson University Hospital
11th and Walnut Streets
Philadelphia, PA 19107

Dear Dr. Vlasses:

Your letter of February 24, 1983 to Dr. Hayes has been
referred to me for response. In that letter you posed the
question whether Doctors of Pharmacy (Pharm.D.s) may serve as
investigators in clinical pharmacological studies of
investigational drugs. You noted that you have received
varying interpretations of our regulations on this point from
different manufacturers who sponsor clinical pharmacological
studies.

It has long been FDA policy to accept Doctors of Pharmacy as
primary investigators of studies of investigational drugs
within their areas of expertise. Because such studies may
require the diagnosis of disease and the recognition and
treatment of adverse reactions or other medical incidents
occurring during the course of the study, we have required
that a person licensed to diagnose and treat disease be
officially associated with the study to be performed. This
is ordinarily done by naming such an individual in item 6(f)
of the Form FD-1572 as being responsible to the principal
investigator of record. Alternatively, both the Doctor of
Pharmacy and the licensed individual may sign the Form
FD-1572 as co-investigators, having equal responsibility in
the performance of the study in question.

I trust that this clarifies FDA policy on the matter.

Sincerely yours,

Stuart L. Nightingale, M.D.
Associate Commissioner for
Health Affairs

DEPARTMENT OF HEALTH & HUMAN SERVICES

Public Health Service

Original dated: April 3, 1990

Food and Drug Administration
Rockville MD 20857

American Association of Colleges of Pharmacy
Attention: Carl E. Trinca, Ph. D.
1426 Prince Street
Alexandria, Virginia 22314

Dear Dr. Trinca:

Your letter of November 28, 1989, asked two questions about the qualifications for clinical investigators. Please excuse my delayed response.

You asked whether FDA would consider pharmacists, especially Pharm.D.'s with adequate training and experience eligible to be principal investigators in 1) pharmacokinetic studies and 2) clinical efficacy studies. This question has been addressed on a number of occasions, beginning in 1980 with Dr. Marion Finkel, then director of the Office of Scientific Evaluation (now called the Offices of Drug Evaluation I and II), and most recently in a memorandum (enclosed) from the Directors of the Offices of Drug Evaluation. In 1980 and at present, the conclusion is the same: pharmacists can serve as principal investigators in any clinical trial. Section 505(i) of the Food, Drug and Cosmetic Act requires that FDA assure that the investigational drug will be provided only to "experts qualified by training and experience to investigate" a new drug. Whether or not FDA will permit a particular pharmacist to be an investigator in a clinical study will be determined on a case by case basis, and may depend on the type of study (pharmacokinetic study, clinical efficacy study) proposed in the IND.

You also asked whether board certification is likely to become an important indicator of whether a person is qualified to be a principal investigator. Certainly, as boards become more widespread, and it becomes more and more probable that well-trained investigators will have them, lack of Boards will become more conspicuous. Nonetheless, the totality of the proposed investigator's experience will be considered and it is improbable that Boards will become necessary.

I hope this is helpful to you. If I can be of further assistance, please contact me.

Sincerely yours,

Carl Peck, M.D
Director
Center for Drug Evaluation and Research
Food and Drug Administration

ENCLOSURE

this point from different manufacturers who sponsor pharmacological studies. It has long been FDA policy to accept Doctors of Pharmacy as primary investigators of studies of investigational drugs within their areas of expertise. Because such studies may require the diagnosis of disease and the recognition and treatment of adverse reactions or other medical incidents occurring during the course of the study, we have required that a person licensed to diagnose and treat disease be officially associated with the study to be performed. This is ordinarily done by naming such an individual in the Form [FDA-1572] as being responsible to the principal investigator of record. Alternatively, both the Doctor of Pharmacy and the licensed individual may sign the form [FDA-1572] as <u>co-investigators</u>, having equal responsibility in the performance of the study in question."

According to an American College of Clinical Pharmacy (ACCP) commentary appearing in *Pharmacotherapy* (2000;20(5):599-608), Nightingale then responded to an ACCP request for clarification on whether the above comments applied only to pharmacokinetic studies:

"Doctors of Pharmacy may serve as clinical investigators for both clinical pharmacology studies and clinical trials of a drug provided they do so in conjunction with a person licensed to diagnose and treat disease." In its commentary, ACCP notes that FDA again emphasized "that a physician be a subinvestigator to assess the patient and make medical decisions."

An April 1990 response from then-CDER Director Carl Peck, M.D., to a similar American Association of Colleges of Pharmacy clarification request stated:

"You asked whether FDA would consider pharmacists, especially Pharm.D.'s with adequate training and experience eligible to be principal investigators in 1) pharmacokinetic studies and 2) clinical efficacy studies. This question has been addressed on a number of occasions, beginning in 1980 with Dr. Marion Finkel, then director of the Office of Scientific Investigations (now called the Offices of Drug Evaluation I and II), and most recently in a [1989] memorandum . . . from the Directors of the Offices of Drug Evaluation. In 1980 and at present, the conclusion is the same: pharmacists can serve as principal investigators in any clinical trial. Section 506(1) of the Food, Drug, and Cosmetic Act requires that FDA assure that the investigational drug will be provided only to 'experts qualified by training and experience to investigate' a new drug. Whether or not FDA will permit a particular pharmacist to be an investigator in a clinical study will be determined on a case by case basis, and may depend on the type of study (pharmacokinetic study, clinical efficacy study) proposed in the IND.

"You also asked whether board certification is likely to become an important indicator of whether a person is qualified to be a principal investigator. Certainly, as boards become more widespread, and it becomes more and more probable that well-trained investigators will have them, lack of boards will become more conspicuous. Nonetheless, the totality of the proposed investigator's experience will be considered and it is improbable that boards will become necessary."

2.2   *Q. Although they do not all appear in the FDA's GCP regulations or the ICH GCP guideline, terms such as "principal investigator," "co-principal investigator," and "co-investigator" are commonly used in the clinical research vernacular. What do these terms mean?*

A. There is much confusion in the field regarding several study-related terms, including principal investigator (PI), co-principal investigator, investigator, and co-investigator. While there may be more of a common understanding of the term "principal investigator" (the responsible leader of the team of individuals involved in a study at a particular site), there remains considerable confusion over how others involved in a trial, such as those mentioned, relate to the principal investigator.

To complicate matters, the term "principal investigator" and related terms traditionally have had somewhat different connotations in the United States and Europe, although the influence of the harmonized ICH GCP guideline (E6) will likely address some of these differences. Within Europe, in fact, there is likely as much confusion about the use of the various terms as there is in the United States. In the glossary of the 1991 European Directive on GCP, the term "principal investigator" was suggested as the term for the coordinating investigator in a multicenter study involving multiple investigators. Where there was more than one coordinator for such studies, these coordinators were called "co-principal investigators."

Because it offers definitions for "investigator," "principal investigator," and "coordinating investigator," the ICH GCP Guideline is likely to encourage consistency in the use of these terms in the future:

Investigator: "A person responsible for the conduct of the clinical trial at a trial site. If a trial is conducted by a team of individuals at a trial site, the investigator is the responsible leader of the team and may be called the principal investigator" (ICH 1.34). While they do not mention or define the term "principal investigator," FDA regulations at 21 CFR 312.3(b) define "investigator" as "an individual who actually conducts a clinical investigation (i.e., under whose immediate direction the drug is administered or dispensed to a subject). In the event an investigation is conducted by a team of individuals, the investigator is the responsible leader of the team."

Coordinating Investigator: "An investigator assigned the responsibility for the coordination of investigators at different centers participating in a multicenter trial" (1.19).

In Europe, the term "co-investigator" was the pre-ICH term that was subsequently replaced by the term "subinvestigator" (see Q2.3 below for further discussion of subinvestigators).

FDA officials openly acknowledge that agency regulations and guidance documents could offer greater clarification on these terms. In recent informal correspondence on this issue, CDER Associate Director for Medical Policy Robert Temple, M.D., stated that "a lot of this needs definition. The term sub-investigator is [also] extremely ambiguous. It's used in the 1572 and it refers to everybody from the nurse to the other doctor who's in charge. I would say that the term is in evolution."

Still, from a regulatory perspective, Temple believes that particular trial-related titles are less important than the idea that trial-related documentation capture the commitments of those assuming important trial-related roles. "What we really want is that any person who functions as an investigator at an institution sign the [Form FDA]1572 [Statement of Investigator], even if that's multiple people. Because we want them to make the commitments that are in the 1572. It can't be somebody who isn't taking responsibility for the study, so you wouldn't have one of the nurses or a fellow do it. But I think our ultimate hope is that every person who is an actual investigator would just sign it, and they can call themselves principal investigator or co-investigator or whatever they feel like."

Many believe that the ideal clinical research model features one principal investigator who serves as the "captain of the ship"—that is, the individual who functions as a single point of control for a particular study at an investigational site. During a study's conduct, all other individuals involved in the study at that trial site would report to this principal investigator. In this model, the investigator's responsibilities are not "shared" or divided between different individuals.

On the Form FDA 1572-Statement of Investigator, this designation is indicated on the "investigator" line. It is worth noting that Block #1 of the 1572 form asks for the "name and address of the investigator," making clear the assumption that this would be a single person. In contrast, Block #6 of the 1572 asks for the "names of the subinvestigators . . . who will be assisting the investigator in the conduct of the investigation(s)," making clear that one or more names may be provided."

Having a single individual serve as the principal investigator may have other advantages. Some FDA field inspectors report being more comfortable when a single name appears in the investigator block on the 1572.

While designations on other documents, such as grants and publications, may use any of the jumble of staff title terminology listed above, the Form FDA 1572, the research agreement, and the staff delegation form should unambiguously identify who is in charge of the study.

2.3   Q. What is a subinvestigator, and how does a subinvestigator relate to a principal investigator? Since subinvestigators conduct important trial-related tasks (e.g., make clinical decisions), must a subinvestigator meet the same "training and experience" qualifications as an investigator? Can nurse coordinators, ARNPs, PAs, Pharm.D.s or Ph.D.s be subinvestigators? And who must be listed as subinvestigators on the FDA Form 1572-Statement of Investigator? Can subinvestigators be investigators that recruit patients at other offices or sites, or must a subinvestigator work at the same office/facility as the investigator?

A. Under FDA regulations (21 CFR Section 312.3(b)), an "investigator" is "an individual who actually conducts a clinical investigation (i.e., under whose immediate direction the drug is administered or dispensed to a subject). In the event an investigation is conducted by a team of individuals, the investigator is the responsible leader of the team. 'Subinvestigator' includes any other individual member of that team." Block #6 in the Form FDA 1572-Statement of Investigator asks for the "names of the subinvestigators (e.g., research fellows, residents, RNs) who will be assisting the investigator in the conduct of the investigation."

In essence, a subinvestigator is any other member (i.e., other than the investigator in charge of the study) of the study team who makes clinical decisions during the study. The ICH GCP guideline defines subinvestigator as, "any individual member of the clinical trial team designated and supervised by the investigator at a trial site to perform critical trial-related procedures and/or to make important trial-related decisions (e.g., residents, research fellows, RNs)." The implication, then, is that the subinvestigator will have a clinical degree and training.

Since the investigator signs the Form FDA 1572 while the subinvestigator does not, it is the investigator who assumes all of the commitments specified in the form, including ensuring "that all associates, colleagues, and employees assisting in the conduct of the study(ies) are informed about their obligations in meeting the above requirements." Confusion frequently arises about who should be listed as subinvestigators on the 1572. Normally, these are the people who make study-related medical decisions regarding the diagnosis and treatment of the disease under investigation. Those who are responsible for completing study paperwork need not be listed on the 1572.

Today, however, FDA officials continue to acknowledge that "subinvestigator" is among several trial-related terms that could use further clarification, despite agency attempts to clarify this area in the past (see Q2.2 above). In the preamble to its 1987 IND regulations, for example, the FDA specifically responded to a request that the agency define the term "subinvestigator," and that it clarify whether the term includes non-physicians, nurses, technicians, and other assistants to the clinical investigator. "Studies frequently are conducted by a team of individuals who share responsibility for designing and conducting the investigation," the agency stated. "The principal investigator is the responsible leader of that team. Subinvestigators include all other professionals who assist the principal investigator in the design and conduct of the investigation. Subinvestigators would not include those technicians and other [assistants] who assume no responsibility for the conduct of the study."

In recent informal correspondence regarding this question, the FDA stated that, "in general, if individuals involved in the conduct of the study are performing functions within the scope of their professional license they would be deemed to be qualified. A subinvestigator may, but does not necessarily have to have the same credentials as the principal investigator . . . However, the investigator is responsible for fulfilling all of the commitments listed in Block #9 [Commitments of Form FDA 1572] at all of the remote sites. If the investigator cannot realistically accomplish these responsibilities, it would be preferred if the subinvestigator at a remote site sign a separate 1572 as investigator for that site."

As a practical matter, NPs, PAs, and other care providers who make clinical decisions regarding study subjects should be listed as subinvestigators. The same advice applies to clinicians who write orders for, or "prescribe," the study drug for each subject. Some sponsors request that pharmacists who prepare a study drug based on patient characteristics such as weight or body mass index also be included as subinvestigators.

2.4   Q. Under FDA regulations (21 CFR Section 312.3), an investigator is "an individual who actually conducts a clinical investigation (i.e., under whose immediate direction the drug is administered or dispensed to a subject). In the event that an investigation is conducted by a team of individuals, the investigator is the responsible leader of the team." Is there a definition for "immediate direction," and specifically, what study duties can an investigator delegate to a subinvestigator or other site staff?

A. An investigator's role in supervising all study-related activities is an area that is of growing concern to the FDA. In fact, at press time, the agency was developing a new guidance on the topic and hoped to release the guidance by mid-2005 (see Q2.7 below).

In earlier informal correspondence on this question, the FDA noted that, "we are not aware of a specific definition of the term 'immediate direction' other than its common definition. Again, if individuals are acting within the scope of their professional license with respect to both the functions they are performing and the level of supervisory medical oversight required under such license, they would be presumed to be qualified. The duties that can or cannot be delegated by the investigator vary from case to case depending upon the study and the professional qualifications of the individual to whom they are delegated. Although investigators may delegate virtually any duty, they may not delegate responsibility, and remain responsible for the overall proper conduct of the study, even for delegated duties."

A best practice suggestion is that a sponsor discuss the delegation of activities with the investigator prior to signing him or her for a trial, and have the specifics of the resultant agreement addressed in clinical trial contractual documents (see Q2.6).

2.5 *Q. In Section 4.1.5, the ICH GCP guideline states that the investigator should maintain a list of appropriately qualified persons to whom the investigator has delegated significant trial-related duties. What are considered significant duties to be included on this list and what are considered non-significant duties that should not be delineated on this list?*

A. In a January 2005 informal response to this question, the FDA stated that, "the ICH guidance doesn't elaborate on what is meant by significant trial related duties, leaving this open to opinion. However, it seems reasonable that in the context of this section of the guidance one can assume that the investigator would be delegating trial related duties for which the investigator would normally be responsible. For example, screening and enrolling subjects, performing protocol required tests and exams, and evaluating subjects' responses to the test article (e.g. assessing AEs, etc.). In general, any duty that would impact significantly on subject safety, protocol compliance and quality and integrity of important study data could be considered significant."

2.6 *Q. To what category of staff may a principal investigator delegate study tasks?*

A. As noted above and in Q2.7 below, a new CDER guidance document on an investigator's supervision of a clinical trial is likely to speak to an investigator's relationship the other site personnel involved in a study.

The principal investigator may delegate many study tasks to site staff—provided that they are qualified to perform the task and it is within the scope of that person's professional licensure if the task requires a license. Such determinations are based not on FDA requirements alone, but on local laws and regulations as well.

The principal investigator, for example, may delegate physical exams to a nurse practitioner, advanced practice nurse, or PA. Most state Nurse Practice Acts do not permit an RN without an advanced practice certification to perform physical exams (not to be confused with physical assessments, which RNs routinely perform). In the same manner, a principal investigator may delegate administration of an intravenous study drug to an RN, but not to a medical assistant. Informed consents should be obtained by staff who are qualified by education and background to adequately explain the details of the study.

In recent industry talks, FDA compliance officials have noted that clinical investigators should not "over-delegate to non-physicians." For example, noted Robert

Shibuya, M.D., a medical officer in the Good Clinical Practice Branch II within CDER's Division of Scientific Investigations in a May 2004 speech, investigators should not delegate responsibility for making a "diagnosis that qualifies/determines eligibility for entry into a clinical study."

Clearly, there are other tasks that a principal investigator cannot delegate. The principal investigator, or another study staff physician, is responsible for determining if a subject must go off study because of an adverse event, for example. In all cases, the principal investigator holds sole responsibility for the general conduct of the study at his or her site, including, but not limited to, ensuring that all study-related processes and procedures are conducted in a safe manner and as specified in the protocol.

2.7 Q. What are CDER's specific concerns and goals in developing this new guidance regarding an investigator's responsibilities in supervising a clinical study?

A. According to CDER officials, a primary goal of the new guidance will be to establish its views of what it means for an investigator to properly "supervise" a clinical study. Signing all the required regulatory forms and simply turning over the study to others is not appropriate, the agency is expected to emphasize in the guidance document.

The second primary goal for the agency will be to establish its views on what it means to protect the rights, safety and welfare of study participants. DSI officials have been frustrated in the past with investigators who claim to have "followed the protocol," but who have been found to have ignored obvious symptoms of illness, failed to identify cases as adverse events, and other important developments. The agency, therefore, will seek to use the guidance to make clear that investigators have an obligation to maintain what one CDER source called "a certain standard of awareness in conducting a clinical study."

2.8 Q. Assume that a sponsor is adding a new investigator and site to an ongoing study in an effort to expedite enrollment. Can the sponsor ship the investigational drug to the new site, and can the investigator enroll and administer the investigational drug or control to subjects, before the FDA is notified about the investigator's addition to the study?

A. Yes, provided the sponsor notifies the agency of the addition of the investigator within 30 days. According to 312.30(c), "A sponsor shall submit a protocol amendment when a new investigator is added to carry out a previously submitted protocol, except that a protocol amendment is not required when a licensed practitioner is added in the case of a treatment protocol under 21 CFR 312.34. Once the investigator is added to the study, the investigational drug may be shipped to the investigator and the investigator may begin participating in the study. The sponsor shall notify FDA of the new investigator within 30 days of the investigator being added."

What does the FDA consider "once the investigator is added to the study" (i.e., the point at which the drug may be shipped and the investigator may participate in the study) to be? In informal correspondence on this issue, agency staffers noted that they would consider this to be the point at which the sponsor had collected all the necessary regulatory documentation from the investigator—in other words, the information listed in 21 CFR 312.53(c), including a signed investigator statement (Form FDA-1572) and curriculum vitae.

2.9 *Q. What are the site affiliation requirements for principal investigators and subinvestigators? And how are these requirements interpreted regarding hospitals/clinics with many satellite offices, or situations in which a site management organization (SMO) has a principal investigator under whom dozens of subinvestigators in multiple states work?*

A. In recent informal correspondence on this question, the FDA stated that, "the principal investigator remains fully responsible for fulfilling the commitments in block #9 [Commitments Section] of the 1572 at all of the remote sites. If the investigator cannot realistically accomplish these responsibilities, as implied in your question, it would be preferred if the subinvestigator at the remote sites each sign a separate 1572 and act as investigator for that site. Also, the ICH GCP guideline (E6) defines investigator as a person responsible for the conduct of the clinical trial at a study site. To the effect that ICH E6 is official FDA guidance, we support this definition."

2.10 *Q. Although much has been written about clinical investigator and institutional conflicts of interest and the regulatory and ethical need to disclose such potential conflicts to research subjects (see Q5.38), there are others in the research process that can have potentially problematic conflicts, including research subjects themselves. What, if any, regulatory responsibilities do clinical investigators have in identifying and responding to such conflicts of interest?*

A. The FDA is not known to have any requirements calling for clinical investigators, IRBs, or sponsors to identify or address possible research subject conflicts of interest. This form of potential financial conflict of interest is just now being discussed more openly. In a May 2004 *Journal of the National Cancer Institute* article, Helft, Ratain, Epstein, and Siegler write that, "in recent years, several research subjects and some family members have told us (via personal communications) that they had bought or intended to buy stock in the company sponsoring the clinical trial in which the research subject was enrolled. Moreover, clinical investigators from other institutions have occasionally recounted that their own research subjects have expressed the same intentions. More recently, and perhaps more ominously, evidence has surfaced that healthy individuals have insinuated themselves into clinical trials to obtain access to private information about drugs that are under clinical trial."

While acknowledging that study subjects with possible financial conflicts of interest may not be common, the authors emphasize that the phenomenon raises legal (e.g., insider trading), ethical, and scientific issues. "In terms of science, such conflicts of interest may interfere with the honest and straightforward reporting of a treatment's toxic effects and participant responses in ways that could compromise the primary scientific goals of early phase clinical trials," they state.

The article authors go on to describe a situation in which a study subject informed them that he owned stock in the company sponsoring the Phase 1 trial in which he was enrolled. Later, the authors stumbled upon an Internet chat room that was dedicated to sharing opinions and information about stocks, including the trial sponsor and that featured a posting in which "real, essentially accurate, and clearly nonpublic information about this research subject's positive clinical response to an investigational agent was being described and discussed . . . , often within days of the information being available to us." Although the information was posted anonymously, the investigators suspected that the subject was attempting to bolster the price of the stock, and became concerned about the accuracy of the research subject's previous reports of his "improving symptoms." They also reported that their communications and interactions with the subject were affected until the source of the "nonpublic information" posted on the Internet was found to be "a contact of the research subject" who learned of the subject's progress from the subject himself.

[see "Inside Information: Financial Conflicts of Interest for Research Subjects in Early Phase Clinical Trials," Helft, Ratain, Epstein, Siegler, *Journal of the National Cancer Institute,* Oxford: May 5, 2004. Vol. 96, Issue 9; p. 656.]

2.11 Q. Increasingly, clinical investigators are contracting with site management organizations (SMO), which assume some of the investigators' clinical study-related regulatory obligations/responsibilities. Although sponsors contract with and transfer certain regulatory responsibilities to CROs (_not_ accountability, which ultimately is the sponsor's), there are specific regulatory provisions for such transfers, unlike the situation for the transfer of investigator obligations to SMOs. Given this, are principal investigators allowed under current GCP standards to transfer certain regulatory obligations to the SMO with which they are working? How is the FDA addressing this area, and how should sponsors/CROs monitor such arrangements?

A. In recent informal correspondence on this question, the FDA emphasized that "clinical investigators remain fully responsible for fulfilling their obligations. As you state, there are no comparable provisions in the regulations for principal investigators to formally transfer these responsibilities to others, as there are for sponsors to transfer obligations to a CRO. Therefore, FDA will continue to hold clinical investigators responsible for the overall conduct of the study at sites for which they are responsible. Sponsors and CROs should fully understand what duties the investigator is performing directly and what duties have been contracted to the SMO to perform. The sponsor/CRO should then monitor performance of those functions, just as they would at a traditional site, regardless of who performs them or where they are performed to determine if they are adequately accomplished. Any problems uncovered should be reported to the principal investigator for correction just as should be done at a traditional site."

When comparing SMOs and CROs, it is important to keep in mind that the latter take on the sponsor's responsibilities, while the former take on some of the investigator's tasks.

2.12 Q. FDA regulations seem to establish that both the sponsor and investigator are responsible for assuring that an IRB that is compliant with agency regulations will be responsible for study-related reviews. How exactly, and to what degree, is a sponsor or an investigator expected to assess whether the

IRB at his or her institution (or the IRB that he or she will use in assessing a proposed study) complies with Part 56, in which the FDA outlines all regulatory requirements for IRBs?

A. 21 CFR 312.23(a)(1)(iv) establishes that a sponsor must submit in an IND "a commitment that an Institutional Review Board (IRB) that complies with requirements set forth in Part 56 will be responsible for the initial and continuing review and approval of each of the studies in the proposed clinical investigation. . . ." Further, FDA regulations state, under 21 CFR 312.66-Assurance of IRB Review, that "an investigator shall assure that an IRB that complies with the requirements set forth in Part 56 will be responsible for the initial and continuing review and approval of the proposed clinical study."

Still, the FDA has both acknowledged and commented on confusion in this area. The requirement that a sponsor assure the FDA that a study will be conducted in compliance with the IRB regulations "has been misinterpreted to mean that it is a sponsor's obligation to determine IRB compliance with the regulations," the agency states in its Information Sheet entitled, "Sponsor-Investigator-IRB Interrelationship." "This is not the case. Sponsors should rely on the clinical investigator, who assures the sponsor on form FDA-1572 for drugs and biologics . . . that the study will be reviewed by an IRB. Because clinical investigators work directly with IRBs, it is appropriate that they assure the sponsor that the IRB is functioning in compliance with the regulations."

The written IRB approval/disapproval/modifications request provided to the investigator "should be made available to the sponsor by the clinical investigator," the agency continues. "In the Agency's view, this required documentation provides the sponsor with reasonable assurance that an IRB complies with 21 CFR part 56 and that it will be responsible for the initial and continuing review." The agency also points out that sponsors can obtain the results of FDA inspections of an IRB through establishment inspection reports (EIR) and, if applicable, Form FDA 483s, under the Freedom of Information Act.

So what, specifically, must the clinical investigator do to assess an IRB? As a practical matter, when the IRB in question is a central IRB, then there is little that a PI can do to perform any kind of thorough assessment. If the IRB in question is a local IRB, then there may be more opportunity for the investigator to conduct a brief assessment of the IRB's compliance (e.g., by discussing the IRB's processes and procedures with one of its members who is also a colleague, asking the principal investigator's study coordinator about his or her experiences with the IRB, having informal discussions with the IRB chair or administrator, judging performance on the basis of the timeliness of previous correspondence, examining the results of previous FDA inspections). An informal survey of other principal investigators and/or study coordinators about their experiences with this IRB might also be helpful. It is doubtful, however, that any of these efforts would in any manner approach a thorough assessment.

As a practical matter, however, there is little a principal investigator can do to assess IRB adherence to regulatory requirements. In fact, despite the regulatory passages cited above, the FDA concedes that it is not the investigator's responsibility to police an IRB, and has never held investigators responsible for IRB compliance or shortcomings. CDER DSI staffers cannot recall ever having cited an investigator for a failure to ensure the adequacy of an IRB. On the other hand, if an investigator becomes aware of IRB problems, the agency would expect the investigator to attempt to address the problems with the IRB or to switch IRBs.

2.13 Q. Must an investigator gain IRB approval before implementing EVERY type of research change (except those to eliminate immediate hazards)?

A. 21 CFR 312.66-Assurance of IRB Review states that an investigator must assure that he or she ". . . will not make any changes in research without IRB approval, except where necessary to eliminate apparent immediate hazards to human subjects." Although the FDA does not provide examples of research changes that require IRB review, agency regulations make clear that even many "minor" changes in research require some form of IRB review and approval. FDA regulations at 21 CFR 56.110, for example, permit IRBs to employ expedited review procedures (e.g., review by IRB chairperson or experienced IRB member) in assessing "minor" changes in ongoing, previously approved research as an alternative to full IRB review.

In addition, IRBs often impose their own reporting requirements that are more demanding than FDA regulations. In these cases, under 21 CFR 56.113 (which grants IRBs the authority to suspend or terminate the approval of research not conducted in accordance with IRB requirements), the IRB directives, in effect, have the same force as FDA regulations.

Changes that are not minor, which the FDA says in a 1998 IRB Information Sheet would include the addition of procedures involving increased risk or discomfort, require review and approval at a convened IRB meeting before an investigator can implement.

As general guidance, the listing below provides several examples of study changes and their implications for IRB review and approval:

- If a test or procedure is added or subtracted from a study, the IRB should approve this change.
- If one manufacturer of a test kit, say a urine pregnancy test, is substituted for another, then IRB approval is not necessary, unless, for example, the sensitivity and/or specificity of the test is dramatically different.
- If the local laboratory changes its equipment for performing certain lab tests, then IRB approval is not necessary.
- Changes in telephone numbers or site staff do not necessarily need approval, although the IRB should be notified in such situations.
- A change from office-based visits to home visits for simple clinical assessments does not require an IRB approval, although an approval may be necessary if tests or procedures such as a blood draws are involved.

The clinical ramifications (so-called spillover effects) of every change should be assessed carefully by the principal investigator. When in doubt, the investigator should always submit the change to the IRB for guidance. An informal telephone call to the IRB administrator or chair might also prove helpful.

2.14 Q. What specific actions must an investigator and site take if a clinical trial subject drops out of a study simply by not returning for follow up visits? Do the GCP regulations spell this out?

A. GCP regulations do not define the steps required to process potential dropouts. Despite this, investigators and sites must undertake and document due diligence in ensuring appropriate follow-up in such cases. To this end, the industry standard for addressing this circumstance involves the following:

- Documented phone calls to the subject; the phone log should describe the outcome of these calls (e.g., "left message on recorder").
- A certified letter (with return receipt requested) sent to subject; the letter should express the site staff's concern for the subject's well-being.
- A subsequent certified letter sent to subject stating that he or she has been officially dropped from the study; the letter should specify if the subject has any further obligations, such as returning unused study medications.

Some study coordinators go even further in attempting to contact potential dropouts. They visit the subjects' homes, hoping to have a face-to-face discussion about the situation. Unannounced visits to the subject's home may carry certain risks, however. A mutually arranged home visit to perform a check of vital signs and collect unused study medication is probably less risky, but suggests that the subject probably could have come to the study facility for a visit.

Some study coordinators attempt to negotiate with potential dropouts over the phone. In some cases, the offer of carfare or childcare removes an obstacle for a return visit, and prevents an unnecessary dropout. In other cases, it is helpful for the principal investigator to discuss the situation with the subject.

There is one other circumstance that should be considered when discussing potential dropouts: If the subject in question has experienced an unresolved serious adverse event, this subject's clinical course must be followed to its resolution. The same principle applies for pregnancies that occur while on study. In both instances, the site must make every reasonable effort to obtain medical records and ensure the subject's safety.

2.15 *Q. In documenting a patient's eligibility for a study, must the investigator obtain the prospective subject's previous medical records, or are history forms completed at the start of a study considered adequate?*

A. Some studies are so complex and have so many complicated inclusion/exclusion criteria that a review of previous medical records is a necessity. A well-written clinical summary prepared by the subject's primary physician, along with relevant lab reports and related documents, would suffice; photocopies of reams of prior medical records are not required.

In more straightforward studies that have few inclusion/exclusion criteria, the completion of a history form alone may be adequate (i.e., without the need to obtain prior medical records). The caveat here is that the history taker must be clinically knowledgeable in order to ask the appropriate questions and adequately probe the study candidate for additional information when needed.

2.16 *Q. Does an investigator have the right to enroll and treat, in a clinical study, a patient who does not meet the protocol's inclusion/exclusion criteria? If so, how should this be handled?*

A. Investigators sometimes disagree with the clinical basis of a protocol's inclusion/exclusion criteria for a particular study. The time for a clinical investigator to object or recommend changes is while the protocol is in draft form or during the investigator meeting, however. Once the study is under way, investigators must follow the inclusion/exclusion criteria in the final protocol.

A principal investigator, however, may occasionally place a patient on study who does not meet these criteria, provided that the investigator receives permission from the study's medical director before beginning the informed consent process, and provided this permission is documented and the documentation is placed in the appropriate files. Further, the investigator must notify the IRB if the applicable IRB requires that protocol inclusion deviations be reported.

2.17 Q. What are the emerging trends in the FDA's GCP inspection and compliance programs for clinical investigators and sites?

A. Continuing increases in clinical investigator inspections driven by voluntary clinical trial-related complaints and foreign inspections is perhaps the most significant trend in this area. After increasing 33% in FY2003, CDER's clinical investigator inspections grew a more modest 3% in FY2004. These figures include both "study-oriented" (routine data audit) and "directed" (for cause) inspectional programs.

The continuing growth in clinical investigator inspections resulted from almost a doubling of the number of foreign inspections (from 44 in FY2003 to about 80 in FY2004), and "directed" CDER inspections undertaken in response to the growing number of voluntary study-related complaints forwarded to the center (a record 200+ in calendar year 2004). Although these voluntary complaints can target any of the parties involved in trials, including sponsor/monitors, hospitals, site staff, IRBs, and others, FDA officials note that clinical investigators are "by far" the most frequent target.

There are hints that the FDA could look more closely at how a clinical investigator supervises a clinical study in the future. In a guidance document that CDER hopes to release by mid-2005, the center will clarify its views on its standards for an investigator's supervision of a clinical trial. Since an investigator agrees to personally conduct and supervise a clinical study, FDA officials are concerned that too many investigators may be signing the required forms and inappropriately turning over day-to-day responsibilities for trial conduct to other site personnel.

In late 2004, CDER had also begun what it calls "linked inspections," which are systematic attempts to look at all elements of a trial's conduct (i.e., investigator/site, sponsor, monitor, IRB) rather than just one element of it. This approach, which the center claims to have used several times by early 2005 in response to evidence of compliance issues or the enrollment of vulnerable populations, will help the agency to gain a more complete picture of a trial's conduct and the precise areas in which the process might have broken down.

2.18 Q. What are the most common deficiencies for which the FDA is citing clinical investigators and sites today?

A. During FY2003 (the latest year for which data are available), CDER found what it considered to be "serious noncompliance"—objectionable practices that represented major departures from GCP regulations—in only 1% of its 368 clinical investigator inspections. In its FY2003 inspections of U.S. clinical sites/investigators,

CDER found that 36% were in full compliance, 63% had objectionable practices that did not represent major departures from federal GCP regulations, and 1% had objectionable practices that represented major departures from GCP regulations.

In its FY2003 inspections of non-U.S. sites, CDER found 22% of the sites to be in full compliance, and 78% to have objectionable practices that did not represent major departures from federal GCP regulations. Preliminary data from FY2004 CDER foreign inspections showed that 36% of foreign sites were in full compliance, while 43% had objectionable practices that did not represent major noncompliance (the remaining 21% of inspections were still pending at this writing). In a separate preliminary analysis of FY2004 CDER inspections of clinical investigators located in the European Union, the center found that 37% were in full compliance and 45% had objectionable practices that did not represent major noncompliance (the remaining 18% of inspections were still pending).

Rather consistently over the years, several general areas have comprised the most common areas of clinical investigator noncompliance. Overall, however, clinical investigator compliance in each of these areas improved in FY2003:

- protocol adherence (25% of sites were deficient compared to 34% in FY2002);
- inadequate/inaccurate records (19% compared to 28% in FY2002);
- inadequate informed consent form (8.5% compared to 11% in FY2002);
- inadequate drug accountability (4.5% compared to 13% in FY2002);
- inappropriate reporting/follow-up of adverse experiences (4.5% compared to 9% in FY2002); and
- other (6.1% in FY2003).

2.19 Q. How do the U.S.-based and foreign-based sites/investigators compare in terms of the breakdown of common GCP deficiencies?

A. According to FY2003 data from CDER's DSI (the latest year for which data are available), both U.S. and foreign clinical trial sites improved in their respective rates of GCP deficiencies. At the same time that it is inspecting more foreign sites (about 80 in FY2004 compared to 44 in FY2003) in response to the more frequent use of clinical data from non-U.S. sites in NDAs, CDER has noted a definite trend toward improved GCP compliance at international sites, particularly those within the ICH regions (EU and Japan).

In contrast to FY2002 inspection results, which showed that U.S. sites had a better compliance rate in the most common areas of GCP noncompliance, FY2003 inspection results indicated that greater percentages of domestic sites had problems in these areas:

- protocol adherence (21% of foreign sites were deficient compared to 26% of U.S. sites);
- inadequate/inaccurate records (19% of both foreign and domestic sites);
- inadequate informed consent form (4% foreign versus 9% domestic);
- inadequate drug accountability (0% foreign versus 5% domestic);
- inappropriate reporting/follow-up of adverse experiences (0% foreign versus 5% domestic); and
- other (34% foreign versus 3% domestic).

Today, however, FDA officials are taking steps to establish GCP-related standards for foreign clinical trial sites that will provide data in U.S. marketing applications. In a June 2004 proposed rule, the FDA proposed to establish U.S. GCP as the standard for its acceptance of data from all non-U.S. clinical trials, even those not conducted under a U.S. IND. Under current regulations, the FDA accepts data from non-IND foreign trials, provided that such trials conform to the Declaration of Helsinki or national requirements, whichever affords the greater protection to study subjects. The FDA says that its GCP requirements now represent the better standard, because they provide "more detail and enumeration of specific responsibilities of various parties, including monitoring of the trial and reporting adverse events." At the same time, FDA's Senior Advisor for Clinical Science David Lepay, M.D., Ph.D., said in September 2004 that, "for those operating under internationally recognized GCP standards such as ICH GCP, the proposed rule should have minimal impact."

2.20 Q. In keeping with ICH GCP Guidelines, how does one interpret "medical decision" making as it applies to the conduct of clinical studies?

A. According to the ICH/GCP Guideline (4.3.1), "a qualified physician (or dentist, when appropriate) who is an investigator or subinvestigator for the trial, should be responsible for all trial-related medical (or dental) decisions." This means that, whenever a clinical trial procedure, finding or activity raises a question or issue the outcome of which will affect a subject's health or safety while on the study, the decision must be made by the physician who is serving as the principal investigator or subinvestigator.

Such decisions, according to the ICH, include those relevant to medical care regarding adverse events and clinically significant lab values, and decisions to inform subjects when care is necessary for an intercurrent illness. These decisions may also include changes in study drug dosing, dropping a subject from the study, and referring a subject out for specialty care or consult, among others.

Unfortunately, in some cases, these decisions are made by a less-qualified person in a clinical trial. All clinical decision-makers should, as best practice, be listed on the 1572.

If the principal investigator is not an M.D., then an M.D. participating as a member of the study team should be involved in these decisions.

2.21 Q. Is it considered acceptable for a study coordinator to sign documentation for an investigator?

A. While it is acceptable for study coordinators to sign certain documentation for an investigator, there are important caveats. Certain documents, such as the Form FDA 1572-Statement of Investigator, financial disclosure forms, and protocols, cannot be signed by the study coordinator on the investigator's behalf. When the study coordinator signs for the principal investigator, the coordinator must initial the signature.

If the investigator gives the study coordinator authority to sign for him or her, the parameters (type of document and special circumstances) must be clearly delineated in a document, which should be maintained in the study binder. The sponsor should be made aware of this practice, and should receive a copy of this documentation. Some IRB correspondence and simple queries and routine, straightforward correspondence with the sponsor or CRO are examples of documents that may be signed by the study coordinator.

All individuals who may make changes to the case report forms or source documents must be identified in study documentation. A signature/delegation log, which is an "essential document" according to the ICH GCP guideline (E6), is used for this purpose.

2.22 Q. In Section 8.3.11 of its listing of essential documents for the conduct of a clinical trial, the ICH GCP Guideline identifies "relevant communications other than site visits" among the items that should be added to the investigator/institution and sponsor files. What study documents constitute "relevant communications"?

A. In collecting documentation during a clinical trial, it is helpful to keep in mind that the purpose of this documentation is to allow someone with the appropriate education and experience to reconstruct the trial. This individual may be a regulatory agency reviewer or an inspector.

Relevant communications include letters, hardcopies and/or emails from a site to the sponsor and/or IRB and vice versa. Notes of face-to-face meetings and teleconferences are also considered relevant. Relevant communications also include letters from subjects to the principal investigator, to the IRB, and to the sponsor about the conduct of the study.

According to the ICH Guideline, the purpose is "to document any agreements or significant discussions regarding trial administration, protocol violations, trial conduct, [and] adverse event reporting." Examples of such communications include the documentation of investigator meeting discussions, communication regarding protocol waivers and/or changes to the protocol, and follow-up communications regarding serious adverse events and letters to subjects who fail to return for study visits.

Some sites maintain a record of every communication in the study binder—including luncheon menus for investigator meetings. Not all of these items are deemed relevant under the ICH GCP standards, however.

2.23 Q. FDA regulations at 21 CFR 312.62(c)—Investigator record retention requirements—call on investigators to retain study-related records "for 2 years following the date a marketing application is approved for the drug for the indication for which it is being investigated; or if no application is to be filed or if the application is not approved for such indication, until 2 years after the investigation is discontinued and FDA is notified." Assuming that no NDA is to be filed or the application is not approved for the indication, how does the FDA interpret "until 2 years after the investigation is discontinued and FDA is notified"?

A. According to staffers in CDER's Division of Scientific Investigations, the FDA interprets this to mean the date on which the sponsor discontinues all studies under the relevant IND. Assume, for example, that a particular site's participation is discontinued while the larger clinical program for the indication continues at other sites. Would the two-year clock begin ticking when that site's participation is discontinued? No, according to CDER's DSI. The two-year clock applicable to record retention would not begin ticking until all studies/sites were discontinued. In effect, that particular site's retention requirements could last for many years depending on how long the other investigations under the IND continue.

Although, in practice, the agency may not split hairs on the precise date that a study "is discontinued and FDA is notified," some at the agency contacted on this issue believe that the date would be the FDA's date of receipt of a sponsor's letter stating that studies are being discontinued for a particular indication or that an entire IND is being withdrawn or inactivated. The FDA is not known to have provided definitive advice on this particular issue, however.

In practice, investigators often must retain these records well beyond the two-year period required by the FDA. In many cases, sponsors require investigators to maintain records for longer periods under clinical protocols. Further, ICH GCP standards may call on investigators to maintain such records for longer periods. Under the ICH's *E6 Guideline for Good Clinical Practice,* for instance, investigators are called on to retain essential study-related documents "until at least 2 years after the last approval of a marketing application in an ICH region and until there are no pending or contemplated marketing applications in an ICH region or at least 2 years have elapsed since the formal discontinuation of clinical development of the investigational products." Depending on the particulars of a drug's development and the sponsor's submission of marketing dossiers, this period could easily extend well beyond the 2-year retention period required under FDA regulations. The E6 guidance goes on to establish that it is the sponsor's responsibility to inform an investigator/institution "as to when these documents no longer need to be retained."

2.24 Q. Under 21 CFR 312.62, a clinical investigator is required to retain study records "for a period of 2 years following the date a marketing application is approved for the drug for the indication for which it is being investigated; or if no application is to be filed or if the application is not approved for such indication, until 2 years after the investigation is discontinued and FDA is notified." Is the FDA's interpretation of this requirement that the site retain these records on-site, or can a site retain these records off site? And can these records be retained through a trusted third party, as suggested by PhRMA in a June 2003 proposal to the agency?

A. Since FDA regulations do not address this issue specifically, there is no regulatory requirement that study records be maintained on-site. In the September 2004 draft guidance entitled, "Computerized Systems Used in Clinical Trials," however, the agency does acknowledge the advantages of on-site storage. "Retaining the original source document or a certified copy of the source document at the site where the investigation was conducted can assist in meeting . . . regulatory requirements [for the maintenance of study records]. It can also assist in the reconstruction and evaluation of the trial throughout and after the completion of the trial."

In practice, the FDA is well aware that many clinical investigational sites do not store their records on site (e.g., due to lack of available space), but possibly in a central location in the larger healthcare facility (e.g., a hospital's central file), or even at an off-site warehouse that may be owned by a data warehousing company.

According to DSI staffers, the agency's policy is that it expects sites to maintain access to such records, that such records be stored under conditions that will preserve their integrity, and that sites be able to retrieve and provide "prompt access" to such records if the FDA requests such records as part of an inspection. In the records retention section of the FDA's Compliance Program Guidance 7348.811 for clinical investigator inspections, the agency acknowledges that a site may not retain "custody" of study-related records, and instructs inspectors to:

"1. Determine who maintains custody of the required records and the means by which prompt access can be assured. Determine whether the investigator has notified the sponsor in writing regarding the custody of required records, if the investigator does not retain them."

2.25 Q. Given that a site might maintain records off-site and may not have immediate access to them, how does the FDA interpret the requirement that an FDA inspector be provided with "prompt access" to required study-related records that will be inspected?

A. Although the FDA's Compliance Program Guidance 7348.811 uses the phrase "prompt access," the agency's regulations do not specify a time period within which FDA inspectors must be provided access to study-related records. FDA regulations at 21 CFR 312.68 (Inspection of investigator's records and reports) state that "An investigator shall upon request from any properly authorized officer or employee of FDA, at reasonable times, permit such officer or employee to have access to, and copy and verify records or reports made by the investigator. . . ."

Given that the FDA generally provides clinical investigators and sites with advance notification of a few days or more for routine inspections and that the agency even identifies the records that it wants to inspect, clinical sites will have time to locate and assemble the records in advance of the inspection itself. Agency inspectors contacted on this question noted their expectation that these pre-identified records be available at the start of an inspection. If such records are not available upon an inspector's arrival or within a brief period of time following that arrival (e.g., a reasonable period to permit site staff to immediately retrieve the records from a nearby office and bring them to the inspector), this could raise suspicions that the site has not maintained adequate access to its own records. The relevant circumstances (e.g., the nature of the records sought, degree of delay) will determine if the delay in access will justify further investigation or even a citation in a Form 483-Inspectional Observations.

Even with advance notification, FDA inspectors sometimes request raw data or other information that the site may not have anticipated and that the site staff has not collected for the inspection. While there is no regulation or guideline that establishes a timeframe within which access to such records must be provided, several present and former FDA inspectors contacted regarding this question suggested that 24 hours is a reasonable timeframe, provided that there are justifiable reasons for such a delay. For example, the specific records may be stored at a distant facility, and the volume of records being requested makes faxing/scanning/emailing impractical. Alternatively, the records may exist only in microfilm/microfiche format, and printouts of these records may be blurry when faxed. In such cases, a site should be able to use an overnight courier service to provide access to the records the following business day.

2.26 Q. Physical exams of study subjects are important in the context of several aspects of clinical studies. Is there a difference between a physical exam and a physical assessment? If so, under what circumstances? Must the protocol state which is required?

A. There is a definite difference between a physical exam and a physical assessment. A physical exam is conducted by a physician, a physician's assistant, or a nurse practitioner. The procedure involves an examination of all or certain body systems (e.g., genito-urinary). The examiner uses auscultation, palpitation, percussion, as well as visual, auditory, and olfactory means, to evaluate the individual. In most states, a registered nurse who performs a physical exam is operating outside his or her scope of practice.

On the other hand, a physical assessment is an abbreviated evaluation, typically performed by a registered nurse. Percussion and palpitation are not routinely employed. The examiner may auscultate heart and lungs, measure vital signs, check pupil size and reaction, and assess skin turgor.

For clinical studies, the protocol should define which of the two procedures will be required. In many cases, protocols are ambiguous and physical assessments are performed in lieu of physical examinations—sometimes to the surprise of the sponsor. There have been studies in which a physical exam was required, but the physical exam source document forms created for the study were actually titled "Physical Assessments." Of course, this creates a conflict between the protocol and study source documents. In other studies, the physical exam source document form was correctly titled, but physical assessments were performed.

In simple studies, nursing assessments may suffice and protocols should reflect this specification. For complex studies, the physical exam is an important activity necessary to demonstrate that the patient's safety is ensured.

Unless specified in a protocol, a physical assessment cannot be submitted for a physical exam.

Further Reading

Hutchinson, David, *12 Golden GCP Rules for Investigators,* Guildford, UK: Canary Publications, 1999.

Mackintosh, D. and Zepp, V., "GCP Responsibilities of Principal Investigators: Beyond the 1572," *Applied Clinical Trials,* 32-40, November 1996.

Mackintosh D., Molloy, V., and DeCherney, G.S., "GCP Responsibilities of Principal Investigators Revisited: Going Far Beyond the 1572," *Applied Clinical Trials,* 9:59-64, March 2000.

Dunn, C.M. and Chadwick, G., *Protecting Study Volunteers in Research: A Manual for Investigative Sites,* Boston, MA: CenterWatch, 1999.

Acknowledgments

Douglas Mackintosh, DrPH, MBA, MS Hyg, and Vernette Molloy, MBA, RN, of GCPA, Inc.; Louis Kirby, MD, President, Pivotal Research Centers, Peoria, Arizona.

Section 3:
Form FDA-1572/Statement of the Investigator

3.1 *Q. Because it is used for a few different purposes, there is uncertainty in some cases about the Form FDA 1572-Statement of Investigator, in particular when its use and submission is mandatory. What is the 1572's regulatory purpose, and in what ways is the form used in practice?*

A. The 1572 itself declares that, "No investigator may participate in an investigation until he/she provides the sponsor with a completed, signed Statement of Investigator, Form FDA 1572." And FDA regulations at 21 CFR 312.53(c)(1) add that, "Before permitting an investigator to begin participation in an investigation, the sponsor shall obtain the following: (1) A signed investigator statement (Form FDA-1572). . . ." Therefore, the Form 1572 is a document that *an investigator* must submit *to the study sponsor.*

Through the 1572 Form and the attachments typically sent with it, an investigator provides a sponsor with, among other things, information on his or her education, training, and experience (CV or other statement of qualifications) that qualifies him or her to undertake the clinical investigation, information on the relevant facility, IRB, and subinvestigators, protocol information, and the investigator's commitment to conduct the study in accordance with the protocol and FDA regulations.

So where is there uncertainty about the 1572's use? In many cases, companies submit the completed and signed 1572s to the FDA in the original IND and subsequently when new investigators are added to a study. IND applicants and holders do this as a convenient way of fulfilling an FDA requirement at 21 CFR 312.23(a)(6)(iii)(b), which calls for a clinical trial protocol submitted in an IND to provide "the name and address and a statement of the qualifications (CV or other statement of qualifications) of each investigator."

Because this has become such a common practice, some incorrectly assume that this is an FDA requirement. In fact, the IND form (Form FDA 1571) explicitly gives sponsors the option of fulfilling 312.23(a)(6)(iii)(b) by submitting either "Investigator data [21 CFR 312.23(a)(6)(iii)(b)] or completed Form(s) FDA 1572."

In informal correspondence on this issue, the FDA stated that, "People seem to obsess over the 1572. We wonder how many people realize that the 1572 is not even required to be submitted to the FDA. In theory, we could never even see it. In practice, however, the 1572 is typically submitted to the IND by the sponsor as an efficient means to provide information required under 21 CFR 312.23(a)(6)(iii)(b)."

3.2 *Q. Since it is such common practice for companies to provide the 1572 and accompanying CV and other information to the FDA in the original IND and subsequently when a new investigator is added to the study, has that become an agency expectation or even a* **de facto** *requirement?*

A. None of several Center for Drug Evaluation and Research review divisions contacted recently claimed that the submission of the 1572 was a divisional expectation. And most did not express even a preference in terms of the format (i.e., a 1572 or alternative format) in which IND applicants should provide investigator qualification-related information.

It is important to note, however, that there are differences between some CDER review divisions, and that applicants should ask about a division's policy in this area. Under a 1992 policy, for example, the Division of Oncologic Drug Products asks that sponsors of commercial INDs (i.e., those submitted by industry) not submit either the 1572 or the investigator's CV for new investigators because such submissions are "inefficient and cumbersome." Rather, in its "no CV letter," the division asks all IND holders to submit summary information, including "the minimum qualifications of investigators selected for the protocol . . . and a statement that each investigator meets or exceeds those qualifications" (see exhibit below).

In the letter, the division emphasizes to applicants that, "You are, of course, also required to maintain the information provided to you by the investigator on the form FDA 1572, which is to be retained by you. In addition, you must maintain in your files a current C.V. of each investigator which must be updated as investigators are added. Only upon request of the Agency, will you be required to submit the current C.V. for a specific investigator."

3.3 *Q. If a subinvestigator leaves a study, must the sponsor complete and file a new Form FDA 1572-Statement of Investigator to delete this person from the list, or is a site signature log with active dates of participation sufficient?*

A. Since most sites maintain a study staff signature/delegation of responsibility form, completing this form is an excellent method for keeping track of who is working on a study and what each person's role is. It is also a good idea to include the dates of service—for example, when a subinvestigator started and when he or she left the project. The 1572 is a very cumbersome method for providing this information.

When subinvestigators are added to the team, they must be added to the 1572. Most sites do not prepare and sign another 1572 when a particular subinvestigator's participation ceases, however. A common industry practice is to remove such a subinvestigator's name from the 1572 when a new subinvestigator is added.

For a study involving residents or fellows who turnover once a year, the 1572 should be modified annually and should include an attachment providing the names of all residents and fellows listed as subinvestigators for the upcoming year. As a practical matter, it is not always possible for a site to specify, in advance, which individuals on the list will be working on a particular study. Once it becomes clear which residents and fellows are staffing the study, however, those individuals should be added to the staff signature/delegation of responsibility form.

3.4 *Q. How does a site/sponsor determine whether a laboratory—for example, a microbiological sampling laboratory or one that will only be used occasionally during the study—should be listed in Block #4 of the Form FDA 1572-Statement of Investigator, which calls for the "name and address of any clinical laboratory facilities to be used in the study"?*

A. Laboratories that are infrequently used need not be included in Block #4. Some companies use the following unofficial rule of thumb: If the lab performs less than 1% of all lab tests performed during the study, they do not include it. If a lab is infrequently but systematically used for very specialized tests whose results are used to change the clinical course of the study subjects as specified in the protocol, however, then sites are advised to list the lab on the 1572. For example, if a protocol

Division of Oncologic Drug Products' "No CV Letter"

Sponsor name and address

Attention: sponsor representative

Dear Dr. name:

The Division of Oncology Drug Products is recommending changes in the policy regarding documentation of investigator qualifications. The changes are intended to streamline the process of submitting and maintaining records regarding qualifications for principal and participating clinical investigators conducting trials under Investigational New Drug Applications (INDs).

Currently, the most prevalent method of complying with those parts of 21 CFR 312.23(a)(6)(iii)(b) and 312.30(d)(1)(iii) pertaining to investigator qualifications is to submit the investigator's curriculum vitae (C.V.). This method has proven to be inefficient and cumbersome. Consequently, the Division requests that C.V.s not be submitted for commercially sponsored INDs.

Instead, for IND submissions that pertain to investigator qualifications, you should include a cover letter along with the completed Form FDA 1571 that provides the following for each clinical protocol submitted, including those in the original submission:

a. The clinical protocol title and number (if applicable);

b. minimum qualifications of investigators selected for the protocol. For example, medical degree, board certification, etc.;

c. a statement that each investigator meets or exceeds those qualifications; and

d. the name and address of each investigator and those subinvestigators working under the supervision of the investigator.

You are, of course, also required to maintain the information provided to you by the investigator on form FDA 1572, which is to be retained by you. In addition, you must maintain in your files a current C.V. of each investigator which must be updated as investigators are added. Only upon request of the Agency, will you be required to submit the current C.V. for a specific investigator.

This policy applies only to appropriate submissions sent to the Division of Oncology Drug Products and may not be appropriate for other Divisions within the Center for Drug Evaluation and Research. This policy does not alter your obligations under 21 CFR 312.53 or other regulations concerning the conduct of clinical investigations. Please note that 21 CFR 312.53(a) states that "A sponsor shall select only investigators qualified by training and experience as appropriate experts to investigate the drug."

Your compliance with this policy is appreciated and will result in a more manageable system of processing IND submissions.

Sincerely yours,

Richard Pazdur, M.D.
Director
Division of Oncology Drug Products
Office of Drug Evaluation 1
Center for Drug Evaluation and Research

cc: Orig. IND
Div. File
HFD-150/CSO
R/D initialed by/SCSO
ADVICE

calls for a specific diagnostic microbiologic test that must be performed if a subject displays certain specific neurologic symptoms, then the lab—one of the few that performs this microbiologic test—should be listed on the 1572.

Labs that are located in cities distant from the clinical site and that perform a few routine tests for one patient on study clearly need not be listed on the 1572.

Although not a regulatory requirement, labs listed on the 1572 should have College of American Pathologists (CAP) or Clinical Laboratories Improvements Amendments (CLIA) certification or, at a minimum, a documented quality assurance procedure, as may be the case for European labs.

3.5 Q. When must a site revise a 1572 for changes in study personnel?

A. FDA regulations are largely silent on the need for revised 1572s to indicate study personnel changes. Since no investigator may participate in a clinical investigation without first completing and signing a 1572 (and since a sponsor must submit an amendment to FDA based on this form for the new investigator, see 312.30(c)), it is clear that a 1572 is a requirement for a new investigator (including a change in the principal investigator or addition of new investigator) who will participate in an ongoing study.

It is important to note, however, that a site should revise an existing 1572 and forward the revised form to the sponsor for other types of changes in the study personnel or other study-related entities identified in previously submitted 1572s, including:

- The addition of a new subinvestigator.
- The addition of a local lab or health care facility to which study patients make visits.
- A change in the IRB or IRB's name.

3.6 Q. Occasionally, European clinical investigators and sites are reluctant to sign the Form FDA 1572-Statement of Investigator. Is this ever acceptable for studies conducted under INDs and, if so, what is done in lieu of the 1572?

A. For a variety of reasons (e.g., the need for an IRB, which some countries do not have), some foreign investigators may refuse to sign the FDA Form 1572-Statement of Investigator, in part because they do not want to enter into a contract directly with the FDA (U.S. government). All study investigators who will participate in studies under an IND must sign the 1572, however. In such scenarios, then, trial sponsors must find other investigators who are willing to sign the form.

3.7 Q. But does this mean that, if a sponsor has an IND under which it is studying a specific drug, then investigators at all non-U.S. sites conducting studies involving that drug must complete and sign a 1572?

A. Not necessarily. Only those sites involved in studies specifically included under the IND are required to sign a 1572.

In a February 2004 informal response to this question, the FDA stated the following:

"There is no FDA requirement that study sites outside of the United States operate under a U.S. IND. FDA regulations (21 CFR Parts 312.120 and 314.106) [establish the criteria under which the agency will accept] non-U.S., non-IND studies/data for purposes of FDA review in support of applications (IND or NDA). The decision to operate under an IND at non-U.S. sites is therefore discretionary on the part of the study sponsor.

"HOWEVER, should a sponsor make the decision that non-U.S. studies/sites [will be conducted] under a U.S. IND, then all FDA IND regulatory requirements must be met. This includes submission of the 1572 with its investigator certification that U.S. IND requirements are understood and will be met.

"On the other hand, a sponsor may decide and indicate that a study's non-U.S. sites [will not be included] under a U.S. IND. In this case, elements of IND regulations (beyond provisions for FDA's acceptance of non-U.S., non-IND studies/data under 312.120/314.106) are not FDA-enforceable requirements per se. That is, there is no FDA regulatory requirement for completion of a 1572 when a sponsor has designated the non-U.S. study or sites as 'non-IND' (although a sponsor may still request completion of the 1572 as part of an internal SOP—and FDA, of course, expects SOP's to be followed).

"The distinction, then, is whether the sponsor has chosen/committed to operate its non-U.S. sites under U.S. regulations (in which case, the 1572 and all IND requirements must be met at non-U.S. sites) or as non-IND (in which case the FDA regulatory requirement for a 1572 does not apply)."

Under a June 2004 proposed regulation, however, the FDA proposed to change its standards for accepting data from foreign, non-IND studies. Although the agency cannot require that foreign studies be conducted under an IND or under U.S. GCP standards (i.e., non-IND studies), the proposed regulation, if implemented, may provide additional reasons why firms may want to include foreign studies under their U.S. INDs.

According to the proposed regulation, the FDA will accept as support for an IND, NDA, or BLA a well-designed and well-conducted non-IND foreign clinical study only if two conditions are met:

- The study was conducted in accordance with U.S. GCP standards, including a review and approval (or provision of a favorable opinion) by an institutional ethics committee (IEC) before study initiation, continuing review of the ongoing study by an IEC, and the obtaining and documenting of a subject's freely given informed consent (or the subject's legally authorized representative) before study initiation.
- The FDA must be able to validate the data from the study through an onsite inspection if the agency deems such an inspection necessary.

While the agency would not accept as support for an IND, NDA, or BLA a foreign study that fails to meet these two criteria, it notes that it "will examine data from such a study."

3.8   *Q. Must the* **curriculum vitae** *or "other statement of qualifications provided for the investigator" with the Form FDA 1572-Statement of Investigator be signed and dated, and must it be updated yearly or periodically? How current should the curriculum vitae (C.V.) provided with the Form FDA 1572 be?*

A. Many sponsors and monitors ask investigators to sign and date their C.V.s. In essence, the signature implies that the information provided is accurate, and the date suggests the C.V.'s applicability to the study enrollment and completion period.

The FDA does not require a signature and date, however. The agency does require that the C.V.s be applicable to the study period and that they be accurate. An investigator's signature is no guarantee of accuracy.

One purpose of the C.V. is to determine if an investigator is qualified to conduct the trial. A second purpose is to determine if any aspects of an investigator's background may suggest a risk or danger to study subjects. Generally, state licensure—and occasionally, board certification—serves as an adequate indicator in both areas.

Therefore, it is important that sponsors and monitors check an investigator's state medical license for the study period under consideration. In Europe, the country registry—a listing of all physicians who can practice in a particular country—should be reviewed. EU countries recognize physicians who are listed on at least one country's registry, and permit them to practice in any EU member state. Most sponsors insist that a copy of the license or registry be placed in the study binder next to the C.V.

Sponsors should note that FDA requirements state only that an investigator be "qualified by training." In practice and according to the laws of all 50 states, an investigator must be licensed if he or she is making medical decisions.

A C.V. should indicate that the investigator actually works at the site listed on the 1572. It should show current state medical licensure and places of employment.

In reviewing an investigator's qualifications, sponsors and monitors should also assess FDA warning letters and the FDA's restricted/disqualified investigator list. One would not expect a warning letter to be mentioned on an investigator's C.V.

3.9 *Q. In many cases, sponsors ask sites to submit the laboratory director's C.V., normal lab ranges, and license/certifications, but do not ask for information on the surgery center, radiology department, pharmacy department, and other departments that may handle study-specific procedures. Why is this so—is it in the GCP regulations?*

A. Although not an FDA regulatory requirement, current U.S. industry practice advocates placing laboratory certifications as well as normal ranges in the study binder. Since Europe does not have similar certification processes, some form of QA documentation is generally sufficient. In about a third of the cases for U.S. studies, lab directors' C.V.s are placed in the binder.

Ironically, for most U.S. and European central labs as well as local labs, normal ranges are printed on each lab report for each lab test result. In its section on essential documents for the conduct of a clinical trial, the ICH GCP guideline (8.2.11 and 8.2.12) calls for normal ranges as well as lab certifications or quality assurance documents that demonstrate that the lab has successfully undergone QA testing. The guideline does not call for the lab director's C.V, however.

Generally, other ancillary departments are not asked to provide certifications or any other documentation of quality performance. In some respects, this is an oversight because substandard clinical performance by these other departments may adversely impact the quality of a clinical study.

3.10 *Q. Should radiology, pharmacy, and surgery departments be addressed in the 1572/investigator agreement if they perform study-specific tasks?*

A. Typically, these ancillary departments are not listed separately on the 1572; instead, the hospital is listed as the entity at which subjects are seen. If surgery is performed on an outpatient basis at a surgical center affiliated with—but physically separate from—the hospital, however, the surgical center probably should be listed on the 1572 in addition to the hospital itself.

The section of the 1572—Block #2-Name and Address of any Medical School, Hospital, or Other Research Facility Where the Clinical Investigation(s) Will Be Conducted—that lists the study's location is designed to help orient FDA staff about study locations. Any locations that study patients visit for study-related tests and procedures should be listed on the 1572 in that section.

3.11 Q. Should third-party blinded assessors, such as radiologists, cardiologists, and pathologists, who evaluate diagnostic media for efficacy parameters be considered as an investigational site or a diagnostic reference laboratory? And how must these individuals be qualified?

A. Third-party blinded assessors do not comprise an investigational site. They are not investigators in the sense that the FDA uses this word. Although x-rays and other diagnostic test results are sent to them, they do not examine or treat study patients. Normally, their assessments are not used to make clinical decisions about subject care, and their evaluations are not shared with principal investigators during the study.

These assessors must be sub-specialists with expertise in a specific area of medicine. For example, they may have read and interpreted thousands of MRIs for a particular organ or part of the body, and published several papers on the topic. Typically, there are only a few individuals with the degree of specialization necessary to meet these qualifications. A C.V. would document this subspecialty, and should be included in the master study file. It would also help if this expert had previously participated in a blinded assessment and understands the ground rules.

If two assessors are used—two radiologists, for example—then the degree of concordance (agreement) on a pre-test should be measured before the actual assessment is performed. In some cases, clinical experts disagree in their interpretation of films, slides, and other study data. Disagreements must be adjudicated according to a predetermined methodology.

It is important to note that these third-party blinded assessors, whose evaluations do not affect patient care, need not be listed on the 1572.

3.12 Q. In signing the Form FDA 1572-Statement of Investigator, clinical investigators agree, in the "Commitments" section, "to conduct the study(ies) in accordance with the relevant, current protocol(s) and will only make changes in a protocol after notifying the sponsor, except when necessary to protect the safety, rights, or welfare of subjects." Is complying with the protocol considered a legal requirement for investigators?

A. It is a legal requirement. When signed, the Form FDA 1572 form is a contract between the investigator and the FDA.

During the testimony of FDA officials at a June 2002 congressional hearing, Representative Ernie Fletcher (R-KY) asked then-CBER Division of Trial Design and Analysis Deputy Director Patricia Keegan, M.D., whether following a protocol is a legal requirement. "All the investigators who conduct studies under INDs sign a statement that is a government form called a 1572 in which they agree basically to conduct the study according to good clinical practice," Keegan responded. "In that sense, it is a legal requirement. I'm not sure that every physician who signs that form understands that, but it is a legal requirement."

3.13 Q. If a sponsor receives a completed Form FDA 1572 with a script (i.e., signed by hand) investigator signature and a computer-generated or typed date, is this acceptable and binding?

A. Although this is acceptable, it is better if the principal investigator personally dates the 1572. Too frequently, documents are dated (and sometimes backdated) by study coordinators before the principal investigator signs them. Also, if the date is typed, then one cannot be reasonably assured that the principal investigator actually signed on that date. Generally, most, if not all, of the other information placed on this form is typed. It is unwise for an investigator to sign a blank 1572 before key information, such as the names of subinvestigators and the name and address of the relevant IRB, is added to the form.

The 1572 does not specifically call for a script date. A typed or rubber-stamped signature is not acceptable, however. In addition, no individual can sign the 1572 for the investigator.

Acknowledgments

Douglas Mackintosh, DrPH, MBA, MS Hyg, and Vernette Molloy, MBA, RN, of GCPA, Inc.; Chris Jepsen, MS, CQA, Quality Director, Genzyme, Cambridge, MA; Joy Littlejohn, Auditor, Regulatory Compliance, Alexion Pharmaceuticals, Cheshire, CT.

Section 4:
Clinical Monitoring

4.1   Q. In past years, FDA officials have claimed that they were studying industry's clinical monitoring practices. Where does this stand today, and on what aspects of monitoring practices is the agency most focused today?

A. Currently, DSI officials claim that they are attempting to identify new ways to examine industry monitoring practices, in particular to determine why many major study-related problems can go undetected or unaddressed in industry-sponsored studies despite the existence of formal monitoring programs. Actually, the division recently undertook a small study to determine if there were factors that would help the agency to predict where or when there would be problems in a clinical study.

In a 2005 interview, DSI officials claimed that the root of the problem appears to be inadequate follow-up from sponsors when monitors do detect study-related issues. In many cases, FDA officials do not believe that sponsors are doing enough to secure investigator/site compliance when problems are found. In response, CDER officials are now considering both increased education and greater enforcement against sponsors.

Further, CDER inspectional practices with regard to sponsor/monitor activities could be affected by a new initiative involving what the agency calls *"linked inspections."* In late 2004, CDER's DSI began conducting "linked inspections," which evaluate all the key entities (sponsor/monitor, investigator, IRB) involved in a particular trial. Instead of looking at the activities and compliance of one of these entities in a particular trial, DSI has decided to take a more systematic look at the way an entire trial is conducted to gain a more complete picture of a trial's conduct and of what in the system might have broken down. As of March 2005, CDER's DSI claims that it had conducted about seven or eight linked inspections, either because the population was vulnerable or because there was an indication (e.g., from an initial inspection) that there were significant problems in study conduct.

The linked inspection effort is really part of a larger FDA initiative to re-examine the bioresearch monitoring (BIMO) programs across the agency's various product centers. An internal FDA working group comprising representatives from CDER, CBER, CDRH and other centers is actively examining the entire BIMO process to re-evaluate how it works currently, what aspects of the program can be improved, how the centers can better coordinate, how the BIMO program can better focus on the highest-risk clinical studies, and how the agency can improve oversight of clinical trials involving special and vulnerable populations, including pediatric populations.

4.2   Q. What has CDER's experience been to date with these so-called "linked inspections"?

A. From about October 2004, when the linked inspection program started, through March 2005, CDER's DSI had conducted about seven or eight linked inspections. According to DSI officials, these inspections have confirmed the theory that, once an issue is detected in one aspect of a study or its monitoring, other problems are found in related areas once agency inspectors follow the relevant "thread."

In one case in early 2005, DSI officials report that a linked inspection resulted in data derived from an extremely large trial not being used as part of the NDA review.

DSI officials claim that although the clinical monitor detected many problems in study conduct, there was inadequate follow-up to ensure that the problems were addressed sufficiently.

4.3 *Q. In the FDA's view, what is an acceptable monitoring frequency for clinical studies?*

A. Industry and even FDA officials often speak of an informal industry standard under which each clinical trial site should be visited, on average, every four to six weeks. At an April 2003 FDA workshop, for example, CDER Office of Medical Policy Director Robert Temple, M.D., mentioned that "the usual industry standard of every four weeks [for] every site [to be inspected]" may not be appropriate for large, simple safety trials, which some agency officials have been advocating in some cases.

The FDA's GCP regulations state only that "the sponsor shall monitor the progress of all clinical investigations under its IND." Although it is far from definitive, the FDA's "Guideline for the Monitoring of Clinical Investigations" (1988) adds, under a section entitled "Periodic Visits," that "the monitor should visit the investigator at the site of the investigation frequently enough to assure that:

- The facilities used by the investigator continue to be acceptable for purposes of the study.
- The study protocol or investigational plan is being followed.
- Changes to the protocol have been approved by the IRB and/or reported to the sponsor and the IRB.
- Accurate, complete, and current records are being maintained.
- Accurate, complete and timely reports are being made to the sponsor and IRB.
- The investigator is carrying out the agreed-upon activities and has not delegated them to other previously unspecified staff."

Although the ICH's GCP guideline says a bit more under Section 5.18.3-Extent and Nature of Monitoring, it does not provide specific advice on monitoring frequency, leaving that determination to the sponsor: "The sponsor should ensure that the trials are adequately monitored. The sponsor should determine the appropriate extent and nature of monitoring. The determination of the extent and nature of monitoring should be based on considerations such as the objective, purpose, design, complexity, blinding, size, and endpoints of the trial. In general there is a need for on-site monitoring before, during, and after the trial; however, in exceptional circumstances the sponsor may determine that central monitoring in conjunction with procedures such as investigators' training and meetings, and extensive written guidance can assure appropriate conduct of the trial in accordance with GCP."

Perhaps the greatest determinant of appropriate monitoring frequency is rate of enrollment. Sites that enroll a large number of patients in a short period of time need to be monitored far more frequently than sites that are low, slow enrollers. Depending on the complexity and frequency of protocol-required study visits, an average enrolling site might have a monitoring visit once per month or once every other month.

The frequency of monitoring visits is less important than the quality of monitoring visits, however. A rushed, perfunctory routine visit that includes only a cursory review of source documents is worthless.

4.4 Q. But in CPG 7348.811 (Inspections of Investigators), FDA instructs agency field inspectors to "briefly describe the method (on-site visit, telephone, contract research organization, etc.) and <u>frequency</u> of monitoring." So obviously, the FDA makes certain assessments in this regard. How does the FDA assess the adequacy of monitoring frequency (i.e., what criteria are used), and what are the typical "red flags" that the FDA looks for in this area?

A. CDER Bioresearch Monitoring (BIMO) Program officials concede that it is extremely difficult for the agency to prospectively determine, for each and every trial, how often monitors should visit sites. For this reason, companies are left to determine what monitoring frequency is appropriate for their specific trials. Admittedly, this does not much help a sponsor wondering what standards it will be held to in terms of monitoring frequency.

In informal correspondence on this question, however, CDER BIMO staff noted that, in assessing the adequacy of monitoring frequency, they will ask several questions, including:

- Was there sufficient early contact between the monitor and investigator to ensure that the study started out well?
- Was monitoring frequency sufficient relative to the rate of enrollment (e.g., did monitoring visits increase in response to extremely rapid enrollment)?
- How many times did the monitor visit a site relative to the study's length?
- If the monitor discovered serious site-related problems, did he or she increase the frequency of visits and/or appropriately follow up?
- How complicated were the study and the records that the monitor had to review?

As a practical matter, however, the agency only truly scrutinizes monitoring frequency when agency inspections uncover specific problems at a clinical site. Therefore, it is the compliance problems that become the "red flag" for possible inappropriate monitoring frequency. In assessing the reasons for such problems, the agency will scrutinize monitoring frequency as a potential cause or contributing factor.

In short, monitoring frequency will not receive significant scrutiny in the absence of compliance problems. Not surprisingly, CDER DSI staffers report that a sponsor has never been cited for inadequate monitoring frequency when no other problems were found with a study. Because most agency inspections are conducted retrospectively (i.e., following a study's completion), monitoring frequency is, by definition, deemed adequate when a study/site is found to be fully compliant.

4.5 Q. Citing HIPAA-related privacy standards, some clinical investigators have attempted to deny sponsor monitors and FDA field inspectors access to study patients' medical records. To what degree, if at all, are such denials of access permissible?

A. Such denials are not permissible in the context of clinical research. In terms of monitor access, to the extent that monitoring activities are required by FDA or other regulation or are for purposes related to adverse events, the HIPAA Privacy Rule permits access without an authorization or waiver of authorization.

Likewise, HIPAA privacy standards in no way affect the FDA's access to study-related records. Because it has encountered such situations at some sites, however, the

FDA has developed specific language that it uses in response to investigator attempts to use HIPAA concerns to block the agency's access to study records:

"The FD&C Act, the FDA-482, and BIMO regulations at CFR 812.145(b), 312.68, and 56.115(b) permit FDA investigators at reasonable times to have access to, copy, and verify records. In addition, the subjects' informed consent forms are to 'include a statement describing the extent, if any, to which confidentiality of records identifying the subjects will be maintained and that notes the possibility that the FDA may inspect the records' [(CFR 50.25(a)(5)]. Additionally, several specific exemptions in the HIPAA privacy rule [45 CFR Parts 160 and 164] expressly permit covered entities to use and disclose protected health information to FDA investigators without the investigator having to sign any kind of agreement. These include uses and disclosures: (1) required by law [45 CFR 164.512(a); (2) to a public health authority authorized by law to collect or receive such information [164.512(b)(1)]; and (3) to a health oversight agency for oversight activities, including audits, investigations and inspections [164.512(d)]. **HIPAA privacy standards are not intended to affect the access that FDA investigators have previously been afforded."**

4.6 *Q. What are the FDA's requirements for and expectations regarding standard operating procedures (SOP) for clinical monitors, clinical trial sites, and others involved in clinical trials?*

A. Interestingly, the FDA's drug regulations include SOP requirements only for IRBs. 21 CFR 56.108 requires IRBs "to follow written procedures" and 21 CFR 56.115(a)(b) requires that these written procedures be retained.

FDA regulations include no specific references to, or requirements for, SOPs for sponsors or clinical investigators. For clinical investigators, in fact, there are no references to SOPs in FDA regulations, site inspectional guidances, or the ICH GCP guidance. It is important to note, however, that FDA compliance-related documents establish a clear agency expectation that sponsors will maintain and follow documented SOPs. And, as an agency official recently noted in informal correspondence regarding sponsor SOPs, "FDA, of course, expects SOPs to be followed" (see Q3.7).

Perhaps the clearest references to the FDA's expectations regarding SOPs for drug sponsors appear in the agency's Compliance Program Guidance (CPG) Manual, Program 7348.810, which provides instructions to FDA field inspectors in conducting compliance inspections of sponsors/monitors and clinical research organizations. Specifically, the document makes references to sponsor SOPs in several areas, including monitoring procedures, data collection and handling procedures, quality assurance auditing/quality assurance unit operations, and electronic trials.

It is interesting to note that although CPG 7348.810 makes reference to a sponsor's SOPs for monitoring procedures and activities, it also allows for the circumstance in which there are no SOPs. In its instructions to FDA field inspectors, CPG 7348.810 states:

- "**Review** the procedures, frequency, scope, and process the sponsor uses to monitor the progress of the clinical investigations. (Device regulations (21 CFR 812.25(e)) require written monitoring procedures as part of the investigational plan.)"

- "**Obtain** a copy of the sponsor's written procedures (SOPs and guidelines) for monitoring and **determine** if the procedures were followed for the selected study. In the absence of written procedures, conduct interviews of the monitors as feasible and **determine** how monitoring was conducted."
- "**Obtain** a copy of any written procedures (SOPs and guidelines) for data verification (i.e., the monitor's review of subject records)."

Although it is assumed that sponsors will be cited if they do not follow SOPs in these areas, it is interesting to note that CGP 7348.810 specifically instructs agency investigators to document deviations only regarding SOPs for data collection and handling procedures: "1. **Review** the sponsor's written procedures (SOPs and guidelines) to assure the integrity of safety and efficacy data collected from clinical investigators (domestic and international). 2. **Verify** that the procedures were followed and **document** any deviations."

As noted, the ICH GCP guidance makes several references to sponsor SOPs, which it defines as "detailed, written instructions to achieve uniformity of the performance of a specific function." Specifically, the ICH GCP guidance states the following:

- "The sponsor is responsible for implementing and maintaining quality assurance and quality control systems with written SOP's to ensure that trials are conducted and data are generated, documented (recorded), and reported in compliance with the protocol, GCP, and the applicable regulatory requirement(s)."
- The sponsor should maintain SOPs for using electronic trial data handling and/or remote electronic trial data systems.
- Monitors should follow and be thoroughly familiar with the sponsor's "established written" SOPs, and should communicate SOP deviations to the investigator.
- The purpose of a sponsor's internal audit of a trial, which is separate from routine monitoring or quality control functions, "should be to evaluate trial conduct and compliance with the protocol, SOPs, GCP, and the applicable regulatory requirements."
- "Noncompliance with the protocol, SOPs, GCP, and/or applicable regulatory requirement(s) by an investigator/institution, or by member(s) of the sponsor's staff should lead to prompt action by the sponsor to secure compliance."

4.7 *Q. Can a monitor review photocopies of medical records, also called "shadow charts," instead of the originals? Which one does the FDA inspector review during site inspections?*

A. As a general rule, site monitors should always review original medical records—for example, actual physician's office notes, clinic notes, and hospital medical records. Monitors often ask site staff to photocopy original records for their review. Unfortunately, this request is often made for the convenience of the monitor—either the monitor does not want to spend the time reviewing the medical records or is not able to navigate through the documentation to find pertinent data.

A fundamental problem in relying on photocopies is that the monitor cannot be certain that the documentation is complete. That is, data may have been advertently or inadvertently deleted from pages (e.g., in the margins or on the back page of the original record). In addition, there may be data in other parts of the record, however small, that may not have been photocopied.

When a specific original record cannot be made available, a certified copy of the original records may be used. A record is considered "certified" when a qualified individual—often in the medical records department—attests that the copies are accurate and complete. In its April 1999 industry guidance entitled, "Computerized Systems Used in Clinical Trials," the FDA defines certified copy as "a copy of original information that has been verified, as indicated by dated signature, as an exact copy having all of the same attributes and information as the original." This same definition appears in a September 2004 draft revision to the April 1999 guidance. [Editor's note: while this guidance addresses certified copies in the context of electronic records, FDA officials maintain that this definition is equally relevant to paper-based records.]

In recent informal correspondence on this issue, the FDA stated that, "obviously, the source documents are the gold standard for study monitoring . . . In general, source documents should be the basis for monitoring. If a sponsor's monitor elects to use 'shadow charts' they are free to do so as the regulations do not specify how monitoring is to be performed. However, in our opinion they would be foolish to rely on shadow charts without establishing that the shadow charts were the equivalent of the source documents—that is, that they are a certified copy, meaning a copy of original information that has been verified, as indicated by dated signature, as an exact copy having all of the same attributes and features and information as the original. That's just an opinion. We instruct FDA investigators to audit against source documents."

In practice, the FDA may accept, for the purpose of an inspection, a photocopy when the original of a specific document is unavailable or has been destroyed. The FDA inspector and the reviewer at the agency's headquarters will decide if a photocopy is acceptable in a particular case. The agency, however, is more likely to accept a photocopy of an isolated record than photocopies of an entire research record.

If FDA field staff decide to rely on a certain number of photocopies during a site inspection, agency officials would expect the inspector to examine the adequacy of the document certification process, including the standard operating procedures for that process.

4.8 Q. Given that clinical monitoring could be viewed as a type of internal auditing activity designed to determine if the clinical investigator and staff, IRB, and others are fulfilling their regulatory responsibilities, are monitoring reports also given equal protection from routine FDA inspection under agency policies?

A. No, a main difference being that clinical monitoring is a specific FDA requirement and sponsor responsibility. This reality has not prevented some companies from attempting to argue, during FDA inspections, that monitoring reports should be afforded such protection, however.

In a June 2004 warning letter, the FDA cited Biotronik, Inc. for, among other things, failing "to allow FDA Investigators to inspect and copy all records relating to an inspection," including monitoring reports. "You refused to allow the FDA investigators direct access to the monitoring reports for the [study] during the inspection, but only allowed examination of correspondence files related to the monitoring visits," the warning letter states. "'Quality audits' or 'internal audits' . . . are *generally* exempt from FDA review, however, monitoring reports for clinical trials are not considered by FDA to be internal audits, and therefore are not exempt from review during FDA inspections.

"Responsibilities of sponsors include ensuring proper monitoring of the investigation . . . in order to secure compliance with the investigational plan. . . . By not allowing FDA to *inspect and copy* all records related to the inspection, including the monitoring reports, the FDA investigators were unable to determine whether the monitoring for this study was adequate to ensure investigator compliance."

When the current monitoring regulations were first proposed, at least one company argued that monitoring, as a quality assurance function, would work more efficiently if it was not made subject to government audit. Further, the company argued that monitors' reports would be more candid and critical, and thus have more value to the sponsor in assuring that appropriate corrective actions are undertaken as needed. The FDA rejected this argument, stating: "FDA believes it should retain the authority to inspect records and reports relating to a sponsor's monitoring of clinical investigations under Part 312. Access to these materials helps the agency both to confirm that monitoring is actually taking place and to determine the nature of such monitoring. FDA also is not persuaded that the prospect of agency inspection of monitoring records and reports should significantly influence monitors in recording their observations and recommendations."

4.9   *Q. Are pre-study, or study initiation, visits required under GCP requirements?*

A. Generally, the pharmaceutical industry splits pre-study monitoring visits into two distinct categories: qualification/selection visits and initiation visits. Qualification/selection visits determine that the site is able to conduct the study, and initiation visits assist the site in its preparation to enroll its first subject. Generally, qualification/selection visits are waived if a sponsor or clinical research organization has recently worked with a site and there remain no questions regarding its capabilities. Initiation visits are waived if a site does not need any assistance in preparing to enroll its first subject. When a site initiation visit is not held, it is always a good idea for the monitor to visit a site after it has enrolled its first few subjects.

Although FDA GCP regulations do not describe a pre-study visit, qualification visits are strongly recommended in the FDA's "Guideline for the Monitoring of Clinical Investigations" (1988). According to the guideline, "a sponsor is responsible for assuring, through personal contact between the monitor and each investigator, that the investigator clearly understands and accepts the obligations incurred in undertaking a clinical investigation. Prior to the initiation of a clinical investigation, the monitor should visit the site of the clinical investigation. . . ."

While the ICH's GCP guideline does not mention "pre-study" or "preinvestigation" visits specifically, it states in its appendix that both a "pretrial monitoring report" and a "trial initiation monitoring report" are considered essential documents. The pretrial monitoring report, which should be maintained in the sponsor's files, should "document that the site is suitable for the trial," says the guideline. The trial initiation monitoring report, which the site should maintain in its files and which can be combined with the pretrial monitoring report, should document that the trial procedures were reviewed with the investigator and the site staff. The ICH guideline also lists several monitoring responsibilities that would be difficult to fulfill without the benefit of a pre-study visit—for example, the monitor is responsible "for verifying that the investigator . . . has resources . . . , including laboratories and equipment . . . adequate to safely and properly conduct the trial. . . ."

Further, the ICH GCP guideline (5.18.3) states that, "in general there is a need for on-site monitoring, before, during, and after the trial; however, in exceptional circumstances the sponsor may determine that central monitoring in conjunction with procedures such as investigators' training and meetings, and extensive written guidance can assure appropriate conduct of the trial in accordance with GCP."

Some companies consider "pre-initiation" investigator meetings, which are group meetings held to educate all participating clinical investigators/study coordinators/ research nurses regarding a study, to be a replacement for individual site initiation visits. Such meetings, however, do not meet the criteria of a "visit" as described in the FDA's 1988 monitoring guideline.

4.10 Q. Should sponsors have their site monitors monitor against the FDA's GCP regulations/guidelines or the ICH GCP guideline, or both?

A. FDA officials emphasize that the 1997 ICH GCP guideline is entirely consistent with the agency's existing GCP regulations and standards. In fact, as a party to the ICH GCP guideline, the FDA states that the harmonized guideline "represents the agency's current thinking on good clinical practices." In addition, FDA officials have stated that they "will consider clinical studies conducted under ICH GCP as meeting GCP standards acceptable to FDA."

Over time, the differences in emphasis and specificity between the FDA standards and ICH GCP guideline should become less evident. FDA officials have stated that the agency will "take into account the ICH GCPs" in developing new or revising existing regulations and guidance as part of routine GCP program maintenance activities.

For now, however, the question is a common one, particularly because the ICH GCP guideline is, in at least several respects, seen as more specific in defining certain GCP standards (see Q1.5). In other areas, FDA GCP standards are more definitive.

Ultimately, the decision regarding whether to monitor against FDA or ICH GCP standards is the sponsor's. A sponsor may also wish to incorporate its own "best practice" standards into its expectations regarding site performance. Since the ICH GCP guideline is more specific than—some would say goes further than—the ICH GCP regulations/guidances in selected areas, conventional wisdom suggests that a company should use the ICH GCP standards for clinical studies that it intends to use in regulatory submissions globally. Compliance with this guideline—and an applicant's statement to this effect in the marketing dossier—as well as the additional regulatory standards of the other ICH participants can only be expected to promote the acceptance of the clinical studies in these other countries.

For studies to be submitted exclusively in the United States, it would seem that either standard would suffice. As noted, FDA officials have stated that the agency will "consider clinical studies conducted under ICH GCP as meeting GCP standards acceptable to FDA."

In terms of FDA clinical investigator and sponsor/monitor compliance inspections, however, it is important to note that, according CDER's Division of Scientific

Investigations (DSI), the center's Bioresearch Monitoring Program (BIMO) is focused primarily on finding deviations from FDA GCP regulations, and not deviations from either FDA or ICH GCP guidelines. Following an FDA inspection of a clinical investigator, sponsor/monitor, or CRO, the Form 483-Inspectional Observations that the inspector leaves with the sponsor/monitor, investigator, or CRO should, according to CDER policy, identify *only* observed deviations from FDA GCP regulations. Although deviations from FDA guidelines *should* be identified and discussed in the later-developed Establishment Inspection Report (EIR) and *may* be discussed in a subsequent inspection-related FDA letter (e.g., untitled letter, warning letter) to the firm or investigator, these deviations will be identified separately from the deviations from FDA regulations. [Editor's Note: an FDA inspector leaves a Form 483 with the investigator/sponsor only if deviations are discovered.] In informal correspondence on this issue, DSI staffers do not recall having seen any EIR or inspection-related CDER letter that identified or discussed any deviation specifically from the ICH GCP guideline.

Still, some within industry believe that adhering to ICH GCP standards in addition to FDA GCP standards increases FDA inspectors' comfort level with site and sponsor performance.

4.11 Q. Can site monitors complete case report forms? If so, under what circumstances?

A. Site monitors perform a quality control function—that is, they verify data that have been entered on case report forms (CRF) by site staff. In this capacity, monitors should never write on original copies of the CRFs. This rule applies both to contracted site monitors (CRO or independents) and to sponsor staff. If a monitor alters or enters original CRF data, it could give the impression that data may have been entered or changed in favor of the sponsor.

At times, CRO or sponsor staff assist site personnel who are functioning in a deadline-driven situation and who may be behind in the completion of CRFs (see Q13.10). In such situations, the CRO/sponsor provides staffing to help the study coordinator enter CRF data. These staff, however, should never be involved in the quality control process—that is, monitoring data at that site. Their work must be strictly independent of the quality control process, and they should not be involved in any source data verification.

In a deadline crunch, it is not unusual for a study coordinator and clinical research associate to sit side-by-side as the study coordinator completes the CRFs. The clinical research associate helps to identify data in source documents, and the study coordinator enters these data on the CRF. Even in the most dire deadline crunch, however, it remains unacceptable for clinical research associates who have quality control or monitoring responsibilities to enter data on CRFs.

4.12 Q. What level of CRF/source documentation verification does FDA require? In other words, must a clinical research associate monitor 100% of the data included in the medical records/charts? If not, what should the clinical research associate focus on monitoring?

A. According to the FDA's "Guideline for the Monitoring of Clinical Investigations" (1988), "during a periodic visit [to a clinical trial site], the monitor should compare a representative number of subject records and other supporting documents with the investigator's reports to determine that:

- The information recorded in the investigator's report is complete, accurate, and legible
- There are no omissions in the reports of specific data elements such as the administration to any subject of concomitant test articles or the development of an intercurrent illness
- Missing visits or examinations are noted in the reports
- Subjects failing to complete the study and the reason for each failure are noted in the reports
- Informed consent has been documented in accordance [with federal regulations]"

Generally, a sponsor will define the "representative number" of CRFs that a monitor should compare against the original source documentation at the site.

In Section 5.18.3, "Nature and Extent of Monitoring," the ICH GCP guideline states only that "statistically controlled sampling may be an acceptable method for selecting the data to be verified."

As noted in Q4.13 below, however, there are two sampling approaches to CRF/source data verification: examining a percentage of all CRFs and examining a percentage of data items on all CRFs. It is difficult to imagine that a monitor would be directed not to review a certain number of CRFs at all.

4.13 Q. But FDA inspectors are instructed, in CDER's Compliance Policy Guide 7348.810, to "determine if all CRFs are verified. If a representative sample was selected, determine how the size and composition of the sample was selected." Therefore, what possible regulatory implications does a CRF/ source verification effort based on representative sampling have in the context of such inspections versus a 100% verification? In other words, how will an FDA inspector approach an inspection differently for studies that were 100% verified versus those that were not?

A. An FDA inspector will not approach an inspection differently based on the CRF verification approach employed. As a practical matter, it is next to impossible for an inspector to determine, assuming there are only a few discrepancies between source documents and CRFs, whether a CRA performed either a 100% verification of CRFs *and* of CRF data items or sampled a lesser percentage. If there are many discrepancies identified during the inspection, then one could conclude that, regardless of the CRF verification approach, the monitoring was unsatisfactory. A sponsor's management team will reach the same conclusion, as will quality assurance auditors.

In practice, most monitors are directed to perform 100% source verification of data items. For a variety of reasons, however, they sometimes take short cuts by not reviewing each data item or by working backwards from CRF data to medical records data. Therefore, the monitor may miss important data that are either "buried" in the medical record or that are contradictory in the medical record.

By separating the NCR paper and submitting copies to data management, the monitor is attesting that, to the best of his or her knowledge, the data on the CRF are accurate and verifiable. For a web-based study, sponsors should specify in a standard operating procedure how monitors are to provide "evidence" that CRFs were source verified.

4.14 Q. Are clinical monitors required to issue follow-up letters to the clinical site after a monitoring visit?

A. There is no FDA requirement that clinical monitors develop and send follow-up letters. The agency's "Guideline for the Monitoring of Clinical Investigations" (1988) focuses on the importance of internal post-inspection monitoring reports rather than follow-up letters. According to the guidance, "the monitor or sponsor should maintain a record of the findings, conclusions, and action taken to correct deficiencies for each on-site visit to an investigator. Such a record may enable FDA to determine that a sponsor's obligations in monitoring the progress of a clinical investigation are being fulfilled."

As a practical matter, however, if a site is experiencing problems that need to be addressed at the site, then there must be documentation in place that demonstrates a sponsor/monitor's good-faith effort to address these problems and have them corrected. In general, a follow-up letter to the principal investigator is an important piece of documentation indicating that corrective action is necessary.

That being said, management teams within some trial sponsors actively discourage including any discussion of GCP problems in either monitoring reports or follow-up letters. They prefer to address issues in oral discussions that leave no trace of these problems. This strategy can backfire, however. If an FDA inspection identifies compliance problems or if a subject initiates a lawsuit alleging that unsafe, non-GCP practices were employed at a site, the sponsor, to avoid regulatory sanctions and/or liability, will be asked to provide evidence that it attempted to correct the specified problems. The conspicuous absence of follow-up letters in such cases will suggest to some that the sponsor did not seek corrective action at the site.

The follow-up letter is also a good vehicle for sponsors to stay in touch with principal investigators and study coordinators and to let them know that they are performing well. Such letters, however, should be carefully crafted and not appear to be form letters. They also need not reiterate all the monitoring activities that took place during a visit. These communications should be helpful, constructive, and above all, truthful. They should, like monitoring reports, also discuss how GCP quality at the site has evolved during the study, for the better or worse.

4.15 Q. If a monitor was once employed by a site, is it permissible for a sponsor or clinical research organization to assign him or her to monitor this site?

A. There are no prohibitions against using a monitor to review records at a site that formerly employed the monitor. Sponsors and CROs, however, would be well advised to let a certain period of time pass—say one year—before making this assignment and thereby avoid the appearance of a conflict of interest. Documenting this prohibition in a standard operating procedure might also be a good idea.

A monitor returning to a clinical site where he or she had previously worked should make a particular effort to remain professional and objective in his or her duties, particularly in recording and correcting data and resolving GCP-related issues.

Obviously, a monitor should not be placed in a situation in which he or she must review records for studies on which he or she previously performed as a study coordinator and/or investigator. The quality control function would then be compromised.

4.16 Q. Must all e-mail (i.e., printouts) and fax (including cover sheets) communications from sponsors to sites and from sites to sponsors be retained and stored at the clinical site or by the clinical trial sponsor? What is FDA's inspectional policy regarding these communications, and does the agency currently review this correspondence to ensure that it matches in the investigator and sponsor files?

A. Although such communications are not addressed specifically in FDA regulations, the ICH GCP guideline seems to suggest, at least indirectly, that such communications should be retained and stored by sites and sponsors. In Section 8-Essential Documents for the Conduct of a Clinical Trial, the guideline states that, "Essential Documents are those documents that individually and collectively permit evaluation of the conduct of a trial and the quality of the data produced. These documents serve to demonstrate the compliance of the investigator, sponsor, and monitor with the standards of GCP and with all applicable regulatory requirements . . . Filing essential documents at the investigator/institution and sponsor sites in a timely manner can greatly assist in the successful management of a trial by the investigator, sponsor, and monitor. These documents are also the ones that are usually audited by the sponsor's independent audit function and inspected by the regulatory authority(ies) as part of the process to confirm the validity of the trial conduct and the integrity of data collected."

Under 8.3.11-Relevant communications other than site visits, the ICH GCP guideline identifies letters, meeting notes, and notes of telephone calls as communications that should be retained "to document any agreements or significant discussions regarding trial administration, protocol violations, trial conduct, [and] adverse event (AE) reporting." It is important to note, however, that some communications are not worth retaining, including e-mails sent to schedule and coordinate visits and flyers with menu choices for meetings. Many sponsors purge these unnecessary communications before storing documents at the end of a trial.

Although it is conceivable that an FDA inspector would visit both a site's and a sponsor/CRO's central files to compare the site's communication records with the same records stored in the sponsor/CRO's investigator files, it is extremely unlikely that the inspector would visit the sponsor's central files. The agency will inspect a sponsor's central files if it suspects that the sponsor/CRO has made changes to data provided by the clinical investigator. An FDA for-cause inspection of central files would, in all likelihood, be conducted by a different agency inspector (i.e., than the one inspecting the site), in part because field inspectors do not generally inspect outside of their assigned districts.

Monitors and auditors should compare records in the central files and site files well before the FDA begins the site inspection process, and throughout the study as part of routine monitoring/auditing practices. Inconsistencies and other problems should be addressed as well. Given the large volume of correspondence, paper work, and record keeping involved in a study, a small number of discrepancies in stored documents, even 1572s, is not unusual.

4.17 Q. Do GCP regulations require that a site establish and maintain a monitor visit log? If so, what happens if a monitor forgets to sign it during a visit? And should a clinical auditor sign the monitor visit log?

A. Neither the FDA GCP regulations nor the ICH GCP guideline identify the need for a "monitor signature log." It is worth noting, however, that the FDA does instruct its field inspectors, during clinical site inspections, to determine whether a log of on-site monitoring visits is included in study records. This determination is part of the inspector's assessment of the sponsor's monitoring practices (e.g., method, frequency) for the study.

Since site monitoring reports are not maintained at sites, a visit log may provide the only site-maintained evidence, with the exception of correspondence, to "prove" that a CRA made routine monitoring visits. In some cases, the study coordinators also sign the monitoring log to further attest to the visit. The log provides a chronological review of the frequency of visits such that an auditor or inspector can quickly comprehend the intensity of monitoring activity.

In addition, a monitor visit log is an excellent means of establishing that monitoring frequency was appropriate given enrollment rates for specific periods of time. The monitoring log can be compared with the enrollment log to evaluate the adequacy of monitoring visit frequency.

If a monitor forgets to sign the log, he or she should sign it at a later date, noting the actual date of the visit and the date of the late entry. The fact that this is a late entry should be made readily apparent.

Clinical auditors do not sign the monitor log unless there is an institutional or sponsor standard operating procedure that requires them to do so. The only evidence that an auditor made a visit might be an auditing certificate placed in the study binder as well as related correspondence.

Originals of the monitor log should remain at the site. Copies should be forwarded to the sponsor central files. Sponsor staff should be alert to discrepancies between dates on the monitor log and dates of visits listed on monitoring reports. Discrepancies should be brought to the monitor's attention and resolved. It is acceptable to annotate explanations of unusual events (earthquakes, hurricanes) on the log to help explain why a visit was cut short. Also, it is acceptable to explain that one of the visitors was co-monitoring or in training or present more as an observer rather than as an "official" monitor.

4.18 Q. For regulatory purposes, when is a site considered formally closed? When a site is closed to new accrual/active subjects, does this change meet the criteria for a "change in research activity" that would require the investigator to notify the IRB?

A. The formal closure of a site occurs beyond the point at which subjects remain on study (see Q4.19). There are several milestones that must be reached before a site is considered formally closed:

- enrollment ceases
- the last subject is off study
- a close-out monitoring visit is completed

In general, most sponsors want to have all major, outstanding queries resolved before formally closing a site. Sites can be closed in spite of open queries that may be irreconcilable, however.

Individual IRBs may have specific rules regarding the reporting of these milestones. Certainly, these milestones should be noted in annual reports to an IRB. In general, investigators are advised to keep an IRB fully informed about study progress and milestones, although many sites, in practice, meet only the minimum IRB requirements and rules.

4.19 Q. What specific actions must a clinical monitor take to "officially" close a clinical trial site?

A. Neither FDA regulations nor the FDA's Guideline on Clinical Trial Monitoring (1988) makes reference to study close out visits by monitors. The ICH GCP guideline, however, refers to a "final trial close-out monitoring report" as an "essential document." It states that the report should "document that all activities required for trial close-out are completed, and copies of essential documents are held in the appropriate files."

In general, three actions are required to "officially" close out a site:

1. The sponsor/CRO conducts a close-out monitoring visit, and the monitor signs the monitoring log.
2. The investigator submits a final report and a letter stating that the site is closed to the IRB.
3. The sponsor sends the investigator a letter stating that the site is closed (the letter may reiterate the investigator's post-closure responsibilities).

If any of these communications are missing, study closure has not been sufficiently documented. Site and sponsor staff should be clear about closure status, and solid documentation reduces the possibility that key staff are uncertain regarding this status.

It is important to keep in mind that individual IRBs may have additional requirements related to the closure of a study site.

4.20 Q. If, due to investigator and study coordinator negligence, an IRB decides that it will not renew the approval for a particular study, what impact does this decision have on site and monitoring activities?

A. An IRB's decision to terminate an approval or deny the renewal of a study's approval is quite serious, in large part because such a decision is based on the safety and well-being of the subjects participating in the study. In this case, without further IRB approval, there can be no further subject visits for the purposes of collecting new protocol-required data, although the study staff can inform subjects that the study has ended. Data clean up and monitoring activities should definitely continue, however.

Incidentally, the IRB is required to report any "serious or continuing non-compliance" to the FDA.

Further Reading

Mackintosh, D. and Zepp, V., "Improving the Quality of Monitoring: Clinical Auditors' Observations," *Applied Clinical Trials* 6:52-58, September 1997.

Woodin, Karen and Schneider, John C., *The CRA's Guide to Monitoring Clinical Research,* Thompson, Centerwatch, 2003.

Acknowledgments

Douglas Mackintosh, DrPH, MBA, MS Hyg, and Vernette Molloy, MBA, RN, of GCPA, Inc.; Lynda Blair, RN, independent GCP consultant, Watertown, MA; Karen Woodin, PhD, President, JKK Consulting, Kalamazoo, MI.

Section 5:
Informed Consent

5.1 *Q. In establishing that federal regulations on informed consent require more than simply "getting the subject to sign a consent document," the FDA states in its information sheets that "the entire informed consent process involves giving the subject adequate information concerning the study, providing adequate opportunity for the subject to consider all options, responding to the subject's questions, ensuring that the subject has comprehended this information, obtaining the subject's voluntary agreement to participate, and continuing to provide information as the subject and situation requires." All but one of these—ensuring that the subject comprehended this information— seem to be addressed in federal regulations. The idea that the informed consent process involves "assuring that the subject has comprehended" the information in the informed consent form was also mentioned in the preamble to FDA's 1981 informed consent regulations. What are the FDA's specific requirements and/or expectations of investigator efforts to ensure that the subject has comprehended the information provided as part of the informed consent process?*

A. There is little direct guidance on the FDA's expectations in this area. In a recent informal response to this question, the FDA stated that, "FDA's regulations do not specify techniques that sites must use to verify if subjects (or their legally authorized representatives) indeed comprehend the information they have been provided about a study. Clearly, if it appears that a subject does not understand some aspect of the study—for example, symptoms that should be reported immediately to the clinical investigator because they could be life-threatening—then it would be important for the clinical investigator and his staff to take additional steps to make sure that the subject clearly understands what is expected before going forward. However, because the regulations do not specify techniques to be used, sponsors and clinical investigators may develop their own methods for ascertaining if subjects comprehend the information they have been given about the study. For example, the clinical investigator's staff may ask the potential subjects follow-up questions to see if they understand what to expect."

To consider this and related issues in the informed consent process, the federal government recently formed an Informed Consent Working Group comprising officials from the FDA, the National Cancer Institute (NCI), and the HHS Office of Human Research Protections. In a document entitled, *Simplification of Informed Consent Documents,* the working group offered the following recommendations to investigators in assessing a prospective subject's understanding of the informed consent information:

"It may be helpful for the researcher to ask the potential research participant short questions after the research has been described and the consent form read, in order to assess that the potential research participant has at least a basic understanding of what the research involves. Example questions include:

- Tell me in your own words what this study is all about.
- Tell me what you think will happen to you in this study.
- What do you expect to gain by taking part in this research?

- What risks might you experience by participating in the research?
- What are your alternatives (other choices or options to participating in this research)?"

Some advanced studies using an on-line consent process are integrating comprehension assessments into the informed consent process. In a 2004 article in the DIA Journal (Vol. 39, pp. 239-251) that describes a study as "an interactive clinical trial conducted using the Internet," the authors note that prospective subjects accessed and reviewed an on-line informed consent document. The subjects were then administered a "quiz consisting of multiple choice and true/false questions on the content of the informed consent. If the patient incorrectly answered a question, the Web site presented to the patient the section in the text where the correct answer could be found. The patient was able to review the informed consent text and reanswer the question. When the quiz was 100% correct, the Web site reminded the patient to ask any questions about the interactive clinical trial to study center personnel."

5.2   *Q. So do FDA inspectors examine this area and cite investigators who fail to assess subjects' understanding and ensure "that the subject has comprehended this information"?*

A. The reality that FDA regulations do not establish specific methods or standards that investigators must use to verify subjects' comprehension of information provided as part of the informed consent process makes this area a difficult one for agency inspectors to address in any meaningful way. In an informal response to this question, the FDA stated that, since "FDA field investigators are trained to include only violations of FDA's regulations on the Form FDA-483 [Inspectional Observations], . . . it would be highly unlikely that any site would be cited for [a] 'failure to ensure that the subject has comprehended the [study] information.' In all likelihood, the issue of a subject's 'comprehension' of information about a study would probably not even arise during an inspection, unless FDA had reason to believe, for example, because of a complaint by a study subject or someone who had witnessed the consent process, that the subject was not given an opportunity to ask questions, or that his questions were ignored. "

5.3   *Q. If a subject is a minor at the beginning of a study and then reaches the age of majority (determined by state law) during the course of the clinical study, must he/she be consented or "reconsented" as an adult (i.e., the very next visit after reaching majority)?*

A. In a recent informal response to this question, the FDA makes the case that the subject should be consented as an adult. The basis for this advice is the fact that, once a person becomes an adult, the parent/legal guardian's trial-related permission for the child to participate would no longer comprise legally effective informed consent for future research.

"FDA's regulations do not specifically address the situation [described]," the agency notes. "However, there is no question that 21 CFR 50.20 requires an investigator to obtain 'the legally effective informed consent of the subject or the subject's legally authorized representative.' Once a child-subject reaches the age of majority (which will vary according to state law), the parent's permission for the child to participate in the trial would no longer constitute 'legally effective informed consent' for research activities that take place in the future because the subject, who is now an adult, can make decisions for him/herself and should be offered the opportunity to do so. This assumes that there are research activities that will be occurring that would require the informed consent of the subject who is now of legal age to consent. That is, [we are] not referring to the defunct concept of deferred consent for what has already occurred; the issue is whether the research will continue and, if it will when the subject has reached majority, then consent of the subject is required."

5.4 *Q. By extension, then, would the same hold if an unconscious patient is entered (i.e., through legal guardian, legally authorized representative) into a clinical trial? Assuming the patient regains consciousness and lucid mentation or capacity is re-established, must he/she be consented for the trial?*

A. In a recent response to this question, the FDA maintained that informed consent should be obtained for trial-related procedures to be undertaken after consciousness/ mentation is regained. "If you have a subject entered into a study who was unable to consent because they were unconscious, and they subsequently regain consciousness, if there are research procedures remaining that would require informed consent, then if the subject is able, the consent of the subject should be sought for those procedures that will occur in the future," the FDA states. "However, consent may not be needed if the emergency has passed at the time the subject regains consciousness (and the investigational product was administered with the consent of a legally authorized representative or exception to informed consent under 50.24). The subject can certainly withdraw from further participation in the research, assuming there is research continuing, but cannot now consent to what has already occurred. IRBs need to look at these situations in relation to the research, state law, institutional commitments, and medical ethics."

5.5 *Q. Under GCP requirements, must the clinical investigator personally be involved in obtaining informed consent from study subjects? Can the principal investigator delegate the administration of informed consent to study staff, such as a nurse?*

A. 21 CFR Section 312.60-General responsibilities of investigators states that "an investigator shall . . . obtain the informed consent of each human subject to whom the drug is administered." The ICH GCP guideline states that, "in obtaining and documenting informed consent, the investigator should comply with the applicable regulatory requirement(s). . . ."

Although the wording of the GCP regulations and ICH GCP guideline seems to imply an investigator's direct involvement in the informed consent process, it is not required. In fact, the ICH GCP guideline makes clear in several other provisions that the person conducting the informed consent discussion can be "a person designated by the investigator." In its Information Sheets, the FDA points notes that "FDA does not specify who this individual should be. Some sponsors and some IRBs require the clinical investigator to personally conduct the consent interview."

Some experts maintain that, particularly for studies that raise issues that are clinically complex, a study physician should be directly involved in the consent process and should participate in a face-to-face discussion with a potential subject.

In some cases, medical assistants who are marginally trained and inexperienced are delegated the responsibility of relating complex clinical issues and study requirements in the consent process without any direct input from a physician. Under these circumstances, many industry professionals would conclude that valid informed consent cannot be obtained.

Regardless of who leads the consent process for a site, it is the principal investigator who is ultimately responsible for the administration of informed consent. As noted, although the investigator may delegate the task to appropriately qualified study staff, such as a registered nurse, there are caveats, most importantly that the individual assuming this responsibility must have the requisite clinical background to provide a thorough description of the study and answer the study candidate's questions. Some studies are so complex that only a physician should administer the consent. In many cases, the administration of the consent is a collaborative effort undertaken by both the principal investigator and the study nurse.

5.6 *Q. In specifying the basic elements of informed consent, 21 CFR 50.25(a)(2), (3), and (4) requires that informed consent forms provide "a description of any reasonably foreseeable risks or discomforts with the drug . . . any benefits to the subject or to others which may reasonably be expected from the research . . . , [and] a disclosure of appropriate alternative procedures or courses of treatment, if any, that might be advantageous to the subject." Are such descriptions and disclosures required to include quantified and comparative estimates of the risks/benefits of the experimental and/or alternative treatments?*

A. Although the FDA acknowledges the value of quantified comparative estimates of risks and benefits in the informed consent process, it has also resisted suggestions that such estimates be mandatory, largely because the quantification of risks and benefits are not possible in all cases. In the preamble to its 1981 informed consent regulations, the FDA stated that it "believes that where such descriptions or disclosures can contain quantified comparative estimates of risks and benefits, they should do so. Where such well-defined estimates are not possible, however, the agency believes that the information required to be disclosed will be sufficient. The agency does not believe that imposing a strict requirement for every case would be realistic or appropriate."

5.7 *Q. Clearly, 21 CFR 56.109(b), which states in part that "An IRB shall require that information given to subjects as part of informed consent is in accordance with 50.25," requires the IRB to review the informed consent form. Today, however, we are beginning to see some clinical programs featuring the use, on a pilot basis, of "interactive multimedia presentations" to supplement the informed consent form and process. These interactive presentations have, according to a recent study, involved the use of tablet PCs and software and interactive video presentations and interactive question and answer sessions to help potential trial subjects understand their disease and the clinical trial. If such presentations are used as part of or to supplement the informed consent process, must the IRB first review and approve the entire presentation* *and everything that the patient will see as part of it? Or can the IRB focus on just the informed consent form itself?*

A. Since such multimedia presentations would be considered part of, or could at least significantly affect, the informed consent process, the IRB must review and approve the presentations before they are used. In an informal communication on this subject, the FDA stated that, based on 21 CFR 56.109(b), "all information presented to subjects as part of the consent process, including that contained in interactive multimedia presentations, would need to be reviewed and approved by the IRB. While these interactive presentations may enhance the consent process, without IRB review of the information conveyed, the presentations may instead cause confusion or convey misinformation. The consent process needs to be seen as being broader than the consent form; it includes other tools used by the researcher to help the subject understand the research."

5.8 *Q. In large part due to the complexity of information conveyed in the informed consent process, the use of research subject advocates or patient advocates to help prospective study participants understand relevant study-related information and options has been advocated and adopted in some cases, in particular for highly complex and high-risk trials. For the AbioCor artificial heart trial, for example, a patient advocate group was established and was made independent of the trial sponsor and the investigators. Since these patient advocates and groups are involved in helping prospective trial subjects understand the risks (and possible benefits) of a clinical study as part of the larger informed consent process, how, if at all, do FDA informed consent requirements and standards apply to these individuals and groups?*

A. Neither FDA regulations nor guidances contemplated patient advocates. Therefore, there are no regulatory provisions that apply either directly or indirectly to such individuals or groups. In addition, none of the CDER officials contacted on this question indicated that the agency is considering any new standards to address the involvement of patient advocates in the informed consent process.

As CDER compliance officials contacted on this question noted, the key issue here is that no element of the investigator's informed consent-related responsibilities is being delegated to the patient advocates. Only if such advocates have been formally delegated specific informed consent-related responsibilities would regulatory requirements become relevant to their activities and involvement. Since it is generally assumed that a clinical investigator will be directly involved in the informed consent process for highly complex and risky trials (i.e., the trials in which patient advocates are typically used), it is particularly unlikely that an investigator would delegate consent-related responsibilities in such cases.

5.9 *Q. FDA regulations at 21 CFR 50.20 require that an investigator seek informed consent "only under circumstances that . . . minimize the possibility of coercion or undue influence." Although it rarely does so (about 1% of routine site inspections in past years), the agency has cited trial investigators for "inappropriate payment to volunteers." What criteria does the FDA apply to determine whether a payment, reimbursement for study-related expenses, credits, or other inducements are coercive or present undue influence?*

A. Neither FDA regulations nor guidance documents provide definitive insights into the criteria or decision processes that agency officials use to determine if a payment to study participants is inappropriate. A general—but perhaps the lengthiest—agency discussion on the topic is provided in an FDA information sheet entitled, "*Payment to Research Subjects,*" which establishes that the IRB must review and approve all payments and payment methods/schedules, and that all payment-related information must be set forth in the informed consent document:

"It is not uncommon for subjects to be paid for their participation in research, especially in the early phases of investigational drug, biologic or device development," the agency's information sheet states. "Payment to research subjects for participation in studies is not considered a benefit, it is a recruitment incentive. Financial incentives are often used when health benefits to subjects are remote or non-existent. The amount and schedule of all payments should be presented to the IRB at the time of initial review. The IRB should review both the amount of payment and the proposed method and timing of disbursement to assure that neither are coercive or present undue influence [21 CFR 50.20]."

Much of the agency's discussion focuses on the scheduling, rather than the amount, of payments to study subjects. "Any credit for payment should accrue as the study progresses and not be contingent upon the subject completing the entire study. Unless it creates undue inconvenience or a coercive practice, payment to subjects who withdraw from the study may be made at the time they would have completed the study (or completed a phase of the study) had they not withdrawn. For example, in a study lasting only a few days, an IRB may find it permissible to allow a single payment date at the end of the study, even to subjects who had withdrawn that date. While the entire payment should not be contingent upon completion of the entire study, payment of a small proportion as an incentive for completion of the study is acceptable to FDA, providing that such incentive is not coercive. The IRB should determine that the amount paid as a bonus for completion is reasonable and not so large as to unduly induce subjects to stay in the study when they would otherwise have withdrawn. All information concerning payment, including the amount and schedule of payment(s), should be set forth in the informed consent document."

Given that the FDA has itself cited studies for "inappropriate payments," however, payments are not just an IRB concern as implied in the passage above, although some agency officials today believe they should be addressed solely by IRBs (see discussion below). It is difficult to get FDA officials to speak candidly about the types and methods of payments that they consider to be inappropriate inducements. In an informal discussion, an FDA field inspector who focuses on bioresearch monitoring issues noted that he will become suspicious if, for example, he notices a study recruitment advertisement that seems to overemphasize financial incentives involved in a study (e.g., a particularly large or frequently recurring "$$$$" sign in the ad, a bolded statement of "money for your time"). The inspector noted, however, that he will not generally include suspected undue influence of financial incentives on the 483-Inspectional Observations form—in fact, he notes that he has never seen such a citation on a 483. Rather, the inspector communicates any suspicions back to headquarters for evaluation, and allows FDA compliance officials to determine if the payments were inappropriate and whether the study should be cited.

In instructions to FDA field staff conducting clinical investigator inspections, FDA Compliance Program Guidance 7348.811 (CPG 7348.811) notes that inspectors should assess "media ads for patient/subject recruitment" and related "promotional material." CPG 7348.811 does not mention payments to trial subjects, however, and instructs FDA inspectors to focus on whether the IRB-approved media recruitment ads or the investigator represented the test article as safe and effective in related promotional materials.

Given the lack of formal FDA guidance or written agency policy on the appropriateness of payments offered to potential subjects, it is not surprising that CDER compliance officials themselves struggle in this area. In some cases, say CDER officials, they will even contact medical officers in CDER's drug review divisions (e.g., an FDA reviewer who is also a board-certified psychiatrist regarding a trial involving an antidepressant) for input on the appropriateness of a particular payment given the nature of the study (e.g., indication, study length, number of visits, medical procedures involved), the things expected of the study subjects, and other relevant factors. Agency officials note, however, that even FDA reviewers struggle with the relevant issues involved (e.g., how can a value or price be put on a study subject's time?).

During internal meetings, agency officials continued to discuss and reassess the agency's role in determining the appropriateness of payments to study subjects. As noted, some within the agency believe that the issue should be left to IRBs alone. Other agency officials point out, however, that IRBs (and even some prospective study subjects) are increasingly seeking FDA guidance on such payments. They add that IRBs only see payments in the context of the studies conducted within their institutions, and that the FDA sees payment-related information and patterns for a much larger sample of trials (e.g., through informed consent forms included in IND submissions). Given this, some FDA officials maintain that the agency should be more proactive in providing guidance regarding such payments, and could, ideally, provide some broad principles or guidance to help IRBs, sponsors, investigators, trial subjects and others address the related issues.

Meanwhile, some government attorneys have claimed that financial inducements paid to clinical study subjects could come under increasing scrutiny by federal prosecutors focused on health care issues. While financial incentives used to recruit healthy patients are unlikely to draw the attention of federal prosecutors, "it gets sticky when you're talking about very vulnerable subjects, either extremely poor subjects or children or the elderly," says Philadelphia Associate U.S. Attorney James Sheehan. "Those I would take a second look at."

5.10 *Q. IRB and sponsor requirements regarding who should sign the informed consent form vary considerably. According to FDA and ICH GCP standards, what specific person(s) should sign the informed consent document? For the site, should the person signing the informed consent form always be the investigator, or should it be the person who led the informed consent process?*

A. In this area, the ICH GCP guideline is more definitive than FDA regulations, although neither document necessarily requires that the investigator sign the informed consent document.

The ICH guideline specifically calls for the written informed consent form to "be signed and personally dated by the subject or by the subject's legally acceptable representative, and by the person who conducted the informed consent discussion." Since the guideline establishes that the individual obtaining the informed consent can be "a person designated by the investigator," the person signing the form could be either the investigator or this designated individual, whomever conducted the informed consent process.

Under FDA regulations at 21 CFR 50.27-Documentation of informed consent, the signatures required on the informed consent form depend on the manner in which informed consent is obtained. In conventional circumstances (i.e., when a written consent document embodying the elements of informed consent is used), FDA regulations require that the IRB-approved written informed consent form be "signed and dated by the subject or the subject's legally authorized representative at the time of consent." Therefore, FDA regulations do not require a second signature in such situations.

Under 21 CFR 50.27, only under specific and rare circumstances—that is, when a short form written consent document stating that the elements of informed consent have been presented orally to the subject or the subject's legally authorized representative is used—must the "person actually obtaining the consent" also sign consent-related documentation. In such a case, the person obtaining the consent and the witness must sign a copy of the IRB-approved written summary of what is to be said to the subject. Furthermore, the short form itself must be signed by the subject or the representative. [Editor's note: because the short form is so rarely used in the United States, the relevance of these requirements is limited.]

5.11 *Q. To date, the only known direct FDA statement on pharmacogenetics-related testing in clinical trials appears in a "note" within a March 2005 FDA guidance ("Pharmacogenomic Data Submissions"), which states that, "regardless of requirements for submission, the fact that samples will be collected for potential [pharmacogenomic] analysis must be noted in any clinical protocol (312.23(a)(6)) and informed consent documents (50.25)." Does this mean that the FDA has determined that it is sufficient for drug companies to specify, in protocols and informed consent documents, that blood/tissue samples will be collected in the trials and that they may be used for future testing without specifying the nature of the possible future testing?*

A. In a recent informal response to this question, the FDA points out that, based on these regulatory passages, the agency would expect both the study protocol and informed consent document to describe the research in the initial study as well as any future research (e.g., pharmacogenomic testing on collected samples) that is contemplated. The agency also makes clear that it is the IRB that will consider such issues and that it will decide how the future research must be addressed in the original and possibly subsequent consent process.

"The applicable regulations in this case include FDA's regulations for study protocols (21 CFR 312.23(a)(6)) and for informed consent (21 CFR 50)," says the agency. "FDA does not have any regulations that are specific to pharmacogenomic studies. FDA's regulations for study protocols require the protocol to "describ[e] all aspects of the study . . ." including a description of the ". . . design of the study . . . , observations and measurements to be made to fulfill the objectives of the study, . . . clinical procedures, laboratory tests, or other measures to be taken to monitor the effects of the drug in human subjects and to minimize risk. . . ." [See 21 CFR 312.23(a)(6)(ii) and (iii)(d), (iii)(f), and (iii)(g)]. FDA's informed consent regulations require the consent form to contain certain basic information, including ". . . an explanation of the purpose of the research and the expected duration of the subject's participation, a description of the procedures to be followed, and identification of any procedures which are experimental . . ." [See 21 CFR 50.25(a)(1).]

"Thus, FDA would expect that both the study protocol and informed consent document should describe any research that is contemplated—not only the research for the initial study, but also the future pharmacogenomic testing as well. In some cases, more information may be available to include in the consent form about the contemplated research than at other times, but that is an issue that the IRB must consider in its review/approval of a protocol and the associated consent document and process. (For example, the IRB could stipulate that the informed consent document indicate that specimens will be collected for future pharmacogenomic research, and the subject will be contacted when more is known, to obtain the subject's consent for that research.)

"In general, however, including as much information in the informed consent document as possible is a way to show respect for the autonomy of the subjects. It provides the subject with an opportunity to question the scope of, or procedures involved in, the study. Further, if a subject believes that what he/she is being asked for is too vague or too broad, then this also provides the subject with an opportunity to opt out."

5.12 Q. Given that the FDA and other regulatory authorities have not provided more substantial guidance on informed consent and pharmacogenetic testing, have any industry groups attempted to provide any guidance or guiding principles in this area?

A. Yes. An industry group called the Pharmacogenetics Working Group (PWG) has published an article to educate the various parties involved in the clinical research process on pharmacogenetics and informed consent-related issues (see below). The PWG describes itself as a voluntary association of 23 major pharmaceutical companies involved in pharmacogenetics research whose goal is to advance the understanding and development of pharmacogenetics by addressing non-competitive ethical, regulatory and legal issues. In November 2001, the PWG developed a position paper on pharmacogenetic terminology in response to interest expressed by the European Medicines Evaluation Agency (EMEA), and followed that by releasing an article on informed consent in 2002. At press time, the group was set to publish a new article on providing pharmacogenetic testing results to clinical trial subjects.

In its 2002 article entitled, "Elements of informed consent for pharmacogenetic research; perspective of the pharmacogenetics working group" (*The Pharmacogenomics Journal* (2002), 2, 284-292), the working group addressed pharmacogenetic research in drug development and some of the associated "special considerations and disclosures in the informed consent process" that such research calls for. In reality, the PWG article was designed to educate not necessarily those in industry, but researchers, IRBs, and regulatory agencies on the informed consent-related issues specific to industry-sponsored pharmacogenetic research. The goal was to help investigators, IRBs, and regulators to protect patients while providing timely review and approval of pharmacogenetic trials.

While acknowledging that "defining the best approach to informed consent for pharmacogenetic research is challenging," the PWG offers many recommendations or "points to consider" in its paper, including the following:

- Because genetic terminology can be difficult to understand, special attention should be paid to the informed document language itself and, when appropriate, consent materials should be given to subjects prior to the research visit so there is sufficient time for review. To avoid possible misconceptions triggered by background information a subject may have received prior to being asked to participate (e.g., from media), the informed consent process should explain not only what pharmacogenetics is, but what it is not (e.g., cloning).

- For pharmacogenomics studies, the subject should be provided with some background information about the biologic function of genes (e.g., that genes affect physical features and health status) and how such studies may help scientists and clinicians learn more about health, disease, and drug treatments. The specific purpose of the pharmacogenetic study should be clearly described, including both short-term objectives and potential long-term applications. Readily understandable study endpoints should be conveyed, such as "to identify genetic reasons why certain individuals respond differently to drugs" or "to identify variations of genes which may cause or modify a disease."

- The informed consent document should identify all intended uses of the pharmacogenetic information and clinical information to be derived from it. The document should disclose plans for archiving the subject's DNA and/or creating immortalized cell lines (which could provide an inexhaustible source of DNA for future studies) and any plans for distributing the subject's genetic materials to secondary users (even if such parties are not yet defined).

- The informed consent process for pharmacogenetics trials should clearly describe the procedures involved in collecting and handling samples, and the options available to the patient once a sample has been acquired and genetic information has been derived.

- Trials involving a pharmacogenetic component often utilize separate informed consent documents for a drug research protocol and a related pharmacogenetic sampling protocol. Frequently, the latter is prepared as an amendment to the main study protocol to enable study subjects to make an informed choice about participating in the pharmacogenetic study independent of their decision to participate in the drug research protocol. A separate informed consent document for pharmacogenetic sampling must provide sufficient information for the subject to make an informed decision to donate genetic materials based on the merits and risks of the pharmacogenetic objectives and procedures alone. In studies in which the pharmacogenetic aspects cannot be separated from the parent trial (e.g., when genotyping is an inclusion criteria), a single consent form is appropriate.

- The informed consent process should include a complete description of sample collection procedures (e.g., phlebotomy, volume of blood and buccal swab technique) as well as an indication of which procedures are part of routine clinical care and which are specifically applicable to the pharmacogenetic research, descriptions of who will be handling the samples, and where and how long the samples will be stored. Subjects should also be informed, if relevant, that enrolment in the pharmacogenetic studies may require a detailed family history of disease or other genetic traits and that such research will require the collection of biological materials used as a source for the extraction of DNA or other genetic materials. Specific plans and timelines for sample destruction and depletion should also be defined, especially in the context of subject protection against informational risks.

- In contrast to standard clinical studies or drug trials, the process of "withdrawal" of subject participation from pharmacogenetic studies may involve a request by the subject (or others) to destroy genetic materials collected. The informed consent process should indicate when sample destruction will not be possible—for example, because of pooling of individual samples in the laboratory—and should also indicate the circumstances under which individual genetic results cannot be retrieved, such as after data pooling or entry into anonymous/anonymized databases.

- The informed consent process should clearly describe any expectation/plan for contact between the subject and the researcher or research sponsor to discuss genetic results or the implications of these results. These must be considered in the context of the specific circumstances of individual studies and the results of genetic assessments, including inadvertent genetic discoveries with health implications (e.g., that a study subject is genetically at risk for a serious disorder).

- The informed consent process should convey the relative risks (e.g., genetic discrimination based solely on public perceptions and societal sensitivities, informational risks associated with the intentional or inadvertent disclosure of genetic data to third parties, physical risks associated with the collection of pharmacogenetic samples) or concerns and should describe the means by which study subjects are protected against such risks, even if these risks are minimal.

- The consent process should include a description (in understandable language) of the coding mechanisms and other procedures designed to ensure that genetic information from a specific pharmacogenetic trial is appropriately protected, disclosed and utilized.

- In the informed consent process for a pharmacogenomics study, the prospective subject should be informed that the contribution of his/her pharmacogenetic sample might result in commercial gains or intellectual property for the sponsoring pharmaceutical company (who should be named) or other designated parties. A disclosure of the researcher's financial interest or affiliation with a research sponsor should be provided, regardless of how clinical samples are obtained or the level of confidentiality that is assigned to them.

Although the PWG and the FDA have worked together on several pharmacogenetics-related workshops, there are no formal ties between the two organizations. While the FDA was made aware of the PWG's work on informed consent and sample collection terminology, it did not have any input on the PWG's recommendations.

[For other PWG recommendations on informed consent for pharmacogenetic testing, see Anderson et al., "Elements of informed consent for pharmacogenetic research; perspective of the pharmacogenetics working group," *The Pharmacogenomics Journal* (2002), 2, 284-292]

5.13 Q. Have any biomedical or scientific associations or societies offered guidance or recommendations on the topic of informed consent issues relevant to pharmacogenomic testing?

A. Yes. Among them is the American Society of Human Genetics (ASHG), which as far back as 1996 issued a document entitled, *Statement on Informed Consent for Genetic Research,* and the Council for International Organizations of Medical Sciences (CIOMS), which issued a document entitled, *Pharmacogenetics: Towards Improving Treatment with Medicines* in early 2005.

Because of advances in genetic research, ASHG emphasized, in its 1996 guidance, that "there is a need to update considerations of informed consent," and addressed consent disclosures, the disposition of samples and test results, the implications of sample coding (e.g., identified vs. anonymous samples), and retrospective studies of existing samples.

Consent Disclosures. "Subjects providing consent to prospective studies should be told about the types of information that could result from genetic research," the ASHG states. "Subjects must be given sufficient information to understand the implications and the limitations of research. Individuals should be told the purpose, limitations, possible outcomes, and means of communicating results and maintaining confidentiality. They should be informed of what information may reasonably be expected to result from the genetic study. Importantly, subjects should also understand that unexpected findings, including identification of medical risk, carrier status, or risk to offspring affected by genetic disease, may arise. During the course of molecular genetic diagnosis, the results may indicate that the child is not the offspring of one or both the presumed parents. The investigator therefore should consider including in the consent form a statement that misidentified parentage will not be disclosed."

Disposition of Samples and Results. "Depending on the study, subjects may be given the opportunity to determine if they want to be informed of the results of their testing. Subjects should be informed if the sample will be stored for later study, but they also need to be told that there is always the possibility of storage failure. Decisions related to disposition of results or samples after the subject's death should be specified by the subject.

"In some studies researchers may wish to disclose results to subjects. If so, it is the obligation of the subjects to keep the investigator informed of how they may be contacted."

"Subjects involved in studies where the samples are identified or identifiable should indicate if their sample should be used exclusively in the study under consideration. If the sample is to be used more generally, subjects should be given options regarding the scope of the subsequent investigations, such as whether the sample can be used only for a specific disease under investigation, or for other unrelated conditions. It is inappropriate to ask a subject to grant blanket consent for all future unspecified genetic research projects on any disease or in any area if the samples are identifiable in those subsequent studies. Subjects involved in studies in which the samples are identified or identifiable should indicate if unused portions of the samples may be shared with other researchers. If the subject is willing to have the sample shared with other researchers, it is the responsibility of the principal investigator to distribute the sample, so as to ensure that the agreement embodied in the informed consent is upheld. Finally, subjects should decide if subsequent researchers may receive their samples as anonymous or identifiable specimens."

Retrospective Studies of Existing Samples. "We endorse the use of anonymous samples for genetic research. Importantly, in retrospective research proposing to use samples collected anonymously or anonymized, there is no possibility, or need, to obtain consent. For many studies, there may be benefits to making identifiable samples anonymous, because this effectively protects subjects from some of the risks of genetic research. Importantly, making samples anonymous will eliminate the need for recontact to obtain informed consent. This will also reduce the chance of introducing bias due to inability to recontact some, or the possible refusal of others to participate. On the other hand, investigators should consider the appropriateness of anonymizing samples, especially when there is available medical intervention for the disorder being tested.

"For research involving identifiable samples, the investigator should be required to recontact the subjects to obtain consent for new studies. However, an investigator may seek a waiver based on the following criteria of 45CFR46.116 [of the Common Rule]:

1. The research involves no more than minimal risk to the subjects;
2. The waiver or alteration will not adversely affect the rights and welfare of the subjects;
3. The research could not practicably be carried out without the waiver or alteration; and
4. Whenever appropriate, the subjects will be provided with additional pertinent information after participation.

For research involving samples that retain identifiers, consent should be obtained. Waivers may be granted, although the waivers will be difficult to justify by the above criteria if identifiers are retained."

5.14 Q. Have European authorities been proactive in issuing guidance and recommendations regarding informed consent and related issues relevant to pharmacogenomics testing?

A. With the Pharmacogenetics Expert Working Group (PWG), a voluntary association of pharmaceutical companies, the European Medicines Evaluation Agency (EMEA) has, in recent years, begun to consider the issues presented by pharmacogenomics testing in the context of clinical research. In 2002, the EMEA adopted a document similar to one developed by the PWG entitled, *Position Paper on Terminology in Pharmacogenetics.*

Implemented in June 2003, this position paper addressed, for the most part, subject privacy issues, the various methods for preserving patient privacy (e.g., sample coding), and the implications of such methods for regulatory inspections, data/subject linkage, and possible actions if a subject withdraws his/her consent.

As does the FDA's draft document, the EMEA's position paper includes only a few sentences that specifically address the informed consent document and process:

"Duration of retention of the [pharmacogenetic] sample or its destruction needs to be defined in the protocol and in the consent form. Otherwise, if and when relevant, the timepoint and the procedure for anonymisation of the sample itself should be defined in these documents."

[Note: the Pharmacogenetics Working Group has since published a paper on informed consent for pharmacogenetic research, see Question 5.12 above]

But the document effectively makes the case for the relevance of several key definitions that relate to the collection of human samples for pharmacogenetic research, the management of the resultant data, the informed consent process, and other communications between the parties involved in the clinical trial. "The set of terms described in this paper are a key to correct handling of the samples and the data and to transparency of communication among industry, ethics committees, regulatory authorities and subjects about the pharmacogenetic approach in clinical research, regulatory assessment of medicinal products and clinical practice," the position paper states. "The processes by which samples and data are collected, labelled and stored have a direct effect on how the samples and the results obtained can be used in the future and on the obligations of the investigator and sponsor to the sample subject. This pertains particularly to situations when a subject withdraws his or her consent to further participation in a study and affects the possibility to return information to the subject or his/her physician, the possibility to withdraw a sample from future analysis and verification of data ascribed to a subject in reports and regulatory submissions…

Five definitions for the labelling and coding of pharmacogenetic samples and data are proposed describing direct implications for the handling methodology of samples for pharmacogenetic testing and corresponding consequences for the level of privacy protection and use of the information for regulatory purposes":

- *Identified samples and data* are those with personal identifiers such as name or social security number.

- *Single coded samples and data* are those to which a single specific code is attributed for protecting individuals.

- *Double-coded samples and data* have an additional privacy safeguard imposed by the use of a second coding system.

- *Anonymised samples and data* are for practical purposes *double coded* samples where the key linking the first and/or second code is deleted.

- *Anonymised samples and data* are those that do not have any link whatsoever between the sample and the individual's identity.

Summary Table of the Five Terms of Pharmacogenetic Sample Labelling

Sample Labeling Category	Link Between Subject Identity and Pharmacogenetic Data	Records Identifiable for Clinical Monitoring	Actions Possible if Subject Withdraws Consent	Return of Individual Results to Subjects	Scope of Subject Privacy Protection
Identified	Yes, directly	Yes	Sample can be withdrawn with immediate effect for any prospective use	Possible	Similar to general healthcare confidentiality
Single coded	Indirectly, via code key	Yes, via protocol-specified procedure	Sample can be withdrawn with immediate effect for any prospective use	Possible	Standard for clinical research conforms to principles of GCP
Double-coded	Very indirectly, via two sets of code keys	Yes, via protocol-specified procedures	Sample can be withdrawn with immediate effect for any prospective use	Possible	Double code offers added privacy protection over single code
Anonymised	No. Key(s) identifying the link between pharmacogenetic data and the identity of the subject is deleted	No	Sample and data are not identifiable. Sample cannot be withdrawn once key is deleted	Not possible	Pharmacogenetic data not linked to individuals
Anonymous	No	No	None	Not possible	Complete

Source: EMEA

5.15 Q. Compared to FDA GCP, does the ICH GCP guideline recommend that additional elements be included in the informed consent form? Does it differ, or is it more specific or detailed, in any respect regarding the informed consent process than FDA GCP?

A. As in other areas, there are differences between ICH and FDA GCP in the area of informed consent.

One of the few respects in which the U.S. GCP standards are more specific than ICH GCP standards is the FDA requirement that the obtaining of informed consent be supported either by source documents or noted on the case report form (21 CFR 312.62(b)). ICH guidelines have no such provisions. The phrase "supported by source documents" can be, and is, interpreted loosely. A progress note need not state that the subject was consented. Instead, it might state that "BZH was here for his screening visit." Alternatively, the fact that BZH's screening labs were drawn as documented by a specimen form might be sufficient. In some respects, a properly signed informed consent is a source document.

Only the ICH GCP guideline requires that the person conducting the informed consent process sign the informed consent form in all cases. Under that guideline, "prior to a subject's participation in the trial, the written informed consent form should be signed and personally dated by the subject or by the subject's legally acceptable representative, and by the person who conducted the informed consent discussion." Also, unlike FDA guidelines, the ICH guideline recommends that the investigator inform the subject's primary physician about the subject's participation in the trial.

Since the ICH GCP guideline was released in 1997, several other differences relevant to the informed consent process have been noted, including the following:

- The ICH GCP guideline explicitly states that the copy of the informed consent form provided to the subject following the informed consent procedure should be a copy of the signed form, while FDA GCP regulations state only that a copy of the form should be provided. In its 1998 Information Sheets for investigators and IRBs, however, the FDA recommends that the copy provided to subjects be a signed copy.
- The ICH GCP guideline calls for an "impartial witness" to be present in those cases in which an informed consent document is read to a trial subject/legally authorized representative (e.g., when the subject/legally authorized representative cannot read). FDA regulations require that a "witness" be present for the oral presentation of the elements of informed consent when the short form is used, but do not specify that the witness be impartial (see Q5.28). [Editor's note: because the short form is so rarely used in the U.S., the relevance of these requirements is limited.]
- FDA regulations require that investigators responsible for key clinical studies complete a financial disclosure form, and that the clinical sponsor collect such information and report on the relevant financial interests of, and compensation paid to, such investigators. The ICH GCP guideline has no such provisions.
- Although both FDA regulations and ICH GCP provisions for the informed consent process call for the disclosure of appropriate alternative procedures or courses of treatment that may be advantageous to subjects, only ICH GCP

standards call for the disclosure of the important potential benefits and risks of the alternatives.

- As part of the informed consent process, ICH GCP calls for a statement that monitors, auditors, the IRB and regulatory authorities will be granted direct access to medical records, and for a statement that, by signing the consent, the subject is authorizing such access. FDA regulations require only a statement that notes the possibility that the agency may inspect the records. It is worth noting that the Privacy Rule, which took effect in April 2003 in the United States, calls for a document that informs the subject of the persons, classes of persons, and organizations that will create, disclose, and/or receive protected health information during research.

- When a subject can only be enrolled with the consent of a legally acceptable representative (e.g., minors, patients with severe dementia), the ICH GCP guideline states that the subject should be informed about the trial to the extent compatible with the subject's understanding and, if capable, the subject should assent, sign and personally date the written informed consent. FDA regulations have no such specific provisions. However, the agency's regulations do require that, when children are involved in a trial, assent of the child is required unless the child is not capable of providing assent or the intervention or procedure is intended to provide direct benefit that is important to the child's well being. In addition, FDA regulations require additional safeguards to protect the rights and welfare of subjects who are vulnerable to coercion or undue influence. While not specifically required by the regulations, the IRB may determine that the assent of those subjects not able to decide for themselves is an appropriate safeguard.

- In the informed consent process, the ICH GCP guideline calls for an explanation as to whether any compensation and any medical treatments will be available if injury occurs for all studies. FDA regulations require such statements only for studies that involve more than minimal risk.

- ICH GCP provisions specifically call for all informed consents to be signed and dated by the person who conducts the informed consent discussion. In most cases, FDA regulations require only one signature, that of the subject or the legally authorized representative. When a short form written consent document is used to establish that the elements of informed consent have been presented orally to the subject or the subject's legally authorized representative, however, FDA regulations require three signatures: the person conducting the consent interview, the witness to the oral presentation, and the subject or legally authorized representative. In such cases, the subject/legally authorized representative signs the short form, the witness signs the short form and a copy of the summary of what was said to the subject/legally authorized representative, and the person obtaining consent signs the copy of the summary. [Editor's note: because the short form is so rarely used in the U.S., the relevance of these requirements is limited.]

Since the consenting process can be such a contentious topic and is one that can trigger care provider and institutional liability, few, if any, U.S. studies rely solely on the short form. Verbal consents lacking a written copy of study procedures and required informed consent elements are no longer used.

5.16 Q. The ICH GCP guideline notes that, following the initial informed consent process and the subject's enrollment in a trial, "the subject or the subject's legally acceptable representative should be informed in a timely manner if new information becomes available that may be relevant to the subject's willingness to continue participation in the trial. The communication of this information should be documented." Specifically, how must the communication of this information be documented? Should the subject be "reconsented"? Should the subject/legal representative and the person informing the subject of the new information sign a document acknowledging the process, as was done in the original informed consent process?

A. The communication of this information must be documented in much the same manner as the original informed consent process was documented. After the written informed consent document is updated/amended to reflect the new information, the subject/legal representative should be informed of the new information and should sign the modified consent. Source documents should reflect that the new information was provided to the subject. In addition, the subject should also receive a copy of the signed and dated consent form updates.

This process represents a reconsenting of the subject and should almost always be done in person unless it is impossible for a patient to return to the investigational site.

5.17 Q. But do FDA regulations or guidance documents provide any insights regarding when and how study subjects must be provided with this information and whether a new consent process must be undertaken in every case?

A. FDA regulations and guidance documents provide little guidance on this topic. Perhaps the most recent discussion of this issue is provided in recommendations developed by an Informed Consent Working Group, which comprises representatives of the FDA, the National Cancer Institute (NCI), and the HHS Office of Human Research Protections. In a document entitled, *Simplification of Informed Consent Documents,* the working group offered the following recommendations:

"When new knowledge that is likely to affect a research participant's willingness to continue participation in the trial or might have affected the decision to enter the trial in the first place, the participant should be informed and written consent may need to be documented again. The urgency of notifying the research participant of new toxicity data, for example, depends on the likelihood and severity of the risk. New information regarding relatively minor risk or low severity may be presented orally at the next routine visit. In any case, the IRB should be notified and consulted as soon as possible to assist the investigator in determining the appropriate form of notification."

5.18 Q. Specifically, what types of situations call for an informed consent form amendment or update?

A. Generally, a revised informed consent is required when there is new information that might affect a subject's willingness to participate in the study. This might include emerging information on the study drug's safety, an increase in the incidence of risks facing study subjects, a change in the subject's rights in the trial, or a change in study procedures.

Administrative changes (which include contact person/phone number, among others) do not necessitate revising the consent form and reconsenting the subjects. However, subjects should be provided with a handout with this new information, and a copy of the handout should be maintained in the regulatory binder.

Both FDA regulations and the ICH GCP guidance address situations in which the informed consent document should be modified. FDA regulations at 21 CFR 50.25(b)(5) make a relatively indirect reference, stating that an informed consent document, when appropriate, should provide "a statement that significant new findings developed during the course of the research which may relate to the subject's willingness to continue participation will be provided to the subject." [Editor's note: FDA officials point out that such a statement would be irrelevant for either a singe-dose study or a study of extremely short duration. It would, therefore, be relevant for studies of sufficient duration, which can be determined by the IRB.]

The ICH GCP guideline (4.8.2) is somewhat more direct: "The written informed consent form and any other written information to be provided to subjects should be revised whenever important new information becomes available that may be relevant to the subject's consent. Any revised written informed consent form, and written information, should receive the IRB/IEC's approval/favorable opinion in advance of use."

5.19 Q. *If a patient has completed the active phase of a clinical trial and is participating in the required follow-up phase (e.g., scheduled questionnaire or telephone interviews), must he or she be reconsented or otherwise be informed of new information? And must subjects who are actively participating in a clinical trial be reconsented if the sponsor/site implements a change that will affect only subsequently enrolled subjects?*

A. According to the FDA's Information Sheets, the agency "does not require the reconsenting of subjects that have completed their active participation in the study, or of subjects who are still actively participating when the change will not affect their participation, for example when the change will be implemented only for subsequently enrolled subjects." However, if there is important, substantive new information, such as discoveries about an increased risk of drug mutagenicity, that will affect subjects in the follow-on phase, then those subjects should be reconsented.

Incidentally, in the opinion of many experts, including several FDA officials, active participation in a study begins when the subject signs the consent form.

5.20 Q. *What are so-called "registry" studies, and what are the specific GCP-related requirements, in particular informed consent requirements, for such studies?*

A. The FDA does not define registry studies in its regulations, although it does address them in at least two guidance documents. In its May 2004 *Good Pharmacovigilance Practices and Pharmacoepidemiologic Assessment* draft guidance, the agency defines a registry as "an organized system for the collection, storage, retrieval, analysis, and dissemination of information on individual persons exposed to a specific medical intervention who have either a particular disease, a condition (e.g., a risk factor) that predisposes [them] to the occurrence of a health-related event, or prior exposure to substances (or circumstances) known or suspected to cause adverse health effects." While a sponsor can initiate a registry at any time, the agency notes that it may be appropriate to initiate a registry at the time of initial marketing, when a new indication is approved, or when there is a need to evaluate safety signals identified from spontaneous case reports. Unlike a highly structured and regulated clinical trial, registry studies are not blinded, and are typically real-world observational studies that examine patient outcomes in normal practice.

In its August 2002 industry guidance entitled, *Establishing Pregnancy Exposure Registries,* the agency states that, "through the creation of registries, a sponsor can follow up on safety signals identified from spontaneous case reports, literature reports, or other sources, and evaluate factors that can affect the risk of adverse outcomes, such as dosing, timing of exposure, or patient characteristics." The agency adds that registries can be particularly useful for collecting outcome information not available in large automated databases and for collecting information from multiple sources (e.g., physician records, hospital summaries, pathology reports, vital statistics).

Not surprisingly, GCP-related guidance regarding registry studies is scarce. This may be due to the reality that it is particularly difficult to outline specific GCP-related requirements for registry-based studies, in large part because they can take several different forms and can involve various information-collection methods, each of which can have different implications for informed consent requirements, for example. In its August 2002 guidance on pregnancy exposure registries, for instance, the FDA discusses several possible research models for registry-based monitoring studies and the informed consent-related implications of each model:

- Most pregnancy exposure registries rely on voluntary reports from health care professionals. In this scenario, patient consent is not required, the agency notes. The guidance adds, however, that some health care providers may be reluctant to seek out and disclose information on pregnancy outcomes without maternal consent, even when no specific patient identifiers are collected.
- A similar model would involve the health care provider obtaining informed consent from the pregnant woman to acquire medical records from both prenatal and pediatric providers.
- Other pregnancy registries recruit and enroll women directly, and typically in such situations informed consent is obtained from the women upon enrollment. While the FDA notes that obtaining informed consent in such cases "may confirm patient motivation" and facilitate cross-validation of information reported by the woman (i.e., by permitting examination of medical records and interviews with health care providers), it adds that "a potential methodological problem with this approach is that the nonparticipation of patients who do not give consent can introduce selection bias."

The FDA's pregnancy-exposure registry guidance, then, ties the need for informed consent to patient confidentiality, access to patient records, and whether patients themselves are enrolled into the registry (i.e., versus voluntary reports by health care professionals). Given the diversity of registry studies and the complexities involved, sponsors should discuss the GCP-related implications of a proposed registry study directly with the relevant FDA review division.

5.21 Q. How is a subject's "active participation" in a study defined for regulatory purposes?

A. As noted in Q5.19 above, the subject's active participation is generally seen as beginning when he or she signs the consent form. The specific point at which active participation concludes is a far more subjective concept, however.

A study's nature can affect the ambiguities associated with the conclusion of a patient's active participation. Many studies, including those for acute diseases, tend to have a clear "active" phase with a relatively well-defined conclusion—that is, when the final drug administration, site visits, and data collection efforts are completed for a patient. Other studies, such as those involving chronic diseases (e.g., cancer), may have what is called a "passive phase," during which there is no drug administration but is some level of patient monitoring and data collection (i.e., less than during active phase) to assess, for example, longer-term efficacy or disease relapses.

In some senses, completing a questionnaire at home or answering questions (e.g., "are your headaches worse than a month ago") over the phone are somewhat passive activities for study subjects, as is providing a stool sample that is mailed to a clinical center. On the other hand, each of these examples of passive participation requires that subjects give up some of their time, that they cooperate, and that they comply with protocol requirements.

In short, there are no hard and fast regulatory rules regarding "active participation." Most protocols do not clearly establish the precise point at which the active participation phase of a study ends and at which the remainder of the study—the passive component, if any—begins. A conservative approach might be for a sponsor to assume that subjects have full rights, including those involving safety reporting and consenting updates, until they are completely finished with a particular study (i.e., completed all protocol-required visits, tests, procedures, and monitoring).

5.22 Q. Both FDA and ICH GCP standards require that informed consent be obtained "prior to" a prospective subject's participation in a clinical study. Does this mean simply that informed consent must be obtained before the experimental therapy or control is administered?

A. From a practical standpoint, it means that consent must be obtained prior to altering the subject's care for the purposes of research, not just the administration of experimental therapy. This includes the following:

- Discontinuing any existing medications the subject is taking for the purpose of determining his or her suitability for the research study (this is termed a "washout period");
- Performing any specific exams or procedures specific to the research study; or
- Administering any study drug.

According to the FDA Information Sheet entitled, "Screening Tests Prior to Study Enrollment," "informed consent must be obtained prior to initiation of any screening procedures that are performed solely for the purpose of determining eligibility for research."

The document adds that, "while an investigator may discuss availability of studies and the possibility of entry into a study with a prospective subject without first obtaining consent, informed consent must be obtained prior to initiation of any clinical procedures that are performed solely for the purpose of determining eligibility for research, including withdrawal from medication (wash-out). When washout is done in anticipation of or in preparation for the research, it is part of the research. Clinical screening procedures for research eligibility are considered part of the subject selection and recruitment process and, therefore, require IRB oversight."

From another perspective, informed consent need not be administered prior to routine tests and procedures that would be administered irrespective of any studies to patients presenting for diagnosis and treatment of their condition or disease.

5.23 Q. The FDA GCP regulations and the ICH GCP guideline require that, during the informed consent process, a potential clinical trial subject be provided with "sufficient opportunity" (FDA GCP regulations) and "ample time and opportunity" (ICH GCP guideline) to decide whether or not to participate in a clinical study. Are there any standards for what amount of time satisfies this requirement?

A. While there are no specific standards in the regulations and guidelines, it is always a good idea to apply the "reasonable man" criterion. Generally accepted standards for what constitutes "reasonable" in this area often include the following:

- Sufficient time for a person with a fifth- or sixth-grade education to read and digest the consent
- Sufficient time for the individual to ask questions of the study staff and to consult with a relative or friend
- Sufficient time, if requested, to review and research some of the provisions in the informed consent form (e.g., alternative therapies)
- Sufficient time to reflect on the decision

If the consent form and the decision-making process are complicated, obviously a reasonable person would require additional time to think through the decision. Children and older adults, as well as learning disabled and other cognitively impaired persons, may require more time.

There are also other factors to consider. A hectic physician waiting room does not provide the proper environment for the consent process. Similarly, a time-pressured care provider who gives the appearance of being hurried and short-tempered during the consenting process may confuse and intimidate potential subjects.

No time constraints should be placed on the consenting process. Patients should not be enrolled in studies if they believe they have been rushed into consenting, and they should be able, unless this is a life-threatening situation, to take as much time as they would like to understand their options and make an informed decision. This principle is the implied intent of both FDA and ICH GCP standards.

5.24 Q. FDA GCP regulations require, and ICH GCP standards recommend, that consent from the subject's legally authorized representative be obtained if the subject is unable to provide consent. Who can serve as a legally authorized representative? And who would need one in the informed consent process? Also, how does the "legally authorized representative" under FDA regulations differ from the "legally acceptable representative" specified for such situations under the ICH GCP guideline?

A. FDA regulations define legally authorized representative as "an individual or juridical or other body authorized under applicable law to consent on behalf of a prospective subject to the subject's participation in the procedure(s) involved in the research." The ICH GCP guideline uses a similar definition, but replaces the phrase "participation in the procedure(s) involved in the research" with the phrase "participation in the clinical trial."

Legally authorized representative is a term that suggests that a person has medical power of attorney for another person, generally a person who is unable to make medical decisions for a variety of reasons. These reasons usually include physical or mental impairment. For an individual to gain medical power of attorney for another person, a court or other judicial proceeding must grant this status.

In an information sheet (see Q44 in Section 20), the FDA states that the agency "defers to state and local laws regarding who is a legally authorized representative. FDA recognizes that a durable power of attorney might suffice as identifying a legally authorized representative under some state and local laws. For example, a subject might have designated an individual to provide consent with regard to health care decisions through a durable power of attorney and have specified that the individual also has the power to make decisions on entry into research . . . Therefore, the IRB should assure that the consent procedures comply with state and local laws, including assurance that the law applies to obtaining informed consent for subjects participating in research as well as for patients who require health care decisions."

Before a person with medical power of attorney signs a study consent for another person, the study staff member obtaining the consent should ask to see documentation that grants this power and should make a note in the source document and/or on the consent that this document was presented and reviewed. A second-best alternative, in a clinically emergent situation, is for the person who has medical power of attorney to present this document at a later time, at which point the clinical staff would enter a note to the source document and/or the consent document.

It is not good clinical practice to have a person who is not the subject sign the consent unless this individual's legal authority to do so is clear. When there is uncertainty, it is better not to enroll a subject under these conditions. For many reasons, including those associated with legal liability, study staff responsible for enrolling subjects should have some training in state law regarding medical power of attorney.

It is worth noting that study staff should also make certain that the adults who sign the consents are either the parents or legal guardians of minors to be enrolled in a trial.

5.25 *Q. FDA GCP regulations state that, during the informed consent process, "the information that is given to the subject or the [legally authorized representative] shall be in language understandable to the subject or the representative." Further, the ICH GCP guideline states that "the language used in the oral and written information about the trial, including the written informed consent form, should be as nontechnical as practical and should be understandable to the subject or the subject's legally acceptable representative and the impartial witness, where applicable." Even if a trial is* *to enroll adults exclusively, the trial population could possess a considerable range of literacy levels. In general, is there a reading level at which informed consent documents must be developed?*

A. In general, industry's approach is to develop consent documents at a fifth- or sixth-grade reading level. According to recommendations made by an Informed Consent Working Group comprising the FDA, NCI, and HHS Office of Human Research Protections, informed consent documents "should be written at an eighth grade or lower reading level" (for task force recommendations, see "Simplification of Informed Consent Documents," including Appendix 3: Checklist for Easy-to-Read Informed Consent Documents at www.cancer.gov/clinicaltrials/understanding/simplification-of-informed-consent-docs).

As a practical matter, however, it is extremely difficult for Ph.D.s, M.D.s, and members of a research team to develop text at this level. It is almost impossible to discuss all the required elements and be, at the same time, succinct. Often, clinical terms do not lend themselves to simplification.

Adults with sixth-grade reading levels read at this level for several reasons. English may not be their native language. They may have reading comprehension problems. Since they may dislike reading any text, a document longer than a single paragraph may not be read.

Nevertheless, study staff, as well as IRBs, must make an effort to consider and address such issues. Over the years, strategies have been devised to improve consent wording, phrasing, and layout.

5.26 Q. If there is a signed informed consent form, are source documents necessary to verify informed consent?

A. Yes, according to FDA GCP regulations. According to 21 CFR 312.62(b), "the case history for each individual shall document that informed consent was obtained prior to participation in the study." Interestingly, the ICH GCP guideline does not specify that the obtaining of informed consent be documented anywhere other in than the consent forms themselves.

Generally, industry fulfills this FDA requirement in one of two ways:
• By documenting consents in source documents; or
• By documenting consents on case report forms.

Whichever method is used, the resulting document falls under the definition of "case history." The problem here is that, to satisfy and be consistent with other GCP standards and guidelines, all data on the case report form should be supported or be verifiable from source data. Some would consider the informed consent form to be a source document and, therefore, would not see the value in repeating this information in a redundant progress note.

To satisfy minimum FDA requirements, site staff may either write a progress note about the consenting process or complete a data item on the case report form that records the date of the consent. Best practices, however, call for a "contextual" statement in a source document regarding exactly how and when the consenting processing occurred (see discussion below and Q5.27).

Ideally, the informed consent process should include: (1) a clear discussion of the information in the informed consent form; (2) a signed and dated informed consent form (by the subject or the subject's legally authorized representative); and (3) a source document containing a progress note or chart note that includes the date of visit and that notes that the informed consent was obtained. The progress or chart note on the source document might state the following, for example: "Following a discussion of the study details and a review of the informed consent form by Dr. Smith, JMW consented to participate in the study and signed/dated the informed consent form. Investigator and witness signatures/dates were obtained and a photocopy of the signed consent form was given to the patient for her records."

5.27 Q. Aside from the informed consent form, is the fact that informed consent was obtained better documented in the subject's medical chart or on the case report form?

A. It is far better to document the consent in the medical record, which as a primary document can easily capture the particulars of the consenting process. Usually, a straightforward progress note should suffice (see exhibit below).

Medical Record Entries

> *10/15/02 Mr. Jones, a white 36 year-old male, presented in clinic today for possible inclusion in study #RK-1672. No history of ETOH or drug abuse. Smoked 1 pack of cigarettes x 5 years, but stopped x 3 years ago. Patient states history of high blood pressure but has been controlled by medication during the past year. No history of carcinoma or pulmonary disease. Explained study protocol and reviewed informed consent form. Patient states he wants to take informed consent form home to discuss with wife. Scheduled to return tomorrow at 10:00 am.*
>
> *J. Rachet, RN*

> *10/16/02 10:00 am Mr. Jones returned today. He and Dr. Smith further discussed the 1672 study and Dr. Smith answered his questions. Mr. Jones, Dr. Smith, and I signed the ICF; Mr. Jones was given a copy.*
>
> *J. Rachet, RN*

It is clear from this example that Mr. Jones has had sufficient time to read, consider, and understand the informed consent form and to ask questions and receive answers about the study.

Typically, a case report form includes a data field only for the date of the consent signing. Although an entry in this field is indicative of consenting, it is not nearly as informative as the entries displayed in the above example.

As the consenting process is subject to increasing external scrutiny, it is imperative that study staff adequately and accurately document the relevant sequence of actions, right down to the informed consent form signing and distribution, directly in the medical record. GCP compliant source documentation is imperative.

5.28 Q. Under FDA GCP standards and the ICH GCP guideline, when specifically must a witness be present for the informed consent process? And must that witness sign the informed consent form?

A. According to both FDA GCP regulations and the ICH GCP guideline, a witness must be present for the entire informed consent process whenever the elements of informed consent are presented orally to the subject or the subject's legally authorized representative.

The ICH GCP guideline states that, "if a subject is unable to read or if a legally acceptable representative is unable to read," an "impartial witness" should be present during the entire informed consent process. The guideline adds that, "after the written informed consent form and any other written information to be provided to subjects is read and explained to the subject or the subject's legally acceptable representative, and after the subject or the subject's legally acceptable representative has orally consented to the subject's participation in the trial, and, if capable of doing so, has signed and personally dated the informed consent form, the witness should sign and personally date the consent form."

The FDA's GCP regulations also require a "witness" when the required elements of informed consent are "presented orally" as part of the "short form" process (i.e., rather than in writing) to a subject or a subject's legally authorized representative (21 CFR Section 50.27). [Editor's note: because the short form is so rarely used in the United States, the relevance of these requirements is limited.]

FDA regulations make no mention of the term "impartial," as the ICH guideline does, although the agency notes in its Information Sheets that, "the intended purpose [of a witness in such cases] . . . is to attest to the accuracy of the presentation and the apparent understanding of the subject." In such cases, FDA regulations state, "the witness shall sign both the short form [written consent document stating that the required elements of informed consent have been presented orally to the subject or the subject's legally authorized representative] and a copy of the [written] summary [of what is to be said to the subject or the representative]."

5.29 Q. What qualifies a person to be a "witness" under the FDA GCP provisions or an "impartial witness" under the ICH GCP guideline for the informed consent process? Can a study coordinator or other site staff be considered impartial?

A. The ICH GCP guideline defines impartial witness as "a person, who is independent of the trial, who cannot be unfairly influenced by people involved with the trial, who attends the informed consent process if the subject or the subject's legally acceptable representative cannot read, and who reads the informed consent form and any other written information supplied to the subject."

FDA regulations/guidelines make no references regarding what qualifies a person to be a witness.

A study coordinator who is being paid to conduct the study in question would not be considered "impartial." Site staff who are not participating in a particular study might be considered "impartial," so long as they could not be unduly influenced by study staff.

A source document or the informed consent form should document exactly why a witness was necessary. For example, a notation in the source document might state that, "Patient BXY is legally blind."

In many cases, informed consent forms have a witness line, but sponsors and IRBs provide no guidance as to whether a signature on this line is mandatory or optional (and if optional, under what conditions it should be used). Generally, the witness line should be used only if the subject has serious vision or comprehension problems or if the consent process is perceived by the primary consentor to be open to future challenge.

It is important to note, however, that some IRBs require a witness signature irrespective of a subject's ability to read the consent. In such cases, obviously, a witness line would be necessary. If the IRB or sponsor places a witness line on the informed consent form, then the IRB or sponsor should provide written guidance to site staff as to when this line should be signed and by whom.

5.30 Q. Would a spouse or immediate family member be classified as an impartial witness under the ICH GCP guideline?

A. A spouse or immediate family member might be considered impartial under the ICH GCP guideline, which defines impartial witness as "a person, who is independent of the trial, who cannot be unfairly influenced by people involved with the trial, who attends the informed consent process if the subject or subject's legally acceptable representative cannot read, and who reads the informed consent form and any other written information supplied to the subject." Because spouses or immediate family members may face challenges similar to those facing the potential subject (e.g., language, education), these individuals may also be more likely to have problems reading certain words in the informed consent form.

Due to complexities inherent in family relations, it also is possible that immediate family members may have certain conflicts of interest. Therefore, they may not be "impartial" at all, and may not necessarily have the patient's best interest as their primary concern.

5.31 Q. When the informed consent process is completed, must the copy of the informed consent form provided to the patient for his or her records be a copy of the signed informed consent form?

A. FDA regulations at 21 CFR 50.27(a) state that, following the informed consent process, "a copy [of the informed consent form] shall be given to the person signing the form." So FDA regulations do not explicitly require that the copy of the informed consent form provided to the patient be the copy that he or she (or that the legally authorized representative) signed. The FDA's Information Sheets note, however, that "the FDA regulations do not require the subject's copy to be a signed copy, although a photocopy with signature(s) is preferred."

The ICH GCP guidance, however, specifically recommends that the patient receive a copy of the signed form: "Prior to participation in the trial, the subject or the subject's legally acceptable representative should receive a copy of the signed and dated written informed consent form and any other written information provided to the subjects" (section 4.8.11).

5.32 Q. Although documenting the precise time of consent is not required by the FDA's GCP regulations or the ICH's consolidated GCP guidance, when is it considered useful and what are the ramifications of documenting the time of consent?

A. The time of consent is sometimes documented when subject consent is obtained on the same day that the subject begins participation in a study. A study may even involve, for example, an emergency room setting in which the patient signs the informed consent form and then the investigative treatment or sedative is administered immediately thereafter. In such cases, the date on the informed consent document would not truly indicate whether the informed consent process actually preceded the investigative procedure (i.e., because the date of informed consent and the procedure itself would be the same). Therefore, companies often require in such cases that the precise time of informed consent be captured to document that it preceded the administration of the investigative drug.

Although the FDA considered, as part of a December 1996 regulation, requiring that the time of consent be documented in such cases, the agency ultimately decided against the requirement. In its Information Sheet entitled, "Guide to Informed Consent," however, the FDA notes that, "if consent is obtained the same day that the subject's involvement in the study begins, the subject's medical records/case report form should document that consent was obtained prior to participation in the research."

GCP standards leave the method of documenting the time of consent to the sponsor/site. The case report form could have a check box asking, "Was consent obtained prior to any study tests/procedures?" Also, a member of the study staff could write a note, including the date and time the note was written, documenting that consent was obtained prior to any study tests/procedures. The best way to document that consenting preceded study procedures, however, is to record it on the informed consent document itself.

When the patient's signing of consent and the investigative procedure occur in rapid succession, site staff must take particular care in the documentation process. Unless the wrist watches (or other time pieces relied upon, such as wall clocks) of those involved in both the consent process and investigative procedure are carefully synchronized, for instance, the recorded times could easily make it appear as though a study procedure preceded the consent process even though it did not.

5.33 *Q. At what age should the assent of children—a child's affirmative agreement to participate in research—be obtained for a clinical trial in addition to parental permission?*

A. State laws regarding consent of minors vary considerably. These laws define the age at which a child's assent is required, thereby specifying those cases calling for the signature of both the child and a parent or legal guardian. Pediatricians and other care providers serving as principal investigators at clinical sites should be aware of the state law governing consent of minors in their states.

Although FDA regulations did not, before April 2002 (see discussion below), address this subject directly, the agency did discuss this topic briefly in its Information Sheet entitled, "A Guide to Informed Consent." "FDA believes that IRBs should consider whether to require the approval of older children [in addition to their parents] before they are enrolled in a research study," the agency states. The FDA notes that some IRBs have required the development of two consent documents: one for parental permission, and another in simplified language for "obtaining the assent of children who can understand the concepts involved."

While the FDA has long recommended the use of HHS regulations for the conduct of studies in children (45 CFR 46, Subpart D) as guidance, the agency issued an April 2001 interim rule to immediately adopt these specific regulations. Therefore, under the interim rule, the safeguards provided by HHS Subpart D now apply to children participating in clinical investigations of FDA-regulated products (i.e., with certain changes to reflect differences in FDA and HHS regulatory authority). These regulations state that "the IRB shall determine that adequate provisions are made for soliciting the assent of the children, when in the judgment of the IRB the children are capable of providing assent. In determining whether children are capable of assenting, the IRB shall take into account the ages, maturity, and psychological state of the children involved. This judgment may be made for all children to be involved in the research under a particular protocol, or for each child, as the IRB deems appropriate. If the IRB determines that the capability of some or all of the children is so limited that they cannot reasonably be consulted or that the intervention or procedure involved in the research holds out a prospect of direct benefit that is important to the health or well-being of the children and is available only in the context of the research, the assent of the children is not a necessary condition for proceeding with the research. Even where the IRB determines that the subjects are capable of assenting, the IRB may still waive the assent requirements [if it finds and documents that: (1) the clinical investigation involves no more than minimal risk to the subjects; (2) the waiver will not adversely affect the rights and welfare of the subjects; (3) the clinical investigation could not practicably be carried out without the waiver; and (4) if appropriate, the subjects will be provided with additional pertinent information after participation]. When the IRB determines that assent is required, it shall also determine whether and how assent must be documented."

Further, Section 4.8.12 of the ICH guideline states that, "when a clinical trial (therapeutic or nontherapeutic) includes subjects who can only be enrolled in the trial with the consent of the subject's legally acceptable representative (e.g., minors, or patients with severe dementia), the subject should be informed about the trial to the extent compatible with the subject's understanding and, if capable, the subject should assent, sign and personally date the written informed consent."

5.34 Q. Are consent documents that will be used in a pediatric trial required to include a space for the assent of children?

A. No. The FDA specifically addresses this in a May 2004 Center for Biologics Evaluation and Research/Center for Devices and Radiological Health guidance entitled, "Premarketing Assessment of Pediatric Medical Devices."

"Although there is no requirement that the informed consent document contain a space for assent by children, many investigators and IRBs consider it standard practice to obtain the agreement of older children who can understand the circumstances before enrolling them in research," the guidance states. "The basic requirement of 21 CFR 50.20 applies, i.e., the legally effective informed consent of the subject or the subject's legally authorized representative must be obtained before enrollment. Parents, legal guardians and/or others may have the ability to give permission to enroll children in research, depending on applicable state and local law of the jurisdiction in which the research is conducted. (Note: permission to enroll in research is not the same as permission to provide medical treatment.) IRBs generally require investigators to obtain the permission of one or both of the parents or guardians (as appropriate) and the assent of children who possess the intellectual and emotional ability to comprehend the concepts involved. Some IRBs require two documents, a fully detailed explanation for parents and older children to read and sign, and a shorter, simpler one for younger children."

5.35 Q. Traditionally, the FDA has always deferred to state law on when individuals may consent for themselves. When the FDA adopted the Common Rule's Subpart D—Additional Safeguards for Children in Clinical Investigations, however, it also adopted the Common Rule's definition of children: "persons who have not attained the legal age for consent to treatments or procedures involved in clinical investigations, under the applicable law of the jurisdiction in which the clinical investigation will be conducted." Some claim that this definition may be problematic because a literal reading of the definition suggests that the FDA/HHS will defer ONLY when an individual has attained "the legal age for consent," and not necessarily in other cases, such as when minors become emancipated under state law. Therefore, does the FDA's adoption of the Subpart D definition represent any type of intentional or unintentional change in agency policy regarding deference to state law in this area?

A. No. In a September 2004 response on this issue, the FDA stated that "FDA has always and continues to defer to state law on issues relating to age of consent, including emancipated minor status."

5.36 Q. Under FDA regulations, what is the difference between a "mature minor" and an "emancipated minor"?

A. The only known FDA reference to the difference between a "mature" and "emancipated" minor appears in an FDA guidance document on testing medical devices in pediatric populations. The guidance document entitled, "Premarket Assessment of Pediatric Medical Devices" (May 2004), defines emancipated minor status as "a legal status conferred upon persons who have not yet attained the age of legal competency as defined by state law, but who are entitled to treatment as if they had by virtue of assuming adult responsibilities, such as self-support, marriage, or procreation." Mature minors, the guidance notes, are "persons who have not reached adulthood (as defined by state law) but who may be treated as an adult for certain purposes (e.g., consenting to medical care). Note that a mature minor is not necessarily an emancipated minor."

From this definition, then, the mature minor is a non-adult who may, under state law, be treated as an adult for limited purposes (possibly consenting to medical care), while an emancipated minor is considered an adult for all purposes under state law.

5.37 Q. In enrolling a child in clinical trials, is one parent's permission considered sufficient?

A. State law again takes precedence in this area. Within the framework of state laws, the IRB and the nature of the clinical trial determine whether both parents' signatures are necessary to enroll a child in a trial. In this area as well, the FDA's April 2001 interim rule incorporating HHS regulations (45 CFR 46, Subpart D) for the conduct of studies in children defines the criteria used in determining the need for parental signatures. "Where parental permission is to be obtained, the IRB may find that the permission of one parent is sufficient, if consistent with State law, for clinical investigations to be conducted under Sec. 50.51 [for clinical investigations involving greater than minimal risk] or Sec. 50.52 [clinical investigations involving greater than minimal risk but presenting the prospect of direct benefit to individual subjects]," the interim rule states.

"Where clinical investigations are covered by Sec. 50.53 [clinical investigations involving greater than minimal risk and no prospect of direct benefit to individual subjects, but likely to yield generalizable knowledge about the subjects' disorder or condition] or Sec. 50.54 [clinical investigations not otherwise approvable that present an opportunity to understand, prevent, or alleviate a serious problem affecting the health or welfare of children] and permission is to be obtained from parents, both parents must give their permission unless one parent is deceased, unknown, incompetent, or not reasonably available, or when only one parent has legal responsibility for the care and custody of the child if consistent with State law."

5.38 Q. What should a consent form indicate about the financial interests of a clinical investigator or medical institution?

A. Currently, there is no requirement that informed consent discuss or address the financial interests of either the investigators or the medical institution in FDA-regulated trials, although government regulators are increasingly recommending or requiring that those conducting trials disclose such information to study participants (see discussion on new NIH policy below and Q13.1). Best practices dictate, however, that an informed consent form should identify the sponsoring agency (e.g., the pharmaceutical manufacturer or self sponsorship (investigator IND)). Potential subjects have a right to know who is paying for a study. Knowledge of sponsorship allows a potential subject, especially one with a bias for or against a particular drug manufacturer, to make an informed decision about participation.

Although there are not currently any formal GCP requirements regarding the disclosure to study subjects of potential conflicts of interest held by clinical investigators, the FDA does emphasize that IRBs should be aware that the informed consent form must describe the study's "reasonably expected" benefits not only for the subject, but for "others" as well. "This may be an issue when benefits accruing to the investigator, the sponsor, or others are different than that normally expected to result from conducting research," the agency states in the Information Sheet entitled, "A Guide to Informed Consent." "Thus, if these benefits may be materially relevant to the subject's decision to participate, they should be disclosed in the informed consent document."

More recent government guidances are also encouraging such disclosures. Following a 2000 HHS "plan of action" designed to strengthen human subject protections in clinical research, HHS ultimately released a May 2004 guidance (superseding a January 2001 draft interim guidance) to help institutions, investigators, and IRBs involved in FDA-regulated and HHS conducted/sponsored research to determine whether specific financial interests in research affect the rights and welfare of human subjects and, if so, what actions should be considered to protect these subjects. Entitled "Financial Relationships and Interests in Research Involving

Human Subjects: Guidance for Human Subject Protection," the document "recommends that in particular, IRBs, institutions engaged in research, and investigators consider whether specific financial relationships create financial interests in research studies that may adversely affect the rights and welfare of subjects." With regard to the informed consent process, the draft guidance recommends that:

- IRBs determine "the kind, amount, and level of detail of information to be provided to research subjects regarding the source of funding, funding arrangements, financial interests of parties involved in the research, and any financial interest management techniques applied."
- Investigators consider "the potential effects that a financial relationship of any kind might have on the research or on interactions with research subjects, and what actions to take." These actions might comprise:
  —"including information in the consent document, such as the source of funding and funding arrangements for the conduct and review of research, or information about a financial arrangement of an institution or an investigator and how it is being managed.
  —using special measures to modify the consent process when a potential or actual financial conflict exists, such as having another individual who does have a potential or actual conflict of interest involved in the consent process, especially when a potential or actual conflict of interest could influence the tone, presentation, or type of information presented during the consent process.
  —using independent monitoring of the research."

In the future, individual IRBs or institutions may require that the amount of a site "grant" be specifically disclosed in consents. Further, in its 2004 voluntary principles for clinical trial conduct, PhRMA encourages clinical investigators "to disclose to potential research subjects during the informal consent process that the investigator and/or institution is receiving payment for the conduct of the clinical trial."

Some are claiming that an evolving liability environment that will hold drug sponsors increasingly responsible for the actions of clinical investigators and clinical research organizations should encourage sponsors to have the financial details and potential conflicts of interest relevant to a trial disclosed to patients. "My view is, and I suspect a jury's view and a judge's view is, when you switch the patient from patient to subject and you get $1,000 for it, that's something the patients ought to know," Assistant U.S. Attorney Jim Sheehan stated at the November 2002 Pharmaceutical Compliance Forum. Even if investigator payments are made by CROs or trial management organizations, sponsors "need to know what's happening at the second tier down from where [they] are."

In general, the financial interests of clinical researchers and potential conflicts of interest within the research community continue to be hot-button issues within U.S. government agencies. In response to controversies regarding potential conflicts of interest among NIH scientists (e.g., consulting arrangements with industry), for example, the federal government issued a February 3, 2005, interim rule in which it prohibited NIH employees from "engaging in certain outside activities" with certain entities, including "biotechnology, pharmaceutical, medical device, and other companies substantially affected by the programs, policies, and operations of the NIH." In addition, the NIH issued a January 4, 2005, policy under which any NIH staff member who participates in clinical research and who has a patent or financial interest in the product under study must ensure that this fact is disclosed to the IRB and to the research subjects (i.e., in the informed consent form) and that the research results are reviewed by an "independent entity," such as a data safety monitoring board. In addition, all principal investigators participating in HHS-sponsored research must review and follow the new policy, entitled *A Guide to Preventing Conflicts of Interest in Human Subjects Research at NIH* (January 4, 2005) and circulate the document to all other investigators whose names appear on a clinical protocol.

5.39 Q. Specifically, how often are informed consent-related issues cited as deficiencies in FDA GCP inspections?

A. Consistently each year, informed consent-related issues are among the most commonly cited deficiencies in CDER's GCP compliance inspections of clinical trial investigators and sites. Unfortunately, CDER's inspectional data do not specify the particular types of informed consent problems cited.

In FY2003 (the latest year for which data are available), 8.5% of the clinical investigators/sites inspected by CDER were cited for informed consent-related issues. This was a slight improvement over the 11% of sites/investigators cited for such violations in FY2002.

Informed consent-related compliance problems are seldom considered significant departures from agency standards. This can be inferred because the FDA cited only 1% of all clinical investigators/sites inspected in FY2003 for what the agency considered major departures from GCP regulations.

While an equal percent—9%—of U.S.-based investigators and sites inspected by FDA were cited for informed consent problems in FY2003 and FY2002, foreign investigators made significant gains in this area. In FY2003, only 4% of foreign investigators/sites were found to have such problems, down from 22% in FY2002.

5.40 Q. Are there any indications that the FDA, in its risk-based GCP inspectional approach, will focus more intently on informed consent-related issues in the future?

A. There are not necessarily any formal indications or data suggesting that the FDA is focusing more intently on informed consent-related issues during its clinical investigator inspections. Since CDER is basing so significant a proportion of its site inspections on voluntary complaints, at least some of the agency's focus is being determined by the exact nature of the complaints (see Q17.2-17.4).

In March 2005, however, Philadelphia Associate U.S. District Attorney James Sheehan warned about what he sees as "the coming storm" in a government focus on clinical research conduct. Sheehan predicted that government investigations into the conduct of clinical trials could focus on institutional review boards and, in particular, on subject protection and informed consent-related disclosures to study subjects. "The biggest problem in the next five years is the subject disclosure and protection issue," said Sheehan. "The law is developing in that area. It's a significant problem. What we're finding out, as there's more intense inspection of institutional review board processes and of studies, is that these problems are not just occasional events."

5.41 Q. But IRBs also have critical informed consent-related responsibilities ("An IRB shall require that information given to subjects as part of informed consent is in accordance with" federal regulations—21 CFR 56.109(b)). How often are IRBs cited for informed consent issues?

A. Given that IRBs do have informed consent-related responsibilities, FDA inspections of IRBs address informed consent issues. In FY2003, 5% of IRBs inspected were cited for deficiencies related to the "elements of informed consent," down from 1% in FY2002.

A December 2004 study (Bramstedt and Kassimatis) of FDA warning letters to IRBs during the period January 1997-June 2004 gives an indication of how often IRB inspections turn up more significant informed-consent related noncompliance (FDA warning letters are sent when the noncompliance is more significant and when a specific action is necessary to correct the noncompliance, see Q10.28). The study authors found that, of 52 FDA warning letters issued to IRBs during this period, 17 (or 33%) were issued for informed consent-related issues. Among the issues cited in the letters were the IRBs' failure to determine that the informed consent forms lacked the essential elements required by federal regulations. Others included informed consent forms that inflated the benefits that research subjects should expect and the use of complex technical language in the consent forms.

Such significant IRB noncompliance in this area remains small, however. Based on general estimates of the number of IRBs inspected from January 1997-June 2004 (the FDA inspects approximately 150-200 IRBs per year), only between 1% to 2% of the IRBs were cited for significant informed consent-related noncompliance in warning letters.

5.42 Q. Given that a significant, if shrinking, number of clinical study sites inspected each year are cited for informed consent issues, including using inadequate informed consent forms, what do we know about the most common deficiencies in the content of informed consent documents?

A. The FDA has not gone on record as to the nature of the detected inadequacies of informed consent forms or their specific frequencies. In all likelihood, these cited problems involve the absence of mandatory consent elements and not more subtle, less well-defined deficiencies.

The exhibit below lists what are generally considered to be common problems with the content and readability of informed consents. The problems cited are for consents that had been approved by IRBs and reviewed by sponsors and their clinical department staff. Items with an asterisk might be cited by the FDA in a Form 483-Inspectional Observations because they violate FDA standards.

Common Problems with Informed Consent Form
Content and Readability

CONTENT	
Problem	**Comments**
No mention of informing subject's primary care MD regarding enrollment in the study	An ICH recommendation; subject should grant permission to contact primary MD
Title is not exact title on protocol	Perhaps an attempt by study staff to make the consent title more understandable
No mention of sponsor by name	Investigator might not want the subject to know that the study is sponsored by a pharmaceutical company
Inadequate discussion of compensation for injury and who will cover these costs (errors and omissions insurance purchased by the sponsor)	Happens frequently. The wording is confusing and often discusses the subject's health insurance
*No IRB/patient advocate contact listed (name and title)	IRB might not want this person named
*Unclear regarding length of time subject will be on study (length of commitment); little mention of the amount of follow-up required	Consent is vague regarding how many weeks, months, or years a subject will have to be followed after receiving drug
*Risks do not match those in investigator's brochure; risks downplayed	Investigator does not want to frighten potential subjects
*No statement of subject payment in benefits or cost reimbursement section	Dollar payments for travel, day care, completing study visits, etc., are not listed
No mention of follow-up of pregnancy to term; use of adequate birth control	Many investigational drugs are too risky to test in pregnant women, but the consent does not strongly state that a woman must use birth control while on study, and does not indicate what happens should she become pregnant
No mention of possible pain associated with procedures, such as blood draws or mammograms	Frequently downplayed
Unclear about % chance of receiving study product (flip of coin)	Needs to be carefully explained, given the study arms and given the potential for harm (going untreated or undiagnosed) of receiving a placebo
No mention of consequences of receiving the placebo and going untreated or undiagnosed	Subjects need to understand natural disease progression and its risks
No mention of access to medical records should subject be hospitalized or receive care at non-study health care facilities	Especially important with the implementation of HIPAA legislation in April 2003
Alternative treatment risks and benefits not described	Sometimes, this is only done orally by a physician during a "recruitment" discussion

Problem	Comments
No mention of responsibility of subject to inform site staff about adverse events, pregnancy, new addresses and phone #s	Subjects have more than just a responsibility to present themselves for visits and submit to procedures
Amount of blood to be collected not specified in lay terms (teaspoons of blood)	Blood draws for lab testing are specified for many studies; their frequency and the amount of blood at each draw and total amount must be specified.
Confidentiality section mentions only that sponsor employees and FDA may review medical records; fails to mention sponsor representatives and other regulators (e.g., EMEA)	CRO monitors, independent auditors, and other agency inspectors may be involved in record review
*Not updated with new safety information	This is a GCP requirement, but like many requirements, it is difficult to determine when it is "triggered"
Number of study participants not specified	Provides an understanding of how many subjects will be exposed
READABILITY	
Layout is poor—no subheadings/ text too dense	Layout can be a formidable obstacle to comprehension
Repetitious	Unless a point is extremely important, it should not be repeated
Too wordy/too long/too many complicated terms/does not follow a logical sequence in describing what will happen while on study	Readers comprehend better with short sentences, logical organization
*Content does not have changes recommended by the IRB	IRBs usually have good reasons for requesting changes and these requests must be honored
Missing signature lines with dates (consenter, and subject; witness if subject is "compromised")	Lines for signatures and dates help complete the process
Absence of a line for time of day of consent (especially if consent signed the same day as dosing or study procedures)	This line helps establish that consent was signed before study tests and procedures were initiated
Confuses study MD with primary care MD by using terms such as, "your physician"	Each reference and each person's specific role should be clear

Despite being widely circulated in 1997, the ICH GCP recommendation that a subject's primary care physician be informed regarding a patient's enrollment in a study is rarely implemented today. This is an important point because subjects sometimes fail to mention critical clinical information about their medical histories that would preclude enrollment. Therefore, a subject's primary care physician might, in certain instances, inform the principal investigator about these conditions, thereby preventing a dangerous situation and non-evaluability.

Subjects may become injured by either the study drug or by study procedures. In such cases, a mechanism should be in place to provide for reimbursement for treatment costs related to medical injury. Often, the informed consent form does not fully describe this mechanism, but features contradictory information that is further confounded by a discussion of the subject's health insurance.

Despite strong statements in study protocols regarding birth control and pregnancy, consents frequently do not have sufficient warnings regarding pregnancy, requirements for pregnancy tests and birth control, and obligations should conception occur while on study. Given related liability issues, one would think that sponsors would insist on strong language in consents.

Revisions to the Declaration of Helsinki in 2000 questioned the ethics of conducting placebo-controlled studies when an approved treatment exists. Yet placebo-controlled trials remain prevalent. It is, therefore, critical that subjects understand their chances of receiving a placebo and what risks they may face if they go undiagnosed or untreated. It is also important for them to fully understand what the alternatives are to enrolling in the study, especially if there is an approved treatment not offered as an arm in the study.

As former HHS Secretary Donna Shalala once wrote, "Full disclosure is a necessary precondition to free choice. Accordingly, subjects who do not understand the potential risks of a trial cannot be said to have chosen freely to face those risks." Risks discussed in the informed consent form must reflect the risks disclosed in the investigator brochure as well as other, more recent information about side effects and contraindications.

In many senses, an informed consent is a type of contract. Both parties to the agreement have obligations. As such, subjects must recognize that they have an obligation to inform study staff about their clinical conditions, even if an abnormality seemingly has little to do with the study.

5.43 Q. What are the FDA's requirements regarding the translation of informed consent for non-English-speaking study candidates?

A. FDA officials continue to develop guidance regarding informed consent issues for non-English-speaking persons. In September 2004, Senior Advisor for Clinical Science David Lepay, M.D., Ph.D., stated that the FDA and HHS are continuing their work to develop a new guidance entitled, "Obtaining and Documenting Informed Consent of Subjects Who Do Not Understand English."

If a site is enrolling a non-English-speaking person, the FDA fully expects that a version of the informed consent form will be provided to the candidate in a language the candidate can understand. A person who reads and speaks this language should administer the consent. Alternatively, a translator should be present; this translator, as best practice, should be a certified translator, but, in practice, frequently is simply fluent in a language rather than certified in that language.

In an Information Sheet entitled, "Guidance for Institutional Review Boards and Clinical Investigators" (1998), the FDA states:

> "To meet the requirements of 21 CFR 50.20, the informed consent document should be in language understandable to the subject (or authorized representative). When the consent interview is conducted in English, the consent

document should be in English. When the study subject population includes non-English speaking people or the clinical investigator or the IRB anticipates that the consent interviews will be conducted in a language other than English, the IRB should require a translated consent document to be prepared and assure that the translation is accurate. As required by 21 CFR 50.27, a copy of the consent document must be given to each subject. In the case of non-English speaking subjects, this would be the translated document. . . .

"If a non-English speaking subject is unexpectedly encountered, investigators will not have a written translation of the consent document and must rely on oral translation. Investigators should carefully consider the ethical/legal ramifications of enrolling subjects when a language barrier exists. If the subject does not clearly understand the information presented, the subject's consent will not truly be informed and may not be legally effective. If investigators enroll subjects without an IRB approved written translation, a 'short form' written consent document, in a language the subject understands, should be used to document that the elements of informed consent required by 21 CFR 50.25 were presented orally. The required signatures on a short form are stated in 21 CFR 50.27(b)(2)."

An unbiased translator should assist in the translation process. A note should be made in the medical record and/or on the consent form about these special consenting procedures. The name of the translator and the relationship between the translator and the consentee should be noted.

Although it might be relatively easy for a site to have on hand a "short form" written in the language understood by non-English speaking subjects even when their participation was not anticipated by the site, it would be more difficult for the site to have the study-specific information readily available in that language.

5.44 Q. Under FDA regulations, the IRB is responsible for reviewing and approving informed consent documents. But to what degree does the FDA review and comment on consent documents?

A. FDA regulations do not require drug sponsors to submit informed consent documents (ICD) in their INDs or any other regulatory submissions. Despite this, many companies routinely submit consent documents in their INDs for FDA review and comment.

And there are now definite signs that the FDA wants to play a greater role in reviewing consent documents in parallel with IRBs. Under a November 2002 policy, CDER formally recommended that its drug review divisions request copies of consent documents and assess them as part of certain IND reviews.

While the CDER policy leaves informed consent document review to the discretion of the review division, the policy emphasizes that, "in most cases, informed consent documents should be reviewed as part of the review of an IND submission when review of the proposed investigational use raises a particular concern about the adequacy of informed consent. For example, review of an informed consent document is warranted when:

- Unusual toxicity is associated with the study drug.
- The study population is particularly vulnerable.
- The study design is unusual for the therapeutic class.

- CDER is in a better position than the IRB to assess whether the informed consent document adequately addresses a particular concern based on proprietary data."

In such cases, drug review divisions are instructed to assess the informed consent document's adequacy in addressing any safety issues or study design matters, and in providing required elements of informed consent. When a division has specific concerns about whether the informed consent document meets regulatory requirements, it is advised to forward the document, the protocol, and relevant supporting documentation to the Division of Scientific Investigations' Human Subject Protection Team for a consultative review.

Due to concerns regarding vulnerable populations, CDER review of the informed consent form is "always recommended" for treatment INDs and protocols and when exceptions to informed consent requirements are sought for emergency research. For such situations, CDER review divisions are advised to seek an assessment by the Division of Scientific Investigations as well. Many CDER divisions already employed such a policy.

While the CDER policy document stops short of recommending that drug review divisions call for the submission of informed consent documents in all cases, it emphasizes that such reviews could be beneficial when the documents are otherwise made available. "If a sponsor has submitted an ICD as part of its IND, but the protocol does not fall under any of the situations [in which ICD review and submission is recommended or warranted], it may still be useful to review the ICD to rule out significant deficiencies," the policy states.

The CDER policy establishes for its review divisions that they have the regulatory authority to request an ICD, which is not identified in the IND regulations or Form FDA-1571 as a submission requirement. Under 21 CFR 312.23(a)(11), an IND sponsor must submit "any other relevant information needed for the review of the application" when requested by the FDA.

Under the policy, CDER provides its review divisions with a range of regulatory options when issues are identified during the ICD review. Generally, review division or DSI comments on ICD content will be what the agency terms "advisory." "They need not specifically prescribe how the sponsor should address the comments, and the investigation need not be put on hold pending submission of a revised ICD," the center states.

"For multicenter trials with local IRB review of the ICD (i.e., for which the content of the ICD may vary somewhat from site to site), the sponsor should be advised to ensure that the ICD for each center is revised to address CDER comments on safety issues."

But the policy does allow CDER review divisions to use the hammer—a formal clinical hold action—in specific cases. "In some situations, the review division or DSI may find an ICD to be misleading, inaccurate, or incomplete in a way that raises a significant safety concern for potential study subjects and requires that specified revisions be made to address the concern before a trial can proceed. In such cases, the review division may place the IND on clinical hold until an acceptable revision of the ICD is received . . . , or may discuss specific modifications with the sponsor to avoid a clinical hold."

5.45 Q. *If a parent is a minor, can she still legally consent for the infant? If not, does she sign an assent form with her parent signing the consent form? If a parent is to give consent for his/her child, but the parent him/herself is a minor, should additional consent be obtained (i.e., from the child's grandparents)?*

A. While this an unusual situation, it can and does occur. Some study sites might refuse to enroll the infant in such cases. The principal investigator may decide that consenting and enrollment are too problematic. Other sites might determine that the minor parent enjoys all the legal rights of parenthood and has standing to enroll her child.

In the United States, state laws vary regarding the age at which a minor becomes an adult and regarding the process of emancipation when a minor becomes an adult. In other countries, such as those in the Pacific Rim, marriage may impact study consenting decision-making, and grandparents have more legal standing regarding decision-making for infants.

5.46 Q. *Assume that a potential subject is a Jehovah's Witness who will not allow any blood products to be transfused, and that he has extremely low blood counts, with a hemoglobin reading around five. Dosing with the study drug poses increased clinical risks in light of the patient's hemoglobin status. What accommodations can be made to enroll this patient, who is eager to start the study?*

A. Most clinical sites and sponsors would not enroll this patient because of the additional clinical risks to an already significantly compromised patient. There have been instances, however, in which investigators and sponsors have permitted this type of patient to be enrolled. In such cases, a modified informed consent that detailed the additional risks is drafted and forwarded for IRB review and approval. The sponsors were also willing to lower the drug dose (which of course had to be noted in the new informed consent form). Not all protocols are flexible enough to accommodate a dosing modification, however, and not all sponsors are willing to take on additional liability exposure.

5.47 Q. *Why are the words "patient" and "subject" and the words "informed consent" and "consent form" debated so much?*

A. A patient is an individual being cared for by a physician who has, as his or her primary objective, the care of that patient. A subject is a person who is agreeing to do something beyond this to allow someone else to answer a question. The subject is a contributor to a greater good. There is also a growing trend to call subjects "participants." Participant implies a more equal relationship between the study team and the person, and should be used only when there is a commitment to balancing the relationship.

"Informed" implies that the study subject was provided with sufficient information so that he or she could make a reasoned decision regarding his or her participation in the study. "Consent" implies agreement. The consent form documents the information that was provided to the subject, and the study subject's agreement, at the time of signing, to become a research subject. It is important to note, however, that a subject's signature on an informed consent form does not, in itself, necessarily mean that the subject was properly informed.

5.48 Q. Although FDA inspectors cite problems regarding missing elements in an informed consent's content, there is also concern among researchers, patient advocates, and IRB members that, due to the complexity of some clinical studies, consent content and the consenting process are too complex for the average subject. Are there measurement tools to assess the complexities inherent in the consenting process?

A. There are three kinds of measurement tools used in this area: those that assess the "readability" of the consent forms; those that evaluate a subject's capability to be adequately consented; and those that survey subjects after consenting has been completed to determine if they understood study procedures, risks, and benefits.

There are commercially available software programs that will analyze text for readability. Even Microsoft Word has a method for assessing document readability. Each of these programs provides statistical output that can help assess the "plain English" characteristics of informed consent forms. They yield results about the reading grade level of the form's content. There is some evidence, however, that a form's reading grade level may not correlate well with reader comprehension. Readability may also be influenced by document-design issues.

A validated tool called the MacArthur Competence Assessment Tool for Clinical Research (MacCAT-CR) measures capacity for consent. This tool divides consent into four aspects: understanding; appreciation; decision-making; and choice. Specifically, MacCAT-CR is intended to help determine if patients who are experiencing pain or stress should be excluded from research participation or, instead, be included after receiving treatment for the pain or stress.

Finally, consent readers can be tested post-consent to determine the effectiveness of the consent process in providing key study-related information. They can undergo survey interviews or they can be administered questionnaires. Some standardized questionnaires include open-ended questions such as, "what is the purpose of this study?" Others delete every fifth word in a consent form and ask the research participant to "fill-in-the-blanks."

For more information about these evaluation tools, see Mark Hochhauser, "The Informed Consent Form: Document Development and Evaluation," *Drug Information Journal,* 34(4), 1309-17, 2000.

Further Reading

Kiev, Ari, "A History of Informed Consent Doctrine," *Applied Clinical Trials,* 2:56-59, May 1993.

Lin, Yeong-Liang, et al, "Compliance of Clinical Trial Consent Forms With International Guidelines," *Drug Information Journal,* 36-17-19, 2002.

Sharp, S. Michael, "Improving the Process of Obtaining Informed Consent," *Applied Clinical Trials,* 10:32-38, January 2001.

Evans, J.P., and Beck, P. "Informed Consent in Medical Research," *Clin Med* 2:267-72, May-June 2002.

Stevens, P.E., and Pletsch, P.K. "Informed Consent and the History of Inclusion of Women in Clinical Research," *Health Care Women Int* 23:809-19, December 2002.

Mackintosh, Douglas, and Molloy, Vernette, "Opportunities to Improve Informed Consent," *Applied Clinical Trials* 12:42-8, May 2003.

Acknowledgments

Douglas Mackintosh, DrPH, MBA, MS Hyg, and Vernette Molloy, MBA, RN, of GCPA, Inc.; Kathy Ford, RN, Senior Director of Clinical Operations, Millennium Pharmaceuticals, Inc., Cambridge, MA.

Section 6:
Source Data/Documentation

6.1   Q. What constitutes valid source documentation in a clinical trial?

A. Source documents in a clinical trial are the hard copies on which clinical observations are first recorded. They are legally valid raw data that support a study's findings. At an investigational site, source documentation is often the medical record, but it can also be a computer printout of lab values, a patient diary, or a physician's notes on a 3x5 card—or even a napkin.

A cardinal rule in good clinical practice (GCP) compliance is that case report forms and the source documents/medical record must match, data point to data point. A patient's medical record should support the data on the case report form, which should, in turn, support the data listings and statistical results provided to regulatory agencies. Source documentation is the beginning of a clean, verifiable audit trail.

The ICH's GCP guideline defines source documents as original records, or certified copies of original records, that contain "clinical findings, observations, or other activities in a clinical trial necessary for the reconstruction and evaluation of the trial" (1.51). Source documents are defined as "original documents, data, and records (e.g., hospital records, clinical and office charts, laboratory notes, memoranda, subjects' diaries or evaluation checklists, pharmacy dispensing records, recorded data from automated instruments, copies or transcriptions certified after verification as being accurate and complete, microfiches, photographic negatives, microfilm or magnetic data, x-rays, subject files, and records kept at the pharmacy, at the laboratories, and at medico-technical departments involved in the clinical trial)" (1.52). The guideline adds that the purpose of source documents is "to document the existence of the subject and substantiate the integrity of trial data collected [and] to include original documents related to the trial, to medical treatment, and history of subject."

In regulatory terms, source documents, along with case report forms, comprise what FDA regulations refer to as "case histories." According to 21 CFR 312.62(b), "an investigator is required to prepare and maintain adequate and accurate case histories that record all observations and other data pertinent to the investigation on each individual administered the investigational drug or employed as a control in the investigation. Case histories include the case report forms and supporting data including, for example, signed and dated consent forms, any medical records, for example, progress notes of the physician, the individual's hospital chart(s), and nurses' notes."

Source documents, then, can include hospital records and medical charts, clinical and office charts, laboratory reports, patient diaries, pharmacy dispensing records, data recorded from automated instruments, diagnostic reports (x-rays and EKGs), and surgical reports. Photocopies of completed case report forms are not valid source documents.

6.2 *Q. Do GCP standards require that 100% of the information recorded on a case report form (CRF) be recorded in a medical record/chart first?*

A. Not necessarily. The ICH GCP guideline specifically acknowledges that data may, in some cases, be recorded directly on case report forms, and FDA GCP standards also permit this practice. "The trial design should include the identification of any data to be recorded directly on the CRFs (i.e., no prior written or electronic record of data), and to be considered source data," the ICH guideline states.

The FDA has discussed situations in which such a practice is permitted. In the preamble to a November 1996 final rule entitled "Protection of Human Subjects; Informed Consent Verification," the FDA states that "if the case report form is made a permanent part of the subject's medical record, then the medical record may not need to contain information that is contained in that case report form. In most instances, the agency thinks that information is typically entered into the subject's medical record first; then, it is entered onto the case report form for transmittal to the research sponsor."

According to ICH guidance, if sections of the CRF are to be considered source documents, these sections or pages should be identified in the protocol prior to study inception (6.4.9). Ideally, in such cases, the documents should be signed and dated.

6.3 *Q. Can completed pages from a case report form serve as valid source documentation?*

A. In general, no. Study observations and evaluations, such as medical history, physical examinations, and study medication accountability, should be recorded first on the medical record, then transcribed into the CRF. The original CRF, however, can be used as a source document when study data that are best captured directly on the CRFs—for example, when a CRF page captures readings directly from automated equipment, such as a continuous blood pressure monitoring device, to promote accuracy.

In addition, the FDA will accept the CRF as a source document in simple trials such as bioequivalency studies. While the use of the CRF as the primary data collection tool and entire source documentation is unacceptable for Phase 2 and 3 studies, such a practice does sometimes occur. More frequently, auditors see the marginally acceptable practice of using hybrid or customized CRFs designed to capture the requisite data. Unfortunately, such forms do not provide an optimal format for describing clinical events in a manner typical of the investigator's routine medical practice. Ideally, data captured on the CRF should be substantiated by corresponding clinical notations written in a chronological format in the medical record. At a minimum, there should be sufficient source documentation to establish the credibility of the CRF in its totality.

The exhibit below lists several typical approaches to documentation found at investigational sites and their corresponding adequacy.

Documentation	Adequacy
No medical record; all raw data recorded directly on CRF	Inadequate for Phase 2 and 3 studies
Raw data recorded on CRF-stamped "source document" then transferred to CRF	Inadequate
Raw data recorded on customized forms provided by monitor, then transferred to CRF	Acceptable, but marginally adequate because not usual medical practice
Raw data recorded in free text form on unlined paper, signed and dated, in chronological order	Adequate

6.4 Q. How often are documentation and records-related issues cited as deficiencies in FDA GCP inspections?

A. Consistently each year, records-related issues (i.e., inadequate/inaccurate records) represent the second most commonly cited deficiency in CDER's GCP compliance inspections of clinical trial investigators and sites (i.e., after failure to adhere to the clinical protocol). In FY2003 (the latest year for which data are available), 19% of the clinical investigators/sites inspected by CDER were cited for records-related issues. This, however, was an improvement over the 28% of sites/investigators cited for such violations in FY2002.

Despite their overall frequency, records-related issues are seldom considered significant departures from agency standards. This can be inferred because the FDA cited only 1% of all clinical investigators/sites inspected in FY2003 for what the agency considered major departures from GCP regulations.

Records-related compliance is an issue with which both U.S. and foreign sites struggle. In FY2003, 19% of U.S. investigators inspected were cited for such problems (compared to 27% in FY2002), while an equal percent of foreign inspectors were cited for such records issues (compared to 36% in FY2002).

6.5 Q. Given the importance of raw data and text as an original record, can clinicians make corrections to, or insertions in, raw data or text?

A. Yes. Source data, however, must be relatively permanent and be protected from unauthorized changes. When changes to raw data are necessary, they must not obscure the original values. Whiteouts, redactions, and similar attempts to obliterate the original data are unacceptable. Although the clinician's intent in making the changes may be benign, an auditor or FDA inspector could view such alterations as an attempt to obscure the real data, and might even suspect fraud.

Four elements must be visible each time a raw data value is changed:
- the old value;
- the new value;
- the date and time of the change; and
- an identification (e.g., initials) of the person making the change.

In making a change, a clinician should simply draw a single line through the original value, record the new value and the date, and initial the change. When raw text must be inserted, it cannot be squeezed between the lines or in the margins. It should be documented as a signed addendum, and a separate, new and dated page that includes the corrections or additions should be added directly after the page to be amended.

6.6 *Q. There are many types of medical records and documents that may include data and information on a patient's medical history and medical course during treatment. In the context of a trial audit or FDA inspection, are all such documents given equal weighting in terms of supporting the data and information in a case report form?*

A. Not necessarily. Certain source documents, by virtue of their being the first record of raw data, hold a higher place in the hierarchy of medical records than later documents that presumably contain the same data. In the exhibit below on the hierarchy of clinical documentation, the left column includes firsthand observations, such as admitting and progress notes. The right column shows secondhand records, such as discharge summaries.

The first recorded value is generally presumed correct. All subsequent transcriptions are considered secondary, and discrepancies may be attributed to transcription errors. In reviewing a medical record for comparisons with a case report form, an auditor or FDA inspector attempts to find the first source documents used to record the original observation of the clinical event.

Hierarchy of Clinical Documentation

Firsthand Documents	Secondhand Documents
Handwritten anesthesia records	Templated "canned" operating room reports
Dictated operating room reports	Lab data handwritten in progress notes
Admission notes	Handwritten lab flow sheets taken from lab reports
Ancillary documents (x-rays, labs, blood gas, physical therapy, pathology reports, etc.)	Discharge summaries
History and physical (H&P) records	
Physician and nurses' progress notes	
Specialist consults	
Emergency room notes	
Ambulance transport records	
Medication administration record	
MD orders	
Death certificates	

Since secondhand documents are created from firsthand documents, mistakes can occur in the transfer of data to these secondary records. It is not unusual to find mistakes in discharge summaries. Study staff, as well as monitors, auditors, and FDA inspectors, rely more on firsthand documents than on secondhand documents.

6.7 *Q. If raw study data are entered directly into a computer system rather than kept on a medical record/chart, what is considered to be the source document?*

A. Section III (General Principles) of the FDA's April 1999 industry guidance entitled, "Computerized Systems Used in Clinical Trials" states that, "when original observations are entered directly into a computerized system, the electronic record is the source document." The same statement appears in the FDA's September 2004 draft revision of the April 1999 guidance (see Section 11).

Raw data as entered into a clinical computer system are considered to be the source data, regardless of whether they are immediately printed out as a hard copy following entry or simply stored as computer files. All rules and conventions regarding the validity and adequacy of source documents apply to electronic transcription.

6.8 Q. FDA regulations at 21 CFR 312.62(c)-Investigator record retention requirements call on investigators to retain study-related records "for 2 years following the date a marketing application is approved for the drug for the indication for which it is being investigated; or if no application is to be filed or if the application is not approved for such indication, until 2 years after the investigation is discontinued and FDA is notified." Assuming that no NDA is to be filed or the application is not approved for the indication, how does the FDA interpret "until 2 years after the investigation is discontinued and FDA is notified"?

A. According to staffers in CDER's Division of Scientific Investigations, the FDA interprets this to mean the date on which the sponsor discontinues all studies under the relevant IND. Assume, for example, that a particular site's participation is discontinued while the larger clinical program for the indication continues at other sites. Would the two-year clock begin ticking when that site's participation is discontinued? No, according to CDER's DSI. The two-year clock applicable to record retention would not begin ticking until all studies/sites were discontinued. In effect, that particular site's retention requirements could last for many years depending on how long the other investigations under the IND continue.

Although, in practice, the agency may not split hairs on the precise date that a study "is discontinued and FDA is notified," some at the agency contacted on this issue believe that the date would be the FDA's date of receipt of a sponsor's letter stating that studies are being discontinued for a particular indication or that an entire IND is being withdrawn or inactivated. The FDA is not known to have provided definitive advice on this particular issue, however.

In practice, investigators often must retain these records well beyond the two-year period required by FDA. In many cases, sponsors require investigators to maintain records for longer periods under clinical protocols. Further, ICH GCP standards may call on investigators to maintain such records for longer periods. Under the ICH's E6 Guideline for Good Clinical Practice, for instance, investigators are called on to retain essential study-related documents "until at least 2 years after the last approval of a marketing application in an ICH region and until there are no pending or contemplated marketing applications in an ICH region or at least 2 years have elapsed since the formal discontinuation of clinical development of the investigational products." Depending on the particulars of a drug's development and the sponsor's submission of marketing dossiers, this period could easily extend well beyond the two-year retention period required under FDA regulations. The E6 guidance goes on to establish that it is the sponsor's responsibility to inform an investigator/institution "as to when these documents no longer need to be retained."

6.9   Q. Under 21 CFR 312.62, a clinical investigator is required to retain study records "for a period of 2 years following the date a marketing application is approved for the drug for the indication for which it is being investigated; or if no application is to be filed or if the application is not approved for such indication, until 2 years after the investigation is discontinued and FDA is notified." Is the FDA's interpretation of this requirement that the site retain these records on-site, or can a site retain these records off site? And can these records be retained through a trusted third party, as suggested by PhRMA in a June 2003 proposal to the agency?

A. Since FDA regulations do not address this issue specifically, there is no regulatory requirement that study records be maintained on-site. In the September 2004 draft guidance entitled, "Computerized Systems Used in Clinical Trials," however, the agency does acknowledge the advantages of on-site storage. "Retaining the original source document or a certified copy of the source document at the site where the investigation was conducted can assist in meeting . . . regulatory requirements [for the maintenance of study records]. It can also assist in the reconstruction and evaluation of the trial throughout and after the completion of the trial."

In practice, the FDA is well aware that many clinical investigational sites do not store their records on site (e.g., due to lack of available space), but possibly in a central location in the larger healthcare facility (e.g., a hospital's central file), or even at an off-site warehouse that may be owned by a data warehousing company.

According to DSI staffers, the agency's policy is that it expects sites to maintain access to such records, that such records be stored under conditions that will preserve their integrity, and that sites be able to retrieve and provide "prompt access" to such records if the FDA requests such records as part of an inspection. In the records retention section of the FDA's Compliance Program Guidance 7348.811 for clinical investigator inspections, the agency acknowledges that a site may not retain "custody" of study-related records, and instructs inspectors to:

"1. Determine who maintains custody of the required records and the means by which prompt access can be assured. Determine whether the investigator has notified the sponsor in writing regarding the custody of required records, if the investigator does not retain them."

6.10   Q. FDA Compliance Policy Guide 7348.811 instructs the agency's inspectors to "determine whether the investigator has notified the sponsor in writing regarding the custody of required records, if the investigator does not retain them." Within the drug regulations for sponsor/investigator record retention, there does not appear to be any regulatory citation for this? Under federal regulations, are investigators REQUIRED to provide such written notification to sponsors in such cases—for example, is this an unwritten, but assumed, element of the "transfer of obligations to a CRO" in 312.23(a)(1)(viii)?

A. Interestingly, the FDA's drug regulations (21 CFR Section 312) offer no specific requirements that clinical investigators notify study sponsors of a transfer in records custody.

In contrast, the FDA's medical device regulations at 812.140(e)—Records custody state that, "an investigator or sponsor may withdraw from the responsibility to maintain records for the period required . . . and transfer custody of the records to any other person who will accept responsibility for them under this part. . . . Notice of a transfer shall be given to FDA not later than 10 working days after transfer occurs." In fact, a June 2004 FDA warning letter to Biotronik, Inc., cited the company for failing to provide such notification to the agency, and for failing to provide a letter from the company assuming custody of the records "indicating their receipt of the clinical data records, and their agreement to accept responsibility for the records under the applicable requirements of 21 CFR Part 812."

6.11 *Q. In some cases, sponsors have standard forms that they use for all their studies, even if some of the information is not needed for a specific study. Can a sponsor collect information on the CRF that will not be data entered or analyzed as part of a specific study?*

A. Sponsors can and frequently do collect information on CRFs that does not become data entered or analyzed. This usually happens because, in the original study design, the sponsor may believe that certain information may be needed for an analysis other than the primary or secondary endpoint analysis. Sponsors may also collect data that will not be analyzed for that study, but that may be used later in sub-group analyses. This is permissible only if the data variables collected in the CRF are listed in the protocol; if they are not, then the sponsor cannot collect it. Some IRBs will review the CRF specifically to verify that only protocol-required information is collected. It is important to keep in mind that a subject in a clinical trial consents only to specific tests and information collection.

In recent informal correspondence on this issue, the FDA commented that, "as to whether it is a violation of the regulations for a sponsor to collect information not required by the protocol, that is an interesting question . . . One could take the position under the informed consent regulations at 21 CFR 50.25(a)(1) that the consent form is to include a description of the procedures to be followed. If the sponsor is requiring the investigator to collect data beyond what the protocol requires, this could involve employing procedures that are not covered in the informed consent, in which case the consent form may be considered inadequate. Likewise, if the protocol does not adequately describe all study procedures, then the IRB may not be able to properly make the determinations required by FDA regulations at CRF 56.111 in approving the study."

6.12 *Q. In some cases, original patient records may not be available at a specific clinical trial site. At a larger hospital or medical facility, for example, original records may be kept in a centralized records department. In such cases, are so-called "shadow charts," which are copies of the original patient records, considered appropriate to monitor against? Must a monitor verify that the information in the shadow chart is the same as that in the original record? If so, how is a monitor to do this?*

A. In recent informal correspondence on this issue, the FDA emphasized that, "obviously, the source documents are the gold standard for study auditing. This is reflected in the ICH guidance, which both defines direct access as:

‘1.21 Direct Access: Permission to examine, analyze, verify, and reproduce any records and reports that are important to evaluation of a clinical trial.’

And directs sponsors to:

'5.15.1 The sponsor should ensure that it is specified in the protocol or other written agreement that the investigator(s)/institution(s) provide direct access to source data/documents for trial-related monitoring, audits, IRB/IEC review, and regulatory inspection.'"

Regarding clinical monitoring activities, the agency adds that, "in general, source documents should be the basis for monitoring. If a sponsor's monitor elects to use 'shadow charts,' they are free to do so as the regulations do not specify how monitoring is to be performed. However, in our opinion they would be foolish to rely on shadow charts without establishing that the shadow charts were the equivalent of the source documents—that is, a certified copy, meaning a copy of original information that has been verified, as indicated by dated signature, as an exact copy having all of the same attributes and information as the original. That's just an opinion. We instruct FDA investigators to audit against source documents."

In keeping with these instructions to audit against source documents, FDA inspectors have, on several occasions, refused to review photocopies of medical records; these inspectors insisted that they be provided access to original hospital medical records during a clinical site inspection. In practice, however, the FDA may accept, for the purpose of an inspection, a photocopy when the original of a specific document is unavailable or has been destroyed. The FDA inspector and the reviewer at the agency's headquarters will decide if a photocopy is acceptable in a particular case. It is important to note that the agency is more likely to accept a photocopy of an isolated record than photocopies of an entire research record.

When shadow charts must be used, the monitor should make every attempt to compare a sample of shadow records against original records to obtain a level of confidence that the shadow charts actually accurately and completely reflect the original records (see Q4.7 and Q6.13). While it takes extra time and effort to review original hospital records, monitors should make a concerted effort to review original records rather than shadow charts.

Clinical trial auditors report that they often find significant medical pathologies "buried" in original hospital records that are not recorded on CRFs. Site personnel claim that one reason for these omissions is that the monitor did not ask for or review original hospital records, and that not all hospital records were photocopied and placed in the "shadow charts."

6.13 Q. What procedures are necessary to ensure that copies of source documents can be considered certified?

A. Copies of source documents are usually considered as valid as originals as long as they are *certified* copies. A certified copy is a document that has been certified by a qualified person to be an exact copy of the original record and to have all the same attributes and information as the original.

This means that an individual, typically a medical records specialist, ensures that the copies represent the totality of the original source documents. Certification means that this individual has verified the integrity of the photocopying process and that no portion of the original has been altered or deleted (e.g., that handwritten notes in the margins and back pages of the original records are accurately captured). The verification process should be documented in a standard operating procedure or operations manual and, of course, should include the dated signature of the individual ensuring the integrity of the process.

In its April 1999 draft industry guidance entitled, "Computerized Systems Used in Clinical Trials," the FDA defines certified copy as "a copy of original information that has been verified, as indicated by dated signature, as an exact copy having all of the same attributes and information as the original." The same definition appears in the agency's September 2004 draft revisions to the April 1999 guidance. [Editor's note: while the April 1999 guidance addresses certified copies in the context of electronic records, FDA officials maintain that this definition is just as relevant to paper-based records.]

Certified copies are typically used in source data verification when original documents are unavailable due to litigation proceedings, or less commonly, when original records are transported from one healthcare facility to another. The key issue in the use of certified copies is the robustness of the verification process as demonstrated by written documentation of both the process and the individual copies.

6.14 Q. Can a site forward original documents, such as x-rays, directly to the sponsor instead of transcribing the findings onto a CRF?

A. Care must be exercised in responding to this question. The question suggests that the x-ray results may not even be source documented at the site, thereby suggesting that their diagnostic interpretations may be of no value to study patients. In this case, however, let's assume, instead, that the local radiologist's report goes into the subject's chart and the x-rays are then forwarded to the sponsor for a third-party, perhaps a blinded, reading. It would be best if the x-rays were "digitized," and if a digitized copy were sent to the sponsor or a copy were placed on tape or some other medium and sent to the sponsor. In either case, the original remains at the site. Alternatively, the sponsor will have to return the original x-rays to the site after the third-party reading.

In short, it is acceptable to bypass the transcription of x-ray findings to the CRF. It avoids the problem of discrepancies in interpretation between the local radiologist and the third-party reader.

6.15 Q. If a sponsor's documentation policies change mid-study (e.g., the sponsor decides that the principal investigator must sign the CRF, and subinvestigators can no longer be delegated this responsibility), should all documents that predated the change be revised to comply with the new policy?

A. Generally, there is no need to revise all documentation that pre-dated a policy revision. The sponsor should have clear documentation as to when and why the policy change was necessary. This should be communicated to all investigators as well.

If a sponsor's prior policy was to permit a subinvestigator to sign the CRF, then there is no need to have the principal investigator countersign the CRFs that were previously signed by the subinvestigator. If CRF changes are implemented after the new policy goes into effect, then the principal investigator should sign these CRFs.

Suppose, for instance, that the subinvestigators did a poor job of reviewing the CRFs, and there are many errors and omissions. In this case, the principal investigator should probably countersign the CRFs after they have been corrected.

In terms of sponsor policies requiring either the principal investigator or subinvestigator to sign the CRF, it is not entirely clear what such policies hope to achieve. Would the principal investigator be any less responsible for errors or omissions if he or she did not sign the CRF? After all, the principal investigator is responsible for the accuracy of these data regardless of whose signature appears. Does the signature increase the likelihood that the responsible individual will spot-check the data or in some way supervise the study coordinator, who usually completes the CRF, more closely? Probably not. In most cases, the signature is perfunctory.

Understandably, many sponsors want to implement multiple GCP safeguards to ensure data accuracy. The investigator's signature on the CRF is one safeguard, albeit an extremely weak one.

6.16 Q. The ICH GCP guideline identifies the staff delegation of authority and responsibility form as an "essential document" in clinical trials. How does the use of this form strengthen a study's source documentation?

A. The purpose of this form is to clearly delineate the name of each individual to whom the principal investigator has delegated authority to perform certain clinical study-related tasks. In this form, the individual's name/title must correspond to one or more specific tasks—in this way, there should be no confusion as to "who did what" during the course of the study.

Staff delegation forms, sometimes known as staff signature forms, support, in part, the validity of source documents. The form, which often contains the staff's initials as well as signatures, can be used to verify clinicians' signatures in source notes. In some cases, clinicians only initial certain source documents, and this form may be able to establish the identity of a clinician based on initials.

Further, in some cases, clinicians use CRF physical exam (PE) pages to directly record their PE findings instead of documenting the findings to a source document first. Frequently, the clinicians do not initial or sign these CRF PE pages. A staff delegation form would provide at least a reasonable suggestion as to who performed the PE. The form could also be helpful in cases in which it is not clear who recorded patient medical histories.

The staff delegation of responsibility form is a multi-purpose tool that serves a valuable purpose in assisting study staff in adhering to ICH GCP and good documentation practices.

6.17 Q. What are the rules regarding the use of a signature stamp in clinical studies?

A. Some clinical settings permit the use of a rubber stamp on medical records. When it is used, however, the impression should be initialed in script, and there must be supporting documentation matching the stamp signature with an original signature.

Rubber stamps may be used in clinical studies in a very limited manner—that is, on hospital medical records if permitted by the hospital and if initialed and dated. As part of the site selection process, the sponsor should evaluate the site's methods for creating and maintaining medical records. If a rubber stamp is routinely used at the investigator's office/clinic or participating hospital, then the rules regarding its use should be discussed with site staff prior to the study's initiation at that site.

A stamp should not be used for key documents such as the Form FDA 1572-Statement of Investigator, protocol signatures, or informed consents.

6.18 Q. Assume that a particular study site conducts numerous studies and enrolls the same patients over and over again in studies after waiting the appropriate amount of time to enroll each patient in the next study. Although study source documents are created for each study, it is the site's policy not to permit monitors or auditors to review source documents from a previous study for a current study under review (i.e., for those subjects who participated in both studies). Is this policy consistent with GCP requirements for source document review?

A. The FDA's "Guideline for the Monitoring of Clinical Investigations" (1998) states that, during a periodic visit to a clinical trial site, the monitor should compare a representative number of subject records and other supporting documents with the investigator's reports to determine, among other things, that the information recorded in the investigator's report is complete, accurate, and legible. This guidance reinforces the need for monitors and auditors to substantiate that a subject meets a protocol's inclusion/exclusion criteria. Typically, this is best accomplished by reviewing *all* available source documentation on a particular study subject.

When investigational site officials sign an agreement with a sponsor, the agreement usually specifies that the sponsor and its agents have access to all subject source documents. Presumably, this includes source documents that reflect a subject's prior medical history, prior treatment, and current medical status.

Site staff, however, might argue that previous study documents have little bearing on the current study, that confidentiality documents signed by the principal investigator prohibit the disclosure of another sponsor's source documents (particularly if templates were used), and that the site's SOPs prohibit access to these documents.

Notwithstanding these arguments, it is unlikely that the site would withhold these source documents from an FDA inspector. A monitor, auditor, or other sponsor representative needs to have the same records access as an FDA inspector to ascertain compliance and regulatory risk. In practice, an FDA inspector and sponsor monitor/auditor may not be aware (i.e., because it has not been disclosed to them) that subjects in the current study participated in previous studies that the site has conducted for other sponsors. In such cases, the inspector and monitor may not have sufficient knowledge on which to base a request for these source documents.

To avoid such confidentiality issues, sites can develop and maintain source documents in charts that include subjects' general medical history and other information, that are not protocol-specific, and that resemble the practice's usual and customary clinic notes. This chart should document clinic subjects' conditions and treatments from study to study, and perhaps between studies if they are seen at that site for a clinical condition or event. The chart should indicate the study or studies in which the subject participated, the investigational drug(s) administered, concomitant medications and AEs. In emergencies, a physician could review this past history, which may be relevant for the emergency treatment. In this manner, the protocol-specific details are not disclosed, while information important to the patient's safety is provided.

The best time to assess a site's charting system is during a pre-study site assessment visit. A site that has no continuous charting system or denies access to historical records is not the ideal choice, since the sponsor may be put at risk if historical documentation cannot be reviewed by the monitor.

6.19 Q. What is the recommended course of action for an investigator if he/she retires and no longer has the ability to store source data and essential documents from a clinical trial? How is this addressed if an institution has a policy of destroying records after a period of time that is shorter than the time period mandated by the FDA?

A. According to 21 CFR 312.62, "An investigator shall retain records required to be maintained under this part for a period of 2 years following the date a marketing application is approved for the drug for the indication for which it is being investigated: or, if no application is to be filed or if the application is not approved for such indication, until 2 years after the investigation is discontinued and FDA is notified."

If an investigator retires and is unable to store the study data, he/she must transfer custody to another person who will accept responsibility for them. The investigator should provide a written notice of this transfer to the sponsor. This notification should be maintained in the investigator file.

If an investigator is conducting a study in an institution that will otherwise destroy records before the FDA-mandatory record-retention period, then the investigator must request that the institution make an exception to its policy to honor the requisite record-maintenance period. In other cases, the sponsor might provide for off-site storage of the study records. In all cases, an investigator should be reminded not to destroy any study records without first checking with the sponsor, and record retention requirements should be specified in the protocol.

Further Reading

Zepp, V. and Mackintosh, D., "Source Documentation: A Key to GCP Compliance in Clinical Trials," *Applied Clinical Trials,* 5:42-46, March 1996.

Molloy, V. and Mackintosh, D., "Source Documentation: Clinical Auditors' Observations," in *The Clinical Audit in Pharmaceutical Development,* Michael R. Hamrell, PhD, Editor, New York, Marcel Dekker, 2000.

Acknowledgments

Douglas Mackintosh, DrPH, MBA, MS Hyg, and Vernette Molloy, MBA, RN, of GCPA, Inc.; G. Stephen DeCherney, MD, MPH, Executive Vice President, Global Clinical Operations, PRA International, McLean, VA.

Section 7:
Clinical Trial Protocols/Protocol Changes/ Protocol Violations

7.1   Q. What is the difference between a protocol deviation and a protocol violation?

A. Neither FDA regulations nor the ICH GCP guideline define the terms "protocol deviation" or "protocol violation," although the ICH GCP document does use the term "protocol deviation" (see discussion below). Because of this, sponsor and IRB standard operating procedures often determine how protocol deviations and violations are differentiated and what specific action is appropriate in each case.

Generally speaking, however, a protocol deviation is an incident involving noncompliance with the protocol, but one that typically does not have a significant effect on the subject's rights, safety, or welfare, or on the integrity of the resultant data. Examples might include obtaining a protocol-required test one day out of the acceptable protocol "window."

Many sponsors consider protocol deviations that are more serious (e.g., involving critical study parameters), or those of which the sponsor was not notified, to be protocol violations. Unlike protocol deviations, protocol violations generally affect the subject's rights, safety, or welfare, or the integrity of the resultant data (i.e., the sponsor's ability to use the data in support of the drug). Examples might include enrolling a subject who did not qualify for the trial without obtaining the sponsor's permission, or repeatedly failing to obtain a protocol-required test.

Again, FDA regulations do not speak directly to protocol deviations or violations. In FDA Form-1572, clinical investigators agree "to conduct the study(ies) in accordance with the relevant, current protocol(s) and will only make changes in a protocol after notifying the sponsor, except when necessary to protect the safety, the rights, or welfare of subjects . . . [and] not to make any changes in the research without IRB approval, except where necessary to eliminate apparent immediate hazards to the human subjects."

Over the years, many have attempted to add clarity to this area. According to G.T. Wolf and R.W. Makuch's 1980 editorial, "Classification System for Protocol Deviations in Clinical Trials" (*Cancer Clinical Trials* 3:101-3), protocol violations are defined as those events that "were caused by or could have been prevented by the investigator and which materially affect the study results." The authors divide protocol deviations into two classes: major deviations are those that "could not be prevented"; minor deviations are those that "are not likely to affect the evaluation of treatment efficacy."

Uncertainty regarding the differences between protocol deviations and violations has been an international phenomenon. In 2001, the European Forum for Good Clinical Practice's (EFGCP) Audit Working Party offered the following definitions:

"Protocol violation: serious non-compliance—may lead to exclusion of patients from eligibility analysis and/or their discontinuation from the study."

"Protocol deviation: less serious non-compliance—may not render a patient ineligible."

Further, in her October 2001 article entitled "Protocol Violations: Implications for Clinical Research" (*CR Focus,* Vol. 12, Number 7, October 2001), Alexandra Hopwood writes that, "many people do not see the point in making a distinction between violations and deviations since ICH E3 (Structure and Content of Clinical Study Reports) makes the statement that all important deviations related to study inclusion or exclusion criteria, conduct of the trial, patient management or patient assessment should be described. However, one should note the use of the word 'important.' Even ICH is expecting us to decide between what's important (violations) and what's not (deviations). Confusion of this terminology on the part of the sponsor and investigator staff does not help in focusing our attention on the important issues. The consequences of one's departure from protocol may not therefore be differentiated from those of another, even where there is a large difference in importance. A better definition of these issues in sponsor SOPs, protocols and guidelines would be most helpful . . . A number of audit findings [including use of prohibited medication, patients do not fulfill inclusion/exclusion criteria, failure to comply with drug dispensing/dosing/storage requirements, and AE reporting procedures not followed] all . . . could be classified as deviations from the investigational plan. Whether or not they could be classified as violations or deviations for your study will largely depend on the nature of the study."

In very general terms, the ICH GCP guideline discusses protocol deviations in section 4.5-Compliance with Protocol, but does not differentiate deviations from violations. Under sections 4.5.1-4.5.4, the guideline states that "the investigator/institution should conduct the trial in compliance with the protocol agreed to by the sponsor and, if required, by the regulatory authority(ies), and which was given approval/favorable opinion by the IRB/IEC. The investigator/institution and the sponsor should sign the protocol, or an alternative contract, as confirmation of their agreement. The investigator should not implement any deviation from, or changes of, the protocol without agreement by the sponsor and prior review and documented approval/favorable opinion from the IRB/IEC of an amendment, except where necessary to eliminate an immediate hazard(s) to trial subjects, or when the change(s) involves only logistical or administrative aspects of the trial (e.g., change of monitor(s), change of telephone number(s)).

"The investigator, or person designated by the investigator, should document and explain any deviation from the appropriate protocol. The investigator may implement a deviation from, or a change in, the protocol to eliminate an immediate hazard(s) to trial subjects without prior IRB/IEC approval/favorable opinion. As soon as possible, the implemented deviation or change, the reasons for it, and, if appropriate, the proposed protocol amendment(s) should be submitted: (a) To the IRB/IEC for review and approval/favorable opinion; (b) To the sponsor for agreement; and if required (c) To the regulatory authority(ies)."

7.2 Q. What is the difference between a protocol revision and a protocol amendment?

A. Protocol revisions are not formally defined in FDA regulations or guidance documents. Generally speaking, a protocol revision refers to a minor change to the protocol—one that has absolutely no impact on risks, clinical decision-making, procedures, or a subject's decision to enroll in a study. Such minor changes might include the correction of spelling mistakes, page renumbering, or changing the name of the corporate medical director. In general, these are administrative housekeeping changes that do not require much, if anything, in the way of an IRB or FDA review. In some cases, such a revised document is called an "administrative amendment."

Protocol amendments, on the other hand, are more significant in nature, and result from sponsor and investigator concerns about deficiencies in the protocol. Such changes would include the removal or addition of an enrollment inclusion/exclusion criterion, the addition of a lab test due to safety concerns, and changes to the definition of what constitutes an adverse event (e.g., certain percentage decreases in platelet counts).

Obviously, distinctions between the significance of certain changes—and whether they are considered revisions or amendments—are not always clear. Is a protocol change that increases the targeted number of enrollees from 500 to 550 a major change, for example? Some would argue that an increase in exposure to risks associated with unapproved drugs is always major, while others might consider the 10 percent increase in patient exposure to be benign and trivial given the universe of other, more significant, changes one might make to a protocol.

All protocol revisions and amendments must be submitted to an IRB, however. Some IRBs merely acknowledge their receipt, while others actively review and approve these changes.

7.3   *Q. What types of protocol changes require that a protocol amendment be submitted to the FDA, and which do not require a protocol amendment?*

A. Every change in a protocol, no matter how major or minor, must be submitted to the FDA. Some protocol revisions or administrative amendments, however, may not require an FDA submission until the annual or semi-annual reporting timeframe. Such an approach requires a definitive prior communication between the sponsor and FDA officials before implementation. In general, absent a prior FDA agreement, every single change in the protocol should be submitted to the FDA (see 21 CFR 312.30).

Protocol amendments are necessary when a sponsor wants to change a previously submitted protocol or to add a study protocol not submitted in the original IND. New protocols and most protocol changes must have been submitted to the FDA and have received IRB approval before being initiated. However, some sponsors may choose to obtain formal FDA review and comment before implementing any new protocols or protocol changes.

Protocol amendments that introduce a new protocol should contain the protocol itself along with a brief description of the most clinically significant differences between the new and previous protocols. In explaining this requirement, the FDA writes that ". . . a detailed and undiscriminating enumeration of the differences would defeat the purpose of this requirement, which is to identify the most important differences between the old and new protocols and to alert FDA reviewers to major changes that may require additional supporting data, such as changes in dose, route of administration, or indication."

Amendments that specify changes to previously submitted protocols are required when a sponsor seeks: (1) to modify a Phase 1 protocol in a manner that significantly affects the safety of clinical subjects; or (2) to modify a Phase 2 or Phase 3 protocol in a manner that significantly affects the safety of the subjects, the scope of the investigation, or the scientific quality of the study. FDA regulations at 21 CFR 312.30(b)(1) provide the following examples of protocol changes requiring amendments:

- any increase in drug dosage or the duration of individual subject exposure to the drug beyond that in the current protocol, or any significant increase in the number of study subjects;
- any significant change in the design of a protocol, such as the addition or deletion of a control group;
- the addition of a new test or procedure that is intended to improve monitoring for, or reduce the risk of, a side effect or adverse event, or the elimination of a test intended to monitor safety;
- the elimination of an apparent, immediate hazard to subjects (such a change may be implemented prior to an amendment submission, provided that the FDA is subsequently notified through a protocol amendment and that the IRB is properly notified); and
- the addition of a new investigator to carry out a previously submitted protocol (the investigational drug may be shipped to the investigator and the investigator may participate in the study prior to the submission of the amendment, provided the sponsor notifies the FDA within 30 days of the investigator's first participation in the study).

Not all protocol changes require the submission of a formal protocol amendment, however. "The sponsor's [reporting] responsibility depends on the nature of the change," the FDA stated in the 1987 preamble to its current IND regulations. "Changes that are not required to be reported in a protocol amendment may still be reportable under another section of these [IND] regulations, or under the regulations governing review of marketing applications (Part 314)." In this preamble and in subsequently published guidance documents, the agency has provided only a few examples of changes for which a protocol amendment is not required:

- Modifications to Phase 1 study designs that do not affect critical safety assessments. These changes must be reported to the FDA in the sponsor's next IND annual report.
- Continuing a subject from one study phase to another (assuming a protocol is in effect for the subsequent phase).
- Other changes—minor modifications of a study design, for example—may not be reportable until the study is submitted in a marketing application, in which it would be reported under the NDA's clinical data section.

In practice, many companies adopt a conservative approach by reporting virtually all protocol changes (ranging from significant study design revisions to minor protocol editing) in formal protocol amendments, CDER staffers report. Among other advantages, doing so may promote the efficient tracking of protocol changes by the sponsor and minimize the chance that the company will be second-guessed by the agency regarding its reporting decisions. Given the nature of the interpretations that must be made and the reporting options available to companies in certain cases, firms are well advised to communicate with the FDA review division responsible for a specific IND in adopting its protocol change reporting strategies.

Protocol amendments for changes to existing protocols must provide a "brief description of the change and reference (date and number) to the submission that contained the protocol." Amendments for a new investigator must include "the investigator's name, the qualifications to conduct the investigation, reference to the previously submitted protocol, and all additional information as is required [for other investigators]."

Protocol amendments must be prominently identified in one of three ways: "Protocol Amendment: New Protocol," "Protocol Amendment: Change in Protocol," or "Protocol Amendment: New Investigator." Amendments for new protocols or changes in existing protocols must be submitted to the FDA before their implementation. The FDA states, however, that "when several submissions of new protocols or protocol changes are anticipated during a short period, the sponsor is encouraged, to the extent feasible, to include these all in a single submission." Amendments to add new investigators or to provide additional information about investigators may be batched and submitted at 30-day intervals.

7.4   *Q. At what point can a protocol violation at a clinical trial site be judged sufficiently serious that a clinical trial sponsor should consider reporting it to the FDA as a problem? For what types of protocol violations does the FDA expect to be contacted?*

A. Both the FDA's GCP regulations and the ICH GCP guideline indicate that sponsors should report an investigator's protocol/GCP noncompliance if the sponsor deems the noncompliance to be sufficiently serious to discontinue the investigator's participation in the trial. According to the ICH's GCP guideline (Sections 5.20.1 and 5.20.2), "noncompliance with the protocol, SOPs, GCP, and/or applicable regulatory requirement(s) by an investigator/institution, or by member(s) of the sponsor's staff should lead to prompt action by the sponsor to secure compliance. If the monitoring and/or auditing identifies serious and/or persistent noncompliance on the part of the investigator/institution, the sponsor should terminate the investigator's/institution's participation in the trial. When an investigator's/institution's participation is terminated because of noncompliance, the sponsor should notify promptly the regulatory authority(ies)."

According to FDA regulations, "A sponsor who discovers that an investigator is not complying with the signed agreement (Form FDA 1572), the general investigational plan, or [GCP or other regulatory] requirements shall promptly either secure compliance or discontinue shipments of the investigational new drug to the investigator and end the investigator's participation in the investigation. If the investigator's participation in the investigation is ended, the sponsor shall require that the investigator dispose of or return the investigational drug in accordance with [federal regulations] and shall notify FDA."

In recent informal correspondence on this issue, the FDA stated that "this question is too case dependent to answer generally. However, there are clearly some situations that should be reported, if not to the FDA, then to the IRB. For example, if the protocol deviations present a serious risk to subjects, they should be reported to the IRB. If they result in such serious noncompliance that the study is terminated, they must be reported to FDA under 312.56(b). Also, if the protocol deviations represent falsification of data, they should be reported."

In recent years, CDER has been encouraging sponsors and others involved in clinical trials to report to the agency on noncompliant sites and activities more actively, particularly in cases that may involve fraud or research misconduct (see Section 17). And, in mid-2001, FDA officials disclosed that they were considering whether to develop a proposed regulation that would require sponsors to report *all* cases of investigator noncompliance or misconduct, including fraud, data falsification, and human subject protection abuses. As discussed above, under existing regulations, a sponsor is required to report investigator misconduct *only* when the investigator is discontinued from a study.

There is increasing evidence indicating that sponsors, study subjects, and others involved in the clinical trial process are voluntarily reporting compliance-related issues to the FDA. After plateauing temporarily at just over 100 complaints annually from FY1999-FY2002, voluntary clinical trial-related complaints to CDER surged to an all-time high of about 210 in FY2004. Although CDER did not provide an analysis of the nature of the complaints, it did note that "failure to follow the protocol" was among the common reasons triggering complaints. Earlier CDER data showed that a full quarter of the complaints received from 1998 to 2001 were for a failure to follow protocol, 24% for possible data falsification, 19% for informed consent noncompliance, 14% for poor AE reporting, and 8% for poor drug accountability. Much of the impetus for voluntarily reporting is that sponsors/CROs, IRBs, site staff, and others with specific clinical trial-related responsibilities do not want to be second guessed later by the FDA for not discovering and reporting possible noncompliance.

7.5 Q. How often are protocol-related issues cited as deficiencies in FDA GCP inspections?

A. Failure to adhere to the clinical protocol is consistently the most commonly cited deficiency in CDER's inspections of clinical investigators each year. In FY2003 (the latest year for which data are available), 25% of the clinical investigators/sites were cited for problems with protocol adherence. This, however, was an improvement over FY2002, when the agency cited 34% of sites for such problems.

Despite representing the most common GCP violation cited in CDER compliance inspections, protocol adherence issues are seldom considered significant departures from agency standards. This can be inferred because the FDA cited only 1% of all clinical investigators/sites inspected in FY2003 for what the agency considered major departures from GCP regulations.

Protocol adherence is an issue with which both U.S. and foreign sites struggle. In FY2003, 26% of U.S. investigators inspected were cited for such problems (compared to 34% in FY2002), while 21% of foreign inspectors were cited (compared to 31% in FY2002).

7.6 Q. Assume that a protocol, as many do today, states that a study was conducted in conformance with the Declaration of Helsinki (and likely other standards). If that protocol has a placebo arm and the experimental therapy is for an indication for which there are marketed alternative treatments, wouldn't the protocol be making an inaccurate statement, both to the FDA and to the research community, regarding its compliance with the Declaration of Helsinki, the 2000 version of which all but prohibits the use of placebos in such cases?

A. This is a complicated question on a variety of levels. As a practical matter, however, such a situation is unlikely to represent a problem for the FDA.

It is true that paragraph 29 of the 2000 amendments to the Declaration of Helsinki states that "the benefits, risks, burdens and effectiveness of a new method should be tested against those of the best current prophylactic, diagnostic, and therapeutic methods. This does not exclude the use of placebo, or no treatment, in studies where no proven prophylactic, diagnostic or therapeutic method exists." Although the World Health Association's General Assembly added a clarification to paragraph 29 in 2002 seemingly liberalizing the 2000 amendment's stance on placebo controls at least to some degree, FDA officials were not swayed by the clarification and are unlikely to adopt the 2000 version of the Declaration of Helsinki.

This does not mean that the Declaration of Helsinki will cease to have relevance as an FDA standard for the acceptance of foreign trials not conducted under an IND. Rather, the agency will continue to include the 1989 version of the Declaration of Helsinki (rather than the 2000 version) in its regulations as a minimum standard for its acceptance of foreign trials not conducted under INDs (see Q1.1).

Editor's note: Under a June 2004 proposed regulation, the FDA is seeking to replace the Declaration of Helsinki with its existing GCP requirements as the standard applicable to foreign clinical trials not conducted under an IND. In the proposed rule, the FDA states that U.S. GCP is now considered a better standard because "it provides more detail and enumeration of specific responsibilities of various parties, including monitoring of the trial and reporting adverse events" (see Q1.2). If finalized, this proposed regulation would delete the references to the Declaration of Helsinki in the FDA's regulation.

In the meantime, if a company has concerns about making references to conformance with the Declaration of Helsinki in its clinical protocols for placebo-controlled studies, it might consider specifying that the protocol complies with the 1989 version included in FDA regulations at 21 CFR 312.120(c)(4).

In view of legal liability concerns, sponsors should exercise care in making a statement in a protocol that could later be cited by a plaintiff's attorney as being blatantly untrue.

7.7   *Q. Are there any regulations or guidelines on whether patients can enter more than one trial?*

A. No provisions in either the FDA regulations or the ICH GCP guideline prohibit a subject's enrollment in more than one study at the same time.

Many protocols stipulate, however, that individuals cannot be enrolled in a clinical study if they were enrolled in another investigational study within the previous 30 days. The reason for this provision is that sponsors want some level of assurance that the study drug has completely washed out of an individual's systems before he or she is enrolled in a new study. The concern focuses on both the subject's safety (i.e., to avoid a possible drug-drug interaction), and the sponsor's desire to avoid any skewing of the efficacy data based on unknown effects of the previously administered drug and its impact on the efficacy of the current investigational product. Generally, an enrollment prohibition carries over to the entire study time period (e.g., while actively enrolled in a study, a patient should not be enrolled in a second drug study).

7.8   *Q. If a sponsor is considering a study for administering a drug under emergency conditions, what steps must be taken to initiate a protocol and protect subjects?*

A. This question addresses a narrow category of clinical trials: when a sponsor seeks to conduct a clinical trial for an investigational drug used to treat a life-threatening condition that requires immediate intervention. In all probability, such a trial would be conducted in an emergency setting, such as at the scene of an accident, in an ambulance, in an operating room, or in an emergency room. The kind of research permitted under 21 CFR 50.24 involves a particularly vulnerable population: persons with life-threatening conditions who can neither give informed consent nor actively refuse enrollment. This type of study, termed "emergency research" by the FDA, is focused on incapacitated patients who will not be able to give their consent as a result of their medical condition.

Three FDA documents apply to emergency research:

- 1998 Information Sheet entitled "Exception from Informed Consent for Studies Conducted in Emergency Settings: Regulatory Language Excerpts from Preamble"
- March 30, 2000 Draft Guidance entitled "Guidance for Institutional Review Boards, Clinical Investigators, and Sponsors: Exception from Informed Consent Requirements for Emergency Research"
- February 2003 CDER's Manual of Policies and Procedures (MAPP) 6030.8 which describes internal center procedures for processing an IND that proposes emergency research

FDA has received comments on the March 30, 2000 draft guidance and has reconvened an agency working group which is actively working to issue a final guidance in the near future. Because this type of research has so many additional requirements imposed by the FDA, this answer only highlights these additional requirements and, in some cases, provisions of the draft guidance. Readers are advised to consult the above referenced documents when planning emergency research.

Before the Study Starts

- This type of research requires written FDA approval prior to subject enrollment. In addition to the applicable drug review division, the Division of Scientific Investigations (DSI) will review all such INDs to ensure the existence of procedures for obtaining informed consent, the informed consent document, and plans for community consultation, among other components described in MAPP 6030.8.
- The IRB reviewing the research must include a licensed physician who is not participating in the research and who independently reviews the protocol and concurs with its contents.
- The IRB must conclude that there is no reasonable way of prospectively identifying the individuals likely to become eligible for participation in the clinical investigation, *and* the IRB must determine that consent from the subject's legally authorized representative is also not feasible.

- The IRB must permit the community from which research subjects are drawn to discuss the research (e.g., a public meeting). The IRB may decide that certain groups within the community should not be enrolled or that wider community discussion is needed.
- Available treatments for the life-threatening condition must be either unproven or unsatisfactory.
- In virtually all cases in which a placebo is used, standard care, if any, would be given to all subjects, with subjects randomized to receive, in addition, the test article or placebo. An exception to this approach would be a study to determine whether standard treatment is, in fact, useful. In this case, there must be a group that does not receive standard care.
- There must be an independent data and safety monitoring committee established to oversee the study. This committee must have the authority to halt the study.
- If an IRB rejects a study of this type, it must notify the principal investigator and sponsor in writing of the reasons for its decision. The sponsor must notify the FDA and other investigators and their IRBs about this rejection.
- Each clinical site must develop an informed consent document and procedure for attempting to find and obtain informed consent from a subject's legally authorized representative.

During the Study

- FDA regulations require the clinical investigator to: (1) inform the subject or the subject's legally authorized representative about the subject's inclusion in the study at the earliest opportunity; and (2) provide an opportunity for the subject or the legally authorized representative to withdraw the subject from the study or sign a consent form agreeing to the subject's continued participation in the study. Thus, the informed consent document and procedures must be developed and available so that they can be used where feasible.
- If a legally authorized representative is not present and if a subject's family member is present before the treatment or intervention is initiated, this individual must be provided an opportunity to object to the potential subject's participation.
- At the earliest feasible opportunity, the subject, his or her legally authorized representative, or a family member must give consent. These individuals can also discontinue the subject's participation at any time.
- In the event of a subject's death, procedures must be in place to provide information about the study to the legally authorized representative or family member.

After the Study Is Completed

- There must be public disclosure of study results including releases to both the research and local community.

Further Reading

Bohaychuk, W., Ball, G., Laurence, G., and Sotirov, K., "Protocol Content and Management," *Applied Clinical Trials,* 8:67-76, March 1999.

Hopwood, Alexandra, "Protocol Violations: Implications for Clinical Research," *CR Focus,* 12:27-33, October 2001.

Acknowledgments

Douglas Mackintosh, DrPH, MBA, MS Hyg, and Vernette Molloy, MBA, RN, of GCPA, Inc.; Fred Ma, MD, Director of Clinical Research, Gliatech, Cleveland, OH.

Section 8:
Institutional Review Boards

8.1 *Q. 21 CFR 56.108 requires that "except when an expedited review procedure is used, [an IRB must] review proposed research at convened meetings at which a majority of the members of the IRB are present. . . ." Can a meeting be considered "convened" if some/all of the necessary members are not present, but are participating via telecon, videocon, or a real-time on-line discussion (real time chat room)? In 21 CFR 56.108, what are FDA's rules for members being "present" and boards being "convened" (i.e., must members be physically present, or can they be located elsewhere, provided they can consider, interact, deliberate, question and vote in real time?)?*

A. It is interesting to note that the FDA addressed the subject of participation via conference calls in discussing its initial IRB regulations back in 1981. "Although FDA, like HHS, encourages meetings to take place with members physically present in the room, FDA also recognizes that in some cases time and commuting expense would favor conference calls," the agency stated in the preamble to the 1981 regulations. "As long as each IRB member can actively participate in any discussion of a protocol and has all pertinent material before the call, FDA has no objection to allowing meetings to occur in such a fashion and will consider meetings that take place by conference call to be 'convened' meetings. These meetings must follow the same requirements (minutes, etc.) as meetings with members physically present."

More recently in March 2000, the HHS issued a similar policy statement on IRB meetings convened via telephone conference calls. "Wherever possible, OPRR strongly recommends that [IRB] meetings take place with all participating IRB members physically present. However, OPRR recognizes that circumstances sometimes warrant conducting IRB meetings vial telephone conference call. Effective immediately, OPRR will recognize as 'convened' those IRB meetings conducted via telephone conference call, provided that each participating IRB member (i) has received all pertinent material prior to the meeting, and (ii) can actively and equally participate in the discussion of all protocols. Minutes of such meetings must clearly document that these two conditions have been satisfied in addition to the usual regulatory requirements. . . ."

8.2 *Q. Would a similar standard be applied to IRBs reviewing protocols on line— for example, in an on line discussion via messages posted to a secure IRB members-only message board (i.e., not a real-time discussion)?*

A. In an informal response to a question on the acceptability of on-line IRB discussions, the FDA suggested that the standards for on-line IRB discussions would be similar. "On-line discussions that do no permit real-time discussion would not substitute for a convened meeting," the agency stated. "The basic rule, if you want to call it that, is that the membership must be able to, as you have stated [in your original question], interact, deliberate, question, and vote in real time."

8.3 *Q. Clearly, 21 CFR 56.109(b), which states in part that "An IRB shall require that information given to subjects as part of informed consent is in accordance with 50.25," requires the IRB to review the informed consent* *form. Today, however, we are beginning to see some clinical programs featuring the use, on a pilot basis, of "interactive multimedia presentations" to supplement the informed consent form and process. These interactive presentations have, according to a recent study, involved the use of tablet PCs and software and interactive video presentations and interactive question and answer sessions to help potential trial subjects understand their disease and the clinical trial. If such presentations are used as part of or to supplement the informed consent process, must the IRB first review and approve the entire presentation and everything that the patient will see as part of it? Or can the IRB focus on just the informed consent form itself?*

A. Since such multimedia presentations would be considered part of, or could at least significantly affect, the informed consent process, the IRB must review and approve the presentations before they are used. In an informal communication on this subject, the FDA stated that, based on 21 CFR 56.109(b), "all information presented to subjects as part of the consent process, including that contained in interactive multimedia presentations, would need to be reviewed and approved by the IRB. While these interactive presentations may enhance the consent process, without IRB review of the information conveyed, the presentations may instead cause confusion or convey misinformation. The consent process needs to be seen as being broader than the consent form; it includes other tools used by the researcher to help the subject understand the research."

8.4 Q. In March 2005, the FDA released a new draft guidance on the use of centralized IRBs in clinical trials. Why does the agency believe that such a guidance is necessary, and what does the guidance accomplish?

A. According to CDER officials, the new draft guidance, entitled "Using a Centralized IRB Review Process in Multicenter Clinical Trials," was developed to address a number of issues, most importantly that the agency wanted to make clear that current regulations allow for the use of alternatives to the use of local IRBs in reviewing and approving clinical studies. Current FDA regulations, say CDER officials, focus almost exclusively on the importance and involvement of local IRBs in study reviews.

But what had really pushed FDA officials to pursue the guidance are the practical challenges presented by large, multi-center trials, particularly oncology trials, in which there may be hundreds of different IRBs evaluating the study. In such cases, each IRB may have different comments or request different changes, some of which may be contradictory to what other IRBs request, leaving the sponsor to deal not only with the inefficiencies of the system, but often contradicting and incompatible IRB comments and change requests regarding the informed consent form and study protocol. In these situations, FDA officials note, it may be more practical to have a central IRB or to consider a number of different options that the agency uses the new guidance to point out are available under current regulations.

In the March 2005 draft guidance, the FDA attempts to facilitate the use of a "centralized IRB review process" for multicenter trials in an effort to reduce IRB burdens and the IRB delays typically found in the conduct of multicenter trials. In the guidance, the agency defines the centralized IRB review process as "an agreement in which multiple study sites in a multicenter trial rely, in whole or in part, on the review of an IRB other than the IRB that ordinarily would be responsible for review of research conducted at that location (i.e., the IRB for the institution with which the site is affiliated)." Although the FDA does not endorse any single mechanism under which IRB review responsibilities are distributed between an institution's IRB and a central IRB, the primary model contemplated by the draft guidance involves IRBs affiliated with the study sites entering into agreements with a central IRB to accept all or some of the findings of the central IRB. Such scenarios might involve so-called joint, or hybrid reviews, under which a central IRB would conduct all scientific reviews of the protocol and ongoing study, while the local IRBs at the various institutions participating in the study would review the study as it related to local requirements, issues and attitudes. The guidance also mentions other possible models, including central IRBs formed to review multicenter trials in a therapeutic category (e.g., the NCI's free-standing central IRB) and regional and nonregional cooperatives.

8.5   *Q. So must the parties involved in clinical research await the issue of a final version of the March 2005 draft guidance before implementing the so-called "centralized IRB reviews"?*

A. No. Although it is only a draft, the March 2005 draft guidance makes clear that "use of a centralized IRB review process is consistent with the existing IRB regulations." The document points out that Section 21 CFR 56.114-Cooperative Research, establishes that "in complying with these [IRB regulations], institutions involved in multi-institutional studies may use joint review, reliance upon the review of another qualified IRB, or similar arrangements aimed at avoidance of duplication of effort."

8.6   *Q. According to some institutions and IRBs, they are sometimes pressured, by their physicians and study sponsors, to permit central IRB reviews of protocols and studies. Is there any regulation or guidance that obligates institutions and IRBs to participate in centralized IRB reviews if a particular study sponsor calls for it?*

A. No. The March 2005 draft guidance makes clear that centralized IRB reviews are an option and not a requirement under existing FDA regulations. In addition, the draft guidance makes clear that the institution can set the parameters of any centralized IRB reviews in which it chooses to participate. Specifically, the agency "recommends that institutions that participate in multi-center clinical investigations develop policies for determining when and which studies conducted in the institution would be appropriate for centralized review and how initial and continuing IRB review would be conducted for such studies. An institution may permit a central IRB to be entirely responsible for initial and continuing review of a study, or the institution may apportion IRB review responsibilities between a central IRB and its own IRB."

Although the March 2005 draft guidance acknowledges that sponsors and investigators can be involved in seeking centralized IRB reviews, it notes that such efforts must defer to a specific institution's policies. "Sponsors can also initiate plans for use of a centralized IRB review process and facilitate agreements and other necessary communications among the parties involved . . . If the investigator is performing this portion of a multicenter study in an institution with its own IRB and the investigator is subject to that institution's policies, those policies would dictate how the investigator will ensure IRB review within the context of a centralized review process. Under these policies, the investigator might ensure review by a central IRB or by the institution's IRB, or with review responsibility apportioned between a central IRB and the institution's IRB."

8.7 Q. In recent years, much has been said about heavy IRB workloads, and about looking for ways to ease the review and paperwork burdens on overworked IRBs. Are there any plans to address such continuing concerns?

A. In early 2005, the FDA appeared to be taking the first substantive steps to address IRB workload issues. On March 21, 2005, the agency held a public hearing to address the issue of clinical trial adverse reaction reporting to IRBs and IRB review of these reports and to consider ways to improve the process. At the meeting, the agency heard testimony from industry sponsors that recommended that sponsors should be given the responsibility of synthesizing, interpreting, and prioritizing all adverse event data and reporting the results to IRBs and investigators. The FDA also heard from IRBs and institution administrators that adverse event over-reporting had become so burdensome for IRBs that some institutions already require sponsors to assume such responsibilities.

Many speakers encouraged the FDA to issue definitive guidance that puts the responsibility for overseeing and reporting clinical trial adverse events on sponsors and investigators and that takes this burden off of overburdened IRBs. Although some suggested that the FDA should require sponsors to employ data safety monitoring boards (DSMB), FDA officials responded that industry would object to such a requirement and that DSMBs would not be appropriate for many studies.

The FDA has acknowledged the problems in the current adverse experience reporting system. "There are many at FDA who believe that this system of shuffling of paper that is really meaningless to the IRB and meaningless in terms of making interpretations about safety has got to stop," FDA GCP Program Director David Lepay, M.D., Ph.D., stated in June 2004. In part, the system suffers from the same problems as the larger AE reporting area—that is, with the flow of paper, the inability to "pick out the noise from the [significant AEs]," says Lepay, who identified adverse experience reporting to IRBs as one of three key priority areas for the FDA's GCP Program in late 2004. To improve the system, Lepay pointed out, the agency may have to reconsider one of the long-standing foundations of GCP: that sponsors should not communicate directly with IRBs. "If we want to ensure subject safety and protection, the only way we are going to effectively do that without swamping the system with paper is to begin having sponsors talk to everyone and start promoting more transparency in this information," he says.

In a March 2005 draft guidance entitled, "Using a Centralized IRB Review Process in Multicenter Clinical Trials," the FDA attempts to facilitate the use of a "centralized IRB review process" for multicenter trials in an effort to reduce IRB burdens and the IRB delays typically found in the conduct of multicenter trials. In the guidance, the agency defines the centralized IRB review process as "an agreement in which multiple study sites in a multicenter trial rely, in whole or in part, on the review of an IRB other than the IRB that ordinarily would be responsible for review of research conducted at that location (i.e., the IRB for the institution with which the site is affiliated)." Although the FDA does not endorse any single mechanism under which IRB review responsibilities are distributed between an institution's IRB and a central IRB, the primary model contemplated by the draft guidance involves IRBs affiliated with the study sites entering into agreements with a central IRB to accept all or some of the findings of the central IRB.

In February 2005, HHS officials also announced plans to release a guidance on standardizing the federal government's requirements for AE reporting across all agencies. The new guidance is expected to address many of the issues mentioned above, including the assessment and handling of AEs from multi-center studies and criteria for determining when AE reports should be shared with other clinical study sites.

8.8 Q. There have also been some rumors about increased government attention to the conduct of clinical trials, in particular the role of IRBs. What is behind this?

A. In March 2005, Philadelphia Associate U.S. District Attorney James Sheehan warned about what he sees as "the coming storm" in a government focus on clinical research conduct. Sheehan predicted that government investigations into the conduct of clinical trials could focus on institutional review boards and, in particular, on subject protection and informed consent-related disclosures to study subjects. "The biggest problem in the next five years is the subject disclosure and protection issue," said Sheehan. "The law is developing in that area. It's a significant problem. What we're finding out, as there's more intense inspection of institutional review board processes and of studies, is that these problems are not just occasional events."

Other U.S. attorneys have spoken about the government using the False Claims Act (Qui Tam) as a basis for assessing clinical trial conduct (see Q17.1). In a February 2005 speech, Philadelphia Assistant U.S. Attorney Virginia Gibson claimed that the government can use the False Claims Act and various fraud statutes "to craft a theory that the overall impact" of clinical trial noncompliance amounts to defrauding the government's Medicare or Medicaid programs. Sheehan predicted that, in three or four years, there will be far more fraud cases and activity related to clinical trials and research.

8.9 Q. Does the ICH GCP guideline (E6) feature any IRB-related provisions different from those in the FDA's existing GCP regulations/standards?

A. Yes. In fact, the ICH guideline does not address several of the specific IRB-related requirements contained in FDA regulations. The ICH guideline, however, states that an IRB "should comply with GCP and with the applicable regulatory requirement(s)," a statement that emphasizes the preeminence of FDA requirements in FDA-regulated studies.

Conversely, there are some IRB-related provisions within the ICH guideline that are not addressed in FDA regulations.

While the FDA emphasizes that the ICH GCP guideline is entirely consistent with its own GCP standards, there are several IRB-related provisions that do differ in emphasis or specificity. Since the ICH GCP guideline was released in 1997, several IRB-related differences have been noted, including the following:

- The ICH guideline specifically calls for an IRB review of subject recruitment procedures, the investigator's brochure, payments and compensation to study subjects, and the curriculum vitae of the investigators. FDA regulations require IRBs to review "all research activities," which is generally understood to include all these elements. The FDA also has guidance documents calling for IRB review of certain recruitment materials and practices.
- FDA regulations allow an expedited initial review of certain types of studies that involve no more than minimal risk. The ICH GCP guideline has no such provision.
- The ICH GCP guideline calls on IRBs, when asked, to provide copies of their written procedures and membership lists to investigators, sponsors, or regulatory authorities. FDA regulations require only that IRBs provide such information to regulatory authorities upon request.
- The ICH GCP guideline calls for IRBs to review investigator qualifications. Although the FDA regulations do not specifically require IRB review of the qualifications of the investigator and the study staff, IRBs consider such a review a necessary part of fulfilling the requirements of 21 CFR 56.111-Criteria for IRB approval of research.
- For subjects who can be enrolled only with the consent of their legally acceptable representative, the ICH GCP guideline calls for the assent of the subjects as well (i.e., if the subject is capable). This includes adults as well as children (4.8.12).
- The ICH GCP guideline recommends that participation in nontherapeutic trials be restricted to those who personally give consent and sign and date the consent form (4.8.13).
- The ICH GCP guideline permits those who cannot personally provide their consent to participate in nontherapeutic trials when all of the following conditions are fulfilled: (a) the objectives of the trial cannot be met by enrolling only subjects who can personally give consent; (b) the foreseeable risks to the subjects are low; (c) the negative impact on the subject's well-being is minimized and low; (d) the trial is not prohibited by law; and (e) the approval/favorable opinion of the IRB/IEC is expressly sought on the inclusion of such subjects, and the written approval/favorable opinion covers this aspect (4.8.14).
- The ICH GCP guideline recommends that the informed consent form be signed and dated by the person conducting the consent interview as well as the subject or legally acceptable representative (4.8.8).
- The ICH GCP guideline specifically recommends that the responsibilities of the study subject be explained in the informed consent form (4.8.10(e)).

8.10 Q. Regarding the general FDA requirements for a quorum, to what degree can "alternate" IRB members be used in IRB meetings?

A. The FDA permits the use of formally appointed alternate IRB members, provided that the IRB's written procedures describe the appointment and function of the alternate members. Ad hoc substitutes are not permissible as IRB members, the FDA has stated. To ensure that an appropriate quorum is maintained, the agency states that the alternate's qualifications should be comparable to those of the primary member being replaced, and that the alternate should review the same materials that the IRB member would have reviewed for a meeting (i.e., sufficiently in advance of the meeting to permit a thorough review).

Assume that an IRB regularly meets once per month, 12 times per year. Dr. X, an IRB member, misses all 12 meetings, and Dr. Y, an alternate member, substitutes for him at all these meetings. Had Dr. Y not stepped in for Dr. X, then quorums would not have been achieved. While this pattern of substitution might be questioned during an FDA inspection, or possibly by the Office for Human Research Protections (DHHS), in a review of the IRB's paperwork, there would not appear to be any indication that the IRB was out of compliance.

As a practical matter, if Dr. Y possesses the same type and caliber of expertise as Dr. X, what harm has occurred as a result of the substitution? The answer depends on the procedures followed by the IRB. If the alternates are provided with all the pre-meeting materials at the same time as the primary members and are normally present at the meetings, there is no discernable difference in whether Dr. X or Dr. Y fills that IRB seat. If Dr. Y is not provided with all materials in a timely manner, however, he would be placed in the position of substituting on short notice when he is not prepared and probably has not read the material.

If the IRB uses a primary reviewer system, under which one committee member reviews the study and presents it to all committee members during a meeting, the primary reviewer could be either Dr. X or Dr. Y, but that assignment should be made well in advance of the meeting. IRBs should consider making member appointments for a short period of time, such as one year. Members who fail to attend meetings or otherwise carry out their duties can then be removed simply by not reappointing them for another term.

Frequent absences by board members and difficulties achieving a quorum may signify that the institution is placing too high a burden on the IRB members and support staff. This burden may be either in terms of the total volume of studies being reviewed or inefficiencies built into the review system.

8.11 Q. Can an IRB function as a HIPAA Privacy Board?

A. According to Mark Barnes and Michael Beauvais of Ropes & Gray, an IRB can also serve as a privacy board under the Privacy Rule (HIPAA), provided that its members meet the qualifications under the Privacy Rule. A privacy board is an entity that may be created under the Privacy Rule to review researchers' requests for alteration or waiver of the Privacy Rule's requirements for individual authorization. In brief, privacy boards must comprise members with varying backgrounds and professional competency, and must include at least one member not affiliated with the research institution or sponsor. Today, most institutions use their IRBs to fulfill privacy board functions.

8.12 Q. What is the nature and level of activity of the FDA's inspectional oversight of IRBs?

A. Under its human subject protection program, CDER conducts routine inspections of approximately 150 IRBs annually. The center conducted only 130 IRB inspections in FY2004, down from the 154 inspections in FY2003. This compares to 69 and 11 IRB inspections by CDRH and CBER, respectively.

CDER DSI officials claim that they are attempting to focus their limited resources on IRBs that are reviewing the highest volume and that are reviewing the most complex and difficult studies. The agency's ability to better focus its resources in these areas will be aided when a new FDA regulation requiring that IRBs register with the agency is finalized (see discussion below).

CDER bases its IRB inspectional program on IRBs that are associated with "active" INDs—that is, INDs under which clinical trials are actively being conducted. The FDA is able to track most IRBs through the Form FDA 1572-Statement of Investigator, in which clinical investigators must provide the name and address of the IRB that is responsible for reviewing and approving the study at that site. So that it can obtain a comprehensive listing of IRBs involved in FDA-regulated research, the agency issued a July 2004 proposed regulation under which IRBs would be required to formally register on an HHS-maintained website.

8.13 Q. The ability of the FDA, HHS, and other government bodies to effectively track the existence and activity of IRBs has been questioned in recent years. Haven't these agencies promised to track IRBs more directly and closely going forward?

A. Yes. In a July 2004 proposed regulation, the FDA proposed to require that IRBs register on a website that will be maintained by HHS. Given that existing FDA regulations require some, but not all, clinical investigators or sponsors of clinical investigations to provide IRB names and addresses to the agency, the FDA has lacked a comprehensive list of IRBs involved in reviewing FDA-regulated clinical trials.

The proposed "electronic registration system" will: (1) enable the FDA to "identify more precisely" the IRBs reviewing FDA-regulated clinical investigations; (2) enable the FDA to send educational information and other information to IRBs; and (3) help the FDA identify IRBs for inspection, because the agency would have a more accurate list of IRBs. So that the system captures all IRBs, those IRBs reviewing research conducted or supported by HHS will be required to register as well.

In registering, IRBs would be required to provide contact information, the number of active protocols involving FDA-regulated products reviewed in the previous calendar year, an indication of whether the IRB is accredited, and a description of the types of FDA-regulated products involved in the protocols reviewed.

8.14 Q. What are the latest trends in FDA findings in terms of IRB GCP compliance?

A. Although CDER had not released formal statistics for FY2004 as of this writing, DSI officials identified, in early 2005, five areas as the continuing areas of "primary IRB deficiencies:" following written procedures; review of the research; expedited reviews; record keeping; and review of informed consent.

In FY2003, CDER found that 30% of the IRBs inspected were in full compliance. The remaining 70% were found to have objectionable practices that did not represent what the agency considered to be "major departures" from GCP regulations. In FY2003, the most common deficiencies involved issues regarding written IRB procedures (29% of IRBs inspected compared to 28% in FY2002), meeting minutes (31% versus 29% in FY2002), quorum (12% compared to 13% in FY2002), research review (5% versus 12% in FY2002), the elements of informed consent (5% versus 11% in FY2002), expedited review (6% versus 6% in FY2002), and IRB membership (4% versus 5% in FY2002).

8.15 Q. Are there any data or studies that identify areas of IRB noncompliance that the FDA categorizes as significant noncompliance?

A. Yes. In a December 2004 study (Bramstedt and Kassimatis, "A study of warning letters issued to institutional review boards by the United States Food and Drug Administration," *Med clin exp,* Vol. 27, No. 6), Bramstedt and Kassimatis found that the FDA had issued 52 warning letters to IRBs during the period January 1997-June 2004. The FDA issues warning letters when the noncompliance is more significant and when a specific action is necessary to correct the noncompliance (see Q10.28).

The most common regulatory violations cited in these 52 IRB warning letters were: the failure to have and follow adequate written procedures on how the IRB was conducting its review of research (50 of 52); the failure to prepare and maintain adequate documentation of IRB activities (e.g., meeting minutes, copies of protocols and consent forms) (47); failing to provide adequate continuing review of approved studies (36); failing to satisfy IRB membership and/or quorum requirements, including member conflicts of interest (30); failure to assure that documentation of and information given to subjects as part of the informed consent process meets federal requirements (19); and failure to provide adequate initial review of studies (11).

It is important to note, however, that the FDA issued warning letters to a small percentage of the IRBs inspected over the study period. Based on general estimates of the number of IRBs inspected from January 1997-June 2004 (the FDA inspects approximately 150-200 IRBs per year), only about 4% of the IRB inspections triggered warning letters.

8.16 Q. Can an IRB function as a data monitoring committee (DMC), also called a data safety and monitoring board?

A. The FDA defines DSMBs as "independent or external panels established by a sponsor to assess at specific intervals the progress of a clinical trial, safety data, and critical efficacy variables and to recommend to the sponsor whether to continue, modify, or terminate a trial based on the panel's reviews/findings." An IRB cannot function as a data safety and monitoring board (DSMB). A physician who is a member of an IRB could also serve as a DSMB member, however.

DSMBs usually comprise three members—two physicians and a statistician. Generally, DSMB members are affiliated with several different academic institutions or private companies. It is important that they are independent of the clinical sites participating in the study that they are monitoring, and that they be free from conflicts of interest. DSMBs must be nimble and able to make recommendations in a timely fashion, sometimes within a day or two in an emergency. They must possess special expertise in reviewing clinical data.

In contrast, IRBs do not function in this way, and sometimes do not have sufficient special expertise.

8.17 Q. If there are no amendments to the clinical protocol and a site has completed enrollment, would a trial site still have to obtain annual IRB approval for the protocol AND the case report form?

A. IRBs approve three kinds of documents: protocols (and amendments); informed consent forms (and revisions); and advertisements. They do not approve or disapprove case report forms. Once a protocol and informed consent are approved, enrollment may begin at a site.

Typically, these approvals require annual renewal. Renewal is contingent on submission of an annual report, reports of serious adverse experiences (SAE) that occurred at the site, and the sponsor's drug safety updates. Assuming that there has been no significant change in the drug safety profile, and the investigator has acted responsibly (e.g., no significant patient complaints, compliance issues), the IRB should permit the study to continue.

Upon the initial review and approval, the IRB determines the interval at which continuing review will be required, although that interval cannot exceed one year. Continuing review should be performed more frequently for higher-risk studies. The IRBs review the protocol, investigator's brochure (if one exists), informed consent form, recruitment advertisements, and the qualifications of the persons conducting the study. The continuing review itself must be completed before the previous review's expiration date. At the time of continuing review, the IRB receives an investigator-submitted report that provides a summary of the study's progress to date. This report includes the number of subjects enrolled and withdrawn, adverse effects, and any study changes. The IRB reviews this information and determines whether the study may be approved for another period.

Even if no changes have been made in the protocol and no new subjects have been enrolled, continuing IRB review is required until all contact with study subjects has been completed. For most studies, IRB-intensive review and scrutiny can taper off when all subjects have completed active involvement as outlined in the protocol. Some studies, such as cancer studies, require a determination of subjects' health status long after the active portion of the study has been completed. The IRB must keep such studies open, although continuing review can be conducted on an expedited means in many cases. On a periodic basis, the FDA publishes in the *Federal Register* a list of the categories of research that IRBs may review in an expedited manner (also, see FDA Information Sheet entitled, "Continuing Review After Study Approval").

8.18 Q. If a sponsor plans to use multiple IRBs for its multicenter study, must an Internet advertisement be approved by all involved IRBs?

A. When sponsors use multiple IRBs for their studies, they must adhere to the requirements of each IRB—no small undertaking at times. If an IRB requires active approval of advertising (some IRBs only require that sponsors send the advertisement to the IRB—a passive type of approval), then the sponsor must wait for the approval of each IRB that requires pre-approval before posting the advertisement on the Internet. To avoid minor changes by each reviewing IRB, the sponsor may include, with the advertisement or telephone script, information about its national use and the IRBs who have or have not granted approval.

Internet postings, which are not the same as advertisements, do not need IRB review, however. According to the FDA Information Sheet entitled, "Recruiting Study

Subjects," "IRB review and approval of listings of clinical trials on the internet would provide no additional safeguard and is not required when the system format limits the information provided to basic trial information, such as: the title; purpose of the study; protocol summary; basic eligibility criteria; study site location (s); and how to contact the site for further information. Examples of clinical trial listing services that do not require prospective IRB approval include the National Cancer Institute's cancer clinical trial listing (PDQ) and the government-sponsored AIDS Clinical Trials Information Service (ACTIS). However, when the opportunity to add additional descriptive information is not precluded by the data base system, IRB review and approval may assure that the additional information does not promise or imply a certainty of cure or other benefit beyond what is contained in the protocol and the informed consent document."

8.19 Q. Should a sponsor conduct a formal audit of an IRB that may be responsible for its study?

A. In the past, sponsors have not routinely performed formal audits of IRBs, but have instead generally relied on FDA reports of inspections or the existence of an assurance from OHRP as evidence of IRB compliance. Due to confidentiality issues, IRBs cannot share meeting minutes and other documentation that includes review summaries of other sponsor's studies. Although the FDA does not prohibit sponsors from requesting IRB records, the regulations are silent on whether IRBs should provide the public or sponsors with copies of pertinent portions of the IRB's records.

Today, sponsors are increasingly performing limited audits of IRBs. The sponsors are seeking assurance that IRBs have adequate written procedures, that these procedures are followed, and that the IRBs maintain adequate meeting minutes and other records. To provide examples of its meetings minutes and other records to sponsors, an IRB can redact confidential information about other sponsor's studies from these documents. Sponsors are then able to audit the IRB's review of these studies without gaining access to confidential information.

8.20 Q. Can a sponsor choose to use a central, or contract, IRB over a local IRB based on its own needs and preferences?

A. Although a sponsor can select clinical trial sites that routinely use, or are willing to use, a central IRB, it cannot require that a site's institution use a central IRB for a particular study. A local IRB that is part of an institution, such as a university or hospital, can define its exclusive domain. Most local IRBs include in this domain studies performed on the institution's premises. Some IRBs also include in their domain studies performed by staff members, regardless of whether these studies are conducted on the institution's premises.

A contract, or central, IRB may not review studies that are to be conducted within a local IRB's expressed domain unless the local IRB or institution agrees to share or relinquish its oversight of the study or class of studies.

According to the FDA, clinical studies will "generally" use the subject institution's IRB, since it will have jurisdiction over all studies conducted within the institution. The agency notes that independent, or central, IRBs may become "the IRB of record" only through the "written agreement" of the institution's administration or the in-house IRB.

Given the demands associated with multi-center IRBs, the FDA facilitated the use of centralized IRBs through a March 2005 draft guidance entitled, "Using a Centralized IRB Review Process in Multicenter Clinical Trials." The draft guidance makes clear, however, that centralized IRB reviews are an option and not a requirement under existing FDA regulations, and that an institution can set the parameters of any centralized IRB reviews in which it chooses to participate.

8.21   Q. In reviewing a study, how do central (national) IRBs fulfill their obligation to consider local community standards and concerns?

A. "Non-local IRBs," as the FDA calls them, must have adequate knowledge of community attitudes, information on the conditions relevant to the conduct of the research, and the study's continuing status. In its Information Sheet entitled, "Non-local IRB Review," the FDA states that "IRBs conducting non-local review need to be knowledgeable about the community from which the subjects are drawn to ensure that subject rights will be protected and that the consent process is appropriate for the subject population involved. The IRB should be sensitive to community laws and mores because state and local laws and community attitudes pertaining to research may be more restrictive than Federal regulations or the prevailing standards of the community where the IRB is located."

To ensure that it can fulfill FDA requirements at 21 CFR 56.107 and 56.111 for each study site, the non-local IRB should have adequate knowledge of community attitudes, information on conditions regarding the conduct of the research, and the continuing status of the research. The non-local IRB must ensure that it meets these requirements for each location at which it has assumed IRB oversight responsibility.

The FDA agrees that these non-local IRBs can attain knowledge of community attitudes through a variety of means, including written materials and site visits by a representative of the IRB, by appointing an IRB member from the community in which a study is to be conducted, or by having a consultant from the community advise the IRB either prior to or during the deliberations.

In addition to the scheduled continuing review of progress reports, non-local IRBs (like local IRBs) must have procedures to ensure that they are made aware of unexpected problems in ongoing studies in a timely manner. "Fulfilling this requirement may call for additional efforts for non-local IRBs, such as visiting the study site, contacting the sponsor's research monitor for information on the monitor's site visits, or arranging for other oversight of the study," the FDA states.

8.22   Q. In practice, however, does the FDA really ever cite centralized or even local IRBs for a failure to consider local community attitudes?

A. Yes. In a December 2004 study (Bramstedt and Kassimatis, "A study of warning letters issued to institutional review boards by the United States Food and Drug Administration," *Med clin exp,* Vol. 27, No. 6) of FDA warning letters forwarded to IRBs during the period January 1997-June 2004, researchers found that the FDA had cited two IRBs for failing to consider community attitudes and cultural backgrounds relevant to the research they reviewed.

According to the study, a university-based "IRB at Great Lakes College of Clinical Medicine (Bluffton, Ohio) had reviewed and approved a study involving 2 sensitive matters: direct injection of blood from one person into another; and administration of live malaria parasites to research subjects. The FDA argued that there was no documentation that indicated the IRB had reflected on how these 2 practices might be perceived in light of the cultural attitudes of these overseas research subjects."

The second IRB to be cited, the Essex Institutional Review Board (Lebanon, NJ), a private IRB, had reviewed and approved two clinical trials conducted in Puerto Rico on research subjects who were potentially "economically disadvantaged." But, the study authors stated, "there was no evidence that any of the IRB members had the expertise to discern the cultural landscape of the population. Furthermore, the IRB did not seek out any consultants to help them assess the cultural landscape."

In a March 2005 draft guidance entitled, "Using a Centralized IRB Review Process in Multicenter Clinical Trials," the FDA makes clear, however, that an IRB's location is not critical to the issue necessarily. "Physical proximity of an IRB to a research site is not necessarily of significance, provided that the IRB is competent to understand the local context of the research," says the agency. "As stated in 21 CFR 56.107(a), this would require sensitivity to community attitudes, familiarity with the standards of professional conduct and practice where the research takes place, and knowledge about local laws and regulations applicable to the study."

8.23 Q. Must quizzes and questionnaires that assess a subject's comprehension of the consent be submitted to and/or approved by an IRB? The purpose of these instruments is to assist the person performing the consent identify those individuals who are experiencing problems understanding a study's procedures and risks (i.e., so that further explanation can be provided).

A. Yes. The IRB is responsible for assessing the consent process, including all tools that may be used to enrich the process. Efforts to ensure comprehension are part of the overall informed consent process.

8.24 Q. How should a principal investigator and sponsor proceed if an IRB administrator refuses the principal investigator's request for a list of IRB members?

A. While most institutions do provide principal investigators with lists of IRB members (who, in turn, provide it to sponsors), some do not. The FDA regulations do not require that the IRB provide sponsors with a membership roster.

Some sponsors will accept a Department of Health and Human Services (DHSS) multiple project assurance (MPA) number or Federal Wide Assurance (FWA) number as evidence of appropriate IRB membership. Institutions with OHRP assurances are listed on the OHRP web site at: http://ohrp.cit.nih.gov/search/asearch.asp#ASUR.

8.25 Q. If the IRB at a potential investigational site has encountered regulatory difficulties with the FDA, should the sponsor of the research take any actions prior to enrolling the site into the study?

A. Most FDA IRB inspections result in recommendations for improvements. The least punitive action would be the verbal comments of an FDA inspector at the close of the inspection. If the FDA inspector believes that an IRB has not met regulatory requirements, the IRB management may be provided with a written notice on a Form FDA 483-Inspectional Observations. A 483 becomes publicly available at the close of an inspection.

Following an inspection, the FDA will issue a letter to the IRB. The majority of these letters do not impose formal sanctions on IRBs. When the regulatory deviations are significant, the FDA issues a warning letter that identifies the deviations and typically requests that the IRB respond in writing by outlining the actions it has taken to correct the problems. Until the IRB takes appropriate corrective action, the FDA may also: (1) withhold approval of new FDA-regulated studies that are conducted at the institution or reviewed by the IRB; (2) direct that no new subjects be added to ongoing FDA-regulated studies; (3) terminate ongoing FDA-regulated studies when doing so would not endanger the subjects; or (4) notify relevant state and federal regulatory agencies and other parties (when apparent noncompliance creates a significant threat to the rights and welfare of human subjects).

Although the FDA can disqualify an IRB (for refusing or repeatedly failing to comply with federal regulations for the protection of the rights or welfare of human subjects in clinical trials), agency officials report that IRBs are rarely if ever disqualified, largely because noncompliant IRBs are typically disbanded or brought into compliance before the enforcement process reaches that point.

Therefore, sponsors may use this information to assure that an IRB is in good standing to review and approve a proposed study. In those cases in which the sponsor interaction with an IRB is handled through the investigator, the study investigator should check with the IRB regarding its regulatory standing. Sponsors can also check with the FDA's various bioresearch monitoring program offices to ensure that the agency has not disqualified or taken administrative actions against a particular IRB.

8.26 Q. Can a central IRB in the United States approve protocols and consents for study sites in other countries? If so, under what conditions?

A. A U.S.-based IRB (central or local) can review studies that will be conducted in foreign jurisdictions. It is important to note, however, that the laws of the foreign jurisdiction may also require review by a local body.

The process for such non-local reviews is similar to that involved in the remote review of U.S.-based studies; most importantly, care must be taken to assess and consider local laws, ethics, and culture. The U.S. IRB should seek information and guidance from local authorities, such as a local IEC, board of health, or university. As is the case for U.S. sites, if there is a local IEC with jurisdiction over the foreign study site, that IRB's authority must be respected.

8.27 Q. Are there any circumstances in which a sponsor or CRO should communicate directly with an IRB?

A. Sponsors and CROs are increasingly communicating with IRBs directly in an effort to expedite the approval process. This process could bypass the investigator, however, who has traditionally maintained the key relationship with the IRB.

This simple, direct flow of information between the IRB and the investigator was adequate when most studies were conducted at single sites or only a small number of sites. Today, however, the practice of having direct communications flow exclusively between investigators and IRBs is being eroded by large site-volume trials that use central IRBs. It has become cumbersome for central IRBs with oversight responsibilities for many sites to route study-wide issues to sponsors through a large number of investigators. While each investigator should be kept current on the progress of study plans, there is no requirement that all information that flows from the IRB to the sponsor pass through the clinical investigator.

Traditionally, investigators have sent communications involving protocol amendments, periodic safety reports, and updates to the investigator's brochure to the IRB. In today's quest to eliminate delays in the review and approval of studies and study changes, however, such documents for multi-site studies are routinely being sent by the sponsor or CRO to the IRB at the same time they are sent to each investigator.

8.28 Q. If a principal investigator is going to participate in a television news interview that may very well generate patient interest in enrolling in the clinical study, would the investigator have to gain IRB approval before participating in the interview?

A. The FDA information sheet entitled, "Guidance for Institutional Review Boards and Clinical Investigators" (1998 update) provides guidance to sponsors and investigators on topics such as media advertising and news stories. The FDA considers direct advertising for study subjects to be "the start of the informed consent and subject selection process," and contends that advertisements be received and approved by the IRB as part of the package for initial review. News stories, on the other hand, are not considered direct advertising, and are not included in the FDA's guidance on direct advertising for clinical trials.

An IRB has no jurisdiction over a news interview. It cannot interfere in a *bona fide* news interview and its free distribution in the public media. It can, however, control the duplication of the interview and the paid distribution of the interview to prospective subjects.

Prospectively, investigators should be reminded of the type of language that can be used in the interview. Language should be consistent with that used in the consent form (e.g., "may provide," "is untested," "experimental"). Since the investigator's language could affect recruitment, he/she should be particularly careful not to overstate possible benefits or understate risks. Generally, large research institutions have a media relations officer and staff who can advise and coach investigators in preparing for the interview.

While press coverage of "new science" is important, care must be taken to avoid creating false hope among patients that an investigational product will provide relief or a cure. The investigator should attempt to provide a fair, accurate, and balanced discussion of the science.

What amount to "infomercials" that appear, only on the surface, to be news interviews with a principal investigator represent an entirely different category of communications. These are paid commercial, scripted venues whose expressed purpose is to recruit subjects. As such, these require IRB approval.

Further Reading

Bohaychuk, Wendy, Ball, Graham, et al, "Ethics Committee and IRB Audit Results," *Applied Clinical Trials,* 7:46-55, November 1998.

Mackintosh, D., Editorial "Ethics Committees Do Not Sufficiently Protect Research Subjects," *European Pharmaceutical Contractor,* August 1999, pp. 16-17.

DHHS Office of the Inspector General, *Institutional Review Boards. Their Role in Reviewing Approved Research,* June 1998.

Acknowledgments

Douglas Mackintosh, DrPH, MBA, MS Hyg, and Vernette Molloy, MBA, RN, of GCPA, Inc.; Erica Heath, MBA, President, Independent Review Consulting, Inc., San Rafael, CA; Paul Goebel, CIP, Vice President, Chesapeake Research Review, Columbia, MD.

Section 9:
Drug/Study Safety and Safety Reporting

by James Nickas, PharmD
Sr. Dir., Development Drug Safety, GCP/GLP Quality Assurance,
Genentech, Inc.

As much as any aspect of clinical trials regulation, safety reporting principles and requirements have been in a state of evolution through much of the last decade. This evolution has been driven by several factors, including international harmonization efforts, continuing efforts to transition to the electronic submission of regulatory filings, and an ever-increasing focus on product safety.

In accordance with GCP and industry standards, investigators participating in clinical trials of an investigational medicinal product (IMP) are generally instructed to expeditiously report all serious adverse events, regardless of causal attribution, to the sponsor. In addition, adverse events and/or laboratory abnormalities identified in the protocol as critical to safety evaluations are also required to be reported to the sponsor in accordance with protocol instructions.

Sponsors are responsible for the ongoing safety evaluation of IMPs and to inform investigators and applicable regulatory authorities of any new information that, based upon appropriate medical judgment, might materially influence the benefit-risk assessment of the IMP or that would be sufficient to consider changes in either product administration or in the overall conduct of a clinical investigation. This includes preclinical findings that suggest significant risk for human subjects, such as reports of mutagenicity, teratogenicity or carcinogenicity.

In the United States (US), requirements for safety reporting during clinical trials involving IMPs are set forth in the Code of Federal Regulations (CFR), specifically sections 21 CFR 312.32, 312.33 and 312.64. In the European Community (EC), requirements for clinical trial safety reporting are set forth in Directive 2001/20/EC, specifically Articles 16 (Notification of adverse events) and 17 (Notification of serious adverse reactions). The sponsor's reporting requirements under Directive 2001/20/EC are further detailed in the European Commission documents entitled, "Detailed guidance on the collection, verification and presentation of adverse reaction reports arising from clinical trials on medicinal products for human use" (ENTR/CT3 revision 1, April 2004) and "Detailed guidance on the European database of Suspected Unexpected Serious Adverse Reactions" (Eudravigilance–Clinical Trial Module) (ENTR.CT4 revision 1, April 2004).

Safety reporting regulations in the United States, ICH directives, and guidance documents in each region refer to and distinguish between several terms that are critical in establishing clinical trial safety reporting requirements: adverse event, adverse drug experience: adverse (drug) reaction: serious adverse event; serious adverse reaction; suspected unexpected serious adverse reaction; and treatment emergent adverse event. These terms are defined below (with commentary) and are used extensively throughout the questions explored in this section.

Adverse Event (AE). The ICH E2A and E6 guidance documents define an AE as "any untoward medical occurrence in a patient or clinical investigation subject administered a pharmaceutical product and which does not necessarily have a causal relationship with this treatment. An AE can therefore be any unfavorable and unintended sign (including an abnormal laboratory finding, for example), symptom, or disease temporally associated with the use of a medicinal product, whether or not considered related to the medicinal product."

This globally accepted definition of an AE implies that, to be regarded as an AE for safety reporting purposes, the unfavorable or unintended event must occur after exposure to a medicinal product. Some protocols define an AE more broadly as any unfavorable or unintended event associated with the research study, which can include untoward events occurring prior to any IMP exposure. Another AE definition commonly found in today's protocols is "any change from baseline."

Adverse Drug Experience (ADE). In post-marketing safety reporting regulations [21 CFR 310.305(b), 314.80(a), 600.80(a)], the FDA defines the term ADE as "Any adverse event associated with the use of a drug/biological product in humans, whether or not considered product related, including the following: An adverse event occurring in the course of the use of a drug/biological product in professional practice; an adverse event occurring from overdose of the product whether accidental or intentional; an adverse event occurring from abuse of the product; an adverse event occurring from withdrawal of the product; and any failure of expected pharmacological action."

In the ADE definition above, the word "associated" simply implies that the adverse event occurs sometime during or after product exposure, regardless of causal attribution. However, in safety reporting regulations pertaining to IMPs (21 CFR 312.32), the FDA actually defines the phrase *associated with the use of the drug* to mean that, "there is a reasonable possibility that the experience may have been caused by the drug."

Adverse Reaction (AR) or Adverse Drug Reaction (AR or ADR). The ICH E2A guideline on clinical safety data management states that "all noxious and unintended responses to a medicinal product related to any dose should be considered adverse drug reactions." In its postmarketing labeling regulation [21 CFR 201.57(g)], the FDA defines an adverse reaction as "an undesirable effect, reasonably associated with the use of the drug, that may occur as part of the pharmacological action of the drug or may be unpredictable in its occurrence."

In clinical trials of IMPs, all AEs judged by either the reporting investigator or the sponsor as having a reasonable causal relationship to the IMP are considered ADRs for regulatory reporting purposes. The expression "reasonable causal relationship" generally implies that there is evidence or plausible arguments to suggest a causal or contributory relationship.

Serious Adverse Event/Reaction (SAE/SAR). The ICH defines a serious adverse event (experience) or reaction as "any untoward medical occurrence that at any dose: results in death, is life-threatening, requires inpatient hospitalization or prolongation of existing hospitalization, results in persistent or significant disability/incapacity, or is a congenital anomaly/birth defect." ICH guidance also recommends that important medical events that may not be immediately life-threatening or result in death or hospitalization should also be considered serious when, based upon appropriate medical judgment, they may jeopardize the patient or may require intervention to prevent one of the other outcomes listed in the serious definition. Examples of such medical events include allergic bronchospasm requiring intensive treatment in an emergency room or at home, blood dyscrasias or convulsions that do not result in inpatient hospitalization, or the development of drug dependency or drug abuse.

In the definition of "serious," the term "life-threatening" refers to an AE that, in the view of the investigator, places the subject at immediate risk of death from the reaction as it occurred. It does not include a reaction that, had it occurred in a more severe form, might have caused death. The term "disability" in the definition of "serious" refers to a substantial disruption of a person's ability to conduct normal life functions.

Suspected Unexpected Serious Adverse Reaction (SUSAR). A SUSAR is a serious adverse drug reaction, the nature or severity of which is not consistent with the applicable product information (e.g., investigator's brochure for an unapproved investigational product or summary of product characteristics for an authorized product). The term is defined in the EU directive and EC guidance documents.

Treatment Emergent Adverse Event (TEAE). A TEAE is an AE that emerges during treatment with a medicinal product having been absent pre-treatment or that worsens relative to the pre-treatment state. The term is defined in both the ICH E9 guideline (Statistical Principles for Clinical Trials) and in the FDA's "Guideline for the Format and Content of the Clinical and Statistical Section of a New Drug Application (1988).

The application of the "treatment emergent" concept when substantial background noise of signs and symptoms is anticipated facilitates the capture of AEs that potentially could be related to treatment, and is probably the most appropriate capture definition for the purposes of safety analyses.

Unexpected Adverse Drug Reaction/Experience. The ICH defines an unexpected adverse drug reaction as an "adverse reaction, the nature or severity of which is not consistent with the applicable product information (e.g., investigator's brochure for an unapproved investigational medicinal product or summary of product characteristics for an authorized product)." In the United States, 21 CFR 312.32(a) defines an unexpected adverse drug experience as "any adverse drug experience, the specificity or severity of which is not consistent with the current investigator brochure; or if an investigator brochure is not required or available, the specificity or severity of which is not consistent with the risk information described in the general investigational plan or elsewhere in the current application, as amended. For example, under this definition, hepatic necrosis would be unexpected (by virtue of greater severity) if the investigator brochure only referred to elevated hepatic enzymes or hepatitis. Similarly, cerebral thromboembolism and cerebral vasculitis would be unexpected (by virtue of greater specificity) if the investigator brochure only listed cerebral vascular accidents. 'Unexpected,' as used in this definition, refers to an adverse drug experience that has not been previously observed (e.g., included in the investigator brochure) rather than from the perspective of such experience not being anticipated from the pharmacological properties of the pharmaceutical product."

In the context of safety reporting, the term "unexpected" refers to an adverse event that is not already characterized in nature or severity as an adverse reaction in the applicable product information document. In other words, only ADRs included in the applicable product information document should be regarded as "expected" for regulatory reporting purposes.

9.1 Q. What are the AE and SAE reporting requirements for investigators and sponsors during clinical trials of investigational products in the United States and Member States of the European Community?

A. In the United States, the requirements for safety reporting during clinical trials conducted under an investigational new drug (IND) application are set forth in 21 CFR 312.32 (IND safety reports) and 312.64 (Investigator reports). Investigators participating in studies conducted under an IND are required to "promptly report to the sponsor any adverse effect that may reasonably be regarded as caused by, or probably caused by, the drug. If the adverse effect is alarming, the investigator shall report the adverse effect immediately." Although the term "alarming" is not defined by regulation, most assume this to mean SAEs.

Although FDA regulations imply that investigators are not required to report AEs that they consider to be unrelated to the study treatment, study protocols typically require investigators to report all protocol-defined AEs and SAEs to the sponsor regardless of causal attribution. Investigators can protect themselves, their studies and their sponsors through such all-inclusive reporting. Sponsors have a responsibility to review all safety information that they receive, essentially because what may appear as an isolated, unrelated AE to an investigator could represent a new safety signal when evaluated against cumulative product experience.

In the EC, Directive 2001/20/EC requires investigators to "report all SAEs immediately to the sponsor except for those that the protocol or investigator's brochure identifies as not requiring immediate reporting." Adverse events and/or laboratory abnormalities identified in the protocol as critical to safety evaluations must also be reported to the sponsor by the investigator within the time periods specified in the protocol. For reported deaths, investigators are required to supply the sponsor and the relevant ethics committee with any additional information requested.

To facilitate compliance with the aforementioned safety reporting requirements, industry sponsors typically require investigators to report all SAEs to the company expeditiously by phone or fax (e.g., within 24 to 48 hours), unless another arrangement is negotiated with applicable regulatory authorities in advance of the study's initiation. In special situations (e.g., when efficacy endpoints are SAEs or when a fatal or other "serious" outcome is the primary efficacy endpoint), the use of an independent data monitoring committee (IDMC) in lieu of expedited reporting may be preferable. For example, when death is an expected outcome of the disease under study (such as in oncology trials) and is an efficacy endpoint, the protocol may instruct investigators to record deaths attributed solely to disease progression as a study endpoint in the case report form (CRF) rather than as an SAE. Such studies will likely require and utilize an IDMC to monitor the frequency of death from all causes in an unblinded manner.

For the purpose of IND safety reporting in the United States, FDA regulations require sponsors to "promptly review all information relevant to the safety of the drug obtained or otherwise received by the sponsor from any source, foreign or domestic, including information derived from any clinical or epidemiological investigations, animal investigations, commercial marketing experience, reports in the scientific literature, and unpublished scientific papers, as well as reports from foreign regulatory authorities that have not already been previously reported to the agency by the sponsor." This means that, for an IMP that has not been approved for US marketing, serious and expected ADRs that are brought to the sponsor's attention via any source are subject to expedited IND safety reporting. However, a sponsor of an IND study of a marketed product is not required to make a safety report for any adverse experience associated with use of the product that is not from the clinical study itself. Such reports from sources other than the IND study itself would likely be subject to post-marketing safety reporting requirements in the United States.

Sponsors of clinical trials conducted under an IND are required to inform the FDA by telephone or a fax report of any unexpected fatal or life-threatening AE that is suspected to be associated with the study treatment. Such notifications must occur within 7 calendar days of the sponsor's initial knowledge of the event. For any serious and unexpected AE suspected to be associated with the study treatment, sponsors must also submit written IND safety reports to the FDA and investigators who are actively participating in studies of the relevant IMP. Such written reports are also required for significant animal study safety-related findings (e.g., mutagenicity, teratogenicity or carcinogenicity) that suggest a potential risk to human subjects.

The sponsor must submit to the FDA written IND safety reports within 15 calendar days of its initial receipt of the information. Written IND safety reports must include a description of the most recent serious and unexpected ADR, a summary of all IND safety reports previously filed with the IND concerning a similar event, and the sponsor's analysis of the significance of the most recent serious and unexpected ADR in light of previous similar reports. Written IND safety reports may be submitted to the FDA on FDA Form 3500A or in an alternative narrative format (foreign events may be submitted either on an FDA Form 3500A or, if preferred, on a CIOMS I form; reports from animal or epidemiological studies shall be submitted in a narrative format), and must prominently declare their contents (i.e., "IND Safety Report"). Important follow-up information to a previously submitted IND safety report must also be submitted. In the United States, investigators are responsible for ensuring that IND safety reports that they receive from sponsors are submitted to the relevant IRB(s)/ethics committee(s) in an expeditious manner.

In the US, sponsors of studies conducted under an IND are also required to submit brief annual reports on the progress of the investigation(s) that include, among other things, a narrative or tabular summary showing the most frequent and most serious adverse experiences by body system, a summary of all IND safety reports submitted during the past year, a list of subjects who died during participation in the investigation(s), and a list of subjects who dropped out of the investigation(s) due to AEs. Sponsors are required to submit these annual progress reports to the FDA but not investigators.

In the EC, sponsors of interventional clinical trials as defined in Directive 2001/20/EC are responsible for ensuring that all SUSARs originating from such trials are promptly reported to the competent authorities in Member States in which the clinical trial is being conducted and also to the relevant ethics committees. The specific and rather complicated requirements are detailed in a pair of European Commission documents: "Detailed guidance on the collection, verification and presentation of adverse reaction reports arising from clinical trials on medicinal products for human use" (ENTR/CT3 revision 1, April 2004) and "Detailed guidance on the European database of Suspected Unexpected Serious Adverse Reactions" (Eudravigilance–Clinical Trial Module) (ENTR.CT4 revision 1, April 2004).

Applicable SUSARs must be sent electronically to the EudraVigilance Clinical Trial Module (EVCTM). Sponsors make a commitment to electronically submit SUSARs that qualify for reporting to the EVCTM in the application that they forward to the competent authority of the European Economic Area (EEA) Member State(s) in seeking approval of the clinical trial. For clinical trials that began before the 1 May 2004 effective date of Directive 2001/20/EC and that have at least one EEA-based investigator site, only SUSARs occurring as of 1 May 2004 are required to be reported electronically to the EVCTM. No retrospective reporting for SUSARs occurring before 1 May 2004 is required.

In the EC, SUSARs that are fatal or life threatening must be reported to the competent authorities in all the Member States concerned and to the relevant ethics committees within 7 calendar days of the sponsor's initial knowledge of the event. Relevant follow-up information that is obtained must be communicated within an additional 8 calendar days. All other SUSARs must be reported to the competent authorities concerned and to the relevant ethics committee as soon as possible, but no later than 15 calendar days of the sponsor's first knowledge of the SUSARs. Each Member State is required to ensure that all investigational medical product-related SUSARs brought to its attention are recorded.

In addition to expeditiously reporting applicable SUSARs, sponsors of interventional clinical trials in the EC are required to provide an annual safety report to the ethics committee and the Member States in whose territory the clinical trial is being conducted. The annual report must include a concise overall safety analysis and benefit-risk evaluation for the clinical trial, a line listing of all suspected serious adverse reactions (including all SUSARs) that occurred in the trial, and an aggregate summary tabulation of suspected adverse reactions that occurred during the trial. More specifics on such annual safety reports are available in the European Commission document entitled, "Detailed guidance on the collection, verification and presentation of adverse reaction reports arising from clinical trials on medicinal products for human use" (ENTR/CT3 revision 1, April 2004).

The EC requirements for informing investigators of individual SUSARs and other potentially important safety information are different than those in the United States. Recall that, for studies conducted under a US IND, sponsors are required to expeditiously inform investigators of all applicable SUSARs in an IND safety report. In addition, each new IND safety report must include an analysis and sponsor assessment of previously submitted IND safety reports of similar events. In the EC, sponsors of interventional clinical trials are required to "inform all investigators concerned on findings that could adversely affect the safety of study subjects. If appropriate, the information can be aggregated in a line listing of SUSARs in periods as warranted by the nature of the clinical development project and the volume of SUSARs generated. This line listing should be accompanied by a concise summary of the evolving safety profile of the investigational medicinal product. In the case of blinded trials the line listing should present data on all SUSARs, regardless of the medication administered (e.g., active/placebo), thereby when possible and appropriate, the blind would be maintained and the risk of inadvertently informing the investigators with regard to the identity of the medication would be avoided. If a significant safety issue is identified, either upon receipt of an individual case report or upon review of aggregate data, the sponsor should issue as soon as possible a communication to all investigators. A safety issue that impacts upon the course of the clinical study or development project, including suspension of the study program or safety-related amendments to study protocols should also be reported to the investigators."

With the continuing emergence of global medical product development programs, sponsors must often develop procedures that comply with both the FDA's IND safety reporting regulations and EC requirements as established in Directive 2001/20/EC.

9.2   Q. Study sites are sometimes instructed to record "treatment emergent" adverse events (TEAE) on adverse event (AE) case report forms (CRF). Are AE and TEAE synonymous terms?

A. The ICH E2A guideline defines an AE is "any untoward medical occurrence in a patient or clinical investigation subject administered a pharmaceutical product and which does not necessarily have a causal relationship with this treatment. An AE can therefore be any unfavorable and unintended sign (including an abnormal laboratory finding, for example), symptom, or disease temporally associated with the use of a medicinal product, whether or not considered related to the medicinal product." This AE definition implies that, to be regarded as an AE for safety analysis purposes, the unfavorable or unintended event must occur after exposure to a medicinal product. However, this definition does not address one of the most difficult issues involved in defining what constitutes a potentially meaningful AE with respect to characterizing the true safety profile of an investigational product—that is, how long-standing medical conditions and/or chronic symptoms that may be part of a patient's medical history should be handled during a clinical trial.

With respect to stable medical conditions, strict application of the ICH AE definition would increase the number of events reported during a clinical trial, but would also increase the likelihood of capturing all potentially important events. On the other hand, reporting events related to stable medical conditions that are part of patient's history might serve only to add superfluous information to databases and potentially obscure the true safety profile of the investigational product. The patient population being studied may influence the perspective taken on this issue. In a study of healthy volunteers, any observed negative event might be relevant to a safety analyses. In studies involving the elderly or populations that suffer from multiple background conditions, however, the reporting of all events can lead to significant extra work and make the process of identifying true safety signals more difficult. In such studies, the application of the "treatment emergent" concept may be appropriate.

The ICH E9 guideline (Statistical Principles for Clinical Trials) defines the phrase "treatment emergent" as: "An event that emerges during treatment having been absent pre-treatment, or worsens relative to the pre-treatment state." This guideline mentions that, when substantial background noise of signs and symptoms is anticipated in a clinical trial, one method to reduce such noise is to make use of the "treatment emergent" concept in which adverse events are recorded only if they emerge or worsen relative to pre-treatment baseline. The application of the "treatment emergent" concept when substantial background noise of signs and symptoms is anticipated facilitates the capture of AEs that potentially could be related to treatment, and is probably the most appropriate capture definition for the purposes of safety analyses.

Protocols that incorporate the treatment emergent concept into reportable AE definitions might instruct investigators to report any: (1) unfavorable or unintended sign, symptom or disease that emerges during a study's defined active phase having been absent pre-study (i.e., anything new), irrespective of the perceived relationship to the study treatment; or (2) any medical condition or chronic symptomatology that was present prior to study participation and that, in the opinion of the investigator, worsens in severity and/or frequency during the study's defined active phase (i.e., any change), irrespective of the perceived relationship to the study treatment.

It is understood that some protocols define an AE more broadly as any unfavorable or unintended event associated with the research study, which could include untoward events occurring prior to any IMP exposure. Such events would not qualify as TEAEs and would be separated out during safety analyses.

9.3 Q. If a patient is randomized to the study but never receives study drug, must site staff report serious adverse events (SAE) for this patient?

A. Commonly, the study period during which all AEs and SAEs must be reported begins after informed consent is obtained and the active or blinded study treatment is administered and continues through the protocol-specified post-treatment follow-up period. By definition, undesirable medical occurrences in subjects who never receive any study treatment (active or blinded) are not treatment emergent AEs and would not be included in safety analyses. Typically, the number of subjects "evaluable for safety" comprises the number of subjects who received at least one dose of the study treatment. This includes subjects who were, for whatever reason, excluded from efficacy analyses, but who received at least one dose of study treatment.

Some protocols may require AEs and/or SAEs to be collected prior to study treatment to establish a baseline against which post-treatment events can be compared, to determine if non-drug interventions mandated by the protocol can be associated with harm to a subject (e.g., medication washout, no treatment run-in, or protocol-mandated invasive procedure), and/or to meet country-specific regulatory requirements. If studies are conducted in France, for example, SAEs associated with any protocol-imposed intervention must be recorded and reported in an expedited manner to the French regulatory authority.

9.4 Q. So how should adverse events observed during a study "washout" period be handled?

A. As discussed above (see Q9.3), some protocols require the recording of AEs and/or SAEs associated with protocol-mandated non-drug interventions because they can be associated with harm to a subject. A protocol-mandated washout period, during which subjects are taken off existing treatments (such as during cross-over trials) that they are receiving before the test article is administered, is an example of such an intervention. Since any withdrawal of treatment can be associated with harm to subjects, the subjects must be monitored closely for AEs during washout periods. If the severity and/or frequency of AEs occurring during washout periods are considered unacceptable, the protocol may have to be modified or the study halted.

Other non-drug interventions that can be associated with harm to study subjects include invasive procedures and no treatment run-in periods.

9.5 *Q. Shouldn't every AE be reported as possibly drug related until its causality relationship is known for sure?*

A. For any individual case safety report (ICSR), it is rarely possible to know with a high level of certainty whether the AE/SAE was caused by the investigational medical product. To date, there are no internationally agreed-upon standards or criteria for assessing causality in ICSRs. Causality judgments will ultimately be based on the sponsor's analyses of aggregate data.

However, investigators are usually asked to assess the relationship between an AE/SAE and the investigational product based on available information (e.g., facts or evidence) and/or their best judgment and to document such assessments in the CRF. Regulatory authorities do not recommend any specific categorization of causality, although the categories of *probable, possible,* and *unlikely* are sometimes used in protocols.

The CIOMS VI Working Group VI, which has addressed issues pertaining to the management of clinical trial safety information, will soon recommend that investigators render a simple binary decision on investigational product causality (related or not related) for SAEs: "Was there a reasonable possibility, Yes or No." The CIOMS VI Working Group will also recommend that investigators should not routinely indicate causality information for non-serious AEs, with the exception of protocol-identified AEs of special interest.

Investigator causality assessments should be based on a number of factors. Those findings that are generally recognized as being supportive of a possible causal/contributory relationship between a product's use and the emergence of the AE include the following:

- Occurrence of the adverse event in the expected time (e.g., type 1 allergic reactions occurring within days of therapy, cancers developing after years of therapy);
- Absence of symptoms related to the event prior to exposure;
- Evidence of positive dechallenge or positive rechallenge;
- Consistency of the event with the established pharmacological/toxicological effects of the product, or for vaccines, consistency with established infectious or immunologic mechanisms of injury;
- Consistency of the event with the known effects of other products in the class;
- Existence of other supporting evidence from preclinical studies, clinical trials, and/or pharmacoepidemiologic studies; and
- Absence of alternative explanations for the event (e.g., no concomitant medications that could contribute to the event, no co- or pre-morbid medical conditions).

[See FDA Guidance for Industry entitled, "Good Pharmacovigilance Practices and Pharmacoepidemiologic Assessment" (March 2005) and Miller, et al., "Approaches for Identifying and Defining Environmentally Associated Rheumatic Disorders," *Arthritis & Rheumatism,* Vol. 43, No. 2, February 2000.]

The investigator's assessment of causality for ICSRs is part of the study documentation process. Regardless of causality assessments for ICSRs, the sponsor is responsible for evaluating all such reports against cumulative product experience to identify and expeditiously communicate possible new safety findings to investigators and applicable regulatory authorities.

9.6 Q. What data elements are important to document when reporting AEs/SAEs?

A. Study sponsors generally instruct investigators to assess the occurrence of protocol-defined AEs and SAEs at all subject evaluation time points during the study. All AEs and SAEs, whether volunteered by the subject, discovered by study personnel during questioning, or detected through physical examination, laboratory test, or other means, must be recorded in the subject's medical record and in the CRF.

Generally, investigators are asked, in recording any AE/SAEs, to document: an accurate characterization/description of the event; date of the onset and cessation of the event; severity/intensity of the event; whether treatment was required and, if so, what treatment or action was taken; outcome (e.g., did the subject recover from the AE?); and the investigator's assessment of the relationship between the AE/SAE and the investigational medical product.

9.7 Q. Should expected clinical outcomes of the disease under study, which are efficacy endpoints, be reported as AEs/SAEs?

A. Traditionally, all expected clinical outcomes observed during a study would be considered AEs/SAEs and reported as such. Advantages of this approach include the ability to directly observe any unexpected increased frequency of events in the treatment and the control groups. The main disadvantage is the burden of reporting in an expedited manner frequent clinical outcomes that are fully expected to be related to the disease under study and not the study treatment.

When appropriately negotiated, regulatory authorities do permit a distinction between AE/SAEs and clinical outcomes defined as efficacy endpoints. The hypothesis underlying this approach is that the study treatment will only decrease (or not affect) the frequency of observed clinical outcomes. If prospectively defined clinical outcomes (e.g., death as a result of disease progression) and/or disease-symptom endpoints are to be assessed only as efficacy variables and not as AEs/SAEs, the methods for recording and analyzing these data should be clearly described in the protocol.

In high morbidity/mortality trials, independent data monitoring committees generally monitor all acquired AE/SAE and clinical outcomes data to detect potential safety issues.

9.8 Q. If investigational sites do not report an SAE as possibly drug related and the SAE is subsequently shown to be an event that is drug related, can the sites be penalized by the sponsor, regulatory authorities or institutional review boards/ethics committees?

A. Generally not. Problems can arise, however, when treatment emergent AEs are not reported to the sponsor because site personnel assume that the AEs are unrelated to the experimental treatment. Study protocols typically require investigators to report all protocol-defined AEs and SAEs to the sponsor regardless of causal attribution. As noted, investigators can protect themselves, their studies and their sponsors through such all-inclusive reporting. Sponsors have a responsibility to review all the safety information that they receive, essentially because what may appear as an isolated, unrelated AE to an investigator could represent a new safety signal when evaluated against cumulative product experience.

It is important to realize that all AEs/SAEs that are reported to the study sponsor will be analyzed and submitted to applicable regulatory authorities expeditiously and/or periodically, regardless of the causality assessment ascribed to ICSRs. The best of both worlds is achieved when investigators record and report all protocol-defined AEs/SAEs and apply their best clinical judgment when ascribing causality assessments to ICSRs.

While the quality of investigator causality assessments can vary, sponsors will generally not downgrade an investigator's positive causality assessment for reporting purposes. According to many companies' standard operating procedures, in fact, if an investigator finds that an SAE is drug-related, then a company will report the event as such, even when the sponsor's medical monitor disagrees. In such cases, sponsors can certainly document their disagreement with an investigator's positive causality assessment in the report to the agency.

Sponsors can also upgrade an investigator's negative causality assessment for regulatory reporting purposes. The sponsor might do so if it has good reason (i.e., based on evidence) to suspect a causal/contributory relationship and/or if it has promised the FDA to report certain events of interest expeditiously.

Current FDA regulations are silent on how SAE reporting should be handled when investigator and sponsor causality assessments differ. Because it is the sponsor's regulatory responsibility to report SAEs, however, it is the sponsor's assessment that takes precedence for reporting purposes, almost by default. In its March 2003 proposed regulation, the FDA proposes that investigator causality assessments be given equal weighting to sponsor assessments for purposes of reporting. Because most companies already report SAEs when investigators make a positive causality assessment (i.e., even when the sponsor assessments disagree), this proposed change will essentially formalize what is already standard industry practice.

If an investigator knowingly and systematically downgrades causality assessments on AE reports without supportive clinical reasoning, that investigator could face significant regulatory sanctions. Under FDA regulations at 21 CFR 312.64, an investigator must "promptly report to the sponsor any adverse effect that may reasonably be regarded as caused by, or probably caused by, the drug. If the adverse effect is alarming, the investigator shall report the adverse effect immediately."

9.9   *Q. For the purposes of safety reporting, are the terms "severe" and "serious" considered synonymous?*

A. The terms "severe" and "serious" are not synonymous. Severity (or intensity) refers to the grade of a specific AE, as in a mild (Grade 1), moderate (Grade 2), or severe (Grade 3) myocardial infarction. "Serious" is a regulatory definition and is based on subject or event outcome or action criteria usually associated with events that pose a threat to a subject's life or functioning. Seriousness (not severity) serves as the guide for defining the sponsor's regulatory reporting obligations (i.e., to the applicable regulatory authorities). Adverse event severity and seriousness should be assessed independently by investigators.

9.10   *Q. Assume that a patient on study was admitted to the hospital for elective surgery, during which he had an unexpected amount of bleeding and required the transfusion of numerous blood products. Since this involved elective surgery, must site staff report any SAEs?*

A. Unless otherwise specified in the protocol, the elective surgery itself or the preexisting condition that required this planned surgery is not an AE and need not be recorded and reported as an AE. However, the unexpected excessive bleeding complication that occurred during the elective surgery is an AE, and should be recorded and reported as such. This AE will be considered an SAE if the situation was life threatening, if hospitalization was extended beyond the time the patient would have been expected to stay had the surgery proceeded as expected, or if the AE met any of the other serious criteria (e.g., if it is considered "medically important").

Any AE that results in hospitalization or prolonged hospitalization should be documented and reported as an SAE. If a subject is hospitalized to undergo a medical or surgical procedure (elective or otherwise) as a result of an on-study AE or SAE, the event responsible for the procedure—and not the procedure itself—should be recorded as the AE/SAE. For example, if a subject is hospitalized to undergo coronary bypass surgery, the heart condition that necessitated the bypass should be recorded on the SAE CRF page. Hospitalizations for the following reasons will generally not be recorded as SAEs.

- Hospitalization or prolonged hospitalization for diagnostic or elective surgical procedures for preexisting conditions;
- Hospitalization or prolonged hospitalization required to allow efficacy measurement for the study; or
- Hospitalization or prolonged hospitalization for scheduled therapy of the target disease of the study.

9.11 Q. If a subject enrolled in a study comes to an emergency room (ER) with chest pain and is hospitalized overnight for observation, must site staff report this as a SAE?

A. Yes. For the seriousness criterion of "inpatient hospitalization" to apply, an overnight stay in the hospital is required. Admission to an ER and release without an overnight stay would not satisfy the "inpatient hospitalization" seriousness criterion. However, there could be other reasons that this event might be classified as serious—for example, the chest pain might be considered "medically important" as defined in the protocol.

9.12 Q. How should site staff report an event if a subject experiences a clinical problem that is determined to be significant enough to be considered "serious," but does not require hospitalization and is not fatal or immediately life threatening?

A. An event that does not require inpatient hospitalization or is not fatal or immediately life threatening may be significant enough to be considered medically serious. The diagnosis of a new malignancy is an example. Such an event might satisfy a protocol-defined criterion establishing that an event is serious if it ". . . may jeopardize the subject and may require medical or surgical intervention to prevent another serious outcome." If so, the aforementioned problem would qualify as an SAE and should be reported as such. If no seriousness criteria apply to an observed clinical event, the event should be recorded and reported as a non-serious AE.

Some protocols define specific events of interest that investigators are required to expeditiously report to the sponsor for real-time monitoring. Examples include events of scientific or medical concern specific to the development program, or events that might be potential precursors or portents of more serious medical conditions. Events of special importance should be consistently defined using standard criteria or in consultation with appropriate experts. If applicable, the definitions and requirements for the use of particular terms should be described in the protocol. Although they are to be reported expeditiously to facilitate the sponsor's real-time review, events of special interest would only be classified as SAEs in safety analyses if the investigator determined that they met established regulatory criteria for serious events.

9.13 Q. What would an SAE's onset date be if a patient on study develops symptoms of congestive heart failure (CHF) on Monday and was admitted to the hospital on Friday?

A. If known, the complete onset date (month-day-year) of the first signs and/or symptoms of the most recent CHF episode should be recorded. In this case, it would be Monday. If the onset date of the first signs and/or symptoms is unknown, the date of hospitalization or diagnosis should be recorded.

9.14 Q. What should site staff do when a subject is hospitalized and has many, many adverse events?

A. There are no industry standards that define one best practice for reporting AEs/SAEs in different situations. The safety objectives of a particular study will generally dictate what investigators are instructed to report. There are a number of common misunderstandings that contribute to imprecise AE reporting during clinical trials, particularly in studies of critically ill patients when substantial background noise of disease-related events is anticipated. In such situations, the "treatment emergent" concept can be applied initially to assess if the observed event represents a change from baseline. If so, the event is most likely a reportable AE/SAE. If not, the event may not be reportable.

A common area of misunderstanding involves the reporting of signs and symptoms versus diagnoses or syndromes. If known at the time of reporting, sponsors usually instruct investigators to report syndromes or diagnoses rather than individual signs and symptoms (e.g., reporting as "flu" as opposed to cough, sniffles and sore throat separately). However, if a constellation of signs and/or symptoms cannot be medically characterized as a single diagnosis or syndrome at the time of reporting, each individual treatment emergent event should be reported. If a diagnosis is subsequently established, it can be reported as follow-up information. Although a case can be made for reporting both syndromes and component signs and symptoms when it is important to define the true incidence of a particular event, an instruction to report only syndromes or diagnoses when applicable is aimed at capturing the most important clinical events and drawing meaningful interpretations from large numbers of AEs.

Another common AE/SAE reporting challenge emerges when events occurring secondary to an initiating AE are observed (e.g., clinical sequelae or cascade events). In general, AEs occurring secondary to other events should be identified by their primary cause. For example, if severe diarrhea is known to have resulted in dehydration, it may be sufficient to record only diarrhea as an AE or SAE in the CRF. This principle generally applies when secondary events emerge at roughly the same time as the initiating event and are considered by the investigator to be linked pathophysiologically. When secondary events occur as a result of an initiating SAE and are known at the time of reporting, investigators are sometimes instructed to report all of the events on a single SAE CRF. For example, a subject admitted to the hospital with congestive heart failure (CHF) may subsequently develop pulmonary edema and cardiogenic shock shortly thereafter. In such a case, the primary event term should be CHF, but pulmonary edema and cardiogenic shock should be described in the event chronology field on the SAE CRF and would be considered secondary events. The CHF leading to pulmonary edema and cardiogenic shock would constitute a single serious report.

If a subject experiences multiple events that do not appear to be temporally related or that cannot be readily linked pathophysiologically, investigators are generally instructed to report such events as separate AEs. If the aforementioned subject went on to develop sepsis as a result of a Swan-Ganz catheter insertion, for example, the sepsis should be recorded and reported as a separate SAE.

Although these AE reporting principles are commonly applied, individual study protocols may have different AE/SAE reporting/recording instructions based on the study objectives.

9.15 Q. When should site staff start collecting safety information on patients, and when should adverse event reporting start?

A. A study subject's signing of the informed consent form is typically designated as the start of safety data collection. Commonly, the study period during which all AEs and SAEs must be reported begins after informed consent is obtained and the initiation of study treatment, and continues through the protocol-specified post-treatment follow-up period.

Some protocols may require certain events to be recorded prior to the initiation of study treatment to establish a baseline against which to compare post-treatment AEs/SAEs, to establish if pre-treatment interventions mandated by the protocol can be associated with harm to a subject (e.g., invasive procedures such as biopsies, medication washout, or no treatment run-in), and/or to meet country-specific regulatory requirements. In studies conducted in France, for example, SAEs associated with any protocol-imposed intervention (pre- or post-treatment) must be documented and reported in an expedited manner to the French regulatory authority.

9.16 Q. With regard to reporting serious adverse events (SAE) to institutional review boards (IRB) or ethics committees, where does the sponsor's responsibility end?

A. In the United States, FDA regulations (21 CFR 312.66) require investigators to communicate with IRBs concerning their clinical studies. Although sponsors are not required to communicate with the reviewing IRBs, they sometimes do (e.g., upon request). It is the investigator's responsibility to provide all necessary information to, and obtain the required approvals from, the IRB. However, the sponsor often prepares some of the safety information that must be submitted to the IRB, such as the summary of relevant safety information in the protocol or investigator's brochure. Investigators, not sponsors, must provide all IND safety reports and any other safety-related information to the IRB upon receiving these materials from the sponsor.

In the European Community, sponsors of interventional clinical trials as defined in Directive 2001/20/EC are responsible for ensuring that all SUSARs originating from such trials are promptly reported to the relevant ethics committees as well as the competent authorities in Member States in which the clinical trial is being conducted. In addition to reporting applicable SUSARs in an expeditious manner, sponsors of interventional clinical trials in the EC are required to provide an annual safety report to the relevant Member States and ethics committees. The annual report must include a concise overall safety analysis and benefit-risk evaluation for the clinical trial, a line listing of all suspected serious adverse reactions (including all SUSARs) that occurred in the trial, and an aggregate summary tabulation of suspected adverse reactions that occurred in the trial.

9.17 Q. After a subject completes a clinical trial's study treatment period, there is often a follow-up visit scheduled for some time later. Are there any guidelines for the length of time during which AEs should be collected after a subject completes the study treatment period?

A. There are no strict guidelines for the length of time that AEs should be collected after a subject completes the study treatment period. The study protocol should clearly define the period of time during which individual trial subjects will be monitored for safety following the treatment period. The duration of the post-treatment follow-up period for safety surveillance purposes should be based on the known pharmacokinetic and pharmacodynamic properties of the investigational product. This may be influenced by such things as the half-life of and previous experience with the investigational product.

Absent specific delayed toxicity concerns or safety hypotheses, a post-treatment follow-up period of at least five half-lives of the product(s) under investigation is recommended. A 30-day post-treatment follow-up period for safety surveillance purposes is common. Ultimately, qualified sponsor personnel in consultation with the principal investigators should decide upon an appropriate post-treatment follow-up period for safety.

9.18 Q. Is there a formal requirement that specifies which fatalities should be included in the "death listing" for a clinical trial?

A. There is no strict rule. Most firms require that all deaths that occur while on study and all deaths that result from an AE that occurred while on study be included in the death listing. Usually, all deaths that are listed are carefully analyzed and explained in narrative text. A common approach involves including all deaths that occur during a period of drug exposure or within a period of up to 30 days following discontinuation of the study drug.

9.19 Q. Should an investigator/site document all AEs in its source documents, even if the sponsor is not collecting reports on selected events?

A. Investigators are required to maintain adequate and complete case histories for all subjects enrolled in a clinical study. These records are commonly referred to as "source documents," and are the basis for information recorded in the case report form (see Section 6). Source documents must verify the accuracy and validity of information recorded in the CRF.

With respect to safety, investigators should record any AE/SAE reported by a subject, discovered by study personnel during questioning, or detected through physical examination, laboratory test, or other means in the subject's medical record. For recorded AEs/SAEs, the source documents should indicate onset and resolution dates, if any treatment was rendered or required, the outcomes, and any follow-up action taken.

It is important that investigators provide as much information about AEs/SAEs to the sponsor as possible, so that an adequate evaluation can be performed.

9.20 Q. If a young adult subject has a history of behavioral problems and received church-provided counseling for these problems, would a single episode of the same counseling while on study constitute an AE?

A. The behavioral problem appears to be a pre-existing medical condition. A pre-existing medical condition is one that is present at the start of the study. Investigators are generally instructed to record such conditions as medical or surgical history in the CRF.

A pre-existing medical condition should be re-assessed throughout the trial and recorded as an AE or SAE only if the frequency, severity, or character of the condition worsens during the study. When reporting such events, it is helpful to convey the concept that the pre-existing condition has changed by including applicable descriptors (e.g., "more frequent headaches").

Applying this guidance, a single episode of counseling, given that the counseling was for the same pre-existing issue, would not constitute an AE. However, if the counseling were for other non-related mental health issues, if there were more intense or multiple sessions, or if the subject was referred to yet another care provider, then an AE should be recorded.

9.21 Q. How does an immediately reportable adverse event (IRAE) differ from a serious adverse event (SAE)?

A. Sponsors sometimes use the term "IRAE" in their protocols. This generally applies to protocol-identified adverse events that are of special interest and that investigators are requested to expeditiously report to the sponsor for real-time monitoring. Examples include events of scientific or medical concern specific to the development program, or events that might be potential precursors or portents of more serious medical conditions.

Although reported expeditiously to the sponsor to facilitate real-time monitoring, AEs of special interest would only be classified as SAEs in safety analyses if the investigator determined that they met established regulatory criteria for serious events.

9.22 Q. If a patient enrolled on study receives an accidental overdose of study medication, how should this be reported?

A. In and of itself, an accidental overdose is not an AE. Any undesirable medical occurrence resulting from an accidental overdose is an AE, however, and should be recorded and reported on the appropriate AE case report form. Since accidental overdoses of study medications could have serious clinical consequences and/or represent product administration confusion, they should be reported to and be evaluated by the sponsor. The site should write a progress note in the subject's medical chart, and should monitor the subject. The principal investigator should decide whether further doses of the study drug should be administered to the subject and discuss these decisions with the patient.

Finally, the study team should discuss steps to prevent future overdoses. Was there a problem with dose calculations, with intravenous equipment, or with the manner in which the nurse administered the drug (e.g., the nurse used the incorrect route of administration, such as injecting the drug in a vein rather than in a muscle)? Did the subject misunderstand dosing instructions? The study team must identify the root cause of the incident and take action to ensure that it is not repeated. These actions should be documented. In addition to capturing and assessing information on overdoses that produce clinical signs and symptoms, some companies also collect and process information about overdoses that do not produce symptomatic adverse events.

9.23 Q. What actions should be taken if a study subject is admitted to another hospital and study staff do not have access to his or her medical record at this outside facility?

A. In many cases, the informed consent form signed previously by the subject is sufficient to help the study site obtain medical records for hospitalization during a clinical trial. If site staff cannot obtain medical records after making routine phone and fax requests, they should speak to the medical records department manager at the admitting hospital. The study site should explain that the patient is a subject in a clinical trial, and that information regarding hospitalization must be obtained to provide FDA-required information. Site staff can offer to fax a copy of the subject's signed consent form to the medical records department.

All attempts to obtain the hospital record should be documented. If all avenues fail, the site staff should write a note-to-the-file documenting attempts to obtain information. Also, an SAE form should be completed with any known information, however minimal, about the hospitalization.

Some study consent forms are not sufficiently explicit regarding a patient's permission to obtain records from outside hospitals. Such records are important in documenting an SAE. An outside hospital's medical records department may have extremely stringent requirements about transmitting copies of its records, however. Unless the consent establishes that the patient granted such permission in a straightforward and detailed manner, the outside medical records department may require that the patient complete a second consent form (generally its own form). This process can take time and cause aggravation.

Alternatively, the study's principal investigator could call the outside hospital's admitting physician to request the physician's help in obtaining copies of the records. The admitting physician can sometimes secure the cooperation of an otherwise uncooperative medical records department administrator. The admitting physician might also make copies of the chart and send them directly to the principal investigator.

9.24 Q. What follow-up, if any, would be necessary if the female partner of a man enrolled in a clinical study becomes pregnant while he is on study? If there were birth defects, what are the sponsor's responsibilities?

A. Follow-up of pregnancies are more likely to be a protocol requirement for Phase 2 or 3 studies in which preclinical and/or Phase 1 data revealed that the drug under study could be mutagenic or otherwise alter the sperm or if the drug itself can be transmitted in seminal fluids. These types of risks should have been identified in the protocol and should be fully explained in the informed consent. In these cases, as soon as the sponsor becomes aware of the pregnancy, the pregnant woman should be monitored throughout the pregnancy until she delivers.

If defects are present, the child may need to be followed as long as it takes for a definitive diagnosis to be made. To capture information on developmental anomalies, some firms follow births for up to six months after delivery.

9.25 Q. Assuming that it is a study exclusion criterion, is a pregnancy while on study considered an AE? Is it considered an SAE?

A. In and of itself, a pregnancy is not considered an AE or SAE. However, abortion, whether accidental, therapeutic, or spontaneous, should always be classified as a SAE and expeditiously reported to the sponsor. Similarly, any congenital anomaly/birth defect in a child born to a female subject exposed to the investigational product should be recorded and reported as an SAE.

If a female subject becomes pregnant while receiving investigational therapy or within a specified time period after the last dose of investigational product, most protocols require prompt notification of the sponsor to facilitate outcome follow-up. Some companies use SAE CRFs to capture reports of pregnancy while others require the completion a special pregnancy CRF.

The important point is that on-study pregnancies should be reported to the sponsor and should be tracked. Ultimately, the sponsor is responsible for following the pregnancy, and the investigator's responsibilities should be defined a priori in the clinical protocol.

9.26 Q. Is an abnormal result from a fetal exam (such as amniocentesis) a congenital anomaly? Is it another adverse event? Or are sponsors interested only in outcomes for pregnancies that have gone to term? Must they be reported in the clinical study report?

A. If a fetal exam reveals a congenital anomaly, the site should report that anomaly to the sponsor and IRB as an SAE. For sponsors who categorize pregnancy while on study as an SAE, then the fetal anomaly would represent a second SAE. The site must report the anomalies to the sponsor and IRB as soon as it becomes aware of them. Waiting until the completion of gestation to report the anomalies would be entirely irresponsible, since the congenital anomalies could be occurring in other fetuses whose mothers became pregnant while on study.

9.27 Q. Under what circumstances is it considered appropriate to unblind a patient in a clinical study?

A. Blinding refers to a procedure in which one or more parties to the trial are kept unaware of the treatment assignment(s). Single-blinding usually refers to the subject(s) being unaware, and double-blinding usually refers to the subject(s), investigator(s), monitor, and, in some cases, data analyst(s) being unaware of the treatment assignment(s).

In general, unblinding of participants during conduct of a clinical trial is not allowed unless there are compelling medical or safety reasons to do so (e.g., knowledge of the blinded information is necessary for treatment of severe adverse events). The conditions and procedures for unblinding should be clearly described in study protocols.

It is recommended that, if at all possible, the investigator always try to contact the sponsor's medical monitor before breaking the blind. This allows the investigator and study monitor to discuss the situation and reach a decision jointly.

9.28 Q. Does the FDA require that sponsors establish and use data safety monitoring boards (DSMB) for clinical studies?

A. All clinical trials require safety monitoring, but not all trials require oversight by an independent committee. A data monitoring committee, sometimes called a data and safety monitoring board (DSMB), is a group of experts established by the sponsor to assess, at specific intervals, the progress of a clinical trial (the safety data and the critical efficacy endpoints), and to recommend to the sponsor whether to continue, modify, or stop a trial. Factors that the DSMB considers in making such recommendations include whether: (1) the potential benefits of the investigational intervention have been established; or (2) the risks are greater than anticipated.

Currently, the FDA requires the establishment and use of DSMBs only when informed consent requirements are waived in emergency research studies (21 CFR 50.24(a)(7)(iv)). In a November 2001 draft guidance entitled, "Guidance for Clinical Trial Sponsors on the Establishment and Operation of Clinical Trial Data Monitoring Committees," however, the FDA recommended that DSMBs be used in all controlled trials employing mortality or major morbidity as a primary or secondary endpoint. Further, the agency notes that DSMBs may also be useful "in settings where trial participants may be at elevated risk of such outcomes even if the study intervention addresses lesser outcomes such as relief of symptoms."

Sponsors should consider using DSMBs when the investigational medicinal product under study is a novel treatment for which little prior clinical safety data exist and when vulnerable populations, such as children or the elderly, will be enrolled in the study in significant numbers. Sponsors often use DSMBs for certain types of trials, including Phase 3 studies, studies involving large populations at multiple sites, and studies that have long durations or that are randomized and double-blinded. Early-stage, unblinded, short and exploratory trials generally do not call for the use of a DSMB.

9.29 Q. When a DSMB is used, are its records considered part of the sponsor's records? Can the FDA inspect, and do IRBs have the authority to require the submission and review of, DSMB meeting minutes and other related records?

A. While the FDA has the authority to inspect any organization participating in a clinical trial conducted under an IND, the agency does not currently inspect DSMBs because it does not have regulations requiring their routine use (see Q9.28). An IRB's reach does not extend to inspecting sponsors or, by extension, DSMBs that may be advising them. Further, DSMBs are not monitored by clinical research associates and are not audited. They are autonomous, independent entities that generally are not subject to external review. Typically, a DSMB's records are considered confidential, and their decisions are disclosed only to sponsors and possibly to a committee of study investigators.

Although the FDA has never inspected a DSMB or its records, it could theoretically seek access to DSMB records as part of a follow-up to a sponsor inspection. The agency might do so, for example, if it suspected that a DSMB made an important safety-related recommendation that a sponsor did not report to the FDA, or if it suspected that a DSMB was being pressured to under-report safety-related concerns to the sponsor. Agency officials concede, however, that the lack of regulations regarding DSMB inspections and the lack of an agency DSMB inspectional program make the FDA's authority in this area less than definitive. The agency would have clear authority to inspect a DSMB if the sponsor formally transferred certain regulatory obligations to the board, however.

9.30 Q. Are hospitalizations that occur more than 30 days after the end of the study period reportable to the FDA? In some conditions, should AEs that occur after a subject has gone off study be captured on case report forms?

A. The study period during which all AEs and SAEs must be reported generally begins after informed consent is obtained and the initiation of study treatment [or initiation of any study procedures] and ends after a protocol-specified post-treatment follow-up period. In the absence of specific delayed toxicity concerns or safety hypotheses, a post-treatment follow-up period of at least five half-lives of the drug under investigation is often recommended. A 30-day post-treatment follow-up period for safety surveillance purposes is common.

After the protocol-specified post-treatment follow-up period, investigators are generally instructed to report only SAEs that they suspect could be attributed to prior study treatment.

Some protocols require post-study survival follow-up or assessments of other post-study clinical outcomes as part of efficacy analyses. These data would not be considered AEs/SAEs.

Further Reading

ICH Guideline: "The Extent of Population Exposure to Assess Clinical Safety" (E1), 1995.

ICH Guideline: "Clinical Safety Data Management: Definitions and Standards for Expedited Reporting" (E2A), 1995.

ICH Guideline: "Standardization of Medical Terminology for Regulatory Purposes" (M1), 1999.

Molloy, V. and Mackintosh, D., "The Importance of Physical Exams in Clinical Trials," *Applied Clinical Trials,* 9:38-44, October 2000.

Mackintosh, D., Molloy, V., and Petty, M., "Good Clinical Practice and Drug Safety: Identification and Documentation of Adverse Events at Clinical Sites," *Applied Clinical Trials,* 11(5):52-62, May 2002.

Brown, Kenneth, Sykes, R. Scott, and Phillips, George, "Is That Adverse Experience Really Expected? Guidelines for Interpreting and Formatting Adverse Experience Information in the United States," *Drug Information Journal,* 35:269-84, 2001.

Gait, John E, Smith, Sandy, and Brown, Sherri L., "Evaluation of Safety Data From Controlled Clinical Trials: The Clinical Principles Explained," *Drug Information Journal,* 34:273-87, 2000.

Section 10:
Quality Assurance Activities/Study Auditing/
FDA Inspections

10.1 Q. In 2005, what are the FDA's current and emerging priorities for its bioresearch monitoring program and GCP compliance?

A. During 2005, CDER will shift its Division of Scientific Investigations (DSI), the unit responsible for the bioresearch monitoring program (BIMO) and GCP compliance, from the Office of Medical Policy to CDER's Office of Compliance, under which it was located until a reorganization several years ago. The decision was made, in part, because so much of DSI's day-to-day activities overlap with the Office of Compliance's compliance-related activities. Although a segment of DSI's work is also related to policy, CDER officials determined that the division would continue to liaison with the Office of Medical Policy when necessary. The move is not expected to be associated with any immediate changes in policies or approaches.

Based on informal communications with CDER officials in March 2005, the center had at least several continuing and emerging priorities for its GCP inspectional and compliance programs:

- *Sponsor/Monitor Initiative.* DSI officials claim that they are attempting to identify new ways to examine industry monitoring practices, in particular to determine how there can be major study-related problems in industry-sponsored studies and that they do not seem to be detected or addressed despite the existence of a monitoring program. Actually, the division recently undertook a small study to determine if there were predictors regarding where the problems were. DSI officials claim that the root of the problem appears to be sponsor follow-up when monitors do detect study-related issues. In response, CDER officials are now considering both increased education and greater enforcement against sponsors.

- *Agency-wide Reassessment of BIMO Program.* In December 2004, the FDA began a major initiative to re-assess its GCP and bioresearch monitoring programs within all of its various program centers, including CDER, CBER, and CDRH. An internal FDA working group comprising representatives from throughout these centers is actively examining the entire BIMO process to re-evaluate how it works currently, what aspects of the program can be improved, how the centers can better coordinate, how the BIMO program can better focus on the highest-risk clinical studies, and how the agency can improve oversight of clinical trials involving special and vulnerable populations, including pediatric populations. In many ways, the BIMO reassessment program is an extension of the FDA's Pharmaceutical cGMPs for the 21st Century Initiative, a two-year effort under which the agency reassessed its regulation of product manufacturing and product quality with the goal of modernizing this area. Since at least mid-2004, FDA officials have been speaking openly about a similar reassessment in the GCP compliance program, in part to better establish inspectional/compliance priorities and possibly reduce regulatory burdens. Although there is no target date for an outcome to the BIMO reassessment, FDA officials claim that the reassessment process will be similar to that undertaken as part of the current good manufacturing practice modernization initiative, which took 24 months to complete.

- *Clinical Investigator Responsibilities.* By mid-2005, CDER hopes to release a new guidance to clarify investigator-related GCP responsibilities. The guidance is being developed due to FDA concern that there it has no regulatory jurisdiction over site staff, third-party vendors, and other individuals who are becoming so involved in the clinical trial process and who are assuming investigator responsibilities. FDA officials suggest that the guidance will emphasize that, although investigators can delegate certain study-related tasks, they cannot under any circumstances delegate their responsibilities. Further, the guidance will clarify the FDA's view of what it means for the investigator to "supervise" a clinical study, and will explore what it means to protect the rights, safety and welfare of subjects. Although FDA officials believe that they need regulatory change to make all the parties involved in clinical trials subject to formal regulatory oversight, they concede that making such changes can take years.

- *Electronic Data Capture.* CDER officials emphasize that they continue to look at several aspects of electronic data capture (EDC) extremely seriously. Of particular concern, they note, are situations in which clinical data are transmitted directly to the sponsor and in which no other parties have a copy of the data, in particular the investigator, who is obligated to maintain study-related records. Center officials are concerned not only because such situations are becoming more common, but because sponsors are now claiming that they are meeting the investigators' obligations by forwarding investigators an archived copy of the data at the completion of the trial. DSI officials disagree entirely that such practices meet current regulatory standards. Also of concern to the agency, particularly FDA statisticians, is that such sponsor-maintained clinical databases provide sponsors with unfettered access to conduct virtually unlimited interim analyses as studies progress. Agency officials, who concede that they continue to attempt to come to terms with current EDC practices and what is and is not acceptable, hope to deal with some of the regulatory issues presented by EDC in a soon-to-be-released guidance document on patient-reported outcomes, which will, in part, address EDC-related issues (e.g., instrument validation, psychometrics).

- *Responding to Voluntary Complaints.* In recent years, CDER's DSI has encouraged the submission of clinical trial-related complaints regarding regulatory noncompliance, fraud, and other issues. The division continues to look at the complaints as a "vital" and "strategically important" element of the DSI program, and as a way to funnel inspectional resources on a risk-based basis toward potential problem areas. In calendar year 2004, DSI received more than 200 voluntary complaints regarding clinical investigators, IRBs, sponsors, and other entities involved in the trial process, about a 50% increase over the number received in 2003. The division also saw the number of "for cause" inspections, which are undertaken in response to specific concerns, remain at near record levels in FY2004, although they were down just slightly from FY2003 levels. CDER's DSI continues to work to make it easier for individuals to submit voluntary complaints: It has established its own website (www.fda.gov/cder/offices/dsi/index.htm), and is working to put its complaint form online.

- *"Linked Inspections."* In late 2004, CDER's DSI began conducting what it terms "linked inspections," which evaluate all the key entities (sponsor/monitor, investigator, IRB) involved in a particular trial. Instead of looking at the activities and compliance of one of these entities in a particular trial, DSI has decided to take a more systematic look at the way an entire trial is conducted to gain a more complete picture of a trial's conduct and of what in the system might have broken down. As of March 2005, CDER's DSI claims that it had conducted about seven or eight linked inspections, either because the population was vulnerable or because there was an indication (e.g., from an inspection) that there were significant problems in study conduct.

- *Focus on Studies Involving Special Populations.* Consistent with the FDA's move to more of a risk-based compliance approach, CDER's DSI claims that it is becoming much more active in identifying clinical studies involving special or vulnerable populations, pediatric populations in particular, and in inspecting these studies.

- *Foreign Inspections.* With foreign inspections nearly doubling in FY2004, to over 80 inspections, CDER's DSI is having to deal with the resource demands that these inspections create as well as the reality that increasing numbers of studies are being done in counties such as India, China, and Russia, which have many sites with less-developed medical infrastructures.

10.2 Q. In what ways is FDA's GCP inspection and compliance program expected to evolve going forward?

A. As is true of other FDA compliance programs in current good manufacturing practices (cGMP) and other areas, CDER is expected to assume "a more risk-management based approach in our inspections, in what we train, in what we focus on at the inspections," FDA Good Clinical Practice Program Director David Lepay, M.D., Ph.D., said in 2004 comments. While noting that CDER's traditional approach has been to "only do inspections of marketing applications, we're going to do three sites and, and they're always going to be the largest sites, that's not where the future of the GCP program lies . . . You will start to see changes as we move towards predominantly looking at what are the highest risk areas, [including] vulnerable populations, high-risk products, high-risk protocols."

Based on more recent comments from CDER DSI officials, the evolution toward more of a risk-based inspectional system is well underway (see Q10.1). As noted, the agency is directing increasing inspectional resources toward responding to voluntary clinical trial-related complaints by sponsors, site staff, study subjects, and private citizens. DSI officials also claim to be focusing more intently on studies involving vulnerable populations, pediatric populations in particular.

In late 2004, the agency also began a reassessment of its GCP and bioresearch monitoring (BIMO) programs. This effort is also likely to influence the future evolution of DSI's GCP inspection and compliance program, and to further accelerate the move to a risk-based program.

10.3 Q. Citing HIPAA-related privacy standards, some clinical investigators have attempted to deny sponsor monitors and FDA field inspectors access to study patients' medical records. To what degree, if at all, are such denials of access permissible?

A. Such denials are not permissible in the context of clinical research. In terms of monitor access, to the extent that monitoring activities are required by FDA or other regulation or are for purposes related to adverse events, the HIPAA Privacy Rule permits access without an authorization or waiver of authorization.

Likewise, HIPAA privacy standards in no way affect the FDA's access to study-related records. Because it has encountered such situations at some sites, however, the FDA has developed specific language that it uses in response to investigator attempts to use HIPAA concerns to block the agency's access to study records:

"The FD&C Act, the FDA-482, and BIMO regulations at CFR 812.145(b), 312.68, and 56.115(b) permit FDA investigators at reasonable times to have access to, copy, and verify records. In addition, the subjects' informed consent forms are to 'include a statement describing the extent, if any, to which confidentiality of records identifying the subjects will be maintained and that notes the possibility that the FDA may inspect the records' [(CFR 50.25(a)(5)]. Additionally, several specific exemptions in the HIPAA privacy rule [45 CFR Parts 160 and 164] expressly permit covered entities to use and disclose protected health information to FDA investigators without the investigator having to sign any kind of agreement. These include uses and disclosures: (1) required by law [45 CFR 164.512(a); (2) to a public health authority authorized by law to collect or receive such information [164.512(b)(1)]; and (3) to a health oversight agency for oversight activities, including audits, investigations and inspections [164.512(d)]. **HIPAA privacy standards are not intended to affect the access that FDA investigators have previously been afforded.**"

10.4 Q. Precisely what documents should a site be prepared to provide to an FDA inspector during an inspection?

A. The FDA has the authority to "have access to and copy and verify any records and reports relating to a clinical investigation" conducted under an IND (21 CFR 312.58(a)). This includes all regulatory files in the study binder, all drug and accountability records, all consents, all medical records, including ancillary tests and procedures, CRFs, and all other documents that relate to a study (except financial records, including payments). The FDA inspector also may examine the qualifications of the clinical investigator and other key staff.

The agency does not have the right to access personnel files (other than qualifications), however, or to obtain personal identifying information about staff, such as social security numbers, home addresses, telephone numbers, and similar information. Therefore, sites should maintain *curricula vitae* for staff that do not include private identifying criteria beyond an individual's name, title, and qualifications.

In many cases, an FDA inspector will voluntarily identify the study and records that will be reviewed during an inspection when he or she first contacts the investigator to schedule an inspection. If the agency inspector does not volunteer that information, the investigator/site staff should specifically ask the inspector for this information so that these records can be made available at the time of the inspection.

Because an FDA inspector provides an advanced notification of case records does not mean that he or she must confine his or her review to these records necessarily. During the site visit, the inspector may request additional records.

10.5 Q. As noted, the FDA has the authority to "have access to, and copy and verify any records or reports made by the investigator" relating to a clinical investigation. These records comprise largely adequate records of the disposition of the drug (312.62(a)) and subjects' "case histories" (312.62(b)). But would an FDA inspector have to be given access to ALL medical records for an enrolled patient, or only those records developed as part of a clinical investigation? In other words, how far back into a patient's medical history and medical record can an FDA inspector look?

A. In its Information Sheets, the FDA states that prospective clinical trial subjects should be notified, in the informed consent process, "that FDA may inspect study records (which include individual medical records) . . . Informed consent documents should make it clear that, by participating in research, the subject's records automatically become part of the research database. Subjects do not have the option to keep their records from being audited/reviewed by FDA."

The FDA's definition of case history refers to study records "pertinent to the investigation:" "An investigator is required to prepare and maintain adequate and accurate case histories that record all observations and other data pertinent to the investigation on each individual administered the investigational drug or employed as a control in the investigation. Case histories include the case report forms and supporting data including, for example, signed and dated consent forms, any medical records, for example, progress notes of the physician, the individual's hospital chart(s), and nurses' notes."

FDA regulations themselves do not set limits on the nature of the records that agency employees can access during clinical site inspections, although they do provide some protection for subject names. 21 CFR 312.68 states that, "the investigator is not required to divulge subject names unless the records of particular individuals require a more detailed study of the cases, or unless there is reason to believe that the records do not represent actual case studies, or do not represent actual results obtained."

While acknowledging that this is a common question that is asked in many variations, the FDA noted in an informal response that the answer is very case-dependent and cautioned that the question addresses legal authority for which an expert legal opinion should be sought. At the same time, the FDA offered the following:

"In general, where there is a question about the scope of FDA's inspection authority, FDA tends to interpret its authority more broadly rather than narrowly. This is done in the interest of serving the public health. Therefore, if necessary to verify information in the case history, we may ask to have access to a subject's prior medical records . . . There may be instances where pre-study information relates to the study."

In fact, the FDA has made clear in its rulemaking process for other regulations that it did not want the regulations to unintentionally imply any limitations in the study-related records to which agency inspectors would have access. When it finalized its current regulations for FDA inspections of a sponsor's records and reports (312.58(a)) in 1987, for example, the agency specifically modified its original proposal for this very reason. "As proposed, 21 CFR 312.58(a) would have required sponsors to make available to FDA's inspectors 'reports required to be maintained under this part and under other applicable parts of this chapter,'" the agency wrote in the preamble to the final regulation. "This might be read as not requiring a sponsor to make available a record or report that is not specifically enumerated in the regulations, even though it is clearly related to the conduct of a clinical investigation. To clarify agency intent, FDA has revised 21 CFR 312.58(a) in the final rule to give the agency explicit authority to inspect and copy any record or report relating to a clinical investigation conducted under Part 312."

10.6 Q. Given that a site might maintain records off-site and may not have immediate access to them, how does the FDA interpret the requirement that an FDA inspector be provided with "prompt access" to required study-related records that will be inspected?

A. Although the FDA's Compliance Program Guidance 7348.811 uses the phrase "prompt access," the agency's regulations do not specify a time period within which FDA inspectors must be provided access to study-related records. FDA regulations at 21 CFR 312.68 (Inspection of investigator's records and reports) state that "An investigator shall upon request from any properly authorized officer or employee of FDA, at reasonable times, permit such officer or employee to have access to, and copy and verify records or reports made by the investigator. . . ."

Given that the FDA generally provides clinical sites with advance notification of a few days or more for routine inspections and that the agency even identifies the records that it wants to inspect, clinical sites have time to locate and assemble the records in advance of the inspection itself. Agency inspectors contacted on this question noted their expectation that these pre-identified records be available at the start of an inspection. If such records are not available upon an inspector's arrival or within a brief period of time following that arrival (e.g., a reasonable period to permit site staff to immediately retrieve the records from a nearby office and bring them to the inspector), this could raise suspicions that the site has not maintained adequate access to its own records. The relevant circumstances (e.g., the nature of the records sought, degree of delay) will determine if the delay in access will justify further investigation or even a citation in a Form 483-Inspectional Observations.

Even with advance notification, FDA inspectors sometimes request raw data or other information that the site may not have anticipated and that the site staff has not collected for the inspection. While there is no regulation or guideline that establishes a timeframe within which access to such records must be provided, several present and former FDA inspectors contacted regarding this question suggested that 24 hours is a reasonable timeframe, provided that there are justifiable reasons for such a delay. For example, the specific records may be stored at a distant facility, and the volume of records being requested makes faxing/scanning/emailing impractical. Alternatively, the records may exist only in microfilm/microfiche format and printouts of these records may be blurry when faxed. In such cases, a site should be able to use an overnight courier service to provide access to the records the following business day.

10.7 Q. Do FDA GCP compliance inspections focus in any way on HIPAA compliance and, if so, can trial sites and sponsors be cited on Form 483s for violations of HIPAA?

A. Since the FDA is not responsible for any aspect of HIPAA compliance, FDA field inspectors do not assess HIPAA compliance or cite firms or investigators for noncompliance with HIPAA requirements. It is conceivable, however, that the FDA could report HIPAA noncompliance to the HHS Office of Civil Rights if it does encounter such noncompliance.

10.8 Q. In what ways is the HHS Office of Civil Rights, which spearheads the federal government's HIPAA-related efforts, enforcing HIPAA in the context of clinical research?

A. Currently, the HHS Office of Civil Rights is focused on HIPAA-related education and on encouraging voluntary compliance with the HIPAA Privacy Rule. The office is, however, actively accepting and investigating voluntary complaints regarding HIPAA-related compliance.

When it receives a complaint, the Office of Civil Rights will assign an investigator, who will review the complaint and related issues. After this review, the investigator will then share the substance of the complaint with the researcher/organization (covered entity) and provide the researcher/organization with an opportunity to respond. If, as is true in virtually all cases, the issue involves unintentional noncompliance, then the Office of Civil Rights will work with the researcher/ organization to address the situation on a voluntary basis.

If a case involves an intent to violate the HIPAA Privacy Rule or a particularly egregious case of noncompliance, then the HHS Office of Civil Rights will forward the case to the Department of Justice for further action.

10.9 Q. Is the Office of Civil Rights receiving any HIPAA-related complaints regarding FDA-regulated clinical trials?

A. According to Office of Civil Rights officials, they have in fact received a small number of complaints regarding industry-sponsored clinical trials. In many cases, however, they point out that such complaints are being made by clinical trial participants who do not understand that HIPAA permits certain access to medical records in the context of clinical research. Specifically, some clinical trial participants have contacted the Office of Civil Rights to report that their medical information is being shared with the clinical trial sponsors.

10.10 Q. Given that clinical monitoring could be viewed as a type of internal auditing activity designed to determine if the clinical investigator and staff, IRB, and others are fulfilling their regulatory responsibilities, are monitoring reports also given equal protection from routine FDA inspection under agency policies?

A. No, a main difference being that clinical monitoring is a specific FDA requirement and sponsor responsibility. This reality has not prevented some companies from attempting to argue, during FDA inspections, that monitoring reports should be afforded such protection, however.

In a June 2004 warning letter, the FDA cited Biotronik, Inc. for, among other things, failing "to allow FDA Investigators to inspect and copy all records relating to an inspection," including monitoring reports. "You refused to allow the FDA investigators direct access to the monitoring reports for the [study] during the inspection, but only allowed examination of correspondence files related to the monitoring visits," the warning letter states. "'Quality audits' or 'internal audits' . . . are *generally* exempt from FDA review, however, monitoring reports for clinical trials are not considered by FDA to be internal audits, and therefore are not exempt from review during FDA inspections.

"Responsibilities of sponsors include ensuring proper monitoring of the investigation . . . in order to secure compliance with the investigational plan . . . By not allowing FDA to *inspect and copy* all records related to the inspection, including the monitoring reports, the FDA investigators were unable to determine whether the monitoring for this study was adequate to ensure investigator compliance."

When the current monitoring regulations were first proposed, at least one company argued that monitoring, as a quality assurance function, would work more efficiently if it was not made subject to government audit. Further, the company argued that monitors' reports would be more candid and critical, and thus have more value to the sponsor in assuring that appropriate corrective actions are undertaken as needed. The FDA rejected this argument, stating: "FDA believes it should retain the authority to inspect records and reports relating to a sponsor's monitoring of clinical investigations under Part 312. Access to these materials helps the agency both to confirm that monitoring is actually taking place and to determine the nature of such monitoring. FDA also is not persuaded that the prospect of agency inspection of monitoring records and reports should significantly influence monitors in recording their observations and recommendations."

10.11 Q. Given the rapidly evolving drug development landscape, which is characterized by an increase in studies and sites, greater volume of activity at each site, the expansion/fluidity of the clinical investigator pool, the emergence of new "players" in new roles (e.g., CROs, SMOs), the use of new technologies, and the global expansion of clinical trials, FDA officials increasingly are speaking about the need for voluntary GCP-related quality assurance of clinical trial activities by industry sponsors. In fact, FDA officials have stated that quality assurance and quality improvement "should become prevailing themes in clinical research." Is quality assurance auditing, beyond what sponsors do in routine monitoring and quality control functions, a formal FDA requirement?

A. Although FDA officials note that quality assurance auditing has always been a "cornerstone of sponsor success in GCP," they concede that the lack of an "explicit regulatory requirement for auditing" has been a "silent topic" at the agency over the years. In the 1980s, the agency actually proposed requiring study auditing, but ultimately backed off such a requirement in favor of requiring that companies specify, in their NDAs/BLAs, whether auditing was conducted and, if so, for which studies. "Knowledge that a sponsor has audited subject records may affect the detail with which FDA conducts its own inspection of the supporting data," the FDA stated in the preamble to its 1987 IND regulations. "Moreover, in those cases where an agency inspection is not conducted, e.g., in some foreign countries, whether the sponsor has audited the study is an important factor to be considered in evaluating the study."

The FDA acknowledges the existence of industry quality assurance units in its compliance program 7348.810, which states that "clinical trial quality control units (QAUs) are not required by regulation. However, many sponsors have clinical QAUs that perform independent audits/data verifications to determine compliance with the study protocol clinical trial SOPs and FDA regulations. QAUs should be independent of, and separate from, routine monitoring or quality control functions."

While not required, sponsor QAU efforts may be reviewed during FDA inspections. During assessments of sponsors/monitors/CROs, FDA inspectors are instructed to determine if a firm conducts QA inspections and audits, to determine how the QAU is organized and operates (if one exists), to obtain a copy of written SOPs for QA audits and QAU operations, and to describe the separation of functions between the QAU and monitoring of clinical trials. Further, inspectors may, in some cases, be asked to compare the list of sponsor-audited trials identified in an NDA/BLA with the sponsor's records—FDA regulations require sponsors, if they have audited original subject records to verify the accuracy of the case reports submitted to them, to forward in the NDA a list identifying each audited clinical study. FDA compliance program 7348.810 notes that "findings that are the product of a written program of QA will not be inspected without prior concurrence of the assigning FDA headquarters unit."

The ICH GCP guidance also addresses clinical quality assurance auditing. In Section 5.19-Audit, the ICH GCP guideline states:

> "If or when sponsors perform audits, as part of implementing quality assurance, they should consider:
> 5.19.1 Purpose.
> > The purpose of a sponsor's audit, which is independent of and separate from routine monitoring or quality control functions, should be to evaluate trial conduct and compliance with the protocol, SOPs, GCP, and the applicable regulatory requirements.
> 5.19.2 Selection and Qualification of Auditors . . .
> 5.19.3 Auditing Procedures . . ."

The ICH GCP guideline establishes, however, that regulators should not routinely review sponsors' audit reports that document the observations and findings. "To preserve the independence and value of the audit function, the regulatory authority(ies) should not routinely request the audit reports. Regulatory authority(ies) may seek access to an audit report on a case-by-case basis, when evidence of serious GCP noncompliance exists, or in the course of legal proceedings."

In addition, the ICH GCP guideline's Section 6.11 identifies "quality control and quality assurance" among the "topics" that the contents of a clinical trial protocol should "generally" address.

10.12 Q. If a sponsor's protocol states that a study is to be conducted consistent with ICH GCP standards, do FDA inspectors audit against ICH standards? If not stated, does the agency audit only against FDA GCP standards?

A. Such statements will not affect the nature or focus of FDA clinical investigator or sponsor/monitor inspections. As a party to the ICH effort, the FDA maintains that its GCP regulations are entirely consistent with the ICH guideline, even though the ICH guideline is clearly more specific in several areas (see Q1.1 and Q1.5). Therefore, the agency does not conduct different types of inspections, or undertake different inspectional approaches, for determining compliance with FDA and ICH GCP standards.

According to CDER's Division of Scientific Investigations (DSI), the center's Bioresearch Monitoring Program (BIMO) is focused primarily on finding deviations from FDA GCP regulations and not deviations from ICH GCP guidelines or FDA guidelines. Following an FDA inspection of a clinical investigator, sponsor/monitor, or CRO, the Form 483-Inspectional Observations that the inspector leaves with the sponsor/monitor, investigator, or CRO should, according to CDER policy, identify *only* observed deviations from FDA GCP regulations. [Editor's note: a 483 is left at the site only if deviations are discovered]. Although deviations from FDA guidelines *should* be identified and discussed in the later-developed establishment inspection report (EIR) and *may* be discussed in a subsequent inspection-related FDA letter (e.g., untitled letter, warning letter) to the firm or investigator, these deviations will be identified separately from the deviations from FDA regulations. DSI staffers do not recall having seen any EIR or inspection-related CDER letter that identified or discussed any deviation specifically from the ICH GCP guideline.

> "We're always looking for ways to do bioresearch monitoring better. When you go out to a site to investigate, the things we're able to look at are relatively few. We compare one record with another. There's a lot of feeling that we're not always capturing the greatest essence of it. For example, we're very interested in how consent is given, but when you go to a place four years after the study was done, you don't learn a lot about that. One of the things we occasionally think about is whether we should do some more contemporaneous investigations of some of these things."
>
> Robert Temple, M.D., CDER's associate director for medical policy and director of Office of Drug Evaluation I, March 16, 2004

10.13 Q. Should companies that have active clinical quality assurance programs file, in the trial master file, documents regarding quality assurance pre-inspection visits, pre-inspection findings, and other documents that refer to any QA audit findings?

A. With one exception, all information regarding QA audits should be locked in file cabinets maintained by the QA or regulatory affairs department. These documents should include audit plans and reports, correspondence, and possibly contracts and non-disclosure agreements.

The only documents that should be stored in the trial master file are audit certificates. Most companies place the following information on such certificates: location, function, or investigator audited, date, auditor(s), and purpose of the audit. The trial master file might contain a number of audit certificates related to that particular study. These certificates may also be placed in study binders at sites, as well as in clinical study reports submitted to regulatory agencies.

Usually, audit reports are not shared with others outside a small cadre of clinical and regulatory staffers. One exception to this rule are "for cause" audit results, which may need to be shared with a wider audience, including the FDA, sponsor and institution upper-level management, and sponsor attorneys. For cause audits are those that focus on a site at which there have been documented GCP irregularities for a particular study.

10.14 Q. Is an investigator or a sponsor responsible for inaccurate data transcribed onto a case report form? In other words, if an FDA inspector cites an investigator for inaccurate case report form data, will the sponsor also be cited for not detecting the error?

A. The investigator is responsible for all study-related activities that take place at his or her site. This includes the transfer of data from medical records to case report forms. FDA inspectors will cite these errors on 483s that are issued to an investigator and on related reports relevant to the inspection (EIRs).

The FDA does note, however, that it may communicate directly with sponsors when serious regulatory deviations are discovered at clinical sites, particularly when site violations may be indicative of ineffective sponsor monitoring (see Q10.25). After issuing a clinical investigator a warning letter regarding regulatory deviations, "the FDA may inform both the study sponsor and the reviewing IRB of the deficiencies," the agency states in an Information Sheet entitled, "FDA Operations." "The Agency may also inform the sponsor if the clinical investigator's procedural deficiencies indicate ineffective monitoring by the sponsor. In addition to issuing these letters, FDA may take other courses of action, i.e., regulatory and/or administrative sanctions."

Data errors and omissions at one site in a multicenter study are not unusual, unexpected, or necessarily a regulatory disaster. What does constitute regulatory risk is a trend across inspected sites that demonstrates that the study was not well controlled. And, as noted above, the FDA's findings across clinical sites can trigger direct agency communication with the study's sponsor, particularly if the findings indicate "ineffective monitoring by the sponsor."

It is prudent for a sponsor to implement the following steps to minimize the chance of being cited for inaccurate CRF data:
- careful site selection and investigator due diligence
- site staff training (including training in what to expect during an FDA inspection)
- high quality monitoring and auditing
- early intervention and corrective action if a site struggles with GCP compliance

This latter step is an important consideration in potential regulatory sanctions against a sponsor.

10.15 Q. During 2004, there was a surge in the number of warning letters that the Center for Devices and Radiological Health (CDRH) issued to clinical investigators for GCP noncompliance. Does this represent a larger agency-wide crackdown, and are CDER and CBER likely to follow suit?

A. It does not appear so. During 2004, CDER did not issue a single warning letter to a clinical investigator (after issuing a few in 2003). Although far off the pace being set by CDRH, which issued 27 warning letters to clinical investigators during 2004, the Center for Biologics Evaluation and Research (CBER) issued eight investigator warning letters over this period.

While CDER is not planning any increase in inspectional or compliance activities involving clinical study investigators, center officials hope that organizational changes—in particular, DSI's pending move to CDER's Office of Compliance, which is expected by summer 2005—will result in at least a modest rise in warning letters to investigators.

10.16 Q. Why has CDER released so few warning letters to clinical investigators, sponsors/monitors, and others involved in the clinical research process during recent years?

A. Although CDER officials claim that they have developed many clinically focused warning letters over the past two years, few have been actually issued. According to some reports, policies and procedures within the FDA's Office of General Counsel (OGC) are preventing the release of the warning letters. Some point to an OGC policy requiring that warning letters be issued no later than four months from the date of a clinical investigator inspection has been particularly problematic.

As noted above, CDER officials hope that DSI's move to the center's Office of Compliance will help the center to issue more clinically focused warning letters going forward.

10.17 Q. How does CDER determine which clinical studies/sites will be inspected as part of a study-oriented inspection regarding a pending NDA?

A. As part of CDER's study-oriented (routine and associated with pending NDAs) inspection program, the FDA inspects a few hundred clinical investigators or clinical sites per year. In FY2004, CDER inspected 380 clinical investigators (over 80 of which were foreign investigators) in its study-oriented and "directed" (for cause) inspectional programs, up from 368 in FY2003 (CBER conducted 71 and CDRH conducted 187 clinical investigator inspections in 2004). Although clinical investigator inspections had declined in FY2001 and FY2002 due largely to the corresponding decline in NDA submissions, site inspections have increased more recently due to factors such as rapid growth in the number of foreign clinical investigator inspections and in the number of CDER directed, or "for cause," inspections undertaken in response to voluntary trial-related complaints reported to the center.

Traditionally, CDER's Division of Scientific Investigations (DSI) has used a sampling method to determine the number of sites and which sites within a particular study will be inspected, although that determination often has been influenced by other factors, including a protocol's complexity. Because of the inspectional program's nature, CDER does not release fine details regarding its criteria for selecting studies and sites for routine inspections. Obviously, however, a particular study's importance (e.g., pivotal) to an NDA and the ultimate approval decision will have a direct bearing on its likelihood of being inspected. CDER drug reviewers and DSI staff will also consider the number of subjects at a site and the number of dropouts at a site. Likewise, the agency will also consider the inspectional history of a site providing key data in making inspectional assignments—sites with problematic inspectional histories are more likely to be inspected. A site may also be selected as a result of a complaint received from a patient or from study staff (see Q10.1 and Q10.20).

In a March 2005 presentation, Joanne Rhoads, M.D., the director of CDER's DSI, noted that the agency, "may inspect from one to several clinical sites per pivotal multicenter trial. For crucial primary efficacy endpoints, FDA may check the accuracy of a sponsor's data listings versus source documents for a sample of up to 100 percent of the subjects. Other elements—for example, the integrity of blinding, drug accountability, etcetera—and safety data such as the reporting of serious adverse events and adverse events to the sponsor and IRB are checked for accuracy in a sample of the subject's records."

Although CDER had been developing an internal policies and procedures manual to describe the study and site selection and assignment process, that project has been on hold since mid-1999.

10.18 Q. Have CDER officials given any recent indications about what inspectors specifically look at and for during today's clinical investigator inspections?

A. Much can be learned about the inspection process by reviewing CDER's various compliance program guides for FDA inspectors, in this case GCP 7348.811—Bioresearch Monitoring: Clinical Investigators. In a March 2005 presentation, Joanne Rhoads, M.D., the director of CDER's DSI, outlined several inspectional focal points during FDA audits of clinical investigator records, which involves a comparison of the source medical record data versus the case report forms versus the data listing submitted in the pending NDA submission.

During her presentation, Rhoads highlighted 11 determinations that an FDA inspector must make during a clinical investigator inspection:

- What was the source of the subjects?
- Did the subjects exist?
- Did they have the disease under study?
- Did they meet inclusion/exclusion criteria?
- Was consent obtained?
- Was IRB review obtained?
- Was the clinical protocol followed?
- Did the subjects receive the assigned study drug in the dose, route and frequency specified by the protocol?
- Are the case report forms complete and in agreement with source data (compare with NDA data listing)?
- Are adverse experiences reported to the sponsor and IRB?
- Are records adequate and complete?

10.19 Q. And what about the selection criteria for foreign inspections? Given the resources involved in conducting inspections of some international trial sites, do they differ at all from those used for domestic inspections?

A. In a March 2005 presentation, Joanne Rhoads, M.D., the director of CDER's DSI, stated that international sites may be audited:

- If there are insufficient domestic clinical data to support a new drug's approval;
- If only foreign clinical data are submitted in support of an application;
- If domestic and foreign data show conflicting results pertinent to decision-making; or
- If there is a serious issue to resolve (e.g., suspicion of fraud, scientific misconduct, significant human subject protection violations).

10.20 Q. How, if at all, is the growing number of voluntary clinical trial-related complaints that the agency is receiving affecting the nature of the FDA's GCP and clinical trial inspection and compliance activities?

A. Within CDER, these voluntary complaints continue to drive significant inspectional activities. And with a new CDER DSI website (www.fda.gov/cder/offices/dsi/index.htm) and the agency's hope to put its compliant form on the website so that trial-related complaints can be forwarded anonymously and more conveniently, CDER continues to view complaints as an important element of its emerging risk-based GCP compliance effort.

In calendar year 2004, CDER received over 200 voluntary complaints, a roughly 50% increase over the number received in 2003. These complaints continue to drive CDER's record levels of "directed" inspections, which are undertaken when the FDA has cause to suspect an issue with study conduct. Although off the record high of 109 in FY2003, the estimated 90 directed inspections undertaken during FY2004 represented a near-record level. It also may reflect the FDA's continuing attempts to use a "risk-based" strategy by focusing its inspections on the highest-risk and highest-impact areas.

While the FDA has not released any formal figures on the nature of the voluntary complaints, DSI officials said in informal comments that most of the complaints are being submitted by drug sponsors and monitors, followed by private citizens. In most cases, the complaints relate to a belief that the trial data are not being collected properly, or that study participants are being put at unnecessary risk.

10.21 Q. Although it conducts far fewer inspections of sponsors/monitors and CROs, how does CDER determine which companies it will inspect?

A. While CDER's sponsor/monitor/CRO inspection program has not been the centerpiece of the BIMO program, inspectional activity in this area has risen due to the FDA's increased focus on monitoring. At the direction of CDER's Division of Scientific Investigations, FDA field inspectors conducted 15 sponsor/monitor/CRO inspections in FY2002 and another 17 in FY2003 (the latest year for which data are available), down significantly from the 27 inspections conducted in FY2001. Like that seen in clinical investigator inspections, this decline is likely due, at least in part, to a downturn in industry drug submissions.

It is important to note that FDA officials believe that, in conducting clinical investigator inspections, the agency is also to a large extent assessing a sponsor/monitor/CRO's performance in monitoring a study. In this sense, the agency's assessment of sponsor/monitor and CRO performance is much more wide-ranging than the 20-some inspections it conducts in this area annually.

Since there are so few sponsor/monitor/CRO inspections, CDER focuses its efforts in two areas: (1) sponsors/monitors/CROs involved in high-priority applications (high profile drugs, new molecular entities, priority NDAs); and (2) sponsors/monitors/CROs that are the subject of a complaint.

10.22 Q. What steps should site staff take to verify that a person claiming to be an FDA inspector is such, and can site staff limit an FDA inspector's access in any way?

A. Although there have always been threats over "imposter" FDA inspectors (e.g., a sponsor's competitor gaining access to proprietary data), there are increased threats today. Recent press reports, for example, disclosed that financial analysts covering the pharmaceutical industry are taking increasingly aggressive steps to gain access to clinical data, including posing as clinical trial subjects and enrolling in trials as well as posing as other prospective investigators to ask clinical investigators and site staff about the perceived utility of experimental drugs.

When the FDA inspector arrives at the clinical site, he or she should be asked to show "FDA credentials," which will include a photo ID that looks similar to a driver's license, and to present a Notice of Inspection (FDA Form-482) to the clinical investigator. (*Note:* the FDA does not issue 482s for foreign inspections.)

Appropriate site staff should accompany the inspector at all times. Because FDA inspections should be limited to the records pertaining to clinical studies, the site may consider storing or keeping all study records in a location separate from other office records. Study-related offices, office equipment, and medical equipment can be inspected as part of the inspector's assessment of their adequacy and proper functioning.

If an inspection is conducted under a search warrant, then any and all records, offices, and equipment must be made available. Search warrants are sought under criminal investigations and are issued by a court only when the agency can show probable cause that a crime (generally fraud) has been committed or is being committed on the premises, or when the "fruits or instrumentalities" of a crime (e.g., study data) may be found on the premises.

10.23 Q. Is the sponsor/monitor or contract research organization (CRO) permitted to be present during an FDA inspection of a clinical trial site?

A. Although there is no FDA prohibition against a sponsor/monitor/CRO representative being present during an FDA site inspection, such a practice would be unconventional. Some sponsors do want to be present during inspections, however.

Sites are advised to alert a sponsor of upcoming inspections so that the company may assist with preparations.

10.24 Q. Are non-FDA site audits ever conducted without a sponsor's knowledge?

A. Occasionally a CRO, SMO, academic institution, or other private entity will conduct an audit of a site without a sponsor's knowledge. These audits are conducted for "self improvement," and to correct deficiencies. In some cases, findings from these "internal" audits should be shared with sponsors, since there may be actions that a sponsor's clinical management should take to inform regulatory agencies, to close sites, and/or to resolve significant GCP problems.

10.25 Q. In the FDA's Information Sheet entitled, "FDA Operations," the agency states that, after issuing a warning letter to a clinical investigator identifying "serious" deviations, the agency "may inform both the study sponsor and the reviewing IRB of the deficiencies. The Agency may also inform the sponsor if the clinical investigator's procedural deficiencies indicate ineffective monitoring by the sponsor." Specifically, according to current agency policy, in what types of situations are sponsors notified by FDA of clinical

investigator inspection results and how? And when investigator inspections reveal/suggest ineffective monitoring and the agency informs the sponsor, how is this done and what generally is the agency's follow-up action?

A. Although it has the option of pro-actively informing sponsors and IRBs of problem investigators, in practice, CDER's DSI does not generally do so until it has issued some type of regulatory letter to the investigator (e.g., warning letter). If CDER does not believe that the problems resulted from inadequate monitoring (see discussion below), it will simply notify the sponsors and IRBs by forwarding them a copy of the agency's letter to the investigator. If the agency is seeking to disqualify the investigator or to recommend that the investigator's data not be considered in a premarketing application's review, CDER will ask the sponsor to evaluate the submission to assess whether the submission is still approvable without the data in question. In some cases, eliminating an investigator's data from an NDA's clinical database has prevented ultimate approval, while in other cases it has not. Theoretically, the agency could also withdraw the approval of a marketed product if that approval was based on data that were later discovered to be false or unverifiable.

If an FDA site inspection reveals seriously inadequate monitoring by the sponsor or CRO, CDER will almost invariably respond with an unannounced "for cause" inspection of the sponsor or CRO to verify the findings at the site and/or gather more data. Although it is not required to do so, CDER generally prefers to determine whether the inadequate monitoring is a systematic problem (i.e., as opposed to an isolated case) before taking formal action against the sponsor or CRO. When such inspections reveal or confirm inadequate monitoring, CDER will then generally issue an untitled or warning letter (see Q10.28).

10.26 Q. Can a clinical investigator or site re-schedule an FDA inspection of the site if the investigator will not be available on that date?

A. For routine inspections, the FDA field inspector contacts the clinical site by telephone to schedule the inspection. The advance notice provided for routine inspections can range from a few days to a few weeks, and can be a function of several factors, including the field inspector's schedule and the time demands associated with the subject NDA's review. Generally, the agency is somewhat more flexible in scheduling inspections with clinical investigators than with sponsors/CROs, since many investigators have demanding daily patient loads.

While it acknowledges the practical difficulties in making pre-arranged inspectional "appointments" with clinical investigators, the FDA also instructs its inspectors not to delay such appointments unnecessarily. "The FDA inspector should, however, keep the time span between initial contact and actual inspection as short as possible," the agency states in Compliance Program 7341.811 on clinical investigator inspections. "What appears to be undue delay (such as more than ten working days without sufficient justification) of the inspection on the part of the clinical investigator shall be reported immediately to the Center."

In practice, there are likely to be, from the FDA's perspective, what might be termed legitimate inconveniences and unacceptable inconveniences:

Legitimate inconvenience: long-standing professional engagement overseas; PI illness; death of family member; facility and case records destroyed by natural disaster.

Unacceptable inconvenience: patients scheduled for all suggested days; must attend son's soccer match; study coordinator scheduled for vacation; cannot get hospital records on such short notice; clinic is moving to a new location; lack of facility space for FDA inspector.

The FDA inspector will listen to a clinical investigator's concerns and will consider the legitimacy of reasons for postponement. Generally, the FDA will not tolerate unacceptable excuses. An FDA supervisor may be brought into the negotiations. Ideally, the principal investigator should not appear to be hostile, evasive, or uncooperative, and should, in most instances, "make room" on his or her schedule to accommodate the inspection. To do otherwise gets the inspection process started under less-than-favorable circumstances, and inspectors, like most human beings, wish to be treated as respected professionals.

It is important to note that the FDA is willing, when faced with tight time demands, to conduct routine inspections when the principal investigator is not present. In such cases, the FDA asks that the investigator ensure that there will be someone there to provide the FDA inspector with access to a work area and to the records. When necessary, the agency can contact the principal investigator following the inspection to ask questions, seek clarifications, or discuss important issues. If an investigator cannot be present for a routine inspection, a situation that FDA staffers emphasize is less than ideal for several reasons, the FDA will present the 482 (Notice of Inspection) to the most senior-level person at the site (e.g., a sub-investigator, study coordinator) upon arrival (FDA inspectors are trained to seek out the "top management official" at the site), and will leave the Form 483-Inspectional Observations with that individual as well following the inspection. In short, for routine FDA audits, the principal investigator's presence is highly preferable, but is not absolutely necessary in all cases.

While the principal investigator's presence is not absolutely necessary for certain routine inspections, the same is not true during for-cause inspections. For such inspections, the investigator's presence probably will be necessary. In addition, his or her convenience and schedule are not likely to be accommodated as willingly by the FDA.

The FDA's willingness to accommodate the principal investigator is likely to depend on several factors. When the FDA is not under tight time constraints, the agency will be more willing to accommodate the investigator and his/her schedule. If the agency is under time constraints or there are questions about the site (e.g., for-cause inspection), the investigator's convenience will be far less significant a factor, and may even be of no significance due to larger issues (e.g., timeline pressures, patient safety).

It is important to bear in mind that advance notification and negotiation of inspection dates are courtesies the FDA extends to sites. Under the law, the FDA may inspect at any "reasonable time," which both the agency and the courts have interpreted as meaning any time the site is in operation. A refusal to permit a legally authorized inspection is a criminal act, and may lead to prosecution or other sanctions. In such cases, the FDA also has the option of obtaining an Administrative Inspection Warrant, which is not the same as a search warrant. An Administrative Inspection Warrant is an affirmation by a Judge or Magistrate of the agency's right to inspect. It does not change the scope of the inspection; however, the FDA serves

Administrative Inspection Warrants in the company of a Deputy United States Marshall. Continued refusal will likely lead to the arrest of the person making the refusal.

10.27 Q. Can the FDA request that a clinical trial site not contact a sponsor regarding an upcoming site inspection?

A. In general, if the FDA is conducting a routine inspection, it anticipates that a sponsor will be notified by site staff and that the sponsor will probably take action to assess GCP compliance prior to the FDA visit. If the FDA is worried that a particular sponsor may "paper over" problems, it can simply show up unannounced. Unannounced "for cause" FDA site inspections rarely occur, however, and all routine inspections are announced.

10.28 Q. There are many types of FDA letters and communications associated with an FDA inspection of a clinical investigator, including Form 483s, establishment inspection reports, "untitled" letters, and warning letters, among others. Following the FDA's inspection of a clinical trial site, what is the sequence of such FDA communications, and what is the sequence of letters and actions if significant noncompliance is found?

A. At the inspectional "close-out" meeting or "exit interview," during which an FDA inspector discusses his or her findings and the inspectional outcome with the clinical investigator at the end of the inspection, the inspector will present a Form 483-Inspectional Observations to the clinical investigator only if apparent violations of FDA regulations were observed during the inspection. If no violations were observed, the FDA inspector will not issue a 483. Although FDA inspectors may note deviations from FDA guidance documents (e.g., FDA GCP guidance) in their inspectional reports, these deviations are not cited on the 483 unless they are also violations of the regulations. The FDA-483 is the FDA investigator's report to the site of those things that, in the opinion of the investigator, may include violations. Form FDA-483 does not represent a final FDA position, and upon internal FDA review, its contents may be overturned in whole or in part.

In February 2003, in fact, the FDA added "standard language" to FDA-483s to emphasize this very point and to discuss the 483 recipient's options immediately following the inspectional observations. According to the FDA's Investigations Operations Manual (2004), FDA-483s must include the following statement: "This document lists observations made by the FDA representative(s) during the inspection of your facility. They are inspectional observations, and do not represent a final Agency determination regarding your compliance. If you have an objection regarding an observation, or have implemented, or plan to implement, corrective action in response to an observation, you may discuss the objection or action with the FDA representative(s) during the inspection or submit this information to FDA at the address above. If you have any questions, please contact FDA at the phone number and address above." While FDA officials did not expect this statement to affect inspections, they felt that it might reduce the frequency with which they must explain why FDA-483 inspection observations do not always appear on subsequent regulatory letters, and why all issues subsequently identified in regulatory letters might not have appeared in the FDA-483.

Upon returning to the FDA district office, the investigator will write an inspectional report, formally called an Establishment Inspection Report (EIR), which will include a more detailed description of the violations of FDA regulations and relevant matters identified during the inspection. It also correlates the narrative findings to the associated documentation (that is, the evidence) obtained by the FDA inspector during the inspection. FDA's Compliance Program 7348.811 regarding inspections of clinical investigators states that, although identified deviations from guidance documents should not be noted in the 483, they "should be discussed with [agency] management and documented in the EIR." In short, the EIR documents all the findings that could significantly impact the FDA's decision-making process, including an NDA/BLA approval decision. Once the EIR is cleared by FDA district office management, it is forwarded to the compliance staff in the relevant center—for inspections of sites conducting studies in support of drug or biologic products, the EIRs would be forwarded to the bioresearch monitoring (BIMO) staff in CDER (Division of Scientific Investigations) or CBER (Bioresearch Monitoring Branch), or to CDRH (Center for Devices and Radiological Health) for medical devices.

The BIMO staff will review the EIR to evaluate the significance of the deviations. As part of this process, the BIMO staff will categorize the deviations, which will in effect determine the nature of the compliance or enforcement action that is necessary, if any (see discussion below). The BIMO staff forwards its recommendations on the inspected study to the relevant review division. This recommendation may be, for example, that the data from the inspected site should or should not be considered in the agency's NDA review process due to the inspectional findings. The division reviewing the NDA or BLA will then consider this recommendation in the context of its overall application approval/non approval decision.

After assessing the violations and deviations found during the inspection, CDER or CBER BIMO staff will then classify the inspection results into one of three categories:

A. NAI (no action indicated)—No objectionable conditions or practices were found during the inspection (or the objectionable conditions found do not justify further regulatory action). In such cases, the FDA will generally forward the site a so-called "untitled letter" indicating that no compliance problems were discovered. (Note: FDA officials point out that the agency's various product centers may employ different practices in communicating NAIs and VAIs with sponsors. The practices depicted here are understood to be the practices of CDER's BIMO).

B. VAI (voluntary action indicated)—Objectionable conditions or practices were found, but the agency is not prepared to take or recommend any administrative or regulatory action. In these cases, the FDA will generally forward an "untitled letter" to identify the areas of non-major noncompliance found during the inspection. In the letter, the FDA will encourage the site to address these areas, and may state that the agency will assess the site's activities in such areas during a future inspection. Increasingly, however, such letters will ask clinical investigators to develop and submit to the agency a remedial action plan to address the noted deficiencies.

C. OAI (official action indicated)—Regulatory and/or administrative actions will be recommended. An OAI classification means that the FDA discovered that a site or investigator was found to have objectionable practices or conditions that represent significant departures from FDA regulations. When inspections trigger OAI classifications, the agency will generally issue a warning letter to the clinical investigator. According to the FDA, a warning letter "is an informal advisory to a firm communicating the Agency's position on a matter but does not commit FDA to taking enforcement action. The agency's policy is that a warning letter should be issued for violations that are of regulatory significance in that failure to adequately and promptly take [corrective action] may be expected to result in enforcement action should the violation(s) continue." Therefore, the FDA takes the position that a warning letter is not a final agency decision to take action. For that reason, courts have refused to extend judicial review to warning letters.

In some cases, the FDA will also notify the relevant IRB and sponsor (e.g., if the findings indicated ineffective monitoring) of the deficiencies. In warning letters, the FDA will ask the clinical investigator to respond, usually with a specific remedial action plan, to address the compliance problems. Generally, clinical investigators (sometimes after additional communication with the agency) are able to develop remedial action plans that are acceptable to the FDA. The agency may re-inspect the site following its implementation of a remedial action plan, but will likely re-inspect the next time that data from that investigator are included in a regulatory submission (i.e., compliance history is a factor in FDA inspectional assignments).

When there is evidence of severe noncompliance, the FDA may issue, instead of a warning letter, a Notice of Initiation of Disqualification Proceedings and Opportunity to Explain, or NIDPOE, letter. According to the FDA, NIDPOE letters "inform the recipient clinical investigator that FDA is initiating an administrative proceeding to determine whether the clinical investigator should be disqualified from receiving investigational products pursuant to FDA's regulations. Generally, the FDA issues a NIDPOE letter when it believes it has evidence that the clinical investigator repeatedly or deliberately violated FDA's regulations governing the proper conduct of clinical studies involving investigational products or submitted false information to the sponsor."

10.29 Q. And how does the enforcement process proceed if the FDA finds the investigator's response to the NIDPOE letter unsatisfactory?

A. Assuming that the FDA still wants to pursue formal regulatory action (e.g., disqualifying or restricting the investigator), the agency will then provide the investigator with a Notice of Opportunity for Hearing (NOOH) letter. At any point in this process (i.e., following the issuance of the NIDPOE letter), the investigator can enter into a "consent agreement," under which the investigator chooses not to dispute the FDA's charges further and agrees to be disqualified. The signing of a consent agreement will put an end to the FDA's administrative processes, but will not shield the investigator from other possible judicial action in the future, including injunction or criminal prosecution if warranted. Disqualified investigators are not eligible to receive investigational drugs, biologics, or devices. In some cases, disqualified investigators can be "reinstated." The FDA's disqualified clinical investigator list is available at www.fda.gov/ora/compliance_ref/bimo/disqlist.htm.

When the clinical investigator provides new information that convinces the agency that disqualification is not warranted, the agency may enter into so-called "restricted agreements." Clinical investigators on the FDA's restricted list remain eligible to receive investigational drugs, provided that they conduct regulated studies in accordance with the restrictions specified in their agreement. Such restrictions, which are case specific and are based on the nature of the violations discovered, may comprise numerous different provisions. The restrictions may, for example, limit the number of studies in which a particular individual can participate as the principal investigator over a specific time period, may permit the investigator to serve only as a co-investigator or sub-investigator, may require the investigator to work under a proctor, or may require the investigator to have direct personal involvement in specific aspects of the trial. In some cases, restrictions can be removed at a later date, and some restrictions apply only for a certain time period (e.g., three years). The FDA's list of restricted investigators is available at www.fda.gov/ora/compliance_ref/biom/restlist.htm.

When a clinical investigator wants to dispute FDA claims (i.e., to avoid disqualification), he or she will be granted a regulatory hearing, during which the investigator will be given the opportunity to explain his or her actions before an impartial "presiding officer" designated by the FDA commissioner. The agency will also present information in support of its proposed decision to disqualify the investigator. Following the hearing, the presiding officer will issue a report with recommendations to the FDA commissioner, who will then review the presiding officer's report and make a decision on the investigator's eligibility to receive investigational articles.

10.30 Q. And how does the sequence of inspectional, compliance, and enforcement actions differ in the case of a sponsor/monitor inspection?

A. The process through which the FDA communicates, and follows up on, the results of sponsor/monitor inspections is virtually identical to the process described above for clinical investigators, except in the final stage of the process—that is, there is no process through which sponsors can be disqualified or restricted.

Although issues regarding sponsor/monitor or CRO GCP noncompliance are almost uniformly addressed earlier in the enforcement process, the so-called Application Integrity Policy (AIP) is, at least theoretically, available to the agency as a last resort in cases of severe noncompliance. Under the AIP, the agency can take certain actions, including deferring a review of a company's applications, when there is evidence of a pattern or practice of wrongful conduct (e.g., submitting a fraudulent application, offering a bribe, making an untrue statement of material fact) that raises questions about the data submitted in an application.

The FDA has invoked the AIP policy for several firms based on severe cases of GCP noncompliance, although such cases have typically been in the medical device area. When a firm is placed under the AIP, the FDA will not consider any further submissions until all issues have been resolved to the agency's satisfaction. The AIP also triggers a wide array of internal activities, including mandated internal investigations by third parties with deliverables to the FDA and possible removal of personnel who are suspected of having committed deliberate wrongful acts.

10.31 Q. And what about debarment? Is debarment relevant to clinical investigators and others involved in clinical trials?

A. Yes it is. Introduced under the Generic Drug Enforcement Act of 1992, debarment is a sanction that the FDA is now using more aggressively against clinical investigators and even research staff. The sanction is reserved, however, for cases in which an individual is convicted of certain crimes or found to have engaged in certain types of severe misconduct (i.e., as opposed to minor regulatory noncompliance). When the FDA debars a person, that individual cannot provide any services to an applicant with an approved or pending drug or biologic product application. For clinical investigators, debarment is a sanction that goes beyond a disqualification (see Q10.29). While a disqualification simply disqualifies a person from serving as a clinical investigator, debarment prevents an individual from "providing any services" to a drug product applicant.

The agency can also debar a firm convicted of certain crimes from obtaining or participating in certain subsequent drug approvals. Applicants for drug product approval are required to certify that they did not and will not use the services of a debarred individual or firm in any capacity in connection with the application.

In a series of separate, but related, debarment actions in late 2002, it was clear that the FDA was sending a message to those involved in clinical trials. The FDA moved to debar not only former clinical investigator Robert Fiddes, M.D., but three members of his clinical study staff as well. This is the first time the agency is known to have debarred clinical research coordinators/study nurses. In 1997, Fiddes was convicted of conspiring to make false statements to the FDA, a conviction based on Fiddes participating in, directing, and encouraging the submission of false information (i.e., falsifying and fabricating clinical data) to sponsors in required clinical study reports used by the FDA in assessing drug safety and effectiveness. The three members of Fiddes' research staff were also convicted of felonies, which served as the basis for their debarments (one of the three debarments was subsequently rescinded, at least temporarily, in early 2003).

10.32 Q. Does the FDA perform routine inspections of sites conducting trials under INDs for which the investigator is the sponsor (i.e., sponsor-investigator)?

A. Typically, no. Generally, what triggers a routine inspection of a site is the submission of clinical or other data in an NDA and the need for the FDA to base important regulatory decision-making on those data. Since the limited data (a few patients per site) collected by a sponsor-investigator are not typically collected for, or submitted in, a marketing application on which the FDA must make a regulatory decision, these sites are not typically inspected. The exception would be the case in which a possible problem comes to light, a situation that would likely trigger a "for cause" inspection.

Events that might trigger a "for cause" inspection include a "whistleblower" (informant) report to the FDA, reports of possible fraud or of serious adverse reactions, or a complaint from the drug's manufacturer that an investigator is inappropriately studying the drug for an off-label purpose, among others.

10.33 Q. How are GCP inspection findings shared with FDA reviewers considering approval of a new drug?

A. Reports of site inspections, which may be conducted by the field offices or directly by CDER's DSI, are written up and sent for a "compliance review" by CDER's DSI. If no major GCP compliance or data problems are found, DSI will author a letter highlighting the findings and minor compliance issues and send the letter to both the site/sponsor and the NDA review division. At the end of the letter, DSI will include a specific "Note to the Medical Reviewer" that will detail what was inspected (site, patients, number of CRFs verified, etc.), and the inspectional results (e.g., minor noncompliance detected). In this "Note" section, DSI will also make a specific recommendation on whether the data that were inspected should or should not be used in the NDA review and decision-making process.

If, in reviewing inspectional results, DSI finds possible major noncompliance regarding a site that provided data for an NDA, the division will immediately (and possibly before the formal review is complete), issue what is called a DEW letter, or distant early warning letter, not only to the division evaluating the NDA, but to all other CDER divisions and other FDA centers to inform them that the data/practices of a specific investigator may be seriously problematic. The issuance of this letter will then trigger a more involved and specific dialogue between DSI officials and the NDA's medical reviewers to assess the potential problem. The quickly issued DEW letter puts everyone at FDA on notice, and ensures that other data from the investigator are not used in pending regulatory decisions while DSI investigates and addresses the key compliance issues.

10.34 Q. What should the sponsor do if, during an FDA audit of a sponsor, the inspector requests copies of the sponsor's internal audit reports?

A. The agency's position is that, while it has the legal right to access these reports, it will exercise enforcement discretion and not ask for them except under specific circumstances. Financial data are specifically exempt from FDA review under the Food, Drug and Cosmetic Act, Section 704(B).

It is the FDA's published policy to not routinely request access to internal audits, as stated in the FDA Compliance Policy Guide No. 7151.02, "FDA access to results of quality assurance program audits and inspections" (March 1979 and revised January 1996) (*Federal Register,* Vol. 54, Vo.56, p.12285, March 24, 1989). In summary, the policy states:

> "During routine inspections and investigations conducted at any regulated entity that has a written quality assurance program, FDA will not review or copy reports and records that result from audits and inspections of the written quality assurance program, including audits conducted under 21 CFR 820.20(b) and written status reports required by 21 CFR 58.35(b)(4).
> "FDA may seek written certification that such audits and inspections have been implemented, performed, and documented and that any required corrective action has been taken. District personnel should consult with the appropriate headquarters office prior to seeking written certification."

The policy goes on to describe specific instances that are not considered "routine," and that, therefore, justify requests for access to internal audit reports. One such instance is the case of a "directed," or "for-cause," inspection.

Therefore, when faced with an FDA inspector who requests access to an internal audit report, the inspected site (or sponsor) should politely point out the content of this agency policy and inquire as to whether the inspection is being conducted on a "for cause" basis (i.e., the stated exception to the rule). Another alternative would be for the site or sponsor to inform the FDA investigator that, while it is not refusing access to the reports, it wishes first to confer with the investigator's supervisor or a District Office Compliance Officer to clarify that the request is in accordance with FDA policy.

10.35 Q. Do the FDA regional offices or even headquarters have written metrics, measures and indicators of efficiency and effectiveness regarding GCP inspector/inspection performance? For example, would the agency expect an investigator to be able to source verify at least two subjects' case records within an eight-hour day? If so, what are these metrics?

A. There are no quantitative metrics of this sort. FDA district offices, however, do implement detailed reviews of FDA-483 observations, narrative establishment inspection reports and accompanying evidence. In addition, agency supervisors occasionally accompany inspectors to observe their performance during actual inspections.

Through management controls exercised along a chain of command (district, regional, and headquarters offices) as well as training standards and programs, the FDA attempts to make its inspections adhere to a uniform approach and to produce findings that are consistent with regulations and issued guidance.

Further Reading

Bruckheimer, Michael, "FDA's Inspections of Clinical Investigators," *Drug Information Journal,* 27:213-16, 1993.

Curran, Charles F., "Preparing a Clinical Site for a Clinical Investigator Inspection by the FDA," *Drug Information Journal,* 33:253-59, 1999.

Mackintosh, D. and Molloy, V., "10 Steps for Improving FDA GCP Inspections," *Applied Clinical Trials,* 11(6):44-48, June 2002.

Acknowledgments

Douglas Mackintosh, DrPH, MBA, MS Hyg, and Vernette Molloy, MBA, RN, of GCPA, Inc.; David Chesney, KMI, Waltham, MA; Margaret Marshall, RN, MS, former Associate Director of Quality Assurance, Wyeth-Lederle Vaccines, Pearl River, NY.

Section 11:
Computerized Systems, e-Clinical Trials, and Part 11
by Lisa A. Olson, John C. McKenney, and Keith Benze
SEC Associates, Inc.

The Internet and World Wide Web continue to transform the way clinical trials are conducted. From small Phase 1 trials to huge, global Phase 3 trials, virtually every aspect of clinical studies is evolving due to technological advances. The introduction of hand-held computers and other technologies for use as patient diaries is having a dramatic impact on the way patient data are collected. Email is replacing the fax machine for query resolution and may ultimately become the preferred method for issuing mandatory notifications to clinical investigators and IRBs. Web-enabled applications are greatly simplifying software and hardware requirements at clinical sites. Recognizing this, the FDA developed and implemented, in August 1997, its electronic records/electronic signatures regulation (21 CFR Part 11) to define the controls and procedures that the agency expects industry to use when it employs electronic records and electronic signatures in regulated activities, such as conducting clinical trials, submitting regulatory applications, and manufacturing pharmaceuticals.

The FDA's interpretation and enforcement of Part 11 requirements have evolved considerably since August 1997. One of the more recent initiatives came in August 2003, when the FDA issued a new Part 11 Scope and Application guidance document. Through this guidance, the FDA considerably liberalized its interpretation of and approach to Part 11. While this has been largely seen as good news for industry, the agency's emerging Part 11 policy and approach has spawned a new generation of issues and questions. In September 2004, the FDA released a draft revision of its 1999 guidance entitled, *Computerized Systems Used in Clinical Trials,* in part to bring the guidance in line with the risk-based regulatory approach espoused in the Scope and Applications guidance.

The questions and answers in this section represent a small subset of those included in a more comprehensive text entitled, *"The "New" Part 11 and Drug Development: A Q&A Reference Guide"* (March 2004). This resource was developed specifically to address the most important and difficult questions following the recent and dramatic shift in the FDA's interpretation of and approach to Part 11 requirements. See www.barnettinternational.com for more information on this reference guide.

11.1 Q. If finalized in its current form, in what ways would the FDA's draft guidance entitled, "Computerized Systems Used in Clinical Trials" (September 2004) change the regulatory/compliance environment for electronic systems used in clinical trials?

A. In 1999, the FDA issued a final guidance entitled, "Computerized Systems Used in Clinical Trials" to provide recommendations on the use of electronic systems for the collection of clinical trial data. This document was helpful to industry, particularly since the predicate regulations relevant to clinical trials for drugs do not mention automation, computer systems, or electronic records. The guidance, however, was fairly prescriptive, and many held that it asked for more than what was readily available to the pharmaceutical industry in most vendor software. Subsequently, the

FDA issued an August 2003 guidance entitled, "Part 11, Electronic Records; Electronic Signatures—Scope and Application," which pointed industry back to the predicate regulations for direction on system requirements. In cases in which the predicates were not clear, the Scope and Application guidance directed industry to take a risk-based approach to determine whether validation and certain Part 11 requirements should be implemented (e.g., based on an assessment of a system's impact on the accuracy, reliability, integrity, availability, and authenticity of required records and signatures, see Q11.3 below).

Certain elements of the FDA's 2003 Part 11 Scope and Application guidance were in conflict with the 1999 computerized systems in clinical trials guidance, however. In September 2004, the FDA issued for public comment a draft revision of the computerized systems guidance. The draft revision is considerably more in line with the risk-based approach recommended in the Scope and Application guidance, and provides more suggestions and alternatives. The draft revision recognizes, for example, that certified copies can be retained in place of original records, and that the collection and processing of clinical data can be reconstructed via a system documentation trail and record controls without retaining original computer hardware and software. The draft also reiterates the importance of security controls, protected access mechanisms, and customer responsibility for the final validation of purchased software. The document references the FDA's January 2002 guidance entitled, "General Principles of Software Validation" as a resource on computer validation concepts.

Given the current emphasis on predicate rules and the lack of GCP references on computer systems, the computer systems guidance is particularly important for the clinical trial community. And with the increasing attention being paid to electronic data capture (EDC) by both industry and the agency, the guidance provides relevant recommendations to help system implementers determine direction and controls.

11.2 Q. There seems to be increasing attention around the subject of electronic patient-reported outcomes (ePRO). Are there any Part 11 implications for ePRO?

A. Electronic patient reported outcomes (ePRO) frequently involve the use of patient diaries to capture information such as symptoms, pain levels, etc. directly from study subjects. These diaries may be implemented through a variety of technologies, including PDA devices, interactive voice response (IVR) systems, or even web-based questionnaires. As such, these systems involve software that implements the study questions, effects branching to other questions, or triggers error-handling routines based on patient responses. Since the software essentially translates the IRB-approved protocol into an electronic format, validation is highly recommended to ensure that the software operates correctly and that mid-study changes do not adversely affect prior functionality or data. Furthermore, some ePRO devices require remote uploading of patient data to a central server. Validation activities should include verification that such data uploads are accurate and complete, and that proper steps are followed in the event of an incomplete transfer. Validation is warranted even absent a specific predicate rule requirement for it, due to the critical nature of ePRO.

Another important consideration is that case history records are required by predicate rule, and the patient diary may be considered part of this case history.

Therefore, if the patient diary is part of the case history and the diary is electronic, then Part 11 applies. In this case, several Part 11 requirements would come into play, such as the attributability of input to the system user. In other words, ePRO systems should include a means of identifying the individual who is entering data, whether it be the patient or a clinical investigator or study coordinator.

Another example of an applicable Part 11 requirement is found in 11.10(i), which requires that individuals using electronic record systems (including PDAs) be properly trained in their use. Since ePRO systems involve users who are not part of the sponsor or clinical organization (i.e., the patients), there are issues with ensuring that they understand how to use the system or device, what is expected in terms of timing of entry, operating the upload process, and contact persons if there is a problem. It is advisable that sites conduct and document this training as each patient is enrolled.

At this writing, CDER was preparing to release its first guidance on so-called patient-reported outcomes (PRO). Although the guidance addresses PRO generally, the push to get the guidance out was fueled, in part, by electronic PRO collection, and by technology vendors that were anxious for the agency to provide guidance in the area (e.g., instrument validation).

11.3 *Q. Increasingly, personal digital assistants (PDAs) are being used as patient diaries in clinical trials. Must the PDAs be compliant with Part 11?*

A. If the PDA contains the source data for the patient diary (i.e., there is no source paper record that is transcribed into the PDA), then the source data is electronic and must comply with Part 11. The fact that the records will be uploaded to a central server on a periodic basis does not negate the requirement that the PDA be Part 11 compliant.

In a July 2001 presentation entitled, "Considerations in the Use of Handheld & Web-Enabled Data Capture," James F. McCormack, Ph.D., then bioresearch monitoring program coordinator within the FDA's Office of Regulatory Affairs, explored many of the critical Part 11 issues that must be considered when using PDAs in clinical trials. McCormack discussed several relevant questions, including:

- Is information in flash RAM storage modules [considered to be] source data?
- What measures should be taken in the event the [PDA] device is damaged prior to the transfer of information?
- Can multiple file conversions between handheld formats and the desktop or server influence the reliability of data?

More recently, comments relevant to this issue were presented at a DIA workshop on electronic patient-reported outcomes (ePRO). Joanne Rhoads, M.D., MPH, director of CDER's Division of Scientific Investigations, reiterated that sponsor and investigator responsibilities (already identified in existing regulations) are not dependent on the method of data collection (whether paper or electronic). She recommended that sponsors assure that appropriate security controls are in place and that there is protection against network attacks. The investigator's brochure for the clinical study is to specify how the ePRO source data will be collected and stored, and investigators must provide the ability to access electronic source documentation during inspections.

Specifically, Rhoads recommended that sponsors:
- avoid direct transmission to one single database that is under the sponsor's control
- ensure that investigator accountability is in no way diminished
- be able to provide copies of electronic source records during an inspection
- ensure that ePRO systems have adequate security controls

It has been argued that, because certain PDAs do not have "durable media" and feature only volatile memory, they are thereby exempt from Part 11. The FDA's previous position indicated that a record was created when it was recorded to durable media. Without recounting all the history, suffice it to say that the FDA has largely shifted its position away from this viewpoint. The agency recognized that trying to define an electronic record by the media on which it resides is inadequate due to rapid changes in technology and the wide variety of media options. Unfortunately, this is likely to be a continuing source of confusion until more specific guidance is issued.

11.4 Q. Is there any evidence that FDA clinical site inspections are resulting in FDA Form-483 citations based on Part 11 issues or noncompliance?

A. Warning letters and Form 483s associated with clinical sponsor and site inspections continue to lack specific citations related to the use of computer systems and electronic records. This is due, in large measure, to the practice of "enforcement discretion" (read non-enforcement) regarding Part 11 requirements as specified by the FDA in its 2003 Scope and Application Guidance. Even before the guidance was issued, there were few Part 11 citations in the GCP environment.

Most of the observations cited in FDA warning letters issued to clinical investigational sites focus, as they have traditionally, on core GCP issues, such as lack of informed consent, not following the protocol, incomplete or inaccurate case histories, lack of adequate accountability of investigational product, and poor documentation practices.

While EDC may have been in use by industry in clinical trials for some time on the front end, it can take years for the results to reach FDA reviewers on the back end. In this regard, EDC is relatively "new" to the review divisions, and we can expect that it will get increased scrutiny as the FDA gains experience with it. This is especially true in instances in which the source documentation is electronic, such as for electronic patient diaries. As agency reviewers gain experience with the exposures and potential risks inherent in electronic record systems, we may see increased emphasis on Part 11 compliance.

11.5 Q. The FDA GCP predicate rules (the underlying requirements in U.S. laws and FDA regulations other than Part 11) do not mention validation of clinical trial data systems. Why, then, is there so much emphasis on validation?

A. It is true that the regulations that comprise FDA GCPs do not explicitly require computer validation, principally because there is no mention of computers or even the word "electronic" in the agency's regulations. It is also true, however, that predicate rule requirements represent only one of the factors that must be considered in determining if a system requires validation. The ICH E6 Guideline for Good Clinical Practice (Section 5.5.3(a)), for example, recommends validation for "electronic trial data handling and/or remote electronic trial data systems."

In some countries, the ICH E6 guideline has served as a foundation for regulations. In the United States, the E6 guideline has been adopted as an FDA guidance document, which means that, while it represents FDA's current thinking on the validation of these systems, its provisions are not legally enforceable. Some companies mandate that their clinical departments and vendors, including contract research organizations (CROs), comply with the provisions of the ICH guideline. Furthermore, the FDA's 1999 guideline entitled, "Computerized Systems Used in Clinical Trials" as well as the agency's September 2004 draft revision to this guidance, indicate that the FDA may request to see documentation demonstrating software validation during an inspection. Therefore, although validation may not be explicitly required in the GCPs, it may still be an expectation. In addition, there may be predicate rules that govern activities involved with clinical trials, but that fall outside the regulations traditionally considered to be part of FDA GCPs. For example, investigational drug supplies used in clinical trials are regulated under FDA GMP regulations, which require the validation of computer systems (21 CFR 211.68).

It should be noted that, in the past, the FDA has questioned the validity of records used to support regulatory requirements. If the integrity of the records is challenged, and further inspection reveals that the system was never validated, this could raise serious doubts about the validity of data associated with the system. Ultimately, this could lead to a records-related citation during an inspection, even if there was no specific predicate requirement for validation. The importance of the records and the degree of uncertainty regarding their validity, of course, will be key factors in determining whether the FDA will issue a records-related citation.

11.6 Q. How should a company decide whether to validate a computer system? Is there any need for validation if there are no predicate rules requiring validation of that system?

A. The FDA's August 2003 Part 11 Scope and Application guidance states that systems must comply with all predicate requirements for validation. This means that, if there is a predicate rule requiring that computer systems be validated (e.g., 21 CFR 211.68(a), 21 CFR 58.61, 21 CFR 820.70(i)), then the system must be validated. The guidance further states that the decision to validate computer systems should also be based on "the impact the systems have on your ability to meet predicate rule requirements," and "the impact those systems might have on the accuracy, reliability, integrity, availability, and authenticity of required records and signatures." Consequently, even if the predicate rules do not explicitly require that a system be validated, validation may still be expected if the system is being used by an organization as a means of complying with a regulatory requirement.

The decision on whether to validate a system should be based on several factors. First, the company must understand how the system is being used as part of the overall process. The firm should determine if there are any predicate rules that, based on the use of the system, would require that the system be validated, or if the system is being used as a means to comply with a regulation. As stated previously, if there is a predicate rule requiring validation, then the system must be validated. If not, it may still be wise to validate the system based on the critical nature of the system to the operation and how the system is used. For example, there may not be a predicate rule requiring the validation of an adverse event reporting system; however, this system should be validated because it can directly affect the safety of the consumer and is being used to comply with a key regulatory requirement.

Another system that presents a strong case for validation is an interactive voice response system (IVRS). Consider an IVRS that delivers dosing information to a clinical site based on the randomization code. In such a case, the IVRS performs a critical function that could result in serious consequences if it fails to function correctly. Note that the FDA's draft revised guidance entitled, "Computerized Systems Used in Clinical Trials" (September 2004) states that clinical data "have broad public health significance" and are expected to be of the "highest quality and integrity." This underscores the importance of ensuring accurate results from computer systems. The purpose of system validation is to ensure that the system functions properly and that the data are reliable and trustworthy. Computer validation, therefore, may be warranted even if there is no predicate requirement for it.

Other factors that should be considered include international standards or guidelines, and internal policies or procedures that may require that systems be validated. If a company decides not to validate a system, the decision should be well documented and be approved by the appropriate level of management.

11.7 Q. Does Part 11 require that users change their passwords to a clinical data entry system every 90 days?

A. For many years, the FDA has steadfastly maintained its position that periodic changes to an individual's password make it more difficult for someone else to impersonate that individual. To some degree, this view assumes that typical password systems may not be strong enough to prevent someone from either gaining access to passwords or guessing them. In other words, if an individual sets a password and never changes it, another individual, given sufficient time, may be able to determine what it is. The perpetrator can then use the "stolen" password to gain system access and impersonate (including possibly electronically signing for) the authorized user without that individual's knowledge. If the password is periodically changed, the period of time that a perpetrator has to use the stolen password is limited.

The frequency with which passwords are changed must be balanced with an individual's ability to remember a password in an often-demanding work environment. For instance, if an individual is asked to change his or her password every week, the frequency of change will make it much more likely that this person will need to write down the password as a way of remembering it. The memory problem is exacerbated if an individual must access multiple systems, each possibly having a different password. In terms of password change frequency, 90 days is often viewed as a good compromise—that is, it represents a reasonably frequent period of change that does not overly burden the user. Some organizations have even gone to 60- or 30-day password changes, while others change only twice annually.

Some security experts take the opposite approach. They argue that it is better to establish an extremely "strong" password (e.g., 8-character minimum, mixed case, alphanumeric, etc.) that is never changed unless it is compromised (they ask, "how often do you change your ATM PIN number?"). The rationale is that, while it may be harder to memorize initially, such a password will be much harder for someone else to find out or guess. Furthermore, if the password never changes, the user will have no need to write down or record the password, where it might be discovered by others.

To date, the FDA has not bought into the "strong password, never changed" theory. The agency still prefers to see periodic password changes. The FDA's concern is that, if the strong password is ever compromised without the owner's knowledge, the password thief may be able to impersonate the owner indefinitely. Regarding passwords that are used as components of electronic signatures, it is important to note that 21 CFR 11.300(b) requires periodic checking, recall, or revision of the electronic signature components. Changing a password is one way through which this requirement can be met.

11.8 Q. Since everyone uses email, why would it be a Part 11 concern in the context of clinical trials?

A. The question of whether or not a particular type of system falls under Part 11 requirements is determined by the use of the system and the type of records that it contains. Email is not exempt from Part 11 consideration merely because it is email. For the most part, it is likely that most email usage falls outside regulatory consideration. However, Part 11 is applicable to regulatory-related records that are "transmitted" (not just stored). Therefore, email systems would be subject to Part 11 requirements when they are used to transmit documents that are required under predicate rules.

For example, the sponsor may send a protocol to the investigator or IRB via email. Since the protocol is required by FDA regulations, this process involves the transmission of a required electronic record via an open system, which means that §11.30 (Controls for Open Systems) applies. Part 11 does not preclude the use of an email system for such a transmission. It merely states that additional controls must be used to protect the integrity of the record in transit. In other words, the sponsor should take steps to ensure that the protocol received by the investigator and the IRB is, in fact, the same protocol that the sponsor sent (i.e., nothing has been changed or deleted). Consider the danger of inconsistent study procedures if the protocol is changed en route or if a protocol amendment never reaches its destination.

There are also cases in which the email message itself may be considered a required record. For example, 56.115(a)(4) notes that "copies of all correspondence between the IRB and the investigators" must be maintained. It is likely that much of this correspondence now takes the form of email communications. Because email is being used to record and transmit predicate rule records, such email systems should feature appropriate Part 11 controls, such as a trail of who created the record, means for ensuring record integrity, and a process for maintaining the record for the required regulatory retention period. Similarly, certain email communications between sponsors and investigators are also likely to invoke predicate record requirements.

Thus, in determining if and how Part 11 controls should be addressed in a system, it is important to consider the specific uses of the particular email system and to examine the predicate requirements for particular records and types of communications.

11.9 Q. In reviewing the GCP predicate rules, the term "audit trail" is not found. Do the predicate rules sometimes use terminology other than "audit trail" that effectively means the same thing?

A. Certain predicate rules do, in fact, call for audit trails without using that specific wording. For example, in the GLP regulations, 21 CFR 58.130 states, "Any change in automated data entries shall be made so as not to obscure the original entry, shall indicate the reason for change, shall be dated, and the responsible individual shall be identified." There are also other predicate examples in which audit trail-type functionality is called for without specifically using the term "audit trail."

Interestingly, FDA GCP regulations do not feature a specific predicate rule requirement for audit trails or for audit trail functionality. However, the ICH's E6 Good Clinical Practice guidance, which the FDA has adopted, does specifically call for the use of audit trails for changes made to case report forms (CRFs). The ICH guidance states in 4.9.3, "Any change or correction to a CRF should be dated, initialed, and explained (if necessary) and should not obscure the original entry (i.e., an audit trail should be maintained); this applies to both written and electronic changes or corrections." For changes made to data, E6 section 5.5.3 states that sponsors should "ensure that the systems are designed to permit data changes in such a way that the data changes are documented and that there is no deletion of entered data (i.e., maintain an audit trail, data trail, edit trail)." Unlike the predicate rules, though, the ICH guidance is not legally binding for FDA-regulated studies. However, the FDA has adopted E6 as a guidance document, and although FDA guidance documents are not legally binding, they do represent FDA's current thinking and expectations.

Even in the absence of a predicate rule requirement, it is important for a company to fully consider the potential impact of the lack of an audit trail for those records. As the FDA states in its August 2003 Part 11 Scope and Application guidance, "we recommend that you base your decision on whether to apply audit trails, or other appropriate measures, on the need to comply with predicate rule requirements, a justified and documented risk assessment, and a determination of the potential effect on product quality and safety and record integrity." Therefore, it would be risky to base the decision purely on predicate rule requirements and to ignore the other two elements of the FDA's compliance equation. Although other mechanisms (such as a manual log of changes) may be allowed, those controls are not as robust as a computerized audit trail that automatically and immediately records user data changes at the time of entry. The FDA's September 2004 draft revised guidance entitled, "Computerized Systems Used in Clinical Trials" states that, "Even if there are no applicable predicate rule requirements, it may be important to have computer-generated, time-stamped audit trails or other physical, logical, or procedural security measures to ensure the trustworthiness and reliability of electronic records. . . . Firms should determine and document the need for audit trails based on a risk assessment that takes into consideration circumstances surrounding system use, the likelihood that information might be compromised, and any system vulnerabilities." The guidance then reiterates the expected types of controls (stated in Part 11) that should be employed when automated audit trails are implemented.

11.10 Q. The FDA wants pharma companies to ensure that users applying electronic signatures understand and intend that their electronic signature is the legally binding equivalent of their handwritten signature. What is acceptable to the FDA as evidence that the user understands the significance of his or her electronic signature?

A. §11.100(c) requires that a certification be sent to the agency declaring that people using electronic signatures understand the legally binding equivalence of electronic signatures to handwritten signatures. As explained in the Part 11 preamble, "The agency is concerned that individuals might disavow an electronic signature as something completely different from a traditional handwritten signature." Consequently, FDA established the requirement that each company must submit a single certification letter (covering its entire organization, including all of its employees at all locations) if the company is using, or intends to use, electronic signatures. By submitting this document, a company is essentially making the following certification to the FDA: "We understand and agree that any electronic signatures used by our employees are as legally binding as handwritten signatures on paper."

The FDA explains in the preamble to Part 11 that the intent is for the certification to be submitted only once in the form of a paper-based letter bearing a single handwritten signature from an authorized company official. The agency provides the following example of acceptable certification wording in the preamble: "Pursuant to Section 11.100 of Title 21 of the Code of Federal Regulations, this is to certify that [name of organization] intends that all electronic signatures executed by our employees, agents, or representatives, located anywhere in the world, are the legally binding equivalent of traditional handwritten signatures." Once submitted, this certification covers all systems, all people, and all locations for as long as the organization remains essentially intact (e.g., a new certification may be warranted if two companies merge and one of them has not submitted a certification).

Further provisions in 11.100(c)(2) note that "additional certification or testimony" might be requested for specific individual electronic signatures. While this does not mean that each person within a company would need to submit a certification letter to FDA, it is critical that all individuals using electronic signatures understand that such signatures are legally equivalent to handwritten signatures. In addition, there should be some evidence to demonstrate that employees who are assigned electronic signatures understand this concept.

FDA does not dictate how employees are to be educated on the subject of electronic signatures. One approach is to provide company-wide training, and to document both the training and participating employees. Stronger evidence is established by requiring employees to read and sign a statement or policy that explains signatures, and that attests to an employee's understanding of the use of electronic signatures. Either approach can be reinforced through the implementation of a pop-up electronic signature box that contains a pre-defined message. In this way, the seriousness of the electronic signature's use should be clear to the individual as each signature is executed.

11.11 Q. Under §11.100(c), are clinical investigators required to certify to FDA if they are using (or planning to use) electronic signatures?

A. This is an area in which FDA has provided no clear written guidance. All persons operating under FDA regulations, including clinical investigators, must establish for the agency their understanding that electronic signatures are legally equivalent to handwritten signatures. This is accomplished through a certification letter to the FDA. For independent investigators and investigators in small practices, it would seem that the safest approach would be for the investigators to submit their own certification letters. In the past, however, FDA officials have indicated in informal comments that they did not envision receiving thousands of letters from individual investigators. If several investigators operate within a larger organization (such as a medical center), a certification could be made at the organizational level, in the same way that sponsor companies do for their employees.

While some have suggested that it may be possible for investigators to be covered under a sponsor's certification, this approach carries with it several risks. One risk is that a particular investigator may conduct studies for more than one sponsor. What if one of the sponsors has not submitted the §11.100(c) certification to the FDA? Another risk is that the sponsor, in its certification letter, may make claims or statements with which the investigator does not agree. A third risk is that a particular sponsor may have no intention of covering the investigators with whom it works, and this could lead to incorrect assumptions by both parties.

A recurring question has been whether it is appropriate or legal for the sponsor company to submit a certification of intent on behalf of clinical investigators when those investigators are not employees of the sponsor. However, as noted above, the FDA does not necessarily expect to receive a signature certification from each individual investigator. More recently, public comments from FDA speakers have indicated that clinical investigators are hired by sponsors to conduct research, and the certification can be submitted on behalf of anyone hired by those sponsors. If a sponsor submits the certification on behalf of its investigators, it is critical that the sponsor clearly communicate to the investigators the instances under which electronic signatures will be required, and the legal implications of the electronic signatures.

11.12 Q. What does Part 11 require regarding the ability of regulated organizations to store, retrieve, and reprocess electronic records for lengthy (i.e., multi-year) retention periods?

A. This is one of the key areas in which the FDA has clarified its expectations considerably. The agency has also substantially eased the burdens that industry faces in complying with the original Part 11 electronic record retention requirements found in §11.10(c) and related preamble comments. Record retention is one of the areas that was identified in the FDA's August 2003 Part 11 Scope and Application guidance and for which the agency does not "intend to devote enforcement resources," according to CDER Office of Compliance Director David Horowitz.

The FDA's August 2003 Part 11 Scope and Application guidance allows firms the flexibility to convert electronic records to other forms in order to meet retention requirements, provided that predicate rule requirements are satisfied. If the record is not required by predicate rules, there are no restrictions on how it can be archived. For records that must be retained under predicate rules, the Part 11 Scope and Application guidance states:

"FDA does not intend to object if you decide to archive required records in electronic format to nonelectronic media such as microfilm, microfiche, and paper, or to a standard electronic file format (examples of such formats include, but are not limited to, PDF, XML, or SGML). Persons must still comply with all predicate rule requirements, and the records themselves and any copies of the required records should preserve their content and meaning."

It is critical that organizations understand which predicate rules apply to their records before making the decision to convert from electronic records to paper or another format. This can be difficult to determine, and firms may want to consult with FDA's Good Clinical Practice Program office (http://www.fda.gov/oc/gcp/) on questions regarding predicate rule requirements for records.

The FDA's draft guidance entitled, "Computerized Systems Used in Clinical Trials" (September 2004) notes that predicate rules 21 CFR 312.62, 511.1(b)(7)(ii), and 812.140 require that the clinical investigator retain required records for the retention time specified in those regulations. The guidance states the expectation that the clinical site will retain either the original or a certified copy of the source document to "assist in the reconstruction and evaluation of the trial throughout and after the completion of the trial." This draft guidance clarified that, although obsolete software and hardware need not be retained to re-process data, available documentation must make it possible to understand the flow and analysis of data during and as a result of the trial. Further, the draft guidance allows records to be retained in forms other than their original form, such as generic electronic formats (PDF, XML), microfilm, microfiche, or even paper.

Keep in mind that many important records are maintained even though there are no explicit predicate regulations requiring such records. For some of these records, there are a variety of reasons why it may be in a firm's best interest to maintain the original electronic records (as discussed in other answers within this section). For many records, however, conversion to paper or PDF format may be perfectly acceptable.

When weighing the factors relevant to this decision, it may be important to consider the likelihood of inspection, or the potential need to answer a regulatory inquiry. It is far easier to search a database than it is to manually review hundreds of paper-based records. On the other hand, if the technology is becoming obsolete, and predicate rules allow it, it may be preferable to print out the records and keep them as paper for the retention period. Realize, however, that the *whole* record must be retained, including any associated audit trails as well as the meaning of all records and data fields (e.g., date formats and reference codes).

11.13 Q. If a company converts hardcopy originals into electronic copies by scanning them into a system, must the firm keep the hardcopy originals?

A. The short answer is that it is acceptable for a firm to delete the hardcopy original records, provided that all predicate requirements are satisfied and provided that the content and meaning of the original records is preserved.

With regard to preserving the content and meaning of the original records, there are several important factors to consider when converting paper records to electronic format. One consideration is the type of paper original that is being converted. The requirements for the scanning system and resolution may need to be carefully specified to address the full range of paper originals that may be converted. For example, significantly higher resolution will be required if an original was handwritten than if it was computer generated using a high-quality printer. Also, if handwritten notes or corrections are made in the margins, perhaps to the very edge of the page, the scanned electronic version must be able to capture all of the content without truncating the margin notes.

Also consider that white-out may have been "illegally" used to correct an error on an original page, thus obscuring the original entry. While this type of correction may be visible when reviewing the paper-based records, it may be undetectable on a scanned copy. Thus, it may not be possible to ascertain whether there had been an attempt at falsification (or whether the writer simply needs training on good GxP documentation practices). If color is an important element in the original (e.g., a chart in which different colors are used to distinguish blood pressure and temperature), part of the original's meaning (metadata) will be lost in a scanned black and white image. Furthermore, scanning documents without conducting a visual inspection of the scanned images may fail to detect skewed or truncated documents. This could result in the loss of original data or notes.

The defensibility of records converted by scanning will depend upon the above factors, the quality of the image and resolution, and the verification checks performed. Before a firm commits to converting paper originals to electronic format, it should conduct tests to confirm that all of the original content and meaning are preserved, including, as appropriate, colors, handwritten notes, and so on. Note also that it should not be possible to change the scanned document. The FDA's Compliance Policy Guide 7150.13 ("Use of Microfiche and/or Microfilm for Method of Records Retention"), which is referenced in the draft FDA guidance entitled, "Computerized Systems Used in Clinical Trials" (September 2004), indicates that a copy must be a "true and accurate" representation of the original record. If the scanned document is changed after scanning, then it is no longer a true and accurate representation of the original record.

As a final precautionary step, individuals should consult their corporate document retention and destruction policies and schedules, and possibly contact their corporate legal departments, before destroying any critical original documents. There may be implications beyond FDA regulatory requirements that could impact decisions regarding whether original documents can be scanned and destroyed.

11.14 Q. A clinical site is using a paperless, web-based electronic data capture (EDC) system in which data are entered directly into the sponsor's database remotely via a web browser interface. There is no local copy of the database at the investigator's site, and there is no paper source documentation (in other words, it is electronic source documentation, or e-source). At the end of the study, the investigator will receive a CD from the sponsor containing copies of all the subject data in PDF files. Does this scenario comply with Part 11 requirements?

A. This is a highly controversial issue that has been actively debated—without a clear resolution—since Part 11 was introduced. The question portrays an interesting scenario in which Part 11 and the ICH's E6 Consolidated GCP guidance seem to support the concept of e-source, but in which the predicate rules hinder the adoption of e-source technologies.

The most significant concern with e-source—and one that has been raised frequently by several agency officials, including James McCormack, Ph.D., director of nonclinical laboratory compliance within FDA's Office of Regulatory Affairs, and Joanne Rhoads, M.D., MPH, the director of CDER's Division of Scientific Investigations—is that this implementation may be in violation of 21 CFR Part

312.62. Specifically, 312.62(b) states that, "an investigator is required to prepare and maintain adequate and accurate case histories. . . ." This has traditionally been interpreted to mean that original source documentation for case histories (or certified copies) must be maintained by the clinical investigator (CI) at his/her site where it is under his/her control.

In an informal June 2002 email response to a similar question posed by the Oracle Clinical Users Group, McCormack responded, "I would caution you that the investigational regulations assign responsibility for maintenance of records to the CI [clinical investigator]. That does not mean that the e-records necessarily have to be on the CI's computer, but it does mean that it has to be under the CI's control and certainly NOT under the sponsor's control." In addition, at an October 2003 DIA conference on the topic of electronic patient reported outcomes (ePRO), an FDA speaker commented that the regulations do not allow for a clinical investigator to transfer his/her regulatory obligations to an outside party in the way that a sponsor is allowed to transfer obligations to a contract research organization under 21 CFR 312.52.

Another concern with this approach is that the investigator receives the complete set of records only at the completion of the study. This may represent a significant volume of data, and it is unlikely that the CI would be able to perform any kind of comprehensive check on the data after the study is complete. Without paper source documents, it would be difficult to ascertain whether the data returned from the sponsor or CRO weeks (or months, or even years) later matched the initially recorded data. Also, if the FDA performs an inspection while the trial is underway, the FDA inspector may not respond positively upon learning that source documents can only be viewed remotely from the sponsor's database. Once again, the issues of record control and accessibility are paramount.

It is also possible that, if the CI receives only static PDF representations of the database, he/she will be lacking potentially critical metadata, such as audit trails of any changes made since original entry. Final printouts of clinical data typically have not shown the whole history of the record.

Much has been written on this topic, and it has been discussed and debated by the FDA and industry at public meetings. Although many in industry have been hoping the FDA would issue formal guidance on this topic to provide a definitive resolution, there is no indication that such guidance is forthcoming. As a result, firms contemplating true e-source implementations between clinical sites and sponsor (or CRO) databases should proceed with caution.

11.15 Q. In the past, the FDA frowned upon the concept of "dual books" (i.e., two sets of records—one paper and one electronic). In such cases, one set of records is often referred to as the "official record" (usually the paper), while the other version (often the electronic record) is considered the "unofficial" record. Has the FDA's position on "dual books" changed?

A. The FDA has modified its position with regard to the "dual books" issue. The FDA's August 2003 Part 11 Scope and Application guidance gives firms the freedom to maintain both paper and electronic versions of records. To comply with this guidance, an organization must determine which version will be used for regulatory purposes, must clearly state this decision in its standard operating procedures (SOPs), and must apply the appropriate procedures and controls. For example, if the online adverse event reporting system will be used to make determinations about product safety profiles, this must be documented in SOPs, and Part 11 and other predicate rules must be applied to the system. Although it is permissible for the company to generate paper printouts from the system, FDA inspectors asking to review adverse event records should be shown the online system and be told that the electronic version is the one used for regulatory decisions and activities. It is not acceptable for a company to use the online system for regulatory activities, and then to provide FDA investigators with only paper records from the system. Organizations must be diligent about determining which format of the records will be used for regulatory purposes, and about ensuring that personnel are properly trained in their use (and on the consequences of not following procedures).

Some organizations encounter a situation in which one department or group uses the electronic form of the record for regulated activities, while a different department uses paper printouts from the same system to perform its regulated tasks. The FDA's August 2003 Part 11 Scope and Application guidance provides adequate leeway to accommodate this dual approach. The keys, once again, are to: (1) carefully document the procedures; (2) apply Part 11 and predicate rules to both record formats as appropriate; and (3) implement controls and procedures to ensure that both groups are working from the correct versions, or levels, of whichever format is used.

11.16 Q. *If it can be demonstrated that paper reports (system output) are used for required processes, rather than the electronic database that created the reports, is it true that Part 11 does not apply?*

A. According to the FDA's 2003 Scope and Application Guidance, the critical point is to be certain that only the paper records are used. If the underlying electronic database is periodically used for regulatory purposes (in addition to the paper records), then a company cannot claim that it relies solely on the paper record, and Part 11 requirements may apply.

Assuming that it is possible for an organization to make the case that it relies solely on paper records, then Part 11 does not apply. Keep in mind, however, that in many cases a computer system is generating the paper reports, including appropriate selection of the records, sorting, formatting, and any calculations and summaries. Because it is important that the output be correct, validation may be warranted to prove that the business requirements are met, that the program code is under control, and that changes are tested and verified. Once again, validation may still be appropriate, even if Part 11 is not required.

A common pitfall occurs when one department uses the paper records (thus thinking that the system is exempt from Part 11), while another department uses the electronic database for regulated purposes. In this scenario, the records in both forms are required records, and Part 11 requirements may apply. See Q11.13 for additional information.

11.17 Q. *My company maintains master copies of standard operating procedures (SOPs) in Microsoft Word format. The SOPs are printed out for management signatures. Once approved, the Word file is converted into Adobe PDF format, and the PDF version of the SOP is made available to employees via*

the company intranet. Subsequent SOP revisions are made to the Word master file, and the process is repeated. Are the Word files and/or PDF files subject to Part 11?

A. Because sponsor or clinical research organization SOPs are not required under FDA GCP predicate regulations, they are not subject to Part 11. In the interest of ensuring that employees follow standard procedures that are approved by management, however, this process should be controlled. Procedures should be written and followed to ensure that the online SOPs (the PDF files) are an accurate and current representation of the signed paper versions, and that appropriate new electronic versions are posted on the intranet once their paper counterparts are updated and approved. Access to the source Word files and their PDF renditions should be carefully controlled to prevent unintended or unauthorized changes. Superseded versions of the SOPs must be available for historical and inspection purposes, although they must be controlled to ensure that they are not inadvertently used after they are retired.

It is interesting to note that SOPs are required records for institutional review boards (IRBs) per predicate regulations. §56.108 indicates that IRBs must follow written procedures, and §56.115(a)(6) requires that written procedures be retained. Therefore, if an IRB uses or maintains electronic SOPs, Part 11 would apply, since these records are required by predicate regulation.

The issue of whether or not particular records are explicitly required by predicate rules (which then triggers Part 11 requirements) is an interesting one. As they do with training records, FDA inspectors expect to see written SOPs at sponsor and CRO sites. In fact, FDA inspectional guides call for agency field personnel to "Obtain a copy of the sponsor's written procedures (SOPs and guidelines) for monitoring [clinical studies]" (FDA Compliance Program Guidance Manual, Program 7348.810, Chapter 48, Bioresearch Monitoring).

Here is the problem: FDA inspectional guides and training, regardless of how detailed they may be, are not considered "predicate rules" as defined in the FDA's August 2003 Part 11 Scope and Application guidance. Furthermore, there is no explicit predicate rule requiring sponsors or CROs to maintain documented SOPs. As stated in the Part 11 Scope and Application guidance (and supported in public statements made by top FDA officials), ". . . records (and any associated signatures) that are not required to be retained under predicate rules, but that are nonetheless maintained in electronic format, are not part 11 records."

Therefore, even if sponsors and CROs maintain (and rely on) SOPs in electronic form, Part 11 will not apply to those electronic records because they have been removed from the narrowed scope of Part 11. In our view, this is a serious gap in the logic of the FDA's August 2003 Part 11 Scope and Application guidance. A better alternative would be to require firms to take a risk-based approach to the application of Part 11 controls to important records that are not required by predicate rules (such as training records and SOPs for sponsors and CROs).

11.18 Q. The sponsor's IT department wants to retire an old clinical data management system (CDMS). As part of this process, records will be migrated from the old system to a new system. The QA department has stated that the transfer should be validated. What does that mean?

A. Stated simply, it means that a defined process should be planned, documented, and implemented to ensure that the records are properly migrated from the old system to the new system. Depending on the size, type, and complexity of the records to be transferred and the availability (or lack thereof) of migration and verification tools, the validation effort can range from quite straightforward to rather involved.

Ordinarily, there should be a validation plan to govern the life cycle activities and deliverables associated with the new system. Validation of the record migration should be included as one of those activities. Documentation should be created to clearly define critical information, including the following: which records are to be transferred; planned or expected data losses, conversions, or transformations; and changes in file or record formats. A verification procedure should be developed, documented, and executed to ensure that the migration occurred as expected, and should include procedures for problem tracking and resolution.

Useful information on data conversion and migration can be found in two of the draft Part 11 guidances that the FDA withdrew in February 2003. At this writing, the withdrawn guidances were still available from the FDA's electronic dockets at the links listed with their respective titles below:

- 21 CFR Part 11; Electronic Records; Electronic Signatures, Validation (http://www.fda.gov/OHRMS/DOCKETS/98fr/001538gd.pdf)
- 21 CFR Part 11; Electronic Records; Electronic Signatures, Maintenance of Electronic Records (http://www.fda.gov/OHRMS/DOCKETS/98fr/00d-1539-gdl0001.pdf)

To access additional information on all of the withdrawn guidances as well as other relevant FDA information on Part 11, visit http://www.fda.gov/ora/compliance_ref/part11/.

11.19 Q. Who is responsible for Part 11 compliance at clinical sites?

A. Every person with access to Part 11 electronic records at a clinical site is responsible for at least some provisions of Part 11. For example, at a minimum, every system user should be assigned a logon (e.g., userid and password that they create), if not an electronic signature (which may consist of the same userid and password as their logon). Part 11 has rules that must be observed by the user, as well as by the person issuing the logon and electronic signature to the user. Persons responsible for system administration, database administration, system security, and other areas will have even greater Part 11-related responsibilities. The FDA's draft guidance entitled, "Use of Computerized Systems in Clinical Trials" (September 2004) states that "staff [should] be kept thoroughly aware of system security measures and the importance of limiting access to authorized personnel."

Ultimately, the principal investigator is accountable for the conduct of a trial, including compliance with all applicable regulations and guidances. While the investigator may delegate responsibility for educating the site team on Part 11 issues and for ensuring that the site's systems and procedures are compliant, the investigator is ultimately responsible for the site.

The situation is more complicated when a sponsor supplies a site with a system (such as an EDC system) for use in a study. Typically in this instance, sponsor staff will act on behalf of site staff in defining, developing, installing, and testing the system (including testing for Part 11 compliance) and in maintaining the validation documentation. A brief summary of the system and the location at which the detailed system and validation documentation are kept should be available at the site in case questions arise during an FDA inspection. Typically, the sponsor would also train the users, although it remains the site's responsibility to ensure that all current users at the site are trained and that system access is properly administered.

It should also be noted that if a site decides to implement its own system for regulated purposes (perhaps an Access database for accountability of investigational product), it is then fully responsible for all Part 11 requirements and should approach validation from a risk-based perspective.

11.20 Q. Must electronic medical records used at clinical sites comply with Part 11?

A. This question touches on an interesting intersection between the world of clinical trial case history records, which fall under FDA regulations, and hospital records (in this case, electronic medical records, or EMRs), which do not.

In a 2003 Forrester Research report entitled, When EMRs Meet Clinical Trials (by Michael J. Barrett, with Bradford J. Holmes and Sara E. McAulay), the authors state, "Due to the problems posed by protocol specificity and 21 CFR Part 11, EMR vendors do not tout their products as suitable for electronic data capture in clinical trials. But double data entry for investigators won't really go away until EMRs do EDC. This is a 10-year project." If Barrett is correct, and investigators are re-entering the data from EMRs into clinical case histories, then EMRs remain outside the scope of Part 11. However, as technology advances and data are transferred electronically from EMRs into clinical case history records, the regulatory boundary begins to blur.

It could be argued that EMR data, if used in a regulatory submission to FDA or if required by GCP predicate rule, may be considered within the scope of Part 11. The reason is that EMRs typically contain source data and source documents that are required as part of the case history per IND regulations in Part 312.62. For example, source data maintained in the EMR may include patients' medical history information, medical examination results, physician's progress notes, nurses' notes, lab results, demographic data, visit dates, and other information. Advanced EMR systems may also include digitized source documents, such as lab reports, X-rays, digital photographs, case report forms, and other records.

As noted above, however, currently there remains a wall of separation (in the form of double data entry) that keeps EMR outside Part 11 controls. As a result, Part 11 has not been a priority with EMR software suppliers. The good news is that this market is heavily influenced and driven by HIPAA requirements. If EMR systems are compliant with the HIPAA privacy and security requirements, at least sponsors (and the FDA) can feel more secure that access controls and data protection are in place. Note, however, that HIPAA regulations do not require evidence that the system actually works correctly (i.e., validation).

11.21 Q. In a particular study, each clinical site is assigned one unique login account that identifies which site is calling in to the IVR (interactive voice response) system. Our company decided that it would be impractical to assign individual logins to each user at all the sites, and then to expect all those users to periodically change their passwords. Are there any Part 11 concerns with shared site login access to the IVR?

A. There are multiple potential uses for an IVR system. It may be used for patient randomization, in which case the clinical site would call in to the IVR to identify patients enrolled. The IVR system could also be used to identify the particular drug kit to be dispensed to a particular patient based on the study randomization code. Further, the IVR system could be used to control drug supply (in other words, to determine when to re-order supply, or even to allow direct order via a pharmacist, for example). In the event of a medical emergency, the system could even be used as an unblinding mechanism to determine whether a particular patient received investigational drug or placebo.

Many IVR functions involve the creation of important records from a study perspective. For such systems, therefore, Part 11 requires that there be a way to determine who created, changed, or deleted a particular record. If multiple individuals at a study site are operating as a single user (by using a shared account), it is impossible to trace the entry of particular records to specific individuals. Therefore, while the concern about burdening users with individual IVR system passwords is understandable, the shared account implementation described would violate Part 11 traceability requirements. In addition, shared accounts can be problematic if one individual leaves the study site. Typically, the password may not be changed, which leaves the system open to access by an unauthorized individual (the terminated employee). Alternatively, if the password <u>is</u> changed, then all site staff must learn a new password because <u>one</u> individual left.

Further Reading

McKenney, Olson, and Benze, *The "New" Part 11 and Drug Development: A Q&A Reference Guide,* March 2004, Barnett International (www.barnettinternational.com).

ICH Guideline: "Electronic Standards for the Transfer of Regulatory Information," (M12), 1997.

FDA "Guidance for Industry: Part 11 Electronic Records; Electronic Signatures – Scope and Application," August 2003.

Alexander, Ian, et al, "Capturing a True Picture of Clinical Trials," *GCPj,* 9:8-11, December 2002.

Stokes, Teri, "Technology Update: Validating Computer Systems, Part 1: A GCP Computer System is a Lifetime Responsibility," *Applied Clinical Trials,* 9:38-43, August 2000.

Stokes, Teri, "Technology Update: Validating Computer Systems, Part 2: GCP Validation of Platform and Infrastructure Systems," *Applied Clinical Trials,* 9:55-66, September 2000.

Stokes, Teri, "Technology Update: Validating Computer Systems, Part 3: GCP Software Verification," *Applied Clinical Trials,* 9:48-58, November 2000.

Section 12:
Patient Recruitment

12.1 Q. In practice, to what degree is there active IRB oversight of various subject recruitment practices?

A. Not much, at least according to a government study several years ago. A 2000 HHS Office of the Inspector General report entitled, "Recruiting Human Subjects: Pressures in Industry-Sponsored Research," for example, concluded that the "oversight of the recruitment of subjects is minimal," and worse, that "IRBs are not reviewing many of the recruitment practices that they and others find most troubling." The study looked at what HHS identified as the "four main strategies" that sponsors and investigators use to recruit human subjects and encourage timely recruitment: (1) sponsor-offered financial and other incentives to investigators to boost enrollment; (2) investigators "target" their own patients as potential subjects; (3) investigators seek additional subjects from other sources, such as physician referrals and disease registries; and (4) sponsor and investigators advertise and promote their studies.

"Although financial incentives given to investigators by sponsors to boost enrollment are among the recruitment practices that IRBs are most concerned about, 75 percent of IRBs that responded to our survey do not review any financial arrangements between sponsors and investigators," the study states. "When IRBs do review subject recruitment practices, they primarily review advertisements and incentives paid to subjects, not practices involving sponsor-investigator interactions."

"In addition, 25 percent of IRB survey respondents do not ask investigators to explain recruiting practices in their application for review. The finding that a significant percentage of IRBs do not gather basic information about recruitment practices on their application for review raises the possibility that some IRBs may not be reviewing recruitment practices at all. In addition, of the 23 applications provided by our surveyed IRBs, 13 ask only general questions about recruitment such as 'How will subjects be recruited for the study?' Few inquire about specific recruitment practices in their application for review."

At the same time, the 2000 HHS report did report some positive trends, including the fact that IRBs reported devoting increasing attention to recruitment-related issues. In addition, 61 percent of the surveyed IRBs reported that they had requested changes in the recruitment practices called for by a protocol during the previous three years, and many said that they were requesting more recruitment-related changes than they had three years earlier.

12.2 Q. Is there any type of definitive guidance from the FDA or other government agencies on controversial recruitment practices such as referral fees paid to physicians who refer patients to clinical studies or the review of patient medical records to search for potential subjects?

A. Although the FDA and HHS have begun to provide guidance in the area of disclosing relevant financial arrangements to study subjects (see Section 13), guidance on specific recruitment practices is still lacking. In its 2000 report entitled, "Recruiting Human Subjects: Pressures in Industry-Sponsored Research," the HHS Office of the Inspector General specifically called on the FDA and NIH work with industry and the research community to develop "a clearer determination of *appropriate* recruiting practices" for sponsors, investigators, and IRBs.

In this recommendation, the HHS OIG asked the FDA and NIH to consider and explore a number of specific unresolved questions, including:

- "Is it acceptable for sponsors to offer bonuses to investigators for successfully recruiting subjects?"
- "Should physicians be allowed to receive fees for referring their patients as potential subjects for a clinical trial?"
- "Does searching medical records for potential subjects constitute a breach of confidentiality?"

12.3 *Q. Although the FDA has established that an IRB should review the methods and materials, including direct advertising, that sponsors/investigators propose to use to recruit clinical trial subjects, are Internet listings of clinical trials subject to IRB review and approval?*

A. It depends. Internet listings, which are not the same as advertisements, do not need IRB review. According to an FDA Information Sheet entitled, "Recruiting Study Subjects" (1998), "IRB review and approval of listings of clinical trials on the Internet would provide no additional safeguard and is not required when the system format limits the information provided to basic trial information, such as: the title; purpose of the study; protocol summary; basic eligibility criteria; study site location(s); and how to contact the site for further information. Examples of clinical trial listing services that do not require prospective IRB approval include the National Cancer Institute's cancer clinical trial listing (PDQ) and the government-sponsored AIDS Clinical Trials Information Service (ACTIS). However, when the opportunity to add additional descriptive information is not precluded by the data base system, IRB review and approval may assure that the additional information does not promise or imply a certainty of cure or other benefit beyond what is contained in the protocol and the informed consent document." Also, see Q8.18.

12.4 *Q. Are subject enrollment incentives that sponsors offer to clinical trial sites permitted under GCP?*

A. Although site enrollment incentives are not addressed explicitly in FDA or GCP standards, FDA Office of Good Clinical Practice officials have recently cited "minimizing the use of enrollment incentives" as one way for sponsors to discourage—or at least not encourage—fraud by clinical investigators. In reviewing the conduct of investigators found guilty of fraudulent research practices, the FDA discovered that maximizing profits was one of the most significant reasons why these investigators created fraudulent records for nonexistent study subjects.

Still, enrollment incentives are very much a fact of life in an environment that places such a premium on development speed, particularly when subject enrollment is seen as one of the key rate-limiting factors. According to PhRMA's June 2002 (updated in 2004) voluntary "Principles for Conduct of Clinical Trials and Communication of Clinical Trial Results," "when enrollment is particularly challenging, reasonable additional payments may be made to compensate the clinical investigator or institution for time and effort spent on extra recruiting efforts to enroll appropriate research participants."

Rather than taking actions to focus site staff so intensely on enrolling subjects (and possibly away from other important tasks and responsibilities), however, sponsors might be better served to ensure that the site has sufficient access to the appropriate patient population and is adequately resourced to conduct the study. Sponsors should also ensure that site budgets adequately compensate the site staff for the time and effort to conduct the study.

Increasingly, enrollment incentives, or recruitment bonuses, are being viewed as potential conflicts of interest for clinical investigators, and as activities that must be managed and, in some cases, disclosed to clinical subjects (see Q13.3).

12.5 *Q. Although it rarely does so (about 1% of routine site inspections in past years), the agency has cited trial investigators for "inappropriate payment to volunteers" in the past. What criteria does the FDA apply to determine whether a payment, reimbursement for study-related expenses, credits, or other inducements are coercive or present undue influence?*

A. Neither FDA regulations nor guidance documents provide definitive insights into the criteria or decision processes that agency officials use to determine if a payment to study participants is inappropriate. A general—but perhaps the lengthiest—agency discussion on the topic is provided in an FDA information sheet entitled, *Payment to Research Subjects,* which establishes that the IRB must review and approve all payments and payment methods/schedules, and that all payment-related information must be set forth in the informed consent document:

"It is not uncommon for subjects to be paid for their participation in research, especially in the early phases of investigational drug, biologic or device development," the agency's information sheet states. "Payment to research subjects for participation in studies is not considered a benefit, it is a recruitment incentive. Financial incentives are often used when health benefits to subjects are remote or non-existent. The amount and schedule of all payments should be presented to the IRB at the time of initial review. The IRB should review both the amount of payment and the proposed method and timing of disbursement to assure that neither are coercive or present undue influence [21 CFR 50.20]."

Much of the agency's discussion focuses on the scheduling, rather than the amount, of payments to study subjects. "Any credit for payment should accrue as the study progresses and not be contingent upon the subject completing the entire study. Unless it creates undue inconvenience or a coercive practice, payment to subjects who withdraw from the study may be made at the time they would have completed the study (or completed a phase of the study) had they not withdrawn. For example, in a study lasting only a few days, an IRB may find it permissible to allow a single payment date at the end of the study, even to subjects who had withdrawn before that date. While the entire payment should not be contingent upon completion of the entire study, payment of a small proportion as an incentive for completion of the study is acceptable to FDA, providing that such incentive is not coercive. The IRB should determine that the amount paid as a bonus for completion is reasonable and not so large as to unduly induce subjects to stay in the study when they would otherwise have withdrawn. All information concerning payment, including the amount and schedule of payment(s), should be set forth in the informed consent document."

Given that the FDA has itself cited studies for "inappropriate payments," however, payments are not just an IRB concern as implied in the passage above, although some agency officials today believe they should be addressed solely by IRBs (see discussion below). It is difficult to get FDA officials to speak candidly about the types and methods of payments that they consider to be inappropriate inducements. In an informal discussion with an FDA field inspector who focuses on bioresearch monitoring issues, the inspector noted that he will become suspicious if, for example, he notices a study recruitment advertisement that seems to overemphasize financial incentives involved in a study (e.g., a particularly large or frequently recurring "$$$$" sign in the ad, a bolded statement of "money for your time"). The inspector noted, however, that he will not generally include suspected undue influence of financial incentives on the 483-Inspectional Observations form—in fact, he notes that he has never seen such a citation on a 483. Rather, the inspector communicates any suspicions back to headquarters for evaluation, and allows FDA compliance officials to determine if the payments were inappropriate and whether the study should be cited.

In instructions to FDA field staff conducting clinical investigator inspections, FDA Compliance Program Guidance 7348.811 (CPG 7348.811) notes that inspectors should assess "media ads for patient/subject recruitment" and related "promotional material." CPG 7348.811 does not mention payments to trial subjects, however, and instructs FDA inspectors to focus on whether the IRB approved media recruitment ads and whether the investigator represented the test article as safe and effective in related promotional materials.

Given the lack of formal FDA guidance or written agency policy on the appropriateness of payments offered to potential subjects, it is not surprising that CDER compliance officials themselves struggle in this area. In some cases, say CDER officials, they will even contact medical officers in CDER's drug review divisions (e.g., an FDA reviewer who is also a board-certified psychiatrist regarding a trial involving an antidepressant) for input on the appropriateness of a particular payment given the nature of the study (e.g., indication, study length, number of visits, medical procedures involved), the things expected of the study subjects, and other relevant factors. Agency officials note, however, that even FDA reviewers struggle with the relevant issues involved (e.g., how can a value or price be put on a study subject's time?).

During internal meetings, agency officials continued to discuss and reassess the agency's role in determining the appropriateness of payments to study subjects. As noted, some within the agency believe that the issue should be left to IRBs alone. Other agency officials point out, however, that IRBs (and even some prospective study subjects) are increasingly seeking FDA guidance on such payments. They add that IRBs only see payments in the context of the studies conducted within their institutions, and that the FDA sees payment-related information and patterns for a much larger sample of trials (e.g., through informed consent forms included in IND submissions). Given this, some FDA officials maintain that the agency should be more proactive in providing guidance regarding such payments, and could, ideally, provide some broad principles or guidance to help IRBs, sponsors, investigators, trial subjects and others address the related issues.

Meanwhile, federal prosecutors have warned that financial inducements paid to clinical study subjects could come under increasing scrutiny. While financial incentives used to recruit healthy patients are unlikely to draw the attention of federal prosecutors, "it gets sticky when you're talking about very vulnerable subjects, either extremely poor subjects or children or the elderly," according to Philadelphia Associate U.S. Attorney James Sheehan. "Those I would take a second look at."

Developed by D. Anderson & Company, the exhibit below highlights key regulatory references regarding patient compensation.

Patient Compensation Regulatory Guidelines
(FDA, ICH, EU, OHRP)

Regulatory References

Note: Those areas in ***bold*** are added for emphasis to highlight key phrases where patient compensation is addressed more specifically.

Source	Item #	Reference (reprinted directly from the source)
21 CFR	50.25 Elements of informed consent	(6) For research involving more than minimal risk, an explanation as to whether ***any compensation*** and an explanation as to whether any medical treatments are ***available if injury occurs*** and, if so, what they consist of, or where further information may be obtained.
INFORMATION SHEETS Guidance for Institutional Review Boards and Clinical Investigators 1998 Update	Payment to Research Subjects	The Institutional Review Board (IRB) should determine that the risks to subjects are reasonable in relation to anticipated benefits [21 CFR 56.111(a)(2)] and that the consent document contains an adequate description of the study procedures [21 CFR 50.25(a)(1)] as well as the risks [21 CFR 50.25(a)(2)] and benefits [21 CFR 50.25(a)(3)]. ***It is not uncommon for subjects to be paid for their participation in research,*** especially in the early phases of investigational drug, biologic or device development. ***Payment to research subjects for participation in studies is not considered a benefit, it is a recruitment incentive. Financial incentives are often used when health benefits to subjects are remote or non-existent. The amount and schedule of all payments should be presented to the IRB at the time of initial review. The IRB should review both the amount of payment and the proposed method and timing of disbursement to assure that neither are coercive or present undue influence [21 CFR 50.20].*** ***Any credit for payment should accrue as the study progresses and not be contingent upon the subject completing the entire study.*** Unless it creates undue inconvenience or a coercive practice, payment to subjects who withdraw from the study may be made at the time they would have completed the study (or completed a phase of the study) had they not withdrawn. For example, in a study lasting only a few days, an IRB may find it permissible to allow a single payment date at the end of the study, even to subjects who had withdrawn before that date. ***While the entire payment should not be contingent upon completion of the entire study, payment of a small proportion as an incentive for completion of the study is acceptable to FDA, providing that such incentive is not coercive. The IRB should determine that the amount paid as a bonus for completion is reasonable and not so large as to unduly induce***

Source	Item #	Reference (reprinted directly from the source)
INFORMATION SHEETS *(cont.)*	Payment to Research Subjects	*subjects to stay in the study when they would otherwise have withdrawn. All information concerning payment, including the amount and schedule of payment(s), should be set forth in the informed consent document.*
INFORMATION SHEETS Guidance for Institutional Review Boards and Clinical Investigators 1998 Update	VI. Informed Consent Document Content	50. May the "compensation" for participation in a trial offered by a sponsor include a coupon good for a discount on the purchase price of the product once it has been approved for marketing? No. This presumes, and inappropriately conveys to the subjects, a certainty of favorable outcome of the study and prompt approval for marketing. Also, if the product is approved, the coupon may financially coerce the subject to insist on that product, even though it may not be the most appropriate medically.
ICH Guideline for Good Clinical Practice	4.8.10 Informed Consent	*(j) The compensation and/or treatment available to the subject in the event of trial-related injury* *(k) The anticipated prorated payment, if any, to the subject for participating in the trial.*
ICH Guideline for Good Clinical Practice	3.18	*The IRB/IEC should review both the amount and method of payment to subjects to assure that neither presents problems of coercion or undue influence on the trial subjects. Payments to a subjects should be prorated and not wholly contingent on completion of the trial by the subject.*
EU Clinical Trials Directive	Article 6: Ethics Committee (j)	In preparing its opinion, the Ethics Committee shall consider in particular: (j) *the amounts and, where appropriate, the arrangements for rewarding or compensating investigators and trial subjects and the relevant aspects* of any agreement between the sponsor and the site
OHRP – IRB Guidebook Chapter III (Research sponsored or conducted by federal government)	G. Incentives for Participation	**INTRODUCTION** Each year, thousands of individuals are paid for participating in biomedical and behavioral research funded either by federal departments and agencies or private institutions. *Although payments are usually monetary, both patients and normal healthy volunteers may be offered other rewards in lieu of or in addition to money. Free medical care, extra vacation time, and academic rewards (in the form of a grade or a letter of recommendation) are examples of alternative rewards. Regardless of the form of remuneration, the issues for IRBs remain the same. IRBs must consider whether paid participants in research are recruited fairly, informed adequately, and paid appropriately.* Taking into consideration the subjects' medical, employment, and educational status, and their financial, emotional and community resources, the IRB must determine whether the rewards offered for participation in research constitute undue inducement.

Source	Item #	Reference (reprinted directly from the source)
OHRP – IRB Guidebook Chapter III *(cont.)*	G. Incentives for Participation	**OVERVIEW** *Federal regulations governing research with human subjects contain no specific guidance for IRB review of payment practices.* One of the primary responsibilities of IRBs, however, is to ensure that a subject's decision to participate in research will be truly voluntary, and that consent will be sought "only under circumstances that provide the prospective subject . . . sufficient opportunity to consider whether or not to participate and that minimize the possibility of coercion or undue influence" [Federal Policy §___.116; 21 CFR 50.20]. Incentives for participation in research are discussed in the FDA's Information Sheet, "Payment to Research Subjects" (February 1989). Clear cases of coercion (*i.e.,* actual threats) are readily identifiable; it is more difficult to recognize undue inducement. An offer one could not refuse is essentially coercive (or "undue"). Undue inducements may be troublesome because: (1) offers that are too attractive may blind prospective subjects to the risks or impair their ability to exercise proper judgment; and (2) they may prompt subjects to lie or conceal information that, if known, would disqualify them from enrolling—or continuing—as participants in a research project. **IRB CONSIDERATIONS** IRBs must attempt to make sure that prospective subjects realize that their participation is voluntary, and that choosing not to participate will not adversely affect their relationship with the institution or its staff in any way. *To make this determination, IRBs should know who the subjects will be, what incentives are being offered, and the conditions under which the offer will be made.* Some institutions have adopted policies regarding the recruitment and payment of volunteers. In general, they attempt to minimize the possibility of coercion or undue influence by requesting that subjects be recruited by open, written invitation rather than by personal solicitation. *Institutions try to ensure that the consent document contains a detailed account of the terms -of payment, including a description of the conditions under which a subject would receive partial or no payment (for example, what will happen if they withdraw part way through the research).* *Determining the appropriateness of the incentive is another matter. For research that requires subjects to undergo only minor inconvenience or discomfort, a modest payment will usually be adequate. Reimbursement for travel, babysitting, and so forth may also be provided. In more complex research projects, IRBs*

Source	Item #	Reference (reprinted directly from the source)
OHRP – IRB Guidebook Chapter III *(cont.)*	G. Incentives for Participation	*tend to base their assessment on the prevailing payment practices within their institution or general locale. Volunteers are often compensated for their participation according to an established fee schedule, based upon the complexity of the study, the type and number of procedures to be performed, the time involved, and the anticipated discomfort or inconvenience. Standard payments may be established for each tissue or fluid sample collected, depending on the type of sample (blood, urine, or saliva) and the time (day or evening) the sample is to be collected. Alternatively, subjects may be paid an hourly rate or a fixed amount, depending on the duration of the study and whether the study requires admission to research ward. Extra payments are usually provided for a variety of additional inconveniences (e.g., the imposition of dietary restrictions). Payments may vary according to a number of factors, and, therefore, IRBs may need to become familiar with the accepted standards within their community as well as the anticipated discomforts and inconveniences involved in a particular study to judge appropriateness of payments. Some institutions have a ceiling on the amount an individual may earn in any one study or during a given length of time (e.g., per year, per semester).*
		One of the most perplexing problems for IRBs is how to assess the appropriateness of payment offers for experiments that involve the assumption of risk or significant discomfort. On a practical level, it is probably impossible for an IRB to determine what amount of money or type of reward would unduly influence a particular individual to accept a given degree of risk. Although our society generally accepts the premise that those assuming risk deserve reward, the application of this rule in establishing payment for subjects in biomedical and behavioral experiments is still being debated. The appropriateness of proposed payments is a matter each institution must address in formulating its policies.
		IRB members tend to approach the problem of assuming risk for pay from one of two positions. One side argues that normal healthy volunteers are able to exercise free choice, and that, since judging the acceptability of risk and weighing the benefits is a personal matter, IRBs should refrain from imposing their own views on potential subjects. On this view, IRB responsibility should be confined to ensuring that consent is properly informed. Other IRB members argue that the IRB should protect potential subjects from inducements that may affect their ability to make an informed, voluntary choice. It should be noted that, in this context, incentives need not be

Source	Item #	Reference (reprinted directly from the source)
OHRP – IRB Guidebook Chapter III *(cont.)*	G. Incentives for Participation	financial to cause problems. Free health care for persons with limited resources and major medical problems may be a significant inducement to participate in research (even if the research activity is nontherapeutic). There is no consensus as to whether this kind of inducement is unacceptable. In assessing this potential problem, IRBs might consider whether only the destitute agree to volunteer or if people who can obtain good medical care on their own agree to participate as well. IRBs may need to monitor subject recruitment to make such determinations. **POINTS TO CONSIDER** 1. Are all conditions in keeping with standards for voluntary and informed consent? 2. Are the incentives offered reasonable, based upon the complexities and inconveniences of the study and the particular subject population? 3. Are there special standards that the IRB ought to apply to the review of research in which volunteers are asked to assume significant risk? 4. Should the IRB monitor subject recruitment to determine whether coercion or undue influence is a problem?

Patient Compensation Regulatory Guidelines: Summary provided by D. Anderson & Company – 2004

12.6 Q. Are all telephone scripts that clinical site staff use to recruit and inform potential subjects who contact the site to inquire about or express an interest in a study subject to IRB approval? If the script instructs the receptionist to say, "Yes, we have a study about XYZ, and you must have symptoms A, B, and C," is that subject to IRB approval?

A. There is a subtle difference between recruiting potential subjects and informing potential subjects. Generally, recruiting and selling are involved when a potential subject hears or reads about a study. Materials used in this phase—an advertisement, a letter, or a "cold call"—must be approved by an IRB.

Once a potential subject knows that a study is being conducted and calls the site, the information provided by the site staff (likely a receptionist) must be straightforward and informative, but need not be scripted or approved by the IRB. Typically, a site receptionist's initial responses may include, "You will be called by Nurse Ratchet," or "Please report to a group meeting at 10:00 a.m. on December 7th in Room 123," or "We will mail you a brief questionnaire to see if you are eligible for our study."

Screening scripts or questionnaires developed to "pre-screen" candidates who respond to clinical trial advertisements via a telephone call to the site personnel or a call center are frequently submitted to IRBs for review as a best practice. This provides the IRB with an opportunity to evaluate the nature and type of information that the potential candidate is being asked to determine study eligibility, and helps ensure that the telephone screeners do not provide potentially misleading or coercive information to the caller.

Any exchange of clinical information, which does not require IRB approval, should be handled by more clinically qualified personnel than the receptionist.

12.7 Q. Is enrolling study staff in a clinical study permissible? How about their children?

A. This practice is highly questionable, and violates, at a minimum, the ICH GCP guideline's (E6) provisions regarding the enrollment of vulnerable subjects. According to the ICH guideline (1.61), vulnerable subjects are "individuals whose willingness to volunteer in a clinical trial may be unduly influenced by the expectation, whether justified or not, of benefits associated with participation, or of a retaliatory response from senior members of a hierarchy in case of refusal to participate. Examples are members of a group within a hierarchical structure, such as medical, pharmacy, dental and nursing students, subordinate hospital and laboratory personnel, employees of the pharmaceutical industry, members of the armed forces, and persons kept in detention."

Special protections must be provided to these subjects because their willingness to volunteer in a clinical trial may be influenced by the expectation, real or perceived, of receiving benefits (e.g., promotion, bonus) associated with participation or of being subjected to a retaliatory response from management (e.g., no promotion, no bonus) if they do not participate.

A clinic secretary, a hospital pharmacist technician, and a health care facility parking lot attendant could all be considered "vulnerable" in this sense. It would be prudent for a health care institution that conducts clinical studies to have policies regarding employee participation in these studies. The policies should address the conditions under which staff may enroll in a study and the safeguards that will be implemented to protect them.

Absent written policies, no employees of the institution should be enrolled. An institution's IRB should make this prohibition known to investigators. Investigators need to be highly sensitive to potential conflicts of interest.

Enrolling the children of clinic staff poses similar ethical conflicts. Minors are already included in the ICH guideline's definition of vulnerable subjects. The fact that their parent—the person legally responsible for them—is also a vulnerable individual only adds additional levels of complexity to enrollment issues. Site staff are well advised to avoid situations that even suggest that they may have enrolled their children based on financial and employment considerations.

12.8 Q. Is it a violation of FDA regulations when a principal investigator posts a note in the emergency room lounge to offer a free dinner to the resident that recruits the most eligible patients for a cardiology study over the next two months?

A. There are no prohibitions on simple recruiting incentives or rewards. These rewards should not be excessive, however. The FDA has not issued any guidelines on this topic. The American Medical Association has issued strongly worded guidance on "fee splitting" (see Q13.12), a practice under which a referring physician shares in the fee paid to the physician who ultimately treats the referred patient.

12.9 *Q. If a clinical investigator prepares a notice describing a trial and soliciting subjects and posts the notice only in employee lounges within the medical center, must the IRB review and approve this notice?*

A. IRBs must receive all advertising for clinical studies, regardless of whether the ads are to appear in newsprint, on radio or television, or in posters in the employees' lounge. Most IRBs prohibit the use of ads until they complete their review of an ad and send an approval letter to the principal investigator. Some IRBs, however, require only that the site submit the ad; since the IRB does not issue an approval letter, this is a type of passive approval.

In general terms, most IRBs want to be assured that advertisements include no coercive language, promises of benefits, or stated monetary rewards for subjects, among other provisions.

Further Reading

Bartruff, Bryce, "Strategies for Effective Subject Recruitment," *Research Practitioner,* 2:141-46, July-August 2001.

Acknowledgments

Douglas Mackintosh, DrPH, MBA, MS Hyg, and Vernette Molloy, MBA, RN, of GCPA, Inc.; Beth Harper, MBA, Vice President of Clinical Services, D. Anderson & Company, Dallas, TX.

Section 13:
Conflicts of Interest/Financial Disclosure

13.1 Q. Under GCP standards, are clinical investigators required to disclose, during the informed consent process, that they or their sites are being compensated for their work in the study?

A. Although there is no FDA GCP requirement or ICH GCP recommendation that clinical investigators disclose that they are being compensated for their work on a study, there is increasing pressure to do so.

In its updated voluntary *Principles for Conduct of Clinical Trials and Communication of Clinical Trial Results (2004)*, PhRMA states that "clinical investigators are encouraged to disclose to potential research participants during the informed consent process that the investigator and/or the institution is receiving payment for the conduct of the clinical trial." The PhRMA document adds that, "payment to clinical investigators or their institutions should be reasonable and based on work performed by the investigator and the investigator's staff, not on any other considerations . . . Payments or compensation of any sort should not be tied to the outcome of clinical trials."

Further, government regulators continue to develop formal guidance documents to address this area as well. In a May 2004 final guidance entitled "Financial Relationships and Interests in Research Involving Human Subjects: Guidance for Human Subject Protection," HHS attempts to help institutions, investigators, and IRBs involved in FDA-regulated and HHS conducted/sponsored research determine whether specific financial interests affect the rights and welfare of human subjects and, if so, what actions should be considered to protect these subjects. The document "recommends that, in particular, IRBs, institutions engaged in research, and investigators consider whether specific financial relationships create financial interests in research studies that may adversely affect the rights and welfare of subjects." With regard to the informed consent process, the guidance recommends that:

- IRBs determine "the kind, amount, and level of detail of information to be provided to research subjects regarding the source of funding, funding arrangements, financial interests of parties involved in the research, and any financial interest management techniques applied."
- Investigators consider "the potential effects that a financial relationship of any kind might have on the research or on interactions with research subjects, and what actions to take." These actions might comprise:
  —"including information in the consent document, such as the source of funding and funding arrangements for the conduct and review of research, or information about a financial arrangement of an institution or an investigator and how it is being managed.
  —using special measures to modify the consent process when a potential or actual financial conflict exists, such as having another individual who does not have a potential or actual conflict of interest involved in the consent process, especially when a potential or actual conflict of interest could influence the tone, presentation, or type of information presented during the consent process.
  —using independent monitoring of the research."

13.2 **Q. *Although much has been written about clinical investigator and institutional conflicts of interest and the regulatory and ethical need to disclose such potential conflicts to research subjects (see Q5.38), there are others in the research process that can have potentially problematic conflicts, including research subjects themselves. What, if any, regulatory responsibilities do clinical investigators have in identifying and responding to such conflicts of interest?***

A. The FDA is not known to have any requirements calling for clinical investigators, IRBs, or sponsors to identify or address possible research subject conflicts of interest. This form of potential financial conflict of interest is just now being discussed more openly. In a May 2004 *Journal of the National Cancer Institute* article, Helft, Ratain, Epstein, and Siegler write that, "in recent years, several research subjects and some family members have told us (via personal communications) that they had bought or intended to buy stock in the company sponsoring the clinical trial in which the research subject was enrolled. Moreover, clinical investigators from other institutions have occasionally recounted that their own research subjects have expressed the same intentions. More recently, and perhaps more ominously, evidence has surfaced that healthy individuals have insinuated themselves into clinical trials to obtain access to private information about drugs that are under clinical trial."

While acknowledging that study subjects with possible financial conflicts of interest may not be common, the authors emphasize that the phenomenon raises legal (e.g., insider trading), ethical, and scientific issues. "In terms of science, such conflicts of interest may interfere with the honest and straightforward reporting of a treatment's toxic effects and participant responses in ways that could compromise the primary scientific goals of early phase clinical trials," they state.

The article authors go on to describe a situation in which a study subject informed them that he owned stock in the company sponsoring the Phase 1 trial in which he was enrolled. Later, the authors stumbled upon an Internet chat room that was dedicate to sharing opinions and information about stocks, including the trial sponsor and that featured a posting in which "real, essentially accurate, and clearly nonpublic information about this research subject's positive clinical response to an investigational agent was being described and discussed . . . , often within days of the information being available to us." Although the information was posted anonymously, the investigators suspected that the subject was attempting to bolster the price of the stock, and became concerned about the accuracy of the research subject's previous reports of his "improving symptoms." They also reported that their communications and interactions with the subject were affected until the source of the "nonpublic information" posted on the Internet was found to be "a contact of the research subject" who learned of the subject's progress from the subject himself.

[see "Inside Information: Financial Conflicts of Interest for Research Subjects in Early Phase Clinical Trials," Helft, Ratain, Epstein, Siegler, *Journal of the National Cancer Institute,* Oxford: May 5, 2004, Vol. 96, Issue 9; p. 656]

13.3 **Q. *Are patient enrollment incentives permitted under GCP and, if so, must they be disclosed to potential subjects during the informed consent process?***

A. GCP standards do not prohibit enrollment incentives, nor do the standards specifically require the disclosure of such incentives to subjects. What are perceived to be overly aggressive patient recruitment efforts in the face of intense competition for trial subjects have been criticized in recent years, however.

Increasingly, enrollment incentives, or recruitment bonuses, are being viewed as potential conflicts of interest for clinical investigators, and as activities that must be managed and, in some cases, disclosed to clinical subjects. Still, such incentives are a fact of life in an environment that places such a premium on development speed, particularly when subject enrollment is seen as one of the key rate-limiting factors. According to PhRMA's voluntary "Principles for Conduct of Clinical Trials and Communication of Clinical Trial Results," "when enrollment is particularly challenging, reasonable additional payments may be made to compensate the clinical investigator or institution for time and effort spent on extra recruiting efforts to enroll appropriate research participants."

The HHS May 2004 final guidance on financial relationships and interests in clinical research (see Q13.1) does address enrollment incentives briefly, recognizing it as one of the factors that IRBs, institutions conducting research, and investigators consider "in establishing and implementing methods to protect the rights and welfare of human subjects from conflicts of interests created by financial relationships of parties involved in research." The guidance recommends that these parties ask whether "individuals or institutions involved in the research…receive payment per participant or incentive payments, and are those payments reasonable?" It is interesting to note, however, that a January 2001 HHS draft interim guidance entitled, "Financial Relationships in Clinical Research: Issues for Institutions, Clinical Investigators, and IRBs to Consider When Dealing with Issues of Financial Interests and Human Subject Protection" discussed these incentives a bit more fully. Specifically, the superseded January 2001 draft interim guidance recommended that these incentives be evaluated as potential conflicts of interest and that they be considered by the IRB and be disclosed to clinical trial subjects. "So-called 'recruitment bonuses' paid per participant, or for reaching an accrual goal within a specific time-frame, and being paid or paying a 'finders fee' for referral of potential participants, might affect one's judgment, or willingness to report adverse reactions possibly related to the study article, or the analysis and interpretation of data . . . ," the now-superseded document stated. "If a financial conflict of interest on the part of the Institution and/or the Clinical Investigator has not been or cannot be eliminated, what the financial arrangement is and how that conflict is being managed should be disclosed in the Consent document. The document should explain what additional protections have been put in place."

Some experts are claiming that an evolving liability environment that will hold drug sponsors increasingly responsible for the actions of clinical investigators and CROs should encourage sponsors to have the financial details and potential conflicts of interest relevant to a trial disclosed to patients. "My view is, and I suspect a jury's view and a judge's view is, when you switch the patient from patient to subject and you get $1,000 for it, that's something the patients ought to know," Assistant U.S. Attorney Jim Sheehan stated at the November 2002 Pharmaceutical Compliance Forum. Even if investigator payments are made by CROs or trial management organizations, sponsors "need to know what's happening at the second tier down from where [they] are."

13.4 Q. Given several recent high profile cases in which clinical researchers have been found to have financial interests in the drugs that they studied, including in a University of Pennsylvania study during which 18-year-old Jesse Gelsinger died tragically in 1999, questions have arisen as to the disclosures of such interests to potential study subjects. Under a regulation that took effect in early 1999, the FDA now requires new drug application (NDA) sponsors to submit information concerning the financial interests of, and compensation paid to, investigators responsible for key clinical studies submitted in NDAs. But that requirement was instituted to permit the FDA to examine submitted clinical data in the context of the financial interests of the clinical investigators who supplied the data. Do GCP standards require clinical investigators who hold financial interests in either a particular drug or a company that is researching that drug to disclose these interests to potential trial subjects during the informed consent process so that the subjects can view their participation in the context of possible investigator conflicts of interest?

A. There are not currently any formal GCP requirements regarding the disclosure to study subjects of potential conflicts of interest held by clinical investigators. The FDA does emphasize, however, that IRBs should be aware that the informed consent form must describe the study's "reasonably expected" benefits not only for the subject, but for "others" as well. "This may be an issue when benefits accruing to the investigator, the sponsor, or others are different than that normally expected to result from conducting research," the agency states in the Information Sheet entitled, "A Guide to Informed Consent." "Thus, if these benefits may be materially relevant to the subject's decision to participate, they should be disclosed in the informed consent document."

Given these high-profile cases, HHS unveiled several initiatives designed "to strengthen human subject protection in clinical research" in May 2000. As part of this effort, HHS released a March 2003 draft guidance followed by a May 2004 final guidance entitled "Financial Relationships and Interests in Research Involving Human Subjects: Guidance for Human Subject Protection," in which it attempts to help institutions, investigators, and IRBs involved in FDA-regulated and HHS conducted/sponsored research determine whether specific financial interests in research affect the rights and welfare of human subjects and, if so, what actions should be considered to protect these subjects. As noted above (see Q13.1), the document "recommends that in particular, IRBs, institutions, and investigators consider whether specific financial relationships create financial interests in research studies that may adversely affect the rights and welfare of subjects."

With regard to disclosing financial arrangements to subjects as part of the informed consent process, the draft guidance recommends that:

- IRBs determine "the kind, amount, and level of detail of information to be provided to research subjects regarding the source of funding, funding arrangements, financial interests of parties involved in the research, and any financial interest management techniques applied."
- Investigators consider "the potential effects that a financial relationship of any kind might have on the research or on interactions with research subjects, and what actions to take." These actions might comprise:

—"including information in the consent document, such as the source of funding and funding arrangements for the conduct and review of research, or information about a financial arrangement of an institution or an investigator and how it is being managed.

—using special measures to modify the consent process when a potential or actual financial conflict exists, such as having another individual who does not have a potential or actual conflict of interest involved in the consent process, especially when a potential or actual conflict of interest could influence the tone, presentation, or type of information presented during the consent process

—using independent monitoring of the research."

Due to the high-profile cases detailed above, some of which have led to lawsuits, increasing numbers of academic and industry groups and officials are looking more closely at whether such disclosures should be made and how they should be made to study subjects. The National Human Research Protections Advisory Committee (NHRPAC), in observing that this "is a largely undefined process with no clear precedents," pointed out that most of its members hold that possible significant conflicts of interest should "be available to, or affirmatively disclosed to, research subjects." And an American Association of Medical Colleges Task Force on Financial Conflicts of Interest recommended that "consent forms should, as a matter of an [academic] institution's COI policy, disclose the existence of . . . significant financial interests" held by researchers involved in clinical studies.

In general, the financial interests of clinical researchers and potential conflicts of interest within the research community continue to be hot-button issues within various U.S. government agencies. In response to controversies regarding potential conflicts of interest among NIH scientists (e.g., consulting arrangements with industry), for example, the federal government issued a February 3, 2005, interim rule in which it prohibited NIH employees from "engaging in certain outside activities" with certain entities, including "biotechnology, pharmaceutical, medical device, and other companies substantially affected by the programs, policies, and operations of the NIH." In addition, the NIH issued a January 4, 2005, policy under which any NIH staff member who participates in clinical research and who has a patent or financial interest in the product under study must ensure that this interest is disclosed to the IRB and to the research subjects (i.e., in the informed consent form) and that the research results are reviewed by an "independent entity," such as a data safety monitoring board. In addition, all principal investigators participating in HHS-sponsored research must review and follow the new policy, entitled *A Guide to Preventing Conflicts of Interest in Human Subjects Research at NIH* (January 4, 2005) and circulate the document to all other investigators whose names appear on a clinical protocol.

13.5 Q. In light of the Gelsinger tragedy, some medical institutions have instituted policies under which clinical investigators who have financial interests in a drug cannot be directly involved in the clinical care of a patient involved in a clinical study of the product. Do FDA or ICH GCP standards prohibit such clinical investigators from participating as either principal or sub-investigators?

A. There is no such prohibition in FDA or ICH standards. Increasing public attention on this area, including sharp criticism of the clinical trial process, is being reflected in emerging industry standards, such as PhRMA's updated "Principles for Conduct of Clinical Trials and Communication of Clinical Trial Results," which PhRMA says "spell out long-established practices for conducting clinical trials [but] also raise the bar by reducing the possibility of conflicts of interest on the part of researchers conducting the trials. . . ."

The PhRMA principles state, for example, that "clinical investigators or their immediate family should not have a direct ownership interest in the specific pharmaceutical product being studied . . . Direct ownership interests in a product (such as patent rights or rights to royalty payments) present an inherent conflict of interest, which could introduce bias into the conduct of the clinical trial. Companies that acquire the rights to products which have arrangements that are in conflict with [this principle] should take reasonable steps to modify the relationship." In addition, PhRMA's voluntary principles add that "clinical investigators and institutions should not be compensated in company stock or stock options for work performed on individual clinical trials."

As noted above, the financial interests of clinical researchers and potential conflicts of interest within the research community continue to be hot-button issues within U.S. government agencies, such as the NIH (Q13.4).

13.6 Q. Under FDA and ICH GCP standards, can a clinical investigator own stock in a pharmaceutical company and be contracted by that company to run a clinical study for one of its investigational drugs?

A. Again, FDA GCP regulations and the ICH GCP guideline do not prohibit clinical investigators from owning the stock of a company for which they are conducting a clinical trial. In certain cases, however, FDA regulations require that investigator financial interests be reported to the agency in marketing applications (see Q13.8).

PhRMA's 2004 "Principles for Conduct of Clinical Trials and Communication of Clinical Trial Results" state that, "ownership of stock in the sponsoring company does not disqualify the investigator from participating in clinical research for the company. However, sponsors may not compensate investigators with stock or stock options for work performed on individual clinical trials."

13.7 Q. A clinical trial for the investigational cancer treatment Erbitux brought greater attention to another type of potential conflict of interest—specifically, "institutional" conflict of interest. In this case, a study at M.D. Anderson Cancer Center enrolled 195 subjects without informing them that John Mendelsohn, the center's president, had a financial stake in, and was on the board of directors of, ImClone Systems, Erbitux's sponsor. Moreover, increasingly today, medical institutions and universities that conduct trials have financial stakes in sponsoring companies and products as well as patent rights to investigative products. Under GCP standards, must these interests be disclosed to potential study subjects during the informed consent process?

A. As noted, neither FDA regulations nor the ICH GCP guideline address potential investigator or institutional conflicts of interest, at least in terms of how such potential conflicts should be handled during clinical trials. Today, however, more and more research institutions, including the M.D. Anderson Cancer Center, are reportedly adopting policies under which potential study subjects must be informed of institutional conflicts of interest (i.e., an equity interest in a company).

And increasingly, regulatory agencies are recommending that those involved in the clinical research process take steps to identify and, where necessary to protect subjects, manage potential conflicts of interest. A May 2004 HHS final guidance entitled, "Financial Relationships and Interests in Research Involving Human Subjects: Guidance for Human Subject Protection" addresses possible conflicts of interest and steps that institutions should take to determine whether specific financial interests in research affect the rights and welfare of human subjects (see Q13.1). "Institutions and individuals involved in human subjects research may establish financial relationships related to or separate from particular research projects," the guidance states. "Those financial relationships may create financial interests of monetary value, such as payments for services, equity interests, or intellectual property rights . . . Financial interests are not prohibited, and not all financial interests cause conflicts of interest or affect the rights and welfare of human subjects. HHS recognizes the complexity of the relationships between government, academia, industry and others, and recognizes that these relationships often legitimately include financial relationships. However, to the extent financial interests may affect the rights and welfare of human subjects in research, IRBs, institutions, and investigators need to consider what actions regarding financial interests may be necessary to protect those subjects."

The May 2004 guidance makes several specific recommendations for those institutions engaged in federally conducted or supported clinical research (i.e., not FDA-regulated research, see note below), including the following:

- Institutions should consider establishing "the independence of institutional responsibility for research activities from the management of the institution's financial interests."
- Institutions should consider establishing conflict of interest committees (COIC), or identify other bodies or persons and procedures to deal with individuals' financial interests in research or verify their absence and to address institutional financial interests in research.
- Institutions should establish criteria to determine what constitutes an institutional conflict of interest, including identifying leadership positions for which the individual's financial interests are such that they may need to be treated as institutional financial interests.
- Institutions should establish policies regarding the types of relationships that may be held by parties involved in the research and circumstances under which those financial relationships and interests may or may not be held.

[Editor's note: the elements of the May 2004 HHS guidance addressing institutional conflicts of interest would not be relevant to FDA-regulated research because the FDA does not believe it has direct authority over medical institutions.]

13.8 Q. How do the FDA regulations requiring that NDA/BLA applicants disclose the financial interests of clinical investigators impact clinical studies?

A. These regulations were not necessarily designed to impact clinical studies directly. The purpose of the regulations, which became effective in February 1999, is to ensure that investigators' financial interests and sponsor/investigator financial arrangements that could affect the reliability of data submitted in pre-marketing applications are disclosed to the agency. The regulations affect sponsors of drug, biologics, and device studies who are submitting marketing applications, including bioequivalency studies. The FDA can refuse to file the application if a sponsor does not include, in its application, either a certification that there are no financial interests that may affect the reliability of the data or a disclosure of any relevant financial interest.

The agency evaluates the information provided by the sponsor to assess the potential of an investigator's financial interests to bias a study. If, upon assessing such information in the NDA, agency reviewers determine that the financial interests raise a serious question about the integrity of the data, the FDA may initiate an audit of the data provided by the clinical investigator in question, request that the applicant conduct further data analyses or that additional studies be conducted to confirm the results of the questioned study, refuse to use the investigator's data as a basis for agency action, or take other appropriate action. According to CDER officials, when reviewers find that an investigator has a financial interest in a sponsor or in the product under review, they will consider such information by more carefully scrutinizing the number of subjects the investigator enrolled and whether there were any outliers in terms of the adverse experiences reported by the investigator.

That being said, there is not yet any evidence that the increased scrutiny of financial interests in NDA reviews has affected the FDA's acceptance of clinical data. FDA officials are not aware of any pivotal study data eliminated from consideration due to the financial interests of clinical investigators.

13.9 Q. Is financial disclosure information about investigators entered into an FDA database? What purpose does this information serve?

A. According to FDA officials contacted on this topic, there is no agency- or center-wide effort to collect or analyze investigator financial disclosure information. Such disclosures are provided by sponsors in their NDAs and other applications, and it is the individual review divisions that use the information in the context of their reviews of the clinical data (see Q13.8).

13.10 Q. Some CROs have developed a relatively new service under which a CRO employee works at an investigational site as a study coordinator. Is there a potential conflict of interest for a company that performs monitoring to also be responsible for the study coordinator's tasks?

A. Potential conflicts of interest and the appearance of conflicts of interest abound in the drug industry, just as they do in science, medicine, law, teaching, and other endeavors. Does this mean that a CRO, by supplying both study coordinators and clinical research associates, is risking the appearance of a potential conflict of interest? Is it violating GCP standards and guidelines?

Study coordinators should answer to principal investigators. They should be paid by the institutions that also employ the principal investigators. When the principal investigator delegates tasks to study coordinators, there must be a considerable degree of assurance and trust that the study coordinator will perform these tasks according to GCP standards and according to the principal investigator's expectations.

A study coordinator who is employed by an organization other than the principal investigator/institution has a divided allegiance, especially if he or she is employed by a CRO. Some SMOs also provide study coordinators for clinical sites.

It is possible that a CRO-appointed monitor could be objective and perform his or her functions without undue or improper influence. There is still, however, the possibility of the perception of a conflict of interest, which should be avoided. Since the study coordinator and clinical research associate functions are so important to clinical study success and GCP compliance, site staff must have independence in fulfilling data collection tasks and monitors must exercise independent and strong quality oversight whenever a CRO employee is serving as a study coordinator.

13.11 Q. Although confidentiality agreements should be signed before study-related materials are sent to a potential clinical trial site, most sponsors send the agreement along with the study documents. What legal risks are associated with this?

A. From a liability standpoint, the safest course for the sponsor (and investigator) is to have, in its possession, a confidentiality agreement signed by the principal investigator before it ships study-related documents and materials to a site. This rule of thumb is equally applicable to other study activities, including contracting with a CRO or auditing firm. The confidentiality, or non-disclosure agreement, protects the sponsor by requiring the signatory to maintain the confidentiality of the sponsor's proprietary information.

13.12 Q. Does the FDA consider it acceptable for an investigator to pay a referral fee to other physicians who do not consent patients but do refer patients to the investigator's clinical site? Can sponsors include such a fee in their institution/investigator agreements/contracts?

A. The FDA's regulations do not strictly regulate fee arrangements between investigators and referring physicians. The bioethics community has a dim view of referral fees, however, and has voiced concern in the past that the practice of giving referral fees compromises professional judgment about trial eligibility. In the past, the Association of Academic Medical Centers (AAMC) and DHHS' Office of Human Research Protections (OHRP) have taken negative stances toward such practices as well.

In a June 2000 HHS Office of the Inspector General report, HHS recommended that the FDA and NIH develop definitive guidelines on appropriate recruiting practices, including whether "physicians should be allowed to receive fees for referring their patients as potential subjects for a clinical trial."

Awarding fees to providers simply for a referral (as opposed to fees related to the fair market value of professional services rendered) could violate the Stark Referral Law if Medicare or Medicaid are involved (however tangential such involvements might be).

Certain IRB members might take exception to the practice of granting referral fees, while others might not. As a practical matter, an IRB would have no knowledge of such fees unless they were disclosed voluntarily by an investigator.

Further Reading

Hockhauser, Mark, "Conflict of Interest Can Result in Research Bias," *Applied Clinical Trials,* 10:58-64, June 2001.

Korn, D., "Industry Academia, Investigator: Managing the Relationships," *Acad Med* 77:1089-95, 2002.

Lo, Bernard, et al, "Conflict-of-Interest Policies for Investigators in Clinical Trials," *NE J Med* 343:1616-20, 30 November 2000.

Acknowledgments

Douglas Mackintosh, DrPH, MBA, MS Hyg, and Vernette Molloy, MBA, RN, of GCPA, Inc.; Judy Newberne, JD, Vice President of Regulatory Affairs, Acambis, Cambridge, MA.

Section 14:
HIPAA and Commercial Clinical Research
by Mark Barnes, J.D. LL.M.
Ropes & Gray

Few other modern regulations have caused as much confusion and uncertainty among drug companies and clinical researchers as the federal government's so-called Privacy Rule. Promulgated under the Health Insurance Portability and Accountability Act of 1996 (HIPAA), these regulations, entitled "Standards for Privacy of Individually Identifiable Health Information" but more commonly referred to as the Privacy Rule, took force on April 14, 2003.

While the Privacy Rule provides individuals with greater control over their own health information, it imposes new limits upon the ways in which health care providers and other regulated entities may use or disclose health information for a variety of purposes, including clinical research.

The section comprises a set of newly updated (in April 2005) questions and answers first published in a text entitled, *HIPAA and Human Subjects Research: A Question & Answer Reference Guide* (March 2003). See www.barnettinternational.com for more information on this new reference guide.

DISCLAIMER: These questions and answers provide general information about the HIPAA Privacy Rule and explain how the Rule may apply to various research activities. They are not intended to provide specific legal advice. Readers should consult their own legal counsel for guidance when applying the Privacy Rule to particular factual situations.

14.1 Q. Who must comply with HIPAA? What is a "covered entity?" Are researchers covered by HIPAA?

A. HIPAA covers health plans, health care clearinghouses, and health care providers (individuals and hospitals or clinics) that transmit health information electronically in connection with certain transactions that are defined in the HIPAA statute. The HIPAA standard transactions include transmittals in connection with health care claims or equivalent encounter information, health care payment or remittance advice, coordination of benefits, health care claims status, enrollment and disenrollment in a health plan, eligibility for a health plan, health plan premium payments, referral certification and authorization, first report of injury, health claims attachments, and other transactions that may be prescribed by regulation. An entity (health plan, clearinghouse or provider) that conducts one or more of these covered transactions is deemed to be a "covered entity" under HIPAA and is bound by the Privacy Rule. A covered entity will also be bound by the related administrative simplification regulations.

Individual health care providers may have more than one status under HIPAA. If they are employees of a covered entity institution (e.g., a hospital), providers are members of the covered entity's workforce, and must follow the entity's privacy policies and procedures; however, in this role they are not themselves covered entities. By contrast, a health care provider who operates a private practice and bills (or engages a third party to bill) electronically on his or her own behalf will be a covered entity. A typical example would be an attending physician who is not a hospital employee and who operates her own private medical practice. This physician must independently meet all the responsibilities of a covered entity with respect to the health information that she creates or maintains in her private practice.

The Privacy Rule governs covered functions that include treatment, payment, and a category of administrative activities termed "health care operations." Research is not a covered function, and therefore researchers are not covered entities under the Privacy Rule by virtue of their research activities, even if those activities involve identifiable health information. If, however, the research involves either the provision of health care by a covered entity (either the researcher or another provider), as is true for most clinical trials, or medical records or archived biological samples maintained by a covered entity and labeled with health information, then the use or disclosure of the information or clinical trial data for research purposes must comply with the Privacy Rule.

14.2 Q. What is "protected health information," or "PHI"?

A. Protected health information ("PHI") is defined in the Privacy Rule as individually identifiable health information transmitted or maintained in any form or medium, unless such information is in the form of education records covered by the Family Educational Rights and Privacy Act or employment records held by a covered entity in its role as an employer.

"Health information" is defined as any information, whether oral or recorded in any form or medium, that: (i) is created or received by a health care provider, health plan, public health authority, employer, life insurer, school or university, or health care clearinghouse; and (ii) relates to the past, present, or future physical or mental health or condition of an individual; the provision of health care to an individual; or the past, present, or future payment for the provision of health care to an individual. Health information is "individually identifiable," and thus is considered to be PHI if there is any reasonable basis to believe that the information can be used to identify an individual. The Privacy Rule governs how covered entities may use or disclose the PHI that they create or maintain.

14.3 Q. What is a "business associate"? Is a business associate contract required before a covered entity may disclose protected health information to a researcher or to sponsors of clinical research?

A. Organizations that (or persons who) perform certain activities on behalf of a covered entity and use or receive PHI in the process are the "business associates" of the covered entity. The services giving rise to a business associate relationship may be functions or activities directly regulated by the Rule (e.g., claims processing or billing), or a defined list of other services that includes legal, administrative, management, accounting, consulting, actuarial, and accreditation services. The Privacy Rule requires a covered entity to enter a "business associate agreement" with each business associate; these agreements must contain specific provisions limiting how the business associate may use or disclose PHI, and spelling out the obligations of the business associate to protect the confidentiality of the PHI and of the covered entity to take certain actions in the event that the covered entity learns the business associate has breached the agreement.

Because research is not a function regulated by the Privacy Rule, a covered entity's disclosures to researchers and sponsors for research purposes do not require a business associate contract, even in those instances where the covered entity has hired the researcher to perform research on the covered entity's own behalf. Note, however, that other provisions in the Privacy Rule limit how covered entities may disclose PHI to researchers and sponsors. In addition, the HHS commentary to the Privacy Rule contemplates that a researcher could become a business associate if the researcher were hired by the covered entity to create de-identified data or a limited data set for the entity's own use or disclosure.

Researchers and sponsors should anticipate that even when business associate agreements are not required, clinical trial sites and covered entities participating in research will likely seek, through provisions in the clinical trial agreement or through data use agreements, to obtain assurances that all data recipients will protect the privacy of research data and will use such data only for agreed-upon purposes.

14.4 Q. What is the relationship between the Privacy Rule, federal research regulations known as the "Common Rule," and the FDA's research regulations that also protect human subjects of research?

A. The Privacy Rule is a separate regulation that applies in addition to and does not replace the federal "Common Rule" or FDA human subjects research regulations. In comparison to the federal Common Rule, which governs federally funded research, or FDA regulations, which govern research involving FDA-regulated products or supporting FDA applications, the Privacy Rule applies more broadly to any research uses or disclosures of PHI by a covered entity. Forms and procedures also differ under the Privacy Rule—for example, the written authorization required by the Privacy Rule for research uses or disclosures is not the same as the consent form required under the FDA and Common Rule regulations (although the two forms may be combined in a single document if that document meets all applicable regulatory requirements).

Additionally, although IRBs are authorized to grant waivers of authorization under the Privacy Rule, such waivers are distinct from the waivers of informed consent that an IRB is authorized to grant under the federal Common Rule. An investigator who is seeking PHI from a covered entity that complies with the Common Rule (e.g., an academic medical center), and who does not want to be required to obtain informed consent and a HIPAA authorization from each patient whose data are to be reviewed, will need to obtain *both* a waiver of informed consent and a waiver of authorization before proceeding with the research. Alternatively, the researcher could seek data in the form of a "limited data set" (data from which a specified list of identifiers have been removed). A limited data set may only be released if the researcher and covered entity enter a data use agreement.

14.5 Q. What are the required elements of an authorization? May the authorization be combined with the informed consent required under the Common Rule and the FDA's research regulations?

A. A valid HIPAA authorization must contain at least the following elements: (1) a "specific and meaningful" description of the information to be used or disclosed; (2) the name or other specific identification of the person (or class of persons) authorized to make the requested use or disclosure; (3) the name or other specific identification of the person (or class of persons) to whom the covered entity may make the requested use or disclosure; (4) a description of each purpose of the requested use or disclosure; (5) an expiration date or an expiration event that relates to the individual or the purpose of the use or disclosure; and (6) the signature of the individual and the date. The authorization must also contain statements adequate to place the individual on notice of all of the following: (1) the individual's right to revoke the authorization in writing (and either the exceptions to the right to revoke and a description of how the individual may revoke the authorization or, in some instances, a reference to the covered entity's notice); (2) the ability or inability of the health care provider or other covered entity to condition treatment, payment, enrollment or eligibility for benefits on the authorization; and (3) the potential for information disclosed pursuant to the authorization to be subject to re-disclosure by the recipient and no longer be protected by the Privacy Rule.

A research authorization may specify an expiration date of "none" (where permitted by state law), and in the case of a clinical trial, participation in the trial may be conditioned upon an authorization. As described above, the authorization to use or disclose PHI in a clinical trial and the informed consent for participation in the trial may be combined in a single document. Importantly, however, recent guidance from the Department of Health and Human Services indicates that an authorization for disclosure of PHI in connection with a clinical trial *may not* be combined with an authorization that would permit PHI collected during the trial to be placed in an archive or database for future research uses, if subjects are required to sign the clinical trial authorization as a condition of participating in the study.

14.6 Q. Can an investigator include the Privacy Rule authorization language in the research informed consent form? What if a potential research subject consents to participate in the research but refuses to sign the authorization?

A. For studies in which both an informed consent form and an authorization are required, the two forms may be combined or presented separately. In either case, investigators should take care to ensure consistency between the new HIPAA language and the traditional confidentiality language in the research informed consent (which is required by the Common Rule). Sponsors and investigators should also be aware that, although an IRB is not required to review a stand-alone authorization form, when the authorization and consent forms are combined the IRB must review the entire form for compliance with federal research regulations.

If a prospective subject refuses to sign the authorization, that person may be excluded from participation in a clinical trial, even if he or she has signed the informed consent form. (Outside the context of a clinical trial, however, a covered entity may not condition treatment upon a subject's willingness to sign an authorization.) This means, for example, that the provision of research-related treatment may not be conditioned upon the subject's willingness to authorize disclosure of PHI to an archive or database for use in future research.

14.7 Q. How does the Privacy Rule affect a researcher's ability to review medical records to identify potential research subjects? May the researcher contact patients whom he or she identifies as potentially eligible for a study?

A. The Privacy Rule allows covered entities to permit researchers to review PHI held in medical records or elsewhere for a "review preparatory to research" for the purpose of assessing the pool of potentially eligible subjects. Whether the researcher may use this PHI to contact potentially eligible subjects depends upon whether the researcher is a member of the covered entity's workforce or is a provider who has a treatment relationship with the patient. Disclosures of a patient's PHI to the patient himself are always permissible; thus, a covered provider who has access to PHI for treatment purposes may use that PHI to contact potential subjects for his or her own research. In addition, HHS guidance indicates that any researcher who is a member of a covered entity's workforce may use PHI obtained during a review preparatory to research to contact prospective subjects for recruitment purposes, so long as no PHI is removed from the covered entity's premises.

If a researcher is not a covered provider or workforce member or his or her research involves the records of individuals with whom the researcher has no treatment relationship, the researcher may apply to an IRB or Privacy Board for a partial waiver of authorization in order to access PHI for recruitment purposes. This is not a "full" waiver of authorization because it does not waive the patient's right to authorize the use or disclosure of his or her protected health information for the research itself. The partial waiver for recruitment may be obtained at the time that the protocol is submitted to the IRB for review, and could potentially be granted on an expedited basis, even if the protocol itself is not eligible for expedited review under the Common Rule.

If a researcher is a covered provider or workforce member conducting recruitment through a review preparatory to research, or if he or she has obtained a partial waiver of authorization for research purposes, the researcher should remember that under the Common Rule, FDA regulations, and most IRB policies, the IRB reserves the right to approve recruitment methods and materials. When the research is subject to IRB oversight, the researcher should not begin the recruitment process until the IRB has approved the recruitment methods and materials as set forth in the protocol.

14.8 Q. In some cases, clinical investigators make adverse event reports to IRBs, data and safety monitoring boards, and/or research sponsors; those adverse event reports often contain PHI. How will the Privacy Rule affect study-related adverse event reporting?

A. The Privacy Rule permits adverse event reporting to research sponsors, public health agencies, and health oversight agencies (e.g., FDA, OHRP) without obtaining an authorization or waiver of authorization. Other recipients of adverse event reports—including an IRB, DSMB, or other investigators in a multi-site trial—should be identified in the authorization form, although in some cases exceptions to the authorization requirement may be invoked to permit disclosures of adverse event information to an IRB without authorization. As a general rule, adverse event reporting should include the fewest possible identifiers, consistent with applicable research regulations.

14.9 Q. What new issues must investigators consider when designing and submitting a research protocol?

A. If an investigator is a covered entity, a workforce member of a covered entity, or requires access to the records of a covered entity for the research, he or she must anticipate how the new requirements of the Privacy Rule will affect his or her research. When designing a research protocol, the investigator should consider whether he or she will need to create or access PHI, and whether it is possible to conduct the study using a limited data set. The IRB or Privacy Officer of each covered entity involved in the study should then be consulted to determine which HIPAA forms or agreements the investigator must use for research involving that entity's PHI. Also, investigators should review their own policies and procedures for protecting the security and confidentiality of research data, as investigators may be asked to describe these safeguards to the IRB or Privacy Board of the covered entity.

If the investigator will be conducting a clinical trial, he or she should make certain that all necessary recipients of PHI generated in the research—including sponsors, sponsor's agents (e.g., CROs), DSMBs, IRBs, and researchers at other participating sites—are listed on the authorization form. If the investigator will be seeking a waiver of authorization or a limited data set, he or she should determine which data elements are necessary for research purposes.

Investigators should also consider whether data (or samples labeled with PHI) collected during a clinical trial will be archived for future research uses. If archiving will occur, the investigator must seek specific authorization for this activity. As noted in Question 14.5, separate authorization must be sought for the compilation of PHI in an archive or database.

Researchers should plan for the additional time required to comply with new Privacy Rule policies and procedures adopted by each covered entity involved in the research.

14.10 Q. Are research sponsors covered by the Privacy Rule?

A. Only to the extent that a sponsor meets the definition of a "covered entity." This would require, for example, that the sponsor act as a health plan, health care clearinghouse, or health care provider transmitting data electronically in connection with one of the standard HIPAA transactions (e.g., billing or claims referrals). It is possible that a sponsor could act as a covered entity if it provided medical products or services to patients and billed third-party payors directly for reimbursement. The HIPAA implications of such activities should be reviewed by legal counsel for each sponsor, and will require a thorough analysis of a sponsor's operations.

With regard to research, however, a sponsor does not become a covered entity when it provides grants to, or enters contracts with, a covered entity for research conducted on the sponsor's behalf, even if the covered entity bills third-party payors for routine clinical care related to the research. By contrast, data created or maintained by the covered entity in connection with a sponsored clinical trial are protected by the Privacy Rule until such data are disclosed to third parties (e.g., sponsors) outside the entity's control. This means that, notwithstanding any provisions to the contrary in the clinical trial agreement, the Privacy Rule will limit how the covered entity may disclose patient information to the research sponsor.

14.11 Q. Are all industry-sponsored research studies subject to the Privacy Rule?

A. Not in every case. The Privacy Rule does not regulate research per se, but instead applies only to the use and disclosure of PHI by covered entities. To the extent that a covered entity, such as a hospital or physician in private practice, conducts research that involves treatment or treatment records, the Privacy Rule applies, even when the research is industry-funded. If, however, neither the research sponsor nor the investigator nor any of the entities involved in conducting the research (e.g., laboratories), is a covered entity or a workforce member of a covered entity, the Privacy Rule does not apply. Also, for research that is "bench science" and involves no human subjects (defined to include samples labeled with identifiers), that research likely would produce no data that would qualify as PHI.

14.12 Q. How will the Privacy Rule impact research sponsors' ability to evaluate and select research sites and investigators for a study?

A. Research sponsors may continue making general inquiries about research sites and investigators. For example, the sponsor can seek—and a covered entity site or investigator may provide—information about whether a research site is appropriately equipped (e.g., whether it has sufficient facilities and administrative resources) and whether an investigator has the requisite experience, training, and patient population to conduct a study.

Research sponsors may review specific information, including PHI, but there will be additional requirements under the Privacy Rule if the site or the investigator is a covered entity. For example, if a sponsor asks to review actual case report forms from a previous study to assess the investigator's recordkeeping, the covered entity investigator or site must first obtain each subject's authorization (or a waiver of authorization from the IRB or Privacy Board) before disclosing such information to the sponsor (see discussion above).

14.13 Q. If a research sponsor is a covered entity, will it be required to enter into a business associate agreement with an investigator?

A. No. Even if a research sponsor is a covered entity, a business associate agreement with an investigator is not required because research is not a function regulated by the Privacy Rule (see discussion above). A business associate agreement would be required if the sponsor engaged a researcher or other contractor to create de-identified data or a limited data set that the sponsor could then use or disclose for research purposes.

14.14 Q. How should the Privacy Rule be addressed in research agreements between sponsors and research sites or investigators?

A. The Privacy Rule does not mandate that particular provisions be included in research agreements. Nonetheless, within the written research agreement, the parties should establish the permissible uses of research data and their respective obligations to protect subjects' privacy and confidentiality.

Thus, a research agreement should include provisions addressing the following issues:

- Each party's obligation to comply with all *applicable* laws and regulations, including HIPAA (since HIPAA is not applicable to most research sponsors anyway, agreeing to such a provision should not disadvantage a research sponsor).
- The research site or investigator's responsibility to obtain the authorization of each research subject or to obtain a waiver of authorization from an IRB or Privacy Board, as applicable.

- If the authorization of each research subject will be obtained, whether the sponsor's or the research site's or investigator's form of authorization will be used.
- Those parties, including the sponsor, who will be permitted to receive PHI as part of the study, and the PHI that they will be permitted to receive.
- Any restrictions on the further use and disclosure of PHI by the sponsor and other parties who receive PHI as part of the study.

14.15 Q. In some clinical trials, research sponsors provide investigators with an informed consent form to be approved by the investigators' Institutional Review Boards. Should research sponsors also provide investigators with a HIPAA authorization form?

A. Depending upon the nature of the clinical site(s) participating in the protocol, sponsors may find it helpful to provide investigators with a model authorization form for the research. This form should meet the requirements of the Privacy Rule while providing sponsors and others involved in the trial (e.g., coordinating centers or data safety monitoring boards) the access to PHI that is necessary to conduct the research. In addition, authorization forms must meet the requirements of any state medical confidentiality laws that have not been preempted by the Privacy Rule. Sponsors should be aware, however, that institutional covered entities (e.g., hospitals and academic medical centers) are likely to have adopted their own authorization forms, along with local policies regarding whether the authorization may be combined with the research informed consent.

If a research sponsor decides to rely upon the authorization forms provided by the investigator or the trial site, the sponsor should consider whether it is advisable to review the forms to determine whether they authorize the range of disclosures to the sponsor and others and the types of uses of PHI that will be necessary to conduct the research. Sponsors should also consider whether issues of data access and use are adequately addressed in the clinical trial agreement, and may wish to consider adding, during the site monitoring process, a check to assure that investigators have obtained the necessary authorizations from study subjects.

14.16 Q. Does the Privacy Rule limit how research sponsors may use and disclose information about research subjects?

A. Because HIPAA applies only to covered entities, the HIPAA Privacy Rule does not limit how research sponsors may use and disclose information about research subjects (except where sponsors are covered entities). Note, however, that a sponsor's use and disclosure of identifiable health information may be limited in other ways. For example, the Privacy Rule only permits a covered entity to disclose PHI to a sponsor pursuant to a waiver of authorization if the purpose is the sponsor's research. Disclosures to a sponsor for marketing purposes require an authorization form from each patient that identifies the marketing purpose. In addition, a research sponsor must abide by any restrictions on its use and disclosure of PHI to which it agreed in the clinical trial agreement. Sponsors of research should note, however, that some state medical privacy laws, including those related to genetic testing results and HIV/AIDS information, may apply to sponsors themselves, and legal counsel should be sought for such state law compliance issues.

14.17 Q. Can research sponsors or their representatives continue to conduct on-site audits and monitoring of interventional clinical trials?

A. Yes. To the extent that such activities are required by FDA or other regulation or are for purposes related to adverse events, the Privacy Rule permits access without an authorization or waiver of authorization. Because auditing and monitoring activities may extend beyond what is expressly required by law or regulation, sponsors should ensure that the authorization form for the trial names sponsors and their agents and representatives as entities that will receive and use PHI for the purposes of the research.

14.18 Q. The Privacy Rule creates a new entity called a "privacy board." What are the distinctions between an Institutional Review Board (IRB) and a Privacy Board?

A. A Privacy Board is an entity that may be created under the Privacy Rule to review researchers' requests for alteration or waiver of the Rule's requirement for individual authorization. A covered entity also has the option of using an IRB to perform these functions. Because some covered entities, both individual physicians and institutions, may lack IRBs, or may feel that their own IRBs lack sufficient expertise in the assessment of risks to privacy, the Privacy Rule permits a covered entity to "reasonably" rely upon a waiver of authorization granted by an external IRB or privacy board.

Unlike an IRB, a Privacy Board is not required to have a minimum number of members, but must include at least one member who is unaffiliated with the covered entity or research sponsor, and no member may participate in the review of a protocol in which the member has a conflict of interest. The Privacy Board must also include members with varying backgrounds and appropriate professional competency to evaluate the effect of the research protocol on the individual's privacy rights and related interests.

14.19 Q. Are there advantages or disadvantages to combining an IRB and Privacy Board into one entity, rather than keeping them separate?

A. HIPAA permits covered entities engaged in research to use an existing affiliated IRB to perform the functions delegated to a privacy board (specifically, reviewing and approving waivers of the authorization requirement). It may be simpler and more efficient for covered entities to rely upon an existing IRB to review requests for waivers of authorization, rather than forming a separate privacy board for this purpose. An institution might also consider forming a privacy board for the limited purpose of reviewing requests to access archives of medical information or identifiable biological samples for research (note that research uses of such archives may also require IRB review under the Common Rule).

If, on the other hand, a covered entity does not have an affiliated IRB or its IRB members lack the expertise necessary to assess risks to privacy and confidentiality, it might be advisable for the entity to form a separate privacy board for the purpose of documenting waivers of authorization. Alternatively, the Privacy Rule permits the covered entity to reasonably rely upon waivers granted by an external IRB or privacy board.

14.20 Q. Does a covered entity need approval by both an IRB and a privacy board in order to use or disclose subjects' protected health information for research purposes?

A. It is important to distinguish between, on the one hand, approval of the research protocol as required by the Common Rule or FDA regulations, and on the other hand, the covered entity's obligation to meet procedural requirements under the Privacy Rule for use or disclosure of PHI in research. When research is subject to the Common Rule or FDA regulations, IRB approval of the research protocol must be sought along with IRB approval of the consent form (or an IRB waiver of informed consent). Federal research regulations also give the IRB a continuing role in the oversight of the research through the continuing review process.

By contrast, the Privacy Rule does not require an IRB or a privacy board to approve a research protocol, nor does the Rule require that an IRB or privacy board continue to oversee research for the duration of the protocol. As noted above, however, under the Privacy Rule the covered entity must ensure that the authorization form contains the necessary disclosures and is properly dated and signed; in practice, such review may often be delegated to the IRB.

Likewise, the Privacy Rule does not require IRB approval of the research protocol before the IRB or privacy board may grant a waiver of authorization for the research, provided that the IRB or privacy board is satisfied that the research meets the Rule's criteria for waiver of authorization. Yet both IRB and privacy board approval would be necessary *before* an investigator could commence a research study in which both informed consent and authorization are to be waived.

Further Reading

Barnes, Mark, and Kulynych, Jennifer, *HIPAA and Human Subjects Research: A Question & Answer Reference Guide,* PAREXEL, 2003. See www.barnettinternational.com for more information.

Kohn, Adam M., "HIPAA Privacy Rule: Effect on Medical Research," *Applied Clinical Trials,* 11:60-62, June 2002.

Section 15:
Drug Accountability, Administration, and Labeling

15.1 Q. Can investigational products be mailed to subjects or must subjects always come in to the site to receive them?

A. Since experimental therapies must always be administered under the investigator's personal supervision or "under the supervision of a subinvestigator responsible to the investigator" (21 CFR 312.61), investigational products should not be mailed directly to subjects. Storage conditions cannot be ensured if products are sent through the mail. Also, the product could possibly end up in the hands of individuals for whom they were not intended, creating the potential for diversion.

Subjects, even those who travel long distances to study sites, must understand that they must show up for study visits to receive these investigational products.

If, in rare cases, a study subject is located a considerable distance from a study site, arrangements could be made to have a family physician or local pharmacy dispense the investigational product to the subject under the direction of an investigator. In this case, the investigational product would be mailed to the family physician or pharmacist along with specific dispensing instructions and, if necessary, a temperature monitor.

15.2 Q. How frequently are drug accountability-related deficiencies cited in FDA GCP inspections?

A. Traditionally, drug accountability is among the more commonly cited deficiencies in CDER's GCP compliance inspections of clinical trial investigators and sites. In FY2003 (the latest year for which data are available), 4.5% of the clinical investigators/sites inspected by CDER were cited for drug accountability issues. This, however, was an improvement over the 13% of sites/investigators cited for such violations in FY2002.

Despite their overall frequency, drug accountability-related issues are seldom considered significant departures from agency standards. This can be inferred because the FDA cited only 1% of all clinical investigators/sites inspected in FY2003 for what the agency considered major departures from GCP regulations.

U.S. and foreign investigators/sites have had somewhat different compliance patterns in this area. In FY2003, 5% of U.S. investigators inspected were cited for such problems compared to no foreign investigators/sites. In FY2002, however, 12% of U.S. sites/investigators were cited for drug accountability issues, compared to 22% of non-U.S. sites/investigators.

15.3 Q. Can approved products used in Phase 4 studies be mailed to subjects to save on subjects' travel time and expense? While it is understood that investigational products cannot be mailed to subjects, shouldn't approved products used in the context of Phase 4 studies be treated differently?

A. Under appropriate mailing conditions, an approved product could be mailed directly to a subject enrolled in a Phase 4 study. At least in terms of the shipping of the drug, this situation is somewhat analogous to a mail order pharmacy supplying a drug product. In a Phase 4 study, however, the study's principal investigator or subinvestigator should be responsible for ordering the study drug so that it may be dispensed through the mail. While there are no special restrictions regarding the mailing of approved drugs, investigators who want to more carefully control the dispensing process may reject this approach.

15.4 Q. What category of study personnel is authorized to administer investigational drugs?

A. Investigational drugs should be administered by the same category of personnel who would ordinarily administer them in general clinical practice. Typically, state licensing boards and clinical institution administrators determine which personnel can dispense drugs. In some states, for example, intramuscular injections can only be administered by an RN or LPN, while in other states they can be administered by any individual under the supervision of a physician. Similarly, there are state regulations and hospital requirements regarding who may prepare and/or administer intravenous drugs.

Unfortunately, these regulations and requirements are not always followed in clinical studies. There have been cases, for example, in which investigators' administrative staff have prepared intravenous investigational drugs for administration. In other cases, medical assistants, who may or may not possess a three-month training certificate, have administered experimental gene therapy products.

In recent informal correspondence on this issue, the FDA noted that site personnel other than the investigator or subinvestigator can administer a study drug, "provided that the appropriate supervision is exercised and provided that drug administration is within the scope of an individual's professional license and state law. These laws regulate clinicians, such as nurses and PAs, in the scope of their practices and may vary from state to state. See Section 505(i)(1)(b) of the FD&C Act, which states that a sponsor must obtain a statement from each investigator that patients to whom the drug is administered will be under his personal supervision, or under the supervision of investigators responsible to him and that he will not supply the drug to any other investigator, or to clinics, for administration to human beings."

For clinical trials, the standard of care should certainly be at least equivalent to the standard exercised in routine medical practice. One could argue, in fact, that it should be higher since clinical trials involve the use of experimental products whose safety and effectiveness profiles are not entirely defined.

15.5 Q. What should be done if, after examining a bottle of study medication, a study coordinator observes that several of the normally white tablets have turned gray?

A. Any time a medication does not look, smell, or feel "normal," it should not be administered. That is the first step—and a simple one.

It is critical, however, that the study coordinator immediately takes additional steps to ensure the safety of the subjects at his or her site as well as all study sites. Most importantly, the study coordinator must immediately notify the principal investigator and the sponsor. Even if other tablets appear normal, the dispensation and administration of study tablets should be suspended from the point at which the "tainted" tablets were noted.

The sponsor must then notify other clinical sites as well as the manufacturer (i.e., if different from the sponsor) and supplier. The tainted tablets, along with other samples, must be analyzed as a first step in determining the cause of the problem. Possible problems could range from product component and/or manufacturing process issues to improper shipment, handling and maintenance of the tablets.

All shipments of study tablets should be halted until the manufacturer provides a written report of the analysis and findings to the sponsor (i.e., if the sponsor is not the manufacturer) and site. The sponsor must ensure that all elements of the manufacturing and shipping process met good manufacturing practice standards. The study sponsor also must ensure that the affected site and all other study sites followed proper storage and handling procedures. Before any additional study drugs are administered to study subjects, the sponsor must be certain that the problem has been addressed and that the integrity of the study product is no longer compromised. In addition, site staff must follow up carefully with subjects who may have received tainted product.

Site staff must make appropriate notations regarding such situations in the subjects' source documents, in regulatory notes to the file, and in drug accountability records.

15.6 Q. At 21 CFR 312.61-Control of the Investigational Drug, FDA regulations state that "an investigator shall administer the drug only to subjects under the investigator's personal supervision or under the supervision of a subinvestigator responsible to the investigator." How is "administer" defined for the purposes of this provision?

A. The term "administer" refers to the act of giving the study drug to the subject; this act may involve the principal investigator or his/her delegate. The purpose of the regulation governing the administration of study drugs is to ensure adequate clinical oversight by the principal investigator over subjects who are receiving investigational products. Oversight can only be ensured if the subjects are under the supervision of the principal investigator or his/her delegates.

As part of hospital in-patient studies, for example, before a nurse administers an intravenous study drug, the principal investigator or subinvestigator must write an order for that drug. Generally, this procedure is in place due to hospital rules. In private physician offices, a physician can verbally instruct an office staff person to administer a drug. In the types of settings in which clinical studies are conducted, staff who give, or administer, study medicines must act under the direct supervision of the principal investigator or subinvestigator.

Often, the terms "administer" and "dispense" are used interchangeably in clinical studies. In general clinical practice, however, nurses administer drugs and pharmacists dispense drugs. In clinical studies, study coordinators often do both: for example, a subject may be administered one study drug capsule to take during the study visit and also be dispensed an additional six capsules to take home. In such cases, the study coordinator is actually performing two different tasks: administration and dispensation. The principal investigator or subinvestigator must exert careful oversight over both of these tasks.

In many clinical studies involving chronic diseases, drugs are dispensed to subjects who thereafter self-administer them at home. As a practical matter, even though a study may employ the use of patient diaries (see Section 18), a principal investigator cannot be absolutely certain that such study drugs were self-administered according to a protocol's specifications.

15.7 *Q. Must an expiration date appear on a test article's labeling?*

A. FDA regulations at 21CFR 312.6-Labeling of an investigational new drug include no provision requiring an expiration date on a test article's label. It is common industry best practice, however, to include an expiration date on the immediate label of an investigational drug product. This permits an investigator and his or her site staff to easily determine if the test article has expired before use.

At 21 CFR 211.137(g), the good manufacturing practice (GMP) regulations provide investigational drugs a specific exemption from expiration dating requirements. These regulations, however, specify that the exemption applies ". . . provided that [investigational drugs] meet appropriate standards or specifications as demonstrated by stability studies during their use in clinical investigations. . . ." Under common industry best practice, sponsors develop stability data demonstrating that the materials will be stable for the expected duration of the clinical trial, at a minimum.

It is important to note that all approved drugs must feature an expiration date on the label.

15.8 *Q. If a particular study site requires additional supply of an investigational product, is it permissible for another investigational site in the same study to forward some of its unused supply to the site?*

A. FDA regulations at 21 CFR 312.59 state that the sponsor may "authorize alternative dispositions of unused supplies . . . provided this alternative disposition does not expose humans to risks from the drugs." The proviso in this regulatory passage was intended primarily to make certain that, if the unused drugs were incinerated or otherwise disposed of, the resulting byproducts would not pose a hazard to humans. On the surface, it would not appear that the transfer of a study drug between sites would expose humans to additional risks.

There are some sponsors whose standard operating procedures prohibit the transfer of study drug from one site to another. Other sponsors will allow a transfer, but only under extremely tight controls. In this case, tight control means regulatory affairs sign-off and completion of the appropriate forms before the transfer can occur. Under no circumstances should one site ship to another without a sponsor's prior written agreement.

Drug accountability records at both clinical sites should accurately reflect the transfer. If problems, such as product damage or diversion, occur in the shipping process, the sponsor's regulatory affairs group should be notified immediately. The principal investigator who shipped the drug to another site must take regulatory responsibility for this action.

There may also be situations in which a site with excess drug supply sends unused drug back to the sponsor who, in turn, sends these supplies to a second site.

As long as the sponsor maintains appropriate drug accountability records as required by 21 CFR 312.57(a) and the FDA can access these records and reconcile drug usage, the agency does not have significant further requirements regarding the disposition of unused drug supplies. In an inter-site drug transfer, however, it is critically important that the site, sponsor, and FDA be able to reconcile drug usage at both sites by reviewing drug accountability records.

From a regulatory perspective, the transfer of investigational drugs between sites operating under different protocols may present additional risks. Even in the face of inadequate drug supply, such transfers should be subjected to even greater scrutiny before they are approved.

Further Reading

Mackintosh, D. and Molloy, V., "Reconciling Drug Accountability Records," *GCPj,* 9(4):24-25, April 2002.

Acknowledgments

Douglas Mackintosh, DrPH, MBA, MS Hyg, and Vernette Molloy, MBA, RN, of GCPA, Inc.; Maryanne Gottfried, President, MVG Consulting Services, Inc., Braintree, MA; Drew Karlan, MS, MBA, Vice President, Regulatory and QA, Wellspring Pharmaceutical Corporation, Neptune, NJ.

Section 16:
Data Management and Statistical Analysis

16.1 Q. What is an acceptable error rate for a study database?

A. After a database has been "cleaned" through the query process and is nearing finalization, a quality control check is performed. In some cases, this process is incorrectly referred to as a "data audit" or "internal quality control audit." While audits are performed by external auditors, this internal review is conducted by individuals within the data management department.

The process involves a comparison of a data sample, usually ten percent, of case report forms with data on line listings from the study's database. The standard generally acceptable within industry is no more than 5 errors per 10,000 data items (0.0005 or 0.05%). Some statistically sophisticated data managers believe that a less-stringent standard (5 errors per 1,000 data items, or 0.5% rate) is acceptable if it reflects the upper bound of a 95% or 99% confidence interval.

The exhibit below displays error rates for five different studies. Study 2A's database has the lowest error rate. Note that the error rate at a 99% confidence bound (2.67 standard deviations) is 21 per 10,000. The error rate for study 4B is 15 per 10,000, which, if the errors involve important study variables, is high.

Results of Internal Quality Control Review

Study	Number of Data Items Reviewed	Number of Errors Detected	Estimated Error Rate per 10,000 Data Items	Error Rate at Upper Bound of 99% Confidence per 10,000 Data Items (2-sided)
01	4222	4	9	27
1B	4010	3	7	25
2A	4005	2	5	21
4A	4062	4	10	28
4B	4012	6	15	36

These quantitative analyses do not specify which variables had errors. Some quality control efforts divide data variables into two types: critical and non-critical variables. Acceptable error rates are lower for critical than for non-critical errors.

QA audits of databases, whether locked (frozen) or unlocked, generally sample a few key critical variables. The exhibit below displays the results of one such audit.

Results of QA Audit of a Study Database

	Patient Number	Visit or Variable	CRF Value	Data Listing Value
Efficacy Measure	1848	Month	two values on one question	entered lower value*
	2029	Day 1	two values on one question	entered lower value*
	1485	Month 1	three questions (#1, 2, and 4)	incorrectly entered
	Total errors = 5			
Adverse Experiences	682	Study Drug caused AE	2	1
	3284	Date stopped	5/17	5/19
	1436	Date stopped	continued	4/7
	Total errors = 3			

*Higher value was to be data entered as specified in the statistical analysis plan.

There were five errors in data listings for the primary efficacy measure and three errors for adverse experiences. While these numbers do not appear to be troubling, error rates, as illustrated in the exhibit below, were 4.8 per 10,000 for the efficacy measures and 7.1 for AE variables. These raw error rates were then adjusted to account for data fields for which, due to CRF skip patterns and other reasons, no data could have or would have been expected to be data entered. The adjusted error rates are 5.2 per 10,000 for the efficacy measure and 10.4 for AEs. Again, these rates appear to be too high.

Summary of Data Listings Audit

	Raw Error Rate (per 10,000)	Adjusted Error Rate (per 10,000)
Efficacy Measure	4.8	5.2
AE	7.1	10.4

Today, industry is moving to a far tougher standard for critical variables, such as key efficacy and safety variables: less than 1 error per 10,000. Some firms expect the error rate to be zero for critical variables. In this case, the review may involve 100% verification of AEs and primary efficacy data.

Company standard operating procedures should define sampling schemes, specify acceptable error rates, and discuss methods for calculating the rates for both QC and QA reviews. In addition, they should define action items when the first review does not meet the standard.

16.2 Q. What are characteristics of well-constructed data queries?

A. First and foremost, queries sent to sites must be understandable to study coordinators (SCs), and must provide an easy method for them to respond. Queries must indicate subject number, visit number, case report form page, variable name, item name, and existing value. Obviously, the query should clearly describe the potential issue with the value being questioned.

The second most important characteristic of a well-constructed data query is wording that highlights the possible issue with the existing value in a neutral, unbiased manner. Biased queries comprise GCP compliance issues, since they might favor or encourage a particular response from site staff.

Care must be taken in programming the wording of queries generated by error-trapping computer programs to ensure that queries are unambiguous, easy to complete, and do not bias responses provided by study coordinators and others.

16.3 Q. Can a database be locked even though all data queries are not addressed or resolved by study site staff?

A. It is not unusual for a database to be locked before all queries are resolved. Before the blind is broken and the efficacy analyses are conducted, however, a clean, locked database is a necessity. If a sponsor waited for all queries to be resolved, it might be unable to perform the statistical analyses and prepare a clinical study report in a timely manner.

In practice, the data query and database lock process generally proceeds as follows. Monitors and project managers try their best to motivate site staff to answer queries. Often, however, a few queries remain unanswered or unresolved by the established deadline. At this point, study staff review and assess these few data problems. As a result, the sponsor's study staff determine, as per data management standard operating procedures, that the outstanding data issues are not significant and that the data, as currently data entered and line listed, are "sufficiently" accurate. Then, they declare these queries "resolved" by consensus, and lock the database.

Given the reality that not even the best of processes is full-proof, there exist procedures through which a database can be unlocked if a "significant" piece of data is modified or becomes available following the database lock. What is important is that the data management and clinical staff make its best effort to resolve as many data queries as possible within the relevant time and resource constraints, and that standard operating procedures are followed in unlocking and relocking the study database.

Clinical site performance is not always optimal. Principal investigators, study coordinators, and other site personnel experience a certain degree of turnover. Source documents are lost. Subjects disappear or are non-compliant. Site staffers neglect to perform tests and collect data. Data values can be spurious and/or significantly out of range. It is simply impractical to expect that every data query can be resolved to the satisfaction of every clinical manager.

If a database is modified after the blind is broken, there should be analyses performed to ascertain the impact of the changes on study results.

16.4 Q. Can a CRO or sponsor write on case report forms, thereby making changes to case report form data?

A. Yes, but only under limited conditions. First, the CRO/sponsor must have a standard operating procedure or a study operations manual that describes what changes can be made, who is authorized to make them, and how these changes will be communicated to the site. Second, changes can only be made on NCR copies, not

on separated white originals. Third, the types of changes must be "self-evident," examples of which include the following:
- CRF header information is blank or incorrect (e.g., the subject's initials are reversed on one page).
- the space for a concomitant medication route of administration is blank, and the particular medication has only one available formulation (tablets taken orally).
- as a result of skip patterns, an entry of 9999 was supposed to have been written in for a data item.

Fourth, the changes should be those that would not require a review of medical records at a site. Fifth, the changes should not reasonably require the concurrence or sign-off of the principal investigator or study coordinator. Lastly, the significance of the changes should not justify a study site's investment of time in responding to a query.

Data management conventions suggest that case report form errors and omissions be divided into two types:
- *Type 1 or Alpha Errors*:* those that can be corrected without queries and site concurrence.
- *Type 2 or Beta Errors*:* those that require queries, site review, and sign-offs.

Type 1 errors can be corrected by designated individuals in the data management department. A company's data management or edit review plan must define, in advance, the process for making these changes and the staff with the authority to implement them.

Forward-thinking data management departments establish specific procedures and standards for triaging errors, for assigning errors as Type 1 or Type 2 errors, and for addressing each error according to its classification.

16.5 Q. Is there a rule of thumb that Phase 2 studies have sample sizes sufficient for 90% power and Phase 3 studies have sample sizes sufficient for a 95% power?

A. There is no best-practice consensus regarding study power, other than a general rule of thumb that studies have a minimum of 80% power. There is a direct association between power and sample sizes.

Phase 2 studies are often designed with 90% power, and conservative Phase 3 trials often have 95% power, although there are many examples in which each study phase has 80% power. If a sponsor plans to use a single pivotal study to support the safety and efficacy of a new drug, it is highly recommended that the pivotal study have at least 90% (preferably 95%) power.

If the power of a study is less than 80%, it diminishes the study's chances of reaching the 0.05 level of confidence, or alpha level, for comparison testing. If an alpha level is 0.05, then a two-sided confidence interval is 95%.

---

*As used in data management context. Should not be confused with the meaning of the terms in the statistical context.

16.6 Q. What are the implications when a particular study's results indicate a statistically significant difference among treatment groups, but no clinically meaningful treatment differences among the groups?

A. Occasionally, a study may have statistically significant results that are not particularly meaningful from the perspective of practicing clinicians. This seemingly contradictory outcome can occur in the following situation, for example:

Assume that a particular study enrolls a large number of subjects. Say that the study detected an extremely small, yet statistically significant, difference in the primary variable—blood pressure in this case—between treatment groups. This difference in blood pressure—say 2 mmHg—would not be large enough for a practicing clinician to consider it clinically meaningful.

In this scenario, there can be considerable disagreement as to whether the primary variable, which is usually selected because the sponsor's clinicians believe it is an important measure of treatment effect, is one that, given a small difference among treatment groups, is sufficiently important to prescribers (i.e., to change their prescribing practices). In some cases, the primary efficacy variable is a composite score of the blinded investigator's opinion of treatment changes from baseline or a standardized behavioral test score; these measures are somewhat subjective or questionable indicators of morbidity and mortality. Although a study may show highly statistically significant results ($p \leq 0.001$), the vast majority of practicing clinicians may be unconvinced that this result matters in the delivery of care to their patients. The sponsor of this study may also make economic and quality-of-life statements to further augment its case for changing prescribing habits.

It is important to note that the FDA may approve a drug based on studies showing a statistically significant difference that is not particularly clinically meaningful. A drug can be approved in such scenarios for several reasons, including that it represents a "first in class" drug for an indication or that it is associated with fewer side effects than established treatments.

In a 1986 decision in the *Warner Lambert v. Margaret Heckler (787 FR 2D Series)* case, however, the U.S. Court of Appeals found that the FDA did not have to approve a drug whose study results were statistically significant but not clinically meaningful. Warner-Lambert sued the FDA claiming, in part, that the agency had erred in failing to approve the company's oral proteolytic enzymes, which were supported by studies showing statistically significant differences between the test and control groups. In its decision, the court wrote that:

"The Commissioner's interpretation of the statute as requiring a showing of clinical significance, rather than merely statistical significance, is persuasive for several reasons."

"The fact that the drug, not chance, can be assumed to have contributed to the factor measured does not necessarily establish that patients will receive a benefit from the drug."

"The largest difference in measurements between the drug group and the placebo group in absolute figures (rather than percentages) was approximately 1/4 inch. Although the percentage difference was statistically significant, the Commissioner rejected the study, in part based on expert testimony that the difference in measurements was 'therapeutically trivial.'"

This court decision made a clear distinction between statistical significance and clinical or therapeutic meaningfulness.

The situation becomes even more complex when the comparative drug is an active approved drug rather than a placebo. In such cases, a study may attempt to show that an experimental therapy is either superior or equivalent to a standard therapy. While a new drug's statistically significant superiority may be very clinically impressive, its statistically significant equivalency may not be particularly meaningful to clinicians.

16.7 Q. The ICH GCP guideline (E6) states that the deletion of entered data is not permitted, and that data edits require the completion of an audit trail. If a data clarification is received from an investigator stating, for example, that an adverse event was really a pre-existing condition before enrollment, is the removal of the adverse event and the addition of the information on the medical history case report form considered an edit or a deletion?

A. What is most important in this case is not losing data that were recorded by the investigator. The key point is considered to be the quality of the audit trail employed and of the initial source document verification. While additions and deletions to the case report form and study database are routine occurrences, they must be supported by source documentation in all cases.

Occasionally, a pre-existing medical condition will not be recorded appropriately on a medical history source document or on the case report form because a patient will forget to tell a care provider about the condition (e.g., recurring headaches). If symptoms of the condition then arise during the study, would this be considered an adverse event? Assuming the symptoms are of the same severity (i.e., as those experienced by the patient pre-study), this probably would not be considered an adverse event. When the subject discloses that he or she neglected to inform the site staff of a pre-existing medical condition, however, then all the documentation regarding the event and the subject's medical history must be corrected.

Further Reading

Senn, Steven, *Statistical Issues in Drug Development,* New York: John Wiley, 1997.

Mackintosh, D., "Quality Assurance of Data Management and Statistical Analysis," *Applied Clinical Trials,* 3:40-50, June 1994.

ICH Guideline: "Statistical Considerations in the Design of Clinical Trials" (E9), 1998.

Esser, Regina, "Biostatistics and Data Management in Global Drug Development," *Drug Information Journal,* 35:643-53, 2001.

Wittes, Janet, "On Changing a Long-Term Clinical Trial Midstream," *Stat Med* 21:2789-95, 15 October 2002.

Society for Clinical Data Management, "The Good Clinical Data Management Practices Guide," Version 2, 2002.

Acknowledgments

Douglas Mackintosh, DrPH, MBA, MS Hyg, and Vernette Molloy, MBA, RN, of GCPA, Inc.; Lukas Makris, PhD, President, BioCor, Yardley, PA; and Mojtaba Noursalehi, PhD, Senior Director of Biometrics, Target Research Associates, New Providence, NJ.

Section 17:
Fraud, Negligence, and Regulatory Non-Compliance

17.1 Q. Recently, various U.S. district attorneys have threatened to more closely examine clinical trial conduct and possible noncompliance. Since the FDA is most directly responsible for regulating clinical trials and enforcing GCP standards, on what regulatory or legal grounds is the Department of Justice basing these warnings?

A. In many cases, the U.S. Department of Justice is using the False Claims Act (Qui Tam) as a basis for evaluating the conduct of clinical trials. First signed into law in 1863 and significantly revamped in 1986, the False Claims Act is designed to permit citizens to sue groups, companies (such as heathcare providers), or individuals that are defrauding the government through, for example, a false or fraudulent claim for payment.

Recently, government attorneys have claimed that the same legal theory that the Department of Justice has used in its off-label drug marketing investigations can be easily extended to clinical trial conduct. Although clinical trial issues "are of great concern to us [but] do not fit into the classic fraud [paradigm] . . . , we can use the False Claims Act and various fraud statutes to craft a theory that the overall impact" of clinical trial noncompliance amounts to a defrauding of the government's Medicare or Medicaid programs, Philadelphia Assistant U.S. Attorney Virginia Gibson stated in a February 2005 speech.

In examining clinical trial practices, Gibson says, the Department of Justice can ask, "has the subject been advised fairly and accurately what is going to happen in the study and what the risks are? Has the protocol been designed properly? Has there been any change in protocol the FDA or IRB was not informed of? Have there been subjects pushed through a protocol that don't really fit? [We can than construct a fraud case if] there's some deception involved there, all looking towards getting a drug approved or keeping a drug on the market that perhaps should not be there.

"At any point in these processes, we can have fraud occurring, we can have kickbacks or inducements to somehow undermine a doctor's prescribing decision, or to undermine the informed consent process for patients who are participating in studies that support either a new drug application or post-marketing studies." Gibson warns that, if the Department of Justice can find that "corners are being cut [in the regulatory process and therefore there are] deceptions occurring in that process," the government can make the case that it was inappropriately billed for the drug involved.

In March 2005, Philadelphia Associate U.S. District Attorney James Sheehan warned about what he sees as "the coming storm" in a government focus on clinical research conduct. Sheehan predicted that government investigations into the conduct of clinical trials could focus on institutional review boards and, in particular, subject protection and informed consent-related disclosures to study subjects.

17.2 Q. In recent years, CDER has actively encouraged all parties involved in clinical trials, including clinical trial sponsors, to report research misconduct and even noncompliance to its Division of Scientific Investigations (DSI). What, specifically, does CDER want sponsors to report, and what does CDER consider to be research misconduct versus noncompliance?

A. The FDA believes that a sponsor should promptly report to the agency whenever it discovers research misconduct, and should provide any information indicating that a person involved in human subject trials committed research misconduct. Agency officials have emphasized that sponsors should make such reports not just regarding clinical investigators, but regarding all parties involved in clinical trials as well.

In addition, FDA officials have disclosed that they are examining whether to pursue new regulations that would require sponsors to report all cases of investigator noncompliance or misconduct, including fraud, data falsification, and human subject protection abuses. Under existing FDA regulations, a sponsor is not "required" to report investigators suspected of misconduct or noncompliance unless the investigator is discontinued from a study. FDA regulations at 21 CFR 312.56(b) state that, "if the investigator's participation is ended, the sponsor shall require that the investigator dispose of or return the investigational drug in accordance with [FDA] requirements . . . and shall notify FDA." Further, this passage is interpreted by some experts to require a report only that the investigator's participation has ended, and not a disclosure of the reasons for the investigator's discontinuation. The agency, however, continues to encourage companies to report all investigator noncompliance or misconduct on a voluntary basis.

In various communications, FDA officials have defined research misconduct as "the falsification of data in proposing, designing, performing, recording, supervising or reviewing research, or in reporting research results." Falsification, they point out, includes acts of both omission, meaning consciously failing to reveal all data (e.g., reportable adverse events, concomitant medications), and commission, meaning consciously altering data or fabricating data (e.g., lab values, blood pressure readings, specimens).

Although the officials noted that "deliberate or repeated noncompliance with the regulations can be considered misconduct," they emphasized that this noncompliance is "secondary to the falsification of data." Agency officials point out that research misconduct does not include "honest error or honest differences of opinion." However, a pattern of errors caused by incompetence, negligence, or inadequate procedures could ultimately trigger the Application Integrity Policy, under which the FDA would suspend scientific review of an application until the irregularity is resolved (see Q17.10 and Q10.30).

In recent informal correspondence regarding when sponsors should report protocol violations to the agency, the FDA stated that "this question is too case dependent to answer generally. However, there are clearly some situations that should be reported, if not to the FDA, then to the IRB. For example, if the protocol deviations present a serious risk to subjects, they should be reported to the IRB. If they result in such serious noncompliance that the study is terminated, they must be reported to FDA under 312.56(b). Also, if the protocol deviations represent falsification of data, they should be reported."

There is now indisputable evidence that sponsors, site staff, study subjects and others involved in the clinical trial process are voluntarily reporting compliance-related issues to the FDA in greater numbers. After the FDA encouraged voluntary reporting several years ago, CDER saw the number of complaints it received annually grow more than 10-fold. And after plateauing at just over 100 complaints annually from FY1999 to FY2002, voluntary complaints surged about 50%, to a record 200+

in calendar year 2004 (from roughly 140 in 2003, itself a record). Much of the impetus for voluntarily reporting is that sponsors/CROs, IRBs, site staff, and others with specific clinical trial-related activities do not want to be second-guessed later by the FDA for not discovering and reporting possible noncompliance.

17.3 Q. So how, if at all, is this growing number of voluntary complaints affecting the FDA's GCP and clinical trial inspection and compliance activities?

A. Within CDER, voluntary complaints continue driving significant GCP inspectional activities. Responding to voluntary clinical trial-related complaints remains a top priority within CDER's Division of Scientific Investigations (DSI) and, during 2004, DSI called complaint follow-up of "vital strategic importance." Unlike many GCP compliance inspections, complaint-related inspections often permit the agency to do real-time follow-up on issues while a clinical trial is ongoing.

According to DSI officials, almost a third of the increase in clinical investigator inspections in recent years was driven by agency inspections initiated in response to voluntary complaints. In calendar year 2004, CDER received just over 200 voluntary complaints, a roughly 50% increase over the number received in 2003.

Not surprisingly, CDER saw its directed, or "for cause," inspections (i.e., those conducted in response to a specific concern) almost double from just over 60 in FY2002 to over 100 in both FY2003 and FY2004. As recently as the late 1990s, CDER was conducting less than 10 directed inspections annually.

Meanwhile, CDER continues to work to increase the visibility and convenience of its voluntary clinical trial complaint program. CDER's DSI now has its own website (www.fda.gov/cder/offices/dsi/index.htm), and is working with OMB to obtain approval to place its anonymous complaint form on the website.

17.4 Q. What is known about who is submitting the voluntary complaints and what they are complaining about specifically?

A. Although the voluntary complaints are confidential, DSI officials claimed, during a 2005 interview, that industry trial sponsors and monitors were submitting the most complaints, followed by private citizens. In the past, agency officials had said that study subjects, IRBs, FDA staff, former employees, health professionals, informants, other government agencies, and the media have all submitted voluntary complaints, some on an anonymous basis.

During the 2005 interview, DSI officials also noted that, in most cases, voluntary complaints focus on either study conduct (e.g., data collection) or patients being put at unnecessary risks. Although CDER has not released any recent data on the nature of the complaints received to date, earlier data indicated that a full quarter of complaints received from 1998 to 2001 involved a failure to follow the protocol, 24% involved possible data falsification, 19% involved informed consent noncompliance, 14% involved poor adverse experience reporting, and 8% involved poor drug accountability. In March 2004, CDER officials disclosed that clinical investigators were easily the target of most complaints, although they noted that complaints have also targeted sponsors, IRBs, monitors/CROs, site management organizations, and hospitals as well. Also, in March 2004, the officials identified the range of issues underlying the complaints received to date:

- Informed consent issues
- Falsification
- Failure to report adverse events
- Failure to follow the protocol
- Inadequate records
- Qualifications of persons performing physicals
- Failure to get IRB approval, report changes in research
- Failure to follow FDA regulations

- Drug accountability
- Recruitment practices
- Poor supervision
- No active IND
- Violations of GLP regs
- Monitoring practices
- Blinding
- Charging for the test article
- Misleading advertisements
- IRB shopping

17.5 Q. With the increasing focus on clinical subject safety and voluntary clinical study-related complaints, has the FDA standard for taking regulatory action against clinical investigators evolved at all?

A. In some ways, the standard for formal regulatory action has evolved recently. In its September 2004 final guidance entitled, *The Use of Clinical Holds Following Investigator Misconduct,* the agency establishes that it can and will impose a clinical hold on a clinical study or investigator immediately based on "preliminary evidence" of an investigator's regulatory misconduct. Through the clinical hold, the FDA can suspend an ongoing study or a particular investigator's participation in the larger study.

Although the agency emphasizes that it expects the use of clinical holds based on misconduct to be "infrequent," it adds that, given the importance of human subject protection, "even preliminary (e.g., pre-inspectional information provided to FDA by the IRB, sponsor, or other parties), but credible evidence raising concerns that subjects may be placed at substantial risk may warrant a clinical hold while further information is being obtained."

While industry had encouraged the agency to base its clinical hold decisions largely on FDA findings in clinical site inspections, the September 2004 final guidance notes that "the grounds for imposition of a clinical hold need not include a finding of misconduct or a violation of a regulation."

17.6 Q. When a sponsor notifies the FDA of investigator noncompliance, can the company obtain any type of FDA documentation as proof that it notified the FDA?

A. A tried and true method is to send a certified letter, return signature requested. The FDA will sign it, which will serve as the proof that the documentation was received. A more polite method is to request, in a cover letter, that the FDA acknowledge its receipt of the documentation; the company can enclose a self-addressed postcard acknowledging receipt and ask that the FDA return it. Yet another method is to have the documentation hand delivered to the agency, and have the courier request that FDA mailroom personnel sign for it.

Somewhere in this process of discovery and reporting, the sponsor with which the investigator is associated will want and need the counsel of a regulatory attorney. This attorney should be familiar with methods for communicating compliance-related problems to the FDA, and with methods for creating a solid record of this communication.

17.7 Q. If, under a contract with a clinical research organization (CRO), a sponsor retained the right/obligation to notify the FDA of noncompliant investigators, would the CRO be cited if the sponsor failed to report a noncompliant investigator?

A. In such a case, the CRO could be cited for regulatory noncompliance if:

- It failed to notify the sponsor of the noncompliance
- It failed to notify the sponsor of the noncompliance in a timely fashion
- It failed to accurately and thoroughly notify the sponsor of the scope and degree of noncompliance (e.g., willfully making the situation appear less serious than it is)
- It failed to immediately address unsafe study subject conditions resulting from the investigator noncompliance

Assuming that the CRO has not failed in any of these areas, however, then it would not be responsible if the sponsor ultimately fails to notify the FDA of the investigator noncompliance.

In a recent informal communication on this subject, the FDA stated that, "we believe both the regulatory requirements for reporting under 312.56(b) and the transfer of obligations from a sponsor to a CRO under 312.52 speak for themselves and are very clear. Simply put, any regulatory obligation that is transferred in writing to the CRO becomes the obligation of the CRO. If the sponsor retains that obligation, they are responsible. The obligation for reporting to FDA should be clearly assigned in the contract."

Ideally, a CRO and sponsor will fully discuss, reach agreement on, and properly document a plan for FDA reporting well in advance of a study's initiation. Again, experienced regulatory attorneys and regulatory affairs professionals should be involved in such decisions.

17.8 Q. Assume that a study coordinator forges the principal investigator's signature on study documents, that the principal investigator has no knowledge of these forgeries until an auditor discovers them, and that the site then discloses the forgeries to the sponsor. What do existing regulations say about reporting this fraud to the FDA, and what penalties can the FDA impose on non-investigators such as site nurses and pharmacists?

A. Although not specifically prescribed by regulation, the FDA advises sponsors to promptly report to the agency any information relating to research misconduct by a person involved in human subject trials. Whenever a sponsor knowingly submits an investigator's fraudulent data, the agency will consider referring the case to the U.S. Department of Justice for prosecution under the False Statements to Government Act (18 U.S.C. § 1001 et seq.).

While the FDA generally holds the designated clinical investigator, rather than employees/agents of the investigator, ultimately responsible for research misconduct (assuming the investigator instituted the misconduct or had knowledge of it and failed to attempt to remedy it), there are recent indications that the FDA will be holding non-investigators accountable as well. In a series of separate, but related prosecutions and debarment actions, it was clear that the FDA was sending a message to those involved in clinical trials. In late 2002, the FDA moved to debar not only former clinical investigator Robert Fiddes, M.D., but three members of his clinical study staff as well. This is the first time the agency is known to have debarred clinical research coordinators/study nurses. When the FDA debars a person, that individual cannot provide any services to an applicant with an approved or pending drug or biologic product application (see Q10.31).

In 1997, Fiddes was convicted of conspiring to make false statements to the FDA, a conviction based on Fiddes participating in, directing, and encouraging the submission of false information (i.e., falsifying and fabricating clinical data) to sponsors in required clinical study reports used by the FDA in assessing drug safety and effectiveness. The three members of Fiddes' research staff were also convicted of felonies, which served as the basis for their debarments (one of the three debarments was subsequently rescinded, at least temporarily, in early 2003).

As an interesting side bar, there is some question as to whether or not the FDA would pursue actions against an investigator who had no knowledge of his or her study coordinator's fraud or gross negligence. The agency's stated policy is to hold the principal investigator responsible for all study activities, including those performed by study coordinators and subinvestigators. Despite this, the agency will, before taking action in some cases, assess how reasonable it is to expect a principal investigator to have known about a specific case of noncompliance or misconduct, particularly in the case of minor noncompliance or misconduct.

Frustrated that they cannot take direct regulatory action against those individuals—often, clinical study coordinators or subinvestigators—when they do not fulfill their trial-related responsibilities or engage in misconduct, FDA officials have considered their options. Among these options, according to some within the agency, was to revise current regulations to require that the Form FDA 1572-Statement of Investigator be signed by a site's clinical study coordinator and subinvestigator(s). Currently, only the investigator is required to sign the form. By signing the Form-1572, the study coordinator and subinvestigator(s) would formally commit, in a legal contract, to fulfill the trial-related tasks that the clinical investigator delegates to them in a study. In turn, these signed commitments would provide the FDA with the regulatory basis it needs to take regulatory action against these key figures in a clinical trial when necessary (see Q2.6 and Q2.7).

17.9 Q. Does a health care institution have any legal obligations to report clinical trial-related physician or nurse fraud to a state regulatory agency, such as the state board of medicine?

A. FDA regulations do not require that a health care institution report trial-related physician or nurse fraud to a state regulatory agency. This does not mean, however, that in practice the agency would not advise a health care institution to refer that information to the state, or that the agency would not refer that information to a relevant state agency (especially if the fraud resulted in a significant risk to a patient's welfare, see Q17.11). Individual states may require that a health care institution report such information (i.e., to the state board of medicine).

17.10 Q. What types of GCP compliance problems would justify the FDA invoking the Application Integrity Policy (AIP) for a particular sponsor? When a sponsor is under the AIP, what sponsor study-related activities are placed on hold? And what steps must a sponsor take to be removed from the AIP?

A. Although most GCP compliance-related issues are resolved well before the point at which the AIP is considered, some cases of severe GCP noncompliance, largely in the medical device area, have resulted in the application of the AIP against product sponsors. Problems that could cause the FDA to place a sponsor under the AIP generally include: submitting a fraudulent application; offering or promising a bribe or illegal gratuity; making an untrue statement of material fact; submitting data that are otherwise unreliable due to, for example, a pattern of errors caused by incompetence, negligence, or an inadequate practice (e.g., SOPs), or a system-wide failure to ensure the integrity of data submissions.[1]

Historically, the FDA has used a "pattern or practice" of data integrity problems as the standard for placing a company under the AIP. "Pattern or practice" has generally meant at least three instances of data integrity problems involving two or more applications.

The imposition of the AIP against a sponsor would result in a moratorium on the further review of applications from the company until the issues leading to the agency's action are resolved. In certain cases, the FDA may allow ongoing stages of the review process to proceed to completion, although no application will be approved while an AIP is in effect. If fraud or other AIP issues are detected at a study site, the study can be halted, and administrative and/or judicial sanctions, up to and including criminal prosecution, may be taken against the investigator.

The corrective actions that the FDA expects an applicant to implement would depend upon the facts and circumstances of each case, the nature of the wrongful acts, the nature of the data under consideration, and the requirements of the particular review process. Generally, the FDA will suspend the review process for any applications subject to the AIP, an action that also could impede a sponsor's ability to obtain federal contracts or grants. Typically, applicants must take the following corrective actions to be removed from the AIP:

1. Cooperate fully with the FDA and other federal investigations to determine the cause and scope of any wrongful acts and to assess the effects of the acts on a product's safety, effectiveness, or quality;
2. Identify all individuals who were involved in, or may have been associated with, the wrongful acts, and ensure that any substantive authority they may have on matters under the jurisdiction of FDA is revoked;
3. Conduct a credible internal review designed to identify all instances of wrongful acts associated with applications submitted to the FDA. Designed to supplement the FDA's ongoing, comprehensive investigation, the investigation should involve qualified outside consultants;

---

[1]FDA Compliance Policy Guide, Sec. 120.100; see also FR 46191, 10 September, 1991.

4. Commit, in writing, to developing and implementing a corrective-action operating plan to assure the safety, effectiveness, and quality of their products. Ordinarily, this commitment will be in the form of a consent decree or agreement, and will be signed by the president or chief executive officer, and submitted to the FDA. The corrective-action operating plan should address procedures and controls to preclude future instances of wrongful acts and noncompliance.

In all likelihood, the FDA will verify that the applicant has satisfactorily completed its internal review and implemented its written corrective-action operating plan. Such inspections should disclose positive evidence (e.g., effective management controls, standard operating procedures, and corroborating documentation) that the applicant's data are reliable.

17.11 Q. If an FDA inspector and the agency's district office determine that an investigator committed fraud and/or endangered the safety of his or her subjects, will the FDA report these findings to the investigator's state licensing board? What about cases in which subjects were in "imminent danger," say from reckless prescribing/dosing.

A. The FDA's regulations and policies do not require that the agency report findings to state boards. Similar to the power that any patient or individual holds to file a complaint with a state licensing board, however, the FDA has the power to report its findings. During recent informal communications on this topic, sources in the FDA's Office of Chief Counsel indicated that the FDA routinely reports its findings to state licensing boards when an investigator's action or lack of action places patients at significant risk. Therefore, a finding that there had been reckless drug ordering, dispensing, and administration in a clinical trial would likely result in an FDA report to the investigator's state licensing board.

If the FDA knew or believed that a particular matter would be of interest to a state agency, the FDA would be expected to inform that agency of its concerns. The timing of this information sharing, however, would have to be such that it would not compromise the FDA's own investigation of the matter.

17.12 Q. Are there legal protections for whistle-blowers, say monitors and study coordinators, who alert the FDA and other government entities about serious GCP violations?

A. State employment law and contract provisions may be important here. Under such laws, for example, an independent contractor may not be as well positioned to benefit from legal protections as a company employee. Further, some companies have corporate compliance programs with policies that require employees to report wrongdoing. Generally, if operating in good faith (even better if they turn out to be right, of course), and especially if they have first notified their employer about the irregularities and permitted the company an opportunity for correction before reporting to the government, whistle-blowers will be reasonably well-positioned to contest a termination following a report, unless their job performance otherwise has been sufficient cause for termination. That said, such individuals may not wish to continue working at the same company, since they are often subjected to various forms of retaliation.

The False Claims Act, which allows a private individual with knowledge that the government is being defrauded to file suit on behalf of the government, contains provisions regarding employer retaliation against employees reporting under the Act. This law can be relevant for research study fraud reporting; it is less clear if simple negligence-type failures that do not aggregate to creating a high level of false trial data could serve as the basis for such a *"qui tam"* action. Other whistleblower laws, including state laws, vary in their protections for whistleblowers.

Further Reading

Mackintosh, D. and Molloy, V., "Detection of Gross Negligence, Fraud, and Other Bad Faith Efforts During Field Auditing of Clinical Trial Sites," *Drug Information Journal,* 30(3):645-653, 1996.

Lock, Stephen and Wells, Frank (eds), *Fraud and Misconduct in Medical Research,* London: BMJ Publishing Group, 1993.

Kanser, E, Ruscan, S., "Research Ethics and Scientific Misconduct in Biomedical Research," *Acta Neurochir Suppl.* 83:11-15, 2002.

Acknowledgments

Douglas Mackintosh, DrPH, MBA, MS Hyg, and Vernette Molloy, MBA, RN, of GCPA, Inc.; Michael D. Petty, JD, MPH, Partner, Ropes & Gray, LLP, Washington, DC.

Section 18:
Subject Diaries

18.1 Q. Given the increasing use of subject diaries and the recognized challenges regarding the reliability of patient-reported data and information, does the FDA have any plans to develop guidance or regulations regarding their use?

A. Yes. At this writing, in fact, CDER was preparing to release its first guidance on so-called patient-reported outcomes (PRO). Although the guidance addresses PRO generally, the push to get the guidance out was fueled, in part, by electronic PRO collection, and by technology vendors that were anxious for the agency to provide guidance in the area (e.g., instrument validation).

18.2 Q. The reliability of data recorded in subject diaries is often questioned, given subjects' propensity for losing the diaries, forgetting to complete them, and falsifying information. Still, given that diaries can be a good source of data on adverse experiences, drug compliance, and daily activities, what steps can clinical research sites take to ensure that the data and information provided in subject diaries will comply with GCP standards?

A. At the beginning of a study, site staff should explain to each subject (or parent) the importance of the diary and how the subject should record data within it. Site staff should review the diary at each visit; deficiencies and attempts to correct these deficiencies should be noted in source records. Site staff must ensure that the diaries are returned at the time designated in the trial protocol. If a patient diary is not returned, the site should make several attempts to retrieve it. These attempts should be documented in the subject's medical record.

Although clinical auditors and FDA inspectors recognize that diaries often pose a source documentation problem, they expect to see documented efforts to minimize these problems. Diaries that are too neat, all look the same, or have been rewritten by the study coordinator are sure to raise suspicions.

18.3 Q. If study coordinators transpose data from diaries onto a case report form, should the site retain copies of the diaries? And are diaries source documents?

A. When diaries are used to record the first observations of a subject's clinical status while on study—even though these observations are made by the subject and not the investigator or site staff—they should be considered source documents. When diary data are transcribed onto a case report form, the diaries must be retained by the site just as any other source documents would be retained. Monitors should review the case report forms against the diaries to check for inconsistencies and/or data omissions.

18.4 Q. If diary data conflict with data recorded on a study visit progress note, which document should be considered the primary source document?

A. Discrepancies between data in diaries and progress notes are not uncommon. When subjects come in for study visits, they sometimes forget to mention the minor discomforts and other experiences that occurred between study visits. Obviously, this is precisely why diaries are used—to provide the subject with a means for documenting these occurrences in "real time." Unless the study coordinator questions the subject about these discrepancies, they may be overlooked.

Typically, it is the monitor who finds the discrepancy during a routine visit and brings it to the attention of the investigator or study coordinator. Care must be taken in questioning the subject regarding the discrepant data—that is, the staff must not bias the subject during the discussion. After a thorough discussion with the subject, the reconciliation should be made and completely documented in the subject's source records.

When there are such discrepancies, the site staff should determine which document makes the most sense clinically and conforms most closely to what the subject remembers about the event under review. This document should be considered the primary source document.

Even if there are no source document discrepancies, study staff should query subjects during each study visit about possible adverse events and treatment interventions. When reviewing diary entries, site staff may also inquire about vague notations, such as "discomfort" or "fatigue," to find out more about their nature, intensity, and duration. Although a diary entry helps with recall, further inquiries can improve the accuracy and specificity of the information recorded in the diary or identified in other source documents.

18.5 Q. Should extraneous information scribbled by the subject in pencil in the margins of the diary (e.g., "left work early") be recorded in the diary case report form page?

A. All the data and information that the subject records in the margins of diaries should be reviewed by site staff with the subject. These data should not automatically be considered extraneous until site staff conduct a thorough discussion with the subject. What may appear to be superfluous information may be, upon further examination and subject input, quite meaningful.

A subject entry such as "left work early" requires clarification and follow up. Why did the subject leave work early—was he/she ill? If the subject was ill, then it could be that the event should be considered an adverse event and be recorded in the case report form's adverse event page as well as the case report form's diary page. A note to explain the subject's margin entry should be made in the subject's source record.

18.6 Q. What should a study coordinator do if she/he observes a subject completing the diary in the office waiting room or parking lot just prior to a study visit?

A. Assuming that the subject is observed entering data that should have been entered in the diary during the previous week or even a day earlier, then the subject was not adhering to the protocol and this behavior should be considered and handled as a protocol violation. As such, the principal investigator or study coordinator should counsel the subject regarding his/her obligations as a study subject. The protocol violation and the discussion with the subject should be documented in the subject's source record.

If the subject's noncompliance continues, site staff should contact the sponsor for advice as to how to proceed. The sponsor may decide that this subject should be dropped from the study because of protocol noncompliance.

18.7 Q. What should a principal investigator do about retention of source documentation at his or her site if electronic patient diaries are used?

A. Predicate rules require that source documents for clinical study data be maintained by the clinical investigator at the investigational site. Regulations also require sites to allow the FDA to inspect, review, and copy records at any time, including while the study is in progress. These expectations are true whether the original source is on paper or is in electronic form. In most current e-diary implementations, the system involves either an immediate original recording in the sponsor's database (if entry by the study subject is web-based or into an interactive voice response system) or short-term capture on some type of device (such as a PDA), with upload to the sponsor's database. Alternatively, the software vendor may be hosting the database.

Unfortunately, neither one of these implementations is compliant with current regulations, which require investigators to maintain source data and do not allow them to transfer their regulatory obligations to another party (as the sponsor can do with a contract research organization). The FDA feels that the "one-database" implementation does not allow for the separation of the originally recorded source data from any changed versions. Also, in most current implementations, sponsors provide a copy of records to the investigator at the completion of the study via a CD. However, investigators do not always have easy access to retrieve or copy these records while the study is in progress, which is another regulatory issue. At the same time, the FDA realizes that it is problematic for some sites to adequately maintain and protect electronic records at the site.

While industry and the agency sort out what is feasible within current regulations and technological availabilities, the key is to ensure that the clinical investigator can demonstrate:

* Complete control over the original recorded data
* Protection of the original recorded data
* Availability of the original recorded data at any point (and for the regulatory retention period)
* Ability to provide copies of data in the event of an inspection

18.8 Q. If a subject provides diary data that are not in the English language, how should these responses be addressed?

A. Such responses recorded in diaries should be translated into English by a certified translator. The site staff should query the subject, using a translator if necessary, to ensure that the subject understood the English diary questions/format.

If the site receives multiple subject diaries completed in a language other than English, then the diary format and instructions/questions should be translated into a language that the subject understands, and this translated diary template should also be back-translated for validation purposes.

Further Reading

Stokes, Teri and Paty, Jean, "What Is a Subject Diary, and How Do Regulations Apply," *Applied Clinical Trials,* 11:38-43, September 2002.

Stone, Arthur, et al, "Subject Non-compliance With Paper Diaries," *British Medical Journal,* 324:1193-4, 2002.

Acknowledgments

Douglas Mackintosh, DrPH, MBA, MS Hyg, and Vernette Molloy, MBA, RN, of GCPA, Inc.; Margaret Marshall, RN, MS, former Associate Director of Quality Assurance, Wyeth-Lederle Vaccines, Pearl River, NY; Joy Littlejohn, Auditor, Regulatory Compliance, Alexion Pharmaceuticals, Cheshire, CT.

Section 19:
Medical Devices and GCP

19.1 Q. Can any IRB approve an investigational device exemption (IDE) protocol?

A. IRBs must review and approve all device clinical studies, including those for devices for which an IDE has been submitted to the FDA. For medical devices, an IDE is roughly the equivalent of an IND for drugs, although there are some significant differences in the submission requirements for the two applications.

Generally, the IRB that approves a device study is the IRB that has jurisdiction for the research site at which the device study is to take place. If no IRB has jurisdiction over the site, a national or central IRB can be approached for approval.

If the reviewing IRB determines that the study is a non-significant risk device study (see note below) and approves it, then the study may begin at that site (i.e., without FDA approval). If the study was presented to the IRB as a non-significant risk device study and the IRB determines that it is a significant risk device study, then the FDA must be notified of this finding under 21 CFR 812.150(b)(9).

[Editor's note: FDA regulations (21 CFR Part 812) define two types of device studies—"significant risk" and "nonsignificant risk" studies. A significant risk device study is a study that presents a potential for serious risk to the health, safety, or welfare of a subject and: (1) is intended as an implant; or (2) is used in supporting or sustaining human life; or (3) is of substantial importance in diagnosing, curing, mitigating or treating disease, or otherwise prevents impairment of human health; or (4) otherwise presents a potential for serious risk to the health, safety, or welfare of a subject. A nonsignificant risk device study is one that does not meet the definition for a significant risk study.]

If the study is a significant risk device study, then a sponsor must obtain approval from both the FDA and the IRB before it initiates the research. Although the sequence in which FDA and IRB approval is obtained is not an important factor, both approvals must be obtained before study initiation. If the FDA, as part of its approval, requires significant changes in a protocol that the IRB had previously approved, then the IRB must approve those changes before study initiation. Similarly, if the IRB requires significant changes to a protocol cleared by the FDA, then the agency must approve those changes before the study may begin.

19.2 Q. Must subinvestigators be listed on the Statement of the Investigator?

A. The FDA does not require that subinvestigators be listed on the Statement of the Investigator. CDRH staff, as well as FDA Good Clinical Practice Program officials, emphasize, however, that listing the subinvestigators is a good idea for a variety of reasons. It is particularly important to list those subinvestigators involved in implanting or injecting an experimental device (see Q2.3 for a discussion about subinvestigators).

19.3 Q. Can the Form FDA 1572-Statement of Investigator be used instead of an investigator agreement?

A. No. For device studies, an investigator agreement must be signed, dated, and placed in the study binder. 1572s are appropriate only for drug, biologic, and some diagnostics studies. *In vitro* diagnostics studies are regulated as devices; however, many studies are exempt from the IDE under 21 CFR 812.2(c)(3). If the study is not exempt, the sponsor needs an investigator agreement.

Although it is not required, it is a good idea to have the principal investigator sign an investigator agreement, even for *in vitro* diagnostic studies. This helps ensure overall compliance, and can be useful when post-study financial disclosure data are requested.

19.4 Q. If five local IRBs approve a device clinical trial and confirm its nonsignificant risk status, but a sixth IRB concludes that it is a significant risk study, what action must the sponsor take?

A. If the sixth IRB finds the study to be a significant risk study, then the sponsor must report this finding to the FDA under 21 CFR 812.150(b)(9). It is not acceptable for a sponsor to just move from IRB to IRB until it finds one that will consider a study to be a non-significant risk study without notifying the FDA of a significant risk finding. Anytime an IRB finds a study to be significant risk study, the FDA must be notified and approve the trial before it begins.

19.5 Q. Is an investigator brochure required for a medical device study?

A. The term "investigator brochure" derives from the IND regulations, and is not relevant to IDEs. The IDE regulation requires a report of prior investigations (21 CFR 812.27) and an investigational plan (21 CFR 812.25). The sponsor is to provide these documents to the study investigators (21 CFR 812.45) and the IRB (FD&C Act, section 520(g)(3)(A)(i)). An investigator brochure is a requirement (per EN 540) for device trials in the European Union.

19.6 Q. Does the ICH GCP guideline apply to device studies?

A. Whenever a device clinical study is conducted, it is industry standard to follow ICH GCP and to adhere to the requirements in FDA regulations at 21 CFR 812. CDRH follows 21 CFR 812, however, and CDRH officials generally are of the opinion that ICH GCP was intended for drug studies and does not include guidelines specific to device studies.

19.7 Q. If a legally marketed device is involved in a study under which it is used for its approved indication (i.e., a Phase 4 trial), is an IDE required? Also, are IRB approval and informed consent required?

A. If a device has an approved indication, then an IDE already exists for it. For subsequent studies of the device for the approved indication, or different indications, IRB approvals of protocols and consents are required. Studies of the device within the cleared indications would be exempt from 21 CFR 812, but studies of different indications would be subject to 21 CFR 812.

19.8 Q. Must the sponsor of a device study directly inform reviewing IRBs of adverse device effects (ADEs), or can the sponsor rely on its investigators to do this?

A. FDA regulations at 21 CFR 812.150(a)(i) establish that investigators are responsible for reporting unexpected adverse device effects (UADEs) to both the sponsor and the IRB. Unanticipated adverse device effect means any serious adverse effect on health or safety or any life-threatening problem or death caused by, or associated with, a device, provided that the effect, problem, or death was not previously identified in nature, severity, or degree of incidence in the investigational plan or application (including a supplementary plan or application). These effects would also include any other unanticipated serious problems that are associated with a device and that relate to the rights, safety, or welfare of subjects (see 21 CFR 812.3(s)).

Sponsors sometimes provide examples of UADEs in their protocols. This does not mean that the sponsor expected the effects, or that they would have been considered "anticipated." Sponsors sometimes include UADEs in their protocols because they want to be informed if these events occur. A sponsor is responsible for alerting investigators about UADEs that occurred at other study sites. UADEs are compiled in IDE safety reports.

Because UADEs are defined as both serious and associated with the device, they differ from drug SAEs, which do not need to be causally related to trigger reporting to the sponsor and the IRB. An IRB may wish to be informed of all serious adverse events that occurred during a device study. In some cases, this discrepancy between sponsor expectations and IRB expectations causes confusion for investigators and others, particularly individuals who also conduct drug studies.

19.9 Q. When do sponsors of IDEs or premarket approval applications (PMAs) need to disclose information on the investigator's financial holdings to the FDA?

A. Sponsors collect this information at the start of the study, and the investigator agreement typically obligates the investigator to update the information during the study if it changes. There is no regulatory requirement for either the investigators or the sponsor to update the information annually. The sponsor only reports the information for each investigator participating in key studies—either in the form of a certification that an investigator has no relevant financial interests or a disclosure of significant financial interests—to the FDA when the 510(k) or PMA is submitted (see http://www.devicelink.com/mddi/archive/00/01/014.html and Q13.8). Financial disclosure information should be obtained for all investigators participating in a device's key clinical studies and identified in the IDE or PMA. The investigator's agreement, which the sponsor obtains at the beginning of the study, should include a provision calling for the investigator to provide the financial disclosure information to the sponsor.

19.10 Q. Must adverse events that occur during non-significant risk studies be reported to the FDA?

A. If the adverse event fits the definition of a UADE (see Q19.8), the investigator should report the event to the sponsor, who in turn must report the UADE to the FDA. A sponsor has ten working days, after first learning or being notified of the UADE, to report the UADE to the FDA. The principal investigator has the responsibility to report the UADE to the local IRB no later than ten working days after he/she learns of the event. Generally, sponsors report UADEs to CDRH's IDE staff in letters providing narrative descriptions of the events or on sponsor-developed reporting forms. Sponsors are also responsible for reporting UADEs to all participating investigators, who in turn submit the UADEs to their IRBs.

19.11 Q. Can the sponsor of a device clinical trial charge the patient for an investigational device?

A. Many implantable devices, especially expensive ones, used in clinical trials are billed to Medicare or the patient's insurance carrier. The amount charged for the device cannot be more than that necessary to recover the costs of manufacture, research, development, and handling (see 21 CFR 812.7(b)). Each IDE approval letter contains what is called a CMS code: B1 for reimbursable devices (the majority) or A for non-reimbursable devices.

Many durable devices are paid for by the investigator and are provided free of charge to the patient. Such devices include those that may be cleared or approved for several indications, but for which new software or accessories have been added for an investigational use.

19.12 Q. Can an investigational device be modified during a clinical trial?

A. To modify an investigational device mid-trial, a sponsor must prepare and submit to the FDA an amended design control dossier and device description with a new risk analysis document. If the FDA grants its permission following discussions with the company, the sponsor can then modify the device. It is unlikely that the FDA would deny approving a device modification and that the sponsor would then decide to discontinue the original study. It is more likely that the FDA would determine that, for purposes of analysis and safety/efficacy/substantial equivalence assessments, the clinical data from the modified device may not be combined with the data from the original device. Sponsors should review the streamlined five-day notification process described in 812.35(a)(3)(iii).

19.13 Q. How should the sponsor design a study involving an investigational device that is used in emergency situations in which the patient may be in considerable distress or unconscious and it is not possible to locate the next of kin prior to inserting, instilling, or applying an experimental device?

A. In these emergency situations, obtaining informed consent from a patient is not possible. As witnessed by the fact that there are products such as defibrillators on the market and widely used today, however, there are ways in which such challenges are addressed in the context of clinical trials.

The FDA has issued guidance regarding studies for drugs, devices, biologics, and diagnostics that are administered under such emergency conditions (i.e., a 1998 Information Sheet entitled, "Exemption from Informed Consent for Studies Conducted in Emergency Settings: Regulatory Language and Excerpts from Preamble"). This guidance establishes that consent can be obtained from uninvolved third parties present during the emergency and/or from the patient or a relative at a later date. It is important that this guidance be followed so as not to compromise patient rights and to accommodate the testing of potentially life-saving technology (see Q7.8 and other FDA draft guidance: http://www.fda.gov/ora/compliance_ref/bimo/err_guide.htm). The reviewing IRB must have procedures in place to process this type of study. Many IRBs do not (see: http://www.devicelink.com/mddi/archive/98/04/014.html).

Further Reading

FDA Information Sheets: "Medical Devices, Frequently Asked Questions about IRB Review of Medical Devices," and "Significant Risk and Non-significant Risk Medical Device Studies."

Feigal, David W., Gardner, Susan N., and McClellan, Mark, "Ensuring Safe and Effective Medical Devices," *New England Journal of Medicine,* 348:191-92, 16 January 2003.

Acknowledgments

Douglas Mackintosh, DrPH, MBA, MS Hyg, and Vernette Molloy, MBA, RN, of GCPA, Inc.; Fred Ma, MD, Director of Clinical Research, Gliatech, Cleveland, OH; Terry McMahon, Manager, Regulatory Affairs, Smith and Nephew, Largo, FL; Will Robinson, RAC, Vice President, Quality Assurance, MedPointe Healthcare, Summit, NJ; Joy Littlejohn, Auditor, Regulatory Compliance, Alexion Pharmaceuticals, Cheshire, CT; and Barry Sall, Senior Regulatory Consultant, PAREXEL International Corporation, Waltham, MA.

Section 20:
The FDA's Frequently Asked GCP Questions

Section 20 comprises the FDA's answers to what the agency characterizes as frequently asked GCP-related questions. Last updated in 1998, these questions and answers largely address institutional review boards, although they also touch on informed consent and certain aspects of clinical investigations.

It is important to note that the FDA is now updating these questions and answers to make them consistent with agency regulations and guidances published since the 1998 update.

I. IRB Organization

1. What is an Institutional Review Board (IRB)?

Under FDA regulations, an IRB is an appropriately constituted group that has been formally designated to review and monitor biomedical research involving human subjects. In accordance with FDA regulations, an IRB has the authority to approve, require modifications in (to secure approval), or disapprove research. This group review serves an important role in the protection of the rights and welfare of human research subjects.

The purpose of IRB review is to assure, both in advance and by periodic review, that appropriate steps are taken to protect the rights and welfare of humans participating as subjects in the research. To accomplish this purpose, IRBs use a group process to review research protocols and related materials (e.g., informed consent documents and investigator brochures) to ensure protection of the rights and welfare of human subjects of research.

2. Do IRBs have to be formally called by that name?

No, "IRB" is a generic term used by FDA (and HHS) to refer to a group whose function is to review research to assure the protection of the rights and welfare of the human subjects. Each institution may use whatever name it chooses. Regardless of the name chosen, the IRB is subject to the Agency's IRB regulations when studies of FDA regulated products are reviewed and approved.

3. Does an IRB need to register with FDA before approving studies?

Currently, FDA does not require IRB registration. The form FDA-1572 "Statement of Investigator" for a study conducted under an IND requires the name and address of the IRB that will be responsible for review of the study. IRBs that approve studies of FDA regulated products must be established and operated in compliance with 21 CFR part 56.

4. What is an "assurance" or a "multiple project assurance"?

An "assurance," is a document negotiated between an institution and the Department of Health and Human Services (HHS) in accordance with HHS regulations. For research involving human subjects conducted by HHS or supported in whole or in part by HHS, the HHS regulations require a written assurance from the performance-site institution that the institution will comply with the HHS protection of human subjects regulations [45 CFR part 46]. The assurance mechanism is described in 45 CFR 46.103. Once an institution's assurance has been approved by HHS, a number is assigned to the assurance. The assurance may be for a single grant or contract (a "single project assurance"); for multiple grants ("multiple project assurances" - formerly called "general assurances"); or for certain types of studies such as oncology group studies and AIDS research group studies ("cooperative project assurances"). The Office for Protection from Research Risks (OPRR), is responsible for implementing the HHS regulations. The address and telephone number for OPRR are: 6100 Executive Boulevard, Suite 3B01 (MSC-7507), Rockville, MD 20892-7507; (301) 496-7041.

5. Is an "assurance" required by FDA?

Currently, FDA regulations do not require an assurance. FDA regulations [21 CFR parts 50 and 56] apply to research involving products regulated by FDA - federal funds and/or support do not need to be involved for the FDA regulations to apply. When research studies involving products regulated by FDA are funded/supported by HHS, the research institution must comply with both the HHS and FDA regulations. Also, see the information sheet entitled "Significant Differences in HHS and FDA Regulations for the protection of Human Subjects."

6. Must an institution establish its own IRB?

No. Although institutions engaged in research involving human subjects will usually have their own IRBs to oversee research conducted within the institution or by the staff of the institution, FDA regulations permit an institution without an IRB to arrange for an "outside" IRB to be responsible for initial and continuing review of studies conducted at the non-IRB institution. Such arrangements should be documented in writing. Individuals conducting research in a non-institutional setting often use established IRBs (independent or institutional) rather than form their own IRBs. Also see the information sheets entitled "Non-local IRB Review" and "Cooperative Research."

7. May a hospital IRB review a study that will be conducted outside of the hospital?

Yes. IRBs may agree to review research from affiliated or unaffiliated investigators, however, FDA does not require IRBs to assume this responsibility. If the IRB routinely conducts these reviews, the IRB policies should authorize such reviews and the process should be described in the IRB's written procedures. A hospital IRB may review outside studies on an individual basis when the minutes clearly show the members are aware of where the study is to be conducted and when the IRB possesses appropriate knowledge about the study site(s).

8. May IRB members be paid for their services?

The FDA regulations do not preclude a member from being compensated for services rendered. Payment to IRB members should not be related to or dependent upon a favorable decision. Expenses, such as travel costs, may also be reimbursed.

9. What is the FDA role in IRB liability in malpractice suits?

FDA regulations do not address the question of IRB or institutional liability in the case of malpractice suits. FDA does not have authority to limit liability of IRBs or their members. Compliance with FDA regulations may help minimize an IRB's exposure to liability.

10. Is the purpose of the IRB review of informed consent to protect the institution or the subject?

The fundamental purpose of IRB review of informed consent is to assure that the rights and welfare of subjects are protected. A signed informed consent document is evidence that the document has been provided to a prospective subject (and presumably, explained) and that the subject has agreed to participate in the research. IRB review of informed consent documents also ensures that the institution has complied with applicable regulations.

11. Does an IRB or institution have to compensate subjects if injury occurs as a result of participation in a research study?

Institutional policy, not FDA regulation, determines whether compensation and medical treatment(s) will be offered and the conditions that might be placed on subject eligibility for compensation or treatment(s). The FDA informed consent regulation on compensation [21 CFR 50.25(a)(6)] requires that, for research involving more than minimal risk, the subject must be told whether any compensation and any medical treatment(s) are available if injury occurs and, if so, what they are, or where further information may be obtained. Any statement that compensation is not offered must avoid waiving or appearing to waive any of the subject's rights or releasing or appearing to release the investigator, sponsor, or institution from liability for negligence [21 CFR 50.20].

II. IRB Membership

12. May a clinical investigator be an IRB member?

Yes, however, the IRB regulations [21 CFR 56.107(e)] prohibit any member from participating in the IRB's initial or continuing review of any study in which the member has a conflicting interest, except to provide information requested by the IRB. When selecting IRB members, the potential for conflicts of interest should be considered. When members frequently have conflicts and must absent themselves from deliberation and abstain from voting, their contributions to the group review process may be diminished and could hinder the review procedure. Even greater disruptions may result if this person is chairperson of the IRB.

13. The IRB regulations require an IRB to have a diverse membership. May one member satisfy more than one membership category?

Yes. For example, one member could be otherwise unaffiliated with the institution and have a primary concern in a non-scientific area. This individual would satisfy two of the membership requirements of the regulations. IRBs should strive, however, for a membership that has a diversity of representative capacities and disciplines. In fact, the FDA regulations [21 CFR 56.107(a)] require that, as part of being qualified as an IRB, the IRB must have "... diversity of members, including consideration of race, gender, cultural backgrounds and sensitivity to such issues as community attitudes ...."

14. When IRB members cannot attend a convened meeting, may they send someone from their department to vote for them?

No. Alternates who are formally appointed and listed in the membership roster may substitute, but ad hoc substitutes are not permissible as members of an IRB. However, a member who is unable to be present at the convened meeting may participate by video-conference or conference telephone call, when the member has received a copy of the documents that are to be reviewed at the meeting. Such members may vote and be counted as part of the quorum. If allowed by IRB procedures, ad hoc substitutes may attend as consultants and gather information for the absent member, but they may not be counted toward the quorum or participate in either deliberation or voting with the board. The IRB may, of course, ask questions of this representative just as they could of any non-member consultant. Opinions of the absent members that are transmitted by mail, telephone, telefax or e-mail may be considered by the attending IRB members but may not be counted as votes or the quorum for convened meetings.

15. May the IRB use alternate members?

The use of formally appointed alternate IRB members is acceptable to the FDA, provided that the IRB's written procedures describe the appointment and function of alternate members. The IRB roster should identify the primary member(s) for whom each alternate member may substitute. To ensure maintaining an appropriate quorum, the alternate's qualifications should be comparable to the primary member to be replaced. The IRB minutes should document when an alternate member replaces a primary member. When alternates substitute for a primary member, the alternate member should have received and reviewed the same material that the primary member received or would have received.

16. Does a non-affiliated member need to attend every IRB meeting?

No. Although 21 CFR 56.108(c) does not specifically require the presence of a member not otherwise affiliated with the institution to constitute a quorum, FDA considers the presence of such members an important element of the IRB's diversity. Therefore, frequent absence of all non-affiliated members is not acceptable to FDA. Acknowledging their important role, many IRBs have appointed more than one member who is not otherwise affiliated with the institution. FDA encourages IRBs to appoint members in accordance with 21 CFR 56.107(a) who will be able to participate fully in the IRB process.

17. Which IRB members should be considered to be scientists and non-scientists?

21 CFR 56.107(c) requires at least one member of the IRB to have primary concerns in the scientific area and at least one to have primary concerns in the non-scientific area. Most IRBs include physicians and Ph.D. level physical or biological scientists. Such members satisfy the requirement for at least one scientist. When an IRB encounters studies involving science beyond the expertise of the members, the IRB may use a consultant to assist in the review, as provided by 21 CFR 56.107(f).

FDA believes the intent of the requirement for diversity of disciplines was to include members who had little or no scientific or medical training or experience. Therefore, nurses, pharmacists and other biomedical health professionals should not be regarded to have "primary concerns in the non-scientific area." In the past, lawyers, clergy and ethicists have been cited as examples of persons whose primary concerns would be in non-scientific areas.

Some members have training in both scientific and non-scientific disciplines, such as a J.D., R.N. While such members are of great value to an IRB, other members who are unambiguously non-scientific should be appointed to satisfy the non-scientist requirement.

III. IRB Procedures

18. The FDA regulations [21 CFR 56.104(c)] exempt an emergency use of a test article from prospective IRB review, however, "... any subsequent use of the test article at the institution is subject to IRB review." What does the phrase "subsequent use" mean?

FDA regulations allow for one emergency use of a test article in an institution without prospective IRB review, provided that such emergency use is reported to the IRB within five working days after such use. An emergency use is defined as a single use (or single course of treatment, e.g., multiple doses of antibiotic) with one subject. "Subsequent use" would be a second use with that subject or the use with another subject.

In its review of the emergency use, if it is anticipated that the test article may be used again, the IRB should request a protocol and consent document(s) be developed so that an approved protocol would be in place when the next need arises. In spite of the best efforts of the clinical investigator and the IRB, a situation may occur where a second emergency use needs to be considered. FDA believes it is inappropriate to deny emergency treatment to an individual when the only obstacle is lack of time for the IRB to convene, review the use and give approval.

19. Are there any regulations that require clinical investigators to report to the IRB when a study has been completed?

IRBs are required to function under written procedures. One of these procedural requirements [21 CFR 56.108(a)(3)] requires ensuring "prompt reporting to the IRB of changes in a research activity." The completion of the study is a change in activity and should be reported to the IRB. Although subjects will no longer be "at risk" under the study, a final report/notice to the IRB allows it to close its files as well as providing information that may be used by the IRB in the evaluation and approval of related studies.

20. What is expedited review?

Expedited review is a procedure through which certain kinds of research may be reviewed and approved without convening a meeting of the IRB. The Agency's IRB regulations [21 CFR 56.110] permit, but do not require, an IRB to review certain categories of research through an expedited procedure if the research involves no more than minimal risk. A list of categories was last published in the *Federal Register* on January 27, 1981 [46 FR 8980]. The list is reproduced as Appendix D of this document.

The IRB may also use the expedited review procedure to review minor changes in previously approved research during the period covered by the original approval. Under an expedited review procedure, review of research may be carried out by the IRB chairperson or by one or more experienced members of the IRB designated by the chairperson. The reviewer(s) may exercise all the authorities of the IRB, except disapproval. Research may only be disapproved following review by the full committee. The IRB is required to adopt a method of keeping all members advised of research studies that have been approved by expedited review.

On November 9, FDA published in the *Federal Register* concurrently with OPRR a new Expedited Review List. The entire *Federal Register* publication, including the FDA preamble, was published on pages 60353 - 60356 of the November 9, 1998 *Federal Register* and is available on the World Wide Web at the Dockets Management Page of the FDA home Page at http://www.fda.gov/ohrms/dockets/98fr/110998b.txt (or use suffix ".pdf" for Adobe Acrobat version) or alternatively at the Government Printing Office site at http://www.access.gpo.gov/su_docs/fedreg/a981109c.html and scroll down to Food and Drug Administration.

21. The number of studies we review has increased, and the size of the package of review materials we send to IRB members is becoming formidable. Must we send the full package to all IRB members?

The IRB system was designed to foster open discussion and debate at convened meetings of the full IRB membership. While it is preferable for every IRB member to have personal copies of all study materials, each member must be provided with sufficient information to be able to actively and constructively participate. Some institutions have developed a "primary reviewer" system to promote a thorough review. Under this system, studies are assigned to one or more IRB members for a full review of all materials. Then, at the convened IRB meeting the study is presented by the primary reviewer(s) and, after discussion by IRB members, a vote for an action is taken.

The "primary reviewer" procedure is acceptable to the FDA if each member receives, at a minimum; a copy of consent documents and a summary of the protocol in sufficient detail to determine the appropriateness of the study-specific statements in the consent documents. In addition, the complete documentation should be available to all members for their review, both before and at the meeting. The materials for review should be received by the membership sufficiently in advance of the meeting to allow for adequate review of the materials.

Some IRBs are also exploring the use of electronic submissions and computer access for IRB members. Whatever system the IRB develops and uses, it must ensure that each study receives an adequate review and that the rights and welfare of the subjects are protected.

22. Are sponsors allowed access to IRB written procedures, minutes and membership rosters?

The FDA regulations do not require public or sponsor access to IRB records. However, FDA does not prohibit the sponsor from requesting IRB records. The IRB and the institution may establish a policy on whether minutes or a pertinent portion of the minutes are provided to sponsors.

Because of variability, each IRB also needs to be aware of State and local laws regarding access to IRB records.

23. Must an investigator's brochure be included in the documentation when an IRB reviews an investigational drug study?

For studies conducted under an investigational new drug application, an investigator's brochure is usually required by FDA [21 CFR 312.23(a)(5) and 312.55]. Even though 21 CFR part 56 does not mention the investigator's brochure by name, much of the information contained in such brochures is clearly required to be reviewed by the IRB. The regulations do outline the criteria for IRB approval of research. 21 CFR 56.111(a)(1) requires the IRB to assure that risks to the subjects are minimized. 21 CFR 56.111(a)(2) requires the IRB to assure that the risks to subjects are reasonable in relation to the anticipated benefits. The risks cannot be adequately evaluated without review of the results of previous animal and human studies, which are summarized in the investigator's brochure.

There is no specific regulatory requirement that the Investigator's Brochure be submitted to the IRB. There are regulatory requirements for submission of information which normally is included in the Investigator's Brochure. It is common that the Investigator's Brochure is submitted to the IRB, and the IRB may establish written procedures which require its submission. Investigator's Brochures may be part of the investigational plan that the IRB reviews when reviewing medical device studies.

24. To what extent is the IRB expected to actively audit and monitor the performance of the investigator with respect to human subject protection issues?

FDA does not expect IRBs to routinely observe consent interviews, observe the conduct of the study or review study records. However, 21 CFR 56.109(f) gives the IRB the authority to observe, or have a third party observe, the consent process and the research. When and if the IRB is concerned about the conduct of the study or the process for obtaining consent, the IRB may consider whether, as part of providing adequate oversight of the study, an active audit is warranted.

25. How can a sponsor know whether an IRB has been inspected by FDA, and the results of the inspection?

The Division of Scientific Investigations, Center for Drug Evaluation and Research, maintains an inventory of the IRBs that have been inspected, including dates of inspection and classification. The Division recently began including the results of inspections assigned by the Center for Biologics Evaluation and Research and the Center for Devices and Radiological Health. This information is available through Freedom of Information Act (FOIA) procedures. Once an investigational file has been closed, the correspondence between FDA and the IRB and the narrative inspectional report are also available under FOI.

26. If an IRB disapproves a study submitted to it, and it is subsequently sent to another IRB for review, should the second IRB be told of the disapproval?

Yes. When an IRB disapproves a study, it must provide a written statement of the reasons for its decision to the investigator and the institution [21 CFR 56.109(e)]. If the study is submitted to a second IRB, a copy of this written statement should be included with the study documentation so that it can make an informed decision about the study. 21 CFR 56.109(a) requires an IRB to "... review ... all research activities [emphasis added] ...." The FDA regulations do not prohibit submission of a study to another IRB following disapproval. However, all pertinent information about the study should be provided to the second IRB.

27. May an independent IRB review a study to be conducted in an institution with an IRB?

Generally, no. Most institutional IRB have jurisdiction over all studies conducted within that institution. An independent IRB may become the IRB of record for such studies only upon written agreement with the administration of the institution or the in-house IRB.

28. Could an IRB lose its quorum when members with a conflict of interest leave the room for deliberation and voting on a study?

Yes. "The quorum is the count of the number of members present. If the number present falls below a majority, the quorum fails. The regulations only require that a member who is conflicted not participate in the deliberations and voting on a study on which he or she is conflicted. The IRB may decide whether an individual should remain in the room."

29. Does FDA expect the IRB chair to sign the approval letters?

FDA does not specify the procedure that IRBs must use regarding signature of the IRB approval letter. The written operating procedures for the IRB should outline the procedure that is followed.

30. Does FDA prohibit direct communication between sponsors and IRBs?

It is important that a formal line of communication be established between the clinical investigator and the IRB. Clinical investigators should report adverse events directly to the responsible IRB, and should send progress reports directly to that IRB. However, FDA does not prohibit direct communication between the sponsor and the IRB, and recognizes that doing so could result in more efficient resolution of some problems.

FDA does require direct communication between the sponsors and the IRBs for certain studies of medical devices and when the 21 CFR 50.24 informed consent waiver has been invoked. Sponsors and IRBs are required to communicate directly for medical device studies under 21 CFR 812.2, 812.66 and 812.150(b). For informed consent waiver studies, direct communication between sponsors and IRBs is required under 21 CFR 50.24(e), 56.109(e), 56.109(g), 312.54(b), 312.130(d), 812.38(b)(4) and 812.47(b).

IV. IRB Records

31. Are annual IRB reviews required when all studies are reviewed by the IRB each quarter?

The IRB records for each study's initial and continuing review should note the frequency (not to exceed one year) for the next continuing review in either months or other conditions, such as after a particular number of subjects are enrolled.

An IRB may decide, to review all studies on a quarterly basis. If every quarterly report contains sufficient information for an adequate continuing review and is reviewed by the IRB under procedures that meet FDA requirements for continuing review, FDA would not require an additional "annual" review.

32. 21 CFR 56.115(a)(1) requires that the IRB maintain copies of "research proposals reviewed." Is the "research proposal" the same as the formal study protocol that the investigator receives from the sponsor of the research?

Yes. The IRB should receive and review all research activities [21 CFR 56.109(a)]. The documents reviewed should include the complete documents received from the clinical investigator, such as the protocol, the investigator's brochure, a sample consent document and any advertising intended to be seen or heard by prospective study subjects. Some IRBs also require the investigator to submit an institutionally-developed protocol summary form. A copy of all documentation reviewed is to be maintained for at least three years after completion of the research at that institution

[21 CFR 56.115(b)]. However, when the IRB makes changes, such as in the wording of the informed consent document, only the finally approved copy needs to be retained in the IRB records.

33. What IRB records are required for studies that are approved but never started?

When an IRB approves a study, continuing review should be performed at least annually. All of the records listed in 21 CFR 56.115(a)(1) - (4) are required to be maintained. The clock starts on the date of approval, whether or not subjects have been enrolled. Written progress reports should be received from the clinical investigator for all studies that are in approved status prior to the date of expiration of IRB approval. If subjects were never enrolled, the clinical investigator's progress report would be brief. Such studies may receive continuing IRB review using expedited procedures. If the study is finally canceled without subject enrollment, records should be maintained for at least three years after cancellation [21 CFR 56.115(b)].

V. Informed Consent Process

34. Is getting the subject to sign a consent document all that is required by the regulations?

No. The consent document is a written summary of the information that should be provided to the subject. Many clinical investigators use the consent document as a guide for the verbal explanation of the study. The subject's signature provides documentation of agreement to participate in a study, but is only one part of the consent process. The entire informed consent process involves giving a subject adequate information concerning the study, providing adequate opportunity for the subject to consider all options, responding to the subject's questions, ensuring that the subject has comprehended this information, obtaining the subject's voluntary agreement to participate and, continuing to provide information as the subject or situation requires. To be effective, the process should provide ample opportunity for the investigator and the subject to exchange information and ask questions.

35. May informed consent be obtained by telephone from a legally authorized representative?

A verbal approval does not satisfy the 21 CFR 56.109(c) requirement for a signed consent document, as outlined in 21 CFR 50.27(a). However, it is acceptable to send the informed consent document to the legally authorized representative (LAR) by facsimile and conduct the consent interview by telephone when the LAR can read the consent as it is discussed. If the LAR agrees, he/she can sign the consent and return the signed document to the clinical investigator by facsimile.

36. 21 CFR 50.27(a) requires that a copy of the consent document be given to the person signing the form. Does this copy have to be a photocopy of the form with the subject's signature affixed?

No. The regulation does not require the copy of the form given to the subject to be a copy of the document with the subject's signature, although this is encouraged. It must, however, be a copy of the IRB approved document that was given to the subject to obtain consent [21 CFR 50.27(a) or 21 CFR 50.27(b)(2)]. One purpose of providing the person signing the form with a copy of the consent document is to allow the subject to review the information with others, both before and after making a decision to participate in the study, as well as providing a continuing reference for items such as scheduling of procedures and emergency contacts.

37. If an IRB uses a standard "fill-in-the-blank" consent format, does the IRB need to review the filled out form for each study?

Yes. A fill-in-the-blank format provides only some standard wording and a framework for organizing the relevant study information. The IRB should review a completed sample form, individualized for each study, to ensure that the consent document, in its entirety, contains all the information required by 21 CFR 50.25 in language the subject can understand. The completed sample form should be typed to enhance its readability by the subjects. The form finally approved by the IRB should be an exact copy of the form that will be presented to the research subjects. The IRB should also review the "process" for conducting the consent interviews, i.e., the circumstances under which consent will be obtained, who will obtain consent, and so forth.

38. The informed consent regulations [21 CFR 50.25 (a)(5)] require the consent document to include a statement that notes the possibility that FDA may inspect the records. Is this statement a waiver of the subject's legal right to privacy?

No. FDA does not require any subject to "waive" a legal right. Rather, FDA requires that subjects be informed that complete privacy does not apply in the context of research involving FDA regulated products. Under the authority of the Federal Food, Drug, and Cosmetic Act, FDA may inspect and copy clinical records to verify information submitted by a sponsor. FDA generally will not copy a subject's name during the inspection unless a more detailed study of the case is required or there is reason to believe that the records do not represent the actual cases studied or results obtained.

The consent document should not state or imply that FDA needs clearance or permission from the clinical investigator, the subject or the IRB for such access. When clinical investigators conduct studies for submission to FDA, they agree to allow FDA access to the study records, as outlined in 21 CFR 312.68 and 812.145. Informed consent documents should make it clear that, by participating in research, the subject's records automatically become part of the research database. Subjects do not have the option to keep their records from being audited/reviewed by FDA.

When an individually identifiable medical record (usually kept by the clinical investigator, not by the IRB) is copied and reviewed by the Agency, proper confidentiality procedures are followed within FDA. Consistent with laws relating to public disclosure of information and the law enforcement responsibilities of the Agency, however, absolute confidentiality cannot be guaranteed.

39. Who should be present when the informed consent interview is conducted?

FDA does not require a third person to witness the consent interview unless the subject or representative is not given the opportunity to read the consent document before it is signed, see 21 CFR 50.27(b). The person who conducts the consent interview should be knowledgeable about the study and able to answer questions. FDA does not specify who this individual should be. Some sponsors and some IRBs require the clinical investigator to personally conduct the consent interview. However, if someone other than the clinical investigator conducts the interview and obtains consent, this responsibility should be formally delegated by the clinical investigator and the person so delegated should have received appropriate training to perform this activity.

40. How do you obtain informed consent from someone who speaks and understands English but cannot read?

Illiterate persons who understand English may have the consent read to them and "make their mark," if appropriate under applicable state law. The 21 CFR 50.27(b)(2) requirements for signature of a witness to the consent process and signature of the person conducting consent interview must be followed, if a "short form" is used. Clinical investigators should be cautious when enrolling subjects who may not truly understand what they have agreed to do. The IRB should consider illiterate persons as likely to be vulnerable to coercion and undue influence and should determine that appropriate additional safeguards are in place when enrollment of such persons is anticipated, see 21 CFR 56.111(b).

41. Must a witness observe the entire consent interview or only the signature of the subject?

FDA does not require the signature of a witness when the subject reads and is capable of understanding the consent document, as outlined in 21 CFR 50.27(b)(1). The intended purpose is to have the witness present during the entire consent interview and to attest to the accuracy of the presentation and the apparent understanding of the subject. If the intent of the regulation were only to attest to the validity of the subject's signature, witnessing would also be required when the subject reads the consent.

42. Should the sponsor prepare a model informed consent document?

Although not required by the IND regulations, the sponsor provides a service to the clinical investigator and the IRB when it prepares suggested study-specific wording for the scientific and technical content of the consent document. However, the IRB has the responsibility and authority to determine the adequacy and appropriateness of all of the wording in the consent, see 21 CFR 56.109(a), 111(a)(4) and 111(a)(5). If an IRB insists on wording the sponsor cannot accept, the sponsor may decide not to conduct the study at that site. For medical device studies that are conducted under an IDE, copies of all forms and informational materials to be provided to subjects to obtain informed consent must be submitted to FDA as part of the IDE, see 21 CFR 812.25(g).

43 . Is the sponsor required to review the consent form approved by the IRB to make sure all FDA requirements are met?

For investigational devices, the informed consent is a required part of the IDE submission. It is, therefore, approved by FDA as part of the IDE application. When an IRB makes substantive changes in the document, FDA reapproval is required and the sponsor is necessarily involved in this process.

FDA regulations for other products do not specifically require the sponsor to review IRB approved consent documents. However, most sponsors do conduct such reviews to assure the wording is acceptable to the sponsor.

44. Are there alternatives to obtaining informed consent from a subject?

The regulations generally require that the investigator obtain informed consent from subjects. Investigators also may obtain informed consent from a legally authorized representative of the subject. FDA recognizes that a durable power of attorney might suffice as identifying a legally authorized representative under some state and local laws. For example, a subject might have designated an individual to provide consent with regard to health care decisions through a durable power of attorney and have specified that the individual also has the power to make decisions on entry into research. FDA defers to state and local laws regarding who is a legally authorized representative. Therefore, the IRB should assure that the consent procedures comply with state and local laws, including assurance that the law applies to obtaining informed consent for subjects participating in research as well as for patients who require health care decisions.

Alternatives 1 and 2 are provided for in the regulations and are appropriate. Alternative 3 allows a designated individual to provide consent for a patient with regard to health care decisions and is appropriate when it specifically includes entry into research. FDA defers to state and local laws regarding substituted consent. Therefore, the IRB must assure itself that the substituted consent procedures comply with state and local law, including assurance the law applies to obtaining informed consent for subjects participating in research as well as for patients who require health care decisions.

45. When should study subjects be informed of changes in the study?

Protocol amendments must receive IRB review and approval before they are implemented, unless an immediate change is necessary to eliminate an apparent hazard to the subjects (21 CFR 56.108(a)(4)). Those subjects who are presently enrolled and actively participating in the study should be informed of the change if it might relate to the subjects' willingness to continue their participation in the study (21 CFR 50.25(b)(5)). FDA does not require reconsenting of subjects that have completed their active participation in the study, or of subjects who are still actively participating when the change will not affect their participation, for example when the change will be implemented only for subsequently enrolled subjects.

VI. Informed Consent Document Content

46. May an IRB require that the sponsor of the study and/or the clinical investigator be identified on the study's consent document?

Yes. The FDA requirements for informed consent are the minimum basic elements of informed consent that must be presented to a research subject [21 CFR 50.25]. An IRB may require inclusion of any additional information which it considers important to a subject's decision to participate in a research study [21 CFR 56.109(b)].

47. Does FDA require the informed consent document to contain a space for assent by children?

No, however, many investigators and IRBs consider it standard practice to obtain the agreement of older children who can understand the circumstances before enrolling them in research. While the FDA regulations do not specifically address enrollment of children (other than to include them as a class of vulnerable subjects), the basic requirement of 21 CFR 50.20 applies, i.e., the legally effective informed consent of the subject or the subject's legally authorized representative must be obtained before enrollment. Parents, legal guardians and/or others may have the ability to give permission to enroll children in research, depending on applicable state and local law of the jurisdiction in which the research is conducted. (Note: permission to enroll in research is not the same as permission to provide medical treatment.) IRBs generally require investigators to obtain the permission of one or both of the parents or guardian (as appropriate) and the assent of children who possess the intellectual and emotional ability to comprehend the concepts involved. Some IRBs require two documents, a fully detailed explanation for parents and older children to read and sign, and a shorter, simpler one for younger children. [For research supported by DHHS, the additional protections at 45 CFR 46 Subpart D are also required. The Subpart D regulations provide appropriate guidance for all other pediatric studies.]

48. Does FDA require the signature of children on informed consent documents?

As indicated above, researchers may seek assent of children of various ages. Older children may be well acquainted with signing documents through prior experience with testing, licensing and/or other procedures normally encountered in their lives. Signing a form to give their assent for research would not be perceived as unusual and would be reasonable. Younger children, however, may never have had the experience of signing a document. For these children requiring a signature may not be appropriate, and some other technique to verify assent could be used. For example, a third party may verify, by signature, that the assent of the child was obtained.

49. Who should be listed on the consent as the contact to answer questions?

21 CFR 50.25(a)(7) requires contacts for questions about the research, the research subject's rights and in case of a research-related injury. It does not specify whom to

contact. The same person may be listed for all three. However, FDA and most IRBs believe it is better to name a knowledgeable person other than the clinical investigator as the contact for study subject rights. Having the clinical investigator as the only contact may inhibit subjects from reporting concerns and/or possible abuses.

50. May the "compensation" for participation in a trial offered by a sponsor include a coupon good for a discount on the purchase price of the product once it has been approved for marketing?

No. This presumes, and inappropriately conveys to the subjects, a certainty of favorable outcome of the study and prompt approval for marketing. Also, if the product is approved, the coupon may financially coerce the subject to insist on that product, even though it may not be the most appropriate medically.

51. Must informed consent documents be translated into the written language native to study subjects who do not understand English?

The signed informed consent document is the written record of the consent interview. Study subjects are given a copy of the consent to be used as a reference document to reinforce their understanding of the study and, if desired, to consult with their physician or family members about the study.

In order to meet the requirements of 21 CFR 50.20, the consent document must be in language understandable to the subject. When the prospective subject is fluent in English, and the consent interview is conducted in English, the consent document should be in English. However, when the study subject population includes non-English speaking people so that the clinical investigator or the IRB anticipates that the consent interviews are likely to be conducted in a language other than English, the IRB should assure that a translated consent form is prepared and that the translation is accurate.

A consultant may be utilized to assure that the translation is correct. A copy of the translated consent document must be given to each appropriate subject. While a translator may be used to facilitate conversation with the subject, routine ad hoc translation of the consent document may not be substituted for a written translation.

Also see FDA Information Sheets: "A Guide to Informed Consent Documents" and "Informed Consent and the Clinical Investigator."

52. Is it acceptable for the consent document to say specimens are "donated"?

What about a separate donation statement? It would be acceptable for the consent to say that specimens are to be used for research purposes. However, the word "donation" implies abandonment of rights to the "property". 21 CFR 50.20 prohibits requiring subjects to waive or appear to waive any rights as a condition for participation in the study. Whether or not the wording is contained in "the actual consent form" is immaterial. All study-related documents must be submitted to the IRB for review. Any separate "donation" agreement is regarded to be part of the informed consent documentation, and must be in compliance with 21 CFR 50.

53. Do informed consent forms have to justify fees charged to study subjects?

FDA does not require the consent to contain justification of charges.

VII. Clinical Investigations

54. Does a physician, in private practice, conducting research with an FDA regulated product, need to obtain IRB approval?

Yes. The FDA regulations require IRB review and approval of regulated clinical investigations, whether or not the study involves institutionalized subjects. FDA has included non-institutionalized subjects because it is inappropriate to apply a double standard for the protection of research subjects based on whether or not they are institutionalized.

An investigator may be able to obtain IRB review by submitting the research proposal to a community hospital, a university/medical school, an independent IRB, a local or state government health agency or other organizations. If IRB review cannot be accomplished by one of these means, investigators may contact the FDA for assistance (Health Assessment Policy Staff 301-827-1685).

55. Does a clinical investigation involving a marketed product require IRB review and approval?

Yes, if the investigation is governed by FDA regulations [see 21 CFR 56.101, 56.102(c), 312.2(b)(1), 361.1, 601.2, and 812.2]. Also, see the information sheet entitled " 'Off-label' and Investigational Use of Marketed Drugs and Biologics" for more information.

VIII. General Questions

56. Which FDA office may an IRB contact to determine whether an investigational new drug application (IND) or investigational device exemption (IDE) is required for a study of a test article?

For drugs, the IRB may contact the Drug Information Branch, Center for Drug Evaluation and Research (CDER), at (301) 827-4573.

For a biological blood product, contact the Office of Blood Research and Review, Center for Biologics Evaluation and Research (CBER), at 301-827-3518.

For a biological vaccine product, contact the Office of Vaccines Research and Review at 301-827-0648.

For a biological Therapeutic product, contact the Office of Therapeutics Research and Review, CBER, at 301-594-2860.

For a medical device, contact the Program Operation Staff, Office of Device Evaluation, Center for Devices and Radiological Health (CDRH), at (301) 594-1190.

If the IRB is unsure about whether a test article is a "drug," a "biologic" or a "device," the IRB may contact the Health Assessment Policy Staff, Office of Health Affairs, at (301) 827-1685.

57. What happens during an FDA inspection of an IRB?

FDA field investigators interview institutional officials and examine the IRB records to determine compliance with FDA regulations. Also, see the information sheet entitled "FDA Institutional Review Board Inspections" for a complete description of the inspection process.

58. Does a treatment IND/IDE [21 CFR 312.34/812.36] require prior IRB approval?

Test articles given to human subjects under a treatment IND/IDE require prior IRB approval, with two exceptions. If a life-threatening emergency exists, as defined by 21 CFR 56.102(d), the procedures described in 56.104(c) ("Exemptions from IRB Requirement") may be followed. In addition, FDA may grant the sponsor or sponsor/investigator a waiver of the IRB requirement in accord with 21 CFR 56.105. An IRB may still choose to review a study even if FDA has granted a waiver. For further information see the information sheets entitled "Emergency Use of an Investigational Drug or Biologic," "Emergency Use of Unapproved Medical Devices," "Waiver of IRB Requirements" and "Treatment use of Investigational Drugs and Biologics."

59. How have the FDA policies on enrollment of special populations changed?

On July 22, 1993, the FDA published the *Guideline for the Study and Evaluation of Gender Differences in the Clinical Evaluation of Drugs,* in the Federal Register [58 FR 39406]. The guideline was developed to ensure that the drug development process provides adequate information about the effects of drugs and biological products in women. For further information, see the information sheet entitled "Evaluation of Gender Differences in Clinical Investigations."

On December 13, 1994, FDA published a final rule on the labeling of prescription drugs for pediatric populations [59 FR 64240]. The rule [21 CFR 201.57] encourages sponsors to include pediatric subjects in clinical trials so that more complete information about the use of drugs and biological products in the pediatric population can be developed.

60. What is a medical device?

A medical device is any instrument, apparatus, or other similar or related article, including component, part, or accessory, which is: (a) recognized in the official National Formulary, or the United States Pharmacopeia, or any supplement to them; (b) intended for use in the diagnosis of disease or other conditions, or in the cure, mitigation, treatment, or prevention of disease, in humans or other animals; **or** (c) intended to affect the structure or any function of the human body or in animals; **and** does not achieve any of its principal intended purposes through chemical action within or on the human body or in animals and is not dependent upon being metabolized for the achievement of its principal intended purposes.

Approximately 1,700 types of medical devices are regulated by FDA. The range of devices is broad and diverse, including bandages, thermometers, ECG electrodes,

IUDs, cardiac pacemakers, and hemodialysis machines. For further information, see the information sheets entitled "Medical Devices," "Frequently Asked Questions about IRB Review of Medical Devices" and "Significant Risk and Nonsignificant Risk Medical Device Studies."

61. Are *in vitro* diagnostic products medical devices?

Yes. The definition of a "device" includes *in vitro* diagnostic products—devices that aid in the diagnosis of disease or medical/physiological conditions (e.g., pregnancy) by using human or animal components to cause chemical reactions, fermentation, and the like. A few diagnostic products are intended for use in controlling other regulated products (such as those used to screen the blood supply for transfusion-transmitted diseases) and are regulated as biological products.

62. What are the IRB's general obligations towards intraocular lens (IOL) clinical investigations?

An IRB is responsible for the initial and continuing review of all IOL clinical investigations. Each individual IOL style is subject to a separate review by the IRB. This does not, however, preclude the IRB from using prior experience with other IOL investigations in considering the comparative merits of a new lens style. All IOL studies are also subject to FDA approval.

63. Considering the large number of IOL studies, how does an IRB approach the review of a new IOL style?

Full IRB review is required for all new IOLs that exhibit major departures from available lenses. Minor changes to existing lenses may be approved through expedited review. FDA designates new IOL styles as either major or minor changes based upon a predetermined classification scheme and advises the sponsor of its determination. The sponsor, through the investigator, should provide the IRB with the investigational plan which indicates the FDA study requirements, as well as the informed consent document and other comparative information on the proposed lens that describes its characteristics. It is the IRB's prerogative to request any relevant information on a new IOL to arrive at a decision or to be more rigorous in its evaluation than FDA considers minimally required.

64. Must a manufacturer comply with 21 CFR 50 and 56 when conducting trials within its own facility using employees as subjects?

Yes. This situation represents a prime example of a vulnerable subject population.

65. Do Radioactive Drug Research Committees (RDRCs) have authority to approve initial clinical studies in lieu of an IND?

No. An IND is required when the purpose of the study is to determine safety and efficacy of the drug or for immediate therapeutic, diagnostic or similar purposes. RDRCs are provided for in 21 CFR 361.1 *Radioactive Drugs for Certain Research Uses*. Radioactive drugs (as defined in 21 CFR 310.3(n)) may be administered to human research subjects without obtaining an IND when the purpose of the research project is to obtain basic information regarding the metabolism (including kinetics, distribution, and localization) of a radioactively labeled drug or regarding human physiology, pathophysiology, or biochemistry. Certain basic research studies, e.g., studies to determine whether a drug localizes in a particular organ or fluid space and to describe the kinetics of that localization, may have eventual therapeutic or diagnostic implications, but the initial studies are considered to be basic research within the meaning of 21 CFR 361.1. Such basic research studies must be conducted under the conditions set forth in 21 CFR 361.1(b).

All RDRC approved studies must also be approved by an IRB prior to initiation of the studies.

66. Does FDA approve RDRCs?

Yes. An RDRC must obtain and maintain approval by the Food and Drug Administration, as outlined in 21 CFR 361.1(c). RDRCs must register with the Division of Medical Imaging and Radiopharmaceutical Drug Products, (HFD-160), Center for Drug Evaluation and Research, FDA, 5600 Fishers Lane, Rockville, Maryland 20857. The FDA contact for compliance issues is the Human Subject Protection Team (HFD-343), CDER, FDA, 7520 Standish Place, Rockville, MD 20855.

Section 21:
Clinical Trials Litigation
by Laura Owens, J.D., and Anna Aven Sumner, J.D.,*
Alston & Bird, LLP

The public landscape of pharmaceutical and medical device development has long been bolstered by the less-noticed building blocks of any approved drug or device: clinical trials. These heretofore essential, but low profile, substructures are now coming into the forefront of modern consciousness, a forefront that includes modern litigation. The proliferation of information on the internet combined with extensive media coverage of clinical trial litigation and potential litigation[1] have resulted in a heightened consciousness of the catch-22 presented by modern clinical trials. A juror who may well understand that clinical trials are necessary may yet be challenged to reconcile the need for this research and development tool with the unavoidable risk that complications—and even death—may result in study participants. Not only is there increased awareness of litigation founded on clinical trials, the scope of suits based on clinical trials has expanded as well, from personal injury claims to False Claims Act suits pursued by the federal government to insurance litigation arising out of clinical trials.[2] Shareholder and derivative suits are entertained as well, based on an alleged failure to adequately disclose negative results from clinical trials.[3]

This new landscape of drug and device development is broader than the eye can see. In the United States annually, there are approximately 80,000 clinical trials enrolling nearly 20 million individuals as participants.[4] The breadth of participation in clinical trials, and the depth of information available about them, are forcing a shift in the way clinical trials are conducted and the way in which the associated risks are assessed.

The Scope of the Problem

No entity—be it an investigator, institutional review board, clinical trial site, or sponsor—is immune from the burgeoning and emerging litigation risks associated with adverse events in clinical trials. At the same time, however, no entity can be absolutely certain of its role in the clinical trial viewed through the all-knowing eye of the judicial system, in large part because of the paucity of reported court decisions.

Those involved in clinical trials should not be comforted by the dearth of case law on liability related to clinical trials. Complaints filed in trial courts are rarely reported to nationwide registries of cases, and quiet settlements of such complaints are even less-frequently reported. Clinical trials are on the trial bar's radar screen, in part because of the perceived deep pockets of sponsoring pharmaceutical and medical device companies, and in part because of recent media attention. Each of these entities, therefore, should arm itself with the available knowledge in an effort to limit exposure to liability while maximizing the utility and safety of the clinical trial process.

---

*The first published version of this section was written by Laura Owens, J.D., and John Crongeyer, M.D., J.D. Dr. Crongeyer, formerly of Alston & Bird, LLP, is now with the law firm of Vroon & Crongeyer, LLP.

21.1 Q. On what traditional legal grounds can participants in clinical trials sue those conducting the clinical trials?

A. Clinical research has long been guided by legal, regulatory, and ethical considerations. In the United States, there is a well-developed body of tort, or personal injury, law that can be applied and has been applied to clinical trial cases. Different duties attach to the various roles played by those involved in conducting clinical trials. The clear definition of who has what responsibilities before a clinical trial is initiated will help the parties present a joint defense in the event of a suit and will minimize finger-pointing at a later stage.

Investigators

Physicians serve as investigators during the clinical trial process. During clinical trials, these physicians protect the rights, safety, and welfare of the participants, control administration of the investigational drug or device, ensure that the trial is conducted in accordance with stated plans and regulations, and obtain informed consent. The investigator, and not the sponsor (discussed below), is responsible for the accuracy of progress reports, safety reports, and final reports.

Physicians conducting clinical trials can be accused of a wide range of legal violations, including: (1) failing to inform the patient of all of the relevant risks of participating in a study; (2) improperly enrolling in clinical trials patients who are at higher risk due to their medical problems or individual characteristics; (3) failing to withdraw a patient from a study once clinical problems became evident; and (4) having or failing to disclose personal bias due to a financial interest in a given drug, device, or clinical trial. These violations can be pleaded as fraud, failure to obtain informed consent, negligence, strict liability, breach of warranty, failure to warn, and violation of ethical duties.

The Institutional Review Board (IRB)

An IRB both leads and follows the investigator/physician. Duties of an IRB include approving, disapproving, or requiring modification of research prior to study initiation, and reviewing informed consents, reviewing the conducted research at least annually, and assuring the safety, rights, and welfare of the subjects during the study.

IRBs that oversee studies can be sued for: (1) failing to examine the design of the study protocol; (2) failing to review the ongoing operation of the trial; (3) failing to review proposed amendments to the informed consent form; (4) failing to review amendments to the study protocol; and (5) failing to ensure proper reporting. In short, a plaintiff's allegations against an IRB usually involve perceived negligence in fulfilling its duties under the terms of the clinical trial.

Clinical Trial Settings

Hospitals at which clinical studies are conducted can be and usually are joined in clinical trials cases under theories of *respondeat superior,* by which employers and institutions are held accountable for the actions and inactions of their employees and agents. In other words, a hospital can be sued for legal violations committed by the doctors, staff, and IRBs, as well as for allowing the use of allegedly unsafe drugs, devices, and treatment practices within the hospital.[5]

Recently, an Illinois appellate court reversed an earlier trial court ruling that had established that a plaintiff could not state a claim against a hospital for inadequate consent.[6] The court determined that, because the hospital and university adopted policies and established an IRB to ensure that the informed consents at issue met FDA and DHHS regulations, a plaintiff could sue the hospital and university for claims arising out of a lack of informed consent.

Sponsors

The sponsor of a clinical trial has responsibilities related to its role as "overseer." That said, the sponsor may transfer its obligations by written agreement to a contract research organization. Regardless of who has these obligations, by contract or otherwise, the entity must select qualified investigators, provide those qualified investigators with sufficient data to conduct their investigation, ensure compliance with the investigational plan and protocols, maintain an effective plan and protocols, and *promptly* inform the FDA or investigators of new adverse events or newly discovered risks associated with the drug or device. In addition, the sponsor must maintain an open channel of communication between the participants, the investigators, and itself.

While much of the attention in the last few years has been focused upon the doctors, IRBs, and hospitals actually conducting the study and enrolling the patients, product sponsors can also be sued on a number of legal grounds. They can be sued for perpetrating a fraud on the FDA if there are allegations that the company was not forthcoming with all pertinent information during the process of obtaining FDA approval of the protocol or in obtaining the agency's approval of the individual drugs, devices, or biologics used in a clinical trial.

Sponsors can also be sued for having an allegedly defective product, either by errant manufacture or errant design. For instance, as was alleged in *In re St. Judge Medical Inc. Silzone Heart Valves Products Liability Litigation,* if an artificial heart valve was found to be prone to paravalvular leak, that device could be the basis of a design defect claim.[7] Alternatively, plaintiffs can allege that a drug or device is defectively manufactured. For instance, if a vaccine intended to be a "killed vaccine" occasionally contained live viruses due to periodic problems in its manufacture, death or injuries from that product could serve as the basis of a "manufacturing defect" claim.

Aside from the risks associated with a product itself, companies can be sued for their corporate activity. If a company assured the public and those conducting a clinical trial that a particular drug could be given without a risk of stroke and this claim was inaccurate, then the company could be sued for breaching a warranty to participants.[8]

In addition to making claims against a sponsoring company or others conducting a clinical trial based on disclosures to participants, plaintiffs also can sue for information that is withheld. Such failure-to-warn and intentional misrepresentation claims are common in products liability cases and were alleged in a Philadelphia clinical trials case, *Gukin v. Nagle.* In the *Gukin* case, plaintiffs claimed that the dangers associated with the medical device exceeded those expected by the average consumer.[9] Typically, failure to warn claims are brought in addition to claims that sponsors violated state-enacted consumer protection laws designed to protect the public health and safety.

21.2 Q. On what other legal grounds can those conducting clinical trials be sued by non-clinical-trial participants?

A. As a recent spate of suits has demonstrated, clinical trial participants are not the only entities who have attempted to enforce their rights vis-à-vis those conducting clinical trials in the legal arena. Non-participant suits can be divided into two general areas: suits by the government, or those acting on the government's behalf; and suits by those with an economic stake in the clinical trial's outcome. Both types of suits have survived attempts at dismissal in the early stages, and these suits may be a harbinger of future trends in clinical trial litigation.

The False Claims Act is a federal whistleblower statute that enables private citizens to bring suit on behalf of the government to recover monies that were erroneously paid by the government. The government may choose to join in such a suit, or may elect to allow the private citizen to pursue the suit alone. In both of the reported False Claims Act cases from 2004, federal district courts permitted claims to go forward against hospitals for acts during clinical trials. The courts concluded that the submission of reimbursement requests by a hospital to Medicare for clinical trials that were not covered or otherwise reimbursable by Medicare was a "false claim."[10] These rulings suggest that if hospitals or other clinical trials sites request and receive reimbursement for clinical trials when that reimbursement is not otherwise due, the federal government, based on the claim of a private citizen, may pursue action against the hospital.

Besides sponsors and investigators, others may have a financial interest in the outcome of clinical trials. One such interested entity is the clinical trial liability insurer. Typically, an insurer's interests would be aligned with those of its client. Conflict between these interests has arisen when the insured and insurer disagree on whether proper disclosures about clinical trial results were made. In *Federal Insurance Company v. Curon Medical, Inc.,* for instance, a California district court rescinded an insurance contract between Federal and Curon, which conducted the clinical trial.[11] The court determined that Curon, as a corporation, had sufficient cumulative knowledge to know that a claim was likely to be made based on a poor outcome of a clinical trial. Curon's failure to disclose this information to Federal was a material misrepresentation sufficient to permit Federal to rescind the contract under California law.[12]

Investors comprise another group with pecuniary interest in the outcome of trials. The New York State Common Retirement Fund has sued Merck over the arthritis drug Vioxx, accusing the pharmaceutical company of misleading shareholders about the drug's safety by withholding information from unfavorable clinical trials.[13] Individual shareholder suits may follow.

21.3 Q. What are the specific types of claims that are most common in clinical trials lawsuits today?

A. In the suits identified above, claims were brought when subjects died, suffered a debilitating injury and a subsequent "premature death," or were injured while participating in a clinical trial.[14] Among the causes of actions raised were: (i) negligence; (ii) strict products liability; (iii) common law fraud and intentional misrepresentation; (iv) intentional and negligent infliction of emotional distress; (v) assault and battery; (vi) lack of informed consent; (vii) fraud on the FDA; (viii) violation of the Common Rule; (ix) violation of federal regulations concerning the manufacture and control of investigational biological drugs for clinical use; (x) violation of subjects' civil rights; (xi) violation of state consumer protection laws; (xii) breach of an agreement to abide by the Belmont Report; and (xiii) breach of the right to be treated with dignity.

The claims that have tended to receive the most significant attention are those based on inadequate consent and conflict of interest. Each of these relatively common claims is addressed further below.

Inadequate Consent

In accordance with basic tort law, as well as with subsequent government regulations such as 45 C.F.R. § 46.116, informed consent is required for all clinical research. Adequate informed consent must describe "any reasonably foreseeable risks or discomforts to the subject,"[15] as well any available alternative treatments.[16] On the basis of these principles, plaintiffs commonly allege that the investigators failed to disclose the known or knowable medical risks of the therapies being studied.

What makes a consent inadequate under the law? Failure to obtain consent *at all* is clearly inadequate in a clinical trial setting. A 1992 Pennsylvania case, *Friter v. Iolab Corp.,* illustrates the inadequacy of a total failure to obtain informed consent in the clinical trials context.[17] The plaintiff-patient received an intraocular lens from a surgeon at Wills Eye Hospital without being informed that the lens was an experimental treatment being tested in an FDA-regulated clinical trial. Prior to surgery, the patient was unaware that he was even a research subject. Following his surgery, he experienced complications, including corneal damage, ocular hemorrhage, and threatened loss of sight in the eye. The jury awarded the plaintiff and his wife $1.75 million in damages, and the hospital itself was found liable for not ensuring that the informed consent was obtained.

Most allegations of failed informed consent, however, focus on situations in which consent is obtained but is nonetheless inadequate. Frequently, to assert a cause of action of this nature, plaintiffs allege that necessary information was not provided in the consent process. In the *Gelsinger* case, for instance, plaintiffs claimed that the informed consent failed to disclose the deaths of monkeys undergoing similar gene therapy experiments or the serious adverse effects in previous human participants in the trial.[18]

Alternatively, a plaintiff may allege that the consent at issue contained inaccurate information. The plaintiffs in *Robertson ex rel. Robertson v. McGee,* a case filed in federal court, alleged that the consent forms used in the clinical trials contained numerous misrepresentations, including a false implication that the FDA had approved the trial vaccine, a false statement that animal and human trials supported the use of the vaccine, and the inaccurate identification of potential side effects.[19]

Plaintiffs can also allege impropriety with respect to the manner in which informed consent was obtained. A class action lawsuit, *Diaz v. Hillsborough County Hospital Authority,* alleged that the informed consent was improper because of the manner in which it was obtained from low-income, high-risk pregnant teenagers during pre-term labor.[20] Specifically, the hospital authority was accused of having patients with a limited knowledge of English sign consent forms that were difficult to understand, and of seeking and obtaining consent at a difficult time (i.e., when patients were medicated or in pre-term labor). Consents obtained in this manner, according to plaintiffs, resulted in violations of the patients' constitutional right to bodily integrity. Therefore, despite the fact that the investigators had obtained a signed consent, the plaintiffs urged the court to find that it was inadequate. For this alleged constitutional violation and with *no* accompanying physical injury, the plaintiffs received a $3.8 million settlement.

To be both informed and a voluntary, informed consent must be substantively accurate in the information it discloses and procedurally fair to participants. The information provided in the consent must be accurate and thorough, and the consent itself must be obtained using a procedure that ensures voluntary acceptance of the risks associated with participating in the clinical trial. Further, any changes in the risks or procedures should be accompanied by a new and updated informed consent.

The fine line between adequate and inadequate consent is evident in the jury verdict in a clinical trial case involving the Fred Hutchinson Cancer Research Center (known as "The Hutch"). In the early 1980s, physicians at The Hutch conducted a study in which the bone marrow of leukemia patients was depleted of T-cells in an attempt to prevent graft-versus-host disease, a potentially fatal complication. Efforts to preserve the lives of the study participants failed, and 83 of 85 patients died. Subsequent litigation charged the doctors with failure to inform patients of the risks involved in participating in this trial. A jury found that the plaintiffs' claims regarding inadequate informed consent were not supported, however, and unanimously agreed that the center had fully informed patients.[21]

Although *lack* of informed consent is often a claim in clinical trial litigation, the presence of an informed consent is a useful shield to litigation as well. Based on the cases filed thus far, attention to the informed consent process is probably the most important step in managing litigation risks for those conducting clinical trials.

Conflicts of Interest

Along with the information disclosed in a fully-informed consent signed by a clinical trial participant, investigators and institutions also need to disclose or eliminate conflicts of interest. This disclosure is of particular importance when financial conflicts of interest may arise. More and more courts are finding that a failure to disclose a conflict of interest is a negligent act that deprives the clinical trial subject of the opportunity to make a truly informed decision about participating in the trial.

Both the Common Rule and FDA regulations prohibit such conflicts with regard to IRB members: "No IRB may have a member participate in the IRB's initial or continuing review of any project in which the member has a conflicting interest, except to provide information requested by the IRB."[22] The term "conflicting interest," however, is not defined by either the Common Rule or relevant FDA regulations.

Other rules implicate the idea of conflicts of interest without better defining the term. For example, research that is funded by the Public Health Service, which includes the NIH, must comply with 42 C.F.R. part 50. These regulations require that designated officials manage conflicting interests.[23] According to the regulations: "A conflict of interest exists when the designated official(s) reasonably determines that a Significant Financial Interest could directly and significantly effect the design, conduct, or reporting of the PHS-funded research."[24]

The regulations provide examples of ways to manage conflicts of interest, including:

(1) Public disclosure of a significant financial interest;

(2) Monitoring of research by an independent reviewer;

(3) Modification of the research plan;

(4) Disqualification from participation in all or a portion of the research funded by the PHS;

(5) Divestiture of the significant financial interest; or

(6) Severance of relationships that create actual or potential conflicts.

Between the jagged edges of these conflict of interest regulations, modern institutions conducting clinical trials may be snagged. The failure to disclose institutional conflicts, as well as those of individuals within the institution, can result in a finding that there was a breach of fiduciary duty to the clinical trial participants.

In two studies performed at The Hutch, investigators allegedly failed to properly inform their patients that they and the institution itself possessed financial interests in the protocols being developed. These researchers allegedly failed to inform patients of their financial interests in the company that owned the commercial rights to the monoclonal antibodies being tested in the study.[25]

The blood cancer study, identified as Protocol 126, was conducted at The Hutch in the early 1980s. No disclosures were made about a potential financial conflict of interest. Although several physicians, including members of the IRB at the Cancer Center, attempted to halt the blood cancer research, the study went forward and resulted in a high mortality rate among the participants.[26]

In Protocol 681, a breast cancer study, researchers analyzed the effects of a combination of drugs designed to protect vital organs during chemotherapy. Again, no disclosures were made about potential financial conflicts of interest. Two of the investigators involved with Protocol 681 founded the company that supplied the drugs for the study. In addition, the cancer center was to receive approximately $20,000 in stock and a minimum of $50,000 per year in licensing fees, plus a percentage of company sales if the research proved successful. As was the case with Protocol 126, Protocol 681 proved harmful to patients and was eventually stopped.[27]

Both studies resulted in lawsuits. The blood cancer study triggered a class-action lawsuit, *Wright v. The Fred Hutchinson Cancer Research Center,* in which the plaintiffs claimed that the "development, initiation, and continuation of [Protocol 126] violated certain federal regulations, lacked informed consent, violated the Washington Consumer Protection Act, and gave rise to strict products liability."[28] As noted above, however, a recent jury verdict sided for the defense on the informed consent claims that formed the heart of that case. The plaintiff in *Berman v. The Fred*

Hutchinson Cancer Research Center, arguing for inadequate consent in Protocol 681, however, won a motion for summary judgment, with the court ruling that the decedent would not have signed the consent had the decedent known of the potential complications.[29]

Whether they are held by investigators or institutions, these types of research-related financial stakes are a reality of modern clinical trials. The relationships between the federal government, medical centers, and the pharmaceutical and medical device industries have grown in complexity over the last 25 years. These complex arrangements have produced great benefits, exponentially increasing the value of research and collaboration.

Despite the obvious benefits of collaboration, conflicts of interest can and do arise. To acknowledge and address the issue of conflicts of interest, HHS sponsored a 2000 conference entitled, "Human Subject and Financial Conflict of Interest," aimed at reviewing the impact of conflicts and the relationship between conflicts and obtaining informed consent. At that conference, the government articulated its position that, at a minimum, physician-investigator and institutional financial interests should be disclosed as part of the informed consent process.[30] OHRP followed this up by issuing a January 2001 document entitled, "Draft Interim Guidance Regarding Financial Relationships and Clinical Research," a March 2003 draft version of the guidance, and a May 2004 final guidance entitled, "Financial Relationships and Interests in Research Involving Human Subjects: Guidance for Human Subject Protection" (see Q13.1). This document serves as a foundation for the disclosure of financial relationships and government prosecution for failures of disclosure.[31]

Although these admonitions in favor of the disclosure of conflicting financial interests are ill-defined, the underlying message is clear. Financial interests create a perception of bias on the part of the investigators and institutions, and their existence certainly can serve as troubling evidence for defendants faced with litigation. Limiting the financial interests of those involved with the clinical trial and adding financial disclosures as another layer of the informed consent will help defend the validity of the trial and the reputations of those conducting it if future litigation arises.[32]

In addition to ownership interests in companies sponsoring clinical research or intellectual property rights, investigators and institutions often receive compensation for their participation in clinical research. These relationships may raise concerns under the federal Anti-Kickback Statute, and should be considered when the financial interests of the parties involved are addressed.[33] In general, payments to researchers should be in line with the fair market value of the services rendered, be for legitimate and necessary services, and not be mere payment for the referral of business. To be prepared for conflict-of-interest challenges, sponsors should take care to document transactions evidencing the necessity of the services and their fair market value.[34]

21.4 *Q. What strategies and arguments may defense attorneys use against these claims?*

A. Despite predictions on the future of clinical trials litigation, the developing legal underpinnings of these suits are not solely within the province of the plaintiffs' bar. Given the dearth of published opinions on these cases, biotech and pharmaceutical companies are in a position to shape arguments that could become case law and provide protection against future claims. Both procedural and substantive arguments are available to the savvy clinical trial entity, although this availability comes with the standard caveat that defenses should be attempted only when the facts of the case reasonably support such arguments. The discussions below highlight some of the major defenses that courts have addressed.

Informed Consent

Informed consent, or the lack thereof, may be one prong of a plaintiff's case. The doctrine of informed consent, however, may at the same time serve as a potential defense in a clinical trials case in which a patient consents to a procedure or agrees to participate in a study after being informed of the nature of the procedure or study, the potential risks involved, and the available therapeutic alternatives. A patient's consent can be established in writing (i.e., when the patient signs a consent form acknowledging receipt of the necessary information), through express words demonstrating consent, or may be implied by the patient's acts or conduct. If a consent form has been signed, a rebuttable presumption is created that the patient provided valid consent. The rebuttable presumption shifts the legal burden to the patient to prove that the consent obtained was not valid.

The first issue with respect to consent is whether consent was obtained. If consent was obtained, the next inquiry is whether the consent obtained was adequate. As noted above, if the consent provides too little information, erroneous information, or is obtained through coercive means, even a signed consent may be deemed inadequate.

Learned Intermediary Doctrine

The learned intermediary doctrine is an exception to the general rule requiring product manufacturers and suppliers to warn consumers of any known or reasonably foreseeable risks associated with their products. This doctrine, when applicable in a clinical trials case, protects manufacturers and suppliers of prescription drugs from liability resulting from a failure to warn ultimate consumers of the dangers and risks associated with their drugs. For the doctrine to apply, however, the drug manufacturer or supplier must provide adequate warnings and information pertaining to the drug to the so-called "learned intermediary"—the prescribing physician for marketed drugs and clinical investigators for clinical trials. The physician, in turn, acts as a liaison between the manufacturer and the ultimate consumer of the drug. The prescribing physician is assumed, due to his or her superior knowledge and training, to be better able to comprehend complex and esoteric drug information and be better able to weigh the risks and benefits of using the drug in a particular patient.

Both physicians and medical clinics participating in investigational drug studies have been held to qualify as learned intermediaries. In *Tracy v. Merrell Dow,* a patient died of cardiac arrest after failing to heed his physician's warning not to smoke or consume alcohol while using an investigational nicotine-replacement patch.[35] The court ruled that because the drug manufacturer did not affect or control the physician's treatment decisions, the physician-patient relationship superseded the physician-manufacturer relationship. Thus, even though the physician received compensation for each of his patients participating in the study, the doctor still qualified as a learned intermediary.

Similarly, in *Kernke v. The Menninger Clinic, Inc.,* a patient died after walking away from a psychiatric clinic where he was a participant in an investigational drug study for the treatment of schizophrenia.[36] The drug manufacturer was absolved from any liability arising from a failure to warn the patient, despite the fact that the manufacturer was allegedly on notice that the clinic's informed consent process was flawed. The court reasoned that a manufacturer is rightfully entitled to rely on the prescribing physician to properly relay drug warnings to study subjects.

Substantive Preemption

The two defenses discussed above are substantive, going to the very factual basis of the plaintiff's case. In contrast, preemption is a procedural legal doctrine of interest for defendants facing clinical trials litigation. The preemption doctrine essentially prevents citizens from suing a company or institution that complies with government regulations when the government specifically undertakes to control or oversee an issue in its entirety. For instance, if the FDA requires that a specific warning appear on a device, then a private citizen cannot sue the company for using that warning.

While preemption is a potent legal tool that can result in defense judgments, its very potency means that it is accepted by courts only in select circumstances. While preemption arguments are only beginning to be advanced in the clinical trials litigation context, the relevant case law over the last decade has clarified, at least to some extent, when the doctrine might be applicable in the clinical trials context. The Supreme Court has addressed preemption in the medical device context in *Medtronic v. Lohr,* ruling that Lohr's manufacturing and labeling claims were not preempted simply because the pacemaker had gone through the FDA's §510 substantial equivalence process.[37] The Supreme Court did not state with a majority opinion whether or not the more rigorous pre-market approval process provided for in §360 preempted state tort actions based on product liability claims, nor did it state clearly whether the classification of products was determinative of preemption at all. Therefore, the door is open for those involved in clinical trials to assert that the clinical research process differs from the marketing of FDA-approved medical devices and drugs and that, because of these differences, courts can and should intervene to prevent litigation claims from chilling much-needed research.[38]

Jurisdiction

Jurisdiction, like preemption, is a potential procedural hurdle for clinical trial plaintiffs. Given the legal novelty of clinical trials cases, it is unsurprising that jurisdictional issues are often the first volleys in a hard-fought litigation-war. Before moving to the substantive merits of legal claims and defenses, both parties in litigation naturally try to gain an advantage by having as favorable a court as possible to decide these issues. Conventional wisdom suggests that, despite tort law reforms in many states, state courts tend to be more favorable to plaintiffs, and federal courts to defendants. The plaintiff has the initial advantage, because he or she is entitled to select the forum in which to file a complaint.

The defendant unhappy with the forum is not without recourse, however, and may remove the case to federal court. Thus far, attempts to remove suits involving clinical trials to federal court have not proved generally successful. Even if a defendant successfully convinces a state court that a federal court properly has jurisdiction, the federal court then may review the removal and determine that jurisdiction is not proper (i.e., and send the case back to state court).

In *Guckin v. Nagle,* for example, the claims in the complaint arose from an alleged personal injury that occurred during the clinical trial of Secca System, a Class III investigational medical device[39] manufactured by Curon Medical, Inc. to remedy fecal incontinence. The plaintiff filed suit in state court, asserting various claims for negligence and fraudulent misrepresentation. The defendant physicians and manufacturer removed the case to federal district court. The district court declined to keep the case, noting that its jurisdiction was limited, despite the fact that the plaintiff alleged violations of the Food, Drug and Cosmetic Act.[40]

21.5 Q. How do federal regulations relate to suits brought by subjects and their families?

A. Non-compliance with the common rule or other government regulations does not create a private right of action for a lawsuit. In other words, a research subject cannot sue an institution or an IRB simply because government regulations were not followed. Rather, the government determines what penalties are imposed for regulatory violations. For instance, if a party breaches a commitment to comply with the common rule, the government can suspend federal funding. If a company or clinical investigator does not comply with FDA regulations, the agency can pursue regulatory or criminal sanctions (see Section 17).[41]

While research subjects cannot directly sue for regulatory violations, the failure to comply with government guidelines and regulations can serve as powerfully suggestive anecdotal evidence that the institutions, IRBs, sponsors, and physician-investigators were negligent in performing their responsibilities. Plaintiffs' attorneys can use agency warning letters or FDA administrative hearing testimony to buttress their cases. Similarly, defendants can cite the lack of FDA citations as persuasive evidence that a clinical trial was designed and conducted properly.

About the Authors

Laura Lewis Owens is a partner of Alston & Bird LLP, where she is the head of the firm's products liability defense practice group. With 20 years of litigation experience, she has successfully defended a wide variety of catastrophic injury and adverse event cases on behalf of the drug and device industry and health care entities. Ms. Owens received a J.D. from the University of Georgia School of Law.

Anna Aven Sumner is an associate in Alston & Bird LLP's products liability group. Her products liability practice focuses on novel causes of action in this arena and likely defenses thereto. Ms. Sumner earned her J.D. degree from the Duke University School of Law.

Footnotes

[1]See, e.g., Barry Meier, "New York's Pension Fund Files Own Suit Against Merck," *N.Y. TIMES,* December 1, 2004, at C1; Gina Kolata, *Johns Hopkins Admits Fault in Fatal Experiment,* N.Y. TIMES, July 17, 2001, at A16; *Grimes v. Kennedy Krieger Inst., Inc.,* 782 A.2d 807 (Md. 2001); *Robertson ex rel. Robertson v. McGee,* No. 01-CV-60-C, 2002 WL 535045 (N.D. Okla., filed Jan. 29, 2001); *Wright v. The Fred Hutchinson Cancer Research Center,* No. 01-2-008376 (Kitsap Co. Wash. Sup. Ct. filed Mar. 29, 2001); *Gelsinger v. Trustees of the Univ. of Pa.,* No. 000901885 (Philadelphia Co. Pa. Ct. Com. Pl. filed 2000 Term); *Berman v. The Fred Hutchinson Cancer Research Center,* No. C01-5217 RSL (W.D. Wash., filed May 18, 2001).

[2]See, e.g., *In re Cardiac Devices Qui Tam Litig.,* 221 F.R.D. 318 (D. Conn. 2004) (suit under False Claims Act survived motion to dismiss for failure to plead with particularity and failure to state a claim); *Cantrell ex rel. United States v. New York Univ.,* 326 F.Supp.2d 468 (S.D. N.Y. 2004) (suit under False Claims Act could be based on separate filings of university); *Federal Ins. Co. v. Curon Med. Inc.,* No. C-03-1356-VRW, 2004 WL 2418318 (N.D. Cal. Oct. 28, 2004) (rescission of insurance policy granted for failure to disclose material facts).

[3]Barry Meier, "New York's Pension Fund Files Own Suit Against Merck," *N.Y. TIMES,* December 1, 2004, at C1.

[4]Michael D. Lemonick & Andrew Goldstein, With reporting by Alice Park/ Baltimore, "At Your Own Risk; Some Patients Join Clinical Trials Out of Desperation, Others to Help Medicine Advance. Who is to Blame if They Get Sick— or Even Die?," *Time Magazine,* April 22, 2002, at 46.

[5]Quite often, these latter claims stem from allegedly inadequate protocols and guidelines in effect at a particular hospital or medical center. For instance, if a particular hospital's protocol for critical care nursing only required vital signs to be checked every six hours, a plaintiff could allege that the adoption and use of this protocol constituted negligence.

[6]*Lenahan v. Univ. of Chicago,* 348 Ill. App.3d 155, 808 N.E.2d 1078 (2004).

[7]*In re St. Jude Medical, Inc., Silzone Heart Valve Products Liability Litig.,* No. 01-1396 (JRT/FLN), 2004 WL 1630786 (D. Minn. July 15, 2004).

[8]In the *Gelsinger* case, breach of warranty claims were brought for "intentionally misrepresenting" the efficacy of the clinical trial treatment.

[9]The plaintiffs in *Guckin v. Nagle,* 259 F.Supp. 2d 406, 408 (E.D. Pa. 2003) brought claims against the sponsor, the investigator, and the hospital for negligence, assault and battery, lack of informed consent, intentional infliction of emotional distress, negligent infliction of emotional distress, common law fraud, intentional misrepresentation, and strict liability in tort.

[10]*Cantrell ex rel. United States v. New York Univ.,* 326 F.Supp.2d 468 (S.D.N.Y. 2004); *In re Cardiac Devices Qui Tam Litig.,* 221 F.R.D. 318 (D. Conn. 2004).

[11]*Federal Ins. Co. v. Curon Med., Inc.,* No. C-03-1356-VRW, 2004 WL 2418318 (N.D. Cal. Oct. 28, 2004).

[12]*Id.* at *9

[13]Barry Meier, "New York's Pension Fund Files Own Suit Against Merck," *N.Y. TIMES,* December 1, 2004, at C1.

[14]*Lenahan v. Univ. of Chicago,* 348 Ill.App.3d 155, 808 N.E.2d 1078 (2004); *Guckin v. Nagle,* 259 F.Supp. 2d 406 (E.D. Pa. 2003); *Grimes v. Kennedy Krieger Inst., Inc.,* 782 A.2d 807 (Md. 2001); *Robertson ex rel. Robertson v. McGee,* No. 01-CV-60-C (N.D. Okla., filed Jan. 29, 2001); *Wright v. The Fred Hutchinson Cancer Research Center,* No. 01-2-008376 (Kitsap Co. Wash. Sup. Ct. filed Mar. 29, 2001); *Gelsinger v. Trustees of the Univ. of Pa.* (Philadelphia Co. Pa. Ct. Com. Pl. filed 2000 Term); *Berman v. The Fred Hutchinson Cancer Research Center,* No. C01-5217 RSL (W.D. Wash. filed May 18, 2001).

[15]45 C.F.R. § 46.116(a)(2).

[16]See 45 C.F.R. § 46.116(a)(4). *See also Diaz v. Hillsborough County Hosp. Auth.,* No. 8:90-CV-120-T-25B, 2000 WL 1682918 (M.D. Fla. Aug. 7, 2000) (noting that plaintiff alleged that consent documents failed to inform participants of available alternative treatments).

[17]*Friter v. Iolab Corp.,* 414 Pa.Super. 622, 607 A.2d 1111 (1992).

[18]*Gelsinger v. Trustees of the Univ. of Pa.,* No. 000901885 (Philadelphia Co. Pa. Ct. Com. Pl. filed Sept. 18, 2000), Complaint at ¶ 60.

[19]*Robertson ex rel. Robertson v. McGee,* No. 01-CV-60-C, 2002 WL 535045 (N.D. Okla. Jan. 28, 2002).

[20]*Diaz v. Hillsborough County Hosp. Auth.,* No. 8:90-CV-120-T-25B, 2000 WL 1682918 (M.D. Fla. Aug. 7, 2000). The published case resolved only whether a consent settlement order was appropriate. The plaintiffs admitted that one of their theories—that of a constitutional violation arising out of a defendant's interference with a plaintiff's bodily integrity—was novel and untested in the class action context.

[21]Tracy Johnson, "Jury Sides With Hutch, Doctors in Deaths of 5 Patients Knew Risks in Leukemia Treatment Study, Panel Decides," *SEATTLE POST-INTELLIGENCER,* April 9, 2004, at A1. Note, however, that the family of a fifth clinical trial participant was given more than $1 million because his donor bone marrow was lost due to a laboratory mistake. David Heath and Luke Timmerman, "Jury Finds Hutch Not Negligent in 4 Deaths," *SEATTLE TIMES,* April 9, 2004, at A1.

[22]7 C.F.R. § 1c.107(e); 10 C.F.R. § 745.107(e); 14 C.F.R. § 1230.107(e); 15 C.F.R. § 27.107(e); 16 C.F.R. § 1028.107(e); 21 C.F.R. § 56.107(e); 22 C.F.R. § 225.107(e); 28 C.F.R. § 46.107(e); 32 C.F.R. § 219.107(e); 34 C.F.R. 97.107(e); 38 C.F.R. § 16.107(e); 40 C.F.R. § 26.107(e); 45 C.F.R. § 46.107(e); 45 C.F.R. § 690.107(e); and 49 C.F.R. § 11.107(e).

[23]42 C.F.R. § 50.605(a).

[24]*Id.* With limited exceptions, Significant Financial Interest means anything of monetary value, including but not limited to, salary or other payments for services (e.g., consulting fees or honoraria); equity interests (e.g., stocks, stock options or other ownership interests); and intellectual property rights (e.g., patents, copyrights and royalties from such rights). 42 C.F.R. § 50.603.

[25]Joseph B. Clamon, "The Search for a Cure: Combating the Problem of Conflicts of Interest that Currently Plagues Biomedical Research," 89 *IOWA L. REV.* 235 (2003).

[26]David Heath and Luke Timmerman, "Jury Finds Hutch Not Negligent in 4 Deaths," *SEATTLE TIMES,* April 9, 2004, at A1.

[27]*Berman v. The Fred Hutchinson Cancer Research Center,* No. C01-5217 RSL (W.D. Wash., filed May 18, 2001), Complaint at ¶¶ 19-63.

[28]*Wright v. The Fred Hutchinson Cancer Research Center,* No. C01-5217L, 2001 WL 1782714 (W.D. Wash. Nov. 19, 2001).

[29]David Heath, "Judge: Hutch Didn't Reveal Study's Risk to Patient," *SEATTLE TIMES,* August 9, 2002, at A1.

[30]Mark Barnes & Sara Krauss, "Conflicts of Interest in Human Research: Risks and Pitfalls of 'Easy Money' in Research Funding," 89 *Health Law Rep.* (BNA) 1378 (Aug. 31, 2000) (citing August 2000 HHS conference on Human Subject Protection & Financial Conflicts of Interest).

[31]Financial Relationships and Clinical Research: Issues for Institutions, Clinical Investigators, and IRBs to Consider When Dealing with Issues of Financial Interest and Human Subject Protection, OHRP, available at http://ohrp.osophs.dhhs.gov/humansubjects/finreltn/fmguid.htm.

[32]See Guidance for Industry: Financial Disclosure by Clinical Investigators, FDA, available at http://www.fda.gov/oc/guidance/financialdis.html.

[33]See 42 U.S.C. § 1320a-7b(b).

[34]Conflicts of interest are not only a problem for current clinical trial investigators. Alleged conflicts may also exist after clinical trial investigation ends; ten out of 32 government drug advisors who voted in favor of continued marketing of Vioxx, Celebrex, and Bextra had consulted with the sponsors of these drugs. Gardiner Harris and Alex Berenson, "10 Voters on Panel Backing Pain Pills Had Industry Ties," *N. Y. TIMES,* February 25, 2005, at A1.

[35]*Tracy v. Merrell Dow Pharm., Inc.* 569 N.E.2d 875 (Ohio 1991).

[36]*Kernke v. The Menninger Clinic, Inc.,* 173 F.Supp. 2d 1117 (D. Kansas 2001).

[37]*Medtronic, Inc. v. Lohr,* 518 U.S. 470 (1996).

[38]The fact that FDA compliance does not guarantee preemption does not mean that FDA compliance goes unnoticed in clinical trial litigation. For instance, FDA compliance may be used as evidence that the duties of the parties to the clinical trial–sponsor, investigator, IRB–were met.

[39]The Food & Drug Administration ("FDA"), through the Food, Drug, and Cosmetic Act ("FDCA"), reserves the most rigorous pre-market approval review for Class III medical devices. These devices are those that "presen[t] a potential unreasonable risk of illness or injury." 21 U.S.C. § 360c(a)(1). The investigational device exemption to the FDCA, however, provides that Class III devices "may proceed to clinical trials, if the FDA preliminarily examines the technical and scientific evidence, and concludes that the device is safe for further testing." *Guckin v. Nagle,* 259 F.Supp. 2d 408, 408 (E.D.Pa. 2003).

[40]*Guckin v. Nagle,* 259 F.Supp. 2d 408 (E.D.Pa. 2003).

[41]For instance, the government pursued a criminal case against a cancer center employee for accessing and using for pecuniary gain a patient's PHI in violation of HIPAA. Because HIPAA deals largely with the privacy of patient health information, it does not fit within the context of this clinical trial discussion, and as such, will not be examined further.

Section 22:
State Laws Affecting Clinical Trials
by John Serio, J.D., R.Ph., Meghan Dilley, J.D., and Jerome Tichner, J.D., Brown Rudnick Berlack Israels LLP

While clinical researchers generally are cognizant of FDA regulations governing the conduct of clinical trials, they are sometimes less aware of a host of state laws and requirements that also impact clinical study activities, particularly those at investigational sites.

This section summarizes some of the more significant differences in state laws and requirements that address clinical trial conduct. This discussion is not intended to be an exhaustive analysis of state laws and requirements, but rather to provide examples of the range and scope of state regulation of clinical trial activities. The section draws upon information in the textbook entitled, *State-by-State Clinical Trial Requirements Reference Guide* (September 2004) published by Barnett Educational Services (see www.barnettinternational.com).

22.1 Q. If a clinical trial is being conducted in full compliance with FDA regulations, why should an investigator be concerned about state laws and regulations?

A. Although many clinical trial sponsors and investigators focus primarily on FDA regulations, any failure to comply with state laws and regulations can expose sponsors and investigators—and in some cases, IRBs—to significant liability risks. Tort actions brought by increasingly aggressive plaintiffs' counsels have alleged numerous arguments centered on state law issues. Negligence, informed consent, battery, wrongful death, and conflicts of interest are among the more prevalent state law theories utilized by plaintiffs' counsels to allege liability of parties conducting clinical trials. Additionally, failure to comply with specific state laws may jeopardize study data and impact FDA approval of a product under clinical investigation.

22.2 Q. How real is the risk of liability for parties, such as investigators and sponsors, involved in the conduct of clinical trails and how does state law compliance affect that risk?

A. Plaintiffs' counsels are becoming particularly creative in their attempts to file suits against organizations and individuals sponsoring and conducting clinical trials (see Section 21). Over the last few years, the increasing visibility of clinical research and subject protection issues as well as significant settlements in favor of clinical trial participants have contributed to the increase in clinical trial lawsuits. While many different theories of tort liability may be brought on behalf of clinical trial participants, it is important to understand that these causes of actions often involve both federal law and state law based claims. Compliance with state informed consent requirements (e.g., age and legal capacity of the clinical trial subject to consent) may significantly impact the ability of a plaintiff's counsel to raise theories of tort liability.

22.3 Q. What are the various causes of action of liability based upon state law?

A. State law theories of liability frequently cited by plaintiffs include battery, negligence based upon a failure to obtain informed consent, and other claims, such as wrongful death. Battery generally is defined as "an uncontested, offensive touching" and traditionally has been applied in the medical treatment context in which no consent (or improper consent) was obtained during a medical procedure, in which the procedure performed is substantially different from the procedure described to the patient, or in which a different doctor is substituted to perform the procedure without the patient's knowledge. This theory of liability also has been raised by plaintiffs seeking to establish that providing inadequate consent leads to unexpected results and aspects of medical procedures that constitute battery.

22.4 Q. What are the significant areas of state law and regulations that differ from federal regulations?

A. A number of states have adopted informed consent standards that differ from the FDA's informed consent requirements. Although many of these state standards are similar to the FDA's regulations, some distinct differences occasionally arise. For example, California clinical trial subjects are required to receive a copy of California's Experimental Subject's Bill of Rights. In addition, some states, such as Delaware, have created prohibitions against obtaining consent from individuals in mental health facilities except under certain circumstances. It is critical that sponsors and investigators understand and follow state laws when attempting to consent special populations (e.g., human subjects in state custody).

22.5 Q. In general terms, which states are the most restrictive in their state laws governing clinical trial conduct? Which are least restrictive?

A. Which states have the most restrictive and least restrictive state laws and standards will typically depend on the nature of study that the principal investigator expects to run and the target population of the study. Every state must offer at least as much protection for human subjects as the federal regulations provide, so the least restrictive states are those that follow only the minimum federal guidelines (see Q22.6).

Determining which states are the most restrictive is a much more difficult exercise. In South Dakota, for example, if the treating medical provider determines that a mental patient is unable to consent to medical treatment, the provider cannot accept the patient's consent, and experimental treatment may only be provided after a circuit court hearing in which the court finds that the patient's mental illness is so severe that he cannot consent and that the experimental treatment is in the patient's best interests. The court must hold a hearing even when the patient is a minor and the patient's parent or guardian consents to the treatment. If a clinical study were going to test the effects of a particular drug on minors with mental illnesses, South Dakota's requirements would be extremely restrictive. However, if the target population for the clinical trial did not include the mentally ill, South Dakota would be no more restrictive than any other state.

As another example, in Wisconsin, informed consent is only valid over a limited time period not to exceed 15 months. In addition, the consent must be approved by a specially appointed consent monitor. If a clinical trial must be conducted over an extended period, then, Wisconsin would present particular challenges, since a new informed consent document would need to be signed at least every 15 months.

Further, California has numerous statutes and regulations related to clinical trials.

While many of them mirror federal requirements, many others go beyond the federal requirements. In particular, sponsors should be aware that California requires proposed research projects involving certain opiates, stimulants, and hallucinogenic drugs classified as Schedule I or Schedule II controlled substances to be pre-reviewed and authorized by the Research Advisory Panel of California (of the Attorney General's Office) prior to initiation.

As is evident from the above examples, state standards tend to be more restrictive in case-specific ways. Therefore, it is extremely difficult to determine which state's policies are the most demanding without first knowing the precise nature of the clinical study to be undertaken.

22.6 Q. Do some states simply require that clinical research conduct conform to FDA regulations?

A. Yes. There are at least 24 states that do not have their own clinical trials laws and regulations and that rely entirely to FDA regulations. These states include Connecticut, Arizona, Colorado, Delaware, Georgia, Michigan, Hawaii, Iowa, Kansas, Kentucky, New Hampshire, Nevada, Nebraska, Montana, Missouri, Vermont, Texas, South Carolina, North Carolina, North Dakota, Oregon, Pennsylvania, Wyoming and Louisiana. At least six of these states have state regulations governing clinical trials involving patients in state-run hospitals, however: Delaware, Georgia, Kentucky, Montana, Missouri and Pennsylvania.

22.7 Q. One of the areas in which FDA requirements defer to state laws is in determining the age of majority—for the purposes of obtaining informed consent, for example. How do states differ in their laws regarding the age of assent and consent? Are there regional differences?

A. Forty-eight states set the age of medical consent at 18. Texas has established the age for medical consent at 16, while Nebraska requires a person to be 19 for medical consent.

Most, if not all, states will also allow emancipated minors to consent to medical care on their own behalf regardless of age. Requirements for becoming an emancipated minor vary from state to state, however.

Further, several states allow individuals who are under the age of 18 but who are married to consent to their own medical care. In some states, these married minors may qualify as emancipated minors, thereby increasing the number of states allowing married minors to consent to medical treatment.

Few states have specified ages of assent—the age at which a child can provide an affirmative agreement to participate in research (see Q5.33). In Mississippi-based psychiatric hospitals, any patient over the age of 12 must give his/her assent before participating in clinical trials. Similarly, in Maine, any potential human subject between the ages of 12 and 18 must consent to participate in the clinical trial unless he or she is unable to do so. (Note: in both Mississippi and Maine, the parent or legal guardian must also give consent.)

22.8 Q. Which states require additional consent forms or addenda, such as a Patient's Bill of Rights?

A. Many states require that a so-called Patient's Bill of Rights be posted in a public place in any medical care facility. California requires that a patient's bill of rights be provided to human subjects involved in any clinical trial conducted in the state.

Few other states require that a Patient's Bill or Rights or other documents accompany the informed consent form. It is important to note, however, that some states require that informed consent documents contain additional information regarding the rights of the patients participating in clinical trials. Virginia, for example, requires that the informed consent document state that there may still be unidentified risks associated with participation in the clinical trial. North Dakota and Pennsylvania follow the federal regulations governing clinical trials, and require that a copy of the applicable regulations be available to potential human subjects while they are considering whether to consent to participation.

22.9 Q. Can physicians, nurses, and pharmacists lose their state licenses to practice for violating GCP standards and guidelines? If so, under what circumstances?

A. Depending on the state licensing laws and medical malpractice standards, it is possible for physicians, nurses, and pharmacists to lose their licenses or face other penalties for failing to comply with good clinical practice standards when such a failure is considered to be below an acceptable professional standard. It is important to note that state licensing authorities have no particular regulations regarding GCP standards. However, a GCP standard may parallel a professional standard of a state licensing board.

22.10 Q. Do any state laws affect the operation of IRBs?

A. Some states have specific regulations on how IRBs should operate. New York, for example, requires that each IRB adopt governing policies, including the state policy on the rights of human subjects; the IRB policy must be approved by the Commissioner of the New York State Health Department before research can begin under that IRB's authority. Massachusetts requires that IRBs comprise no fewer than five individuals from varying backgrounds, and that they document the committee members' backgrounds.

Other states require that IRBs evaluate specific issues prior to approving clinical trials. For example, Florida requires, among other things, that IRBs specifically determine: that the subject population is appropriate in terms of characteristics and size; that subjects are recruited without coercion; that the potential benefits of the research are maximized; and that the form of consent is ethically sound.

Some states require IRBs that review state-sponsored or funded research to follow special procedures. Montana requires that if the clinical trial will enroll patients at state-run mental health institutions, the trial must receive enhanced board review. Similarly, Arizona requires that any clinical research in which the Department of Health Services collaborated or that the department conducted, funded, or sponsored must be reviewed by an IRB established specifically for that purpose; in such cases, the IRB requires a more detailed description of the clinical trial than is mandated by federal law.

In contrast, Oklahoma requires that all clinical studies not specifically exempted from state IRB approval under federal law be approved both by an IRB affiliated with a specific institution and by a special IRB established by the State Department of Health. Massachusetts has a similar, but less demanding, policy—it requires that any IRB approving research have an affiliation with the state, the Department of Public Health, or the Department of Mental Health, but does not require principal investigators to seek approval from two separate IRBs.

Some states also impose additional requirements on the composition of the IRB or the internal operations of the IRB. In Ohio, for example, a number of minority members must sit on the IRB so that the ratio of minorities to non-minorities is proportionate to the corresponding ratio in the targeted service population. Maryland requires that all IRBs have their minutes available for inspection (properly redacted) within 30 days of each IRB meeting.

22.11 Q. Do some states have laws or regulations that, in effect, encourage research on certain types of therapeutic classes or indications for drugs or devices?

A. Many states have legislation that requires insurance companies to offer health insurance that provides coverage for patients entering clinical trials for cancer therapies. Some of these states also require insurance coverage for other clinical trials targeted at life-threatening diseases. Most of these states require that the clinical trials be reviewed and approved by the NIH, a National Cancer Institute-affiliated group (NCE cooperative groups), the FDA, or the Federal Department of Defense or Veterans Affairs before insurance coverage can be mandated. They also typically require that the study be in Phase 2, Phase 3, or Phase 4.

In terms of insurance coverage, most states fall into one of several possible categories. California has special rules concerning the development of AIDS vaccines and the testing of AIDS-related drugs. The state also has regulations that encourage research involving cancer therapeutics. Specifically, California's "Cancer Act" allows cancer-related clinical trials to proceed based upon a notification provided to, and reviewed by, the California Department of Health Services. The Cancer Act is unusual in that it allows clinical studies to be conducted within California outside of the traditional FDA IND requirements.

In Connecticut and Nevada, insurance companies must provide coverage for routine patient care costs associated with cancer clinical trials; insurance is not, however, required to cover costs that could be reimbursed from other sources. Delaware and North Carolina require insurance coverage for general patient care costs associated with clinical trials designed to treat any previously diagnosed life-threatening disease. New Hampshire requires insurance coverage of medically necessary routine patient care costs associated with a clinical trial for treating cancer or another life-threatening disease. Missouri requires that insurance companies cover routine patient care costs only for Phase 3 and Phase 4 clinical trials for cancer treatments.

Georgia and Washington, among other states, allow the use of marijuana for certain types of clinical trials related to the substance's ability to ease nausea and vomiting in chemotherapy patients.

Some states maintain special cancer patient-associated records that could be useful in the context of a clinical trial. For example, Oregon maintains a list of patients diagnosed with cancer in a registry, which principal investigators may access after receiving approval from the Oregon Department of Human Services. Access to such a registry may allow the principal investigator to select a specific geographic location for the study (i.e., in which there exists a substantial population of cancer patients).

22.12 Q. How do most states address the issue of the provision of, and discussions about, birth control for minors participating in a clinical study? Consider protocols that require that a subject not be pregnant at the time of enrollment and that require that a subject not become pregnant during these studies.

A. There are no special state rules governing the provision of birth control to minors as part of a clinical trial. This type of situation would be governed by relevant state laws on birth control, age of consent and parental notification. However, other state regulations may apply in situations in which minors are receiving birth control as part of a clinical trial. California, for example, allows that if the patient is a minor (under the age of 18), a treating medical professional may, with or without the patient's consent, notify the minor's parent or guardian of the treatment given. This regulation would allow a medical professional administering a clinical trial to reveal to a minor human subject's parents that birth control was distributed as part of the clinical trial.

22.13 Q. Are there state laws that govern either the compassionate use or emergency use of investigational drugs for clinical study purposes?

A. In most states, if a patient is incompetent during an emergency, Federal regulations on the use of legal representatives would apply, and the legal representative could consent on the patient's behalf. Very few states have specific rules for obtaining informed consent in emergency situations. California has special rules on who may give informed consent for a prospective study patient in a medical emergency in which the patient cannot provide consent. These requirements are less strict than those imposed in a non-emergency situation. California also has policies allowing the emergency use of an investigational drug without informed consent if no legal representative is available to consent, the patient's life is in danger, and the investigational treatment is the best available treatment method.

States have no particular statutes or regulations governing the compassionate use of investigational drugs.

22.14 Q. Do states have criminal penalties that can be assessed related to the conduct of clinical studies? If so, which members of the research team might be impacted?

A. Most states do not have specific criminal penalties linked to clinical trials; however, state criminal laws and medical malpractice laws will apply to clinical trial staff as they do to other medical professionals and care providers.

California is a state that has detailed criminal penalties for any person who is responsible for a clinical experiment and who fails to obtain informed consent, including employees of a pharmaceutical company who contract with someone else to perform the clinical trial. In contrast, a few states explicitly limit criminal liability for doctors and other professionals working in clinical trials in particular circumstances. Colorado, for example, will not hold physicians, health care providers, or health care facilities liable for the lack of informed consent if they make reasonable efforts to contact a legal representative to consent on behalf of any patient who is unable to consent on his or her own behalf. Nevada also has such liability limitations for insurers. An insurer that covers expenses associated with a clinical trial is also immune from liability for any injury caused by the medical treatment received in a clinical trial, an act or omission by the medical provider in a clinical trial, or any adverse result stemming from involvement in the clinical trial.

22.15 *Q. Do state-legislated medical malpractice award ceilings have an impact on clinical trials litigation? How do these ceilings vary from state to state?*

A. To the extent that clinical trial staff are subject to medical malpractice regulations in general, state legislation on medical malpractice awards will impact litigation involving clinical trials. Medical malpractice award ceilings are currently in a state of flux. In 2003, 34 state legislatures considered measures aimed at limiting medical malpractice liability. Of these states, 11 of them, including Arkansas, Florida, Idaho, Nevada, New Hampshire, New York, Texas, Utah, West Virginia, Montana, and Ohio, enacted legislation capping medical malpractice awards or heightening the legal burdens in medical malpractice cases. Ultimately, these limits may have little effect on where clinical trials are held because injured study subjects are able to commence actions against trial sponsors in multiple forums based upon procedural rights available to the plaintiff's bar.

About the Authors

John C. Serio, senior counsel with Brown Rudnick Berlack Israels LLP, is a registered patent attorney concentrating his practice in the area of intellectual property concerning biotechnology, pharmaceuticals, medical devices and analytical scientific equipment. With expertise in food and drug law involving pharmaceuticals and medical devices, Mr. Serio also assists clients in preparing and filing regulatory documents, compliance with FDA regulations and regulatory matters arising from the conduct of clinical trials. He earned his J.D. degree from the Western New England School of Law and his pharmacy degree from the University of Rhode Island.

Meghan E. Dilley, an associate with Brown Rudnick Berlack Israels LLP, focuses her practice in corporate law. She earned her J.D. degree from the Georgetown University Law Center.

Jerome B. Tichner, Jr., an associate with Brown Rudnick Berlack Israels LLP, focuses his practice in the areas of corporate health care transactions and regulatory compliance. He earned a J.D. degree from the Boston University School of Law.

Appendices

PART 11 — ELECTRONIC RECORDS; ELECTRONIC SIGNATURES

Subpart A — General Provisions

Subpart B — Electronic Records

Subpart C — Electronic Signatures

AUTHORITY: 21 U.S.C. 321–393; 42 U.S.C. 262.

SOURCE: 62 FR 13464, Mar. 20, 1997, unless otherwise noted.

Subpart A — General Provisions

§ 11.1 Scope.

(a) The regulations in this part set forth the criteria under which the agency considers electronic records, electronic signatures, and handwritten signatures executed to electronic records to be trustworthy, reliable, and generally equivalent to paper records and handwritten signatures executed on paper.

(b) This part applies to records in electronic form that are created, modified, maintained, archived, retrieved, or transmitted, under any records requirements set forth in agency regulations. This part also applies to electronic records submitted to the agency under requirements of the Federal Food, Drug, and Cosmetic Act and the Public Health Service Act, even if such records are not specifically identified in agency regulations. However, this part does not apply to paper records that are, or have been, transmitted by electronic means.

(c) Where electronic signatures and their associated electronic records meet the requirements of this part, the agency will consider the electronic signatures to be equivalent to full handwritten signatures, initials, and other general signings as required by agency regulations, unless specifically excepted by regulation(s) effective on or after August 20, 1997.

(d) Electronic records that meet the requirements of this part may be used in lieu of paper records, in accordance with § 11.2, unless paper records are specifically required.

(e) Computer systems (including hardware and software), controls, and attendant documentation maintained under this part shall be readily available for, and subject to, FDA inspection.

(f) This part does not apply to records required to be established or maintained by §§ 1.326 through 1.368 of this chapter. Records that satisfy the requirements of part 1, subpart J of this chapter, but that also are required under other applicable statutory provisions or regulations, remain subject to this part.

[as amended at 69 FR 71655, Dec. 9, 2005]

§ 11.2 Implementation.

(a) For records required to be maintained but not submitted to the agency, persons may use electronic records in lieu of paper records or electronic signatures in lieu of traditional signatures, in whole or in part, provided that the requirements of this part are met.

(b) For records submitted to the agency, persons may use electronic records in lieu of paper records or electronic signatures in lieu of traditional signatures, in whole or in part, provided that:

(1) The requirements of this part are met; and

(2) The document or parts of a document to be submitted have been identified in public docket No. 92S–0251 as being the type of submission the agency accepts in electronic form. This docket will identify specifically what types of documents or parts of documents are acceptable for submission in electronic form without paper records and the agency receiving unit(s) (e.g., specific center, office, division, branch) to which such submissions may be made. Documents to agency receiving unit(s) not specified in the public docket will not be considered as official if they are submitted in electronic form; paper forms of such documents will be considered as official and must accompany any electronic records. Persons are expected to consult with the intended agency receiving unit for details on how (e.g., method of transmission, media, file formats, and technical protocols) and whether to proceed with the electronic submission.

§ 11.3 Definitions.

(a) The definitions and interpretations of terms contained in section 201 of the act apply to those terms when used in this part.

(b) The following definitions of terms also apply to this part:

(1) *Act* means the Federal Food, Drug, and Cosmetic Act (secs. 201–903 (21 U.S.C. 321–393)).

(2) *Agency* means the Food and Drug Administration.

(3) *Biometrics* means a method of verifying an individual's identity based on measurement of the individual's physical feature(s) or repeatable action(s) where those features and/or actions are both unique to that individual and measurable.

(4) *Closed system* means an environment in which system access is controlled by persons who are responsible for the content of electronic records that are on the system.

(5) *Digital signature* means an electronic signature based upon cryptographic methods of originator authentication, computed by using a set of rules and a set of parameters such that the identity of the signer and the integrity of the data can be verified.

(6) *Electronic record* means any combination of text, graphics, data, audio, pictorial, or other information representation in digital form that is created, modified, maintained, archived, retrieved, or distributed by a computer system.

(7) *Electronic signature* means a computer data compilation of any symbol or series of symbols executed, adopted, or authorized by an individual to be the legally binding equivalent of the individual's handwritten signature.

(8) *Handwritten signature* means the scripted name or legal mark of an individual handwritten by that individual and executed or adopted with the present intention to authenticate a writing in a permanent form. The act of signing with a writing or marking instrument such as a pen or stylus is preserved. The scripted name or legal mark, while conventionally applied to paper, may also be applied to other devices that capture the name or mark.

(9) *Open system* means an environment in which system access is not controlled by persons who are responsible for the content of electronic records that are on the system.

Subpart B — Electronic Records

§ 11.10 Controls for closed systems.

Persons who use closed systems to create, modify, maintain, or transmit electronic records shall employ procedures and controls designed to ensure the authenticity, integrity, and, when appropriate, the confidentiality of electronic records, and to ensure that the signer cannot readily repudiate the signed record as not genuine. Such procedures and controls shall include the following:

(a) Validation of systems to ensure accuracy, reliability, consistent intended performance, and the ability to discern invalid or altered records.

(b) The ability to generate accurate and complete copies of records in both human readable and electronic form suitable for inspection, review, and copying by the agency. Persons should contact the agency if there are any questions regarding the ability of the agency to perform such review and copying of the electronic records.

(c) Protection of records to enable their accurate and ready retrieval throughout the records retention period.

(d) Limiting system access to authorized individuals.

(e) Use of secure, computer-generated, time-stamped audit trails to independently record the date and time of operator entries and actions that create, modify, or delete electronic records. Record changes shall not obscure previously recorded information. Such audit trail documentation shall be retained for a period at least as long as that required for the subject electronic records and shall be available for agency review and copying.

(f) Use of operational system checks to enforce permitted sequencing of steps and events, as appropriate.

(g) Use of authority checks to ensure that only authorized individuals can use the system, electronically sign a record, access the operation or computer system input or output device, alter a record, or perform the operation at hand.

(h) Use of device (e.g., terminal) checks to determine, as appropriate, the validity of the source of data input or operational instruction.

(i) Determination that persons who develop, maintain, or use electronic record/electronic signature systems have the education, training, and experience to perform their assigned tasks.

(j) The establishment of, and adherence to, written policies that hold individuals accountable and responsible for actions initiated under their electronic signatures, in order to deter record and signature falsification.

(k) Use of appropriate controls over systems documentation including:

(1) Adequate controls over the distribution of, access to, and use of documentation for system operation and maintenance.

(2) Revision and change control procedures to maintain an audit trail that documents time-sequenced development and modification of systems documentation.

§ 11.30 Controls for open systems.

Persons who use open systems to create, modify, maintain, or transmit electronic records shall employ procedures and controls designed to ensure the authenticity, integrity, and, as appropriate, the confidentiality of electronic records from the point of their creation to the point of their receipt. Such procedures and controls shall include those identified in § 11.10, as appropriate, and additional measures such as document encryption and use of appropriate digital signature standards to ensure, as necessary under the circumstances, record authenticity, integrity, and confidentiality.

§ 11.50 Signature manifestations.

(a) Signed electronic records shall contain information associated with the signing that clearly indicates all of the following:

(1) The printed name of the signer;

(2) The date and time when the signature was executed; and

(3) The meaning (such as review, approval, responsibility, or authorship) associated with the signature.

(b) The items identified in paragraphs (a)(1), (a)(2), and (a)(3) of this section shall be subject to the same controls as for electronic records and shall be included as part of any human readable form of the electronic record (such as electronic display or printout).

§ 11.70 Signature/record linking.

Electronic signatures and handwritten signatures executed to electronic records shall be linked to their respective electronic records to ensure that the signatures cannot be excised, copied, or otherwise transferred to falsify an electronic record by ordinary means.

Subpart C — Electronic Signatures

§ 11.100 General requirements.

(a) Each electronic signature shall be unique to one individual and shall not be reused by, or reassigned to, anyone else.

(b) Before an organization establishes, assigns, certifies, or otherwise sanctions an individual's electronic signature, or any element of such electronic signature, the organization shall verify the identity of the individual.

(c) Persons using electronic signatures shall, prior to or at the time of such use, certify to the agency that the electronic signatures in their system, used on or after August 20, 1997, are intended to be the legally binding equivalent of traditional handwritten signatures.

(1) The certification shall be submitted in paper form and signed with a traditional handwritten signature, to the Office of Regional Operations (HFC–100), 5600 Fishers Lane, Rockville, MD 20857.

(2) Persons using electronic signatures shall, upon agency request, provide additional certification or testimony that a specific electronic signature is the legally binding equivalent of the signer's handwritten signature.

§ 11.200 Electronic signature components and controls.

(a) Electronic signatures that are not based upon biometrics shall:

(1) Employ at least two distinct identification components such as an identification code and password.

(i) When an individual executes a series of signings during a single, continuous period of controlled system access, the first signing shall be executed using all electronic signature components; subsequent signings shall be executed using at least one electronic signature component that is only executable by, and designed to be used only by, the individual.

(ii) When an individual executes one or more signings not performed during a single, continuous period of controlled system access, each signing shall be executed using all of the electronic signature components.

(2) Be used only by their genuine owners; and

(3) Be administered and executed to ensure that attempted use of an individual's electronic signature by anyone other than its genuine owner requires collaboration of two or more individuals.

(b) Electronic signatures based upon biometrics shall be designed to ensure that they cannot be used by anyone other than their genuine owners.

§ 11.300 Controls for identification codes/passwords.

Persons who use electronic signatures based upon use of identification codes in combination with passwords shall employ controls to ensure their security and integrity. Such controls shall include:

(a) Maintaining the uniqueness of each combined identification code and password, such that no two individuals have the same combination of identification code and password.

(b) Ensuring that identification code and password issuances are periodically checked, recalled, or revised (e.g., to cover such events as password aging).

(c) Following loss management procedures to electronically deauthorize lost, stolen, missing, or otherwise potentially compromised tokens, cards, and other devices that bear or generate identification code or password information, and to issue temporary or permanent replacements using suitable, rigorous controls.

(d) Use of transaction safeguards to prevent unauthorized use of passwords and/or identification codes, and to detect and report in an immediate and urgent manner any attempts at their unauthorized use to the system security unit, and, as appropriate, to organizational management.

(e) Initial and periodic testing of devices, such as tokens or cards, that bear or generate identification code or password information to ensure that they function properly and have not been altered in an unauthorized manner.

PART 50 — PROTECTION OF HUMAN SUBJECTS

Subpart A — General Provisions

Subpart B — Informed Consent of Human Subjects

Subpart C [Reserved]

Subpart D — Additional Safeguards for Children in Clinical Investigations

AUTHORITY: 21 U.S.C. 321, 343, 346, 346a, 348, 350a, 350b, 352, 353, 355, 360, 360c-360f, 360h-360j, 371, 379e, 381; 42 U.S.C. 216, 241, 262, 263b-263n.

SOURCE: 45 FR 36390, May 30, 1980, unless otherwise noted.

Subpart A — General Provisions

§ 50.1 Scope.

(a) This part applies to all clinical investigations regulated by the Food and Drug Administration under sections 505(I), and 520(g) of the Federal Food and Drug Administration under sections 505(i), and 520(g) of the Federal Food, Drug, and Cosmetic Act, as well as clinical investigations that support applications for research or marketing permits for products regulated by the Food and Drug Administration, including foods, including dietary supplements, that bear a nutrient content claim or a health claim, infant formulas, food and color additives, drugs for human use, and electronic products. Additional specific obligations and commitments of, and standards of conduct for, persons who sponsor or monitor clinical investigations involving particular test articles may also be found in other parts (e.g., parts 312 and 812). Compliance with these parts is intended to protect the rights and safety of subjects involved in investigations filed with the Food and Drug Administration pursuant to sections 403, 406, 409, 412, 413, 502, 503, 505, 510, 513-516, 518-520, 721, and 801 of the Federal Food, Drug, and Cosmetic Act and sections 351 and 354-360F of the Public Health Service Act.

(b) References in this part to regulatory sections of the Code of Federal Regulations are to chapter I of title 21, unless otherwise noted.

[45 FR 36390, May 30, 1980; 46 FR 8979, Jan. 27, 1981, as amended at 63 FR 26697, May 13, 1998; 64 FR 399, Jan. 5, 1999; 66 FR 20597, Apr. 24, 2001]

§ 50.3 Definitions.

As used in this part:

(a) *Act* means the Federal Food, Drug, and Cosmetic Act, as amended (secs. 201-902, 52 Stat. 1040 *et seq.* as amended (21 U.S.C. 321-392)).

(b) *Application for research or marketing permit* includes:

(1) A color additive petition, described in part 71.

(2) A food additive petition, described in parts 171 and 571.

(3) Data and information about a substance submitted as part of the procedures for establishing that the substance is generally recognized as safe for use that results or may reasonably be expected to result, directly or indirectly, in its becoming a component or otherwise affecting the characteristics of any food, described in §§ 170.30 and 570.30.

(4) Data and information about a food additive submitted as part of the procedures for food additives permitted to be used on an interim basis pending additional study, described in § 180.1.

(5) Data and information about a substance submitted as part of the procedures for establishing a tolerance for unavoidable contaminants in food and food-packaging materials, described in section 406 of the act.

(6) An investigational new drug application, described in part 312 of this chapter.

(7) A new drug application, described in part 314.

(8) Data and information about the bioavailability or bioequivalence of drugs for human use submitted as part of the procedures for issuing, amending, or repealing a bioequivalence requirement, described in part 320.

(9) Data and information about an over-the-counter drug for human use submitted as part of the procedures for classifying these drugs as generally recognized as safe and effective and not misbranded, described in part 330.

(10) Data and information about a prescription drug for human use submitted as part of the procedures for classifying these drugs as generally recognized as safe and effective and not misbranded, described in this chapter.

(11) [Reserved]

(12) An application for a biologics license, described in part 601 of this chapter.

(13) Data and information about a biological product submitted as part of the procedures for determining that licensed biological products are safe and effective and not misbranded, described in part 601.

(14) Data and information about an in vitro diagnostic product submitted as part of the procedures for establishing, amending, or repealing a standard for these products, described in part 809.

(15) An *Application for an Investigational Device Exemption,* described in part 812.

(16) Data and information about a medical device submitted as part of the procedures for classifying these devices, described in section 513.

(17) Data and information about a medical device submitted as part of the procedures for establishing, amending, or repealing a standard for these devices, described in section 514.

(18) An application for premarket approval of a medical device, described in section 515.

(19) A product development protocol for a medical device, described in section 515.

(20) Data and information about an electronic product submitted as part of the procedures for establishing, amending, or repealing a standard for these products, described in section 358 of the Public Health Service Act.

(21) Data and information about an electronic product submitted as part of the procedures for obtaining a variance from any electronic product performance standard, as described in § 1010.4.

(22) Data and information about an electronic product submitted as part of the procedures for granting, amending, or extending an exemption from a radiation safety performance standard, as described in § 1010.5.

(23) Data and information about a clinical study of an infant formula when submitted as part of an infant formula notification under section 412(c) of the Federal Food, Drug, and Cosmetic Act.

(24) Data and information submitted in a petition for a nutrient content claim, described in § 101.69 of this chapter, or for a health claim, described in § 101.70 of this chapter.

(25) Data and information from investigations involving children submitted in a new dietary ingredient notification, described in § 190.6 of this chapter.

(c) *Clinical investigation* means any experiment that involves a test article and one or more human subjects and that either is subject to requirements for prior submission to the Food and Drug Administration under section 505(i), or 520(g) of the act, or is not subject to requirements for prior submission to the Food and Drug Administration under these sections of the act, but the results of which are intended to be submitted later to, or held for inspection by, the Food and Drug Administration as part of an application for a research or marketing permit. The term does not include experiments that are subject to the provisions of part 58 of this chapter, regarding nonclinical laboratory studies.

(d) *Investigator* means an individual who actually conducts a clinical investigation, i.e., under whose immediate direction the test article is administered or dispensed to, or used involving, a subject, or, in the event of an investigation conducted by a team of individuals, is the responsible leader of that team.

(e) *Sponsor* means a person who initiates a clinical investigation, but who does not actually conduct the investigation, i.e., the test article is administered or dispensed to or used involving, a subject under the immediate direction of another individual. A person other than an individual (e.g., corporation or agency) that uses one or more of its own employees to conduct a clinical investigation it has initiated is considered to be a sponsor (not a sponsor-investigator), and the employees are considered to be investigators.

(f) *Sponsor-investigator* means an individual who both initiates and actually conducts, alone or with others, a clinical investigation, i.e., under whose immediate direction the test article is administered or dispensed to, or used involving, a subject. The term does not include any person other than an individual, e.g., corporation or agency.

(g) *Human subject* means an individual who is or becomes a participant in research, either as a recipient of the test article or as a control. A subject may be either a healthy human or a patient.

(h) *Institution* means any public or private entity or agency (including Federal, State, and other agencies). The word *facility* as used in section 520(g) of the act is deemed to be synonymous with the term *institution* for purposes of this part.

(i) *Institutional review board* (IRB) means any board, committee, or other group formally designated by an institution to review biomedical research involving humans as subjects, to approve the initiation of and conduct periodic review of such research. The term has the same meaning as the phrase *institutional review committee* as used in section 520(g) of the act.

(j) *Test article* means any drug (including a biological product for human use), medical device for human use, human food additive, color additive, electronic product, or any other article subject to regulation under the act or under sections 351 and 354-360F of the Public Health Service Act (42 U.S.C. 262 and 263b-263n).

(k) *Minimal risk* means that the probability and magnitude of harm or discomfort anticipated in the research are not greater in and of themselves than those ordinarily encountered in daily life or during the performance of routine physical or psychological examinations or tests.

(l) *Legally authorized representative* means an individual or judicial or other body authorized under applicable law to consent on behalf of a prospective subject to the subject's participation in the procedure(s) involved in the research.

(m) *Family member* means any one of the following legally competent persons: Spouse; parents; children (including adopted children); brothers, sisters, and spouses of brothers and sisters; and any individual related by blood or affinity whose close association with the subject is the equivalent of a family relationship.

(n) *Assent* means a child's affirmative agreement to participate in a clinical investigation. Mere failure to object may not, absent affirmative agreement, be construed as assent.

(o) *Children* means persons who have not attained the legal age for consent to treatments or procedures involved in clinical investigations, under the applicable law of the jurisdiction in which the clinical investigation will be conducted.

(p) *Parent* means a child's biological or adoptive parent.

(q) *Ward* means a child who is placed in the legal custody of the State or other agency, institution, or entity, consistent with applicable Federal, State, or local law.

(r) *Permission* means the agreement of parent(s) or guardian to the participation of their child or ward in a clinical investigation. Permission must be obtained in compliance with subpart B of this part and must include the elements of informed consent described in § 50.25.

(s) *Guardian* means an individual who is authorized under applicable State or local law to consent on behalf of a child to general medical care when general medical care includes participation in research. For purposes of subpart D of this part, a guardian also means an individual who is authorized to consent on behalf of a child to participate in research.

[45 FR 36390, May 30, 1980, as amended at 46 FR 8950, Jan. 27, 1981; 54 FR 9038, Mar. 3, 1989; 56 FR 28028, June 18, 1991; 61 FR 51528, Oct. 2, 1996; 62 FR 39440, July 23, 1997; 64 FR 399, Jan. 5, 1999; 64 FR 56448, Oct. 20, 1999; 66 FR 20597, Apr. 24, 2001]

Subpart B — Informed Consent of Human Subjects

SOURCE: 46 FR 8951, Jan. 27, 1981, unless otherwise noted.

§ 50.20 General requirements for informed consent.

Except as provided in §§ 50.23 and 50.24, no investigator may involve a human being as a subject in research covered by these regulations unless the investigator has obtained the legally effective informed consent of the subject or the subject's legally authorized representative. An investigator shall seek such consent only under circumstances that provide the prospective subject or the representative sufficient opportunity to consider whether or not to participate and that minimize the possibility of coercion or undue influence. The information that is given to the subject or the representative shall be in language understandable to the subject or the representative. No informed consent, whether oral or written, may include any exculpatory language through which the subject or the representative is made to waive or appear to waive any of the subject's legal rights, or releases or appears to release the investigator, the sponsor, the institution, or its agents from liability for negligence.

[46 FR 8951, Jan. 27, 1981, as amended at 64 FR 10942, Mar. 8, 1999]

§ 50.23 Exception from general requirements.

(a) The obtaining of informed consent shall be deemed feasible unless, before use of the test article (except as provided in paragraph (b) of this section), both the investigator and a physician who is not otherwise participating in the clinical investigation certify in writing all of the following:

(1) The human subject is confronted by a life-threatening situation necessitating the use of the test article.

(2) Informed consent cannot be obtained from the subject because of an inability to communicate with, or obtain legally effective consent from, the subject.

(3) Time is not sufficient to obtain consent from the subject's legal representative.

(4) There is available no alternative method of approved or generally recognized therapy that provides an equal or greater likelihood of saving the life of the subject.

(b) If immediate use of the test article is, in the investigator's opinion, required to preserve the life of the subject, and time is not sufficient to obtain the independent determination required in paragraph (a) of this section in advance of using the test article, the determinations of the clinical investigator shall be made and, within 5 working days after the use of the article, be reviewed and evaluated in writing by a physician who is not participating in the clinical investigation.

(c) The documentation required in paragraph (a) or (b) of this section shall be submitted to the IRB within 5 working days after the use of the test article.

(d)(1) Under 10 U.S.C. 1107(f) the President may waive the prior consent requirement for the administration of an investigational new drug to a member of the armed forces in connection with the member's participation in a particular military operation. The statute specifies that only the President may waive informed consent in this connection and the President may grant such a waiver only if the President determines in writing that obtaining consent: Is not feasible; is contrary to the best interests of the military member; or is not in the interests of national security. The statute further provides that in making a determination to waive prior informed consent on the ground that it is not feasible or the ground that it is contrary to the best interests of the military members involved, the President shall apply the standards and criteria that are set forth in the relevant FDA regulations for a waiver of the prior informed consent requirements of section 505(i)(4) of the Federal Food, Drug, and Cosmetic Act (21 U.S.C. 355(i)(4)). Before such a determination may be made that obtaining informed consent from military personnel prior to the use of an investigational drug (including an antibiotic or biological product) in a specific protocol under an investigational new drug application (IND) sponsored by the Department of Defense (DOD) and limited to specific military personnel involved in a particular military operation is not feasible or is contrary to the best interests of the military members involved the Secretary of Defense must first request such a determination from the President, and certify and document to the President that the following standards and criteria contained in paragraphs (d)(1) through (d)(4) of this section have been met.

(i) The extent and strength of evidence of the safety and effectiveness of the investigational new drug in relation to the medical risk that could be encountered during the military operation supports the drug's administration under an IND.

(ii) The military operation presents a substantial risk that military personnel may be subject to a chemical, biological, nuclear, or other exposure likely to produce death or serious or life-threatening injury or illness.

(iii) There is no available satisfactory alternative therapeutic or preventive treatment in relation to the intended use of the investigational new drug.

(iv) Conditioning use of the investigational new drug on the voluntary participation of each member could significantly risk the safety and health of any individual member who would decline its use, the safety of other military personnel, and the accomplishment of the military mission.

(v) A duly constituted institutional review board (IRB) established and operated in accordance with the requirements of paragraphs (d)(2) and (d)(3) of this section, responsible for review of the study, has reviewed and approved the investigational new drug protocol and the administration of the investigational new drug without informed consent. DOD's request is to include the documentation required by Sec. 56.115(a)(2) of this chapter.

(vi) DOD has explained:

(A) The context in which the investigational drug will be administered, e.g., the setting or whether it will be self-administered or it will be administered by a health professional;

(B) The nature of the disease or condition for which the preventive or therapeutic treatment is intended; and

(C) To the extent there are existing data or information available, information on conditions that could alter the effects of the investigational drug.

(vii) DOD's recordkeeping system is capable of tracking and will be used to track the proposed treatment from supplier to the individual recipient.

(viii) Each member involved in the military operation will be given, prior to the administration of the investigational new drug, a specific written information sheet (including information required by 10 U.S.C. 1107(d)) concerning the investigational new drug, the risks and benefits of its use, potential side effects, and other pertinent information about the appropriate use of the product.

(ix) Medical records of members involved in the military operation will accurately document the receipt by members of the notification required by paragraph (d)(1)(viii) of this section.

(x) Medical records of members involved in the military operation will accurately document the receipt by members of any investigational new drugs in accordance with FDA regulations including part 312 of this chapter.

(xi) DOD will provide adequate followup to assess whether there are beneficial or adverse health consequences that result from the use of the investigational product.

(xii) DOD is pursuing drug development, including a time line, and marketing approval with due diligence.

(xiii) FDA has concluded that the investigational new drug protocol may proceed subject to a decision by the President on the informed consent waiver request.

(xiv) DOD will provide training to the appropriate medical personnel and potential recipients on the specific investigational new drug to be administered prior to its use.

(xv) DOD has stated and justified the time period for which the waiver is needed, not to exceed one year, unless separately renewed under these standards and criteria.

(xvi) DOD shall have a continuing obligation to report to the FDA and to the President any changed circumstances relating to these standards and criteria (including the time period referred to in paragraph (d)(1)(xv) of this section) or that otherwise might affect the determination to use an investigational new drug without informed consent.

(xvii) DOD is to provide public notice as soon as practicable and consistent with classification requirements through notice in the FEDERAL REGISTER describing each waiver of informed consent determination, a summary of the most updated scientific information on the products used, and other pertinent information.

(xviii) Use of the investigational drug without informed consent otherwise conforms with applicable law.

(2) The duly constituted institutional review board, described in paragraph (d)(1)(v) of this section, must include at least 3 nonaffiliated members who shall not be employees or officers of the Federal Government (other than for purposes of membership on the IRB) and shall be required to obtain any necessary security clearances. This IRB shall review the proposed IND protocol at a convened meeting at which a majority of the members are present including at least one member whose primary concerns are in nonscientific areas and, if feasible, including a majority of the nonaffiliated members. The information required by Sec. 56.115(a)(2) of this chapter is to be provided to the Secretary of Defense for further review.

(3) The duly constituted institutional review board, described in paragraph (d)(1)(v) of this section, must review and approve:

(i) The required information sheet;

(ii) The adequacy of the plan to disseminate information, including distribution of the information sheet to potential recipients, on the investigational product (e.g., in forms other than written);

(iii) The adequacy of the information and plans for its dissemination to health care providers, including potential side effects, contraindications, potential interactions, and other pertinent considerations; and

(iv) An informed consent form as required by part 50 of this chapter, in those circumstances in which DOD determines that informed consent may be obtained from some or all personnel involved.

(4) DOD is to submit to FDA summaries of institutional review board meetings at which the proposed protocol has been reviewed.

(5) Nothing in these criteria or standards is intended to preempt or limit FDA's and DOD's authority or obligations under applicable statutes and regulations.

[46 FR 8951, Jan. 27, 1981, as amended at 55 FR 52817, Dec. 21, 1990; 64 FR 399, Jan. 5, 1999; 64 FR 54188, Oct. 5, 1999]

§ 50.24 Exception from informed consent requirements for emergency research.

(a) The IRB responsible for the review, approval, and continuing review of the clinical investigation described in this section may approve that investigation without requiring that informed consent of all research subjects be obtained if the IRB (with the concurrence of a licensed physician who is a member of or consultant to the IRB and who is not otherwise participating in the clinical investigation) finds and documents each of the following:

(1) The human subjects are in a life-threatening situation, available treatments are unproven or unsatisfactory, and the collection of valid scientific evidence, which may include evidence

obtained through randomized placebo-controlled investigations, is necessary to determine the safety and effectiveness of particular interventions.

(2) Obtaining informed consent is not feasible because:

(i) The subjects will not be able to give their informed consent as a result of their medical condition;

(ii) The intervention under investigation must be administered before consent from the subjects' legally authorized representatives is feasible; and

(iii) There is no reasonable way to identify prospectively the individuals likely to become eligible for participation in the clinical investigation.

(3) Participation in the research holds out the prospect of direct benefit to the subjects because:

(i) Subjects are facing a life-threatening situation that necessitates intervention;

(ii) Appropriate animal and other preclinical studies have been conducted, and the information derived from those studies and related evidence support the potential for the intervention to provide a direct benefit to the individual subjects; and

(iii) Risks associated with the investigation are reasonable in relation to what is known about the medical condition of the potential class of subjects, the risks and benefits of standard therapy, if any, and what is known about the risks and benefits of the proposed intervention or activity.

(4) The clinical investigation could not practicably be carried out without the waiver.

(5) The proposed investigational plan defines the length of the potential therapeutic window based on scientific evidence, and the investigator has committed to attempting to contact a legally authorized representative for each subject within that window of time and, if feasible, to asking the legally authorized representative contacted for consent within that window rather than proceeding without consent. The investigator will summarize efforts made to contact legally authorized representatives and make this information available to the IRB at the time of continuing review.

(6) The IRB has reviewed and approved informed consent procedures and an informed consent document consistent with § 50.25. These procedures and the informed consent document are to be used with subjects or their legally authorized representatives in situations where use of such procedures and documents is feasible. The IRB has reviewed and approved procedures and information to be used when providing an opportunity for a family member to object to a subject's participation in the clinical investigation consistent with paragraph (a)(7)(v) of this section.

(7) Additional protections of the rights and welfare of the subjects will be provided, including, at least:

(i) Consultation (including, where appropriate, consultation carried out by the IRB) with representatives of the communities in which the clinical investigation will be conducted and from which the subjects will be drawn;

(ii) Public disclosure to the communities in which the clinical investigation will be conducted and from which the subjects will be drawn, prior to initiation of the clinical investigation, of plans for the investigation and its risks and expected benefits;

(iii) Public disclosure of sufficient information following completion of the clinical investigation to apprise the community and researchers of the study, including the demographic characteristics of the research population, and its results;

(iv) Establishment of an independent data monitoring committee to exercise oversight of the clinical investigation; and

(v) If obtaining informed consent is not feasible and a legally authorized representative is not reasonably available, the investigator has committed, if feasible, to attempting to contact within the therapeutic window the subject's family member who is not a legally authorized representative, and asking whether he or she objects to the subject's participation in the clinical investigation. The investigator will summarize efforts made to contact family members and make this information available to the IRB at the time of continuing review.

(b) The IRB is responsible for ensuring that procedures are in place to inform, at the earliest feasible opportunity, each subject, or if the subject remains incapacitated, a legally authorized representative of the subject, or if such a representative is not reasonably available, a family member, of the subject's inclusion in the clinical investigation, the details of the investigation and other information contained in the informed consent document. The IRB shall also ensure that there is a procedure to inform the subject, or if the subject remains incapacitated, a legally authorized representative of the subject, or if such a representative is not reasonably available, a family member, that he or she may discontinue the subject's participation at any time without penalty or loss of benefits to which the subject is otherwise entitled. If a legally authorized representative or family member is told about the clinical investigation and the subject's condition improves, the subject is also to be informed as soon as feasible. If a subject is entered into a clinical investigation with waived consent and the subject dies before a legally authorized representative or family member can be contacted, information about the clinical investigation is to be provided to the subject's legally authorized representative or family member, if feasible.

(c) The IRB determinations required by paragraph (a) of this section and the documentation required by paragraph (e) of this section are to be retained by the IRB for at least 3 years after completion of the clinical investigation, and the records shall be accessible for inspection and copying by FDA in accordance with § 56.115(b) of this chapter.

(d) Protocols involving an exception to the informed consent requirement under this section must be performed under a separate investigational new drug application (IND) or investigational device exemption (IDE) that clearly identifies such protocols as protocols that may include subjects who are unable to consent. The submission of those protocols in a separate IND/IDE is required even if an IND for the same drug product or an IDE for the same device already exists. Applications for investigations under this section may not be submitted as amendments under §§ 312.30 or 812.35 of this chapter.

(e) If an IRB determines that it cannot approve a clinical investigation because the investigation does not meet the criteria in the exception provided under paragraph (a) of this section or because of other relevant ethical concerns, the IRB must document its findings and provide these findings promptly in writing to the clinical investigator and to the sponsor of the clinical investigation. The sponsor of the clinical investigation must promptly disclose this information to FDA and to the sponsor's clinical investigators who are participating or are asked to participate in this or a substantially equivalent clinical investigation of the sponsor, and to other IRB's that have been, or are, asked to review this or a substantially equivalent investigation by that sponsor.

[61 FR 51528, Oct. 2, 1996]

§ 50.25 Elements of informed consent.

(a) *Basic elements of informed consent.* In seeking informed consent, the following information shall be provided to each subject:

(1) A statement that the study involves research, an explanation of the purposes of the research and the expected duration of the subject's participation, a description of the procedures to be followed, and identification of any procedures which are experimental.

(2) A description of any reasonably foreseeable risks or discomforts to the subject.

(3) A description of any benefits to the subject or to others which may reasonably be expected from the research.

(4) A disclosure of appropriate alternative procedures or courses of treatment, if any, that might be advantageous to the subject.

(5) A statement describing the extent, if any, to which confidentiality of records identifying the subject will be maintained and that notes the possibility that the Food and Drug Administration may inspect the records.

(6) For research involving more than minimal risk, an explanation as to whether any compensation and an explanation as to whether any medical treatments are available if injury occurs and, if so, what they consist of, or where further information may be obtained.

(7) An explanation of whom to contact for answers to pertinent questions about the research and research subjects' rights, and whom to contact in the event of a research-related injury to the subject.

(8) A statement that participation is voluntary, that refusal to participate will involve no penalty or loss of benefits to which the subject is otherwise entitled, and that the subject may discontinue participation at any time without penalty or loss of benefits to which the subject is otherwise entitled.

(b) *Additional elements of informed consent.* When appropriate, one or more of the following elements of information shall also be provided to each subject:

(1) A statement that the particular treatment or procedure may involve risks to the subject (or to the embryo or fetus, if the subject is or may become pregnant) which are currently unforeseeable.

(2) Anticipated circumstances under which the subject's participation may be terminated by the investigator without regard to the subject's consent.

(3) Any additional costs to the subject that may result from participation in the research.

(4) The consequences of a subject's decision to withdraw from the research and procedures for orderly termination of participation by the subject.

(5) A statement that significant new findings developed during the course of the research which may relate to the subject's willingness to continue participation will be provided to the subject.

(6) The approximate number of subjects involved in the study.

(c) The informed consent requirements in these regulations are not intended to preempt any applicable Federal, State, or local laws which require additional information to be disclosed for informed consent to be legally effective.

(d) Nothing in these regulations is intended to limit the authority of a physician to provide emergency medical care to the extent the physician is permitted to do so under applicable Federal, State, or local law.

§ 50.27 Documentation of informed consent.

(a) Except as provided in § 56.109(c), informed consent shall be documented by the use of a written consent form approved by the IRB and signed and dated by the subject or the subject's legally authorized representative at the time of consent. A copy shall be given to the person signing the form.

(b) Except as provided in § 56.109(c), the consent form may be either of the following:

(1) A written consent document that embodies the elements of informed consent required by § 50.25. This form may be read to the subject or the subject's legally authorized representative, but, in any event, the investigator shall give either the subject or the representative adequate opportunity to read it before it is signed.

(2) A *short form* written consent document stating that the elements of informed consent required by § 50.25 have been presented orally to the subject or the subject's legally authorized representative. When this method is used, there shall be a witness to the oral

presentation. Also, the IRB shall approve a written summary of what is to be said to the subject or the representative. Only the short form itself is to be signed by the subject or the representative. However, the witness shall sign both the short form and a copy of the summary, and the person actually obtaining the consent shall sign a copy of the summary. A copy of the summary shall be given to the subject or the representative in addition to a copy of the short form.

[46 FR 8951, Jan. 27, 1981, as amended at 61 FR 57280, Nov. 5, 1996]

Subpart C [Reserved]

Subpart D — Additional Safeguards for Children in Clinical Investigations

SOURCE: 66 FR 20598, Apr. 24, 2001, unless otherwise noted.

§ 50.50 IRB duties.

In addition to other responsibilities assigned to IRBs under this part and part 56 of this chapter, each IRB must review clinical investigations involving children as subjects covered by this subpart D and approve only those clinical investigations that satisfy the criteria described in § 50.51, § 50.52, or § 50.53 and the conditions of all other applicable sections of this subpart D.

§ 50.51 Clinical investigations not involving greater than minimal risk.

Any clinical investigation within the scope described in §§ 50.1 and 56.101 of this chapter in which no greater than minimal risk to children is presented may involve children as subjects only if the IRB finds and documents that adequate provisions are made for soliciting the assent of the children and the permission of their parents or guardians as set forth in § 50.55.

§ 50.52 Clinical investigations involving greater than minimal risk but presenting the prospect of direct benefit to individual subjects.

Any clinical investigation within the scope described in §§ 50.1 and 56.101 of this chapter in which more than minimal risk to children is presented by an intervention or procedure that holds out the prospect of direct benefit for the individual subject, or by a monitoring procedure that is likely to contribute to the subject's well-being, may involve children as subjects only if the IRB finds and documents that:

(a) The risk is justified by the anticipated benefit to the subjects;

(b) The relation of the anticipated benefit to the risk is at least as favorable to the subjects as that presented by available alternative approaches; and

(c) Adequate provisions are made for soliciting the assent of the children and permission of their parents or guardians as set forth in § 50.55.

§ 50.53 Clinical investigations involving greater than minimal risk and no prospect of direct benefit to individual subjects, but likely to yield generalizable knowledge about the subjects' disorder or condition.

Any clinical investigation within the scope described in §§ 50.1 and 56.101 of this chapter in which more than minimal risk to children is presented by an intervention or procedure that does not hold out the prospect of direct benefit for the individual subject, or by a monitoring procedure that is not likely to contribute to the well-being of the subject, may involve children as subjects only if the IRB finds and documents that:

(a) The risk represents a minor increase over minimal risk;

(b) The intervention or procedure presents experiences to subjects that are reasonably commensurate with those inherent in their actual or expected medical, dental, psychological, social, or educational situations;

(c) The intervention or procedure is likely to yield generalizable knowledge about the subjects' disorder or condition that is of vital importance for the understanding or amelioration of the subjects' disorder or condition; and

(d) Adequate provisions are made for soliciting the assent of the children and permission of their parents or guardians as set forth in § 50.55.

§ 50.54 Clinical investigations not otherwise approvable that present an opportunity to understand, prevent, or alleviate a serious problem affecting the health or welfare of children.

If an IRB does not believe that a clinical investigation within the scope described in §§ 50.1 and 56.101 of this chapter and involving children as subjects meets the requirements of § 50.51, § 50.52, or § 50.53, the clinical investigation may proceed only if:

(a) The IRB finds and documents that the clinical investigation presents a reasonable opportunity to further the understanding, prevention, or alleviation of a serious problem affecting the health or welfare of children; and

(b) The Commissioner of Food and Drugs, after consultation with a panel of experts in pertinent disciplines (for example: science, medicine, education, ethics, law) and following opportunity for public review and comment, determines either:

(1) That the clinical investigation in fact satisfies the conditions of § 50.51, § 50.52, or § 50.53, as applicable, or

(2) That the following conditions are met:

(i) The clinical investigation presents a reasonable opportunity to further the understanding, prevention, or alleviation of a serious problem affecting the health or welfare of children;

(ii) The clinical investigation will be conducted in accordance with sound ethical principles; and

(iii) Adequate provisions are made for soliciting the assent of children and the permission of their parents or guardians as set forth in § 50.55.

§ 50.55 Requirements for permission by parents or guardians and for assent by children.

(a) In addition to the determinations required under other applicable sections of this subpart D, the IRB must determine that adequate provisions are made for soliciting the assent of the children when in the judgment of the IRB the children are capable of providing assent.

(b) In determining whether children are capable of providing assent, the IRB must take into account the ages, maturity, and psychological state of the children involved. This judgment may be made for all children to be involved in clinical investigations under a particular protocol, or for each child, as the IRB deems appropriate.

(c) The assent of the children is not a necessary condition for proceeding with the clinical investigation if the IRB determines:

(1) That the capability of some or all of the children is so limited that they cannot reasonably be consulted, or

(2) That the intervention or procedure involved in the clinical investigation holds out a prospect of direct benefit that is important to the health or well-being of the children and is available only in the context of the clinical investigation.

(d) Even where the IRB determines that the subjects are capable of assenting, the IRB may still waive the assent requirement if it finds and documents that:

(1) The clinical investigation involves no more than minimal risk to the subjects;

(2) The waiver will not adversely affect the rights and welfare of the subjects;

(3) The clinical investigation could not practicably be carried out without the waiver; and

(4) Whenever appropriate, the subjects will be provided with additional pertinent information after participation.

(e) In addition to the determinations required under other applicable sections of this subpart D, the IRB must determine that the permission of each child's parents or guardian is granted.

(1) Where parental permission is to be obtained, the IRB may find that the permission of one parent is sufficient, if consistent with State law, for clinical investigations to be conducted under § 50.51 or § 50.52.

(2) Where clinical investigations are covered by § 50.53 or § 50.54 and permission is to be obtained from parents, both parents must give their permission unless one parent is deceased, unknown, incompetent, or not reasonably available, or when only one parent has legal responsibility for the care and custody of the child if consistent with State law.

(f) Permission by parents or guardians must be documented in accordance with and to the extent required by § 50.27.

(g) When the IRB determines that assent is required, it must also determine whether and how assent must be documented.

§ 50.56 Wards.

(a) Children who are wards of the State or any other agency, institution, or entity can be included in clinical investigations approved under § 50.53 or § 50.54 only if such clinical investigations are:

(1) Related to their status as wards; or

(2) Conducted in schools, camps, hospitals, institutions, or similar settings in which the majority of children involved as subjects are not wards.

(b) If the clinical investigation is approved under paragraph (a) of this section, the IRB must require appointment of an advocate for each child who is a ward.

(1) The advocate will serve in addition to any other individual acting on behalf of the child as guardian or in loco parentis.

(2) One individual may serve as advocate for more than one child.

(3) The advocate must be an individual who has the background and experience to act in, and agrees to act in, the best interest of the child for the duration of the child's participation in the clinical investigation.

(4) The advocate must not be associated in any way (except in the role as advocate or member of the IRB) with the clinical investigation, the investigator(s), or the guardian organization.

PART 54 — FINANCIAL DISCLOSURE BY CLINICAL INVESTIGATORS

AUTHORITY: 21 U.S.C. 321, 331, 351, 352, 353, 355, 360, 360c-360j, 371, 372, 373, 374, 375, 376, 379; 42 U.S.C. 262.

SOURCE: 63 FR 5250, Feb. 2, 1998, unless otherwise noted.

§ 54.1 Purpose.

(a) The Food and Drug Administration (FDA) evaluates clinical studies submitted in marketing applications, required by law, for new human drugs and biological products and marketing applications and reclassification petitions for medical devices.

(b) The agency reviews data generated in these clinical studies to determine whether the applications are approvable under the statutory requirements. FDA may consider clinical studies inadequate and the data inadequate if, among other things, appropriate steps have not been taken in the design, conduct reporting, and analysis of the studies to minimize bias. One potential source of bias in clinical studies is a financial interest of the clinical investigator in the outcome of the study because of the way payment is arranged (e.g., a royalty) or because the investigator has a proprietary interest in the product (e.g., a patent) or because the investigator has an equity interest in the sponsor of the covered study. This section and conforming regulations require an applicant whose submission relies in part on clinical data to disclose certain financial arrangements between sponsor(s) of the covered studies and the clinical investigators and certain interests of the clinical investigators in the product under study or in the sponsor of the covered studies. FDA will use this information, in conjunction with information about the design and purpose of the study, as well as information obtained through on-site inspections, in the agency's assessment of the reliability of the data.

§ 54.2 Definitions.

For the purposes of this part:

(a) *Compensation affected by the outcome of clinical studies* means compensation that could be higher for a favorable outcome than for an unfavorable outcome, such as compensation that is explicitly greater for a favorable result or compensation to the investigator in the form of an equity interest in the sponsor of a covered study or in the form of compensation tied to sales of the product, such as the royalty interest.

(b) *Significant equity interest in the sponsor of a covered study* means any ownership interest, stock options, or other financial interest whose value cannot be readily determined through reference to public prices (generally, interests in a nonpublicly traded corporation), or any equity interest in a publicly traded corporation that exceeds $50,000 during the time the clinical investigator is carrying out the study and for 1 year following completion of the study.

(c) *Proprietary interest in the tested product* means property or other financial interest in the product including, but not limited to, a patent, trademark, copyright or licensing agreement.

(d) *Clinical investigator* means only a listed or identified investigator or subinvestigator who is directly involved in the treatment or evaluation of research subjects. The term also includes the spouse and each dependent child of the investigator.

(e) *Covered clinical study* means any study of a drug or device in humans submitted in a marketing application or reclassification petition subject to this part that the applicant or FDA relies on to establish that the product is effective (including studies that show equivalence to an effective product) or any study in which a single investigator makes a significant contribution to the demonstration of safety. This would, in general, not include phase 1 tolerance studies or pharmacokinetic studies, most clinical pharmacology studies (unless they are critical to an efficacy determination), large open safety studies conducted at multiple sites, treatment protocols, and parallel track protocols. An applicant may consult with FDA as to which clinical studies constitute "covered clinical studies" for purposes of complying with financial disclosure requirements.

(f) *Significant payments of other sorts* means payments made by the sponsor of a covered study to the investigator or the institution to support activities of the investigator that have a monetary value of more than $25,000, exclusive of the costs of conducting the clinical study or other clinical studies, (e.g., a grant to fund ongoing research, compensation in the form of equipment or retainers for ongoing consultation or honoraria) during the time the clinical investigator is carrying out the study and for 1 year following completion of the study.

(g) *Applicant* means the party who submits a marketing application to FDA for approval of a drug, device, or biologic product. The applicant is responsible for submitting the appropriate certification and disclosure statements required in this part.

(h) *Sponsor of the covered clinical study* means the party supporting a particular study at the time it was carried out.

[63 FR 5250, Feb. 20, 1998, as amended at 63 FR 72181, Dec. 31, 1998]

§ 54.3 Scope.

The requirements of this part apply to any applicant who submits a marketing application for a human drug, biological product, or device and who submits covered clinical studies. The applicant is responsible for making the appropriate certification or disclosure statement where the applicant either contracted with one or more clinical investigators to conduct the studies or submitted studies conducted by others not under contract with the applicant.

§ 54.4 Certification and disclosure requirements.

For purposes of this part, an applicant must submit a list of all clinical investigators who conducted covered clinical studies to determine whether the applicant's product meets FDA's marketing requirements, identifying those clinical investigators who are full-time or part-time employees of the sponsor of each covered study. The applicant must also completely and accurately disclose or certify information concerning the financial interests of a clinical investigator who is not a full-time or part-time employee of the sponsor for each covered clinical study. Clinical investigators subject to investigational new drug or investigational device exemption regulations must provide the sponsor of the study with sufficient accurate information needed to allow subsequent disclosure or certification. The applicant is required to submit for each clinical investigator who participates in a covered study, either a certification that none of the financial arrangements described in § 54.2 exist, or disclose the nature of those arrangements to the agency. Where the applicant acts with due diligence to obtain the information required in this section but is unable to do so, the applicant shall certify that despite the applicant's due diligence in attempting to obtain the information, the applicant was unable to obtain the information and shall include the reason.

(a) The applicant (of an application submitted under sections 505, 506, 510(k), 513, or 515 of the Federal Food, Drug, and Cosmetic Act, or section 351 of the Public Health Services Act) that relies in whole or in part on clinical studies shall submit, for each clinical investigator who participated in a covered clinical study, either a certification described in paragraph (a)(1) of this section or a disclosure statement described in paragraph (a)(3) of this section.

(1) Certification: The applicant covered by this section shall submit for all clinical investigators (as defined in § 54.2 (d)), to whom the certification applies, a completed Form FDA 3454 attesting to the absence of financial interests and arrangements described in paragraph (a)(3) of this section. The form shall be dated and signed by the chief financial officer or other responsible corporate representative.

(2) If the certification covers less than all covered clinical data in the application, the applicant shall include in the certification a list of the studies covered by this certification.

(3) Disclosure Statement: For any clinical investigator defined in § 54.2 (d) for whom the applicant does not submit the certification described in paragraph (a)(1) of this section, the applicant shall submit a completed Form FDA 3455 disclosing completely and accurately the following:

(i) Any financial arrangements entered into between the sponsor of the covered study and the clinical investigator involved in the conduct of a covered clinical trial, whereby the value of the compensation to the clinical investigator for conducing the study could be influenced by the outcome of the study;

(ii) Any significant payments of other sorts from the sponsor of the covered study, such as a grant to fund ongoing research, compensation in the form of equipment, retainer for ongoing consultation, or honoraria;

(iii) Any proprietary interest in the tested product held by any clinical investigator involved in a study;

(iv) Any significant equity interest in the sponsor of the covered study held by any clinical investigator involved in any clinical study; and

(v) Any steps taken to minimize the potential for bias resulting from any of the disclosed arrangements, interests, or payments.

(b) The clinical investigator shall provide to the sponsor of the covered study sufficient accurate financial information to allow the sponsor to submit complete and accurate financial certification or disclosure statements as required in paragraph (a) of this section. The investigator shall promptly update this information if any relevant changes occur in the course of the investigation or for 1 year following completion of the study.

(c) Refusal to file application. FDA may refuse to file any marketing application described in paragraph (a) of this section that does not contain the information required by this section or a certification by the applicant that the applicant has acted with due diligence to obtain the information but was unable to do so and stating the reason.

[63 FR 5250, Feb. 2, 1998, as amended at 63 FR 35134, June 29, 1998; 64 FR 399, Jan. 5, 1999]

§ 54.5 Agency evaluation of financial interests.

(a) *Evaluation of disclosure statement.* FDA will evaluate the information disclosed under § 54.4 (a)(2) about each covered clinical study in an application to determine the impact of any disclosed financial interests on the reliability of the study. FDA may consider both the size and the nature of a disclosed financial interest (including the potential increase in the value of the interest if the product is approved) and steps that have been taken to minimize the potential for bias.

(b) *Effect of study design.* In assessing the potential of an investigator's financial interests to bias a study, FDA will take into account the design and purpose of the study. Study designs that utilize such approaches as multiple investigators (most of whom do not have a disclosable interest), blinding, objective endpoints, or measurement of endpoints by someone other than the investigator may adequately protect against any bias created by a disclosable financial interest.

(c) *Agency actions to ensure reliability of data.* If FDA determines that the financial interests of any clinical investigator raise a serious question about the integrity of the data, FDA will take any action it deems necessary to ensure the reliability of the data including:

(1) Initiating agency audits of the data derived from the clinical investigator in question;

(2) Requesting that the applicant submit further analyses of data, e.g., to evaluate the effect of the clinical investigator's data on overall study outcome;

(3) Requesting that the applicant conduct additional independent studies to confirm the results of the questioned study; and

(4) Refusing to treat the covered clinical study as providing data that can be the basis for an agency action.

§ 54.6 Recordkeeping and record retention.

(a) *Financial records of clinical investigators to be retained.* An applicant who has submitted a marketing application containing covered clinical studies shall keep on file certain information pertaining to the financial interests of clinical investigators who conducted studies on which the application relies and who are not full or part-time employees of the applicant, as follows:

(1) Complete records showing any financial interest or arrangement as described in § 54.4 (a)(3)(i) paid to such clinical investigators by the sponsor of the covered study.

(2) Complete records showing significant payments of other sorts, as described in § 54.4 (a)(3)(ii) made by the sponsor of the covered clinical study to the clinical investigator.

(3) Complete records showing any financial interests held by clinical investigators as set forth in § 54.4 (a)(3)(iii) and (a)(3)(iv).

(b) *Requirements for maintenance of clinical investigators' financial records.*

(1) For any application submitted for a covered product, an applicant shall retain records as described in paragraph (a) of this section for 2 years after the date of approval of the application.

(2) The person maintaining these records shall, upon request from any properly authorized officer or employee of FDA, at reasonable times, permit such officer or employee to have access to and copy and verify these records.

PART 56 — INSTITUTIONAL REVIEW BOARDS

Subpart A — General Provisions

AUTHORITY: 21 U.S.C. 321, 343, 346, 346a, 348, 350a, 350b, 351, 352, 353, 355, 360, 360c-360f, 360h-360j, 371, 379e, 381; 42 U.S.C. 216, 241, 262, 263b-263n.

SOURCE: 46 FR 8975, Jan. 27, 1981, unless otherwise noted.

Subpart A — General Provisions

§ 56.101 Scope.

(a) This part contains the general standards for the composition, operation, and responsibility of an Institutional Review Board (IRB) that reviews clinical investigations regulated by the Food and Drug Administration under sections 505(i) and 520(g) of the act, as well as clinical investigations that support applications for research or marketing permits for products regulated by the Food and Drug Administration, including foods, including dietary supplements, that bear a nutrient content claim or a health claim, infant formulas, food and color additives, drugs for human use, medical devices for human use, biological products for human use, and electronic products. Compliance with this part is intended to protect the rights and welfare of human subjects involved in such investigations.

(b) References in this part to regulatory sections of the Code of Federal Regulations are to chapter I of title 21, unless otherwise noted.

[46 FR 8975, Jan. 27, 1981, as amended at 64 FR 399, Jan. 5, 1999]

§ 56.102 Definitions.

As used in this part:

(a) *Act* means the Federal Food, Drug, and Cosmetic Act, as amended (secs. 201-902, 52 Stat. 1040 et seq., as amended (21 U.S.C. 321-392)).

(b) *Application for research or marketing permit* includes:

(1) A color additive petition, described in part 71.

(2) Data and information regarding a substance submitted as part of the procedures for establishing that a substance is generally recognized as safe for a use which results or may reasonably be expected to result, directly or indirectly, in its becoming a component or otherwise affecting the characteristics of any food, described in § 170.35.

(3) A food additive petition, described in part 171.

(4) Data and information regarding a food additive submitted as part of the procedures regarding food additives permitted to be used on an interim basis pending additional study, described in § 180.1.

(5) Data and information regarding a substance submitted as part of the procedures for establishing a tolerance for unavoidable contaminants in food and food-packaging materials, described in section 406 of the act.

(6) An investigational new drug application, described in part 312 of this chapter.

(7) A new drug application, described in part 314.

(8) Data and information regarding the bioavailability or bioequivalence of drugs for human use submitted as part of the procedures for issuing, amending, or repealing a bioequivalence requirement, described in part 320.

(9) Data and information regarding an over-the-counter drug for human use submitted as part of the procedures for classifying such drugs as generally recognized as safe and effective and not misbranded, described in part 330.

(10) An application for a biologics license, described in part 601 of this chapter.

(11) Data and information regarding a biological product submitted as part of the procedures for determining that licensed biological products are safe and effective and not misbranded, as described in part 601 of this chapter.

(12) An *Application for an Investigational Device Exemption,* described in parts 812 and 813.

(13) Data and information regarding a medical device for human use submitted as part of the procedures for classifying such devices, described in part 860.

(14) Data and information regarding a medical device for human use submitted as part of the procedures for establishing, amending, or repealing a standard for such device, described in part 861.

(15) An application for premarket approval of a medical device for human use, described in section 515 of the act.

(16) A product development protocol for a medical device for human use, described in section 515 of the act.

(17) Data and information regarding an electronic product submitted as part of the procedures for establishing, amending, or repealing a standard for such products, described in section 358 of the Public Health Service Act.

(18) Data and information regarding an electronic product submitted as part of the procedures for obtaining a variance from any electronic product performance standard, as described in § 1010.4.

(19) Data and information regarding an electronic product submitted as part of the procedures for granting, amending, or extending an exemption from a radiation safety performance standard, as described in § 1010.5.

(20) Data and information regarding an electronic product submitted as part of the procedures for obtaining an exemption from notification of a radiation safety defect or failure of compliance with a radiation safety performance standard, described in subpart D of part 1003.

(21) Data and information about a clinical study of an infant formula when submitted as part of an infant formula notification under section 412(c) of the Federal Food, Drug, and Cosmetic Act.

(22) Data and information submitted in a petition for a nutrient content claim, described in §101.69 of this chapter, and for a health claim, described in §101.70 of this chapter.

(23) Data and information from investigations involving children submitted in a new dietary ingredient notification, described in §190.6 of this chapter.

(c) *Clinical investigation* means any experiment that involves a test article and one or more human subjects, and that either must meet the requirements for prior submission to the Food and Drug Administration under section 505(i) or 520(g) of the act, or need not meet the requirements for prior submission to the Food and Drug Administration under these sections of the act, but the results of which are intended to be later submitted to, or held for inspection by, the Food and Drug Administration as part of an application for a research or marketing permit. The term does not include experiments that must meet the provisions of part 58, regarding nonclinical laboratory studies. The terms *research, clinical research, clinical study, study, and clinical investigation* are deemed to be synonymous for purposes of this part.

(d) *Emergency use* means the use of a test article on a human subject in a life-threatening situation in which no standard acceptable treatment is available, and in which there is not sufficient time to obtain IRB approval.

(e) *Human subject* means an individual who is or becomes a participant in research, either as a recipient of the test article or as a control. A subject may be either a healthy individual or a patient.

(f) *Institution* means any public or private entity or agency (including Federal, State, and other agencies). The term facility as used in section 520(g) of the act is deemed to be synonymous with the term *institution* for purposes of this part.

(g) *Institutional Review Board (IRB)* means any board, committee, or other group formally designated by an institution to review, to approve the initiation of, and to conduct periodic review of, biomedical research involving human subjects. The primary purpose of such review is to assure the protection of the rights and welfare of the human subjects. The term has the same meaning as the phrase *institutional review committee* as used in section 520(g) of the act.

(h) *Investigator* means an individual who actually conducts a clinical investigation (i.e., under whose immediate direction the test article is administered or dispensed to, or used involving, a subject) or, in the event of an investigation conducted by a team of individuals, is the responsible leader of that team.

(i) *Minimal risk* means that the probability and magnitude of harm or discomfort anticipated in the research are not greater in and of themselves than those ordinarily encountered in daily life or during the performance of routine physical or psychological examinations or tests.

(j) *Sponsor* means a person or other entity that initiates a clinical investigation, but that does not actually conduct the investigation, i.e., the test article is administered or dispensed to, or used involving, a subject under the immediate direction of another individual. A person other than an individual (e.g., a corporation or agency) that uses one or more of its own employees to conduct an investigation that it has initiated is considered to be a sponsor (not a sponsor-investigator), and the employees are considered to be investigators.

(k) *Sponsor-investigator* means an individual who both initiates and actually conducts, alone or with others, a clinical investigation, i.e., under whose immediate direction the test article is administered or dispensed to, or used involving, a subject. The term does not include any person other than an individual, e.g., it does not include a corporation or agency. The obligations of a sponsor-investigator under this part include both those of a sponsor and those of an investigator.

(l) *Test article* means any drug for human use, biological product for human use, medical device for human use, human food additive, color additive, electronic product, or any other article subject to regulation under the act or under sections 351 or 354-360F of the Public Health Service Act.

(m) *IRB approval* means the determination of the IRB that the clinical investigation has been reviewed and may be conducted at an institution within the constraints set forth by the IRB and by other institutional and Federal requirements.

[46 FR 8975, Jan. 27, 1981, as amended at 54 FR 9038, Mar. 3, 1989; 56 FR 28028, June 18, 1991; 64 FR 399, Jan. 5, 1999; 64 FR 56448, Oct. 20, 1999; 65 FR 52302, Aug. 29, 2000]

§ 56.103 Circumstances in which IRB review is required.

(a) Except as provided in §§ 56.104 and 56.105, any clinical investigation which must meet the requirements for prior submission (as required in parts 312, 812, and 813) to the Food and Drug Administration shall not be initiated unless that investigation has been reviewed and approved by, and remains subject to continuing review by, an IRB meeting the requirements of this part.

(b) Except as provided in §§ 56.104 and 56.105, the Food and Drug Administration may decide not to consider in support of an application for a research or marketing permit any data or information that has been derived from a clinical investigation that has not been approved by, and that was not subject to initial and continuing review by, an IRB meeting the requirements of this part. The determination that a clinical investigation may not be considered in support of an application for a research or marketing permit does not, however, relieve the applicant for such a permit of any obligation under any other applicable regulations to submit the results of the investigation to the Food and Drug Administration.

(c) Compliance with these regulations will in no way render inapplicable pertinent Federal, State, or local laws or regulations.

[46 FR 8975, Jan. 27, 1981; 46 FR 14340, Feb. 27, 1981]

§ 56.104 Exemptions from IRB requirement.

The following categories of clinical investigations are exempt from the requirements of this part for IRB review:

(a) Any investigation which commenced before July 27, 1981 and was subject to requirements for IRB review under FDA regulations before that date, provided that the investigation remains subject to review of an IRB which meets the FDA requirements in effect before July 27, 1981.

(b) Any investigation commenced before July 27, 1981 and was not otherwise subject to requirements for IRB review under Food and Drug Administration regulations before that date.

(c) Emergency use of a test article, provided that such emergency use is reported to the IRB within 5 working days. Any subsequent use of the test article at the institution is subject to IRB review.

(d) Taste and food quality evaluations and consumer acceptance studies, if wholesome foods without additives are consumed or if a food is consumed that contains a food ingredient at or below the level and for a use found to be safe, or agricultural, chemical, or environmental contaminant at or below the level found to be safe, by the Food and Drug Administration or approved by the Environmental Protection Agency or the Food Safety and Inspection Service of the U.S. Department of Agriculture.

[46 FR 8975, Jan. 27, 1981, as amended at 56 FR 28028, June 18, 1991]

§ 56.105 Waiver of IRB requirement.

On the application of a sponsor or sponsor-investigator, the Food and Drug Administration may waive any of the requirements contained in these regulations, including the requirements for IRB review, for specific research activities or for classes of research activities, otherwise covered by these regulations.

Subpart B — Organization and Personnel

§ 56.107 IRB membership.

(a) Each IRB shall have at least five members, with varying backgrounds to promote complete and adequate review of research activities commonly conducted by the institution. The IRB shall be sufficiently qualified through the experience and expertise of its members, and the diversity of the members, including consideration of race, gender, cultural backgrounds, and sensitivity to such issues as community attitudes, to promote respect for its advice and counsel in safeguarding the rights and welfare of human subjects. In addition to possessing the professional competence necessary to review the specific research activities, the IRB shall be able to ascertain the acceptability of proposed research in terms of institutional commitments and regulations, applicable law, and standards or professional conduct and practice. The IRB shall therefore include persons knowledgeable in these areas. If an IRB regularly reviews research that involves a vulnerable category of subjects, such as children, prisoners, pregnant women, or handicapped or mentally disabled persons, consideration shall be given to the inclusion of one or more individuals who are knowledgeable about and experienced in working with those subjects.

(b) Every nondiscriminatory effort will be made to ensure that no IRB consists entirely of men or entirely of women, including the institution's consideration of qualified persons of both sexes, so long as no selection is made to the IRB on the basis of gender. No IRB may consist entirely of members of one profession.

(c) Each IRB shall include at least one member whose primary concerns are in the scientific area and at least one member whose primary concerns are in nonscientific areas.

(d) Each IRB shall include at least one member who is not otherwise affiliated with the institution and who is not part of the immediate family of a person who is affiliated with the institution.

(e) No IRB may have a member participate in the IRB's initial or continuing review of any project in which the member has a conflicting interest, except to provide information requested by the IRB.

(f) An IRB may, in its discretion, invite individuals with competence in special areas to assist in the review of complex issues which require expertise beyond or in addition to that available on the IRB. These individuals may not vote with the IRB.

[46 FR 8975, Jan. 27, 1981, as amended at 56 FR 28028, June 18, 1991; 56 FR 29756, June 28, 1991]

Subpart C — IRB Functions and Operations

§ 56.108 IRB functions and operations.

In order to fulfill the requirements of these regulations, each IRB shall:

(a) Follow written procedures: (1) For conducting its initial and continuing review of research and for reporting its findings and actions to the investigator and the institution; (2) for determining which projects require review more often than annually and which projects need verification from sources other than the investigator that no material changes have occurred since previous IRB review; (3) for ensuring prompt reporting to the IRB of changes in research activity; and (4) for ensuring that changes in approved research, during the period for which IRB approval has already been given, may not be initiated without IRB review and approval except where necessary to eliminate apparent immediate hazards to the human subjects.

(b) Follow written procedures for ensuring prompt reporting to the IRB, appropriate institutional officials, and the Food and Drug Administration of: (1) Any unanticipated problems involving risks to human subjects or others; (2) any instance of serious or continuing noncompliance with these regulations or the requirements or determinations of the IRB; or (3) any suspension or termination of IRB approval.

(c) Except when an expedited review procedure is used (see § 56.110), review proposed research at convened meetings at which a majority of the members of the IRB are present, including at least one member whose primary concerns are in nonscientific areas. In order for the research to be approved, it shall receive the approval of a majority of those members present at the meeting.

[46 FR 8975, Jan. 27, 1981, as amended at 56 FR 28028, June 18, 1991]

§ 56.109 IRB review of research.

(a) An IRB shall review and have authority to approve, require modifications in (to secure approval), or disapprove all research activities covered by these regulations.

(b) An IRB shall require that information given to subjects as part of informed consent is in accordance with § 50.25. The IRB may require that information, in addition to that specifically mentioned in § 50.25, be given to the subjects when in the IRB's judgment the information would meaningfully add to the protection of the rights and welfare of subjects.

(c) An IRB shall require documentation of informed consent in accordance with § 50.27 of this chapter, except as follows:

(1) The IRB may, for some or all subjects, waive the requirement that the subject or the subject's legally authorized representative sign a written consent form if it finds that the research presents no more than minimal risk of harm to subjects and involves no procedures for which written consent is normally required outside the research context; or

(2) The IRB may, for some or all subjects, find that the requirements in § 50.24 of this chapter for an exception from informed consent for emergency research are met.

(d) In cases where the documentation requirement is waived under paragraph (c)(1) of this section, the IRB may require the investigator to provide subjects with a written statement regarding the research.

(e) An IRB shall notify investigators and the institution in writing of its decision to approve or disapprove the proposed research activity, or of modifications required to secure IRB approval of the research activity. If the IRB decides to disapprove a research activity, it shall include in its written notification a statement of the reasons for its decision and give the investigator an opportunity to respond in person or in writing. For investigations involving an exception to informed consent under § 50.24 of this chapter, an IRB shall promptly notify in writing the investigator and the sponsor of the research when an IRB determines that it cannot approve the research because is does not meet the criteria in the exception provided under § 50.24(a) of this chapter or because of other relevant ethical concerns. The written notification shall include a statement of the reasons for the IRB's determination.

(f) An IRB shall conduct continuing review of research covered by these regulations at intervals appropriate to the degree of risk, but not less than once per year, and shall have authority to observe or have a third party observe the consent process and the research.

(g) An IRB shall provide in writing to the sponsor of research involving an exception to informed consent under § 50.24 of this chapter a copy of information that has been publicly disclosed under § 50.24(a)(7)(ii) and (a)(7)(iii) of this chapter. The IRB shall provide this information to the sponsor promptly so that the sponsor is aware that such disclosure has occurred. Upon receipt, the sponsor shall provide copies of the information disclosed to FDA.

(h) When some or all of the subjects in a study are children, an IRB must determine that the research study is in compliance with part 50, subpart D of this chapter, at the time of its initial review of the research. When some or all of the subjects in a study that is ongoing on April 30, 2001 are children, an IRB must conduct a review of the research to determine compliance with part 50, subpart D of this chapter, either at the time of continuing review or, at the discretion of the IRB, at an earlier date.

[46 FR 8975, Jan. 27, 1981 as amended at 61 FR 51529, Oct. 2, 1996]

§ 56.110 Expedited review procedures for certain kinds of research involving no more than minimal risk, and for minor changes in approved research.

(a) The Food and Drug Administration has established, and published in the FEDERAL REGISTER, a list of categories of research that may be reviewed by the IRB through an expedited review procedure. The list will be amended, as appropriate, through periodic republication in the FEDERAL REGISTER.

(b) An IRB may use the expedited review procedure to review either or both of the following: (1) Some or all of the research appearing on the list and found by the reviewer(s) to involve no more than minimal risk, (2) minor changes in previously approved research during the period (of 1 year or less) for which approval is authorized. Under an expedited review procedure, the review may be carried out by the IRB chairperson or by one or more experienced reviewers designated by the IRB chairperson from among the members of the IRB. In reviewing the research, the reviewers may exercise all of the authorities of the IRB except that the reviewers may not disapprove the research. A research activity may be disapproved only after review in accordance with the nonexpedited review procedure set forth in § 56.108(c).

(c) Each IRB which uses an expedited review procedure shall adopt a method for keeping all members advised of research proposals which have been approved under the procedure.

(d) The Food and Drug Administration may restrict, suspend, or terminate an institution's or IRB's use of the expedited review procedure when necessary to protect the rights or welfare of subjects.

[46 FR 8975, Jan. 27, 1981, as amended at 56 FR 28029, June 18, 1991]

§ 56.111 Criteria for IRB approval of research.

(a) In order to approve research covered by these regulations the IRB shall determine that all of the following requirements are satisfied:

(1) Risks to subjects are minimized: (i) By using procedures which are consistent with sound research design and which do not unnecessarily expose subjects to risk, and (ii) whenever appropriate, by using procedures already being performed on the subjects for diagnostic or treatment purposes.

(2) Risks to subjects are reasonable in relation to anticipated benefits, if any, to subjects, and the importance of the knowledge that may be expected to result. In evaluating risks and benefits, the IRB should consider only those risks and benefits that may result from the research (as distinguished from risks and benefits of therapies that subjects would receive even if not participating in the research). The IRB should not consider possible long-range effects of applying knowledge gained in the research (for example, the possible effects of the research on public policy) as among those research risks that fall within the purview of its responsibility.

(3) Selection of subjects is equitable. In making this assessment the IRB should take into account the purposes of the research and the setting in which the research will be conducted and should be particularly cognizant of the special problems of research involving vulnerable populations, such as children, prisoners, pregnant women, handicapped, or mentally disabled persons, or economically or educationally disadvantaged persons.

(4) Informed consent will be sought from each prospective subject or the subject's legally authorized representative, in accordance with and to the extent required by part 50.

(5) Informed consent will be appropriately documented, in accordance with and to the extent required by § 50.27.

(6) Where appropriate, the research plan makes adequate provision for monitoring the data collected to ensure the safety of subjects.

(7) Where appropriate, there are adequate provisions to protect the privacy of subjects and to maintain the confidentiality of data.

(b) When some or all of the subjects, such as children, prisoners, pregnant women, handicapped, or mentally disabled persons, or economically or educationally disadvantaged persons, are likely to be vulnerable to coercion or undue influence additional safeguards have been included in the study to protect the rights and welfare of these subjects.

(c) In order to approve research in which some or all of the subjects are children, an IRB must determine that all research is in compliance with part 50, subpart D of this chapter.

[46 FR 8975, Jan. 27, 1981, as amended at 56 FR 28029, June 18, 1991]

§ 56.112 Review by institution.

Research covered by these regulations that has been approved by an IRB may be subject to further appropriate review and approval or disapproval by officials of the institution. However, those officials may not approve the research if it has not been approved by an IRB.

§ 56.113 Suspension or termination of IRB approval of research.

An IRB shall have authority to suspend or terminate approval of research that is not being conducted in accordance with the IRB's requirements or that has been associated with unexpected serious harm to subjects. Any suspension or termination of approval shall include a statement of the reasons for the IRB's action and shall be reported promptly to the investigator, appropriate institutional officials, and the Food and Drug Administration.

§ 56.114 Cooperative research.

In complying with these regulations, institutions involved in multi-institutional studies may use joint review, reliance upon the review of another qualified IRB, or similar arrangements aimed at avoidance of duplication of effort.

Subpart D — Records and Reports

§ 56.115 IRB records.

(a) An institution, or where appropriate an IRB, shall prepare and maintain adequate documentation of IRB activities, including the following:

(1) Copies of all research proposals reviewed, scientific evaluations, if any, that accompany the proposals, approved sample consent documents, progress reports submitted by investigators, and reports of injuries to subjects.

(2) Minutes of IRB meetings which shall be in sufficient detail to show attendance at the meetings; actions taken by the IRB; the vote on these actions including the number of members voting for, against, and abstaining; the basis for requiring changes in or disapproving research; and a written summary of the discussion of controverted issues and their resolution.

(3) Records of continuing review activities.

(4) Copies of all correspondence between the IRB and the investigators.

(5) A list of IRB members identified by name; earned degrees; representative capacity; indications of experience such as board certifications, licenses, etc., sufficient to describe each member's chief anticipated contributions to IRB deliberations; and any employment or other relationship between each member and the institution; for example: full-time employee, part-time employee, a member of governing panel or board, stockholder, paid or unpaid consultant.

(6) Written procedures for the IRB as required by § 56.108 (a) and (b).

(7) Statements of significant new findings provided to subjects, as required by § 50.25.

(b) The records required by this regulation shall be retained for at least 3 years after completion of the research, and the records shall be accessible for inspection and copying by authorized representatives of the Food and Drug Administration at reasonable times and in a reasonable manner.

(c) The Food and Drug Administration may refuse to consider a clinical investigation in support of an application for a research or marketing permit if the institution or the IRB that reviewed the investigation refuses to allow an inspection under this section.

[46 FR 8975, Jan. 27, 1981, as amended at 56 FR 28029, June 18, 1991]

Subpart E — Administrative Actions for Noncompliance

§ 56.120 Lesser administrative actions.

(a) If apparent noncompliance with these regulations in the operation of an IRB is observed by an FDA investigator during an inspection, the inspector will present an oral or written summary of observations to an appropriate representative of the IRB. The Food and Drug Administration may subsequently send a letter describing the noncompliance to the IRB and to the parent institution. The agency will require that the IRB or the parent institution respond to this letter within a time period specified by FDA and describe the corrective actions that will be taken by the IRB, the institution, or both to achieve compliance with these regulations.

(b) On the basis of the IRB's or the institution's response, FDA may schedule a reinspection to confirm the adequacy of corrective actions. In addition, until the IRB or the parent institution takes appropriate corrective action, the agency may:

(1) Withhold approval of new studies subject to the requirements of this part that are conducted at the institution or reviewed by the IRB;

(2) Direct that no new subjects be added to ongoing studies subject to this part;

(3) Terminate ongoing studies subject to this part when doing so would not endanger the subjects; or

(4) When the apparent noncompliance creates a significant threat to the rights and welfare of human subjects, notify relevant State and Federal regulatory agencies and other parties with a direct interest in the agency's action of the deficiencies in the operation of the IRB.

(c) The parent institution is presumed to be responsible for the operation of an IRB, and the Food and Drug Administration will ordinarily direct any administrative action under this subpart against the institution. However, depending on the evidence of responsibility for deficiencies, determined during the investigation, the Food and Drug Administration may restrict its administrative actions to the IRB or to a component of the parent institution determined to be responsible for formal designation of the IRB.

§ 56.121 Disqualification of an IRB or an institution.

(a) Whenever the IRB or the institution has failed to take adequate steps to correct the noncompliance stated in the letter sent by the agency under § 56.120(a), and the Commissioner of Food and Drugs determines that this noncompliance may justify the disqualification of the IRB or of the parent institution, the Commissioner will institute proceedings in accordance with the requirements for a regulatory hearing set forth in part 16.

(b) The Commissioner may disqualify an IRB or the parent institution if the Commissioner determines that:

(1) The IRB has refused or repeatedly failed to comply with any of the regulations set forth in this part, and

(2) The noncompliance adversely affects the rights or welfare of the human subjects in a clinical investigation.

(c) If the Commissioner determines that disqualification is appropriate, the Commissioner will issue an order that explains the basis for the determination and that prescribes any actions to be taken with regard to ongoing clinical research conducted under the review of the IRB. The Food and Drug Administration will send notice of the disqualification to the IRB and the parent institution. Other parties with a direct interest, such as sponsors and clinical investigators, may also be sent a notice of the disqualification. In addition, the agency may elect to publish a notice of its action in the FEDERAL REGISTER.

(d) The Food and Drug Administration will not approve an application for a research permit for a clinical investigation that is to be under the review of a disqualified IRB or that is to be conducted at a disqualified institution, and it may refuse to consider in support of a marketing permit the data from a clinical investigation that was reviewed by a disqualified IRB as conducted at a disqualified institution, unless the IRB or the parent institution is reinstated as provided in § 56.123.

§ 56.122 Public disclosure of information regarding revocation.

A determination that the Food and Drug Administration has disqualified an institution and the administrative record regarding that determination are disclosable to the public under part 20.

§ 56.123 Reinstatement of an IRB or an institution.

An IRB or an institution may be reinstated if the Commissioner determines, upon an evaluation of a written submission from the IRB or institution that explains the corrective action that the institution or IRB plans to take, that the IRB or institution has provided adequate assurance that it will operate in compliance with the standards set forth in this part. Notification of reinstatement shall be provided to all persons notified under § 56.121(c).

§ 56.124 Actions alternative or additional to disqualification.

Disqualification of an IRB or of an institution is independent of, and neither in lieu of nor a precondition to, other proceedings or actions authorized by the act. The Food and Drug Administration may, at any time, through the Department of Justice institute any appropriate judicial proceedings (civil or criminal) and any other appropriate regulatory action, in addition to or in lieu of, and before, at the time of, or after, disqualification. The agency may also refer pertinent matters to another Federal, State, or local government agency for any action that that agency determines to be appropriate.

PART 312 — INVESTIGATIONAL NEW DRUG APPLICATION

Subpart A — General Provisions

Subpart B — Investigational New Drug Application (IND)

Subpart C — Administrative Actions

PART 312 — INVESTIGATIONAL NEW DRUG APPLICATION (continued)

Subpart D — Responsibilities of Sponsors and Investigators

Subpart E — Drugs Intended to Treat Life-threatening and Severely-debilitating Illnesses

PART 312 — INVESTIGATIONAL NEW DRUG APPLICATION (continued)

Subpart F — Miscellaneous

Subpart G — Drugs for Investigational Use in Laboratory Research Animals or in Vitro Tests

AUTHORITY: 21 U.S.C. 321, 331, 351, 352, 353, 355, 371; 42 U.S.C. 262.

SOURCE: 52 FR 8831, Mar. 19, 1987, unless otherwise noted.

Subpart A — General Provisions

§ 312.1 Scope.

(a) This part contains procedures and requirements governing the use of investigational new drugs, including procedures and requirements for the submission to, and review by, the Food and Drug Administration of investigational new drug applications (IND). An investigational new drug for which an IND is in effect in accordance with this part is exempt from the premarketing approval requirements that are otherwise applicable and may be shipped lawfully for the purpose of conducting clinical investigations of that drug.

(b) References in this part to regulations in the Code of Federal Regulations are to chapter I of title 21, unless otherwise noted.

§ 312.2 Applicability.

(a) *Applicability*. Except as provided in this section, this part applies to all clinical investigations of products that are subject to section 505 of the Federal Food, Drug, and Cosmetic Act or to the licensing provisions of the Public Health Service Act (58 Stat. 632, as amended (42 U.S.C. 201 *et seq.*)).

(b) *Exemptions*. (1) The clinical investigation of a drug product that is lawfully marketed in the United States is exempt from the requirements of this part if all the following apply:

(i) The investigation is not intended to be reported to FDA as a well-controlled study in support of a new indication for use nor intended to be used to support any other significant change in the labeling for the drug;

(ii) If the drug that is undergoing investigation is lawfully marketed as a prescription drug product, the investigation is not intended to support a significant change in the advertising for the product;

(iii) The investigation does not involve a route of administration or dosage level or use in a patient population or other factor that significantly increases the risks (or decreases the acceptability of the risks) associated with the use of the drug product;

(iv) The investigation is conducted in compliance with the requirements for institutional review set forth in part 56 and with the requirements for informed consent set forth in part 50; and

(v) The investigation is conducted in compliance with the requirements of § 312.7.

(2)(i) A clinical investigation involving an in vitro diagnostic biological product listed in paragraph (b)(2)(ii) of this section is exempt from the requirements of this part if *(a)* it is intended to be used in a diagnostic procedure that confirms the diagnosis made by another, medically established, diagnostic product or procedure and *(b)* it is shipped in compliance with § 312.160.

(ii) In accordance with paragraph (b)(2)(i) of this section, the following products are exempt from the requirements of this part: *(a)* blood grouping serum; *(b)* reagent red blood cells; and *(c)* anti-human globulin.

(3) A drug intended solely for tests in vitro or in laboratory research animals is exempt from the requirements of this part if shipped in accordance with § 312.160.

(4) FDA will not accept an application for an investigation that is exempt under the provisions of paragraph (b)(1) of this section.

(5) A clinical investigation involving use of a placebo is exempt from the requirements of this part if the investigation does not otherwise require submission of an IND.

(6) A clinical investigation involving an exception from informed consent under § 50.24 of this chapter is not exempt from the requirements of this part.

(c) *Bioavailability studies.* The applicability of this part to in vivo bioavailability studies in humans is subject to the provisions of § 320.31.

(d) *Unlabeled indication.* This part does not apply to the use in the practice of medicine for an unlabeled indication of a new drug product approved under part 314 or of a licensed biological product.

(e) *Guidance.* FDA may, on its own initiative, issue guidance on the applicability of this part to particular investigational uses of drugs. On request, FDA will advise on the applicability of this part to a planned clinical investigation.

[52 FR 8831, Mar. 19, 1987, as amended at 61 FR 51529, Oct. 2, 1996; 64 FR 401, Jan. 5, 1999]

§ 312.3 Definitions and interpretations.

(a) The definitions and interpretations of terms contained in section 201 of the Act apply to those terms when used in this part:

(b) The following definitions of terms also apply to this part:

Act means the Federal Food, Drug, and Cosmetic Act (secs. 201-902, 52 Stat. 1040 *et seq.*, as amended (21 U.S.C. 301-392)).

Clinical investigation means any experiment in which a drug is administered or dispensed to, or used involving, one or more human subjects. For the purposes of this part, an experiment is any use of a drug except for the use of a marketed drug in the course of medical practice.

Contract research organization means a person that assumes, as an independent contractor with the sponsor, one or more of the obligations of a sponsor, e.g., design of a protocol, selection or monitoring of investigations, evaluation of reports, and preparation of materials to be submitted to the Food and Drug Administration.

FDA means the Food and Drug Administration.

IND means an investigational new drug application. For purposes of this part, "IND" is synonymous with "Notice of Claimed Investigational Exemption for a New Drug."

Investigational new drug means a new drug or biological drug that is used in a clinical investigation. The term also includes a biological product that is used in vitro for diagnostic purposes. The terms "investigational drug" and "investigational new drug" are deemed to be synonymous for purposes of this part.

Investigator means an individual who actually conducts a clinical investigation (i.e., under whose immediate direction the drug is administered or dispensed to a subject). In the event an investigation is conducted by a team of individuals, the investigator is the responsible leader of the team. "Subinvestigator" includes any other individual member of that team.

Marketing application means an application for a new drug submitted under section 505(b) of the act or a biologics license application for a biological product submitted under the Public Health Service Act.

Sponsor means a person who takes responsibility for and initiates a clinical investigation. The sponsor may be an individual or pharmaceutical company, governmental agency, academic institution, private organization, or other organization. The sponsor does not actually conduct the investigation unless the sponsor is a sponsor-investigator. A person other than an individual that uses one or more of its own employees to conduct an investigation that it has initiated is a sponsor, not a sponsor-investigator, and the employees are investigators.

Sponsor-Investigator means an individual who both initiates and conducts an investigation, and under whose immediate direction the investigational drug is administered or dispensed. The term does not include any person other than an individual. The requirements applicable to a sponsor-investigator under this part include both those applicable to an investigator and a sponsor.

Subject means a human who participates in an investigation, either as a recipient of the investigational new drug or as a control. A subject may be a healthy human or a patient with a disease.

[52 FR 8831, Mar. 19, 1987, as amended at 64 FR 401, Jan. 5, 1999; 64 FR 56449, Oct. 20, 1999]

§ 312.6 Labeling of an investigational new drug.

(a) The immediate package of an investigational new drug intended for human use shall bear a label with the statement "Caution: New Drug-Limited by Federal (or United States) law to investigational use."

(b) The label or labeling of an investigational new drug shall not bear any statement that is false or misleading in any particular and shall not represent that the investigational new drug is safe or effective for the purposes for which it is being investigated.

§ 312.7 Promotion and charging for investigational drugs.

(a) *Promotion of an investigational new drug.* A sponsor or investigator, or any person acting on behalf of a sponsor or investigator, shall not represent in a promotional context that an investigational new drug is safe or effective for the purposes for which it is under investigation or otherwise promote the drug. This provision is not intended to restrict the full exchange of scientific information concerning the drug, including dissemination of scientific findings in scientific or lay media. Rather, its intent is to restrict promotional claims of safety or effectiveness of the drug for a use for which it is under investigation and to preclude commercialization of the drug before it is approved for commercial distribution.

(b) *Commercial distribution of an investigational new drug.* A sponsor or investigator shall not commercially distribute or test market an investigational new drug.

(c) *Prolonging an investigation.* A sponsor shall not unduly prolong an investigation after finding that the results of the investigation appear to establish sufficient data to support a marketing application.

(d) *Charging for and commercialization of investigational drugs-*

(1) *Clinical trials under an IND.* Charging for an investigational drug in a clinical trial under an IND is not permitted without the prior written approval of FDA. In requesting such approval, the sponsor shall provide a full written explanation of why charging is necessary in order for the sponsor to undertake or continue the clinical trial, e.g., why distribution of the drug to test subjects should not be considered part of the normal cost of doing business.

(2) *Treatment protocol or treatment IND.* A sponsor or investigator may charge for an investigational drug for a treatment use under a treatment protocol or treatment IND provided: (i) There is adequate enrollment in the ongoing clinical investigations under the authorized IND; (ii) charging does not constitute commercial marketing of a new drug for which a marketing application has not been approved; (iii) the drug is not being commercially promoted or advertised; and (iv) the sponsor of the drug is actively pursuing marketing approval with due diligence. FDA must be notified in writing in advance of commencing any such charges, in an information amendment submitted under § 312.31. Authorization for charging goes into effect automatically 30 days after receipt by FDA of the information amendment, unless the sponsor is notified to the contrary.

(3) *Noncommercialization of investigational drug.* Under this section, the sponsor may not commercialize an investigational drug by charging a price larger than that necessary to recover costs of manufacture, research, development, and handling of the investigational drug.

(4) *Withdrawal of authorization.* Authorization to charge for an investigational drug under this section may be withdrawn by FDA if the agency finds that the conditions underlying the authorization are no longer satisfied.

[52 FR 8831, Mar. 19, 1987, as amended at 52 FR 19476, May 22, 1987; 67 FR 9585, Mar. 4, 2002]

§ 312.10 Waivers.

(a) A sponsor may request FDA to waive applicable requirement under this part. A waiver request may be submitted either in an IND or in an information amendment to an IND. In an emergency, a request may be made by telephone or other rapid communication means. A waiver request is required to contain at least one of the following:

(1) An explanation why the sponsor's compliance with the requirement is unnecessary or cannot be achieved;

(2) A description of an alternative submission or course of action that satisfies the purpose of the requirement; or

(3) Other information justifying a waiver.

(b) FDA may grant a waiver if it finds that the sponsor's noncompliance would not pose a significant and unreasonable risk to human subjects of the investigation and that one of the following is met:

(1) The sponsor's compliance with the requirement is unnecessary for the agency to evaluate the application, or compliance cannot be achieved;

(2) The sponsor's proposed alternative satisfies the requirement; or

(3) The applicant's submission otherwise justifies a waiver.

[52 FR 8831, Mar. 19, 1987, as amended at 52 FR 23031, June 17, 1987; 67 FR 9585, Mar. 4, 2002]

Subpart B — Investigational New Drug Application (IND)

§ 312.20 Requirement for an IND.

(a) A sponsor shall submit an IND to FDA if the sponsor intends to conduct a clinical investigation with an investigational new drug that is subject to § 312.2(a).

(b) A sponsor shall not begin a clinical investigation subject to § 312.2(a) until the investigation is subject to an IND which is in effect in accordance with § 312.40.

(c) A sponsor shall submit a separate IND for any clinical investigation involving an exception from informed consent under § 50.24 of this chapter. Such a clinical investigation is not permitted to proceed without the prior written authorization from FDA. FDA shall provide a written determination 30 days after FDA receives the IND or earlier.

[52 FR 8831, Mar. 19, 1987, as amended at 61 FR 51529, Oct. 2, 1996; 62 FR 32479, June 16, 1997.]

§ 312.21 Phases of an investigation.

An IND may be submitted for one or more phases of an investigation. The clinical investigation of a previously untested drug is generally divided into three phases. Although in general the phases are conducted sequentially, they may overlap. These three phases of an investigation are a follows:

(a) *Phase 1.* (1) Phase 1 includes the initial introduction of an investigational new drug into humans. Phase 1 studies are typically closely monitored and may be conducted in patients or normal volunteer subjects. These studies are designed to determine the metabolism and pharmacologic actions of the drug in humans, the side effects associated with increasing doses, and, if possible, to gain early evidence on effectiveness. During Phase 1, sufficient information about the drug's pharmacokinetics and pharmacological effects should be obtained to permit the design of well-controlled, scientifically valid, Phase 2 studies. The total number of subjects and patients included in Phase 1 studies varies with the drug, but is generally in the range of 20 to 80.

(2) Phase 1 studies also include studies of drug metabolism, structure-activity relationships, and mechanism of action in humans, as well as studies in which investigational drugs are used as research tools to explore biological phenomena or disease processes.

(b) *Phase 2.* Phase 2 includes the controlled clinical studies conducted to evaluate the effectiveness of the drug for a particular indication or indications in patients with the disease or condition under study and to determine the common short-term side effects and risks associated with the drug. Phase 2 studies are typically well controlled, closely monitored, and conducted in a relatively small number of patients, usually involving no more than several hundred subjects.

(c) *Phase 3.* Phase 3 studies are expanded controlled and uncontrolled trials. They are performed after preliminary evidence suggesting effectiveness of the drug has been obtained, and are intended to gather the additional information about effectiveness and safety that is needed to evaluate the overall benefit-risk relationship of the drug and to provide an adequate basis for physician labeling. Phase 3 studies usually include from several hundred to several thousand subjects.

§ 312.22 General principles of the IND submission.

(a) FDA's primary objectives in reviewing an IND are, in all phases of the investigation, to assure the safety and rights of subjects, and, in Phase 2 and 3, to help assure that the quality of the scientific evaluation of drugs is adequate to permit an evaluation of the drug's effectiveness and safety. Therefore, although FDA's review of Phase 1 submissions will focus on assessing the safety of Phase 1 investigations, FDA's review of Phases 2 and 3 submissions will also include an assessment of the scientific quality of the clinical investigations and the likelihood that the investigations will yield data capable of meeting statutory standards for marketing approval.

(b) The amount of information on a particular drug that must be submitted in an IND to assure the accomplishment of the objectives described in paragraph (a) of this section depends upon such factors as the novelty of the drug, the extent to which it has been studied previously, the known or suspected risks, and the developmental phase of the drug.

(c) The central focus of the initial IND submission should be on the general investigational plan and the protocols for specific human studies. Subsequent amendments to the IND that contain new or revised protocols should build logically on previous submissions and should be supported by additional information, including the results of animal toxicology studies or other human studies as appropriate. Annual reports to the IND should serve as the focus for reporting the status of studies being conducted under the IND and should update the general investigational plan for the coming year.

(d) The IND format set forth in § 312.23 should be followed routinely by sponsors in the interest of fostering an efficient review of applications. Sponsors are expected to exercise considerable discretion, however, regarding the content of information submitted in each section, depending upon the kind of drug being studied and the nature of the available information. Section 312.23 outlines the information needed for a commercially sponsored IND for a new molecular entity. A sponsor-investigator who uses, as a research tool, an investigational new drug that is already subject to a manufacturer's IND or marketing application should follow the same general format, but ordinarily may, if authorized by the manufacturer, refer to the manufacturer's IND or marketing application in providing the technical information supporting the proposed clinical investigation. A sponsor-investigator who uses an investigational drug not subject to a manufacturer's IND or marketing application is ordinarily required to submit all technical information supporting the IND, unless such information may be referenced from the scientific literature.

§ 312.23 IND content and format.

(a) A sponsor who intends to conduct a clinical investigation subject to this part shall submit an "Investigational New Drug Application" (IND) including, in the following order:

(1) *Cover sheet* (Form FDA-1571). A cover sheet for the application containing the following:

(i) The name, address, and telephone number of the sponsor, the date of the application, and the name of the investigational new drug.

(ii) Identification of the phase or phases of the clinical investigation to be conducted.

(iii) A commitment not to begin clinical investigations until an IND covering the investigations is in effect.

(iv) A commitment that an Institutional Review Board (IRB) that complies with the requirements set forth in part 56 will be responsible for the initial and continuing review and approval of each of the studies in the proposed clinical investigation and that the investigator will report to the IRB proposed changes in the research activity in accordance with the requirements of part 56.

(v) A commitment to conduct the investigation in accordance with all other applicable regulatory requirements.

(vi) The name and title of the person responsible for monitoring the conduct and progress of the clinical investigations.

(vii) The name(s) and title(s) of the person(s) responsible under § 312.32 for review and evaluation of information relevant to the safety of the drug.

(viii) If a sponsor has transferred any obligations for the conduct of any clinical study to a contract research organization, a statement containing the name and address of the contract research organization, identification of the clinical study, and a listing of the obligations transferred. If all obligations governing the conduct of the study have been transferred, a general statement of this transfer-in lieu of a listing of the specific obligations transferred-may be submitted.

(ix) The signature of the sponsor or the sponsor's authorized representative. If the person signing the application does not reside or have a place of business within the United States, the IND is required to contain the name and address of, and be countersigned by, an attorney, agent, or other authorized official who resides or maintains a place of business within the United States.

(2) *A table of contents.*

(3) *Introductory statement and general investigational plan.* (i) A brief introductory statement giving the name of the drug and all active ingredients, the drug's pharmacological class, the structural formula of the drug (if known), the formulation of the dosage form(s) to be used, the route of administration, and the broad objectives and planned duration of the proposed clinical investigation(s).

(ii) A brief summary of previous human experience with the drug, with reference to other INDs if pertinent, and to investigational or marketing experience in other countries that may be relevant to the safety of the proposed clinical investigation(s).

(iii) If the drug has been withdrawn from investigation or marketing in any country for any reason related to safety or effectiveness, identification of the country(ies) where the drug was withdrawn and the reasons for the withdrawal.

(iv) A brief description of the overall plan for investigating the drug product for the following year. The plan should include the following: *(a)* The rationale for the drug or the research study; *(b)* the indication(s) to be studied; *(c)* the general approach to be followed in evaluating the drug; *(d)* the kinds of clinical trials to be conducted in the first year following the submission (if plans are not developed for the entire year, the sponsor should so indicate); *(e)* the estimated number of patients to be given the drug in those studies; and *(f)* any risks of particular severity or seriousness anticipated on the basis of the toxicological data in animals or prior studies in humans with the drug or related drugs.

(4) [Reserved]

(5) *Investigator's brochure*. If required under § 312.55, a copy of the investigator's brochure, containing the following information:

(i) A brief description of the drug substance and the formulation, including the structural formula, if known.

(ii) A summary of the pharmacological and toxicological effects of the drug in animals and, to the extent known, in humans.

(iii) A summary of the pharmacokinetics and biological disposition of the drug in animals and, if known, in humans.

(iv) A summary of information relating to safety and effectiveness in humans obtained from prior clinical studies. (Reprints of published articles on such studies may be appended when useful.)

(v) A description of possible risks and side effects to be anticipated on the basis of prior experience with the drug under investigation or with related drugs, and of precautions or special monitoring to be done as part of the investigational use of the drug.

(6) *Protocols*. (i) A protocol for each planned study. (Protocols for studies not submitted initially in the IND should be submitted in accordance with § 312.30(a).) In general, protocols for Phase 1 studies may be less detailed and more flexible than protocols for Phase 2 and 3 studies. Phase 1 protocols should be directed primarily at providing an outline of the investigation-an estimate of the number of patients to be involved, a description of safety exclusions, and a description of the dosing plan including duration, dose, or method to be used in determining dose-and should specify in detail only those elements of the study that are critical to safety, such as necessary monitoring of vital signs and blood chemistries. Modifications of the experimental design of Phase 1 studies that do not affect critical safety assessments are required to be reported to FDA only in the annual report.

(ii) In Phases 2 and 3, detailed protocols describing all aspects of the study should be submitted. A protocol for a Phase 2 or 3 investigation should be designed in such a way that, if the sponsor anticipates that some deviation from the study design may become necessary as the investigation progresses, alternatives or contingencies to provide for such deviation are built into the protocols at the outset. For example, a protocol for a controlled short-term study might include a plan for an early crossover of nonresponders to an alternative therapy.

(iii) A protocol is required to contain the following, with the specific elements and detail of the protocol reflecting the above distinctions depending on the phase of study:

(a) A statement of the objectives and purpose of the study.

(b) The name and address and a statement of the qualifications (curriculum vitae or other statement of qualifications) of each investigator, and the name of each subinvestigator (e.g., research fellow, resident) working under the supervision of the investigator; the name and address of the research facilities to be used; and the name and address of each reviewing Institutional Review Board.

(c) The criteria for patient selection and for exclusion of patients and an estimate of the number of patients to be studied.

(d) A description of the design of the study, including the kind of control group to be used, if any, and a description of methods to be used to minimize bias on the part of subjects, investigators, and analysts.

(e) The method for determining the dose(s) to be administered, the planned maximum dosage, and the duration of individual patient exposure to the drug.

(f) A description of the observations and measurements to be made to fulfill the objectives of the study.

(g) A description of clinical procedures, laboratory tests, or other measures to be taken to monitor the effects of the drug in human subjects and to minimize risk.

(7) *Chemistry, manufacturing, and control information.* (i) As appropriate for the particular investigations covered by the IND, a section describing the composition, manufacture, and control of the drug substance and the drug product. Although in each phase of the investigation sufficient information is required to be submitted to assure the proper identification, quality, purity, and strength of the investigational drug, the amount of information needed to make that assurance will vary with the phase of the investigation, the proposed duration of the investigation, the dosage form, and the amount of information otherwise available. FDA recognizes that modifications to the method of preparation of the new drug substance and dosage form and changes in the dosage form itself are likely as the investigation progresses. Therefore, the emphasis in an initial Phase 1 submission should generally be placed on the identification and control of the raw materials and the new drug substance. Final specifications for the drug substance and drug product are not expected until the end of the investigational process.

(ii) It should be emphasized that the amount of information to be submitted depends upon the scope of the proposed clinical investigation. For example, although stability data are required in all phases of the IND to demonstrate that the new drug substance and drug product are within acceptable chemical and physical limits for the planned duration of the proposed clinical investigation, if very short-term tests are proposed, the supporting stability data can be correspondingly limited.

(iii) As drug development proceeds and as the scale or production is changed from the pilot-scale production appropriate for the limited initial clinical investigations to the larger-scale production needed for expanded clinical trials, the sponsor should submit information amendments to supplement the initial information submitted on the chemistry, manufacturing, and control processes with information appropriate to the expanded scope of the investigation.

(iv) Reflecting the distinctions described in this paragraph (a)(7), and based on the phase(s) to be studied, the submission is required to contain the following:

(a) Drug substance. A description of the drug substance, including its physical, chemical, or biological characteristics; the name and address of its manufacturer; the general method of preparation of the drug substance; the acceptable limits and analytical methods used to assure the identity, strength, quality, and purity of the drug substance; and information sufficient to support stability of the drug substance during the toxicological studies and the planned clinical studies. Reference to the current edition of the United States Pharmacopeia-National Formulary may satisfy relevant requirements in this paragraph.

(b) Drug product. A list of all components, which may include reasonable alternatives for inactive compounds, used in the manufacture of the investigational drug product, including both those components intended to appear in the drug product and those which may not appear but which are used in the manufacturing process, and, where applicable, the quantitative composition of the investigational drug product, including any reasonable variations that may be expected during the investigational stage; the name and address of the drug product manufacturer; a brief general description of the manufacturing and packaging procedure as appropriate for the product; the acceptable limits and analytical methods used to assure the

identity, strength, quality, and purity of the drug product; and information sufficient to assure the product's stability during the planned clinical studies. Reference to the current edition of the United States Pharmacopeia-National Formulary may satisfy certain requirements in this paragraph.

(c) A brief general description of the composition, manufacture, and control of any placebo used in a controlled clinical trial.

(d) Labeling. A copy of all labels and labeling to be provided to each investigator.

(e) Environmental analysis requirements. A claim for categorical exclusion under § 25.30 or 25.31 or an environmental assessment under § 25.40.

(8) *Pharmacology and toxicology information.* Adequate information about pharmacological and toxicological studies of the drug involving laboratory animals or in vitro, on the basis of which the sponsor has concluded that it is reasonably safe to conduct the proposed clinical investigations. The kind, duration, and scope of animal and other tests required varies with the duration and nature of the proposed clinical investigations. Guidance documents are available from FDA that describe ways in which these requirements may be met. Such information is required to include the identification and qualifications of the individuals who evaluated the results of such studies and concluded that it is reasonably safe to begin the proposed investigations and a statement of where the investigations were conducted and where the records are available for inspection. As drug development proceeds, the sponsor is required to submit informational amendments, as appropriate, with additional information pertinent to safety.

(i) *Pharmacology and drug disposition.* A section describing the pharmacological effects and mechanism(s) of action of the drug in animals, and information on the absorption, distribution, metabolism, and excretion of the drug, if known.

(ii) *Toxicology.*

(a) An integrated summary of the toxicological effects of the drug in animals and in vitro. Depending on the nature of the drug and the phase of the investigation, the description is to include the results of acute, subacute, and chronic toxicity tests; tests of the drug's effects on reproduction and the developing fetus; any special toxicity test related to the drug's particular mode of administration or conditions of use (e.g., inhalation, dermal, or ocular toxicology); and any in vitro studies intended to evaluate drug toxicity.

(b) For each toxicology study that is intended primarily to support the safety of the proposed clinical investigation, a full tabulation of data suitable for detailed review.

(iii) For each nonclinical laboratory study subject to the good laboratory practice regulations under part 58, a statement that the study was conducted in compliance with the good laboratory practice regulations in part 58, or, if the study was not conducted in compliance with those regulations, a brief statement of the reason for the noncompliance.

(9) *Previous human experience with the investigational drug.* A summary of previous human experience known to the applicant, if any, with the investigational drug. The information is required to include the following:

(i) If the investigational drug has been investigated or marketed previously, either in the United States or other countries, detailed information about such experience that is relevant to the safety of the proposed investigation or to the investigation's rationale. If the drug has been the subject of controlled trials, detailed information on such trials that is relevant to an assessment of the drug's effectiveness for the proposed investigational use(s) should also be provided. Any published material that is relevant to the safety of the proposed investigation or to an assessment of the drug's effectiveness for its proposed investigational use should be provided in full. Published material that is less directly relevant may be supplied by a bibliography.

(ii) If the drug is a combination of drugs previously investigated or marketed, the information required under paragraph (a)(9)(i) of this section should be provided for each active drug component. However, if any component in such combination is subject to an approved marketing application or is otherwise lawfully marketed in the United States, the sponsor is not required to submit published material concerning that active drug component unless such material relates directly to the proposed investigational use (including publications relevant to component-component interaction).

(iii) If the drug has been marketed outside the United States, a list of the countries in which the drug has been marketed and a list of the countries in which the drug has been withdrawn from marketing for reasons potentially related to safety or effectiveness.

(10) *Additional information.* In certain applications, as described below, information on special topics may be needed. Such information shall be submitted in this section as follows:

(i) *Drug dependence and abuse potential.* If the drug is a psychotropic substance or otherwise has abuse potential, a section describing relevant clinical studies and experience and studies in test animals.

(ii) *Radioactive drugs.* If the drug is a radioactive drug, sufficient data from animal or human studies to allow a reasonable calculation of radiation-absorbed dose to the whole body and critical organs upon administration to a human subject. Phase 1 studies of radioactive drugs must include studies which will obtain sufficient data for dosimetry calculations.

(iii) *Pediatric studies.* Plans for assessing pediatric safety and effectiveness.

(iv) *Other information.* A brief statement of any other information that would aid evaluation of the proposed clinical investigations with respect to their safety or their design and potential as controlled clinical trials to support marketing of the drug.

(11) *Relevant information.* If requested by FDA, any other relevant information needed for review of the application.

(b) *Information previously submitted.* The sponsor ordinarily is not required to resubmit information previously submitted, but may incorporate the information by reference. A reference to information submitted previously must identify the file by name, reference number, volume, and page number where the information can be found. A reference to information submitted to the agency by a person other than the sponsor is required to contain a written statement that authorizes the reference and that is signed by the person who submitted the information.

(c) *Material in a foreign language.* The sponsor shall submit an accurate and complete English translation of each part of the IND that is not in English. The sponsor shall also submit a copy of each original literature publication for which an English translation is submitted.

(d) *Number of copies.* The sponsor shall submit an original and two copies of all submissions to the IND file, including the original submission and all amendments and reports.

(e) *Numbering of IND submissions.* Each submission relating to an IND is required to be numbered serially using a single, three-digit serial number. The initial IND is required to be numbered 000; each subsequent submission (e.g., amendment, report, or correspondence) is required to be numbered chronologically in sequence.

(f) *Identification of exception from informed consent.* If the investigation involves an exception from informed consent under § 50.24 of this chapter, the sponsor shall prominently identify on the cover sheet that the investigation is subject to the requirements in § 50.24 of this chapter.

[52 FR 8831, Mar. 19, 1987, as amended at 52 FR 23031, June 17, 1987; 53 FR 1918, Jan. 25, 1988; 61 FR 51529, Oct. 2, 1996; 62 FR 40599, July 29, 1997; 63 FR 66669, Dec. 2, 1998; 65 FR 56479, Sept. 19, 2000; 67 FR 9585, Mar. 4, 2002]

§ 312.30 Protocol amendments.

Once an IND is in effect, a sponsor shall amend it as needed to ensure that the clinical investigations are conducted according to protocols included in the application. This section sets forth the provisions under which new protocols may be submitted and changes in previously submitted protocols may be made. Whenever a sponsor intends to conduct a clinical investigation with an exception from informed consent for emergency research as set forth in § 50.24 of this chapter, the sponsor shall submit a separate IND for such investigation.

(a) *New protocol.* Whenever a sponsor intends to conduct a study that is not covered by a protocol already contained in the IND, the sponsor shall submit to FDA a protocol amendment containing the protocol for the study. Such study may begin provided two conditions are met: (1) The sponsor has submitted the protocol to FDA for its review; and (2) the protocol has been approved by the Institutional Review Board (IRB) with responsibility for review and approval of the study in accordance with the requirements of part 56. The sponsor may comply with these two conditions in either order.

(b) *Changes in a protocol.* (1) A sponsor shall submit a protocol amendment describing any change in a Phase 1 protocol that significantly affects the safety of subjects or any change in a Phase 2 or 3 protocol that significantly affects the safety of subjects, the scope of the investigation, or the scientific quality of the study. Examples of changes requiring an amendment under this paragraph include:

(i) Any increase in drug dosage or duration of exposure of individual subjects to the drug beyond that in the current protocol, or any significant increase in the number of subjects under study.

(ii) Any significant change in the design of a protocol (such as the addition or dropping of a control group).

(iii) The addition of a new test or procedure that is intended to improve monitoring for, or reduce the risk of, a side effect or adverse event; or the dropping of a test intended to monitor safety.

(2)(i) A protocol change under paragraph (b)(1) of this section may be made provided two conditions are met:

(*a*) The sponsor has submitted the change to FDA for its review; and

(*b*) The change has been approved by the IRB with responsibility for review and approval of the study. The sponsor may comply with these two conditions in either order.

(ii) Notwithstanding paragraph (b)(2)(i) of this section, a protocol change intended to eliminate an apparent immediate hazard to subjects may be implemented immediately provided FDA is subsequently notified by protocol amendment and the reviewing IRB is notified in accordance with § 56.104(c).

(c) *New investigator.* A sponsor shall submit a protocol amendment when a new investigator is added to carry out a previously submitted protocol, except that a protocol amendment is not required when a licensed practitioner is added in the case of a treatment protocol under § 312.34. Once the investigator is added to the study, the investigational drug may be shipped to the investigator and the investigator may begin participating in the study. The sponsor shall notify FDA of the new investigator within 30 days of the investigator being added.

(d) *Content and format.* A protocol amendment is required to be prominently identified as such (i.e., "Protocol Amendment: New Protocol", "Protocol Amendment: Change in Protocol", or "Protocol Amendment: New Investigator"), and to contain the following:

(1)(i) In the case of a new protocol, a copy of the new protocol and a brief description of the most clinically significant differences between it and previous protocols.

(ii) In the case of a change in protocol, a brief description of the change and reference (date and number) to the submission that contained the protocol.

(iii) In the case of a new investigator, the investigator's name, the qualifications to conduct the investigation, reference to the previously submitted protocol, and all additional information about the investigator's study as is required under § 312.23(a)(6)(iii)*(b)*.

(2) Reference, if necessary, to specific technical information in the IND or in a concurrently submitted information amendment to the IND that the sponsor relies on to support any clinically significant change in the new or amended protocol. If the reference is made to supporting information already in the IND, the sponsor shall identify by name, reference number, volume, and page number the location of the information.

(3) If the sponsor desires FDA to comment on the submission, a request for such comment and the specific questions FDA's response should address.

(e) *When submitted.* A sponsor shall submit a protocol amendment for a new protocol or a change in protocol before its implementation. Protocol amendments to add a new investigator or to provide additional information about investigators may be grouped and submitted at 30-day intervals. When several submissions of new protocols or protocol changes are anticipated during a short period, the sponsor is encouraged, to the extent feasible, to include these all in a single submission.

[52 FR 8831, Mar. 19, 1987, as amended at 52 FR 23031, June 17, 1987; 53 FR 1918, Jan. 25, 1988; 61 FR 51530, Oct. 2, 1996; 67 FR 9585, Mar. 4, 2002]

§ 312.31 Information amendments.

(a) *Requirement for information amendment.* A sponsor shall report in an information amendment essential information on the IND that is not within the scope of a protocol amendment, IND safety reports, or annual report. Examples of information requiring an information amendment include:

(1) New toxicology, chemistry, or other technical information; or

(2) A report regarding the discontinuance of a clinical investigation.

(b) *Content and format of an information amendment.* An information amendment is required to bear prominent identification of its contents (e.g., "Information Amendment: Chemistry, Manufacturing, and Control", "Information Amendment: Pharmacology-Toxicology", "Information Amendment: Clinical"), and to contain the following:

(1) A statement of the nature and purpose of the amendment.

(2) An organized submission of the data in a format appropriate for scientific review.

(3) If the sponsor desires FDA to comment on an information amendment, a request for such comment.

(c) *When submitted.* Information amendments to the IND should be submitted as necessary but, to the extent feasible, not more than every 30 days.

[52 FR 8831, Mar. 19, 1987, as amended at 52 FR 23031, June 17, 1987; 53 FR 1918, Jan. 25, 1988; 67 FR 9585, Mar. 4, 2002]

§ 312.32 IND safety reports.

(a) *Definitions.* The following definitions of terms apply to this section:

Associated with the use of the drug. There is a reasonable possibility that the experience may have been caused by the drug.

Disability. A substantial disruption of a person's ability to conduct normal life functions.

Life-threatening adverse drug experience. Any adverse drug experience that places the patient or subject, in the view of the investigator, at immediate risk of death from the reaction as it occurred, i.e., it does not include a reaction that, had it occurred in a more severe form, might have caused death.

Serious adverse drug experience. Any adverse drug experience occurring at any dose that results in any of the following outcomes: Death, a life-threatening adverse drug experience, inpatient hospitalization or prolongation of existing hospitalization, a persistent or significant disability/incapacity, or a congenital anomaly/birth defect. Important medical events that may not result in death, be life-threatening, or require hospitalization may be considered a serious adverse drug experience when, based upon appropriate medical judgment, they may jeopardize the patient or subject and may require medical or surgical intervention to prevent one of the outcomes listed in this definition. Examples of such medical events include allergic bronchospasm requiring intensive treatment in an emergency room or at home, blood dyscrasias or convulsions that do not result in inpatient hospitalization, or the development of drug dependency or drug abuse.

Unexpected adverse drug experience: Any adverse drug experience, the specificity or severity of which is not consistent with the current investigator brochure; or, if an investigator brochure is not required or available, the specificity or severity of which is not consistent with the risk information described in the general investigational plan or elsewhere in the current application, as amended. For example, under this definition, hepatic necrosis would be unexpected (by virtue of greater severity) if the investigator brochure only referred to elevated hepatic enzymes or hepatitis. Similarly, cerebral thromboembolism and cerebral vasculitis would be unexpected (by virtue of greater specificity) if the investigator brochure only listed cerebral vascular accidents. "Unexpected," as used in this definition, refers to an adverse drug experience that has not been previously observed (e.g., included in the investigator brochure) rather than from the perspective of such experience not being anticipated from the pharmacological properties of the pharmaceutical product.

(b) *Review of safety information.* The sponsor shall promptly review all information relevant to the safety of the drug obtained or otherwise received by the sponsor from any source, foreign or domestic, including information derived from any clinical or epidemiological investigations, animal investigations, commercial marketing experience, reports in the scientific literature, and unpublished scientific papers as well as reports from foreign regulatory authorities that have not already been previously reported to the agency by the sponsor.

(c) *IND safety reports.* (1) *Written reports* – (i) The sponsor shall notify FDA and all participating investigators in a written IND safety report of:

(A) Any adverse experience associated with use of the drug that is both serious and unexpected; or

(B) Any finding from tests in laboratory animals that suggests a significant risk for human subjects including reports of mutagenicity, teratogenicity, or carcinogenicity. Each notification shall be made as soon as possible and in no event later than 15 calendar days after the sponsor's initial receipt of the information. Each written notification may be submitted on FDA Form 3500A or in a narrative format (foreign events may be submitted either on an FDA Form 3500A or, if preferred, on a CIOMS I form; reports from animal or epidemiological studies shall be submitted in a narrative format) and shall bear prominent identification of its contents, i.e., "IND Safety Report." Each written notification to FDA shall be transmitted to the FDA new drug review division in the Center for Drug Evaluation and Research or the product review division in the Center for Biologics Evaluation and Research that has responsibility for review of the IND. If FDA determines that additional data are needed, the agency may require further data to be submitted.

(ii) In each written IND safety report, the sponsor shall identify all safety reports previously filed with the IND concerning a similar adverse experience, and shall analyze the significance of the adverse experience in light of the previous, similar reports.

(2) *Telephone and facsimile transmission safety reports.* The sponsor shall also notify FDA by telephone or by facsimile transmission of any unexpected fatal or life-threatening experience associated with the use of the drug as soon as possible but in no event later than 7 calendar days

after the sponsor's initial receipt of the information. Each telephone call or facsimile transmission to FDA shall be transmitted to the FDA new drug review division in the Center for Drug Evaluation and Research or the product review division in the Center for Biologics Evaluation and Research that has responsibility for review of the IND.

(3) *Reporting format or frequency.* FDA may request a sponsor to submit IND safety reports in a format or at a frequency different than that required under this paragraph. The sponsor may also propose and adopt a different reporting format or frequency if the change is agreed to in advance by the director of the new drug review division in the Center for Drug Evaluation and Research or the director of the product review division in the Center for Biologics Evaluation and Research which is responsible for review of the IND.

(4) A sponsor of a clinical study of a marketed drug is not required to make a safety report for any adverse experience associated with use of the drug that is not from the clinical study itself.

(d) *Followup.* (1) The sponsor shall promptly investigate all safety information received by it.

(2) Followup information to a safety report shall be submitted as soon as the relevant information is available.

(3) If the results of a sponsor's investigation show that an adverse drug experience not initially determined to be reportable under paragraph (c) of this section is so reportable, the sponsor shall report such experience in a written safety report as soon as possible, but in no event later than 15 calendar days after the determination is made.

(4) Results of a sponsor's investigation of other safety information shall be submitted, as appropriate, in an information amendment or annual report.

(e) *Disclaimer.* A safety report or other information submitted by a sponsor under this part (and any release by FDA of that report or information) does not necessarily reflect a conclusion by the sponsor or FDA that the report or information constitutes an admission that the drug caused or contributed to an adverse experience. A sponsor need not admit, and may deny, that the report or information submitted by the sponsor constitutes an admission that the drug caused or contributed to an adverse experience.

[52 FR 8831, Mar. 19, 1987, as amended at 52 FR 23031, June 17, 1987; 55 FR 11579, Mar. 29, 1990; 62 FR 52250, Oct. 7, 1997; 67 FR 9585, Mar. 4, 2002]

§ 312.33 Annual reports.

A sponsor shall within 60 days of the anniversary date that the IND went into effect, submit a brief report of the progress of the investigation that includes:

(a) *Individual study information.* A brief summary of the status of each study in progress and each study completed during the previous year. The summary is required to include the following information for each study:

(1) The title of the study (with any appropriate study identifiers such as protocol number), its purpose, a brief statement identifying the patient population, and a statement as to whether the study is completed.

(2) The total number of subjects initially planned for inclusion in the study, the number entered into the study to date, tabulated by age group, gender, and race; the number whose participation in the study was completed as planned; and the number who dropped out of the study for any reason.

(3) If the study has been completed, or if interim results are known, a brief description of any available study results.

(b) *Summary information.* Information obtained during the previous year's clinical and nonclinical investigations, including:

(1) A narrative or tabular summary showing the most frequent and most serious adverse experiences by body system.

(2) A summary of all IND safety reports submitted during the past year.

(3) A list of subjects who died during participation in the investigation, with the cause of death for each subject.

(4) A list of subjects who dropped out during the course of the investigation in association with any adverse experience, whether or not thought to be drug related.

(5) A brief description of what, if anything, was obtained that is pertinent to an understanding of the drug's actions, including, for example, information about dose response, information from controlled trials, and information about bioavailability.

(6) A list of the preclinical studies (including animal studies) completed or in progress during the past year and a summary of the major preclinical findings.

(7) A summary of any significant manufacturing or microbiological changes made during the past year.

(c) A description of the general investigational plan for the coming year to replace that submitted 1 year earlier. The general investigational plan shall contain the information required under § 312.23(a)(3)(iv).

(d) If the investigator brochure has been revised, a description of the revision and a copy of the new brochure.

(e) A description of any significant Phase 1 protocol modifications made during the previous year and not previously reported to the IND in a protocol amendment.

(f) A brief summary of significant foreign marketing developments with the drug during the past year, such as approval of marketing in any country or withdrawal or suspension from marketing in any country.

(g) If desired by the sponsor, a log of any outstanding business with respect to the IND for which the sponsor requests or expects a reply, comment, or meeting.

[52 FR 8831, Mar. 19, 1987, as amended at 52 FR 23031, June 17, 1987; 63 FR 6862, Feb. 11, 1998; 67 FR 9585, Mar. 4, 2002]

§ 312.34 Treatment use of an investigational new drug.

(a) *General*. A drug that is not approved for marketing may be under clinical investigation for a serious or immediately life-threatening disease condition in patients for whom no comparable or satisfactory alternative drug or other therapy is available. During the clinical investigation of the drug, it may be appropriate to use the drug in the treatment of patients not in the clinical trials, in accordance with a treatment protocol or treatment IND. The purpose of this section is to facilitate the availability of promising new drugs to desperately ill patients as early in the drug development process as possible, before general marketing begins, and to obtain additional data on the drug's safety and effectiveness. In the case of a serious disease, a drug ordinarily may be made available for treatment use under this section during Phase 3 investigations or after all clinical trials have been completed; however, in appropriate circumstances, a drug may be made available for treatment use during Phase 2. In the case of an immediately life-threatening disease, a drug may be made available for treatment use under this section earlier than Phase 3, but ordinarily not earlier than Phase 2. For purposes of this section, the "treatment use" of a drug includes the use of a drug for diagnostic purposes. If a protocol for an investigational drug meets the criteria of this section, the protocol is to be submitted as a treatment protocol under the provisions of this section.

(b) *Criteria*. (1) FDA shall permit an investigational drug to be used for a treatment use under a treatment protocol or treatment IND if:

(i) The drug is intended to treat a serious or immediately life-threatening disease;

(ii) There is no comparable or satisfactory alternative drug or other therapy available to treat that stage of the disease in the intended patient population;

(iii) The drug is under investigation in a controlled clinical trial under an IND in effect for the trial, or all clinical trials have been completed; and

(iv) The sponsor of the controlled clinical trial is actively pursuing marketing approval of the investigational drug with due diligence.

(2) *Serious disease.* For a drug intended to treat a serious disease, the Commissioner may deny a request for treatment use under a treatment protocol or treatment IND if there is insufficient evidence of safety and effectiveness to support such use.

(3) *Immediately life-threatening disease.* (i) For a drug intended to treat an immediately life-threatening disease, the Commissioner may deny a request for treatment use of an investigational drug under a treatment protocol or treatment IND if the available scientific evidence, taken as a whole, fails to provide a reasonable basis for concluding that the drug:

(A) May be effective for its intended use in its intended patient population; or

(B) Would not expose the patients to whom the drug is to be administered to an unreasonable and significant additional risk of illness or injury.

(ii) For the purpose of this section, an "immediately life-threatening" disease means a stage of a disease in which there is a reasonable likelihood that death will occur within a matter of months or in which premature death is likely without early treatment.

(c) *Safeguards.* Treatment use of an investigational drug is conditioned on the sponsor and investigators complying with the safeguards of the IND process, including the regulations governing informed consent (21 CFR part 50) and institutional review boards (21 CFR part 56) and the applicable provisions of part 312, including distribution of the drug through qualified experts, maintenance of adequate manufacturing facilities, and submission of IND safety reports.

(d) *Clinical hold.* FDA may place on clinical hold a proposed or ongoing treatment protocol or treatment IND in accordance with § 312.42.

[52 FR 19476, May 22, 1987, as amended at 57 FR 13248, Apr. 15, 1992]

§ 312.35 Submissions for treatment use.

(a) *Treatment protocol submitted by IND sponsor.* Any sponsor of a clinical investigation of a drug who intends to sponsor a treatment use for the drug shall submit to FDA a treatment protocol under § 312.34 if the sponsor believes the criteria of § 312.34 are satisfied. If a protocol is not submitted under § 312.34, but FDA believes that the protocol should have been submitted under this section, FDA may deem the protocol to be submitted under § 312.34. A treatment use under a treatment protocol may begin 30 days after FDA receives the protocol or on earlier notification by FDA that the treatment use described in the protocol may begin.

(1) A treatment protocol is required to contain the following:

(i) The intended use of the drug.

(ii) An explanation of the rationale for use of the drug, including, as appropriate, either a list of what available regimens ordinarily should be tried before using the investigational drug or an explanation of why the use of the investigational drug is preferable to the use of available marketed treatments.

(iii) A brief description of the criteria for patient selection.

(iv) The method of administration of the drug and the dosages.

(v) A description of clinical procedures, laboratory tests, or other measures to monitor the effects of the drug and to minimize risk.

(2) A treatment protocol is to be supported by the following:

(i) Informational brochure for supplying to each treating physician.

(ii) The technical information that is relevant to safety and effectiveness of the drug for the intended treatment purpose. Information contained in the sponsor's IND may be incorporated by reference.

(iii) A commitment by the sponsor to assure compliance of all participating investigators with the informed consent requirements of 21 CFR part 50.

(3) A licensed practitioner who receives an investigational drug for treatment use under a treatment protocol is an "investigator" under the protocol and is responsible for meeting all applicable investigator responsibilities under this part and 21 CFR parts 50 and 56.

(b) *Treatment IND submitted by licensed practitioner.* (1) If a licensed medical practitioner wants to obtain an investigational drug subject to a controlled clinical trial for a treatment use, the practitioner should first attempt to obtain the drug from the sponsor of the controlled trial under a treatment protocol. If the sponsor of the controlled clinical investigation of the drug will not establish a treatment protocol for the drug under paragraph (a) of this section, the licensed medical practitioner may seek to obtain the drug from the sponsor and submit a treatment IND to FDA requesting authorization to use the investigational drug for treatment use. A treatment use under a treatment IND may begin 30 days after FDA receives the IND or on earlier notification by FDA that the treatment use under the IND may begin. A treatment IND is required to contain the following:

(i) A cover sheet (Form FDA 1571) meeting § 312.23(g)(1).

(ii) Information (when not provided by the sponsor) on the drug's chemistry, manufacturing, and controls, and prior clinical and nonclinical experience with the drug submitted in accordance with § 312.23. A sponsor of a clinical investigation subject to an IND who supplies an investigational drug to a licensed medical practitioner for purposes of a separate treatment clinical investigation shall be deemed to authorize the incorporation-by-reference of the technical information contained in the sponsor's IND into the medical practitioner's treatment IND.

(iii) A statement of the steps taken by the practitioner to obtain the drug under a treatment protocol from the drug sponsor.

(iv) A treatment protocol containing the same information listed in paragraph (a)(1) of this section.

(v) A statement of the practitioner's qualifications to use the investigational drug for the intended treatment use.

(vi) The practitioner's statement of familiarity with information on the drug's safety and effectiveness derived from previous clinical and nonclinical experience with the drug.

(vii) Agreement to report to FDA safety information in accordance with § 312.32.

(2) A licensed practitioner who submits a treatment IND under this section is the sponsor-investigator for such IND and is responsible for meeting all applicable sponsor and investigator responsibilities under this part and 21 CFR parts 50 and 56.

[52 FR 19477, May 22, 1987, as amended at 57 FR 13249, Apr. 15, 1992; 67 FR 9585, Mar. 4, 2002]

§ 312.36 Emergency use of an investigational drug (IND).

Need for an investigational drug may arise in an emergency situation that does not allow time for submission of an IND in accordance with § 312.23 or § 312.34. In such a case, FDA may authorize shipment of the drug for a specified use in advance of submission of an IND. A request for such authorization may be transmitted to FDA by telephone or other rapid communication means. For investigational biological drugs regulated by the Center for Biologics Evaluation and Research, the request should be directed to the Office of Communication, Training and

Manufacturers Assistance (HFM-40), Center for Biologics Evaluation and Research, 301-827-2000. For all other investigational drugs, the request for authorization should be directed to the Division of Drug Information (HFD-240), Center for Drug Evaluation and Research, 301-827-4570. After normal working hours, eastern standard time, the request should be directed to the FDA Office of Emergency Operations (HFA-615), 301-443-1240. Except in extraordinary circumstances, such authorization will be conditioned on the sponsor making an appropriate IND submission as soon as practicable after receiving the authorization.

[52 FR 8831, Mar. 19, 1987, as amended at 52 FR 23031, June 17, 1987; 55 FR 11579, Mar. 29, 1990; 67 FR 9585, Mar. 4, 2002; 69 FR 17927, Apr. 6, 2004]

§ 312.38 Withdrawal of an IND.

(a) At any time a sponsor may withdraw an effective IND without prejudice.

(b) If an IND is withdrawn, FDA shall be so notified, all clinical investigations conducted under the IND shall be ended, all current investigators notified, and all stocks of the drug returned to the sponsor or otherwise disposed of at the request of the sponsor in accordance with § 312.59.

(c) If an IND is withdrawn because of a safety reason, the sponsor shall promptly so inform FDA, all participating investigators, and all reviewing Institutional Review Boards, together with the reasons for such withdrawal.

[52 FR 8831, Mar. 19, 1987, as amended at 52 FR 23031, June 17, 1987; 67 FR 9586, Mar. 4, 2002]

Subpart C — Administrative Actions

§ 312.40 General requirements for use of an investigational new drug in a clinical investigation.

(a) An investigational new drug may be used in a clinical investigation if the following conditions are met:

(1) The sponsor of the investigation submits an IND for the drug to FDA; the IND is in effect under paragraph (b) of this section; and the sponsor complies with all applicable requirements in this part and parts 50 and 56 with respect to the conduct of the clinical investigations; and

(2) Each participating investigator conducts his or her investigation in compliance with the requirements of this part and parts 50 and 56.

(b) An IND goes into effect:

(1) Thirty days after FDA receives the IND, unless FDA notifies the sponsor that the investigations described in the IND are subject to a clinical hold under § 312.42; or

(2) On earlier notification by FDA that the clinical investigations in the IND may begin. FDA will notify the sponsor in writing of the date it receives the IND.

(c) A sponsor may ship an investigational new drug to investigators named in the IND:

(1) Thirty days after FDA receives the IND; or

(2) On earlier FDA authorization to ship the drug.

(d) An investigator may not administer an investigational new drug to human subjects until the IND goes into effect under paragraph (b) of this section.

§ 312.41 Comment and advice on an IND.

(a) FDA may at any time during the course of the investigation communicate with the sponsor orally or in writing about deficiencies in the IND or about FDA's need for more data or information.

(b) On the sponsor's request, FDA will provide advice on specific matters relating to an IND. Examples of such advice may include advice on the adequacy of technical data to support an investigational plan, on the design of a clinical trial, and on whether proposed investigations are likely to produce the data and information that is needed to meet requirements for a marketing application.

(c) Unless the communication is accompanied by a clinical hold order under § 312.42, FDA communications with a sponsor under this section are solely advisory and do not require any modification in the planned or ongoing clinical investigations or response to the agency.

[52 FR 8831, Mar. 19, 1987, as amended at 52 FR 23031, June 17, 1987; 67 FR 9586, Mar. 4, 2002]

§ 312.42 Clinical holds and requests for modification.

(a) *General.* A clinical hold is an order issued by FDA to the sponsor to delay a proposed clinical investigation or to suspend an ongoing investigation. The clinical hold order may apply to one or more of the investigations covered by an IND. When a proposed study is placed on clinical hold, subjects may not be given the investigational drug. When an ongoing study is placed on clinical hold, no new subjects may be recruited to the study and placed on the investigational drug; patients already in the study should be taken off therapy involving the investigational drug unless specifically permitted by FDA in the interest of patient safety.

(b) *Grounds for imposition of clinical hold*–(1) *Clinical hold of a Phase 1 study under an IND.* FDA may place a proposed or ongoing Phase 1 investigation on clinical hold if it finds that:

(i) Human subjects are or would be exposed to an unreasonable and significant risk of illness or injury;

(ii) The clinical investigators named in the IND are not qualified by reason of their scientific training and experience to conduct the investigation described in the IND;

(iii) The investigator brochure is misleading, erroneous, or materially incomplete; or

(iv) The IND does not contain sufficient information required under § 312.23 to assess the risks to subjects of the proposed studies.

(v) The IND is for the study of an investigational drug intended to treat a life-threatening disease or condition that affects both genders, and men or women with reproductive potential who have the disease or condition being studied are excluded from eligibility because of a risk or potential risk from use of the investigational drug of reproductive toxicity (i.e., affecting reproductive organs) or developmental toxicity (i.e., affecting potential offspring). The phrase "women with reproductive potential" does not include pregnant women. For purposes of this paragraph, "life-threatening illnesses or diseases" are defined as "diseases or conditions where the likelihood of death is high unless the course of the disease is interrupted." The clinical hold would not apply under this paragraph to clinical studies conducted:

(A) Under special circumstances, such as studies pertinent only to one gender (e.g., studies evaluating the excretion of a drug in semen or the effects on menstrual function);

(B) Only in men or women, as long as a study that does not exclude members of the other gender with reproductive potential is being conducted concurrently, has been conducted, or will take place within a reasonable time agreed upon by the agency; or

(C) Only in subjects who do not suffer from the disease or condition for which the drug is being studied.

(2) *Clinical hold of a Phase 2 or 3 study under an IND.* FDA may place a proposed or ongoing Phase 2 or 3 investigation on clinical hold if it finds that:

(i) Any of the conditions in paragraph (b)(1)(i) through (b)(1)(v) of this section apply; or

(ii) The plan or protocol for the investigation is clearly deficient in design to meet its stated objectives.

(3) Clinical hold of a treatment IND or treatment protocol.

(i) *Proposed use.* FDA may place a proposed treatment IND or treatment protocol on clinical hold if it is determined that:

(A) The pertinent criteria in § 312.34(b) for permitting the treatment use to begin are not satisfied; or

(B) The treatment protocol or treatment IND does not contain the information required under § 312.35 (a) or (b) to make the specified determination under § 312.34(b).

(ii) *Ongoing use.* FDA may place an ongoing treatment protocol or treatment IND on clinical hold if it is determined that:

(A) There becomes available a comparable or satisfactory alternative drug or other therapy to treat that stage of the disease in the intended patient population for which the investigational drug is being used;

(B) The investigational drug is not under investigation in a controlled clinical trial under an IND in effect for the trial and not all controlled clinical trials necessary to support a marketing application have been completed, or a clinical study under the IND has been placed on clinical hold:

(C) The sponsor of the controlled clinical trial is not pursuing marketing approval with due diligence;

(D) If the treatment IND or treatment protocol is intended for a serious disease, there is insufficient evidence of safety and effectiveness to support such use; or

(E) If the treatment protocol or treatment IND was based on an immediately life-threatening disease, the available scientific evidence, taken as a whole, fails to provide a reasonable basis for concluding that the drug:

(1) May be effective for its intended use in its intended population; or

(2) Would not expose the patients to whom the drug is to be administered to an unreasonable and significant additional risk of illness or injury.

(iii) FDA may place a proposed or ongoing treatment IND or treatment protocol on clinical hold if it finds that any of the conditions in paragraph (b)(4)(i) through (b)(4)(viii) of this section apply.

(4) *Clinical hold of any study that is not designed to be adequate and well-controlled.* FDA may place a proposed or ongoing investigation that is not designed to be adequate and well-controlled on clinical hold if it finds that:

(i) Any of the conditions in paragraph (b)(1) or (b)(2) of this section apply; or

(ii) There is reasonable evidence the investigation that is not designed to be adequate and well-controlled is impeding enrollment in, or otherwise interfering with the conduct or completion of, a study that is designed to be an adequate and well-controlled investigation of the same or another investigational drug; or

(iii) Insufficient quantities of the investigational drug exist to adequately conduct both the investigation that is not designed to be adequate and well-controlled and the investigations that are designed to be adequate and well-controlled; or

(iv) The drug has been studied in one or more adequate and well-controlled investigations that strongly suggest lack of effectiveness; or

(v) Another drug under investigation or approved for the same indication and available to the same patient population has demonstrated a better potential benefit/risk balance; or

(vi) The drug has received marketing approval for the same indication in the same patient population; or

(vii) The sponsor of the study that is designed to be an adequate and well-controlled investigation is not actively pursuing marketing approval of the investigational drug with due diligence; or

(viii) The Commissioner determines that it would not be in the public interest for the study to be conducted or continued. FDA ordinarily intends that clinical holds under paragraphs (b)(4)(ii), (b)(4)(iii) and (b)(4)(v) of this section would only apply to additional enrollment in nonconcurrently controlled trials rather than eliminating continued access to individuals already receiving the investigational drug.

(5) *Clinical hold of an investigation involving an exception from informed consent under § 50.24 of this chapter.* FDA may place a proposed or ongoing investigation involving an exception from this informed consent under § 50.24 of this chapter on clinical hold if it is determined that:

(i) Any of the conditions in paragraphs (b)(1) or (b)(2) of this section apply; or

(ii) The pertinent criteria in § 50.24 of this chapter for such an investigation to begin or continue are not submitted or not satisfied.

(6) Clinical hold of any investigation involving an exception from informed consent under § 50.23(d) of this chapter. FDA may place a proposed or ongoing investigation involving an exception from informed consent under § 50.23 (d) of this chapter on clinical hold if it is determined that:

(i) Any of the conditions in paragraphs (b)(1) or (b)(2) of this section apply; or

(ii) A determination by the President to waive the prior consent requirement for the administration of an investigational new drug has not been made.

(c) *Discussion of deficiency.* Whenever FDA concludes that a deficiency exists in a clinical investigation that may be grounds for the imposition of clinical hold FDA will, unless patients are exposed to immediate and serious risk, attempt to discuss and satisfactorily resolve the matter with the sponsor before issuing the clinical hold order.

(d) *Imposition of clinical hold.* The clinical hold order may be made by telephone or other means of rapid communication or in writing. The clinical hold order will identify the studies under the IND to which the hold applies, and will briefly explain the basis for the action. The clinical hold order will be made by or on behalf of the Division Director with responsibility for review of the IND. As soon as possible, and no more than 30 days after imposition of the clinical hold, the Division Director will provide the sponsor a written explanation of the basis for the hold.

(e) *Resumption of clinical investigations.* An investigation may only resume after FDA (usually the Division Director, or the Director's designee, with responsibility for review of the IND) has notified the sponsor that the investigation may proceed. Resumption of the affected investigation(s) will be authorized when the sponsor corrects the deficiency(ies) previously cited or otherwise satisfies the agency that the investigation(s) can proceed. FDA may notify a sponsor of its determination regarding the clinical hold by telephone or other means of rapid communication. If a sponsor of an IND that has been placed on clinical hold requests in writing that the clinical hold be removed and submits a complete response to the issue(s) identified in the clinical hold order, FDA shall respond in writing to the sponsor within 30-calendar days of receipt of the request and the complete response. FDA's response will either remove or maintain the clinical hold, and will state the reasons for such determination. Notwithstanding the 30-calendar day response time, a sponsor may not proceed with a clinical trial on which a clinical hold has been imposed until the sponsor has be notified by FDA that the hold has been lifted.

(f) *Appeal.* If the sponsor disagrees with the reasons cited for the clinical hold, the sponsor may request reconsideration of the decision in accordance with § 312.48.

(g) *Conversion of IND on clinical hold to inactive status.* If all investigations covered by an IND remain on clinical hold for 1 year or more, the IND may be placed on inactive status by FDA under § 312.45.

[52 FR 8831, Mar 19, 1987, as amended at 52 FR 19477, May 22, 1987; 57 FR 13249, Apr. 15, 1992; 61 FR 51530, Oct. 2, 1996; 63 FR 68678, Dec. 14, 1998; 64 FR 54189, Oct. 5, 1999; 65 FR 34971, June 1, 2000]

§ 312.44 Termination.

(a) *General.* This section describes the procedures under which FDA may terminate an IND. If an IND is terminated, the sponsor shall end all clinical investigations conducted under the IND and recall or otherwise provide for the disposition of all unused supplies of the drug. A termination action may be based on deficiencies in the IND or in the conduct of an investigation under an IND. Except as provided in paragraph (d) of this section, a termination shall be preceded by a proposal to terminate by FDA and an opportunity for the sponsor to respond. FDA will, in general, only initiate an action under this section after first attempting to resolve differences informally or, when appropriate, through the clinical hold procedures described in § 312.42.

(b) *Grounds for termination*–(1) *Phase 1.* FDA may propose to terminate an IND during Phase 1 if it finds that:

(i) Human subjects would be exposed to an unreasonable and significant risk of illness or injury.

(ii) The IND does not contain sufficient information required under § 312.23 to assess the safety to subjects of the clinical investigations.

(iii) The methods, facilities, and controls used for the manufacturing, processing, and packing of the investigational drug are inadequate to establish and maintain appropriate standards of identity, strength, quality, and purity as needed for subject safety.

(iv) The clinical investigations are being conducted in a manner substantially different than that described in the protocols submitted in the IND.

(v) The drug is being promoted or distributed for commercial purposes not justified by the requirements of the investigation or permitted by § 312.7.

(vi) The IND, or any amendment or report to the IND, contains an untrue statement of a material fact or omits material information required by this part.

(vii) The sponsor fails promptly to investigate and inform the Food and Drug Administration and all investigators of serious and unexpected adverse experiences in accordance with § 312.32 or fails to make any other report required under this part.

(viii) The sponsor fails to submit an accurate annual report of the investigations in accordance with § 312.33.

(ix) The sponsor fails to comply with any other applicable requirement of this part, part 50, or part 56.

(x) The IND has remained on inactive status for 5 years or more.

(xi) The sponsor fails to delay a proposed investigation under the IND or to suspend an ongoing investigation that has been placed on clinical hold under § 312.42(b)(4).

(2) *Phase 2 or 3.* FDA may propose to terminate an IND during Phase 2 or Phase 3 if FDA finds that:

(i) Any of the conditions in paragraphs (b)(1)(i) through (b)(1)(xi) of this section apply; or

(ii) The investigational plan or protocol(s) is not reasonable as a bona fide scientific plan to determine whether or not the drug is safe and effective for use; or

(iii) There is convincing evidence that the drug is not effective for the purpose for which it is being investigated.

(3) FDA may propose to terminate a treatment IND if it finds that:

(i) Any of the conditions in paragraphs (b)(1)(i) through (x) of this section apply; or

(ii) Any of the conditions in § 312.42(b)(3) apply.

(c) *Opportunity for sponsor response.* (1) If FDA proposes to terminate an IND, FDA will notify the sponsor in writing, and invite correction or explanation within a period of 30 days.

(2) On such notification, the sponsor may provide a written explanation or correction or may request a conference with FDA to provide the requested explanation or correction. If the sponsor does not respond to the notification within the allocated time, the IND shall be terminated.

(3) If the sponsor responds but FDA does not accept the explanation or correction submitted, FDA shall inform the sponsor in writing of the reason for the nonacceptance and provide the sponsor with an opportunity for a regulatory hearing before FDA under Part 16 on the question of whether the IND should be terminated. The sponsor's request for a regulatory hearing must be made within 10 days of the sponsor's receipt of FDA's notification of nonacceptance.

(d) *Immediate termination of IND.* Notwithstanding paragraphs (a) through (c) of this section, if at any time FDA concludes that continuation of the investigation presents an immediate and substantial danger to the health of individuals, the agency shall immediately, by written notice to the sponsor from the Director of the Center for Drug Evaluation and Research or the Director of the Center for Biologics Evaluation and Research, terminate the IND. An IND so terminated is subject to reinstatement by the Director on the basis of additional submissions that eliminate such danger. If an IND is terminated under this paragraph, the agency will afford the sponsor an opportunity for a regulatory hearing under part 16 on the question of whether the IND should be reinstated.

[52 FR 8831, Mar. 19, 1987, as amended at 52 FR 23031, June 17, 1987; 55 FR 11579, Mar. 29, 1990; 57 FR 13249, Apr. 15, 1992; 67 FR 9586, Mar. 4, 2002]

§ 312.45 Inactive status.

(a) If no subjects are entered into clinical studies for a period of 2 years or more under an IND, or if all investigations under an IND remain on clinical hold for 1 year or more, the IND may be placed by FDA on inactive status. This action may be taken by FDA either on request of the sponsor or on FDA's own initiative. If FDA seeks to act on its own initiative under this section, it shall first notify the sponsor in writing of the proposed inactive status. Upon receipt of such notification, the sponsor shall have 30 days to respond as to why the IND should continue to remain active.

(b) If an IND is placed on inactive status, all investigators shall be so notified and all stocks of the drug shall be returned or otherwise disposed of in accordance with § 312.59.

(c) A sponsor is not required to submit annual reports to an IND on inactive status. An inactive IND is, however, still in effect for purposes of the public disclosure of data and information under § 312.130.

(d) A sponsor who intends to resume clinical investigation under an IND placed on inactive status shall submit a protocol amendment under § 312.30 containing the proposed general investigational plan for the coming year and appropriate protocols. If the protocol amendment relies on information previously submitted, the plan shall reference such information. Additional information supporting the proposed investigation, if any, shall be submitted in an information amendment. Notwithstanding the provisions of § 312.30, clinical investigations under an IND on inactive status may only resume (1) 30 days after FDA receives the protocol amendment, unless FDA notifies the sponsor that the investigations described in the amendment are subject to a clinical hold under § 312.42, or (2) on earlier notification by FDA that the clinical investigations described in the protocol amendment may begin.

(e) An IND that remains on inactive status for 5 years or more may be terminated under § 312.44.

[52 FR 8831, Mar. 19, 1987, as amended at 52 FR 23031, June 17, 1987; 67 FR 9586, Mar. 4, 2002]

§ 312.47 Meetings.

(a) *General.* Meetings between a sponsor and the agency are frequently useful in resolving questions and issues raised during the course of a clinical investigation. FDA encourages such meetings to the extent that they aid in the evaluation of the drug and in the solution of scientific problems concerning the drug, to the extent that FDA's resources permit. The general principle underlying the conduct of such meetings is that there should be free, full, and open communication about any scientific or medical question that may arise during the clinical investigation. These meetings shall be conducted and documented in accordance with part 10.

(b) *"End-of-Phase 2" meetings and meetings held before submission of a marketing application.* At specific times during the drug investigation process, meetings between FDA and a sponsor can be especially helpful in minimizing wasteful expenditures of time and money and thus in speeding the drug development and evaluation process. In particular, FDA has found that meetings at the end of Phase 2 of an investigation (end-of-Phase 2 meetings) are of considerable assistance in planning later studies and that meetings held near completion of Phase 3 and before submission of a marketing application ("pre-NDA" meetings) are helpful in developing methods of presentation and submission of data in the marketing application that facilitate review and allow timely FDA response.

(1) *End-of-Phase 2 meetings*–(i) *Purpose.* The purpose of an end-of-Phase 2 meeting is to determine the safety of proceeding to Phase 3, to evaluate the Phase 3 plan and protocols and the adequacy of current studies and plans to assess pediatric safety and effectiveness, and to identify any additional information necessary to support a marketing application for the uses under investigation.

(ii) *Eligibility for meeting.* While the end-of-Phase 2 meeting is designed primarily for IND's involving new molecular entities or major new uses of marketed drugs, a sponsor of any IND may request and obtain an end-of-Phase 2 meeting.

(iii) *Timing.* To be most useful to the sponsor, end-of-Phase 2 meetings should be held before major commitments of effort and resources to specific Phase 3 tests are made. The scheduling of an end-of-Phase 2 meeting is not, however, intended to delay the transition of an investigation from Phase 2 to Phase 3.

(iv) *Advance information.* At least 1 month in advance of an end-of-Phase 2 meeting, the sponsor should submit background information on the sponsor's plan for Phase 3, including summaries of the Phase 1 and 2 investigations, the specific protocols for Phase 3 clinical studies, plans for any additional nonclinical studies, plans for pediatric studies, including a time line for protocol finalization, enrollment, completion, and data analysis, or information to support any planned request for waiver or deferral of pediatric studies, and, if available, tentative labeling for the drug. The recommended contents of such a submission are described more fully in FDA Staff Manual Guide 4850.7 that is publicly available under FDA's public information regulations in Part 20.

(v) *Conduct of meeting.* Arrangements for an end-of-Phase 2 meeting are to be made with the division in FDA's Center for Drug Evaluation and Research or the Center for Biologics Evaluation and Research which is responsible for review of the IND. The meeting will be scheduled by FDA at a time convenient to both FDA and the sponsor. Both the sponsor and FDA may bring consultants to the meeting. The meeting should be directed primarily at establishing agreement between FDA and the sponsor of the overall plan for Phase 3 and the objectives and design of particular studies. The adequacy of the technical information to support Phase 3 studies and/or a marketing application may also be discussed. FDA will also provide its best judgment, at that time, of the pediatric studies that will be required for the drug product and whether their submission will be deferred until after approval. Agreements reached at the meeting on these matters will be recorded in minutes of the conference that will be taken by FDA in accordance with § 10.65 and provided to the sponsor. The minutes along with any other written material provided to the sponsor will serve as a permanent record of any agreements reached. Barring a significant scientific development that requires otherwise, studies conducted in accordance with the agreement shall be presumed to be sufficient in objective and design for the purpose of obtaining marketing approval for the drug.

(2) *"Pre-NDA" and "pre-BLA" meetings.* FDA has found that delays associated with the initial review of a marketing application may be reduced by exchanges of information about a proposed marketing application. The primary purpose of this kind of exchange is to uncover any major unresolved problems, to identify those studies that the sponsor is relying on as adequate and well-controlled to establish the drug's effectiveness, to identify the status of ongoing or needed studies adequate to assess pediatric safety and effectiveness, to acquaint FDA reviewers with the general information to be submitted in the marketing application (including technical information), to discuss appropriate methods for statistical analysis of the data, and to discuss the best approach to the presentation and formatting of data in the marketing application. Arrangements for such a meeting are to be initiated by the sponsor with the division responsible for review of the IND. To permit FDA to provide the sponsor with the most useful advice on preparing a marketing application, the sponsor should submit to FDA's reviewing division at least 1 month in advance of the meeting the following information:

(i) A brief summary of the clinical studies to be submitted in the application.

(ii) A proposed format for organizing the submission, including methods for presenting the data.

(iii) Information on the status of needed or ongoing pediatric studies.

(iv) Any other information for discussion at the meeting.

[52 FR 8831, Mar. 19, 1987, as amended at 52 FR 23031, June 17, 1987; 55 FR 11580, Mar. 29, 1990; 63 FR 66669, Dec. 2, 1998; 67 FR 9586, Mar. 4, 2002]

§ 312.48 Dispute resolution.

(a) *General.* The Food and Drug Administration is committed to resolving differences between sponsors and FDA reviewing divisions with respect to requirements for INDs as quickly and amicably as possible through the cooperative exchange of information and views.

(b) *Administrative and procedural issues.* When administrative or procedural disputes arise, the sponsor should first attempt to resolve the matter with the division in FDA's Center for Drug Evaluation and Research or Center for Biologics Evaluation and Research which is responsible for review of the IND, beginning with the consumer safety officer assigned to the application. If the dispute is not resolved, the sponsor may raise the matter with the person designated as ombudsman, whose function shall be to investigate what has happened and to facilitate a timely and equitable resolution. Appropriate issues to raise with the ombudsman include resolving difficulties in scheduling meetings and obtaining timely replies to inquiries. Further details on this procedure are contained in FDA Staff Manual Guide 4820.7 that is publicly available under FDA's public information regulations in part 20.

(c) *Scientific and medical disputes.* (1) When scientific or medical disputes arise during the drug investigation process, sponsors should discuss the matter directly with the responsible reviewing officials. If necessary, sponsors may request a meeting with the appropriate reviewing officials and management representatives in order to seek a resolution. Requests for such meetings shall be directed to the director of the division in FDA's Center for Drug Evaluation and Research or Center for Biologics Evaluation and Research which is responsible for review of the IND. FDA will make every attempt to grant requests for meetings that involve important issues and that can be scheduled at mutually convenient times.

(2) The "end-of-Phase 2" and "pre-NDA" meetings described in § 312.47(b) will also provide a timely forum for discussing and resolving scientific and medical issues on which the sponsor disagrees with the agency.

(3) In requesting a meeting designed to resolve a scientific or medical dispute, applicants may suggest that FDA seek the advice of outside experts, in which case FDA may, in its discretion, invite to the meeting one or more of its advisory committee members or other consultants, as designated by the agency. Applicants may rely on, and may bring to any meeting, their own consultants. For major scientific and medical policy issues not resolved by informal meetings, FDA may refer the matter to one of its standing advisory committees for its consideration and recommendations.

[52 FR 8831, Mar. 19, 1987, as amended at 55 FR 11580, Mar. 29, 1990]

Subpart D — Responsibilities of Sponsors and Investigators

§ 312.50 General responsibilities of sponsors.

Sponsors are responsible for selecting qualified investigators, providing them with the information they need to conduct an investigation properly, ensuring proper monitoring of the investigation(s), ensuring that the investigation(s) is conducted in accordance with the general investigational plan and protocols contained in the IND, maintaining an effective IND with respect to the investigations, and ensuring that FDA and all participating investigators are promptly informed of significant new adverse effects or risks with respect to the drug. Additional specific responsibilities of sponsors are described elsewhere in this part.

§ 312.52 Transfer of obligations to a contract research organization.

(a) A sponsor may transfer responsibility for any or all of the obligations set forth in this part to a contract research organization. Any such transfer shall be described in writing. If not all obligations are transferred, the writing is required to describe each of the obligations being assumed by the contract research organization. If all obligations are transferred, a general statement that all obligations have been transferred is acceptable. Any obligation not covered by the written description shall be deemed not to have been transferred.

(b) A contract research organization that assumes any obligation of a sponsor shall comply with the specific regulations in this chapter applicable to this obligation and shall be subject to the same regulatory action as a sponsor for failure to comply with any obligation assumed under these regulations. Thus, all references to "sponsor" in this part apply to a contract research organization to the extent that it assumes one or more obligations of the sponsor.

§ 312.53 Selecting investigators and monitors.

(a) *Selecting investigators.* A sponsor shall select only investigators qualified by training and experience as appropriate experts to investigate the drug.

(b) *Control of drug.* A sponsor shall ship investigational new drugs only to investigators participating in the investigation.

(c) *Obtaining information from the investigator.* Before permitting an investigator to begin participation in an investigation, the sponsor shall obtain the following:

(1) A signed investigator statement (Form FDA-1572) containing:

(i) The name and address of the investigator;

(ii) The name and code number, if any, of the protocol(s) in the IND identifying the study(ies) to be conducted by the investigator;

(iii) The name and address of any medical school, hospital, or other research facility where the clinical investigation(s) will be conducted;

(iv) The name and address of any clinical laboratory facilities to be used in the study;

(v) The name and address of the IRB that is responsible for review and approval of the study(ies);

(vi) A commitment by the investigator that he or she:

(a) Will conduct the study(ies) in accordance with the relevant, current protocol(s) and will only make changes in a protocol after notifying the sponsor, except when necessary to protect the safety, the rights, or welfare of subjects;

(b) Will comply with all requirements regarding the obligations of clinical investigators and all other pertinent requirements in this part;

(c) Will personally conduct or supervise the described investigation(s);

(d) Will inform any potential subjects that the drugs are being used for investigational purposes and will ensure that the requirements relating to obtaining informed consent (21 CFR part 50) and institutional review board review and approval (21 CFR part 56) are met;

(e) Will report to the sponsor adverse experiences that occur in the course of the investigation(s) in accordance with § 312.64;

(f) Has read and understands the information in the investigator's brochure, including the potential risks and side effects of the drug; and

(g) Will ensure that all associates, colleagues, and employees assisting in the conduct of the study(ies) are informed about their obligations in meeting the above commitments.

(vii) A commitment by the investigator that, for an investigation subject to an institutional review requirement under part 56, an IRB that complies with the requirements of that part will be responsible for the initial and continuing review and approval of the clinical investigation and that the investigator will promptly report to the IRB all changes in the research activity and all unanticipated problems involving risks to human subjects or others, and will not make any changes in the research without IRB approval, except where necessary to eliminate apparent immediate hazards to the human subjects.

(viii) A list of the names of the subinvestigators (e.g., research fellows, residents) who will be assisting the investigator in the conduct of the investigation(s).

(2) *Curriculum vitae.* A curriculum vitae or other statement of qualifications of the investigator showing the education, training, and experience that qualifies the investigator as an expert in the clinical investigation of the drug for the use under investigation.

(3) *Clinical protocol.* (i) For Phase 1 investigations, a general outline of the planned investigation including the estimated duration of the study and the maximum number of subjects that will be involved.

(ii) For Phase 2 or 3 investigations, an outline of the study protocol including an approximation of the number of subjects to be treated with the drug and the number to be employed as controls, if any; the clinical uses to be investigated; characteristics of subjects by age, sex, and condition; the kind of clinical observations and laboratory tests to be conducted; the estimated duration of the study; and copies or a description of case report forms to be used.

(4) *Financial disclosure information.* Sufficient accurate financial information to allow the sponsor to submit complete and accurate certification or disclosure statements required under part 54 of this chapter. The sponsor shall obtain a commitment from the clinical investigator to promptly update this information if any relevant changes occur during the course of the investigation and for 1 year following the completion of the study.

(d) *Selecting monitors.* A sponsor shall select a monitor qualified by training and experience to monitor the progress of the investigation.

[52 FR 8831, Mar. 19, 1987, as amended at 52 FR 23031, June 17, 1987; 61 FR 57280, Nov. 5, 1996; 63 FR 5252, Feb. 2, 1998; 67 FR 9586, Mar. 4, 2002]

§ 312.54 Emergency research under § 50.24 of this chapter.

(a) The sponsor shall monitor the progress of all investigations involving an exception from informed consent under § 50.24 of this chapter. When the sponsor receives from the IRB information concerning the public disclosures required by § 50.24 (a)(7)(ii) and (a)(7)(iii) of this chapter, the sponsor promptly shall submit to the IND file and to Docket Number 95S-0158 in the Dockets Management Branch (HFA-305), Food and Drug Administration, 5630 Fishers Lane, rm. 1061, Rockville, MD 20852, copies of the information that was disclosed, identified by the IND number.

(b) The sponsor also shall monitor such investigations to identify when an IRB determines that it cannot approve the research because it does not meet the criteria in the exception in § 50.24(a) of this chapter or because of other relevant ethical concerns. The sponsor promptly shall provide this information in writing to FDA, investigators who are asked to participate in this or a substantially equivalent clinical investigation, and other IRB's that are asked to review this or a substantially equivalent investigation.

[61 FR 51530, Oct. 2, 1996, as amended at 68 FR 24879, May 9, 2003]

§ 312.55 Informing investigators.

(a) Before the investigation begins, a sponsor (other than a sponsor-investigator) shall give each participating clinical investigator an investigator brochure containing the information described in § 312.23(a)(5).

(b) The sponsor shall, as the overall investigation proceeds, keep each participating investigator informed of new observations discovered by or reported to the sponsor on the drug, particularly with respect to adverse effects and safe use. Such information may be distributed to investigators by means of periodically revised investigator brochures, reprints or published studies, reports or letters to clinical investigators, or other appropriate means. Important safety information is required to be relayed to investigators in accordance with § 312.32.

[52 FR 8831, Mar. 19, 1987, as amended at 52 FR 23031, June 17, 1987; 67 FR 9586, Mar. 4, 2002]

§ 312.56 Review of ongoing investigations.

(a) The sponsor shall monitor the progress of all clinical investigations being conducted under its IND.

(b) A sponsor who discovers that an investigator is not complying with the signed agreement (Form FDA-1572), the general investigational plan, or the requirements of this part or other applicable parts shall promptly either secure compliance or discontinue shipments of the investigational new drug to the investigator and end the investigator's participation in the investigation. If the investigator's participation in the investigation is ended, the sponsor shall require that the investigator dispose of or return the investigational drug in accordance with the requirements of § 312.59 and shall notify FDA.

(c) The sponsor shall review and evaluate the evidence relating to the safety and effectiveness of the drug as it is obtained from the investigator. The sponsors shall make such reports to FDA regarding information relevant to the safety of the drug as are required under § 312.32. The sponsor shall make annual reports on the progress of the investigation in accordance with § 312.33.

(d) A sponsor who determines that its investigational drug presents an unreasonable and significant risk to subjects shall discontinue those investigations that present the risk, notify FDA, all institutional review boards, and all investigators who have at any time participated in the investigation of the discontinuance, assure the disposition of all stocks of the drug outstanding as required by § 312.59, and furnish FDA with a full report of the sponsor's actions. The sponsor shall discontinue the investigation as soon as possible, and in no event later than 5 working days after making the determination that the investigation should be discontinued. Upon request, FDA will confer with a sponsor on the need to discontinue an investigation.

[52 FR 8831, Mar. 19, 1987, as amended at 52 FR 23031, June 17, 1987; 67 FR 9586, Mar. 4, 2002]

§ 312.57 Recordkeeping and record retention.

(a) A sponsor shall maintain adequate records showing the receipt, shipment, or other disposition of the investigational drug. These records are required to include, as appropriate, the name of the investigator to whom the drug is shipped, and the date, quantity, and batch or code mark of each such shipment.

(b) A sponsor shall maintain complete and accurate records showing any financial interest in § 54.4(a)(3)(i), (a)(3)(ii), (a)(3)(iii), and (a)(3)(iv) of this chapter paid to clinical investigators by the sponsor of the covered study. A sponsor shall also maintain complete and accurate records concerning all other financial interests of investigators subject to part 54 of this chapter.

(c) A sponsor shall retain the records and reports required by this part for 2 years after a marketing application is approved for the drug; or, if an application is not approved for the drug, until 2 years after shipment and delivery of the drug for investigational use is discontinued and FDA has been so notified.

(d) A sponsor shall retain reserve samples of any test article and reference standard identified in, and used in any of the bioequivalence or bioavailability studies described in, § 320.38 or § 320.63 of this chapter, and release the reserve samples to FDA upon request, in accordance with, and for the period specified in § 320.38.

[52 FR 8831, Mar. 19, 1987, as amended at 52 FR 23031, June 17, 1987; 58 FR 25926, Apr. 28, 1993; 63 FR 5252, Feb. 2, 1998; 67 FR 9586, Mar. 4, 2002]

§ 312.58 Inspection of sponsor's records and reports.

(a) *FDA inspection.* A sponsor shall upon request from any properly authorized officer or employee of the Food and Drug Administration, at reasonable times, permit such officer or employee to have access to and copy and verify any records and reports relating to a clinical investigation conducted under this part. Upon written request by FDA, the sponsor shall submit the records or reports (or copies of them) to FDA. The sponsor shall discontinue shipments of the drug to any investigator who has failed to maintain or make available records or reports of the investigation as required by this part.

(b) *Controlled substances.* If an investigational new drug is a substance listed in any schedule of the Controlled Substances Act (21 U.S.C. 801; 21 CFR part 1308), records concerning shipment, delivery, receipt, and disposition of the drug, which are required to be kept under this part or other applicable parts of this chapter shall, upon the request of a properly authorized employee of the Drug Enforcement Administration of the U.S. Department of Justice, be made available by the investigator or sponsor to whom the request is made, for inspection and copying. In addition, the sponsor shall assure that adequate precautions are taken, including storage of the investigational drug in a securely locked, substantially constructed cabinet, or other securely locked, substantially constructed enclosure, access to which is limited, to prevent theft or diversion of the substance into illegal channels of distribution.

§ 312.59 Disposition of unused supply of investigational drug.

The sponsor shall assure the return of all unused supplies of the investigational drug from each individual investigator whose participation in the investigation is discontinued or terminated. The sponsor may authorize alternative disposition of unused supplies of the investigational drug provided this alternative disposition does not expose humans to risks from the drug. The sponsor shall maintain written records of any disposition of the drug in accordance with § 312.57.

[52 FR 8831, Mar. 19, 1987, as amended at 52 FR 23031, June 17, 1987; 67 FR 9586, Mar. 4, 2002]

§ 312.60 General responsibilities of investigators.

An investigator is responsible for ensuring that an investigation is conducted according to the signed investigator statement, the investigational plan, and applicable regulations; for protecting the rights, safety, and welfare of subjects under the investigator's care; and for the control of drugs under investigation. An investigator shall, in accordance with the provisions of part 50 of this chapter, obtain the informed consent of each human subject to whom the drug is administered, except as provided in §§ 50.23 or 50.24 of this chapter. Additional specific responsibilities of clinical investigators are set forth in this part and in parts 50 and 56 of this chapter.

[52 FR 8831, Mar. 19, 1987, as amended at 61 FR 51530, Oct. 2, 1996]

§ 312.61 Control of the investigational drug.

An investigator shall administer the drug only to subjects under the investigator's personal supervision or under the supervision of a subinvestigator responsible to the investigator. The investigator shall not supply the investigational drug to any person not authorized under this part to receive it.

§ 312.62 Investigator recordkeeping and record retention.

(a) *Disposition of drug.* An investigator is required to maintain adequate records of the disposition of the drug, including dates, quantity, and use by subjects. If the investigation is terminated, suspended, discontinued, or completed, the investigator shall return the unused supplies of the drug to the sponsor, or otherwise provide for disposition of the unused supplies of the drug under § 312.59.

(b) *Case histories.* An investigator is required to prepare and maintain adequate and accurate case histories that record all observations and other data pertinent to the investigation on each individual administered the investigational drug or employed as a control in the investigation. Case histories include the case report forms and supporting data including, for example, signed and dated consent forms, any medical records, for example, progress notes of the physician, the individual's hospital chart(s), and nurses' notes. The case history for each individual shall document that informed consent was obtained prior to participation in the study.

(c) *Record retention.* An investigator shall retain records required to be maintained under this part for a period of 2 years following the date a marketing application is approved for the drug for the indication for which it is being investigated; or, if no application is to be filed or if the application is not approved for such indication, until 2 years after the investigation is discontinued and FDA is notified.

[52 FR 8831, Mar. 19, 1987, as amended at 52 FR 23031, June 17, 1987; 61 FR 57280, Nov. 5, 1996; 67 FR 9586, Mar. 4, 2002]

§312.64 Investigator reports.

(a) *Progress reports.* The investigator shall furnish all reports to the sponsor of the drug who is responsible for collecting and evaluating the results obtained. The sponsor is required under §312.33 to submit annual reports to FDA on the progress of the clinical investigations.

(b) *Safety reports.* An investigator shall promptly report to the sponsor any adverse effect that may reasonably be regarded as caused by, or probably caused by, the drug. If the adverse effect is alarming, the investigator shall report the adverse effect immediately.

(c) *Final report.* An investigator shall provide the sponsor with an adequate report shortly after completion of the investigator's participation in the investigation.

(d) *Financial disclosure reports.* The clinical investigator shall provide the sponsor with sufficient accurate financial information to allow an applicant to submit complete and accurate certification or disclosure statements as required under part 54 of this chapter. The clinical investigator shall promptly update this information if any relevant changes occur during the course of the investigation and for 1 year following the completion of the study.

[52 FR 8831, Mar. 19, 1987, as amended at 52 FR 23031, June 17, 1987; 63 FR 5252, Feb. 2, 1998; 67 FR 9586, Mar. 4, 2002]

§312.66 Assurance of IRB review.

An investigator shall assure that an IRB that complies with the requirements set forth in Part 56 will be responsible for the initial and continuing review and approval of the proposed clinical study. The investigator shall also assure that he or she will promptly report to the IRB all changes in the research activity and all unanticipated problems involving risk to human subjects or others, and that he or she will not make any changes in the research without IRB approval, except where necessary to eliminate apparent immediate hazards to human subjects.

[52 FR 8831, Mar. 19, 1987, as amended at 52 FR 23031, June 17, 1987; 67 FR 9586, Mar. 4, 2002]

§312.68 Inspection of investigator's records and reports.

An investigator shall upon request from any properly authorized officer or employee of FDA, at reasonable times, permit such officer or employee to have access to, and copy and verify any records or reports made by the investigator pursuant to §312.62. The investigator is not required to divulge subject names unless the records of particular individuals require a more detailed study of the cases, or unless there is reason to believe that the records do not represent actual case studies, or do not represent actual results obtained.

§312.69 Handling of controlled substances.

If the investigational drug is subject to the Controlled Substances Act, the investigator shall take adequate precautions, including storage of the investigational drug in a securely locked, substantially constructed cabinet, or other securely locked, substantially constructed enclosure, access to which is limited, to prevent theft or diversion of the substance into illegal channels of distribution.

§312.70 Disqualification of a clinical investigator.

(a) If FDA has information indicating that an investigator (including a sponsor-investigator) has repeatedly or deliberately failed to comply with the requirements of this part, part 50, or part 56 of this chapter, or has submitted to FDA or to the sponsor false information in any required report, the Center for Drug Evaluation and Research or the Center for Biologics Evaluation and Research will furnish the investigator written notice of the matter complained of and offer the investigator an opportunity to explain the matter in writing, or, at the option of the investigator, in an informal conference. If an explanation is offered but not accepted by the Center for Drug Evaluation and Research or the Center for Biologics Evaluation and Research, the investigator will be given an opportunity for a regulatory hearing under part 16 on the question of whether the investigator is entitled to receive investigational new drugs.

(b) After evaluating all available information, including any explanation presented by the investigator, if the Commissioner determines that the investigator has repeatedly or deliberately failed to comply with the requirements of this part, part 50, or part 56 of this chapter, or has deliberately or repeatedly submitted false information to FDA or to the sponsor in any required report, the Commissioner will notify the investigator and the sponsor of any investigation in which the investigator has been named as a participant that the investigator is not entitled to receive investigational drugs. The notification will provide a statement of basis for such determination.

(c) Each IND and each approved application submitted under part 314 containing data reported by an investigator who has been determined to be ineligible to receive investigational drugs will be examined to determine whether the investigator has submitted unreliable data that are essential to the continuation of the investigation or essential to the approval of any marketing application.

(d) If the Commissioner determines, after the unreliable data submitted by the investigator are eliminated from consideration, that the data remaining are inadequate to support a conclusion that it is reasonably safe to continue the investigation, the Commissioner will notify the sponsor who shall have an opportunity for a regulatory hearing under part 16. If a danger to the public health exists, however, the Commissioner shall terminate the IND immediately and notify the sponsor of the determination. In such case, the sponsor shall have an opportunity for a regulatory hearing before FDA under part 16 on the question of whether the IND should be reinstated.

(e) If the Commissioner determines, after the unreliable data submitted by the investigator are eliminated from consideration, that the continued approval of the drug product for which the data were submitted cannot be justified, the Commissioner will proceed to withdraw approval of the drug product in accordance with the applicable provisions of the act.

(f) An investigator who has been determined to be ineligible to receive investigational drugs may be reinstated as eligible when the Commissioner determines that the investigator has presented adequate assurances that the investigator will employ investigational drugs solely in compliance with the provisions of this part and of parts 50 and 56.

[52 FR 8831, Mar. 19, 1987, as amended at 52 FR 23031, June 17, 1987; 55 FR 11580, Mar. 29, 1990; 62 FR 46876, Sept. 5, 1997; 67 FR 9586, Mar. 4, 2002]

Subpart E — Drugs Intended to Treat Life-Threatening and Severely-debilitating Illnesses

AUTHORITY: 21 U.S.C. 351, 352, 353, 355, 371; 42 U.S.C. 262.

SOURCE: 53 FR 41523, Oct. 21, 1988, unless otherwise noted.

§ 312.80 Purpose.

The purpose of this section is to establish procedures designed to expedite the development, evaluation, and marketing of new therapies intended to treat persons with life-threatening and severely-debilitating illnesses, especially where no satisfactory alternative therapy exists. As stated § 314.105(c) of this chapter, while the statutory standards of safety and effectiveness apply to all drugs, the many kinds of drugs that are subject to them, and the wide range of uses for those drugs, demand flexibility in applying the standards. The Food and Drug Administration (FDA) has determined that it is appropriate to exercise the broadest flexibility in applying the statutory standards, while preserving appropriate guarantees for safety and effectiveness. These procedures reflect the recognition that physicians and patients are generally willing to accept greater risks or side effects from products that treat life-threatening and severely-debilitating illnesses, than they would accept from products that treat less serious illnesses. These procedures also reflect the recognition that the benefits of the drug need to be evaluated in light of the severity of the disease being treated. The procedure outlined in this section should be interpreted consistent with that purpose.

§ 312.81 Scope.

This section applies to new drug and biological products that are being studied for their safety and effectiveness in treating life-threatening or severely-debilitating diseases.

(a) For purposes of this section, the term "life-threatening" means:

(1) Diseases or conditions where the likelihood of death is high unless the course of the disease is interrupted; and

(2) Diseases or conditions with potentially fatal outcomes, where the end point of clinical trial analysis is survival.

(b) For purposes of this section, the term "severely-debilitating" means diseases or conditions that cause major irreversible morbidity.

(c) Sponsors are encouraged to consult with FDA on the applicability of these procedures to specific products.

[53 FR 41523, Oct. 21, 1988, as amended at 64 FR 401, Jan. 5, 1999]

§ 312.82 Early consultation.

For products intended to treat life-threatening or severely-debilitating illnesses, sponsors may request to meet with FDA-reviewing officials early in the drug development process to review and reach agreement on the design of necessary preclinical and clinical studies. Where appropriate, FDA will invite to such meetings one or more outside expert scientific consultants or advisory committee members. To the extent FDA resources permit, agency reviewing officials will honor requests for such meetings.

(a) *Pre-investigational new drug (IND) meetings.* Prior to the submission of the initial IND, the sponsor may request a meeting with FDA-reviewing officials. The primary purpose of this meeting is to review and reach agreement on the design of animal studies needed to initiate human testing. The meeting may also provide an opportunity for discussing the scope and design of phase 1 testing, plans for studying the drug product in pediatric populations, and the best approach for presentation and formatting of data in the IND.

(b) *End-of-phase 1 meetings.* When data from phase 1 clinical testing are available, the sponsor may again request a meeting with FDA-reviewing officials. The primary purpose of this meeting is to review and reach agreement on the design of phase 2 controlled clinical trials, with the goal that such testing will be adequate to provide sufficient data on the drug's safety and effectiveness to support a decision on its approvability for marketing, and to discuss the need for, as well as the design and timing of, studies of the drug in pediatric patients. For drugs for life-threatening diseases, FDA will provide its best judgment, at that time, whether pediatric studies will be required and whether their submission will be deferred until after approval. The procedures outlined in § 312.47(b)(1) with respect to end-of-phase 2 conferences, including documentation of agreements reached, would also be used for end-of-phase 1 meetings.

[53 FR 41523, Oct. 21, 1988, as amended at 63 FR 66669, Dec. 2, 1998]

§ 312.83 Treatment protocols.

If the preliminary analysis of phase 2 test results appears promising, FDA may ask the sponsor to submit a treatment protocol to be reviewed under the procedures and criteria listed in §§ 312.34 and 312.35. Such a treatment protocol, if requested and granted, would normally remain in effect while the complete data necessary for a marketing application are being assembled by the sponsor and reviewed by FDA (unless grounds exist for clinical hold of ongoing protocols, as provided in § 312.42(b)(3)(ii)).

§ 312.84 Risk-benefit analysis in review of marketing applications for drugs to treat life-threatening and severely-debilitating illnesses.

(a) FDA's application of the statutory standards for marketing approval shall recognize the need for a medical risk-benefit judgment in making the final decision on approvability. As part of this evaluation, consistent with the statement of purpose in § 312.80, FDA will consider whether the benefits of the drug outweigh the known and potential risks of the drug and the need to answer remaining questions about risks and benefits of the drug, taking into consideration the severity of the disease and the absence of satisfactory alternative therapy.

(b) In making decisions on whether to grant marketing approval for products that have been the subject of an end-of-phase 1 meeting under § 312.82, FDA will usually seek the advice of outside expert scientific consultants or advisory committees. Upon the filing of such a marketing application under § 314.101 or part 601 of this chapter, FDA will notify the members of the relevant standing advisory committee of the application's filing and its availability for review.

(c) If FDA concludes that the data presented are not sufficient for marketing approval, FDA will issue (for a drug) a not approvable letter pursuant to § 314.120 of this chapter, or (for a biologic) a deficiencies letter consistent with the biological product licensing procedures. Such letter, in describing the deficiencies in the application, will address why the results of the research design agreed to under § 312.82, or in subsequent meetings, have not provided sufficient evidence for marketing approval. Such letter will also describe any recommendations made by the advisory committee regarding the application.

(d) Marketing applications submitted under the procedures contained in this section will be subject to the requirements and procedures contained in part 314 or part 600 of this chapter, as well as those in this subpart.

§ 312.85 Phase 4 studies.

Concurrent with marketing approval, FDA may seek agreement from the sponsor to conduct certain postmarketing (phase 4) studies to delineate additional information about the drug's risks, benefits, and optimal use. These studies could include, but would not be limited to, studying different doses or schedules of administration than were used in phase 2 studies, use of the drug in other patient populations or other stages of the disease, or use of the drug over a longer period of time.

§ 312.86 Focused FDA regulatory research.

At the discretion of the agency, FDA may undertake focused regulatory research on critical rate-limiting aspects of the preclinical, chemical/manufacturing, and clinical phases of drug development and evaluation. When initiated, FDA will undertake such research efforts as a means for meeting a public health need in facilitating the development of therapies to treat life-threatening or severely-debilitating illnesses.

§ 312.87 Active monitoring of conduct and evaluation of clinical trials.

For drugs covered under this section, the Commissioner and other agency officials will monitor the progress of the conduct and evaluation of clinical trials and be involved in facilitating their appropriate progress.

§ 312.88 Safeguards for patient safety.

All of the safeguards incorporated within parts 50, 56, 312, 314, and 600 of this chapter designed to ensure the safety of clinical testing and the safety of products following marketing approval apply to drugs covered by this section. This includes the requirements for informed consent (part 50 of this chapter) and institutional review boards (part 56 of this chapter). These safeguards further include the review of animal studies prior to initial human testing (§ 312.23), and the monitoring of adverse drug experiences through the requirements of IND safety reports (§ 312.32), safety update reports during agency review of a marketing application (§ 314.50 of this chapter), and postmarketing adverse reaction reporting (§ 314.80 of this chapter).

Subpart F — Miscellaneous

§ 312.110 Import and export requirements.

(a) *Imports*. An investigational new drug offered for import into the United States complies with the requirements of this part if it is subject to an IND that is in effect for it under § 312.40 and: (1) The consignee in the United States is the sponsor of the IND; (2) the consignee is a qualified investigator named in the IND; or (3) the consignee is the domestic agent of a foreign sponsor, is responsible for the control and distribution of the investigational drug, and the IND identifies the consignee and describes what, if any, actions the consignee will take with respect to the investigational drug.

(b) *Exports*. An investigational new drug intended for export from the United States complies with the requirements of this part as follows:

(1) If an IND is in effect for the drug under § 312.40 and each person who receives the drug is an investigator named in the application; or

(2) If FDA authorizes shipment of the drug for use in a clinical investigation. Authorization may be obtained as follows:

(i) Through submission to the International Affairs Staff (HFY-50), Associate Commissioner for Health Affairs, Food and Drug Administration, 5600 Fishers Lane, Rockville, MD 20857, of a written request from the person that seeks to export the drug. A request must provide adequate information about the drug to satisfy FDA that the drug is appropriate for the proposed investigational use in humans, that the drug will be used for investigational purposes only, and that the drug may be legally used by that consignee in the importing country for the proposed investigational use. The request shall specify the quantity of the drug to be shipped per shipment and the frequency of expected shipments. If FDA authorizes exportation under this paragraph, the agency shall concurrently notify the government of the importing country of such authorization.

(ii) Through submission to the International Affairs Staff (HFY-50), Associate Commissioner for Health Affairs, Food and Drug Administration, 5600 Fishers Lane, Rockville, MD 20857, of a formal request from an authorized official of the government of the country to which the drug is proposed to be shipped. A request must specify that the foreign government has adequate information about the drug and the proposed investigational use, that the drug will be used for investigational purposes only, and that the foreign government is satisfied that the drug may legally be used by the intended consignee in that country. Such a request shall specify the quantity of drug to be shipped per shipment and the frequency of expected shipments.

(iii) Authorization to export an investigational drug under paragraph (b)(2)(i) or (ii) of this section may be revoked by FDA if the agency finds that the conditions underlying its authorization are no longer met.

(3) This paragraph applies only where the drug is to be used for the purpose of clinical investigation.

(4) This paragraph does not apply to the export of new drugs (including biological products, antibiotic drugs, and insulin) approved or authorized for export under section 802 of the act (21 U.S.C. 382) or section 351 (h)(1)(A) of the Public Health Service Act (42 U.S.C. 262(h)(1)(A)).

[52 FR 8831, Mar. 19, 1987, as amended at 52 FR 23031, June 17, 1987; 64 FR 401, Jan. 5, 1999; 67 FR 9586, Mar. 4, 2002]

§ 312.120 Foreign clinical studies not conducted under an IND.

(a) *Introduction.* This section describes the criteria for acceptance by FDA of foreign clinical studies not conducted under an IND. In general, FDA accepts such studies provided they are well designed, well conducted, performed by qualified investigators, and conducted in accordance with ethical principles acceptable to the world community. Studies meeting these criteria may be utilized to support clinical investigations in the United States and/or marketing approval. Marketing approval of a new drug based solely on foreign clinical data is governed by § 314.106.

(b) *Data submissions.* A sponsor who wishes to rely on a foreign clinical study to support an IND or to support an application for marketing approval shall submit to FDA the following information:

(1) A description of the investigator's qualifications;

(2) A description of the research facilities;

(3) A detailed summary of the protocol and results of the study, and, should FDA request, case records maintained by the investigator or additional background data such as hospital or other institutional records;

(4) A description of the drug substance and drug product used in the study, including a description of components, formulation, specifications, and bioavailability of the specific drug product used in the clinical study, if available; and

(5) If the study is intended to support the effectiveness of a drug product, information showing that the study is adequate and well controlled under § 314.126.

(c) *Conformance with ethical principles.* (1) Foreign clinical research is required to have been conducted in accordance with the ethical principles stated in the "Declaration of Helsinki" (see paragraph (c)(4) of this section) or the laws and regulations of the country in which the research was conducted, whichever represents the greater protection of the individual.

(2) For each foreign clinical study submitted under this section, the sponsor shall explain how the research conformed to the ethical principles contained in the "Declaration of Helsinki" or the foreign country's standards, whichever were used. If the foreign country's standards were used, the sponsor shall explain in detail how those standards differ from the "Declaration of Helsinki" and how they offer greater protection.

(3) When the research has been approved by an independent review committee, the sponsor shall submit to FDA documentation of such review and approval, including the names and qualifications of the members of the committee. In this regard, a "review committee" means a committee composed of scientists and, where practicable, individuals who are otherwise qualified (e.g., other health professionals or laymen). The investigator may not vote on any aspect of the review of his or her protocol by a review committee.

(4) The "Declaration of Helsinki" states as follows:

Recommendations Guiding Physicians in Biomedical Research Involving Human Subjects

Introduction

It is the mission of the physician to safeguard the health of the people. His or her knowledge and conscience are dedicated to the fulfillment of this mission.

The Declaration of Geneva of the World Medical Association binds the physician with the words, "The health of my patient will be my first consideration," and the International Code of Medical Ethics declares that, "A physician shall act only in the patient's interest when providing medical care which might have the effect of weakening the physical and mental condition of the patient."

The purpose of biomedical research involving human subjects must be to improve diagnostic, therapeutic and prophylactic procedures and the understanding of the aetiology and pathogenesis of disease.

In current medical practice most diagnostic, therapeutic or prophylactic procedures involve hazards. This applies especially to biomedical research.

Medical progress is based on research which ultimately must rest in part on experimentation involving human subjects.

In the field of biomedical research a fundamental distinction must be recognized between medical research in which the aim is essentially diagnostic or therapeutic for a patient, and medical research, the essential object of which is purely scientific and without implying direct diagnostic or therapeutic value to the person subjected to the research.

Special caution must be exercised in the conduct of research which may affect the environment, and the welfare of animals used for research must be respected.

Because it is essential that the results of laboratory experiments be applied to human beings to further scientific knowledge and to help suffering humanity, the World Medical Association has prepared the following recommendations as a guide to every physician in biomedical research involving human subjects. They should be kept under review in the future. It must be stressed that the standards as drafted are only a guide to physicians all over the world. Physicians are not relieved from criminal, civil and ethical responsibilities under the laws of their own countries.

I. Basic Principles

1. Biomedical research involving human subjects must conform to generally accepted scientific principles and should be based on adequately performed laboratory and animal experimentation and on a thorough knowledge of the scientific literature.

2. The design and performance of each experimental procedure involving human subjects should be clearly formulated in an experimental protocol which should be transmitted for consideration, comment and guidance to a specially appointed committee independent of the investigator and the sponsor provided that this independent committee is in conformity with the laws and regulations of the country in which the research experiment is performed.

3. Biomedical research involving human subjects should be conducted only by scientifically qualified persons and under the supervision of a clinically competent medical person. The responsibility for the human subject must always rest with a medically qualified person and never rest on the subject of the research, even though the subject has given his or her consent.

4. Biomedical research involving human subjects cannot legitimately be carried out unless the importance of the objective is in proportion to the inherent risk to the subject.

5. Every biomedical research project involving human subjects should be preceded by careful assessment of predictable risks in comparison with foreseeable benefits to the subject or to others. Concern for the interests of the subject must always prevail over the interests of science and society.

6. The right of the research subject to safeguard his or her integrity must always be respected. Every precaution should be taken to respect the privacy of the subject and to minimize the impact of the study on the subject's physical and mental integrity and on the personality of the subject.

7. Physicians should abstain from engaging in research projects involving human subjects unless they are satisfied that the hazards involved are believed to be predictable. Physicians should cease any investigation if the hazards are found to outweigh the potential benefits.

8. In publication of the results of his or her research, the physician is obliged to preserve the accuracy of the results. Reports of experimentation not in accordance with the principles laid down in this Declaration should not be accepted for publication.

9. In any research on human beings, each potential subject must be adequately informed of the aims, methods, anticipated benefits and potential hazards of the study and the discomfort it may entail. He or she should be informed that he or she is at liberty to abstain from participation in the study and that he or she is free to withdraw his or her consent to participation at any time. The physician should then obtain the subject's freely-given informed consent, preferably in writing.

10. When obtaining informed consent for the research project the physician should be particularly cautious if the subject is in a dependent relationship to him or her or may consent under duress. In that case the informed consent should be obtained by a physician who is not engaged in the investigation and who is completely independent of this official relationship.

11. In case of legal incompetence, informed consent should be obtained from the legal guardian in accordance with national legislation. Where physical or mental incapacity makes it impossible to obtain informed consent, or when the subject is a minor, permission from the responsible relative replaces that of the subject in accordance with national legislation.

Whenever the minor child is in fact able to give a consent, the minor's consent must be obtained in addition to the consent of the minor's legal guardian.

12. The research protocol should always contain a statement of the ethical considerations involved and should indicate that the principles enunciated in the present Declaration are complied with.

II. Medical Research Combined with Professional Care
(Clinical Research)

1. In the treatment of the sick person, the physician must be free to use a new diagnostic and therapeutic measure, if in his or her judgment it offers hope of saving life, reestablishing health or alleviating suffering.

2. The potential benefits, hazards and discomfort of a new method should be weighed against the advantages of the best current diagnostic and therapeutic methods.

3. In any medical study, every patient-including those of a control group, if any-should be assured of the best proven diagnostic and therapeutic method.

4. The refusal of the patient to participate in a study must never interfere with the physician-patient relationship.

5. If the physician considers it essential not to obtain informed consent, the specific reasons for this proposal should be stated in the experimental protocol for transmission to the independent committee (I, 2).

6. The physician can combine medical research with professional care, the objective being the acquisition of new medical knowledge, only to the extent that medical research is justified by its potential diagnostic or therapeutic value for the patient.

III. Non-Therapeutic Biomedical Research Involving Human Subjects
(Non-Clinical Biomedical Research)

1. In the purely scientific application of medical research carried out on a human being, it is the duty of the physician to remain the protector of the life and health of that person on whom biomedical research is being carried out.

2. The subjects should be volunteers-either healthy persons or patients for whom the experimental design is not related to the patient's illness.

3. The investigator or the investigating team should discontinue the research if in his/her or their judgment it may, if continued, be harmful to the individual.

4. In research on man, the interest of science and society should never take precedence over considerations related to the well-being of the subject.

[52 FR 8831, Mar. 19, 1987, as amended at 52 FR 23031, June 17, 1987; 56 FR 22113, May 14, 1991; 64 FR 401, Jan. 5, 1999; 67 FR 9586, Mar. 4, 2002]

§ 312.130 Availability for public disclosure of data and information in an IND.

(a) The existence of an investigational new drug application will not be disclosed by FDA unless it has previously been publicly disclosed or acknowledged.

(b) The availability for public disclosure of all data and information in an investigational new drug application for a new drug will be handled in accordance with the provisions established in § 314.430 for the confidentiality of data and information in applications submitted in part 314. The availability for public disclosure of all data and information in an investigational new drug application for a biological product will be governed by the provisions of §§ 601.50 and 601.51.

(c) Notwithstanding the provisions of § 314.430, FDA shall disclose upon request to an individual to whom an investigational new drug has been given a copy of any IND safety report relating to the use in the individual.

(d) The availability of information required to be publicly disclosed for investigations involving an exception from informed consent under § 50.24 of this chapter will be handled as follows: Persons wishing to request the publicly disclosable information in the IND that was required to be filed in Docket Number 95S-0158 in the Dockets Management Branch (HFA-305), Food and Drug Administration, 5630 Fishers Lane, Rm. 1061, Rockville, MD 20852, shall submit a request under the Freedom of Information Act.

[52 FR 8831, Mar. 19, 1987. Redesignated at 53 FR 41523, Oct. 21, 1988, as amended at 61 FR 51530, Oct. 2, 1996; 64 FR 401, Jan. 5, 1999; 68 FR 24879, May 9, 2003]

§ 312.140 Address for correspondence.

(a) A sponsor must send an initial IND submission to the Center for Drug Evaluation and Research (CDER) or to the Center for Biologics Evaluation and Research (CBER), depending on the Center responsible for regulating the product as follows:

(1) For drug products regulated by CDER. Send the IND submission to the Central Document Room, Center for Drug Evaluation and Research, Food and Drug Administration, 5901-B Ammendale Rd., Beltsville, MD 20705-1266.

(2) For biological products regulated by CDER. Send the IND submission to the CDER Therapeutic Biological Products Document Room, Center for Drug Evaluation and Research, Food and Drug Administration, 12229 Wilkins Ave., Rockville, MD 20852.

(3) For biological products regulated by CBER. Send the IND submission to the Document Control Center (HFM-99), Center for Biologics Evaluation and Research, Food and Drug Administration, 1401 Rockville Pike, suite 200N, Rockville, MD 20852-1448.

(b) On receiving the IND, the responsible Center will inform the sponsor which one of the divisions in CDER or CBER is responsible for the IND. Amendments, reports, and other correspondence relating to matters covered by the IND should be directed to the appropriate Center and division. The outside wrapper of each submission shall state what is contained in the submission, for example, "IND Application", "Protocol Amendment", etc.

(c) All correspondence relating to export of an investigational drug under § 312.110(b)(2) shall be submitted to the International Affairs Staff (HFY-50), Office of Health Affairs, Food and Drug Administration, 5600 Fishers Lane, Rockville, MD 20857.

[52 FR 8831, Mar. 19, 1987, as amended at 52 FR 23031, June 17, 1987; 55 FR 11580, Mar. 29, 1990; 67 FR 9586, Mar. 4, 2002; 69 FR 13473, Mar. 23, 2004; 56 FR 14981, Mar. 24, 2005]

§ 312.145 Guidance Documents.

(a) FDA has made available guidance documents under § 10.115 of this chapter to help you to comply with certain requirements of this part.

(b) The Center for Drug Evaluation and Research (CDER) and the Center for Biologics Evaluation and Research (CBER) maintain lists of guidance documents that apply to the centers' regulations. The lists are maintained on the Internet and are published annually in the FEDERAL REGISTER. A request for a copy of the CDER list should be directed to the Office of Training and Communications, Division of Communications Management, Drug Information Branch (HFD–210), Center for Drug Evaluation and Research, Food and Drug Administration, 5600 Fishers Lane, Rockville, MD 20857. A request for a copy of the CBER list should be directed to the Office of Communication, Training, and Manufacturers Assistance (HFM–40), Center for Biologics Evaluation and Research, Food and Drug Administration, 1401 Rockville Pike, Rockville, MD 20852-1448.

[52 FR 8831, Mar. 19, 1987, as amended at 55 FR 11580, Mar. 29, 1990; 56 FR 3776, Jan. 31, 1991; 57 FR 10814, Mar. 31, 1992; 65 FR 56479, Sep. 19, 2000]

Subpart G — Drugs for Investigational Use in Laboratory Research Animals or In Vitro Tests

§ 312.160 Drugs for investigational use in laboratory research animals or in vitro tests.

(a) *Authorization to ship.* (1)(i) A person may ship a drug intended solely for tests in vitro or in animals used only for laboratory research purposes if it is labeled as follows:

CAUTION: Contains a new drug for investigational use only in laboratory research animals, or for tests in vitro. Not for use in humans.

(ii) A person may ship a biological product for investigational in vitro diagnostic use that is listed in § 312.2(b)(2)(ii) if it is labeled as follows:

CAUTION: Contains a biological product for investigational in vitro diagnostic tests only.

(2) A person shipping a drug under paragraph (a) of this section shall use due diligence to assure that the consignee is regularly engaged in conducting such tests and that the shipment of the new drug will actually be used for tests in vitro or in animals used only for laboratory research.

(3) A person who ships a drug under paragraph (a) of this section shall maintain adequate records showing the name and post office address of the expert to whom the drug is shipped and the date, quantity, and batch or code mark of each shipment and delivery. Records of shipments under paragraph (a)(1)(i) of this section are to be maintained for a period of 2 years after the

shipment. Records and reports of data and shipments under paragraph (a)(1)(ii) of this section are to be maintained in accordance with § 312.57(b). The person who ships the drug shall upon request from any properly authorized officer or employee of the Food and Drug Administration, at reasonable times, permit such officer or employee to have access to and copy and verify records required to be maintained under this section.

(b) *Termination of authorization to ship.* FDA may terminate authorization to ship a drug under this section if it finds that:

(1) The sponsor of the investigation has failed to comply with any of the conditions for shipment established under this section; or

(2) The continuance of the investigation is unsafe or otherwise contrary to the public interest or the drug is used for purposes other than bona fide scientific investigation. FDA will notify the person shipping the drug of its finding and invite immediate correction. If correction is not immediately made, the person shall have an opportunity for a regulatory hearing before FDA pursuant to part 16.

(c) *Disposition of unused drug.* The person who ships the drug under paragraph (a) of this section shall assure the return of all unused supplies of the drug from individual investigators whenever the investigation discontinues or the investigation is terminated. The person who ships the drug may authorize in writing alternative disposition of unused supplies of the drug provided this alternative disposition does not expose humans to risks from the drug, either directly or indirectly (e.g., through food-producing animals). The shipper shall maintain records of any alternative disposition.

[Redesignated at 53 FR 41523, Oct. 21, 1988] [52 FR 8831, Mar. 19, 1987, as amended at 52 FR 23031, June 17, 1987. Redesignated at 53 FR 41523, Oct. 21, 1988; 67 FR 9586, Mar. 4, 2002]

ICH
Guideline for
Good Clinical Practice

As published in the
Federal Register May 9, 1997

SUMMARY: The Food and Drug Administration (FDA) is publishing a guideline entitled "Good Clinical Practice: Consolidated Guideline." The guideline was prepared under the auspices of the International Conference on Harmonisation of Technical Requirements for Registration of Pharmaceuticals for Human Use (ICH). The guideline is intended to define "Good Clinical Practice" and to provide a unified standard for designing, conducting, recording, and reporting trials that involve the participation of human subjects. The guideline also describes the minimum information that should be included in an Investigator's Brochure (IB) and provides a suggested format. In addition, the guideline describes the essential documents that individually and collectively permit evaluation of the conduct of a clinical study and the quality of the data produced.

DATES: Effective May 9, 1997. Written comments may be submitted at any time.

ADDRESSES: Submit written requests for single copies of "Good Clinical Practice: Consolidated Guideline" to the Drug Information Branch (HFD-210), Center for Drug Evaluation and Research, Food and Drug Administration, 5600 Fishers Lane, Rockville, MD 20857, 301-827-4573. Send two self-addressed adhesive labels to assist that office in processing your requests. Submit written comments on the guideline to the Dockets Management Branch (HFA-305), Food and Drug Administration, 12420 Parklawn Dr., rm. 1-23, Rockville. MD 20857. Two copies of any comments are to be submitted, except that individuals may submit one copy. The "Good Clinical Practice: Consolidated Guideline" and received comments are available for public examination in the Dockets Management Branch (address above) between 9 a.m. and 4 p.m., Monday through Friday.

FOR FURTHER INFORMATION CONTACT: Regarding the guideline: Bette L. Barton, Center for Drug Evaluation and Research (HFD-344), Food and Drug Administration, 7500 Standish Pl., Rockville, MD 20855, 301-594-1032.

Regarding ICH: Janet J. Showalter, Office of Health Affairs (HFY-20), Food and Drug Administration, 5600 Fishers Lane, Rockville, MD 20857, 301-827-0864.

SUPPLEMENTARY INFORMATION: In recent years, many important initiatives have been undertaken by regulatory authorities and industry associations to promote international harmonization of regulatory requirements. FDA has participated in many meetings designed to enhance harmonization and is committed to seeking scientifically based harmonized technical procedures for pharmaceutical development. One of the goals of harmonization is to identify and then reduce differences in technical requirements for drug development among regulatory agencies.

ICH was organized to provide an opportunity for tripartite harmonization initiatives to be developed with input from both regulatory and industry representatives. FDA also seeks input from consumer representatives and others. ICH is concerned with harmonization of technical requirements for the registration of pharmaceutical products among three regions: The European Union, Japan, and the United States. The six ICH sponsors are the European Commission, the European Federation of Pharmaceutical Industries Associations, the Japanese Ministry of Health and Welfare. the Japanese Pharmaceutical Manufacturers Association, the Centers for Drug Evaluation and Research and Biologics Evaluation and Research, FDA, and the Pharmaceutical Research and Manufacturers of America. The ICH Secretariat, which coordinates the preparation of documentation, is provided by the International Federation of Pharmaceutical Manufacturers Associations (IFPMA).

The ICH Steering Committee includes representatives from each of the ICH sponsors and the IFPMA, as well as observers from the World Health Organization, the Canadian Health Protection Branch, and the European Free Trade Area.

In the Federal Register of August 17, 1995 (60 FR 42948), FDA published a draft tripartite guideline entitled "Good Clinical Practice." In the Federal Register of August 9, 1994, FDA published draft tripartite guidelines entitled "Guideline for the Investigator's Brochure (59 FR 40772) and "Guideline for Essential Documents for the Conduct of a Clinical Study" (59 FR 40774). The notices gave interested persons an opportunity to submit comments.

After consideration of the comments received and revisions to the guidelines, the three guidelines were consolidated into one guideline on good clinical practice. The consolidated guideline was submitted to the ICH Steering Committee and endorsed by the three participating regulatory agencies at the ICH meeting held on April 30, 1996.

The guideline defines "Good Clinical Practice" and provides a unified standard for designing, conducting, recording, and reporting trials that involve the participation of human subjects. Compliance with Good Clinical Practice provides public assurance that the rights, well-being, and confidentiality of trial subjects are protected and that trial data are credible. The guideline should be followed when generating clinical data that are intended to be submitted to regulatory authorities. The principles established in this guideline should also be applied to other investigations that involve therapeutic intervention in, or observation of, human subjects.

The guideline also describes the minimum information that should be included in an IB, such as information on the drug's physical, chemical, and pharmaceutical properties, and its effect in humans; a suggested format for the IB is also provided. The guideline also describes the purpose of essential documents in a clinical study and explains whether the documents should be filed in the investigator's files or the sponsor's files.

This guideline represents the agency's current thinking on good clinical practices. It does not create or confer any rights for or on any person and does not operate to bind FDA or the public. An alternative approach may be used if such approach satisfies the requirements of the applicable statutes, regulations, or both.

GOOD CLINICAL PRACTICE: CONSOLIDATED GUIDELINE

TABLE OF CONTENTS

6. CLINICAL TRIAL PROTOCOL AND PROTOCOL AMENDMENT(S)

GUIDELINE FOR GOOD CLINICAL PRACTICE

INTRODUCTION

Good clinical practice (GCP) is an international ethical and scientific quality standard for designing, conducting, recording, and reporting trials that involve the participation of human subjects. Compliance with this standard provides public assurance that the rights, safety, and well-being of trial subjects are protected, consistent with the principles that have their origin in the Declaration of Helsinki, and that the clinical trial data are credible.

The objective of this ICH GCP Guideline is to provide a unified standard for the European Union (EU), Japan, and the United States to facilitate the mutual acceptance of clinical data by the regulatory authorities in these jurisdictions.

The guideline was developed with consideration of the current good clinical practices of the European Union, Japan, and the United States, as well as those of Australia, Canada, the Nordic countries, and the World Health Organization (WHO).

This guideline should be followed when generating clinical trial data that are intended to be submitted to regulatory authorities.

The principles established in this guideline may also be applied to other clinical investigations that may have an impact on the safety and well-being of human subjects.

1. GLOSSARY

1.1 Adverse Drug Reaction (ADR)

In the preapproval clinical experience with a new medicinal product or its new usages, particularly as the therapeutic dose(s) may not be established, all noxious and unintended responses to a medicinal product related to any dose should be considered adverse drug reactions. The phrase "responses to a medicinal product" means that a causal relationship between a medicinal product and an adverse event is at least a reasonable possibility, i.e., the relationship cannot be ruled out.

Regarding marketed medicinal products: A response to a drug that is noxious and unintended and that occurs at doses normally used in man for prophylaxis, diagnosis, or therapy of diseases or for modification of physiological function (see the ICH Guideline for Clinical Safety Data Management: Definitions and Standards for Expedited Reporting).

1.2 Adverse Event (AE)

An AE is any untoward medical occurrence in a patient or clinical investigation subject administered a pharmaceutical product and that does not necessarily have a causal relationship with this treatment. An AE can therefore be any unfavorable and unintended sign (including an abnormal laboratory finding), symptom, or disease temporally associated with the use of a medicinal (investigational) product, whether or not related to the medicinal (investigational) product (see the ICH Guideline for Clinical Safety Data Management: Definitions and Standards for Expedited Reporting).

1.3 Amendment (to the protocol)

See Protocol Amendment.

1.4 Applicable Regulatory Requirement(s)

Any law(s) and regulation(s) addressing the conduct of clinical trials of investigational products of the jurisdiction where a trial is conducted.

1.5 Approval (in relation to Institutional Review Boards (IRB's))

The affirmative decision of the IRB that the clinical trial has been reviewed and may be conducted at the institution site within the constraints set forth by the IRB, the institution, good clinical practice (GCP), and the applicable regulatory requirements.

1.6 Audit

A systematic and independent examination of trial-related activities and documents to determine whether the evaluated trial-related activities were conducted, and the data were recorded, analyzed, and accurately reported according to the protocol, sponsor's standard operating procedures (SOP's), good clinical practice (GCP), and the applicable regulatory requirement(s).

1.7 Audit Certificate

A declaration of confirmation by the auditor that an audit has taken place.

1.8 Audit Report

A written evaluation by the sponsor's auditor of the results of the audit.

1.9 Audit Trail

Documentation that allows reconstruction of the course of events.

1.10 Blinding/Masking

A procedure in which one or more parties to the trial are kept unaware of the treatment assignment(s). Single blinding usually refers to the subject(s) being unaware, and double blinding usually refers to the subject(s), investigator(s), monitor, and, in some cases, data analyst(s) being unaware of the treatment assignment(s).

1.11 Case Report Form (CRF)

A printed, optical, or electronic document designed to record all of the protocol-required information to be reported to the sponsor on each trial subject.

1.12 Clinical Trial/Study

Any investigation in human subjects intended to discover or verify the clinical, pharmacological, and/or other pharmacodynamic effects of an investigational product(s), and/or to identify any adverse reactions to an investigational product(s), and/or to study absorption, distribution, metabolism, and excretion of an investigational product(s) with the object of ascertaining its safety and/or efficacy. The terms clinical trial and clinical study are synonymous.

1.13 Clinical Trial/Study Report

A written description of a trial/study of any therapeutic, prophylactic, or diagnostic agent conducted in human subjects, in which the clinical and statistical description, presentations, and analyses are fully integrated into a single report (see the ICH Guideline for Structure and Content of Clinical Study Reports).

1.14 Comparator (Product)

An investigational or marketed product (i.e., active control), or placebo, used as a reference in a clinical trial.

1.15 Compliance (in relation to trials)

Adherence to all the trial-related requirements, good clinical practice (GCP) requirements, and the applicable regulatory requirements.

1.16 Confidentiality

Prevention of disclosure, to other than authorized individuals, of a sponsor's proprietary information or of a subject's identity.

1.17 Contract

A written, dated, and signed agreement between two or more involved parties that sets out any arrangements on delegation and distribution of tasks and obligations and, if appropriate, on financial matters. The protocol may serve as the basis of a contract.

1.18 Coordinating Committee

A committee that a sponsor may organize to coordinate the conduct of a multicenter trial.

1.19 Coordinating Investigator

An investigator assigned the responsibility for the coordination of investigators at different centers participating in a multicenter trial.

1.20 Contract Research Organization (CRO)

A person or an organization (commercial, academic, or other) contracted by the sponsor to perform one or more of a sponsor's trial-related duties and functions.

1.21 Direct Access

Permission to examine, analyze, verify, and reproduce any records and reports that are important to evaluation of a clinical trial. Any party (e.g., domestic and foreign regulatory authorities, sponsors, monitors, and auditors) with direct access should take all reasonable precautions within the constraints of the applicable regulatory requirement(s) to maintain the confidentiality of subjects' identities and sponsor's proprietary information.

1.22 Documentation

All records, in any form (including, but not limited to, written, electronic, magnetic, and optical records; and scans, x-rays, and electrocardiograms) that describe or record the methods, conduct, and/or results of a trial, the factors affecting a trial, and the actions taken.

1.23 Essential Documents

Documents that individually and collectively permit evaluation of the conduct of a study and the quality of the data produced (see section 8. "Essential Documents for the Conduct of a Clinical Trial").

1.24 Good Clinical Practice (GCP)

A standard for the design, conduct, performance, monitoring, auditing, recording, analyses, and reporting of clinical trials that provides assurance that the data and reported results are credible and accurate, and that the rights, integrity, and confidentiality of trial subjects are protected.

1.25 Independent Data Monitoring Committee (IDMC) (Data and Safety Monitoring Board, Monitoring Committee, Data Monitoring Committee)

An independent data monitoring committee that may be established by the sponsor to assess at intervals the progress of a clinical trial, the safety data, and the critical efficacy endpoints, and to recommend to the sponsor whether to continue, modify, or stop a trial.

1.26 Impartial Witness

A person, who is independent of the trial, who cannot be unfairly influenced by people involved with the trial, who attends the informed consent process if the subject or the subject's legally acceptable representative cannot read, and who reads the informed consent form and any other written information supplied to the subject.

1.27 Independent Ethics Committee (IEC)

An independent body (a review board or a committee, institutional, regional, national, or supranational), constituted of medical/ scientific professionals and nonmedical/nonscientific members, whose responsibility it is to ensure the protection of the rights, safety, and well-being of human subjects involved in a trial and to provide public assurance of that protection, by, among other things, reviewing and approving/providing favorable opinion on the trial protocol, the suitability of the investigator(s), facilities, and the methods and material to be used in obtaining and documenting informed consent of the trial subjects.

The legal status, composition, function, operations, and regulatory requirements pertaining to Independent Ethics Committees may differ among countries, but should allow the Independent Ethics Committee to act in agreement with GCP as described in this guideline.

1.28 Informed Consent

A process by which a subject voluntarily confirms his or her willingness to participate in a particular trial, after having been informed of all aspects of the trial that are relevant to the subject's decision to participate. Informed consent is documented by means of a written, signed, and dated informed consent form.

1.29 Inspection

The act by a regulatory authority(ies) of conducting an official review of documents, facilities, records, and any other resources that are deemed by the authority(ies) to be related to the clinical trial and that may be located at the site of the trial, at the sponsor's and/or contract research organization's (CRO's) facilities, or at other establishments deemed appropriate by the regulatory authority(ies).

1.30 Institution (medical)

Any public or private entity or agency or medical or dental facility where clinical trials are conducted.

1.31 Institutional Review Board (IRB)

An independent body constituted of medical, scientific, and nonscientific members, whose responsibility it is to ensure the protection of the rights, safety, and well-being of human subjects involved in a trial by, among other things, reviewing, approving, and providing continuing review of trials, of protocols and amendments, and of the methods and material to be used in obtaining and documenting informed consent of the trial subjects.

1.32 Interim Clinical Trial/Study Report

A report of intermediate results and their evaluation based on analyses performed during the course of a trial.

1.33 Investigational Product

A pharmaceutical form of an active ingredient or placebo being tested or used as a reference in a clinical trial, including a product with a marketing authorization when used or assembled (formulated or packaged) in a way different from the approved form, or when used for an unapproved indication, or when used to gain further information about an approved use.

1.34 Investigator

A person responsible for the conduct of the clinical trial at a trial site. If a trial is conducted by a team of individuals at a trial site, the investigator is the responsible leader of the team and may be called the principal investigator. See also Subinvestigator.

1.35 Investigator/Institution

An expression meaning "the investigator and/or institution, where required by the applicable regulatory requirements."

1.36 Investigator's Brochure

A compilation of the clinical and nonclinical data on the investigational product(s) that is relevant to the study of the investigational product(s) in human subjects (see section 7. "Investigator's Brochure").

1.37 Legally Acceptable Representative

An individual or juridical or other body authorized under applicable law to consent, on behalf of a prospective subject, to the subject's participation in the clinical trial.

1.38 Monitoring

The act of overseeing the progress of a clinical trial, and of ensuring that it is conducted, recorded, and reported in accordance with the protocol, standard operating procedures (SOP's), GCP, and the applicable regulatory requirement(s).

1.39 Monitoring Report

A written report from the monitor to the sponsor after each site visit and/or other trial-related communication according to the sponsor's SOP's.

1.40 Multicenter Trial

A clinical trial conducted according to a single protocol but at more than one site, and, therefore, carried out by more than one investigator.

1.41 Nonclinical Study

Biomedical studies not performed on human subjects.

1.42 Opinion (in relation to Independent Ethics Committee)

The judgment and/or the advice provided by an Independent Ethics Committee (IEC).

1.43 Original Medical Record

See Source Documents.

1.44 Protocol

A document that describes the objective(s), design, methodology, statistical considerations, and organization of a trial. The protocol usually also gives the background and rationale for the trial, but these could be provided in other protocol referenced documents. Throughout the ICH GCP Guideline, the term protocol refers to protocol and protocol amendments.

1.45 Protocol Amendment

A written description of a change(s) to or formal clarification of a protocol.

1.46 Quality Assurance (QA)

All those planned and systematic actions that are established to ensure that the trial is performed and the data are generated, documented (recorded), and reported in compliance with GCP and the applicable regulatory requirement(s).

1.47 Quality Control (QC)

The operational techniques and activities undertaken within the quality assurance system to verify that the requirements for quality of the trial-related activities have been fulfilled.

1.48 Randomization

The process of assigning trial subjects to treatment or control groups using an element of chance to determine the assignments in order to reduce bias.

1.49 Regulatory Authorities

Bodies having the power to regulate. In the ICH GCP guideline, the expression "Regulatory Authorities" includes the authorities that review submitted clinical data and those that conduct inspections (see 1.29). These bodies are sometimes referred to as competent authorities.

1.50 Serious Adverse Event (SAE) or Serious Adverse Drug Reaction (Serious ADR)

Any untoward medical occurrence that at any dose:
- Results in death,
- Is life-threatening,
- Requires inpatient hospitalization or prolongation of existing hospitalization,
- Results in persistent or significant disability/incapacity,

or
- Is a congenital anomaly/birth defect,

(See the ICH Guideline for Clinical Safety Data Management: Definitions and Standards for Expedited Reporting.)

1.51 Source Data

All information in original records and certified copies of original records of clinical findings, observations, or other activities in a clinical trial necessary for the reconstruction and evaluation of the trial. Source data are contained in source documents (original records or certified copies).

1.52 Source Documents

Original documents, data, and records (e.g., hospital records, clinical and office charts, laboratory notes, memoranda, subjects' diaries or evaluation checklists, pharmacy dispensing records, recorded data from automated instruments, copies or transcriptions certified after verification as being accurate and complete, microfiches, photographic negatives, microfilm or magnetic media, x-rays, subject files, and records kept at the pharmacy, at the laboratories, and at medico-technical departments involved in the clinical trial).

1.53 Sponsor

An individual, company, institution, or organization that takes responsibility for the initiation, management, and/or financing of a clinical trial.

1.54 Sponsor-Investigator

An individual who both initiates and conducts, alone or with others, a clinical trial, and under whose immediate direction the investigational product is administered to, dispensed to, or used by a subject. The term does not include any person other than an individual (e.g., it does not include a corporation or an agency). The obligations of sponsor-investigator include both those of a sponsor and those of an investigator.

1.55 Standard Operating Procedures (SOP's)

Detailed, written instructions to achieve uniformity of the performance of a specific function.

1.56 Subinvestigator

Any individual member of the clinical trial team designated and supervised by the investigator at a trial site to perform critical trial-related procedures and/or to make important trial-related decisions (e.g., associates, residents, research fellows). See also Investigator.

1.57 Subject/Trial Subject

An individual who participates in a clinical trial, either as a recipient of the investigational product(s) or as a control.

1.58 Subject Identification Code

A unique identifier assigned by the investigator to each trial subject to protect the subject's identity and used in lieu of the subject's name when the investigator reports adverse events and/or other trial-related data.

1.59 Trial Site

The location(s) where trial-related activities are actually conducted.

1.60 Unexpected Adverse Drug Reaction

An adverse reaction, the nature or severity of which is not consistent with the applicable product information (e.g., Investigator's Brochure for an unapproved investigational product or package insert/summary of product characteristics for an approved product). (See the ICH Guideline for Clinical Safety Data Management: Definitions and Standards for Expedited Reporting.)

1.61 Vulnerable Subjects

Individuals whose willingness to volunteer in a clinical trial may be unduly influenced by the expectation, whether justified or not, of benefits associated with participation, or of a retaliatory response from senior members of a hierarchy in case of refusal to participate. Examples are members of a group with a hierarchical structure, such as medical, pharmacy, dental, and nursing students, subordinate hospital and laboratory personnel, employees of the pharmaceutical industry, members of the armed forces, and persons kept in detention. Other vulnerable subjects include patients with incurable diseases, persons in nursing homes, unemployed or impoverished persons, patients in emergency situations, ethnic minority groups, homeless persons, nomads, refugees, minors, and those incapable of giving consent.

1.62 Well-being (of the trial subjects)

The physical and mental integrity of the subjects participating in a clinical trial.

2. THE PRINCIPLES OF ICH GCP

2.1 Clinical trials should be conducted in accordance with the ethical principles that have their origin in the Declaration of Helsinki, and that are consistent with GCP and the applicable regulatory requirement(s).

2.2 Before a trial is initiated, foreseeable risks and inconveniences should be weighed against the anticipated benefit for the individual trial subject and society. A trial should be initiated and continued only if the anticipated benefits justify the risks.

2.3 The rights, safety, and well-being of the trial subjects are the most important considerations and should prevail over interests of science and society.

2.4 The available nonclinical and clinical information on an investigational product should be adequate to support the proposed clinical trial.

2.5 Clinical trials should be scientifically sound, and described in a clear, detailed protocol.

2.6 A trial should be conducted in compliance with the protocol that has received prior institutional review board (IRB)/independent ethics committee (IEC) approval/favorable opinion.

2.7 The medical care given to, and medical decisions made on behalf of, subjects should always be the responsibility of a qualified physician or, when appropriate, of a qualified dentist.

2.8 Each individual involved in conducting a trial should be qualified by education, training, and experience to perform his or her respective task(s).

2.9 Freely given informed consent should be obtained from every subject prior to clinical trial participation.

2.10 All clinical trial information should be recorded, handled, and stored in a way that allows its accurate reporting, interpretation, and verification.

2.11 The confidentiality of records that could identify subjects should be protected, respecting the privacy and confidentiality rules in accordance with the applicable regulatory requirement(s).

2.12 Investigational products should be manufactured, handled, and stored in accordance with applicable good manufacturing practice (GMP). They should be used in accordance with the approved protocol.

2.13 Systems with procedures that assure the quality of every aspect of the trial should be implemented.

3. INSTITUTIONAL REVIEW BOARD/ INDEPENDENT ETHICS COMMITTEE (IRB/IEC)

3.1 Responsibilities

3.1.1 An IRB/IEC should safeguard the rights, safety, and well-being of all trial subjects. Special attention should be paid to trials that may include vulnerable subjects.

3.1.2 The IRB/IEC should obtain the following documents:

Trial protocol(s)/amendment(s), written informed consent form(s) and consent form updates that the investigator proposes for use in the trial, subject recruitment procedures (e.g., advertisements), written information to be provided to subjects, Investigator's Brochure (IB), available safety information, information about payments and compensation available to subjects, the investigator's current curriculum vitae and/or other documentation evidencing qualifications, and any other documents that the IRB/IEC may require to fulfill its responsibilities.

The IRB/IEC should review a proposed clinical trial within a reasonable time and document its views in writing, clearly identifying the trial, the documents reviewed, and the dates for the following:

- Approval/favorable opinion;
- Modifications required prior to its approval/favorable opinion;
- Disapproval/negative opinion; and
- Termination/suspension of any prior approval/favorable opinion.

3.1.3 The IRB/IEC should consider the qualifications of the investigator for the proposed trial, as documented by a current curriculum vitae and/or by any other relevant documentation the IRB/IEC requests.

3.1.4 The IRB/IEC should conduct continuing review of each ongoing trial at intervals appropriate to the degree of risk to human subjects, but at least once per year.

3.1.5 The IRB/IEC may request more information than is outlined in paragraph 4.8.10 be given to subjects when, in the judgment of the IRB/IEC, the additional information would add meaningfully to the protection of the rights, safety, and/or well-being of the subjects.

3.1.6 When a nontherapeutic trial is to be carried out with the consent of the subject's legally acceptable representative (see sections 4.8.12, 4.8.14), the IRB/IEC should determine that the proposed protocol and/or other document(s) adequately addresses relevant ethical concerns and meets applicable regulatory requirements for such trials.

3.1.7 Where the protocol indicates that prior consent of the trial subject or the subject's legally acceptable representative is not possible (see 4.8.15), the IRB/IEC should determine that the proposed protocol and/or other document(s) adequately addresses relevant ethical concerns and meets applicable regulatory requirements for such trials (i.e., in emergency situations).

3.1.8 The IRB/IEC should review both the amount and method of payment to subjects to assure that neither presents problems of coercion or undue influence on the trial subjects. Payments to a subject should be prorated and not wholly contingent on completion of the trial by the subject.

3.1.9 The IRB/IEC should ensure that information regarding payment to subjects, including the methods, amounts, and schedule of payment to trial subjects, is set forth in the written informed consent form and any other written information to be provided to subjects. The way payment will be prorated should be specified.

3.2 Composition, Functions, and Operations

3.2.1 The IRB/IEC should consist of a reasonable number of members, who collectively have the qualifications and experience to review and evaluate the science, medical aspects, and ethics of the proposed trial. It is recommended that the IRB/IEC should include:

(a) At least five members.

(b) At least one member whose primary area of interest is in a nonscientific area.

(c) At least one member who is independent of the institution/trial site.

Only those IRB/IEC members who are independent of the investigator and the sponsor of the trial should vote/provide opinion on a trial-related matter.

A list of IRB/IEC members and their qualifications should be maintained.

3.2.2 The IRB/IEC should perform its functions according to written operating procedures, should maintain written records of its activities and minutes of its meetings, and should comply with GCP and with the applicable regulatory requirement(s).

3.2.3 An IRB/IEC should make its decisions at announced meetings at which at least a quorum, as stipulated in its written operating procedures, is present.

3.2.4 Only members who participate in the IRB/IEC review and discussion should vote/provide their opinion and/or advise.

3.2.5 The investigator may provide information on any aspect of the trial, but should not participate in the deliberations of the IRB/IEC or in the vote/opinion of the IRB/IEC.

3.2.6 An IRB/IEC may invite nonmembers with expertise in special areas for assistance.

3.3 Procedures

The IRB/IEC should establish, document in writing, and follow its procedures, which should include:

3.3.1 Determining its composition (names and qualifications of the members) and the authority under which it is established.

3.3.2 Scheduling, notifying its members of, and conducting its meetings.

3.3.3 Conducting initial and continuing review of trials.

3.3.4 Determining the frequency of continuing review, as appropriate.

3.3.5 Providing, according to the applicable regulatory requirements, expedited review and approval/favorable opinion of minor change(s) in ongoing trials that have the approval/favorable opinion of the IRB/IEC.

3.3.6 Specifying that no subject should be admitted to a trial before the IRB/IEC issues its written approval/favorable opinion of the trial.

3.3.7 Specifying that no deviations from, or changes of, the protocol should be initiated without prior written IRB/IEC approval/favorable opinion of an appropriate amendment, except when necessary to eliminate immediate hazards to the subjects or when the change(s) involves only logistical or administrative aspects of the trial (e.g., change of monitor(s), telephone number(s)) (see section 4.5.2).

3.3.8 Specifying that the investigator should promptly report to the IRB/IEC:

(a) Deviations from, or changes of, the protocol to eliminate immediate hazards to the trial subjects (see sections 3.3.7, 4.5.2, 4.5.4).

(b) Changes increasing the risk to subjects and/or affecting significantly the conduct of the trial (see section 4.10.2).

(c) All adverse drug reactions (ADRs) that are both serious and unexpected.

(d) New information that may affect adversely the safety of the subjects or the conduct of the trial.

3.3.9 Ensuring that the IRB/IEC promptly notify in writing the investigator/institution concerning:

    (a) Its trial-related decisions/opinions.

    (b) The reasons for its decisions/opinions.

    (c) Procedures for appeal of its decisions/opinions.

3.4 Records

The IRB/IEC should retain all relevant records (e.g., written procedures, membership lists, lists of occupations/affiliations of members, submitted documents, minutes of meetings, and correspondence) for a period of at least 3 years after completion of the trial and make them available upon request from the regulatory authority(ies).

The IRB/IEC may be asked by investigators, sponsors, or regulatory authorities to provide copies of its written procedures and membership lists.

4. INVESTIGATOR

4.1 Investigator's Qualifications and Agreements

4.1.1 The investigator(s) should be qualified by education, training, and experience to assume responsibility for the proper conduct of the trial, should meet all the qualifications specified by the applicable regulatory requirement(s), and should provide evidence of such qualifications through up-to-date curriculum vitae and/or other relevant documentation requested by the sponsor, the IRB/IEC, and/or the regulatory authority(ies).

4.1.2 The investigator should be thoroughly familiar with the appropriate use of the investigational product(s), as described in the protocol, in the current Investigator's Brochure, in the product information, and in other information sources provided by the sponsor.

4.1.3 The investigator should be aware of, and should comply with, GCP and the applicable regulatory requirements.

4.1.4 The investigator/institution should permit monitoring and auditing by the sponsor, and inspection by the appropriate regulatory authority(ies).

4.1.5 The investigator should maintain a list of appropriately qualified persons to whom the investigator has delegated significant trial-related duties.

4.2 Adequate Resources

4.2.1 The investigator should be able to demonstrate (e.g., based on retrospective data) a potential for recruiting the required number of suitable subjects within the agreed recruitment period.

4.2.2 The investigator should have sufficient time to properly conduct and complete the trial within the agreed trial period.

4.2.3 The investigator should have available an adequate number of qualified staff and adequate facilities for the foreseen duration of the trial to conduct the trial properly and safely.

4.2.4 The investigator should ensure that all persons assisting with the trial are adequately informed about the protocol, the investigational product(s), and their trial-related duties and functions.

4.3 Medical Care of Trial Subjects

4.3.1 A qualified physician (or dentist, when appropriate), who is an investigator or a subinvestigator for the trial, should be responsible for all trial-related medical (or dental) decisions.

4.3.2 During and following a subject's participation in a trial, the investigator/institution should ensure that adequate medical care is provided to a subject for any adverse events, including clinically significant laboratory values, related to the trial. The investigator/institution should inform a subject when medical care is needed for intercurrent illness(es) of which the investigator becomes aware.

4.3.3 It is recommended that the investigator inform the subject's primary physician about the subject's participation in the trial if the subject has a primary physician and if the subject agrees to the primary physician being informed.

4.3.4 Although a subject is not obliged to give his/her reason(s) for withdrawing prematurely from a trial, the investigator should make a reasonable effort to ascertain the reason(s), while fully respecting the subject's rights.

4.4 Communication with IRB/IEC

4.4.1 Before initiating a trial, the investigator/institution should have written and dated approval/favorable opinion from the IRB/IEC for the trial protocol, written informed consent form, consent form updates, subject recruitment procedures (e.g., advertisements), and any other written information to be provided to subjects.

4.4.2 As part of the investigator's/institution's written application to the IRB/IEC, the investigator/institution should provide the IRB/IEC with a current copy of the Investigator's Brochure. If the Investigator's Brochure is updated during the trial, the investigator/institution should supply a copy of the updated Investigator's Brochure to the IRB/IEC.

4.4.3 During the trial the investigator/institution should provide to the IRB/IEC all documents subject to its review.

4.5 Compliance with Protocol

4.5.1 The investigator/institution should conduct the trial in compliance with the protocol agreed to by the sponsor and, if required, by the regulatory authority(ies), and which was given approval/favorable opinion by the IRB/IEC. The investigator/institution and the sponsor should sign the protocol, or an alternative contract, to confirm their agreement.

4.5.2 The investigator should not implement any deviation from, or changes of, the protocol without agreement by the sponsor and prior review and documented approval/favorable opinion from the IRB/IEC of an amendment, except where necessary to eliminate an immediate hazard(s) to trial subjects, or when the change(s) involves only logistical or administrative aspects of the trial (e.g., change of monitor(s), change of telephone number(s)).

4.5.3 The investigator, or person designated by the investigator, should document and explain any deviation from the approved protocol.

4.5.4 The investigator may implement a deviation from, or a change in, the protocol to eliminate an immediate hazard(s) to trial subjects without prior IRB/IEC approval/favorable opinion. As soon as possible, the implemented deviation or change, the reasons for it, and, if appropriate, the proposed protocol amendment(s) should be submitted:

(a) To the IRB/IEC for review and approval/favorable opinion;

(b) To the sponsor for agreement; and, if required;

(c) To the regulatory authority(ies).

4.6 Investigational Product(s)

4.6.1 Responsibility for investigational product(s) accountability at the trial site(s) rests with the investigator/institution.

4.6.2 Where allowed/required, the investigator/institution may/should assign some or all of the investigator's/institution's duties for investigational product(s) accountability at the trial site(s) to an appropriate pharmacist or another appropriate individual who is under the supervision of the investigator/institution.

4.6.3 The investigator/institution and/or a pharmacist or other appropriate individual, who is designated by the investigator/institution, should maintain records of the product's delivery to the trial site, the inventory at the site, the use by each subject, and the return to the sponsor or alternative disposition of unused product(s). These records should include dates, quantities, batch/serial numbers, expiration dates (if applicable), and the unique code numbers assigned to the investigational product(s) and trial subjects. Investigators should maintain records that document adequately that the subjects were provided the doses specified by the protocol and reconcile all investigational product(s) received from the sponsor.

4.6.4 The investigational product(s) should be stored as specified by the sponsor (see sections 5.13.2 and 5.14.3) and in accordance with applicable regulatory requirement(s).

4.6.5 The investigator should ensure that the investigational product(s) are used only in accordance with the approved protocol.

4.6.6 The investigator, or a person designated by the investigator/institution, should explain the correct use of the investigational product(s) to each subject and should check, at intervals appropriate for the trial, that each subject is following the instructions properly.

4.7 Randomization Procedures and Unblinding

The investigator should follow the trial's randomization procedures, if any, and should ensure that the code is broken only in accordance with the protocol. If the trial is blinded, the investigator should promptly document and explain to the sponsor any premature unblinding (e.g., accidental unblinding, unblinding due to a serious adverse event) of the investigational product(s).

4.8   Informed Consent of Trial Subjects

4.8.1   In obtaining and documenting informed consent, the investigator should comply with the applicable regulatory requirement(s), and should adhere to GCP and to the ethical principles that have their origin in the Declaration of Helsinki. Prior to the beginning of the trial, the investigator should have the IRB/IEC's written approval/favorable opinion of the written informed consent form and any other written information to be provided to subjects.

4.8.2   The written informed consent form and any other written information to be provided to subjects should be revised whenever important new information becomes available that may be relevant to the subject's consent. Any revised written informed consent form, and written information should receive the IRB/IEC's approval/favorable opinion in advance of use. The subject or the subject's legally acceptable representative should be informed in a timely manner if new information becomes available that may be relevant to the subject's willingness to continue participation in the trial. The communication of this information should be documented.

4.8.3   Neither the investigator, nor the trial staff, should coerce or unduly influence a subject to participate or to continue to participate in a trial.

4.8.4   None of the oral and written information concerning the trial, including the written informed consent form, should contain any language that causes the subject or the subject's legally acceptable representative to waive or to appear to waive any legal rights, or that releases or appears to release the investigator, the institution, the sponsor, or their agents from liability for negligence.

4.8.5   The investigator, or a person designated by the investigator, should fully inform the subject or, if the subject is unable to provide informed consent, the subject's legally acceptable representative, of all pertinent aspects of the trial including the written information given approval/favorable opinion by the IRB/IEC.

4.8.6   The language used in the oral and written information about the trial, including the written informed consent form, should be as nontechnical as practical and should be understandable to the subject or the subject's legally acceptable representative and the impartial witness, where applicable.

4.8.7   Before informed consent may be obtained, the investigator, or a person designated by the investigator, should provide the subject or the subject's legally acceptable representative ample time and opportunity to inquire about details of the trial and to decide whether or not to participate in the trial. All questions about the trial should be answered to satisfaction of the subject or the subject's legally acceptable representative.

4.8.8   Prior to a subject's participation in the trial, the written informed consent form should be signed and personally dated by the subject or by the subject's legally acceptable representative, and by the person who conducted the informed consent discussion.

4.8.9   If a subject is unable to read or if a legally acceptable representative is unable to read, an impartial witness should be present during the entire informed consent discussion. After the written informed consent form and any other written information to be provided to subjects is read and explained to the subject or the subject's legally acceptable representative, and after the subject or the subject's legally acceptable representative has orally consented to the subject's participation in the trial, and, if capable of doing so, has signed and personally dated the informed consent form, the witness should sign and personally date the consent form. By signing the consent form, the witness attests that the information in the consent form and any other written information was accurately explained to, and apparently understood by, the subject or the subject's legally acceptable representative, and that informed consent was freely given by the subject or the subject's legally acceptable representative.

4.8.10 Both the informed consent discussion and the written informed consent form and any other written information to be provided to subjects should include explanations of the following:

(a) That the trial involves research.

(b) The purpose of the trial.

(c) The trial treatment(s) and the probability for random assignment to each treatment.

(d) The trial procedures to be followed, including all invasive procedures.

(e) The subject's responsibilities.

(f) Those aspects of the trial that are experimental.

(g) The reasonably foreseeable risks or inconveniences to the subject and, when applicable, to an embryo, fetus, or nursing infant.

(h) The reasonably expected benefits. When there is no intended clinical benefit to the subject, the subject should be made aware of this.

(i) The alternative procedure(s) or course(s) of treatment that may be available to the subject, and their important potential benefits and risks.

(j) The compensation and/of treatment available to the subject in the event of trial-related injury.

(k) The anticipated prorated payment, if any, to the subject for participating in the trial.

(l) The anticipated expenses, if any, to the subject for participating in the trial.

(m) That the subject's participation in the trial is voluntary and that the subject may refuse to participate or withdraw from the trial, at any time, without penalty or loss of benefits to which the subject is otherwise entitled.

(n) That the monitor(s), the auditor(s), the IRB/IEC, and the regulatory authority(ies) will be granted direct access to the subject's original medical records for verification of clinical trial procedures and/or data, without violating the confidentiality of the subject, to the extent permitted by the applicable laws and regulations and that, by signing a written informed consent form, the subject or the subject's legally acceptable representative is authorizing such access.

(o) That records identifying the subject will be kept confidential and, to the extent permitted by the applicable laws and/or regulations, will not be made publicly available. If the results of the trial are published, the subject's identity will remain confidential.

    (p) That the subject or the subject's legally acceptable representative will be informed in a timely manner if information becomes available that may be relevant to the subject's willingness to continue participation in the trial.

    (q) The person(s) to contact for further information regarding the trial and the rights of trial subjects, and whom to contact in the event of trial-related injury.

    (r) The foreseeable circumstances and/or reasons under which the subject's participation in the trial may be terminated.

    (s) The expected duration of the subject's participation in the trial.

    (t) The approximate number of subjects involved in the trial.

4.8.11 Prior to participation in the trial, the subject or the subject's legally acceptable representative should receive a copy of the signed and dated written informed consent form and any other written information provided to the subjects. During a subject's participation in the trial, the subject or the subject's legally acceptable representative should receive a copy of the signed and dated consent form updates and a copy of any amendments to the written information provided to subjects.

4.8.12 When a clinical trial (therapeutic or nontherapeutic) includes subjects who can only be enrolled in the trial with the consent of the subject's legally acceptable representative (e.g., minors, or patients with severe dementia), the subject should be informed about the trial to the extent compatible with the subject's understanding and, if capable, the subject should assent, sign and personally date the written informed consent.

4.8.13 Except as described in 4.8.14, a nontherapeutic trial (i.e., a trial in which there is no anticipated direct clinical benefit to the subject) should be conducted in subjects who personally give consent and who sign and date the written informed consent form.

4.8.14 Nontherapeutic trials may be conducted in subjects with consent of a legally acceptable representative provided the following conditions are fulfilled:

    (a) The objectives of the trial cannot be met by means of a trial in subjects who can give informed consent personally.

    (b) The foreseeable risks to the subjects are low.

    (c) The negative impact on the subject's well-being is minimized and low.

    (d) The trial is not prohibited by law.

    (e) The approval/favorable opinion of the IRB/IEC is expressly sought on the inclusion of such subjects, and the written approval/ favorable opinion covers this aspect.

Such trials, unless an exception is justified, should be conducted in patients having a disease or condition for which the investigational product is intended. Subjects in these trials should be particularly closely monitored and should be withdrawn if they appear to be unduly distressed.

4.8.15 In emergency situations, when prior consent of the subject is not possible, the consent of the subject's legally acceptable representative, if present, should be requested. When prior consent of the subject is not possible, and the subject's legally acceptable representative is not available, enrollment of the subject should require measures described in the protocol and/or elsewhere, with documented approval/favorable opinion by the IRB/IEC, to protect the rights, safety, and well-being of the subject and to ensure compliance with applicable regulatory requirements. The subject or the subject's legally acceptable representative should be informed about the trial as soon as possible and consent to continue and other consent as appropriate (see section 4.8.10) should be requested.

4.9 Records and Reports

4.9.1 The investigator should ensure the accuracy, completeness, legibility, and timeliness of the data reported to the sponsor in the CRFs and in all required reports.

4.9.2 Data reported on the CRF, which are derived from source documents, should be consistent with the source documents or the discrepancies should be explained.

4.9.3 Any change or correction to a CRF should be dated, initialed, and explained (if necessary) and should not obscure the original entry (i.e., an audit trail should be maintained); this applies to both written and electronic changes or corrections (see section 5.18.4(n)). Sponsors should provide guidance to investigators and/or the investigators' designated representatives on making such corrections. Sponsors should have written procedures to assure that changes or corrections in CRFs made by sponsor's designated representatives are documented, are necessary, and are endorsed by the investigator. The investigator should retain records of the changes and corrections.

4.9.4 The investigator/institution should maintain the trial documents as specified in Essential Documents for the Conduct of a Clinical Trial (see section 8.) and as required by the applicable regulatory requirement(s). The investigator/institution should take measures to prevent accidental or premature destruction of these documents.

4.9.5 Essential documents should be retained until at least 2 years after the last approval of a marketing application in an ICH region and until there are no pending or contemplated marketing applications in an ICH region or at least 2 years have elapsed since the formal discontinuation of clinical development of the investigational product. These documents should be retained for a longer period, however, if required by the applicable regulatory requirements or by an agreement with the sponsor. It is the responsibility of the sponsor to inform the investigator/institution as to when these documents no longer need to be retained (see section 5.5.12).

4.9.6 The financial aspects of the trial should be documented in an agreement between the sponsor and the investigator/institution.

4.9.7 Upon request of the monitor, auditor, IRB/IEC, or regulatory authority, the investigator/institution should make available for direct access all requested trial-related records.

4.10 Progress Reports

4.10.1 Where required by the applicable regulatory requirements, the investigator should submit written summaries of the trial's status to the institution. The investigator/institution should submit written summaries of the status of the trial to the IRB/IEC annually, or more frequently, if requested by the IRB/IEC.

4.10.2 The investigator should promptly provide written reports to the sponsor, the IRB/IEC (see section 3.3.8), and, where required by the applicable regulatory requirements, the institution on any changes significantly affecting the conduct of the trial, and/or increasing the risk to subjects.

4.11 Safety Reporting

4.11.1 All serious adverse events (SAEs) should be reported immediately to the sponsor except for those SAEs that the protocol or other document (e.g., Investigator's Brochure) identifies as not needing immediate reporting. The immediate reports should be followed promptly by detailed, written reports. The immediate and follow-up reports should identify subjects by unique code numbers assigned to the trial subjects rather than by the subjects' names, personal identification numbers, and/or addresses. The investigator should also comply with the applicable regulatory requirement(s) related to the reporting of unexpected serious adverse drug reactions to the regulatory authority(ies) and the IRB/IEC.

4.11.2 Adverse events and/or laboratory abnormalities identified in the protocol as critical to safety evaluations should be reported to the sponsor according to the reporting requirements and within the time periods specified by the sponsor in the protocol.

4.11.3 For reported deaths, the investigator should supply the sponsor and the IRB/IEC with any additional requested information (e.g., autopsy reports and terminal medical reports).

4.12 Premature Termination or Suspension of a Trial

If the trial is terminated prematurely or suspended for any reason, the investigator/institution should promptly inform the trial subjects, should assure appropriate therapy and follow-up for the subjects, and, where required by the applicable regulatory requirement(s), should inform the regulatory authority(ies). In addition:

4.12.1 If the investigator terminates or suspends a trial without prior agreement of the sponsor, the investigator should inform the institution, where required by the applicable regulatory requirements, and the investigator/institution should promptly inform the sponsor and the IRB/IEC, and should provide the sponsor and the IRB/IEC a detailed written explanation of the termination or suspension.

4.12.2 If the sponsor terminates or suspends a trial (see section 5.21), the investigator should promptly inform the institution, where required by the applicable regulatory requirements, and the investigator/institution should promptly inform the IRB/IEC and provide the IRB/IEC a detailed written explanation of the termination or suspension.

4.12.3 If the IRB/IEC terminates or suspends its approval/favorable opinion of a trial (see sections 3.1.2 and 3.3.9), the investigator should inform the institution, where required by the applicable regulatory requirements, and the investigator/institution should promptly notify the sponsor and provide the sponsor with a detailed written explanation of the termination or suspension.

4.13 Final Report(s) by Investigator/Institution

Upon completion of the trial, the investigator should, where required by the applicable regulatory requirements, inform the institution, and the investigator/institution should provide the sponsor with all required reports, the IRB/IEC with a summary of the trial's outcome, and the regulatory authority(ies) with any report(s) they require of the investigator/institution.

5. SPONSOR

5.1 Quality Assurance and Quality Control

5.1.1 The sponsor is responsible for implementing and maintaining quality assurance and quality control systems with written SOP's to ensure that trials are conducted and data are generated, documented (recorded), and reported in compliance with the protocol, GCP, and the applicable regulatory requirement(s).

5.1.2 The sponsor is responsible for securing agreement from all involved parties to ensure direct access (see section 1.21) to all trial-related sites, source data/documents, and reports for the purpose of monitoring and auditing by the sponsor, and inspection by domestic and foreign regulatory authorities.

5.1.3 Quality control should be applied to each stage of data handling to ensure that all data are reliable and have been processed correctly.

5.1.4 Agreements, made by the sponsor with the investigator/institution and/or with any other parties involved with the clinical trial, should be in writing, as part of the protocol or in a separate agreement.

5.2 Contract Research Organization (CRO)

5.2.1 A sponsor may transfer any or all of the sponsor's trial-related duties and functions to a CRO, but the ultimate responsibility for the quality and integrity of the trial data always resides with the sponsor. The CRO should implement quality assurance and quality control.

5.2.2 Any trial-related duty and function that is transferred to and assumed by a CRO should be specified in writing.

5.2.3 Any trial-related duties and functions not specifically transferred to and assumed by a CRO are retained by the sponsor.

5.2.4 All references to a sponsor in this guideline also apply to a CRO to the extent that a CRO has assumed the trial-related duties and functions of a sponsor.

5.3 Medical Expertise

The sponsor should designate appropriately qualified medical personnel who will be readily available to advise on trial-related medical questions or problems. If necessary, outside consultant(s) may be appointed for this purpose.

5.4 Trial Design

5.4.1 The sponsor should utilize qualified individuals (e.g., biostatisticians, clinical pharmacologists, and physicians) as appropriate, throughout all stages of the trial process, from designing the protocol and CRF's and planning the analyses to analyzing and preparing interim and final clinical trial/study reports.

5.4.2 For further guidance: Clinical Trial Protocol and Protocol Amendment(s) (see section 6.), the ICH Guideline for Structure and Content of Clinical Study Reports, and other appropriate ICH guidance on trial design, protocol, and conduct.

5.5 Trial Management, Data Handling, Recordkeeping, and Independent Data Monitoring Committee

5.5.1 The sponsor should utilize appropriately qualified individuals to supervise the overall conduct of the trial, to handle the data, to verify the data, to conduct the statistical analyses, and to prepare the trial reports.

5.5.2 The sponsor may consider establishing an independent data monitoring committee (IDMC) to assess the progress of a clinical trial, including the safety data and the critical efficacy endpoints at intervals, and to recommend to the sponsor whether to continue, modify, or stop a trial. The IDMC should have written operating procedures and maintain written records of all its meetings.

5.5.3 When using electronic trial data handling and/or remote electronic trial data systems, the sponsor should:

(a) Ensure and document that the electronic data processing system(s) conforms to the sponsor's established requirements for completeness, accuracy, reliability, and consistent intended performance (i.e., validation).

(b) Maintain SOP's for using these systems.

(c) Ensure that the systems are designed to permit data changes in such a way that the data changes are documented and that there is no deletion of entered data (i.e., maintain an audit trail, data trail, edit trail).

(d) Maintain a security system that prevents unauthorized access to the data.

(e) Maintain a list of the individuals who are authorized to make data changes (see sections 4.1.5 and 4.9.3).

(f) Maintain adequate backup, of the data.

(g) Safeguard the blinding, if any (e.g., maintain the blinding during data entry and processing).

5.5.4 If data are transformed during processing, it should always be possible to compare the original data and observations with the processed data.

5.5.5 The sponsor should use an unambiguous subject identification code (see section 1.58) that allows identification of all the data reported for each subject.

5.5.6 The sponsor, or other owners of the data, should retain all of the sponsor-specific essential documents pertaining to the trial. (See section 8. "Essential Documents for the Conduct of a Clinical Trial.")

5.5.7 The sponsor should retain all sponsor-specific essential documents in conformance with the applicable regulatory requirement(s) of the country(ies) where the product is approved, and/or where the sponsor intends to apply for approval(s).

5.5.8 If the sponsor discontinues the clinical development of an investigational product (i.e., for any or all indications, routes of administration, or dosage forms), the sponsor should maintain all sponsor-specific essential documents for at least 2 years after formal discontinuation or in conformance with the applicable regulatory requirement(s).

5.5.9 If the sponsor discontinues the clinical development of an investigational product, the sponsor should notify all the trial investigators/institutions and all the appropriate regulatory authorities.

5.5.10 Any transfer of ownership of the data should be reported to the appropriate authority(ies), as required by the applicable regulatory requirement(s).

5.5.11 The sponsor-specific essential documents should be retained until at least 2 years after the last approval of a marketing application in an ICH region and until there are no pending or contemplated marketing applications in an ICH region or at least 2 years have elapsed since the formal discontinuation of clinical development of the investigational product. These documents should be retained for a longer period, however, if required by the applicable regulatory requirement(s) or if needed by the sponsor.

5.5.12 The sponsor should inform the investigator(s)/institution(s) in writing of the need for record retention and should notify the investigator(s)/institution(s) in writing when the trial-related records are no longer needed (see section 4.9.5).

5.6 Investigator Selection

5.6.1 The sponsor is responsible for selecting the investigator(s)/institution(s). Each investigator should be qualified by training and experience and should have adequate resources (see sections 4.1, 4.2) to properly conduct the trial for which the investigator is selected. If a coordinating committee and/or coordinating investigator(s) are to be utilized in multicenter trials, their organization and/or selection are the sponsor's responsibility.

5.6.2 Before entering an agreement with an investigator/institution to conduct a trial, the sponsor should provide the investigator(s)/institution(s) with the protocol and an up-to-date Investigator's Brochure, and should provide sufficient time for the investigator/institution to review the protocol and the information provided.

5.6.3 The sponsor should obtain the investigator's/institution's agreement:

    (a) To conduct the trial in compliance with GCP, with the applicable regulatory requirement(s), and with the protocol agreed to by the sponsor and given approval/favorable opinion by the IRB/IEC;

    (b) To comply with procedures for data recording/reporting: and

    (c) To permit monitoring, auditing, and inspection (see section 4.1.4).

    (d) To retain the essential documents that should be in the investigator/institution files (see section 8.) until the sponsor informs the investigator/institution these documents are no longer needed (see sections 4.9.4, 4.9.5, and 5.5.12).

The sponsor and the investigator/institution should sign the protocol, or an alternative document, to confirm this agreement.

5.7   Allocation of Duties and Functions

Prior to initiating a trial, the sponsor should define, establish, and allocate all trial-related duties and functions.

5.8   Compensation to Subjects and Investigators

5.8.1   If required by the applicable regulatory requirement(s), the sponsor should provide insurance or should indemnify (legal and financial coverage) the investigator/the institution against claims arising from the trial, except for claims that arise from malpractice and/or negligence.

5.8.2   The sponsor's policies and procedures should address the costs of treatment of trial subjects in the event of trial-related injuries in accordance with the applicable regulatory requirement(s).

5.8.3   When trial subjects receive compensation, the method and manner of compensation should comply with applicable regulatory requirement(s).

5.9   Financing

The financial aspects of the trial should be documented in an agreement between the sponsor and the investigator/institution.

5.10   Notification/Submission to Regulatory Authority(ies)

Before initiating the clinical trial(s), the sponsor (or the sponsor and the investigator, if required by the applicable regulatory requirement(s)), should submit any required application(s) to the appropriate authority(ies) for review, acceptance, and/or permission (as required by the applicable regulatory requirement(s)) to begin the trial(s). Any notification/submission should be dated and contain sufficient information to identify the protocol.

5.11   Confirmation of Review by IRB/IEC

5.11.1 The sponsor should obtain from the investigator/institution:

(a)   The name and address of the investigator's/institution's IRB/IEC.

(b)   A statement obtained from the IRB/IEC that it is organized and operates according to GCP and the applicable laws and regulations.

(c)   Documented IRB/IEC approval/favorable opinion and, if requested by the sponsor, a current copy of protocol, written informed consent form(s) and any other written information to be provided to subjects, subject recruiting procedures, and documents related to payments and compensation available to the subjects, and any other documents that the IRB/IEC may have requested.

5.11.2 If the IRB/IEC conditions its approval/favorable opinion upon change(s) in any aspect of the trial, such as modification(s) of the protocol, written informed consent form and any other written information to be provided to subjects, and/or other procedures, the sponsor should obtain from the investigator/institution a copy of the modification(s) made and the date approval/favorable opinion was given by the IRB/IEC.

5.11.3 The sponsor should obtain from the investigator/institution documentation and dates of any IRB/IEC reapprovals/reevaluations with favorable opinion, and of any withdrawals or suspensions of approval/favorable opinion.

5.12 Information on Investigational Product(s)

5.12.1 When planning trials, the sponsor should ensure that sufficient safety and efficacy data from nonclinical studies and/or clinical trials are available to support human exposure by the route, at the dosages, for the duration, and in the trial population to be studied.

5.12.2 The sponsor should update the Investigator's Brochure as significant new information becomes available. (See section 7. "Investigator's Brochure.")

5.13 Manufacturing, Packaging, Labeling, and Coding Investigational Product(s)

5.13.1 The sponsor should ensure that the investigational product(s) (including active comparator(s) and placebo, if applicable) is characterized as appropriate to the stage of development of the product(s), is manufactured in accordance with any applicable GMP, and is coded and labeled in a manner that protects the blinding, if applicable. In addition, the labeling should comply with applicable regulatory requirement(s).

5.13.2 The sponsor should determine, for the investigational product(s), acceptable storage temperatures, storage conditions (e.g., protection from light), storage times, reconstitution fluids and procedures, and devices for product infusion, if any. The sponsor should inform all involved parties (e.g., monitors, investigators, pharmacists, storage managers) of these determinations.

5.13.3 The investigational product(s) should be packaged to prevent contamination and unacceptable deterioration during transport and storage.

5.13.4 In blinded trials, the coding system for the investigational product(s) should include a mechanism that permits rapid identification of the product(s) in case of a medical emergency, but does not permit undetectable breaks of the blinding.

5.13.5 If significant formulation changes are made in the investigational or comparator product(s) during the course of clinical development, the results of any additional studies of the formulated product(s) (e.g., stability, dissolution rate, bioavailability) needed to assess whether these changes would significantly alter the pharmacokinetic profile of the product should be available prior to the use of the new formulation in clinical trials.

5.14 Supplying and Handling Investigational Product(s)

5.14.1 The sponsor is responsible for supplying the investigator(s)/ institution(s) with the investigational product(s).

5.14.2 The sponsor should not supply an investigator/institution with the investigational product(s) until the sponsor obtains all required documentation (e.g., approval/favorable opinion from IRB/IEC and regulatory authority(ies)).

5.14.3 The sponsor should ensure that written procedures include instructions that the investigator/institution should follow for the handling and storage of investigational product(s) for the trial and documentation thereof. The procedures should address adequate and safe receipt, handling, storage, dispensing, retrieval of unused product from subject, and return of unused investigational product(s) to the sponsor (or alternative disposition if authorized by the sponsor and in compliance with the applicable regulatory requirement(s)).

5.14.4 The sponsor should:

    (a) Ensure timely delivery of investigational product(s) to the investigator(s).

    (b) Maintain records that document shipment, receipt, disposition, return, and destruction of the investigational product(s). (See section 8. "Essential Documents for the Conduct of a Clinical Trial.")

    (c) Maintain a system for retrieving investigational products and documenting this retrieval (e.g., for deficient product recall, reclaim after trial completion, expired product reclaim).

    (d) Maintain a system for the disposition of unused investigational product(s) and for the documentation of this disposition.

5.14.5 The sponsor should:

    (a) Take steps to ensure that the investigational product(s) are stable over the period of use.

    (b) Maintain sufficient quantities of the investigational product(s) used in the trials to reconfirm specifications, should this become necessary, and maintain records of batch sample analyses and characteristics. To the extent stability permits, samples should be retained either until the analyses of the trial data are complete or as required by the applicable regulatory requirement(s), whichever represents the longer retention period.

5.15 Record Access

5.15.1 The sponsor should ensure that it is specified in the protocol or other written agreement that the investigator(s)/institution(s) provide direct access to source data/documents for trial-related monitoring, audits, IRB/IEC review, and regulatory inspection.

5.15.2 The sponsor should verify that each subject has consented, in writing, to direct access to his/her original medical records for trial-related monitoring, audit, IRB/IEC review, and regulatory inspection.

5.16 Safety Information

5.16.1 The sponsor is responsible for the ongoing safety evaluation of the investigational product(s).

5.16.2 The sponsor should promptly notify all concerned investigator(s)/institution(s) and the regulatory authority(ies) of findings that could affect adversely the safety of subjects, impact the conduct of the trial, or alter the IRB/IEC's approval/favorable opinion to continue the trial.

5.17 Adverse Drug Reaction Reporting

5.17.1 The sponsor should expedite the reporting to all concerned investigator(s)/ institutions(s), to the IRB(s)/IEC(s), where required, and to the regulatory authority(ies) of all adverse drug reactions (ADR's) that are both serious and unexpected.

5.17.2 Such expedited reports should comply with the applicable regulatory requirement(s) and with the ICH Guideline for Clinical Safety Data Management: Definitions and Standards for Expedited Reporting.

5.17.3 The sponsor should submit to the regulatory authority(ies) all safety updates and periodic reports, as required by applicable regulatory requirement(s).

5.18 Monitoring

5.18.1 Purpose. The purposes of trial monitoring are to verify that:

    (a) The rights and well-being of human subjects are protected.

    (b) The reported trial data are accurate, complete, and verifiable from source documents.

    (c) The conduct of the trial is in compliance with the currently approved protocol/amendment(s), with GCP, and with applicable regulatory requirement(s).

5.18.2 Selection and Qualifications of Monitors.

    (a) Monitors should be appointed by the sponsor.

    (b) Monitors should be appropriately trained, and should have the scientific and/or clinical knowledge needed to monitor the trial adequately. A monitor's qualifications should be documented.

    (c) Monitors should be thoroughly familiar with the investigational product(s), the protocol, written informed consent form and any other written information to be provided to subjects, the sponsor's SOPs, GCP, and the applicable regulatory requirement(s).

5.18.3 Extent and Nature of Monitoring.

The sponsor should ensure that the trials are adequately monitored. The sponsor should determine the appropriate extent and nature of monitoring. The determination of the extent and nature of monitoring should be based on considerations such as the objective, purpose, design, complexity, blinding, size, and endpoints of the trial. In general there is a need for on-site monitoring, before, during, and after the trial; however, in exceptional circumstances the sponsor may determine that central monitoring in conjunction with procedures such as investigators' training and meetings, and extensive written guidance can assure appropriate conduct of the trial in accordance with GCP. Statistically controlled sampling may be an acceptable method for selecting the data to be verified.

5.18.4 Monitor's Responsibilities.

The monitor(s), in accordance with the sponsor's requirements, should ensure that the trial is conducted and documented properly by carrying out the following activities when relevant and necessary to the trial and the trial site:

    (a) Acting as the main line of communication between the sponsor and the investigator.

    (b) Verifying that the investigator has adequate qualifications and resources (see sections 4.1, 4.2, 5.6) and these remain adequate throughout the trial period, and that the staff and facilities, including laboratories and equipment, are adequate to safely and properly conduct the trial and these remain adequate throughout the trial period.

(c) Verifying, for the investigational product(s):

    (i)   That storage times and conditions are acceptable, and that supplies are sufficient throughout the trial.

    (ii)   That the investigational product(s) are supplied only to subjects who are eligible to receive it and at the protocol specified dose(s).

    (iii)   That subjects are provided with necessary instruction on properly using, handling, storing, and returning the investigational product(s).

    (iv)   That the receipt, use, and return of the investigational product(s) at the trial sites are controlled and documented adequately.

    (v)   That the disposition of unused investigational product(s) at the trial sites complies with applicable regulatory requirement(s) and is in accordance with the sponsor's authorized procedures.

(d) Verifying that the investigator follows the approved protocol and all approved amendment(s), if any.

(e) Verifying that written informed consent was obtained before each subject's participation in the trial.

(f) Ensuring that the investigator receives the current Investigator's Brochure, all documents, and all trial supplies needed to conduct the trial properly and to comply with the applicable regulatory requirement(s).

(g Ensuring that the investigator and the investigator's trial staff are adequately informed about the trial.

(h) Verifying that the investigator and the investigator's trial staff are performing the specified trial functions, in accordance with the protocol and any other written agreement between the sponsor and the investigator/institution, and have not delegated these functions to unauthorized individuals.

(i) Verifying that the investigator is enrolling only eligible subjects.

(j) Reporting the subject recruitment rate.

(k) Verifying that source data/documents and other trial records are accurate, complete, kept up-to-date, and maintained.

(l) Verifying that the investigator provides all the required reports, notifications, applications, and submissions, and that these documents are accurate, complete, timely, legible, dated, and identify the trial.

(m) Checking the accuracy and completeness of the CRF entries, source data/documents, and other trial-related records against each other. The monitor specifically should verify that:

    (i)   The data required by the protocol are reported accurately on the CRFs and are consistent with the source data/documents.

    (ii)   Any dose and/or therapy modifications are well documented for each of the trial subjects.

    (iii)   Adverse events, concomitant medications, and intercurrent illnesses are reported in accordance with the protocol on the CRFs.

(iv) Visits that the subjects fail to make, tests that are not conducted, and examinations that are not performed are clearly reported as such on the CRFs.

(v) All withdrawals and dropouts of enrolled subjects from the trial are reported and explained on the CRFs.

(n) Informing the investigator of any CRF entry error, omission, or illegibility. The monitor should ensure that appropriate corrections, additions, or deletions are made, dated, explained (if necessary), and initialed by the investigator or by a member of the investigator's trial staff who is authorized to initial CRF changes for the investigator. This authorization should be documented.

(o) Determining whether all adverse events (AEs) are appropriately reported within the time periods required by GCP, the ICH Guideline for Clinical Safety Data Management: Definitions and Standards for Expedited Reporting, the protocol, the IRB/IEC, the sponsor, and the applicable regulatory requirement(s).

(p) Determining whether the investigator is maintaining the essential documents. (See section 8. "Essential Documents for the Conduct of a Clinical Trial.")

(q) Communicating deviations from the protocol, SOPs, GCP, and the applicable regulatory requirements to the investigator and taking appropriate action designed to prevent recurrence of the detected deviations.

5.18.5 Monitoring Procedures.

The monitor(s) should follow the sponsor's established written SOPs as well as those procedures that are specified by the sponsor for monitoring a specific trial.

5.18.6 Monitoring Report.

(a) The monitor should submit a written report to the sponsor after each trial-site visit or trial-related communication.

(b) Reports should include the date, site, name of the monitor, and name of the investigator or other individual(s) contacted.

(c) Reports should include a summary of what the monitor reviewed and the monitor's statements concerning the significant findings/facts, deviations and deficiencies, conclusions, actions taken or to be taken, and/or actions recommended to secure compliance.

(d) The review and follow-up of the monitoring report by the sponsor should be documented by the sponsor's designated representative.

5.19 Audit

If or when sponsors perform audits, as part of implementing quality assurance, they should consider:

5.19.1 Purpose.

The purpose of a sponsor's audit, which is independent of and separate from routine monitoring or quality control functions, should be to evaluate trial conduct and compliance with the protocol, SOPs, GCP, and the applicable regulatory requirements.

5.19.2 Selection and Qualification of Auditors.

(a) The sponsor should appoint individuals, who are independent of the clinical trial/data collection system(s), to conduct audits.

(b) The sponsor should ensure that the auditors are qualified by training and experience to conduct audits properly. An auditor's qualifications should be documented.

5.19.3 Auditing Procedures.

(a) The sponsor should ensure that the auditing of clinical trials/systems is conducted in accordance with the sponsor's written procedures on what to audit, how to audit, the frequency of audits, and the form and content of audit reports.

(b) The sponsor's audit plan and procedures for a trial audit should be guided by the importance of the trial to submissions to regulatory authorities, the number of subjects in the trial, the type and complexity of the trial, the level of risks to the trial subjects, and any identified problem(s).

(c) The observations and findings of the auditor(s) should be documented.

(d) To preserve the independence and value of the audit function, the regulatory authority(ies) should not routinely request the audit reports. Regulatory authority(ies) may seek access to an audit report on a case-by-case basis, when evidence of serious GCP noncompliance exists, or in the course of legal proceedings.

(e) Where required by applicable law or regulation, the sponsor should provide an audit certificate.

5.20 Noncompliance

5.20.1 Noncompliance with the protocol, SOPs, GCP, and/or applicable regulatory requirement(s) by an investigator/institution, or by member(s) of the sponsor's staff should lead to prompt action by the sponsor to secure compliance.

5.20.2 If the monitoring and/or auditing identifies serious and/or persistent noncompliance on the part of an investigator/institution, the sponsor should terminate the investigator's/institution's participation in the trial. When an investigator's/institution's participation is terminated because of noncompliance, the sponsor should notify promptly the regulatory authority(ies).

5.21 Premature Termination or Suspension of a Trial

If a trial is terminated prematurely or suspended, the sponsor should promptly inform the investigators/institutions, and the regulatory authority(ies) of the termination or suspension and the reason(s) for the termination or suspension. The IRB/IEC should also be informed promptly and provided the reason(s) for the termination or suspension by the sponsor or by the investigator/institution, as specified by the applicable regulatory requirement(s).

5.22 Clinical Trial/Study Reports

Whether the trial is completed or prematurely terminated, the sponsor should ensure that the clinical trial/study reports are prepared and provided to the regulatory agency(ies) as required by the applicable regulatory requirement(s). The sponsor should also ensure that the clinical trial/study reports in marketing applications meet the standards of the ICH Guideline for

Structure and Content of Clinical Study Reports. (NOTE: The ICH Guideline for Structure and Content of Clinical Study Reports specifies that abbreviated study reports may be acceptable in certain cases.)

5.23 Multicenter Trials

For multicenter trials, the sponsor should ensure that:

> **5.23.1** All investigators conduct the trial in strict compliance with the protocol agreed to by the sponsor and, if required, by the regulatory authority(ies), and given approval/favorable opinion by the IRB/IEC.
>
> **5.23.2** The CRFs are designed to capture the required data at all multicenter trial sites. For those investigators who are collecting additional data, supplemental CRFs should also be provided that are designed to capture the additional data.
>
> **5.23.3** The responsibilities of the coordinating investigator(s) and the other participating investigators are documented prior to the start of the trial.
>
> **5.23.4** All investigators are given instructions on following the protocol, on complying with a uniform set of standards for the assessment of clinical and laboratory findings, and on completing the CRFs.
>
> **5.23.5** Communication between investigators is facilitated.

6. CLINICAL TRIAL PROTOCOL AND PROTOCOL AMENDMENT(S)

The contents of a trial protocol should generally include the following topics. However, site specific information may be provided on separate protocol page(s), or addressed in a separate agreement, and some of the information listed below may be contained in other protocol referenced documents, such as an Investigator's Brochure.

6.1 General Information

> **6.1.1** Protocol title, protocol identifying number, and date. Any amendment(s) should also bear the amendment number(s) and date(s).
>
> **6.1.2** Name and address of the sponsor and monitor (if other than the sponsor).
>
> **6.1.3** Name and title of the person(s) authorized to sign the protocol and the protocol amendment(s) for the sponsor.
>
> **6.1.4** Name, title, address, and telephone number(s) of the sponsor's medical expert (or dentist when appropriate) for the trial.
>
> **6.1.5** Name and title of the investigator(s) who is (are) responsible for conducting the trial, and the address and telephone number(s) of the trial site(s).
>
> **6.1.6** Name, title, address, and telephone number(s) of the qualified physician (or dentist, if applicable) who is responsible for all trial-site related medical (or dental) decisions (if other than investigator).
>
> **6.1.7** Name(s) and address(es) of the clinical laboratory(ies) and other medical and/or technical department(s) and/or institutions involved in the trial.

6.2   Background Information

   6.2.1   Name and description of the investigational product(s).

   6.2.2   A summary of findings from nonclinical studies that potentially have clinical significance and from clinical trials that are relevant to the trial.

   6.2.3   Summary of the known and potential risks and benefits, if any, to human subjects.

   6.2.4   Description of and justification for the route of administration, dosage, dosage regimen, and treatment period(s).

   6.2.5   A statement that the trial will be conducted in compliance with the protocol, GCP, and the applicable regulatory requirement(s).

   6.2.6   Description of the population to be studied.

   6.2.7   References to literature and data that are relevant to the trial, and that provide background for the trial.

6.3   Trial Objectives and Purpose

A detailed description of the objectives and the purpose of the trial.

6.4   Trial Design

The scientific integrity of the trial and the credibility of the data from the trial depend substantially on the trial design. A description of the trial design should include:

   6.4.1   A specific statement of the primary endpoints and the secondary endpoints, if any, to be measured during the trial.

   6.4.2   A description of the type/design of trial to be conducted (e.g., double-blind, placebo-controlled, parallel design) and a schematic diagram of trial design, procedures, and stages.

   6.4.3   A description of the measures taken to minimize/avoid bias, including (for example):
   (a) Randomization.
   (b) Blinding.

   6.4.4   A description of the trial treatment(s) and the dosage and dosage regimen of the investigational product(s). Also include a description of the dosage form, packaging, and labeling of the investigational product(s).

   6.4.5   The expected duration of subject participation, and a description of the sequence and duration of all trial periods, including follow-up, if any.

   6.4.6   A description of the "stopping rules" or "discontinuation criteria" for individual subjects, parts of trial, and entire trial.

   6.4.7   Accountability procedures for the investigational product(s), including the placebo(s) and comparator(s), if any.

6.4.8 Maintenance of trial treatment randomization codes and procedures for breaking codes.

6.4.9 The identification of any data to be recorded directly on the CRFs (i.e., no prior written or electronic record of data), and to be considered to be source data.

6.5 Selection and Withdrawal of Subjects

6.5.1 Subject inclusion criteria.

6.5.2 Subject exclusion criteria.

6.5.3 Subject withdrawal criteria (i.e., terminating investigational product treatment/trial treatment) and procedures specifying:

(a) When and how to withdraw subjects from the trial/ investigational product treatment.

(b) The type and timing of the data to be collected for withdrawn subjects.

(c) Whether and how subjects are to be replaced.

(d) The follow-up for subjects withdrawn from investigational product treatment/ trial treatment.

6.6 Treatment of Subjects

6.6.1 The treatment(s) to be administered, including the name(s) of all the product(s), the dose(s), the dosing schedule(s), the route/mode(s) of administration, and the treatment period(s), including the follow-up period(s) for subjects for each investigational product treatment/trial treatment group/arm of the trial.

6.6.2 Medication(s)/treatment(s) permitted (including rescue medication) and not permitted before and/or during the trial.

6.6.3 Procedures for monitoring subject compliance.

6.7 Assessment of Efficacy

6.7.1 Specification of the efficacy parameters.

6.7.2 Methods and timing for assessing, recording, and analyzing efficacy parameters.

6.8 Assessment of Safety

6.8.1 Specification of safety parameters.

6.8.2 The methods and timing for assessing, recording, and analyzing safety parameters.

6.8.3 Procedures for eliciting reports of and for recording and reporting adverse event and intercurrent illnesses.

6.8.4 The type and duration of the follow-up of subjects after adverse events.

6.9 Statistics

6.9.1 A description of the statistical methods to be employed, including timing of any planned interim analysis(ses).

6.9.2 The number of subjects planned to be enrolled. In multicenter trials, the number of enrolled subjects projected for each trial site should be specified. Reason for choice of sample size, including reflections on (or calculations of) the power of the trial and clinical justification.

6.9.3 The level of significance to be used.

6.9.4 Criteria for the termination of the trial.

6.9.5 Procedure for accounting for missing, unused, and spurious data.

6.9.6 Procedures for reporting any deviation(s) from the original statistical plan (any deviation(s) from the original statistical plan should be described and justified in the protocol and/or in the final report, as appropriate).

6.9.7 The selection of subjects to be included in the analyses (e.g., all randomized subjects, all dosed subjects, all eligible subjects, evaluate-able subjects).

6.10 Direct Access to Source Data/Documents

The sponsor should ensure that it is specified in the protocol or other written agreement that the investigator(s)/institution(s) will permit trial-related monitoring, audits IRB/IEC review, and regulatory inspection(s) by providing direct access to source data/documents.

6.11 Quality Control and Quality Assurance

6.12 Ethics

Description of ethical considerations relating to the trial.

6.13 Data Handling and Recordkeeping

6.14 Financing and Insurance

Financing and insurance if not addressed in a separate agreement.

6.15 Publication Policy

Publication policy, if not addressed in a separate agreement.

6.16 Supplements

(NOTE: Since the protocol and the clinical trial/study report are closely related, further relevant information can be found in the ICH Guideline for Structure and Content of Clinical Study Reports.)

7. INVESTIGATOR'S BROCHURE

7.1 Introduction

The Investigator's Brochure (IB) is a compilation of the clinical and nonclinical data on the investigational product(s) that are relevant to the study of the product(s) in human subjects. Its purpose is to provide the investigators and others involved in the trial with the information to facilitate their understanding of the rationale, for, and their compliance with, many key features of the protocol, such as the dose, dose frequency/interval, methods of administration, and safety monitoring procedures. The IB also provides insight to support the clinical management of the study subjects during the course of the clinical trial. The information should be presented in a concise, simple, objective, balanced, and nonpromotional form that enables a clinician, or potential investigator, to understand it and make his/her own unbiased risk-benefit assessment of the appropriateness of the proposed trial. For this reason, a medically qualified person should generally participate in the editing of an IB, but the contents of the IB should be approved by the disciplines that generated the described data.

This guideline delineates the minimum information that should be included in an IB and provides suggestions for its layout. It is expected that the type and extent of information available will vary with the stage of development of, the investigational product. If the investigational product is marketed and its pharmacology is widely understood by medical practitioners, an extensive IB may not be necessary. Where permitted by regulatory authorities, a basic product information brochure, package leaflet, or labeling may be an appropriate alternative, provided that it includes current, comprehensive, and detailed information on all aspects of the investigational product that might be of importance to the investigator. If a marketed product is being studied for a new use (i.e., a new indication), an IB specific to that new use should be prepared. The IB should be reviewed at least annually and revised as necessary in compliance with a sponsor's written procedures. More frequent revision may be appropriate depending on the stage of development and the generation of relevant new information. However, in accordance with GCP, relevant new information may be so important that it should be communicated to the investigators, and possibly to the Institutional Review Boards (IRB's)/Independent Ethics Committees (IEC's) and/or regulatory authorities before it is included in a revised IB.

Generally, the sponsor is responsible for ensuring that an up-to-date IB is made available to the investigator(s) and the investigators are responsible for providing the up-to-date IB to the responsible IRB's/ IEC's. In the case of an investigator-sponsored trial, the sponsor-investigator should determine whether a brochure is available from the commercial manufacturer. If the investigational product is provided by the sponsor-investigator, then he or she should provide the necessary information to the trial personnel. In cases where preparation of a formal IB is impractical, the sponsor-investigator should provide, as a substitute, an expanded background information section in the trial protocol that contains the minimum current information described in this guideline.

7.2 General Considerations

The IB should include:

> **7.2.1** Title Page. This should provide the sponsor's name, the identity of each investigational product (i.e., research number, chemical or approved generic name, and trade name(s) where legally permissible and desired by the sponsor), and the release date. It is also suggested that an edition number, and a reference to the number and date of the edition it supersedes, be provided. An example is given in Appendix 1.

> **7.2.2** Confidentiality Statement. The sponsor may wish to include a statement instructing the investigator/recipients to treat the IB as a confidential document for the sole information and use of the investigator's team and the IRB/IEC.

7.3 Contents of the Investigator's Brochure.

The IB should contain the following sections, each with literature references where appropriate:

7.3.1 Table of Contents. An example of the Table of Contents is given in Appendix 2.

7.3.2 Summary. A brief summary (preferably not exceeding two pages) should be given, highlighting the significant physical, chemical, pharmaceutical, pharmacological, toxicological, pharmacokinetic, metabolic, and clinical information available that is relevant to the stage of clinical development of the investigational product.

7.3.3 Introduction. A brief introductory statement should be provided that contains the chemical name (and generic and trade name(s) when approved) of the investigational product(s), all active ingredients, the investigational product(s) pharmacological class and its expected position within this class (e.g., advantages), the rationale for performing research with the investigational product(s), and the anticipated prophylactic, therapeutic, or diagnostic indication(s). Finally, the introductory statement should provide the general approach to be followed in evaluating the investigational product.

7.3.4 Physical, Chemical, and Pharmaceutical Properties and Formulation. A description should be provided of the investigational product substance(s) (including the chemical and/or structural formula(e)), and a brief summary should be given of the relevant physical, chemical, and pharmaceutical properties.

To permit appropriate. safety measures to be taken in the course of the trial, a description of the formulation(s) to be used, including excipients, should be provided and justified if clinically relevant. Instructions for the storage and handling of the dosage form(s) should also be given.

Any structural similarities to other known compounds should be mentioned.

7.3.5 Nonclinical Studies.

Introduction:

The results of all relevant nonclinical pharmacology, toxicology, pharmacokinetic, and investigational product metabolism studies should be provided in summary form. This summary should address the methodology used, the results, and a discussion of the relevance of the findings to the investigated therapeutic and the possible unfavorable and unintended effects in humans.

The information provided may include the following, as appropriate, if known/available:

Species tested;

Number and sex of animals in each group;

Unit dose (e.g., milligram/kilogram (mg/kg));

Dose interval;

Route of administration;

Duration of dosing;

Information on systemic distribution;

Duration of post-exposure follow-up;

Results, including the following aspects:

- Nature and frequency of pharmacological or toxic effects;

- Severity or intensity of pharmacological or toxic effects;

- Time to onset of effects;
- Reversibility of effects;
- Duration of effects;
- Dose response.

Tabular format/listings should be used whenever possible to enhance the clarity of the presentation.

The following sections should discuss the most important findings from the studies, including the dose response of observed effects, the relevance to humans, and any aspects to be studied in humans. If applicable, the effective and nontoxic dose findings in the same animal species should be compared (i.e., the therapeutic index should be discussed). The relevance of this information to the proposed human dosing should be addressed. Whenever possible, comparisons should be made in terms of blood/tissue levels rather than on a mg/kg basis.

(a) Nonclinical Pharmacology

A summary of the pharmacological aspects of the investigational product and, where appropriate, its significant metabolites studied in animals should be included. Such a summary should incorporate studies that assess potential therapeutic activity (e.g., efficacy models, receptor binding, and specificity) as well as those that assess safety (e.g., special studies to assess pharmacological actions other than the intended therapeutic effect(s)).

(b) Pharmacokinetics and Product Metabolism in Animals

A summary of the pharmacokinetics and biological transformation and disposition of the investigational product in all species studied should be given. The discussion of the findings should address the absorption and the local and systemic bioavailability of the investigational product and its metabolites, and their relationship to the pharmacological and toxicological findings in animal species.

(c) Toxicology

A summary of the toxicological effects found in relevant studies conducted in different animal species should be described under the following headings where appropriate:

Single dose;

Repeated dose;

Carcinogenicity;

Special studies (e.g., irritancy and sensitization);

Reproductive toxicity;

Genotoxicity (mutagenicity).

7.3.6 Effects in Humans.

Introduction:

A thorough discussion of the known effects of the investigational product(s) in humans should be provided, including information on pharmacokinetics, metabolism, pharmacodynamics, dose response, safety, efficacy, and other pharmacological activities. Where possible, a summary of each completed clinical trial should be provided.

Information should also be provided regarding results from any use of the investigational product(s) other than in clinical trials, such as from experience during marketing.

(a) Pharmacokinetics and Product Metabolism in Humans

A summary of information on the pharmacokinetics of the investigational product(s) should be presented, including the following, if available:

Pharmacokinetics (including metabolism, as appropriate, and absorption, plasma protein binding, distribution, and elimination).

Bioavailability of the investigational product (absolute, where possible, and/or relative) using a reference dosage form.

Population subgroups (e.g., gender, age, and impaired organ function).

Interactions (e.g., product-product interactions and effects of food).

Other pharmacokinetic data (e.g., results of population studies performed within clinical trial(s)).

(b) Safety and Efficacy

A summary of information should be provided about the investigational product's/products' (including metabolites, where appropriate) safety, pharmacodynamics, efficacy, and dose response that were obtained from preceding trials in humans (healthy volunteers and/or patients). The implications of this information should be discussed. In cases where a number of clinical trials have been completed, the use of summaries of safety and efficacy across multiple trials by indications in subgroups may provide a clear presentation of the data. Tabular summaries of adverse drug reactions for all the clinical trials (including those for all the studied indications) would be useful. Important differences in adverse drug reaction patterns/incidences across indications or subgroups should be discussed.

The IB should provide a description of the possible risks and adverse drug reactions to be anticipated on the basis of prior experiences with the product under investigation and with related products. A description should also be provided of the precautions or special monitoring to be done as part of the investigational use of the product(s).

(c) Marketing Experience

The IB should identify countries where the investigational product has been marketed or approved. Any significant information arising from the marketed use should be summarized (e.g., formulations, dosages, routes of administration, and adverse product reactions). The IB should also identify all the countries where the investigational product did not receive approval/registration for marketing or was withdrawn from marketing/registration.

7.3.7 Summary of Data and Guidance for the Investigator.

This section should provide an overall discussion of the nonclinical and clinical data, and should summarize the information from various sources on different aspects of the investigational product(s), wherever possible. In this way, the investigator can be provided with the most informative interpretation of the available data and with an assessment of the implications of the information for future clinical trials.

Where appropriate, the published reports on related products should be discussed. This could help the investigator to anticipate adverse drug reactions or other problems in clinical trials.

The overall aim of this section is to provide the investigator with a clear understanding of the possible risks and adverse reactions, and of the specific tests, observations, and precautions that may be needed for a clinical trial. This understanding should be based on the available physical, chemical, pharmaceutical, pharmacological, toxicological, and clinical information on the investigational product(s). Guidance should also be provided to the clinical investigator on the recognition and treatment of possible overdose and adverse drug reactions that is based on previous human experience and on the pharmacology of the investigational product.

7.4 Appendix 1:

TITLE PAGE OF INVESTIGATOR'S BROCHURE (Example)

> Sponsor's Name:
>
> Product:
>
> Research Number:
>
> Name(s): Chemical, Generic (if approved)
>
> > Trade Name(s) (if legally permissible and desired by the sponsor)
>
> Edition Number:
>
> Release Date:
>
> Replaces Previous Edition Number:
>
> Date:

7.5 Appendix 2:

TABLE OF CONTENTS OF INVESTIGATOR'S BROCHURE (Example)

- Confidentiality Statement (optional)
- Signature Page (optional)
1. Table of Contents
2. Summary
3. Introduction
4. Physical, Chemical, and Pharmaceutical Properties and Formulation
5. Nonclinical Studies
    - 5.1 Nonclinical Pharmacology
    - 5.2 Pharmacokinetics and Product Metabolism in Animals
    - 5.3 Toxicology
6. Effects in Humans
    - 6.1 Pharmacokinetics and Product Metabolism in Humans
    - 6.2 Safety and Efficacy
    - 6.3 Marketing Experience

7.   Summary of Data and Guidance for the Investigator

NB: References on

  1. Publications

  2. Reports

These references should be found at the end of each chapter.

Appendices (if any)

8.   ESSENTIAL DOCUMENTS FOR THE CONDUCT OF A CLINICAL TRIAL

8.1   Introduction

Essential Documents are those documents that individually and collectively permit evaluation of the conduct of a trial and the quality of the data produced. These documents serve to demonstrate the compliance of the investigator, sponsor, and monitor with the standards of GCP and with all applicable regulatory requirements.

Essential Documents also serve a number of other important purposes. Filing essential documents at the investigator/institution and sponsor sites in a timely manner can greatly assist in the successful management of a trial by the investigator, sponsor, and monitor. These documents are also the ones that are usually audited by the sponsor's independent audit function and inspected by the regulatory authority(ies) as part of the process to confirm the validity of the trial conduct and the integrity of data collected.

The minimum list of essential documents that has been developed follows. The various documents are grouped in three sections according to the stage of the trial during which they will normally be generated: (1) Before the clinical phase of the trial commences, (2) during the clinical conduct of the trial, and (3) after completion or termination of the trial. A description is given of the purpose of each document, and whether it should be filed in either the investigator/institution or sponsor files, or both. It is acceptable to combine some of the documents, provided the individual elements are readily identifiable.

Trial master files should be established at the beginning of the trial, both at the investigator/institution's site and at the sponsor's office. A final close-out of a trial can only be done when the monitor has reviewed both investigator/institution and sponsor files and confirmed that all necessary documents are in the appropriate files.

Any or all of the documents addressed in this guideline may be subject to, and should be available for, audit by the sponsor's auditor and inspection by the regulatory authority(ies).

8.2 Before the Clinical Phase of the Trial Commences

During this planning stage the following documents should be generated and should be on file before the, trial formally starts.

	Title of Document	Purpose	Located in Files of	
			Investigator/ Instituition	Sponsor
8.2.1	Investigator's brochure	To document that relevant and current scientific information about the investigational product has been provided to the investigator	X	X
8.2.2	Signed protocol and amendments, if any, and sample case report form (CRF)	To document investigator and sponsor agreement to the protocol/amendment(s) and CRF	X	X
8.2.3	Information given to trial subject • Informed consent form (Including all applicable translations) • Any other written information	• To document the informed consent • To document that subjects will be given appropriate written information (content and wording) to support their ability to give fully informed consent	X X	X X
	• Advertisement for subject recruitment (if used)	• To document that recruitment measures are appropriate and not coercive	X	
8.2.4	Financial aspects of the trial	To document the financial agreement between the investigator/institution and the sponsor for the trial	X	X
8.2.5	Insurance statement (where required)	To document that compensation to subject(s) for trial-related injury will be available	X	X
8.2.6	Signed agreement between involved parties, e.g.: • Investigator/institution and sponsor • Investigator/institution and CRO • Sponsor and CRO • Investigator/institution and authority(ies) (where required)	To document agreements	X X X	X X (where required) X X

	Title of Document	Purpose	Located in Files of	
			Investigator/ Institution	Sponsor
8.2.7	Dated, documented approval/favorable opinion of IRB/IEC of the following: • Protocol and any amendments • CRF (if applicable) • Informed consent form(s) • Any other written information to be provided to the subject(s) • Advertisement for subject recruitment (if used) • Subject compensation (if any) • Any other documents given approval/favorable opinion	To document that the trial has been subject to IRB/IEC review and given approval/favorable opinion. To identify the version number and date of the document(s).	X	X
8.2.8	Institutional review board/ independent ethics committee composition	To document that the IRB/IEC is constituted in agreement with GCP	X	X (where required)
8.2.9	Regulatory authority(ies) authorization/approval/notification of protocol (where required)	To document appropriate authorization/approval/ notification by the regulatory authority(ies) has been obtained prior to initiation of the trial in compliance with the applicable regulatory requirement(s)	X (where required)	X (where required)
8.2.10	Curriculum vitae and/or other relevant documents evidencing qualifications of investigator(s) and subinvestigators	To document qualifications and eligibility to conduct trial and/or provide medical supervision of subjects	X	X
8.2.11	Normal value(s)/range(s) for medical/ laboratory/technical procedure(s) and/or test(s) included in the protocol	To document normal values and/or ranges of the tests	X	X
8.2.12	Medical/laboratory/technical procedures/tests • Certification or accreditation or • Established quality control and/or external quality assessment or • Other validation (where required)	To document competence of facility to perform required test(s), and support reliability of results	X (where required)	X

	Title of Document	Purpose	Located in Files of	
			Investigator/ Institution	Sponsor
8.2.13	Sample of label(s) attached to investigational product container(s)	To document compliance with applicable labeling regulations and appropriateness of instructions provided to the subjects		X
8.2.14	Instructions for handling of investigational product(s) and trial-related materials (if not included in protocol or Investigator's Brochure)	To document instructions needed to ensure proper storage, packaging, dispensing, and disposition of investigational products and trial-related materials	X	X
8.2.15	Shipping records for investigational product(s) and trial-related materials	To document shipment dates, batch numbers, and method of shipment of investigational product(s) and trial-related materials. Allows tracking of product batch, review of shipping conditions, and accountability	X	X
8.2.16	Certificate(s) of analysis of investigational product(s) shipped	To document identity, purity, and strength of investigational products to be used in the trial.		X
8.2.17	Decoding procedures for blinded trials	To document how, in case of an emergency, identity of blinded investigational product can be revealed without breaking the blind for the remaining subjects' treatment	X	X (3rd party if applicable)
8.2.18	Master randomization list	To document method for randomization of trial population		X (3rd party if applicable)
8.2.19	Pretrial monitoring report	To document that the site is suitable for the trial (may be combined with 8.2.20)		X
8.2.20	Trial initiation monitoring report	To document that trial procedures were reviewed with the investigator and investigators trial staff (may be combined with 8.2.19)	X	X

8.3 During the Clinical Conduct of the Trial

In addition to having on file the above documents, the following should be added to the files during the trial as evidence that all new relevant information is documented as it becomes available.

	Title of Document	Purpose	Located in Files of Investigator/Institution	Located in Files of Sponsor
8.3.1	Investigator's Brochure updates	To document that investigator is informed in a timely manner of relevant information as it becomes available	X	X
8.3.2	Any revisions to: • Protocol/amendment(s) and CRF • Informed consent form • Any other written information provided to subjects • Advertisement for subject recruitment (if used)	To document revisions of these trial-related documents that take effect during trial	X	X

8.3.3	Dated, documented approval/favorable opinion of institutional review board (IRB)/Independent ethics committee (IEC) of the following:
	• Protocol amendment(s)
	• Revision(s) of:
	  • Informed consent form
	  • Any other written information to be provided to the subject
	  • Advertisement for subject recruitment (if used)
	• Any other documents given approval/favorable opinion
	• Continuing review of trial (see section 3.1.4)
		To document that the amendment(s) and/or revision(s) have been subject to IRB/IEC review and were given approval/favorable opinion. To identify the version number and date of the document(s)	X	X

8.3.4	Regulatory authority(ies) authorizations/approvals/notifications where required for: • Protocol amendment(s) and other documents	To document compliance with applicable regulatory requirements	X (where required)	X

| | Title of Document | Purpose | Located in Files of | |
			Investigator/ Institution	Sponsor
8.3.5	Curriculum vitae for new investigator(s) and/or subinvestigators	(See section 8.2.10)	X	X
8.3.6	Updates to normal value(s)/range(s) for medical laboratory/technical procedure(s)/test(s) included in the protocol	To document normal values and ranges that are revised during the trial (see section 8.2.11)	X	X
8.3.7	Updates of medical/laboratory/ technical procedures/tests • Certification or • Accreditation or • Established quality control and/or external quality assessment or • Other validation (where required)	To document that tests remain adequate throughout the trial period (see section 8.2.12)	X (where required)	X
8.3.8	Documentation of investigational product(s) and trial-related materials shipment	(See section 8.2.15)	X	X
8.3.9	Certificate(s) of analysis for new batches of investigational products	(See section 8.2.16)		X
8.3.10	Monitoring visit reports	To document site visits by, and findings of, the monitor		X
8.3.11	Relevant communications other than site visits • Letters • Meeting notes • Notes of telephone calls	To document any agreements or significant discussions regarding trial administration, protocol violations, trial conduct, adverse event (AE) reporting	X	X
8.3.12	Signed informed consent forms	To document that consent is obtained in accordance with GCP and protocol and dated prior to participation of each subject in trial. Also to document direct access permission (see section 8.2.3)	X	

	Title of Document	Purpose	Located in Files of	
			Investigator/ Institution	Sponsor
8.3.13	Source documents	To document the existence of the subject and substantiate integrity of trial data collected. To include original documents related to the trial, to medical treatment, and history of subject	X	
8.3.14	Signed, dated, and completed case report forms (CRFs)	To document that the investigator or authorized member of the investigators staff confirms the observations recorded	X (copy)	X (original)
8.3.15	Documentation of CRF corrections	To document all changes/additions or corrections made to CRF after initial data were recorded	X (copy)	X (original)
8.3.16	Notification by originating investigator to sponsor of serious adverse events and related reports	Notification by originating investigator to sponsor of serious adverse events and related reports in accordance with 4.11	X	X
8.3.17	Notification by sponsor and/or investigator, where applicable, to regulatory authority(ies) and IRB(s)/IEC(s) of unexpected serious adverse drug reactions and of other safety information	Notification by sponsor and/or investigator, where applicable, to regulatory authority(ies) and IRB(s)/IEC(s) of unexpected serious adverse drug reactions in accordance with 5.17 and 4.11.1 and of other safety information in accordance with 4.11.2 and 5.16.2	X (where required)	X
8.3.18	Notification by sponsor to investigators of safety information	Notification by sponsor to investigators of safety information in accordance with 5.16.2	X	X
8.3.19	Interim or annual reports to IRB/IEC and authority(ies)	Interim or annual reports provided to IRB/IEC in accordance with 4.10 and to authority(ies) in accordance with 5.17.3	X	X (where required)
8.3.20	Subject screening log	To document identification of subjects who entered pretrial screening	X	X (where required)

	Title of Document	Purpose	Located in Files of	
			Investigator/ Institution	Sponsor
8.3.21	Subject identification code list	To document that investigator/institution keeps a confidential list of names of all subjects allocated to trial numbers on enrolling in the trial. Allows investigator/institution to reveal identity of any subject	X	
8.3.22	Subject enrollment log	To document chronological enrollment of subjects by trial number	X	
8.3.23	Investigational product(s) accountability at the site	To document that investigational product(s) have been used according to the protocol	X	X
8.3.24	Signature sheet	To document signatures and initials of all persons authorized to make entries and/or corrections on CRFs	X	X
8.3.25	Record of retained body fluids/tissue samples (if any)	To document location and identification of retained samples if assays need to be repeated	X	X

8.4 After Completion or Termination of the Trial

After completion or termination of the trial, all of the documents identified in sections 8.2 and 8.3 should be in the file together with the following:

	Title of Document	Purpose	Located in Files of — Investigator/Institution	Located in Files of — Sponsor
8.4.1	Investigational product(s) accountability at site	To document that the investigational product(s) have been used according to the protocol. To document the final accounting of investigational product(s) received at the site, dispensed to subjects, returned by the subjects, and returned to sponsor	X	X
8.4.2	Documentation of investigational product(s) destruction	To document destruction of unused investigational product(s) by sponsor or at site	X (if destroyed at site)	X
8.4.3	Completed subject identification code list	To permit identification of all subjects enrolled in the trial in case follow-up is required. List should be kept in a confidential manner and for agreed upon time	X	
8.4.4	Audit certificate (if required)	To document that audit was performed (if required) (see section 5.19.3(e))		X
8.4.5	Final trial close-out monitoring report	To document that all activities required for trial close-out are completed, and copies of essential documents are held in the appropriate files		X
8.4.6	Treatment allocation and decoding documentation	Returned to sponsor to document any decoding that may have occurred		X
8.4.7	Final report by investigator/institution to IRB/IEC where required, and where applicable, to the regulatory authority(ies) (see section 4.13)	To document completion of the trial	X	
8.4.8	Clinical study report (see section 5.22)	To document results and interpretation of trial	X (if applicable)	X

ICH Guideline

Clinical Safety Data Management: Definitions and Standards for Expedited Reporting

as published in the Federal Register
March 1, 1995

SUMMARY: The Food and Drug Administration (FDA) is publishing a final guideline entitle "Clinical Safety Data Management: Definitions and Standards for Expedited Reporting." Th guideline was prepared under the auspices of the International Conference on Harmonisation Technical Requirements for Registration of Pharmaceuticals for Human Use (ICH). The guideli provides standard definitions and terms for key aspects of clinical safety reporting. The guideli also discusses mechanisms for expedited reporting. This guideline is intended to help harmoni methods for gathering and evaluating clinical safety data.

DATES: Effective March 1, 1995. Submit written comments at any time.

ADDRESSES: Submit written comments on the guideline to the Dockets Management Bran (HFA-305), Food and Drug Administration, rm. 1-23, 12420 Parklawn Dr., Rockville, MD 2085 Copies of the guideline are available from CDER Executive Secretariat Staff (HFD-8), Center f Drug Evaluation and Research, Food and Drug Administration, 7500 Standish Pl., Rockville, M 20855.

FOR FURTHER INFORMATION CONTACT: Regarding the guideline: Murray M. Lumpki Center for Drug Evaluation and Research (HFD-2), Food and Drug Administration, 14! Rockville Pike, Rockville, MD 20852, 301-594-6740.

Regarding ICH: Janet J. Showalter, Office of Health Affairs (HFY-20), Food and Dru Administration, 5600 Fishers Lane, Rockville, MD 20857, 301-443-1382.

SUPPLEMENTARY INFORMATION: In recent years, many important initiatives have bee undertaken by regulatory authorities and industry associations to promote internation harmonization of regulatory requirements. FDA has participated in many meetings designed t enhance harmonization and is committed to seeking scientifically based harmonized technic procedures for pharmaceutical development. One of the goals of harmonization is to identify an then reduce differences in technical requirements for drug development among regulato agencies.

ICH was organized to provide an opportunity for tripartite harmonization initiatives to t developed with input from both regulatory and industry representatives. FDA also seeks input fro consumer representatives and others. ICH is concerned with harmonization of technic requirements for the registration of pharmaceutical products among three regions: The Europea Union, Japan, and the United States. The six ICH sponsors are the European Commission; th European Federation of Pharmaceutical Industry Associations; the Japanese Ministry of Heal and Welfare; the Japanese Pharmaceutical Manufacturers Association; the Centers for Dru Evaluation and Research and Biologics Evaluation and Research, FDA; and the Pharmaceutic Research and Manufacturers of America. The ICH Secretariat, which coordinates the preparatio of documentation, is provided by the International Federation of Pharmaceutical Manufacturer Association (IFPMA).

The ICH Steering Committee includes representatives from each of the ICH sponsors and IFPMA as well as observers from the World Health Organization, the Canadian Health Protection Branc and the European Free Trade Area.

Harmonization of clinical safety data management was selected as a priority topic during the earl stages of the ICH initiative. In the Federal Register of July 9, 1993 (58 FR 37408), FDA publishe a draft tripartite guideline entitled, "Clinical Safety Data Management: Definitions and Standard for Expedited Reporting." The notice gave interested persons an opportunity to submit comment by August 9, 1993.

After consideration of the comments received and revisions to the guideline, a final draft of the guideline was submitted to the ICH Steering Committee and endorsed by the three participating regulatory agencies at the ICH meeting held in October 1994.

The guideline defines basic terms, such as "adverse event," "adverse drug reaction," and "unexpected adverse drug reaction." The guideline also provides guidance on determining whether an adverse drug reaction is "expected," and contains standards for expedited reporting, describing what information should be reported, recommending reporting timeframes and the use of the CIOMS-I form for reporting information or, alternatively, suggesting that basic information or data elements be used. The guideline also discusses: Whether and when the blind should be broken for a patient; reporting reactions associated with comparison drug or placebo treatments; products with more than one dosage form, route of administration, or use; and adverse events that occur after the patient has completed the clinical study.

In the past, guidelines have generally been issued under Sec. 10.90(b) (21 CFR 10.90(b)), which provides for the use of guidelines to state procedures or standards of general applicability that are not legal requirements but are acceptable to FDA. The agency is now in the process of revising Sec. 10.90(b). Therefore, this guideline is not being issued under the authority of Sec. 10.90(b), and it does not create or confer any rights, privileges, or benefits for or on any person, nor does it operate to bind FDA in any way.

TABLE OF CONTENTS

GUIDELINE FOR INDUSTRY[1]

CLINICAL SAFETY DATA MANAGEMENT: DEFINITIONS AND STANDARDS FOR EXPEDITED REPORTING[2]

I.   INTRODUCTION

It is important to harmonize the way to gather and, if necessary, to take action on important clinical safety information arising during clinical development. Thus, agreed definitions and terminology, as well as procedures, will ensure uniform Good Clinical Practice standards in this area. The initiatives already undertaken for marketed medicines through the CIOMS-1 and CIOMS-2 Working Groups on expedited (alert) reports and periodic safety update reporting, respectively, are important precedents and models. However, there are special circumstances involving medicinal products under development, especially in the early stages and before any marketing experience is available. Conversely, it must be recognized that a medicinal product will be under various stages of development and/or marketing in different countries, and safety data from marketing experience will ordinarily be of interest to regulators in countries where the medicinal product is still under investigational only (Phase 1, 2, or 3) status. For this reason, it is both practical and well-advised to regard premarketing and post-marketing clinical safety reporting concepts and practices as interdependent, while recognizing that responsibility for clinical safety within regulatory bodies and companies may reside with different departments, depending on the status of the product (investigational vs. marketed).

---

[1]This guideline was developed within the Expert Working Group (Efficacy) of the International Conference on Harmonisation of Technical Requirements for Registration of Pharmaceuticals for Human Use (ICH) and has been subject to consultation by the regulatory parties, in accordance with the ICH process. This document has been endorsed by the ICH Steering Committee at *Step 4* of the ICH process, October 27, 1994. At *Step 4* of the process, the final draft is recommended for adoption to the regulatory bodies of the European Union, Japan and the USA. This guidance was published in the Federal Register on March 1, 1995 (60 FR 11284) and is applicable to both drug and biological products. In the past, guidelines have generally been issued under § 10.90(b) [21 CFR 10.90(b)], which provides for the use of guidelines to state procedures or standards of general applicability that are not legal requirements but that are acceptable to FDA. The agency is now in the process of revising §10.90(b). Therefore, this guideline is not being issued under the authority of §10.90(b), and it does not create or confer any rights, privileges or benefits for or on any person, nor does it operate to bind FDA in any way. For additional copies of this guideline contact the Executive Secretariat Staff, HFD-8, Center for Drug Evaluation and Research, 7500 Standish Place, Rockville, MD 20855, 301-594-1012. An electronic version of this guideline is also available via Internet by connecting to the CDER FTP server (CDVS2.CDER.FDA.GOV) using the FTP protocol.

[2]The time frames and definitions in this guideline differ from those in the Code of Federal Regulations [21 CFR 314.80]. Until the regulations are revised, the time frames and definitions in the CFR should be followed.

There are two issues within the broad subject of clinical safety data management that are appropriate for harmonization at this time:

- the development of standard definitions and terminology for key aspects of clinical safety reporting, and

- the appropriate mechanism for handling expedited (rapid) reporting, in the investigational (i.e., pre-approval) phase.

The provisions of this guideline should be used in conjunction with other ICH Good Clinical Practice guidelines.

II. DEFINITIONS AND TERMINOLOGY ASSOCIATED WITH CLINICAL SAFETY EXPERIENCE

A. Basic Terms

Definitions for the terms adverse event (or experience), adverse reaction, and unexpected adverse reaction have previously been agreed to by consensus of the more than 30 Collaborating Centers of the WHO International Drug Monitoring Centre (Uppsala, Sweden). [Edwards, I.R., et al, "Harmonisation in Pharmacovigilance," *Drug Safety* 10(2): 93-102, 1994.] Although those definitions can pertain to situations involving clinical investigations, some minor modifications are necessary, especially to accommodate the pre-approval, development environment.

The following definitions, with input from the WHO Collaborative Centre, have been agreed:

1. Adverse Event (or Adverse Experience)

Any untoward medical occurrence in a patient or clinical investigation subject administered a pharmaceutical product and which does not necessarily have to have a causal relationship with this treatment.

An adverse event (AE) can therefore be any unfavorable and unintended sign (including an abnormal laboratory finding, for example), symptom, or disease temporally associated with the use of a medicinal product, whether or not considered related to the medicinal product.

2. Adverse Drug Reaction (ADR)

In the *pre-approval clinical experience* with a new medicinal product or its new usages, particularly as the therapeutic dose(s) may not be established:

all noxious and unintended responses to a medicinal product related to any dose should be considered adverse drug reactions.

The phrase "responses to a medicinal products" means that a causal relationship between a medicinal product and an adverse event is at least a reasonable possibility, i.e., the relationship cannot be ruled out.

Regarding *marketed medicinal products*, a well-accepted definition of an adverse drug reaction in the post-marketing setting is found in WHO Technical Report 498 [1972] and reads as follows:

> A response to a drug which is noxious and unintended and which occurs at doses normally used in man for prophylaxis, diagnosis, or therapy of disease or for modification of physiological function.

The old term "side effect" has been used in various ways in the past, usually to describe negative (unfavorable) effects, but also positive (favorable) effects. It is recommended that this term no longer be used and particularly should not be regarded as synonymous with adverse event or adverse reaction.

3. Unexpected Adverse Drug Reaction

An adverse reaction, the nature or severity of which is not consistent with the applicable product information (e.g., Investigator's Brochure for an unapproved investigational medicinal product). See section III.C.

B. Serious Adverse Event or Adverse Drug Reaction

During clinical investigations, adverse events may occur which, if suspected to be medicinal product-related (adverse drug reactions), might be significant enough to lead to important changes in the way the medicinal product is developed (e.g., change in dose, population, needed monitoring, consent forms). This is particularly true for reactions which, in their most severe forms, threaten life or function. Such reactions should be reported promptly to regulators.

Therefore, special medical or administrative criteria are needed to define reactions that, either due to their nature ("serious") or due to the significant, unexpected information they provide, justify expedited reporting.

To ensure no confusion or misunderstanding exist of the difference between the terms "serious" and "severe," which are not synonymous, the following note of clarification is provided:

> The term "severe" is often used to describe the intensity (severity) of a specific event (as in mild, moderate, or severe myocardial infarction); the event itself, however, may be of relatively minor medical significance (such as severe headache). This is *not* the same as "serious," which is based on patient/event *outcome or action* criteria usually associated with events that pose a threat to a patient's life or functioning. Seriousness (not severity) serves as a guide for defining regulatory reporting obligations.

After reviewing the various regulatory and other definitions in use or under discussion elsewhere, the following definition is believed to encompass the spirit and meaning of them all:

> A serious adverse event (experience) or reaction is any untoward medical occurrence that at any dose:

- Results in death,
- Is life-threatening,

NOTE: The term "life-threatening" in the definition of "serious" refers to an event in which the patient was at risk of death at the time of the event; it does not refer to an event which hypothetically might have caused death if it were more severe.

- Requires inpatient hospitalization or prolongation of existing hospitalization,

- Results in persistent or significant disability/incapacity, or

- Is a congenital anomaly/birth defect.

Medical and scientific judgment should be exercised in deciding whether expedited reporting is appropriate in other situations, such as important medical events that may not be immediately life-threatening or result in death or hospitalization but may jeopardize the patient or may require intervention to prevent one of the other outcomes listed in the definition above. These should also usually be considered serious.

Examples of such events are intensive treatment in an emergency room or at home for allergic bronchospasm; blood dyscrasias or convulsions that do not result in hospitalization; or development of drug dependency or drug abuse.

C. Expectedness of an Adverse Drug Reaction

The purpose of expedited reporting is to make regulators, investigators, and other appropriate people aware of new, important information on serious reactions. Therefore, such reporting will generally involve events previously unobserved or undocumented, and a guideline is needed on how to define an event as "unexpected" or "expected" (expected/unexpected from the perspective of previously observed, *not* on the basis of what might be anticipated from the pharmacological properties of a medicinal product).

As stated in the definition (II.A.3.), an "unexpected" adverse reaction is one, the nature or severity of which is not consistent with information in the relevant source document(s). Until source documents are amended, expedited reporting is required for additional occurrences of the reaction.

The following documents or circumstances will be used to determine whether an adverse event/reaction is expected:

1. For a medicinal product not yet approved for marketing in a country, a company's Investigator's Brochure will serve as the source document in that country. See section III.F. and ICH Guideline for the Investigator's Brochure.

2. Reports which add significant information on specificity or severity of a known, already documented serious ADR constitute unexpected events. For example, an event more specific or more severe than described in the Investigator's Brochure would be considered "unexpected." Specific examples would be (a) acute renal failure as a labeled ADR with a subsequent new report of interstitial nephritis and (b) hepatitis with a first report of fulminant hepatitis.

III. STANDARDS FOR EXPEDITED REPORTING

A. What Should be Reported?

1. Single Cases of Serious, Unexpected ADRs

All ADRs that are both serious and unexpected are subject to expedited reporting. This applies to reports from spontaneous sources and from any type of clinical or epidemiological investigation, independent of design or purpose. It also applies to cases not reported directly to a sponsor or manufacturer (for example, those found in regulatory authority generated ADR registries or in publications). The source of a report (investigation, spontaneous, other) should always be specified.

Expedited reporting of reactions that are serious but *expected* will ordinarily be inappropriate. Expedited reporting is also inappropriate for serious events from clinical investigations that are considered *not* related to study product, whether the event is expected or not. Similarly, nonserious adverse reactions, whether expected or not, will ordinarily not be subject to *expedited* reporting.

Information obtained by a sponsor or manufacturer on serious, unexpected reports from any source should be submitted on an expedited basis to appropriate regulatory authorities if the minimum criteria for expedited reporting can be met. See section III.B.

Causality assessment is required for clinical investigation cases. All cases judged by either the reporting health care professional or the sponsor as having a reasonable suspected causal relationship to the medicinal product qualify as ADRs. For purposes of reporting, adverse event reports associated with marketed drugs (spontaneous reports) usually imply causality.

Many terms and scales are in use to describe the degree of causality (attributability) between a medicinal product and an event, such as certainly, definitely, probably, possibly or likely related or not related. Phrases such as "plausible relationship," "suspected causality," or "causal relationship cannot be ruled out" are also invoked to describe cause and effect. However, there is currently no standard international nomenclature. The expression "reasonable causal relationship" is meant to convey in general that there are facts (evidence) or arguments to suggest a causal relationship.

2. Other Observations

There are situations in addition to single case reports of "serious" adverse events or reactions that may necessitate rapid communication to regulatory authorities; appropriate medical and scientific judgment should be applied for each situation. In general, information that might materially influence the benefit-risk assessment of a medicinal product or that would be sufficient to consider changes in medicinal product administration or in the overall conduct of a clinical investigation represents such situations. Examples include:

a. For an "expected," serious ADR, an increase in the rate of occurrence which is judged to be clinically important.

   b.   A significant hazard to the patient population, such as lack of efficacy with a medicinal product used in treating life-threatening disease.

   c.   A major safety finding from a newly completed animal study (such as carcinogenicity).

B.   Reporting Time Frames

1.   Fatal or Life-Threatening Unexpected ADRs

Certain ADRs may be sufficiently alarming so as to require very rapid notification to regulators in countries where the medicinal product or indication, formulation, or population for the medicinal product are still not approved for marketing, because such reports may lead to consideration of suspension of, or other limitations to, a clinical investigation program. Fatal or life-threatening, unexpected ADRs occurring in clinical investigations qualify for very rapid reporting. Regulatory agencies should be notified (e.g., by telephone, facsimile transmission, or in writing) as soon as possible but no later than 7 calendar days after first knowledge by the sponsor that a case qualifies, followed by as complete a report as possible within 8 additional calendar days. This report should include an assessment of the importance and implication of the findings, including relevant previous experience with the same or similar medicinal products.

2.   All Other Serious, Unexpected ADRs

Serious, unexpected reactions (ADRs) that are not fatal or life-threatening must be filed as soon as possible but no later than 15 calendar days after first knowledge by the sponsor that the case meets the minimum criteria for expedited reporting.

3.   Minimum Criteria for Reporting

Information for final description and evaluation of a case report may not be available within the required time frames for reporting outlined above. Nevertheless, for regulatory purposes, initial reports should be submitted within the prescribed time as long as the following minimum criteria are met: an identifiable patient; a suspect medicinal product; an identifiable reporting source; and an event or outcome that can be identified as serious and unexpected, and for which, in clinical investigation cases, there is a reasonable suspected causal relationship. Follow-up information should be actively sought and submitted as it becomes available.

C.   How to Report

The CIOMS-I form has been a widely accepted standard for expedited adverse event reporting. However, no matter what the form or format used, it is important that certain basic information/data elements, when available, be included with any expedited report, whether in a tabular or narrative presentation. The listing in Attachment 1 addresses those data elements regarded as desirable; if all are not available at the time of expedited reporting, efforts should be made to obtain them. See section III.B.

All reports must be sent to those regulators or other official parties requiring them (as appropriate for the local situation) in countries where the drug is under development.

D. Managing Blinded Therapy Cases

When the sponsor and investigator are blinded to individual patient treatment (as in a double-blind study), the occurrence of a serious event requires a decision on whether to open (break) the code for the specific patient. If the investigator breaks the blind, then it is assumed the sponsor will also know the assigned treatment for that patient. Although it is advantageous to retain the blind for all patients prior to final study analysis, when a serious adverse reaction is judged reportable on an expedited basis, it is recommended that the blind be broken only for that specific patient by the sponsor even if the investigator has not broken the blind. It is also recommended that, when possible and appropriate, the blind be maintained for those persons, such as biometrics personnel, responsible for analysis and interpretation of results at the study's conclusion.

There are several disadvantages to maintaining the blind under the circumstances described which outweigh the advantages. By retaining the blind, placebo and comparator (usually a marketed product) cases are filed unnecessarily. When the blind is eventually opened, which may be many weeks or months after reporting to regulators, it must be ensured that company and regulatory data bases are revised. If the event is serious, new, and possibly related to the medicinal product, then if the Investigator's Brochure is updated, notifying relevant parties of the new information in a blinded fashion is inappropriate and possibly misleading. Moreover, breaking the blind for a single patient usually has little or no significant implications for the conduct of the clinical investigation or on the analysis of the final clinical investigation data.

However, when a fatal or other "serious" outcome is the primary efficacy endpoint in a clinical investigation, the integrity of the clinical investigation may be compromised if the blind is broken. Under these and similar circumstances, it may be appropriate to reach agreement with regulatory authorities in advance concerning serious events that would be treated as disease-related and not subject to routine expedited reporting.

E. Miscellaneous Issues

1. Reactions Associated with Active Comparator or Placebo Treatment

It is the sponsor's responsibility to decide whether active comparator drug reactions should be reported to the other manufacturer and/or directly to appropriate regulatory agencies. Sponsors should report such events to either the manufacturer of the active control or to appropriate regulatory agencies. Events associated with placebo will usually not satisfy the criteria for an ADR and, therefore, for expedited reporting.

2. Products with More Than One Presentation or Use

To avoid ambiguities and uncertainties, an ADR that qualifies for expedited reporting with one presentation of a product (e.g., a dosage form, formulation, delivery system) or product use (e.g., for an indication or population), should be reported or referenced to regulatory filings across other product presentations and uses.

It is not uncommon that more than one dosage form, formulation, or delivery system (oral, IM, IV, topical, etc.) of the pharmacologically active compound(s) is under study or marketed; for these different presentations there may be some marked differences in the clinical safety profile. The same may apply for a given product used in different indications or populations (single dose vs. chronic administration, for example). Thus, "expectedness" may be product or product use specific, and separate Investigator's Brochures may be used accordingly. However, such documents are expected to cover ADR information that applies to all affected product presentations and uses. When relevant, separate discussions of pertinent product-specific or use-specific safety information will also be included.

It is recommended that any adverse drug reactions that qualify for expedited reporting observed with one product dosage form or use be cross referenced to regulatory records for all other dosage forms and uses for that product. This may result in a certain amount of overreporting or unnecessary reporting in obvious situations (for example, a report of phlebitis on IV injection sent to authorities in a country where only an oral dosage form is studied or marketed). However, underreporting is completely avoided.

3. Post-study Events

    Although such information is not routinely sought or collected by the sponsor, serious adverse events that occurred after the patient had completed a clinical study (including any protocol required post-treatment follow-up) will possibly be reported by an investigator to the sponsor. Such cases should be regarded for expedited reporting purposes as though they were study reports. Therefore, a causality assessment and determination of expectedness are needed for a decision on whether or not expedited reporting is required.

F. Informing Investigators and Ethics Committees/Institutional Review Boards of New Safety Information

    International standards regarding such communication are discussed within the ICH GCP Guidelines, including the addendum on "Guideline for the Investigator's Brochure." In general, the sponsor of a study should amend the Investigator's Brochure as needed, and in accord with any local regulatory requirements, so as to keep the description of safety information updated.

IV. REFERENCE

<u>Federal Register</u>. Vol.60, No. 40, Wednesday, March 1, 1995, pages 11284-11287.

KEY DATA ELEMENTS FOR INCLUSION IN EXPEDITED REPORTS OF SERIOUS ADVERSE DRUG REACTIONS

The following list of items has its foundation in several established precedents, including those of CIOMS-I, the WHO International Drug Monitoring Centre, and various regulatory authority forms and guidelines. Some items may not be relevant depending on the circumstances. The minimum information required for expedited reporting purposes is: an identifiable patient, the name of a suspect medicinal product, an identifiable reporting source, and an event or outcome that can be identified as serious and unexpected and for which, in clinical investigation cases, there is a reasonable suspected causal relationship. Attempts should be made to obtain follow-up information on as many other listed items pertinent to the case.

1.   Patient Details:

- •   Initials,
- •   Other relevant identifier (clinical investigation number, for example),
- •   Gender,
- •   Age and/or date of birth,
- •   Weight,
- •   Height.

2.   Suspected Medicinal Product(s):

- •   Brand name as reported,
- •   International Non-Proprietary Name (INN),
- •   Batch number,
- •   Indication(s) for which suspect medicinal product was prescribed or tested,
- •   Dosage form and strength,
- •   Daily dose and regimen (specify units - e.g., mg, mL, mg/kg),
- •   Route of administration,
- •   Starting date and time of day,
- •   Stopping date and time, or duration of treatment.

3.   Other Treatment(s):

- •   For concomitant medicinal products (including non-prescription/OTC medicinal products) and non-medicinal product therapies, provide the same information as for the suspected product.

4. Details of Suspected Adverse Drug Reaction(s):

- Full description of reaction(s) including body site and severity, as well as the criterion (or criteria) for regarding the report as serious should be given. In addition to a description of the reported signs and symptoms, whenever possible, attempts should be made to establish a specific diagnosis for the reaction.

- Start date (and time) of onset of reaction,

- Stop date (and time) or duration of reaction,

- Dechallenge and rechallenge information,

- Setting (e.g., hospital, out-patient clinic, home, nursing home),

- Outcome: Information on recovery and any sequelae; what specific tests and/or treatment may have been required and their results; for a fatal outcome, cause of death and a comment on its possible relationship to the suspected reaction should be provided. Any autopsy or other post-mortem findings (including a coroner's report) should also be provided when available. Other information: anything relevant to facilitate assessment of the case, such as medical history including allergy, drug or alcohol abuse; family history; findings from special investigations.

5. Details on Reporter of Event (Suspected ADR):

- Name,

- Address,

- Telephone number,

- Profession (speciality).

6. Administrative and Sponsor/Company Details:

- Source of report: Was it spontaneous, from a clinical investigation (provide details), from the literature (provide copy), other?

- Date event report was first received by sponsor/manufacturer,

- Country in which event occurred,

- Type of report filed to authorities: initial or follow-up (first, second, etc.),

- Name and address of sponsor/manufacturer/company,

- Name, address, telephone number, and FAX number of contact person in reporting company or institution,

- Identifying regulatory code or number for marketing authorization dossier or clinical investigation process for the suspected product (for example IND or CTX number, NDA number),

- Sponsor/manufacturer's identification number for the case (This number should be the same for the initial and follow-up reports on the same case).

EUROPEAN UNION CLINICAL TRIALS DIRECTIVE

Directive 2001/20/EC of the European Parliament and of the Council of 4 April 2001 on the approximation of the laws, regulations and administrative provisions of the Member States relating to the implementation of good clinical practice in the conduct of clinical trials on medicinal products for human use.

THE EUROPEAN PARLIAMENT AND THE COUNCIL OF THE EUROPEAN UNION,

Having regard to the Treaty establishing the European Community, and in particular Article 95 thereof,

Having regard to the proposal from the Commission[1],

Having regard to the opinion of the Economic and Social Committee[2],

Acting in accordance with the procedure laid down in Article 251 of the Treaty[3],

Whereas:

(1) Council Directive 65/65/EEC of 26 January 1965 on the approximation of provisions laid down by law, regulation or administrative action relating to medicinal products[4] requires that applications for authorisation to place a medicinal product on the market should be accompanied by a dossier containing particulars and documents relating to the results of tests and clinical trials carried out on the product. Council Directive 75/318/EEC of 20 May 1975 on the approximation of the laws of Member States relating to analytical, pharmaco-toxicological and clinical standards and protocols in respect of the testing of medicinal products[5] lays down uniform rules on the compilation of dossiers including their presentation.

(2) The accepted basis for the conduct of clinical trials in humans is founded in the protection of human rights and the dignity of the human being with regard to the application of biology and medicine, as for instance reflected in the 1996 version of the Helsinki Declaration. The clinical trial subject's protection is safeguarded through risk assessment based on the results of toxicological experiments prior to any clinical trial, screening by ethics committees and Member States' competent authorities, and rules on the protection of personal data.

(3) Persons who are incapable of giving legal consent to clinical trials should be given special protection. It is incumbent on the Member States to lay down rules to this effect. Such persons may not be included in clinical trials if the same results can be obtained using persons capable of giving consent. Normally these persons should be included in clinical trials only when there are grounds for expecting that the administering of the medicinal product would be of direct benefit to the patient, thereby outweighing the risks. However, there is a need for clinical trials involving children to improve the treatment available to them. Children represent a vulnerable population with developmental, physiological and psychological differences from adults, which make age- and development-related research important for their benefit. Medicinal products, including vaccines, for children need to be tested

---

[1]OJ C 306, 8.10.1997, p. 9 and OJ C 161, 8.6.1999, p. 5.

[2]OJ C 95, 30.3.1998, p. 1.

[3]Opinion of the European Parliament of 17 November 1998 (OJ C 379, 7. 12. 1998, p. 27). Council Common Position of 20 July 2000 (OJ C 300, 20.10.2000, p. 32) and Decision of the European Parliament of 12 December 2000. Council Decision of 26 February 2001.

[4]OJ 22, 9.2.1965, p. 1/65. Directive as last amended by Council Directive 93/39/EEC (OJ L 214, 24.8.1993, p. 22).

[5]OJ L 147, 9.6.1975, p. 1. Directive as last amended by Commission Directive 1999/83/EC (OJ L 243, 15.9.1999, p. 9).

scientifically before widespread use. This can only be achieved by ensuring that medicinal products which are likely to be of significant clinical value for children are fully studied. The clinical trials required for this purpose should be carried out under conditions affording the best possible protection for the subjects. Criteria for the protection of children in clinical trials therefore need to be laid down.

(4) In the case of other persons incapable of giving their consent, such as persons with dementia, psychiatric patients, etc., inclusion in clinical trials in such cases should be on an even more restrictive basis. Medicinal products for trial may be administered to all such individuals only when there are grounds for assuming that the direct benefit to the patient outweighs the risks. Moreover, in such cases the written consent of the patient's legal representative, given in cooperation with the treating doctor, is necessary before participation in any such clinical trial.

(5) The notion of legal representative refers back to existing national law and consequently may include natural or legal persons, an authority and/or a body provided for by national law.

(6) In order to achieve optimum protection of health, obsolete or repetitive tests will not be carried out, whether within the Community or in third countries. The harmonisation of technical requirements for the development of medicinal products should therefore be pursued through the appropriate fora, in particular the International Conference on Harmonisation.

(7) For medicinal products falling within the scope of Part A of the Annex to Council Regulation (EEC) No 2309/93 of 22 July 1993 laying down Community procedures for the authorisation and supervision of medicinal products for human and veterinary use and establishing a European Agency for the Evaluation of Medicinal Products[6], which include products intended for gene therapy or cell therapy, prior scientific evaluation by the European Agency for the Evaluation of Medicinal Products (hereinafter referred to as the "Agency"), assisted by the Committee for Proprietary Medicinal Products, is mandatory before the Commission grants marketing authorisation. In the course of this evaluation, the said Committee may request full details of the results of the clinical trials on which the application for marketing authorisation is based and, consequently, on the manner in which these trials were conducted and the same Committee may go so far as to require the applicant for such authorisation to conduct further clinical trials. Provision must therefore be made to allow the Agency to have full information on the conduct of any clinical trial for such medicinal products.

(8) A single opinion for each Member State concerned reduces delay in the commencement of a trial without jeopardising the well-being of the people participating in the trial or excluding the possibility of rejecting it in specific sites.

(9) Information on the content, commencement and termination of a clinical trial should be available to the Member States where the trial takes place and all the other Member States should have access to the same information. A European database bringing together this information should therefore be set up, with due regard for the rules of confidentiality.

(10) Clinical trials are a complex operation, generally lasting one or more years, usually involving numerous participants and several trial sites, often in different Member States. Member States' current practices diverge considerably on the rules on commencement and conduct of the clinical trials and the requirements for carrying them out vary widely. This therefore results in delays and complications detrimental to effective conduct of such trials in the Community. It is therefore necessary to simplify and harmonise the administrative

---

[6]OJ L 214, 24.8.1993, p. 1. Regulation as amended by Commission Regulation (EC) No 649/98 (OJ L 88, 24.3.1998, p. 7)

provisions governing such trials by establishing a clear, transparent procedure and creating conditions conducive to effective coordination of such clinical trials in the Community by the authorities concerned.

(11) As a rule, authorisation should be implicit, i.e. if there has been a vote in favour by the Ethics Committee and the competent authority has not objected within a given period, it should be possible to begin the clinical trials. In exceptional cases raising especially complex problems, explicit written authorisation should, however, be required.

(12) The principles of good manufacturing practice should be applied to investigational medicinal products.

(13) Special provisions should be laid down for the labelling of these products.

(14) Non-commercial clinical trials conducted by researchers without the participation of the pharmaceuticals industry may be of great benefit to the patients concerned. The Directive should therefore take account of the special position of trials whose planning does not require particular manufacturing or packaging processes, if these trials are carried out with medicinal products with a marketing authorisation within the meaning of Directive 65/65/EEC, manufactured or imported in accordance with the provisions of Directives 75/319/EEC and 91/356/EEC, and on patients with the same characteristics as those covered by the indication specified in this marketing authorisation. Labelling of the investigational medicinal products intended for trials of this nature should be subject to simplified provisions laid down in the good manufacturing practice guidelines on investigational products and in Directive 91/356/EEC.

(15) The verification of compliance with the standards of good clinical practice and the need to subject data, information and documents to inspection in order to confirm that they have been properly generated, recorded and reported are essential in order to justify the involvement of human subjects in clinical trials.

(16) The person participating in a trial must consent to the scrutiny of personal information during inspection by competent authorities and properly authorised persons, provided that such personal information is treated as strictly confidential and is not made publicly available.

(17) This Directive is to apply without prejudice to Directive 95/46/EEC of the European Parliament and of the Council of 24 October 1995 on the protection of individuals with regard to the processing of personal data and on the free movement of such data[7].

(18) It is also necessary to make provision for the monitoring of adverse reactions occurring in clinical trials using Community surveillance (pharmacovigilance) procedures in order to ensure the immediate cessation of any clinical trial in which there is an unacceptable level of risk.

(19) The measures necessary for the implementation of this Directive should be adopted in accordance with Council Decision 1999/468/EC of 28 June 1999 laying down the procedures for the exercise of implementing powers conferred on the Commission[8],

HAVE ADOPTED THIS DIRECTIVE:

Article 1. Scope

1. This Directive establishes specific provisions regarding the conduct of clinical trials, including multi-centre trials, on human subjects involving medicinal products as defined in Article 1 of Directive 65/65/EEC, in particular relating to the implementation of good clinical practice. This Directive does not apply to non-interventional trials.

---

[7]OJ L 281, 23.11.1995, p. 31.
[8]OJ L 184, 17.7.1999, p. 23.

2. Good clinical practice is a set of internationally recognised ethical and scientific quality requirements which must be observed for designing, conducting, recording and reporting clinical trials that involve the participation of human subjects. Compliance with this good practice provides assurance that the rights, safety and well-being of trial subjects are protected, and that the results of the clinical trials are credible.

3. The principles of good clinical practice and detailed guidelines in line with those principles shall be adopted and, if necessary, revised to take account of technical and scientific progress in accordance with the procedure referred to in Article 21(2).

These detailed guidelines shall be published by the Commission.

4. All clinical trials, including bioavailability and bioequivalence studies, shall be designed, conducted and reported in accordance with the principles of good clinical practice.

Article 2. Definitions

For the purposes of this Directive the following definitions shall apply:

(a) "clinical trial": any investigation in human subjects intended to discover or verify the clinical, pharmacological and/or other pharmacodynamic effects of one or more investigational medicinal product(s), and/or to identify any adverse reactions to one or more investigational medicinal product(s) and/or to study absorption, distribution, metabolism and excretion of one or more investigational medicinal product(s) with the object of ascertaining its (their) safety and/or efficacy;

This includes clinical trials carried out in either one site or multiple sites, whether in one or more than one Member State;

(b) "multi-centre clinical trial": a clinical trial conducted according to a single protocol but at more than one site, and therefore by more than one investigator, in which the trial sites may be located in a single Member State, in a number of Member States and/or in Member States and third countries;

(c) "non-interventional trial": a study where the medicinal product(s) is (are) prescribed in the usual manner in accordance with the terms of the marketing authorisation. The assignment of the patient to a particular therapeutic strategy is not decided in advance by a trial protocol but falls within current practice and the prescription of the medicine is clearly separated from the decision to include the patient in the study. No additional diagnostic or monitoring procedures shall be applied to the patients and epidemiological methods shall be used for the analysis of collected data;

(d) "investigational medicinal product": a pharmaceutical form of an active substance or placebo being tested or used as a reference in a clinical trial, including products already with a marketing authorisation but used or assembled (formulated or packaged) in a way different from the authorised form, or when used for an unauthorised indication, or when used to gain further information about the authorised form;

(e) "sponsor": an individual, company, institution or organisation which takes responsibility for the initiation, management and/or financing of a clinical trial;

(f) "investigator": a doctor or a person following a profession agreed in the Member State for investigations because of the scientific background and the experience in patient care it requires. The investigator is responsible for the conduct of a clinical trial at a trial site. If a trial is conducted by a team of individuals at a trial site, the investigator is the leader responsible for the team and may be called the principal investigator;

(g) "investigator's brochure": a compilation of the clinical and non-clinical data on the investigational medicinal product or products which are relevant to the study of the product or products in human subjects;

(h) "protocol": a document that describes the objective(s), design, methodology, statistical considerations and organisation of a trial. The term protocol refers to the protocol, successive versions of the protocol and protocol amendments;

(i) "subject": an individual who participates in a clinical trial as either a recipient of the investigational medicinal product or a control;

(j) "informed consent": decision, which must be written, dated and signed, to take part in a clinical trial, taken freely after being duly informed of its nature, significance, implications and risks and appropriately documented, by any person capable of giving consent or, where the person is not capable of giving consent, by his or her legal representative; if the person concerned is unable to write, oral consent in the presence of at least one witness may be given in exceptional cases, as provided for in national legislation.

(k) "ethics committee": an independent body in a Member State, consisting of healthcare professionals and non-medical members, whose responsibility it is to protect the rights, safety and wellbeing of human subjects involved in a trial and to provide public assurance of that protection, by, among other things, expressing an opinion on the trial protocol, the suitability of the investigators and the adequacy of facilities, and on the methods and documents to be used to inform trial subjects and obtain their informed consent;

(l) "inspection": the act by a competent authority of conducting an official review of documents, facilities, records, quality assurance arrangements, and any other resources that are deemed by the competent authority to be related to the clinical trial and that may be located at the site of the trial, at the sponsor's and/or contract research organisation's facilities, or at other establishments which the competent authority sees fit to inspect;

(m) "adverse event": any untoward medical occurrence in a patient or clinical trial subject administered a medicinal product and which does not necessarily have a causal relationship with this treatment;

(n) "adverse reaction": all untoward and unintended responses to an investigational medicinal product related to any dose administered;

(o) "serious adverse event or serious adverse reaction": any untoward medical occurrence or effect that at any dose results in death, is life-threatening, requires hospitalisation or prolongation of existing hospitalisation, results in persistent or significant disability or incapacity, or is a congenital anomaly or birth defect;

(p) "unexpected adverse reaction": an adverse reaction, the nature or severity of which is not consistent with the applicable product information (e.g. investigator's brochure for an unauthorised investigational product or summary of product characteristics for an authorised product).

Article 3. Protection of clinical trial subjects

1. This Directive shall apply without prejudice to the national provisions on the protection of clinical trial subjects if they are more comprehensive than the provisions of this Directive and consistent with the procedures and time-scales specified therein. Member States shall, insofar as they have not already done so, adopt detailed rules to protect from abuse individuals who are incapable of giving their informed consent.

2. A clinical trial may be undertaken only if, in particular:

(a) the foreseeable risks and inconveniences have been weighed against the anticipated benefit for the individual trial subject and other present and future patients. A clinical trial may be initiated only if the Ethics Committee and/or the competent authority comes to the conclusion that the anticipated therapeutic and public health benefits justify the risks and may be continued only if compliance with this requirement is permanently monitored;

(b) the trial subject or, when the person is not able to give informed consent, his legal representative has had the opportunity, in a prior interview with the investigator or a member of the investigating team, to understand the objectives, risks and inconveniences of the trial, and the conditions under which it is to be conducted and has also been informed of his right to withdraw from the trial at any time;

(c) the rights of the subject to physical and mental integrity, to privacy and to the protection of the data concerning him in accordance with Directive 95/46/EC are safeguarded;

(d) the trial subject or, when the person is not able to give informed consent, his legal representative has given his written consent after being informed of the nature, significance, implications and risks of the clinical trial; if the individual is unable to write, oral consent in the presence of at least one witness may be given in exceptional cases, as provided for in national legislation;

(e) the subject may without any resulting detriment withdraw from the clinical trial at any time by revoking his informed consent;

(f) provision has been made for insurance or indemnity to cover the liability of the investigator and sponsor.

3. The medical care given to, and medical decisions made on behalf of, subjects shall be the responsibility of an appropriately qualified doctor or, where appropriate, of a qualified dentist.

4. The subject shall be provided with a contact point where he may obtain further information.

Article 4. Clinical trials on minors

In addition to any other relevant restriction, a clinical trial on minors may be undertaken only if:

(a) the informed consent of the parents or legal representative has been obtained; consent must represent the minor's presumed will and may be revoked at any time, without detriment to the minor;

(b) the minor has received information according to its capacity of understanding, from staff with experience with minors, regarding the trial, the risks and the benefits;

(c) the explicit wish of a minor who is capable of forming an opinion and assessing this information to refuse participation or to be withdrawn from the clinical trial at any time is considered by the investigator or where appropriate the principal investigator;

(d) no incentives or financial inducements are given except compensation;

(e) some direct benefit for the group of patients is obtained from the clinical trial and only where such research is essential to validate data obtained in clinical trials on persons able to give informed consent or by other research methods; additionally, such research should either relate directly to a clinical condition from which the minor concerned suffers or be of such a nature that it can only be carried out on minors;

(f) the corresponding scientific guidelines of the Agency have been followed;

(g) clinical trials have been designed to minimise pain, discomfort, fear and any other foreseeable risk in relation to the disease and developmental stage; both the risk threshold and the degree of distress have to be specially defined and constantly monitored;

(h) the Ethics Committee, with paediatric expertise or after taking advice in clinical, ethical and psychosocial problems in the field of paediatrics, has endorsed the protocol; and

(i) the interests of the patient always prevail over those of science and society.

Article 5. Clinical trials on incapacitated adults not able to give informed legal consent

In the case of other persons incapable of giving informed legal consent, all relevant requirements listed for persons capable of giving such consent shall apply. In addition to these requirements, inclusion in clinical trials of incapacitated adults who have not given or not refused informed consent before the onset of their incapacity shall be allowed only if:

(a) the informed consent of the legal representative has been obtained; consent must represent the subject's presumed will and may be revoked at any time, without detriment to the subject;

(b) the person not able to give informed legal consent has received information according to his/her capacity of understanding regarding the trial, the risks and the benefits;

(c) the explicit wish of a subject who is capable of forming an opinion and assessing this information to refuse participation in, or to be withdrawn from, the clinical trial at any time is considered by the investigator or where appropriate the principal investigator;

(d) no incentives or financial inducements are given except compensation;

(e) such research is essential to validate data obtained in clinical trials on persons able to give informed consent or by other research methods and relates directly to a life-threatening or debilitating clinical condition from which the incapacitated adult concerned suffers;

(f) clinical trials have been designed to minimise pain, discomfort, fear and any other foreseeable risk in relation to the disease and developmental stage; both the risk threshold and the degree of distress shall be specially defined and constantly monitored;

(g) the Ethics Committee, with expertise in the relevant disease and the patient population concerned or after taking advice in clinical, ethical and psychosocial questions in the field of the relevant disease and patient population concerned, has endorsed the protocol;

(h) the interests of the patient always prevail over those of science and society; and

(i) there are grounds for expecting that administering the medicinal product to be tested will produce a benefit to the patient outweighing the risks or produce no risk at all.

Article 6. Ethics Committee

1. For the purposes of implementation of the clinical trials, Member States shall take the measures necessary for establishment and operation of Ethics Committees.

2. The Ethics Committee shall give its opinion, before a clinical trial commences, on any issue requested.

3. In preparing its opinion, the Ethics Committee shall consider, in particular:

(a) the relevance of the clinical trial and the trial design;

(b) whether the evaluation of the anticipated benefits and risks as required under Article 3(2)(a) is satisfactory and whether the conclusions are justified;

(c) the protocol;

(d) the suitability of the investigator and supporting staff;

(e) the investigator's brochure;

(f) the quality of the facilities;

(g) the adequacy and completeness of the written information to be given and the procedure to be followed for the purpose of obtaining informed consent and the justification for the research on persons incapable of giving informed consent as regards the specific restrictions laid down in Article 3;

(h) provision for indemnity or compensation in the event of injury or death attributable to a clinical trial;

(i) any insurance or indemnity to cover the liability of the investigator and sponsor;

(j) the amounts and, where appropriate, the arrangements for rewarding or compensating investigators and trial subjects and the relevant aspects of any agreement between the sponsor and the site;

(k) the arrangements for the recruitment of subjects.

4. Notwithstanding the provisions of this Article, a Member State may decide that the competent authority it has designated for the purpose of Article 9 shall be responsible for the consideration of, and the giving of an opinion on, the matters referred to in paragraph 3(h), (i) and (j) of this Article.

When a Member State avails itself of this provision, it shall notify the Commission, the other Member States and the Agency.

5. The Ethics Committee shall have a maximum of 60 days from the date of receipt of a valid application to give its reasoned opinion to the applicant and the competent authority in the Member State concerned.

6. Within the period of examination of the application for an opinion, the Ethics Committee may send a single request for information supplementary to that already supplied by the applicant. The period laid down in paragraph 5 shall be suspended until receipt of the supplementary information.

7. No extension to the 60-day period referred to in paragraph 5 shall be permissible except in the case of trials involving medicinal products for gene therapy or somatic cell therapy or medicinal products containing genetically modified organisms. In this case, an extension of a maximum of 30 days shall be permitted. For these products, this 90-day period may be extended by a further 90 days in the event of consultation of a group or a committee in accordance with the regulations and procedures of the Member States concerned. In the case of xenogenic cell therapy, there shall be no time limit to the authorisation period.

Article 7. Single opinion

For multi-centre clinical trials limited to the territory of a single Member State, Member States shall establish a procedure providing, notwithstanding the number of Ethics Committees, for the adoption of a single opinion for that Member State.

In the case of multi-centre clinical trials carried out in more than one Member State simultaneously, a single opinion shall be given for each Member State concerned by the clinical trial.

Article 8. Detailed guidance

The Commission, in consultation with Member States and interested parties, shall draw up and publish detailed guidance on the application format and documentation to be submitted in an application for an ethics committee opinion, in particular regarding the information that is given to subjects, and on the appropriate safeguards for the protection of personal data.

Article 9. Commencement of a clinical trial

1. Member States shall take the measures necessary to ensure that the procedure described in this Article is followed for commencement of a clinical trial.

The sponsor may not start a clinical trial until the Ethics Committee has issued a favourable opinion and inasmuch as the competent authority of the Member State concerned has not informed the sponsor of any grounds for non-acceptance. The procedures to reach these decisions can be run in parallel or not, depending on the sponsor.

2. Before commencing any clinical trial, the sponsor shall be required to submit a valid request for authorisation to the competent authority of the Member State in which the sponsor plans to conduct the clinical trial.

3. If the competent authority of the Member State notifies the sponsor of grounds for non-acceptance, the sponsor may, on one occasion only, amend the content of the request referred to in paragraph 2 in order to take due account of the grounds given. If the sponsor fails to amend the request accordingly, the request shall be considered rejected and the clinical trial may not commence.

4. Consideration of a valid request for authorisation by the competent authority as stated in paragraph 2 shall be carried out as rapidly as possible and may not exceed 60 days. The Member States may lay down a shorter period than 60 days within their area of responsibility if that is in compliance with current practice. The competent authority can nevertheless notify the sponsor before the end of this period that it has no grounds for non-acceptance.

No further extensions to the period referred to in the first subparagraph shall be permissible except in the case of trials involving the medicinal products listed in paragraph 6, for which an extension of a maximum of 30 days shall be permitted. For these products, this 90-day period may be extended by a further 90 days in the event of consultation of a group or a committee in accordance with the regulations and procedures of the Member States concerned. In the case of xenogenic cell therapy there shall be no time limit to the authorisation period.

5. Without prejudice to paragraph 6, written authorisation may be required before the commencement of clinical trials for such trials on medicinal products which do not have a marketing authorisation within the meaning of Directive 65/65/EEC and are referred to in Part A of the Annex to Regulation (EEC) No 2309/93, and other medicinal products with special characteristics, such as medicinal products the active ingredient or active ingredients of which is or are a biological product or biological products of human or animal origin, or contains biological components of human or animal origin, or the manufacturing of which requires such components.

6. Written authorisation shall be required before commencing clinical trials involving medicinal products for gene therapy, somatic cell therapy including xenogenic cell therapy and all medicinal products containing genetically modified organisms. No gene therapy trials may be carried out which result in modifications to the subject's germ line genetic identity.

7. This authorisation shall be issued without prejudice to the application of Council Directives 90/219/EEC of 23 April 1990 on the contained use of genetically modified micro-organisms[9] and 90/220/EEC of 23 April 1990 on the deliberate release into the environment of genetically modified organisms[10].

8. In consultation with Member States, the Commission shall draw up and publish detailed guidance on:

(a) the format and contents of the request referred to in paragraph 2 as well as the documentation to be submitted to support that request, on the quality and manufacture of the investigational medicinal product, any toxicological and pharmacological tests, the protocol and clinical information on the investigational medicinal product including the investigator's brochure;

(b) the presentation and content of the proposed amendment referred to in point (a) of Article 10 on substantial amendments made to the protocol;

(c) the declaration of the end of the clinical trial.

---

[9]OJ L 117, 8.5.1990, p. 1. Directive as last amended by Directive 98/81/EC (OJ L 330, 5.12.1998, p. 13).

[10]OJ L 117, 8.5.1990, p. 15. Directive as last amended by Commission Directive 97/35/EC (OJ L 169, 27.6.1997, p. 72).

Article 10. Conduct of a clinical trial

Amendments may be made to the conduct of a clinical trial following the procedure described hereinafter:

(a) after the commencement of the clinical trial, the sponsor may make amendments to the protocol. If those amendments are substantial and are likely to have an impact on the safety of the trial subjects or to change the interpretation of the scientific documents in support of the conduct of the trial, or if they are otherwise significant, the sponsor shall notify the competent authorities of the Member State or Member States concerned of the reasons for, and content of, these amendments and shall inform the ethics committee or committees concerned in accordance with Articles 6 and 9.

On the basis of the details referred to in Article 6(3) and in accordance with Article 7, the Ethics Committee shall give an opinion within a maximum of 35 days of the date of receipt of the proposed amendment in good and due form. If this opinion is unfavourable, the sponsor may not implement the amendment to the protocol.

If the opinion of the Ethics Committee is favourable and the competent authorities of the Member States have raised no grounds for non-acceptance of the abovementioned substantial amendments, the sponsor shall proceed to conduct the clinical trial following the amended protocol. Should this not be the case, the sponsor shall either take account of the grounds for non-acceptance and adapt the proposed amendment to the protocol accordingly or withdraw the proposed amendment;

(b) without prejudice to point (a), in the light of the circumstances, notably the occurrence of any new event relating to the conduct of the trial or the development of the investigational medicinal product where that new event is likely to affect the safety of the subjects, the sponsor and the investigator shall take appropriate urgent safety measures to protect the subjects against any immediate hazard. The sponsor shall forthwith inform the competent authorities of those new events and the measures taken and shall ensure that the Ethics Committee is notified at the same time;

(c) within 90 days of the end of a clinical trial the sponsor shall notify the competent authorities of the Member State or Member States concerned and the Ethics Committee that the clinical trial has ended. If the trial has to be terminated early, this period shall be reduced to 15 days and the reasons clearly explained.

Article 11. Exchange of information

1. Member States in whose territory the clinical trial takes place shall enter in a European database, accessible only to the competent authorities of the Member States, the Agency and the Commission:

(a) extracts from the request for authorisation referred to in Article 9(2);

(b) any amendments made to the request, as provided for in Article 9(3);

(c) any amendments made to the protocol, as provided for in point a of Article 10;

(d) the favourable opinion of the Ethics Committee;

(e) the declaration of the end of the clinical trial; and

(f) a reference to the inspections carried out on conformity with good clinical practice.

2. At the substantiated request of any Member State, the Agency or the Commission, the competent authority to which the request for authorisation was submitted shall supply all further information concerning the clinical trial in question other than the data already in the European database.

3. In consultation with the Member States, the Commission shall draw up and publish detailed guidance on the relevant data to be included in this European database, which it operates with the assistance of the Agency, as well as the methods for electronic

communication of the data. The detailed guidance thus drawn up shall ensure that the confidentiality of the data is strictly observed.

Article 12. Suspension of the trial or infringements

1. Where a Member State has objective grounds for considering that the conditions in the request for authorisation referred to in Article 9(2) are no longer met or has information raising doubts about the safety or scientific validity of the clinical trial, it may suspend or prohibit the clinical trial and shall notify the sponsor thereof.

Before the Member State reaches its decision it shall, except where there is imminent risk, ask the sponsor and/or the investigator for their opinion, to be delivered within one week.

In this case, the competent authority concerned shall forthwith inform the other competent authorities, the Ethics Committee concerned, the Agency and the Commission of its decision to suspend or prohibit the trial and of the reasons for the decision.

2. Where a competent authority has objective grounds for considering that the sponsor or the investigator or any other person involved in the conduct of the trial no longer meets the obligations laid down, it shall forthwith inform him thereof, indicating the course of action which he must take to remedy this state of affairs. The competent authority concerned shall forthwith inform the Ethics Committee, the other competent authorities and the Commission of this course of action.

Article 13. Manufacture and import of investigational medicinal products

1. Member States shall take all appropriate measures to ensure that the manufacture or importation of investigational medicinal products is subject to the holding of authorisation. In order to obtain the authorisation, the applicant and, subsequently, the holder of the authorisation, shall meet at least the requirements defined in accordance with the procedure referred to in Article 21(2).

2. Member States shall take all appropriate measures to ensure that the holder of the authorisation referred to in paragraph 1 has permanently and continuously at his disposal the services of at least one qualified person who, in accordance with the conditions laid down in Article 23 of the second Council Directive 75/319/EEC of 20 May 1975 on the approximation of provisions laid down by law, regulation or administrative action relating to proprietary medicinal products[11], is responsible in particular for carrying out the duties specified in paragraph 3 of this Article.

3. Member States shall take all appropriate measures to ensure that the qualified person referred to in Article 21 of Directive 75/319/EEC, without prejudice to his relationship with the manufacturer or importer, is responsible, in the context of the procedures referred to in Article 25 of the said Directive, for ensuring:

(a) in the case of investigational medicinal products manufactured in the Member State concerned, that each batch of medicinal products has been manufactured and checked in compliance with the requirements of Commission Directive 91/356/EEC of 13 June 1991 laying down the principles and guidelines of good manufacturing practice for medicinal products for human use[12], the product specification file and the information notified pursuant to Article 9(2) of this Directive;

(b) in the case of investigational medicinal products manufactured in a third country, that each production batch has been manufactured and checked in accordance with standards of

---

[11]OJ L 147, 9.6.1975, p. 13. Directive as last amended by Council Directive 93/39/EC (OJ L 214, 24.8.1993, p. 22).

[12]OJ L 193, 17.7.1991, p. 30.

good manufacturing practice at least equivalent to those laid down in Commission Directive 91/356/EEC, in accordance with the product specification file, and that each production batch has been checked in accordance with the information notified pursuant to Article 9(2) of this Directive;

(c) in the case of an investigational medicinal product which is a comparator product from a third country, and which has a marketing authorisation, where the documentation certifying that each production batch has been manufactured in conditions at least equivalent to the standards of good manufacturing practice referred to above cannot be obtained, that each production batch has undergone all relevant analyses, tests or checks necessary to confirm its quality in accordance with the information notified pursuant to Article 9(2) of this Directive.

Detailed guidance on the elements to be taken into account when evaluating products with the object of releasing batches within the Community shall be drawn up pursuant to the good manufacturing practice guidelines, and in particular Annex 13 to the said guidelines. Such guidelines will be adopted in accordance with the procedure referred to in Article 21(2) of this Directive and published in accordance with Article 19a of Directive 75/319/EEC.

Insofar as the provisions laid down in (a), (b) or (c) are complied with, investigational medicinal products shall not have to undergo any further checks if they are imported into another Member State together with batch release certification signed by the qualified person.

4. In all cases, the qualified person must certify in a register or equivalent document that each production batch satisfies the provisions of this Article. The said register or equivalent document shall be kept up to date as operations are carried out and shall remain at the disposal of the agents of the competent authority for the period specified in the provisions of the Member States concerned. This period shall in any event be not less than five years.

5. Any person engaging in activities as the qualified person referred to in Article 21 of Directive 75/319/EEC as regards investigational medicinal products at the time when this Directive is applied in the Member State where that person is, but without complying with the conditions laid down in Articles 23 and 24 of that Directive, shall be authorised to continue those activities in the Member State concerned.

Article 14. Labelling

The particulars to appear in at least the official language(s) of the Member State on the outer packaging of investigational medicinal products or, where there is no outer packaging, on the immediate packaging, shall be published by the Commission in the good manufacturing practice guidelines on investigational medicinal products adopted in accordance with Article 19a of Directive 75/319/EEC.

In addition, these guidelines shall lay down adapted provisions relating to labelling for investigational medicinal products intended for clinical trials with the following characteristics:

- the planning of the trial does not require particular manufacturing or packaging processes;
- the trial is conducted with medicinal products with, in the Member States concerned by the study, a marketing authorisation within the meaning of Directive 65/65/EEC, manufactured or imported in accordance with the provisions of Directive 75/319/EEC;
- the patients participating in the trial have the same characteristics as those covered by the indication specified in the abovementioned authorisation.

Article 15. Verification of compliance of investigational medicinal products with good clinical and manufacturing practice

1. To verify compliance with the provisions on good clinical and manufacturing practice, Member States shall appoint inspectors to inspect the sites concerned by any clinical trial

conducted, particularly the trial site or sites, the manufacturing site of the investigational medicinal product, any laboratory used for analyses in the clinical trial and/or the sponsor's premises.

The inspections shall be conducted by the competent authority of the Member State concerned, which shall inform the Agency; they shall be carried out on behalf of the Community and the results shall be recognised by all the other Member States. These inspections shall be coordinated by the Agency, within the framework of its powers as provided for in Regulation (EEC) No 2309/93. A Member State may request assistance from another Member State in this matter.

2. Following inspection, an inspection report shall be prepared. It must be made available to the sponsor while safeguarding confidential aspects. It may be made available to the other Member States, to the Ethics Committee and to the Agency, at their reasoned request.

3. At the request of the Agency, within the framework of its powers as provided for in Regulation (EEC) No 2309/93, or of one of the Member States concerned, and following consultation with the Member States concerned, the Commission may request a new inspection should verification of compliance with this Directive reveal differences between Member States.

4. Subject to any arrangements which may have been concluded between the Community and third countries, the Commission, upon receipt of a reasoned request from a Member State or on its own initiative, or a Member State may propose that the trial site and/or the sponsor's premises and/or the manufacturer established in a third country undergo an inspection. The inspection shall be carried out by duly qualified Community inspectors.

5. The detailed guidelines on the documentation relating to the clinical trial, which shall constitute the master file on the trial, archiving, qualifications of inspectors and inspection procedures to verify compliance of the clinical trial in question with this Directive shall be adopted and revised in accordance with the procedure referred to in Article 21(2).

Article 16. Notification of adverse events

1. The investigator shall report all serious adverse events immediately to the sponsor except for those that the protocol or investigator's brochure identifies as not requiring immediate reporting. The immediate report shall be followed by detailed, written reports. The immediate and follow-up reports shall identify subjects by unique code numbers assigned to the latter.

2. Adverse events and/or laboratory abnormalities identified in the protocol as critical to safety evaluations shall be reported to the sponsor according to the reporting requirements and within the time periods specified in the protocol.

3. For reported deaths of a subject, the investigator shall supply the sponsor and the Ethics Committee with any additional information requested.

4. The sponsor shall keep detailed records of all adverse events which are reported to him by the investigator or investigators. These records shall be submitted to the Member States in whose territory the clinical trial is being conducted, if they so request.

Article 17. Notification of serious adverse reactions

1. (a) The sponsor shall ensure that all relevant information about suspected serious unexpected adverse reactions that are fatal or life-threatening is recorded and reported as soon as possible to the competent authorities in all the Member States concerned, and to the Ethics Committee, and in any case no later than seven days after knowledge by the sponsor of such a case, and that relevant follow-up information is subsequently communicated within an additional eight days.

(b) All other suspected serious unexpected adverse reactions shall be reported to the competent authorities concerned and to the Ethics Committee concerned as soon as possible but within a maximum of fifteen days of first knowledge by the sponsor.

(c) Each Member State shall ensure that all suspected unexpected serious adverse reactions to an investigational medicinal product which are brought to its attention are recorded.

(d) The sponsor shall also inform all investigators.

2. Once a year throughout the clinical trial, the sponsor shall provide the Member States in whose territory the clinical trial is being conducted and the Ethics Committee with a listing of all suspected serious adverse reactions which have occurred over this period and a report of the subjects' safety.

3. (a) Each Member State shall see to it that all suspected unexpected serious adverse reactions to an investigational medicinal product which are brought to its attention are immediately entered in a European database to which, in accordance with Article 11(1), only the competent authorities of the Member States, the Agency and the Commission shall have access.

(b) The Agency shall make the information notified by the sponsor available to the competent authorities of the Member States.

Article 18. Guidance concerning reports

The Commission, in consultation with the Agency, Member States and interested parties, shall draw up and publish detailed guidance on the collection, verification and presentation of adverse event/reaction reports, together with decoding procedures for unexpected serious adverse reactions.

Article 19. General provisions

This Directive is without prejudice to the civil and criminal liability of the sponsor or the investigator. To this end, the sponsor or a legal representative of the sponsor must be established in the Community.

Unless Member States have established precise conditions for exceptional circumstances, investigational medicinal products and, as the case may be, the devices used for their administration shall be made available free of charge by the sponsor.

The Member States shall inform the Commission of such conditions.

Article 20. Adaptation to scientific and technical progress

This Directive shall be adapted to take account of scientific and technical progress in accordance with the procedure referred to in Article 21(2).

Article 21. Committee procedure

1. The Commission shall be assisted by the Standing Committee on Medicinal Products for Human Use, set up by Article 2b of Directive 75/318/EEC (hereinafter referred to as the Committee).

2. Where reference is made to this paragraph, Articles 5 and 7 of Decision 1999/468/EC shall apply, having regard to the provisions of Article 8 thereof.

The period referred to in Article 5(6) of Decision 1999/468/EC shall be set at three months.

3. The Committee shall adopt its rules of procedure.

Article 22. Application

1. Member States shall adopt and publish before 1 May 2003 the laws, regulations and administrative provisions necessary to comply with this Directive. They shall forthwith inform the Commission thereof.

They shall apply these provisions at the latest with effect from 1 May 2004.

When Member States adopt these provisions, they shall contain a reference to this Directive or shall be accompanied by such reference on the occasion of their official publication. The methods of making such reference shall be laid down by Member States.

2. Member States shall communicate to the Commission the text of the provisions of national law which they adopt in the field governed by this Directive.

Article 23. Entry into force

This Directive shall enter into force on the day of its publication in the Official Journal of the European Communities.

Article 24. Addressees

This Directive is addressed to the Member States.

Done at Luxembourg, 4 April 2001.

For the European Parliament
The President
N. Fontaine

For the Council
The President
B. Rosengren

Glossary of Abbreviations

A

AAMC	Association of Academic Medical Centers
ACCP	American College of Clinical Pharmacy
ACTIS	AIDS Clinical Trials Information Service
AE	Adverse event
AIDS	Acquired Immune Deficiency Syndrome
AIMD	Active Implantable Medical Devices
AIP	Application Integrity Policy
AMA	American Medical Association
AR	Adverse reaction

B

BIMO	Bioresearch Monitoring Program
BLA	Biologics License Application

C

CAP	College of American Pathologists
CBER	Center for Biologics Evaluation and Research
CCPPRB	Consultation Committees for the Protection of Persons Undergoing Biomedical Research
CD	Compact disc
CDER	Center for Drug Evaluation and Research
CDRH	Center for Devices and Radiological Health
CFR	Code of Federal Regulations
CHF	Congestive heart failure
CI	Clinical investigator
CIOMS	Council for International Organizations of Medical Sciences
CLIA	Clinical Laboratory Improvements Amendments
COI	Conflict of Interest
CPG	Compliance Policy Guide
CPMP	Committee for Proprietary Medicinal Products
CRA	Clinical research associate
CRF	Case report form
CRO	Contract research organization
CV	*Curriculum Vitae*

D

DDS	Doctor of Dental Science
DHHS	Department of Health and Human Services
DO	Doctor of Osteopathy
DSI	Division of Scientific Investigations
DSMB	Data safety monitoring board

E

ECG	Electrocardiogram (aka EKG)
EIR	Establishment Inspection Report
EMEA	European Agency for the Evaluation of Medicinal Products
EMT	Emergency medical technician
ER	Emergency room
ETOH	Ethyl alcohol
EU	European Union

F

FDA	Food and Drug Administration
FOI	Freedom of Information
FWA	Federal Wide Assurance
FY	Fiscal Year

G

GCP	Good Clinical Practice
GMP	Good Manufacturing Practice

H

HHS	Health and Human Services, Department of
HIPAA	Health Insurance Portability and Accountability Act
HIV	Human Immunodeficiency Virus
HMO	Health maintenance organization

I

IC	Informed consent
ICD	Informed consent document
ICF	Informed consent form
ICH	International Conference on Harmonization
IDB	Investigator's drug brochure
IDE	Investigational Device Exemption
IEC	Independent ethics committee
IM	Intramuscular
IMP	Investigational medicinal product
IND	Investigational New Drug Application
IRAE	Immediately reportable adverse event
IRB	Institutional review board
IT	Information technology
IUD	Intra-uterine device
IV	Intravenous

L

LAR	Legally authorized representative
LPN	Licensed practical nurse
LREC	Local Research Ethics Committees

M

MDD	General Medical Devices
MM	Medical monitor
MPA	Multiple Project Assurance
MREC	Multi-centre Research Ethics Committees
MRI	Magnetic resonance imaging
MS	Member States

N

NAI	No action indicated
NCI	National Cancer Institute
NCR	National Cash Register
NDA	New Drug Application
NHLBI	National Heart, Lung, and Blood Institute
NHRPAC	National Human Research Protection Advisory Committee
NIDPOE	Notice of Initiation of Disqualification Proceedings and Opportunity to Explain
NIH	National Institutes of Health
NOOH	Notice of Opportunity for Hearing
NP	Nurse practitioner

O

OAI	Official action indicated
OB-GYN	Obstetrics and Gynecology
ODE	Office of Drug Evaluation
OHRP	Office for Human Research Protection
OTC	Over-the-counter

P

PA	Physician assistant
PC	Personal computer
PDQ	Physicians Data Query
PE	Physical exam
PhD	Doctor of Philosophy
PHI	Protected health information (described in the HIPAA Privacy Rule)
PhRMA	Pharmaceutical Research and Manufacturers of America
PI	Principal investigator

PLA	Product License Application
PMA	Pre-Market Approval Application
PMD	Private medical doctor
PSR	Periodic safety report

Q

QA	Quality assurance
QAU	Quality assurance unit
QC	Quality control

R

| RN | Registered nurse |
| ROPI | Report of Prior Investigation |

S

SAE	Serious adverse event
SAS	Statistical Analysis Software
SC	Study coordinator
SI	Subinvestigator
SMO	Site management organization
SOP	Standard operating procedure
SUSAR	Suspected unexpected serious adverse reaction

T

| TEAE | Treatment emergent adverse event |

U

| UADE | Unexpected adverse device effect |

V

| VAI | Voluntary action indicated |
| VP | Vice President |

W

| WHO | World Health Organization |
| WMA | World Medical Association |

Acknowledgment

Eric Mackintosh, Peace Corps Volunteer, Dominican Republic.

Notes

Notes